THE ✦ TIMES
ATLAS OF THE
WORLD
MINI EDITION

W0007833

THE TIMES

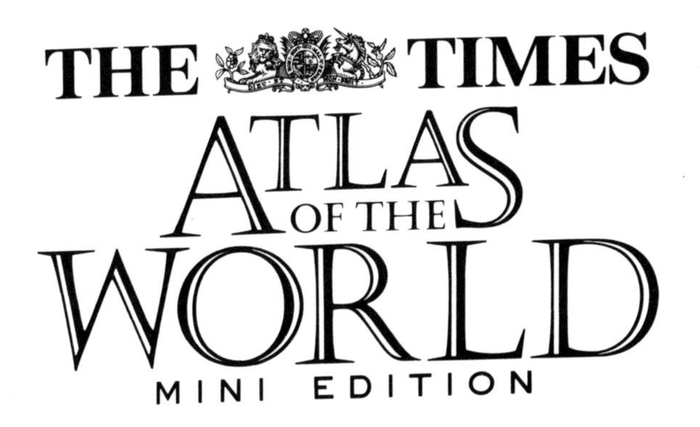

ATLAS OF THE WORLD

MINI EDITION

TIMES BOOKS

A Division of HarperCollins*Publishers*

This edition published 1994 by Times Books
A Division of HarperCollins Publishers
77-85 Fulham Palace Road, London W6 8JB

© Times Books and Bartholomew 1994

First published by Bartholomew 1991
Revised 1992, 1993

ISBN 0 7230 0669 5

Printed in Great Britain by Bartholomew, The Edinburgh Press Limited.

Details included in this atlas are subject to change without notice. Whilst every
effort is made to keep information up to date Bartholomew will not be
responsible for any loss, damage or inconvenience caused by inaccuracies in
this atlas. The publishers are always pleased to acknowledge any corrections
brought to their notice, and record their appreciation of the valuable services
rendered in the past by map users in assisting to maintain the accuracy of their
publications

GH7783

CONTENTS

viii-ix World Physical
x-xi World Political
xii-xiii World Time Zones
xiv-xv World Environment
xvi Key to Symbols

1 Arctic Ocean
2-3 North America
4-5 Canada, West
6-7 Canada, East
8-9 USA, West
10-11 USA, East
12 USA, Alaska
13 Canada Pacific
14-15 Lower Canada, USA North-East
16 Washington – New York – Boston
17 USA, South-East
18-19 USA, South-Central
20 USA, Pacific NW
21 USA, Pacific S
22 San Francisco & Los Angeles
23 Central Mexico
24-25 Mexico & Central America
26-27 Caribbean
28 South America
29 South America, South
30 South America, Central
31 South America, NE

32–33	South America, North
34	Central Argentina
35	South-East Brazil
36–37	Europe
38–39	Scandinavia
40–41	British Isles
42–43	England & Wales
44	Scotland, North
45	Ireland
46	Paris – Brussels – Ruhr
47	Alps
48–49	France
50–51	Spain & Portugal
52–53	Italy
54–55	The Balkans
56–57	Germany & Austria
58–59	East-Central Europe
60–61	European Russia, Ukraine & Baltic States
62	North Asia
63	Russian Federation, East
64–65	Russian Federation, West
66–67	South Asia
68–69	East Asia
70–71	South-East Asia
72–73	Central China
74	Japan & Korea
75	Central Japan
76–77	Indo-China & Singapore

78	Indonesia, Central
79	Philippines
80–81	Middle East
82–83	India & West China
84–85	India, NW & Pakistan
86	India, NE & Bangladesh
87	India, South & Sri Lanka
88–89	Africa
90–91	Iran and the Gulf
92–93	Turkey, Syria & Iraq
94	Israel & Lebanon
95	Africa, North-East
96–97	Africa, West
98–99	Africa, Central
100–101	Africa, South
102–103	Atlantic Ocean
104–105	Australasia
106–107	Australia
108–109	Australia South-East
110–111	New Zealand
112	Antarctica

Index

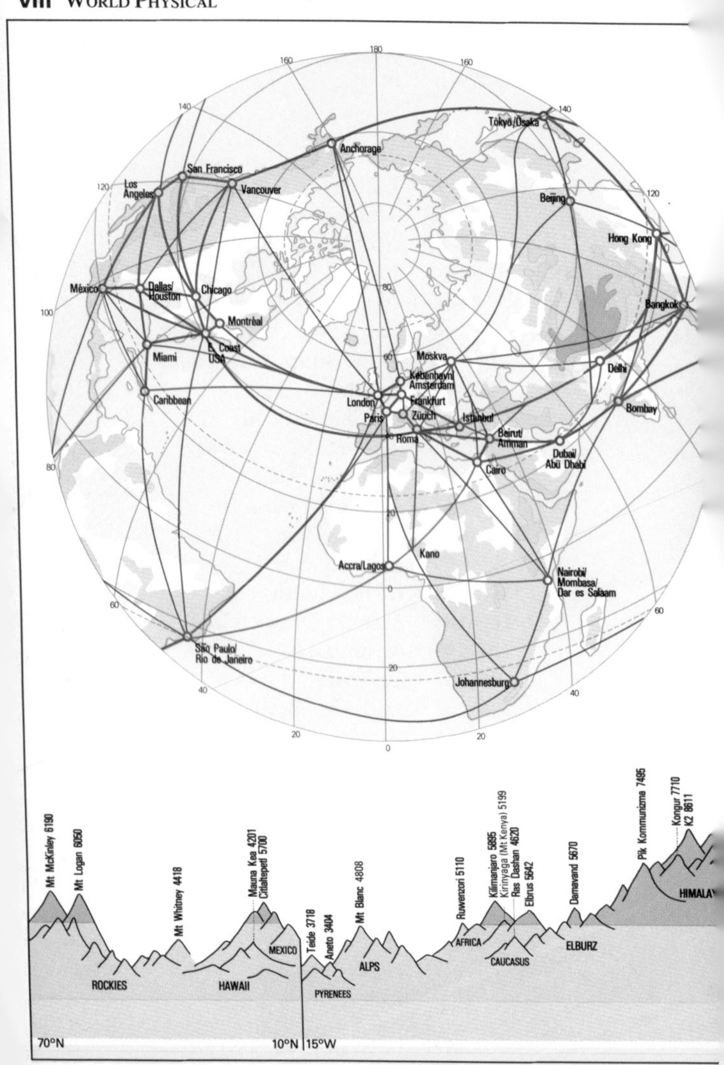
Anchorage
Tōkyō/Ōsaka
San Francisco
Los Angeles
Vancouver
Beijing
Hong Kong
México
Dallas/ Houston
Chicago
Montréal
E. Coast USA
Miami
Caribbean
Bangkok
Moskva
København/ Amsterdam
Frankfurt
London
Paris
Zürich
Istanbul
Roma
Bairut/ Amman
Cairo
Dubai/ Abū Dhabi
Delhi
Bombay
Kano
Accra/Lagos
Nairobi/ Mombasa/ Dar es Salaam
São Paulo/ Rio de Janeiro
Johannesburg
Mt McKinley 6190
Mt Logan 6050
Mt Whitney 4418
Mauna Kea 4201
Citlaltepetl 5700
Teide 3718
Aneto 3404
Mt Blanc 4808
Ruwenzori 5110
Kilimanjaro 5895
Kirinyaga (Mt Kenya) 5199
Ras Dashan 4620
Elbrus 5642
Damavand 5670
Pik Kommunizma 7495
Kongur 7710
K2 8611
ROCKIES
HAWAII
MEXICO
PYRENEES
ALPS
AFRICA
CAUCASUS
ELBURZ
70°N
10°N
15°W

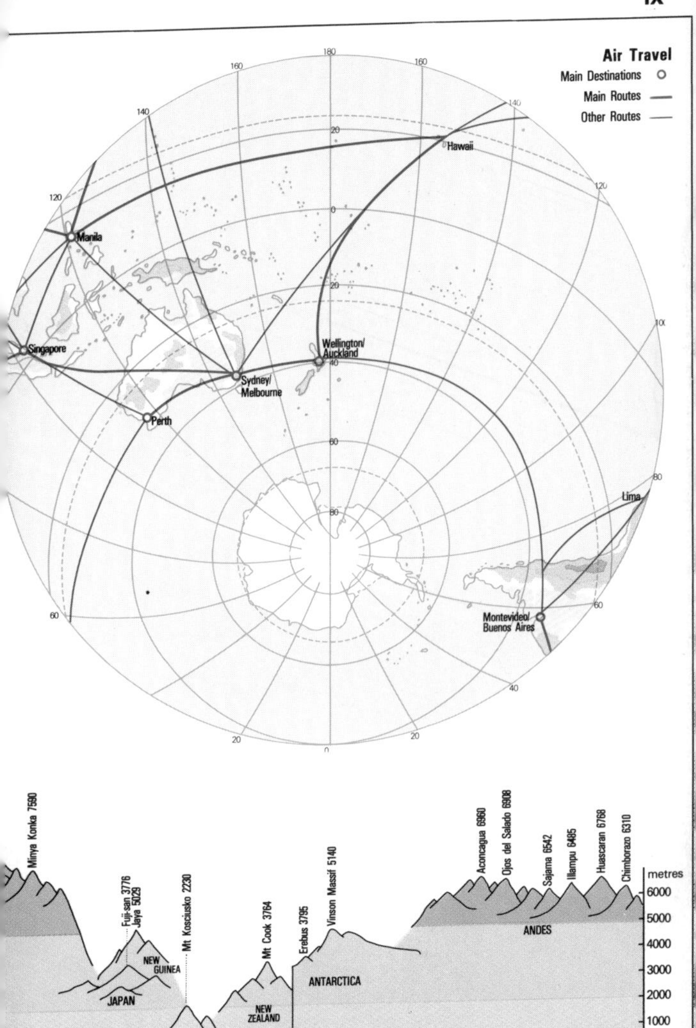

Air Travel

Main Destinations ○
Main Routes ——
Other Routes ——

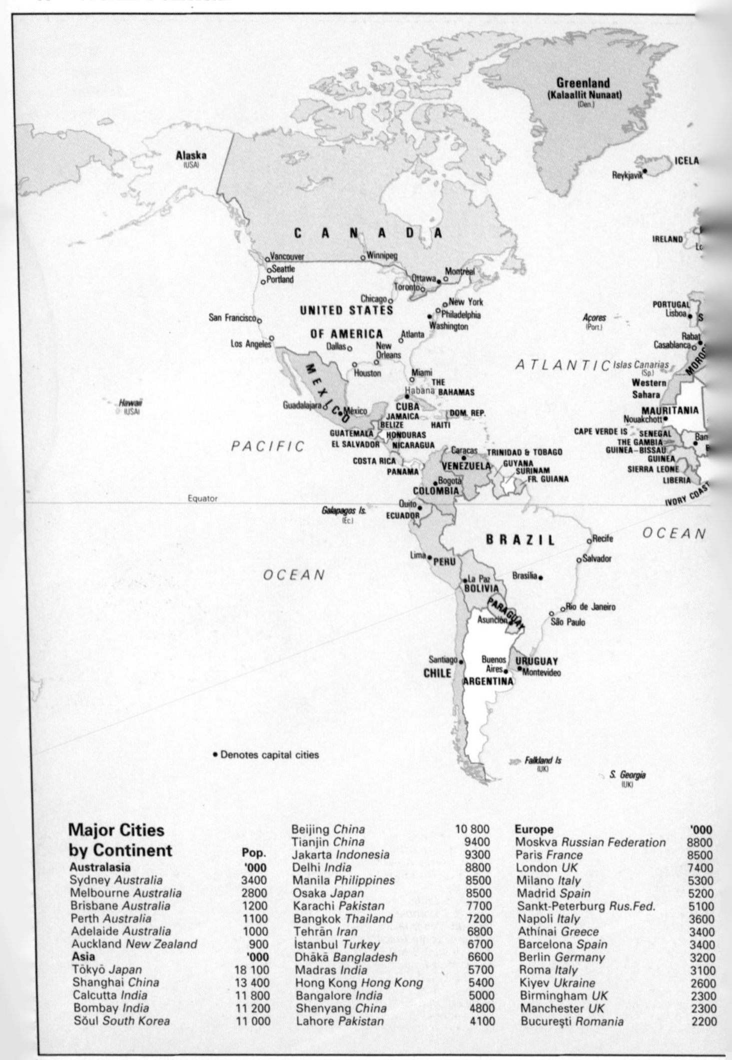

• Denotes capital cities

Major Cities by Continent		Beijing *China*	10 800	Europe	'000
		Tianjin *China*	9400	Moskva *Russian Federation*	8800
	Pop.	Jakarta *Indonesia*	9300	Paris *France*	8500
Australasia	**'000**	Delhi *India*	8800	London *UK*	7400
Sydney *Australia*	3400	Manila *Philippines*	8500	Milano *Italy*	5300
Melbourne *Australia*	2800	Osaka *Japan*	8500	Madrid *Spain*	5200
Brisbane *Australia*	1200	Karachi *Pakistan*	7700	Sankt-Peterburg *Rus.Fed.*	5100
Perth *Australia*	1100	Bangkok *Thailand*	7200	Napoli *Italy*	3600
Adelaide *Australia*	1000	Tehrān *Iran*	6800	Athínai *Greece*	3400
Auckland *New Zealand*	900	Istanbul *Turkey*	6700	Barcelona *Spain*	3400
Asia	**'000**	Dhākā *Bangladesh*	6600	Berlin *Germany*	3200
Tōkyō *Japan*	18 100	Madras *India*	5700	Roma *Italy*	3100
Shanghai *China*	13 400	Hong Kong *Hong Kong*	5400	Kiyev *Ukraine*	2600
Calcutta *India*	11 800	Bangalore *India*	5000	Birmingham *UK*	2300
Bombay *India*	11 200	Shenyang *China*	4800	Manchester *UK*	2300
Sŏul *South Korea*	11 000	Lahore *Pakistan*	4100	Bucureşti *Romania*	2200

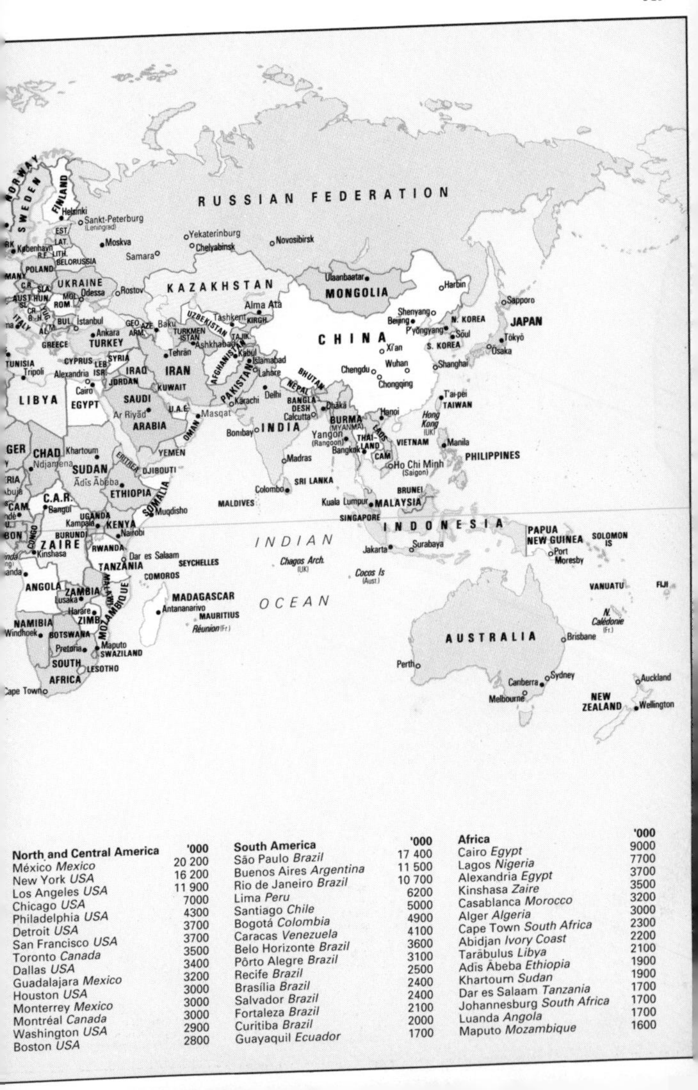

North and Central America	'000
México *Mexico*	20 200
New York *USA*	16 200
Los Angeles *USA*	11 900
Chicago *USA*	7000
Philadelphia *USA*	4300
Detroit *USA*	3700
San Francisco *USA*	3700
Toronto *Canada*	3500
Dallas *USA*	3400
Guadalajara *Mexico*	3200
Houston *USA*	3000
Monterrey *Mexico*	3000
Montréal *Canada*	3000
Washington *USA*	2900
Boston *USA*	2800

South America	'000
São Paulo *Brazil*	17 400
Buenos Aires *Argentina*	11 500
Rio de Janeiro *Brazil*	10 700
Lima *Peru*	6200
Santiago *Chile*	5000
Bogotá *Colombia*	4900
Caracas *Venezuela*	4100
Belo Horizonte *Brazil*	3600
Pôrto Alegre *Brazil*	3100
Recife *Brazil*	2500
Brasília *Brazil*	2400
Salvador *Brazil*	2400
Fortaleza *Brazil*	2100
Curitiba *Brazil*	2000
Guayaquil *Ecuador*	1700

Africa	'000
Cairo *Egypt*	9000
Lagos *Nigeria*	7700
Alexandria *Egypt*	3700
Kinshasa *Zaire*	3500
Casablanca *Morocco*	3200
Alger *Algeria*	3000
Cape Town *South Africa*	2300
Abidjan *Ivory Coast*	2200
Adis Abeba *Ethiopia*	2100
Tarābulus *Libya*	1900
Khartoum *Sudan*	1900
Dar es Salaam *Tanzania*	1700
Johannesburg *South Africa*	1700
Luanda *Angola*	1700
Maputo *Mozambique*	1600

| 22 +10 | 23 +11 | 24 | 1 −11 | 2 −10 | 3 −9 | 4 −8 | 5 −7 | 6 −6 | 7 −5 | 8 −4 | 9 −3 | 10 −2 | 11 −1 |

DATE LINE

Monday
Sunday

Anchorage

Vancouver
Winnipeg
Ottawa
8.30
Lon

Denver
Washington

Los Angeles
New Orleans
Ro

México
Miami

Dakar

Panama
Caracas
Abi

Equator

2.30

Lima

3.00
La Paz
São Paulo

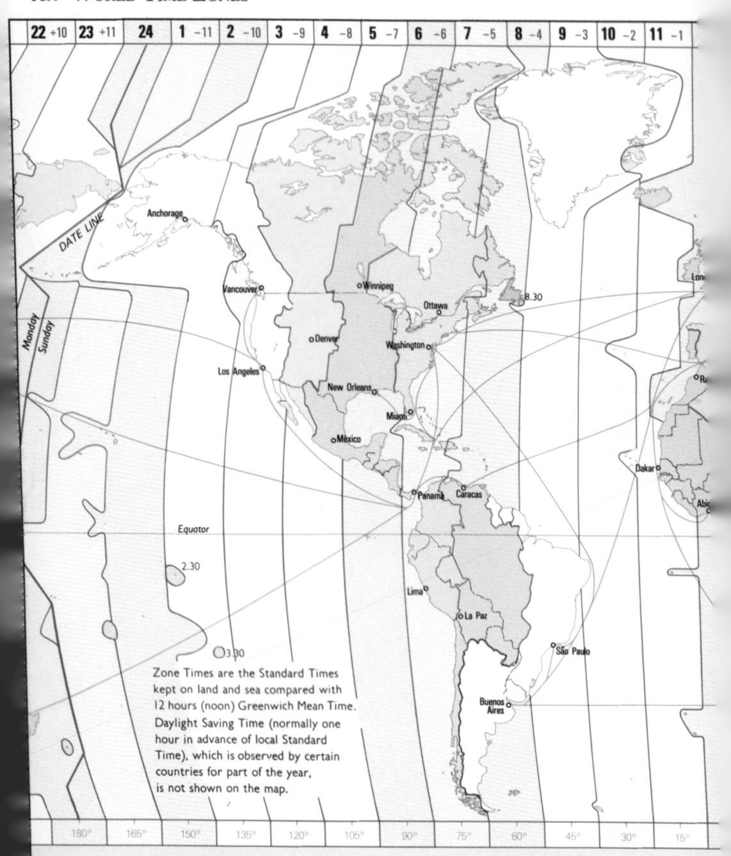

Zone Times are the Standard Times
kept on land and sea compared with
12 hours (noon) Greenwich Mean Time.
Daylight Saving Time (normally one
hour in advance of local Standard
Time), which is observed by certain
countries for part of the year,
is not shown on the map.

Buenos
Aires

| 180° | 165° | 150° | 135° | 120° | 105° | 90° | 75° | 60° | 45° | 30° | 15° |

Journey Times

Sail (via Cape)
164 days

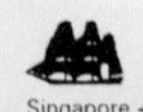

Steam (via Cape)
43 days

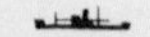

Steam (via Suez)
30 days

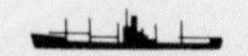

Supertanker
(via Cape)
28 days

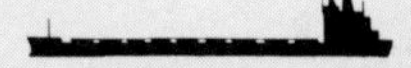

Singapore ←

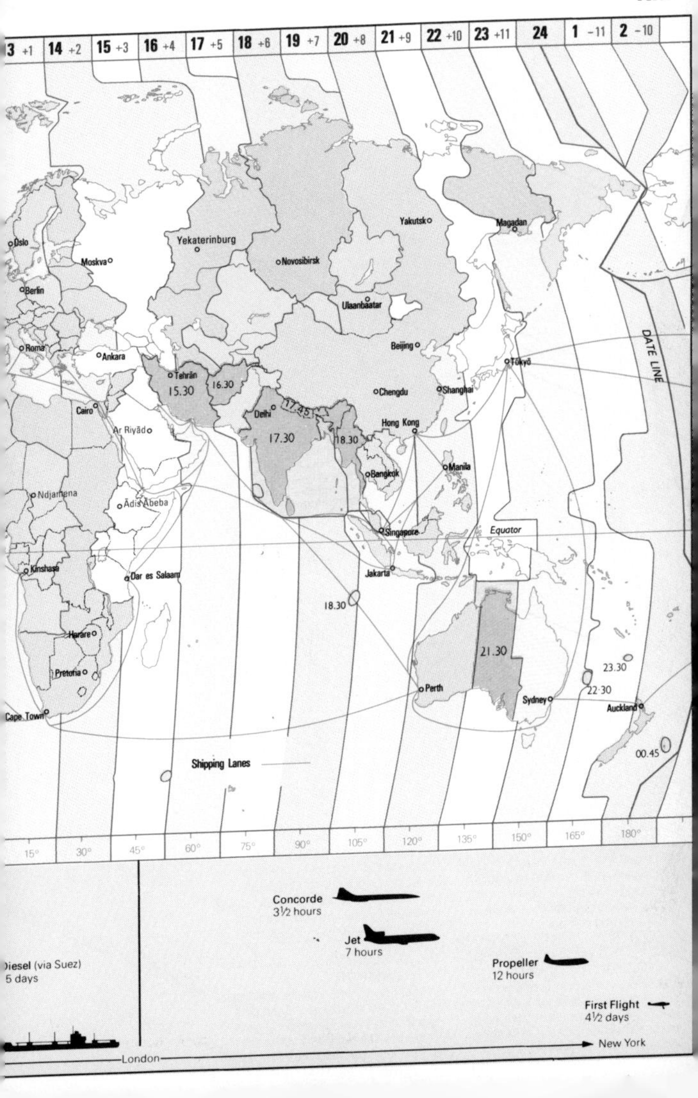

13 +1 14 +2 15 +3 16 +4 17 +5 18 +6 19 +7 20 +8 21 +9 22 +10 23 +11 24 1 −11 2 −10

DATE LINE

Oslo

Moskva

Berlin

Roma

Ankara

Cairo

Ar Riyād

Ndjamena

Adis Abeba

Kinshasa

Dar es Salaam

Harare

Pretoria

Cape Town

Yekaterinburg

Novosibirsk

Yakutsk

Magadan

Ulaanbaatar

Beijing

Chengdu

Shanghai

Tōkyō

Tehrān 15.30

16.30

Delhi 17.30

18.30

Hong Kong

Bangkok

Manila

Singapore

Equator

Jakarta

18.30

21.30

Perth

Sydney 22:30

23.30

Auckland

00.45

Shipping Lanes

15° 30° 45° 60° 75° 90° 105° 120° 135° 150° 165° 180°

Concorde
3½ hours

Jet
7 hours

Propeller
12 hours

First Flight
4½ days

Diesel (via Suez)
5 days

London ➤ New York

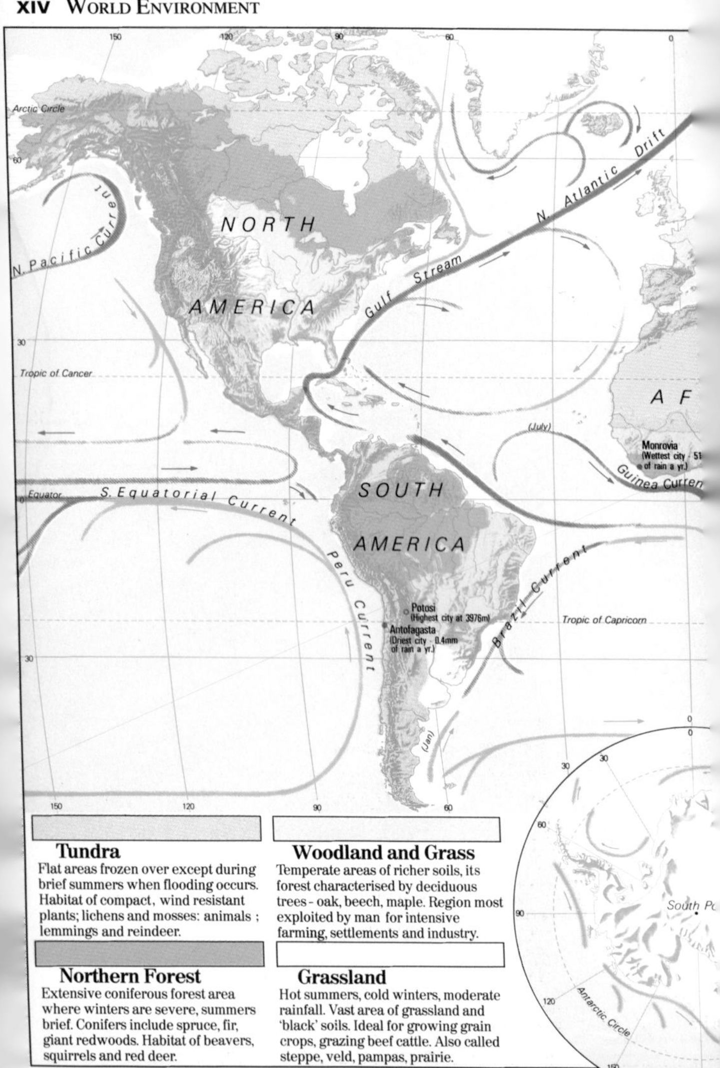

Arctic Circle

N. Pacific Current

NORTH

AMERICA

Gulf Stream

N. Atlantic Drift

Tropic of Cancer

A F

Monrovia
(Wettest city - 51
of rain a yr.)

Guinea Current

Equator

S. Equatorial Current

SOUTH

AMERICA

(July)

Peru Current

Brazil Current

Potosi
Highest city at 3976m)
Antofagasta
(Driest city 0.4mm
of rain a yr.)

Tropic of Capricorn

(July)

South Po

Antarctic Circle

Tundra
Flat areas frozen over except during brief summers when flooding occurs. Habitat of compact, wind resistant plants; lichens and mosses: animals ; lemmings and reindeer.

Northern Forest
Extensive coniferous forest area where winters are severe, summers brief. Conifers include spruce, fir, giant redwoods. Habitat of beavers, squirrels and red deer.

Woodland and Grass
Temperate areas of richer soils, its forest characterised by deciduous trees - oak, beech, maple. Region most exploited by man for intensive farming, settlements and industry.

Grassland
Hot summers, cold winters, moderate rainfall. Vast area of grassland and 'black' soils. Ideal for growing grain crops, grazing beef cattle. Also called steppe, veld, pampas, prairie.

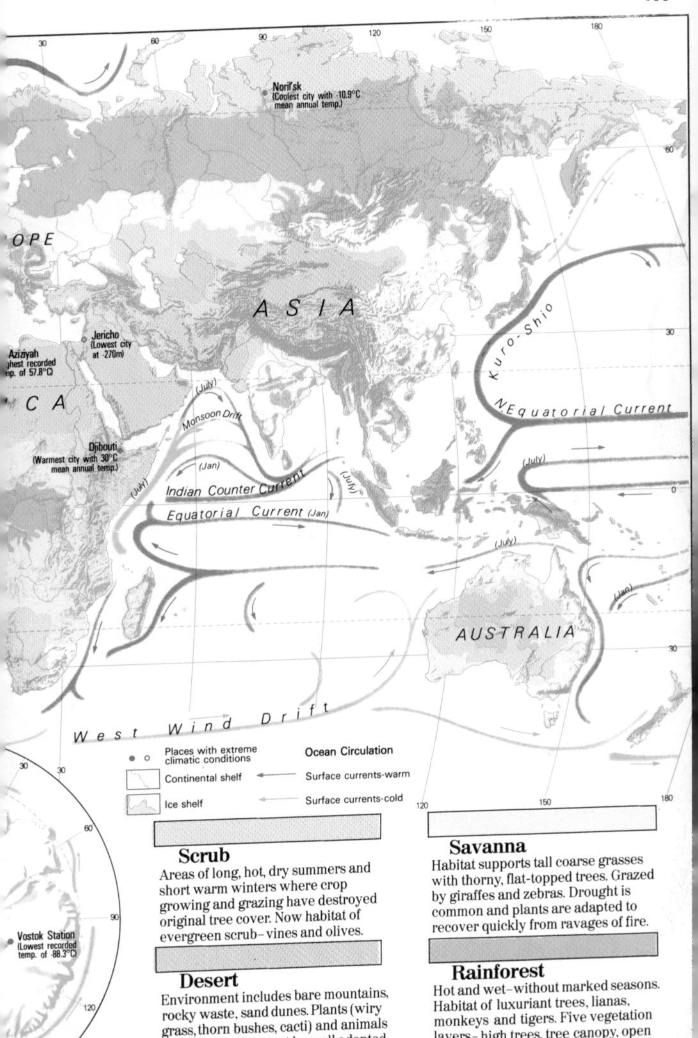

Norilsk
(Coolest city with -10.9°C
mean annual temp.)

O P E

A S I A

Kuro-Shio

N Equatorial Current

C A

Jericho
(Lowest city
at -270m)

Azizīyah
(highest recorded
temp. of 57.8°C)

Djibouti
(Warmest city with 30°C
mean annual temp.)

(July)

Monsoon Drift

(Jan)

Indian Counter Current

Equatorial Current (Jan)

(July)

(July)

(July)

(July)

AUSTRALIA

W e s t   W i n d   D r i f t

30

60

90

Vostok Station
(Lowest recorded
temp. of 88.3°C)

120

150

● ● Places with extreme
climatic conditions

Continental shelf

Ice shelf

Ocean Circulation

⟵ Surface currents-warm

⟵ Surface currents-cold

Scrub
Areas of long, hot, dry summers and
short warm winters where crop
growing and grazing have destroyed
original tree cover. Now habitat of
evergreen scrub–vines and olives.

Desert
Environment includes bare mountains,
rocky waste, sand dunes. Plants (wiry
grass, thorn bushes, cacti) and animals
(lizards, camels) must be well adapted
to extremes of heat and drought.

Savanna
Habitat supports tall coarse grasses
with thorny, flat-topped trees. Grazed
by giraffes and zebras. Drought is
common and plants are adapted to
recover quickly from ravages of fire.

Rainforest
Hot and wet–without marked seasons.
Habitat of luxuriant trees, lianas,
monkeys and tigers. Five vegetation
layers - high trees, tree canopy, open
canopy, shrubs, ground herbs.

BOUNDARIES

▬▬▬▬	International
▬ ▬ ▬ ▬	International under Dispute
· · · · · · ·	Cease Fire Line
▬▬▬▬	Autonomous or State
▬▬▬▬	Administrative
▬▬▬▬	Maritime (National)

LETTERING STYLES

CANADA	Independent Nation
FLORIDA	State, Province or Autonomous Region
Gibraltar (U.K.)	Sovereignty of Dependent Territory
Lothian	Administrative Area
LANGUEDOC	Historic Region
Loire **Vosges**	Physical Feature or Physical Region

TOWNS AND CITIES

Square Symbols denote capital cities. Each settlement is given a symbol according to its relative importance, with type size to match.

▪	●	**New York**	Major City
▪	●	**Montréal**	City
▫	○	Ottawa	Small City
▪	●	**Québec**	Large Town
▫	○	St John's	Town
▫	○	Yorkton	Small Town
○	○	Jasper	Village
			Built-up-area

LAKE FEATURES

	Permanent
	Seasonal

OTHER FEATURES

	River
	Seasonal River
=	Pass, Gorge
	Dam, Barrage
	Waterfall, Rapid
	Aqueduct
	Reef
▲4231	Summit, Peak
.217	Spot Height, Depth
‿	Well
△	Oil Field
▲	Gas Field
Gas / Oil	Oil/Natural Gas Pipeline
Gemsbok Nat Pk	National Park
∴UR	Historic Site
	Main Railway
	Other Railway
- - - - - -	Under Construction
→···→	Rail Tunnel
- - - - - -	Rail Ferry
	Canal
⊕	International Airport
✦	Other Airport

For pages 102-103, 104-105 only:

0	Sea Level
200m	
2000m	
4000m	
6000m	
	Depth

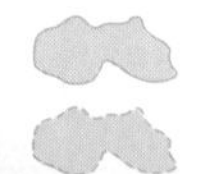

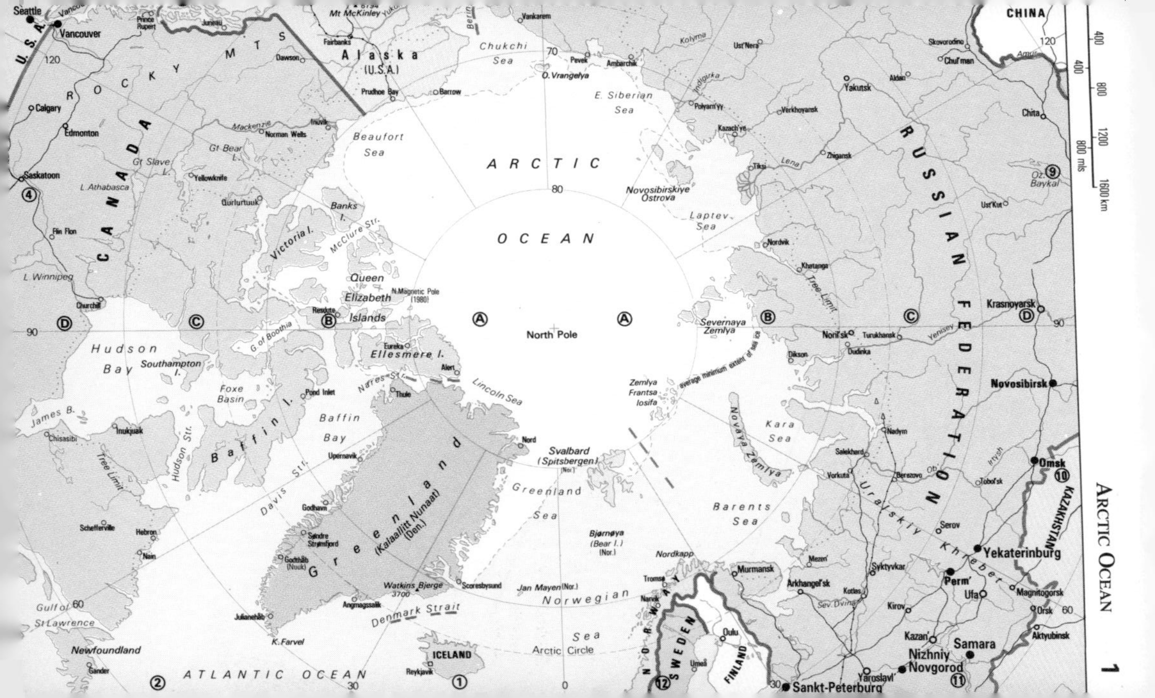
400 800 1200 1600 km
400 800 mls
ARCTIC OCEAN
North Pole
RUSSIAN FEDERATION
CHINA
KAZAKHSTAN
FINLAND
SWEDEN
NORWAY
ICELAND
CANADA
ROCKY MTS
U.S.A.
Alaska (U.S.A.)
Greenland (Kalaallit Nunaat) (Den.)
Chukchi Sea
E. Siberian Sea
Laptev Sea
Kara Sea
Barents Sea
Beaufort Sea
Lincoln Sea
Greenland Sea
Norwegian Sea
Baffin Bay
Hudson Bay
Foxe Basin
ATLANTIC OCEAN
Arctic Circle
Tree Limit
average minimum extent of sea ice
Novaya Zemlya
Severnaya Zemlya
Zemlya Frantsa Iosifa
Novosibirskiye Ostrova
O. Vrangelya
Svalbard (Spitsbergen) (Nor.)
Bjørnøya (Bear I.) (Nor.)
Jan Mayen (Nor.)
Queen Elizabeth Islands
Ellesmere I.
Banks I.
Victoria I.
Baffin I.
Southampton I.
Newfoundland
Uralskiy Khrebet
Davis Str.
Hudson Str.
Denmark Strait
Nares Str.
McClure Str.
G. of Boothia
Gulf of St Lawrence
James B.
N. Magnetic Pole (1980)
Watkins Bjerge 3700
Mt McKinley
Seattle
Vancouver
Prince Rupert
Juneau
Fairbanks
Dawson
Prudhoe Bay
Barrow
Inuvik
Norman Wells
Calgary
Edmonton
Saskatoon
Flin Flon
Churchill
Yellowknife
Qurlurtuuk
Resolute
Eureka
Alert
Thule
Pond Inlet
Nord
Upernavik
Godhavn
Søndre Strømfjord
Godthåb (Nuuk)
Angmagssalik
Julianehåb
K. Farvel
Scoresbysund
Inukjuak
Chisasibi
Schefferville
Hebron
Nain
Gander
Reykjavik
L. Athabasca
L. Winnipeg
Gt Slave L.
Gt Bear L.
Mackenzie
Vankarem
Pevek
Ambarchik
Kolyma
Indigirka
Ust'Nera
Polyarnyy
Kazach'ye
Verkhoyansk
Yakutsk
Aldan
Skovorodino
Chul'man
Amur
Chita
Zhigansk
Tiksi
Lena
Oz. Baykal
Ust'Kut
Nordvik
Khatanga
Noril'sk
Turukhansk
Dudinka
Dikson
Yenisey
Krasnoyarsk
Novosibirsk
Nadym
Salekhard
Vorkuta
Berezovo
Ob'
Irtysh
Tobol'sk
Omsk
Serov
Yekaterinburg
Perm'
Ufa
Magnitogorsk
Orsk
Aktyubinsk
Samara
Kazan'
Nizhniy Novgorod
Yaroslavl'
Kirov
Kotlas
Syktyvkar
Mezen'
Arkhangel'sk
Sev. Dvina
Murmansk
Nordkapp
Tromsø
Narvik
Oulu
Umeå
Sankt-Peterburg

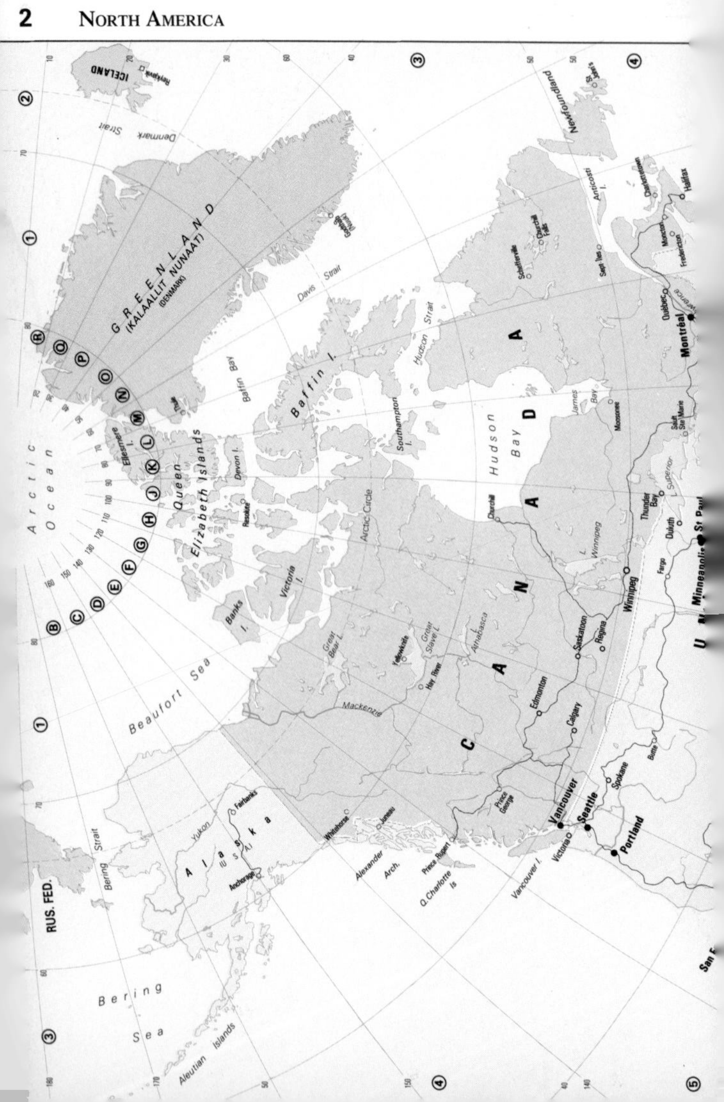

Arctic Ocean
GREENLAND
(KALAALLIT NUNAAT)
(DENMARK)
ICELAND
Reykjavik
Denmark Strait
Davis Strait
Baffin Bay
Baffin I.
Thule
Ellesmere I.
Queen Elizabeth Islands
Devon I.
Resolute
Banks I.
Victoria I.
Southampton I.
Hudson Strait
Hudson Bay
James Bay
Moosonee
Arctic Circle
Beaufort Sea
Great Bear L.
Great Slave L.
Yellowknife
Hay River
Mackenzie
L. Athabasca
CANADA
Churchill
L. Winnipeg
Winnipeg
Edmonton
Calgary
Saskatoon
Regina
Thunder Bay
L. Superior
Sault Ste Marie
Duluth
Fargo
Minneapolis
St Paul
Montréal
Québec
Fredericton
Moncton
Charlottetown
Halifax
Anticosti I.
Sept Iles
Schefferville
Churchill Falls
Newfoundland
St John's
RUS. FED.
Bering Strait
Bering Sea
Aleutian Islands
Alaska
U S A
Yukon
Fairbanks
Anchorage
Whitehorse
Juneau
Alexander Arch.
Prince Rupert
Q. Charlotte Is
Prince George
Vancouver
Vancouver I.
Victoria
Seattle
Portland
Spokane
Butte

250 500 750 1000 1250 km
250 500 750 mls

⑤ ⑥ ⑦ BARBADOS ⑧

ATLANTIC OCEAN

Bermuda (UK)

Philadelphia
Washington
Baltimore
Norfolk

Indianapolis
Atlanta
Memphis
Nashville
Birmingham
Charleston
Jacksonville

St Louis
Kansas City

A M E R I C A

O F

Ohio

Mississippi

New Orleans
Houston
Dallas
Fort Worth
San Antonio

THE BAHAMAS
Miami
Tampa
Nassau

CUBA
Habana

DOMINICAN REP.
Sto Domingo
HAITI
Port-au-Prince
Guantánamo
Kingston
JAMAICA

Pto. Rico (U.S.A.)

Netherlands Antilles

DOMINICA
ST LUCIA
ST VINCENT & THE GRENADINES
GRENADA
TRINIDAD & TOBAGO

CARIBBEAN SEA

Caracas
Maracaibo
VENEZUELA

BRAZIL

Gulf of Mexico

Mérida

BELIZE
Belmopan
HONDURAS
Tegucigalpa
GUATEMALA
Guatemala
S.Salvador
EL SALVADOR
NICARAGUA
Managua
COSTA RICA
S.José

Panamá
PANAMA
Barranquilla
Sta Marta
Medellín
Bogotá
COLOMBIA

Quito
ECUADOR
PERU

I. del Coco (CR)

Tampico
Veracruz
Rio Grande
Monterrey
Torreón
Chihuahua
El Paso
Albuquerque
México
Acapulco

M E X I C O

Guadalajara
Mazatlán

Phoenix
Tucson

Los Angeles
San Diego

G. de California

Guadalupe (Mex.)
Is Revilla Gigedo (Mex.)

Clipperton (Fr.)

Malpelo (Col.)

Galápagos Is (Ec.)

PACIFIC OCEAN

Tropic of Cancer

Equator

⑥ ⑦ ⑧

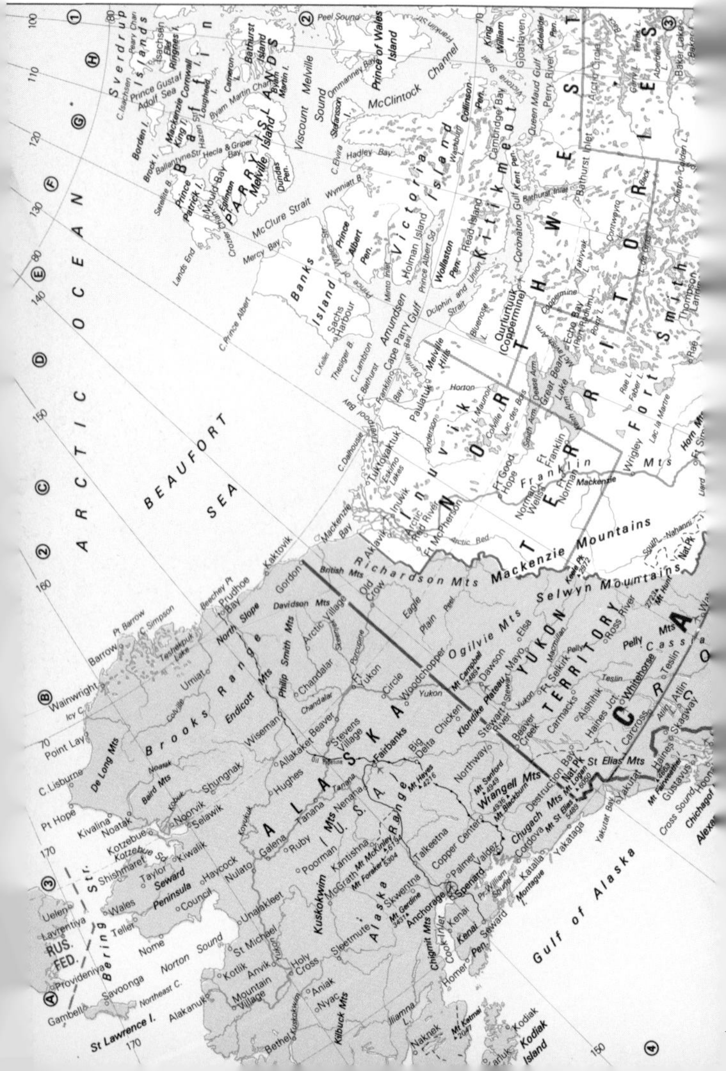

ARCTIC OCEAN

BEAUFORT SEA

Sverdrup Islands

PARRY ISLANDS

Prince of Wales Island

Banks Island

Victoria Island

NORTHWEST TERRITORIES

Mackenzie Mountains

Selwyn Mountains

Richardson Mts

Brooks Range

Endicott Mts

ALASKA U.S.A.

Alaska Range

Mt McKinley

YUKON TERRITORY

St Elias Mts

Wrangell Mts

Chugach Mts

CANADA

Gulf of Alaska

Kodiak Island

Bering Strait

RUS. FED.

St Lawrence I.

200   400   600 km
100   200   300 mls

MANITOBA
SASKATCHEWAN
ALBERTA
BRITISH COLUMBIA
NORTH DAKOTA
SOUTH DAKOTA
WYOMING
MONTANA
IDAHO
OREGON
WASHINGTON

CANADA
U.S.

Winnipeg
Portage la Prairie
Brandon
Grand Rapids
The Pas
Flin Flon
Prince Albert
Saskatoon
Regina
Moose Jaw
Swift Current
Medicine Hat
Lethbridge
Calgary
Red Deer
Edmonton
Prince George
Kamloops
Kelowna
Penticton
Vancouver
Victoria
Nanaimo
Prince Rupert
Kitimat
Queen Charlotte Islands
Seattle
Tacoma
Olympia
Portland
Salem
Eugene
Astoria
Aberdeen
Spokane
Yakima
Walla Walla
Pendleton
Boise
Twin Falls
Pocatello
Idaho Falls
Butte
Helena
Missoula
Great Falls
Billings
Bozeman
Bismarck
Fargo
Grand Forks
Minot
Williston
Aberdeen
Pierre
Rapid City
Huron
Sioux Falls
Watertown
Mitchell

Wood Buffalo National Park

PACIFIC OCEAN

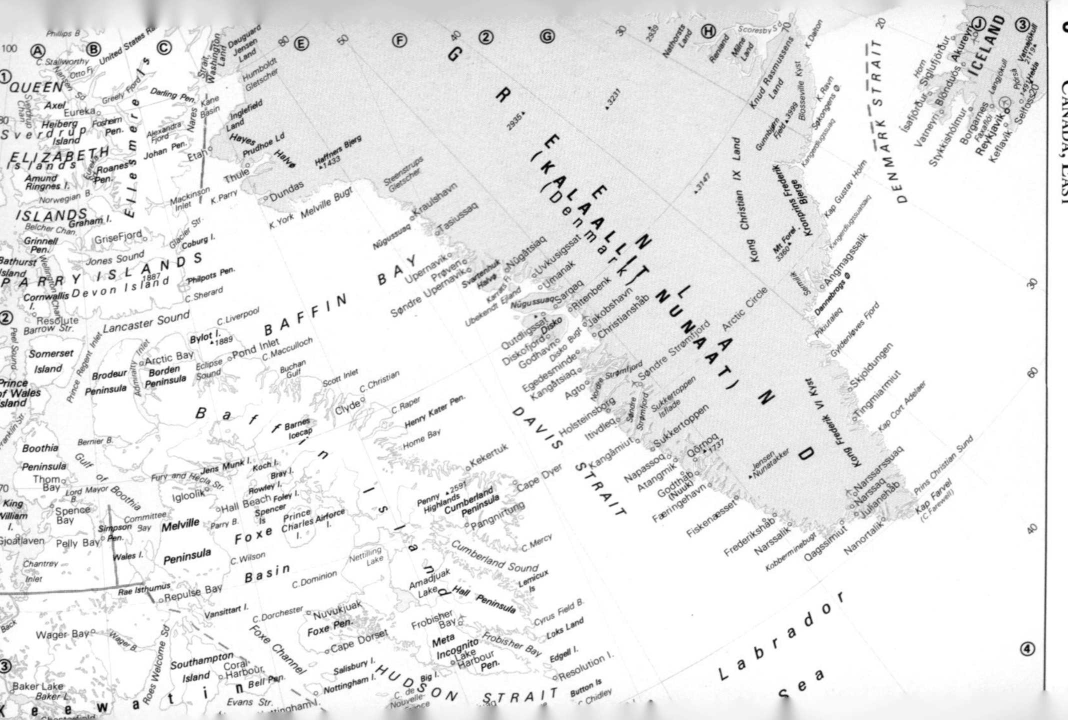
GREENLAND
(KALAALLIT NUNAAT)
(Denmark)
ICELAND
DENMARK STRAIT
DAVIS STRAIT
Labrador Sea
BAFFIN BAY
Baffin Island
Foxe Basin
Foxe Channel
HUDSON STRAIT
QUEEN ELIZABETH ISLANDS
PARRY ISLANDS
Sverdrup Islands
Ellesmere Is
Devon Island
Axel Heiberg Island
Somerset Island
Prince of Wales Island
Boothia Peninsula
Melville Peninsula
Southampton Island
Keewatin
Gulf of Boothia
Lancaster Sound
Jones Sound
Cumberland Sound
Frobisher Bay
Arctic Circle
Reykjavík
Keflavík
Akureyri
Thule
Dundas
Upernavik
Godthåb (Nuuk)
Jakobshavn
Christianshåb
Holsteinsborg
Frederikshåb
Julianehåb
Angmagssalik
Kong Christian IX Land
Kong Frederik VI Kyst
Knud Rasmussens Land
Kronprins Frederik Bjerge
Melville Bugt
Pond Inlet
Clyde
Igloolik
Hall Beach
Resolute
GriseFjord
Eureka
Coral Harbour
Cape Dorset
Repulse Bay
Pangnirtung
Pelly Bay
Spence Bay
Gjoa Haven
Baker Lake
Wager Bay
Roes Welcome Sd
Nettilling Lake
Amadjuak Lake
Barnes Icecap
Bylot I.
Resolution I.
Arctic Bay
Cape Dyer
Prins Christian Sund
Kap Farvel (C. Farewell)
Nares
Kane Basin

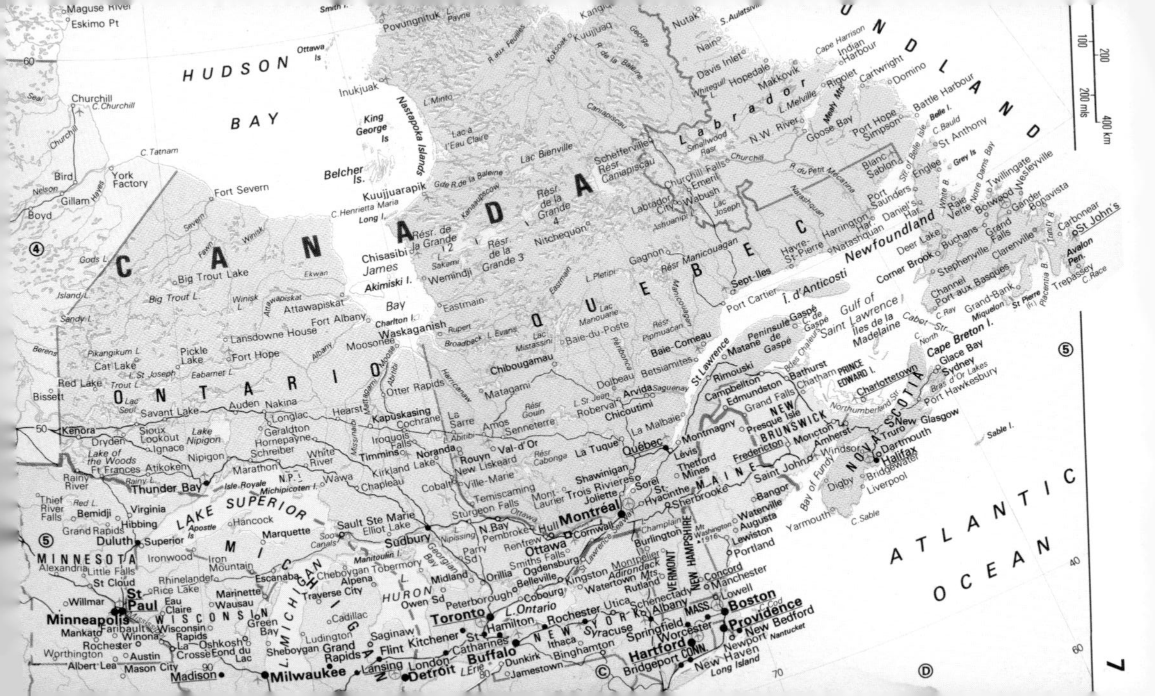
200
400 km
100
200 mls
HUDSON BAY
CANADA
NEWFOUNDLAND
Labrador
ONTARIO
QUEBEC
ATLANTIC OCEAN
James Bay
Akimiski I.
Belcher Is.
King George Is
Nastapoka Islands
Newfoundland
Gulf of Saint Lawrence
Î. d'Anticosti
Cape Breton I.
PRINCE EDWARD I.
NEW BRUNSWICK
NOVA SCOTIA
Bay of Fundy
MAINE
NEW HAMPSHIRE
VERMONT
NEW YORK
MASS.
CONN.
MINNESOTA
WISCONSIN
MICHIGAN
LAKE SUPERIOR
L. HURON
L. Ontario
L. Erie
Québec
Montréal
Ottawa
Toronto
Hamilton
Buffalo
Detroit
Milwaukee
Minneapolis
St Paul
Duluth
Thunder Bay
Sudbury
Sault Ste Marie
Timmins
Boston
Providence
Hartford
Albany
Halifax
St John's
Charlottetown
Sept-Îles
Churchill
Kenora
Madison
Sable I.

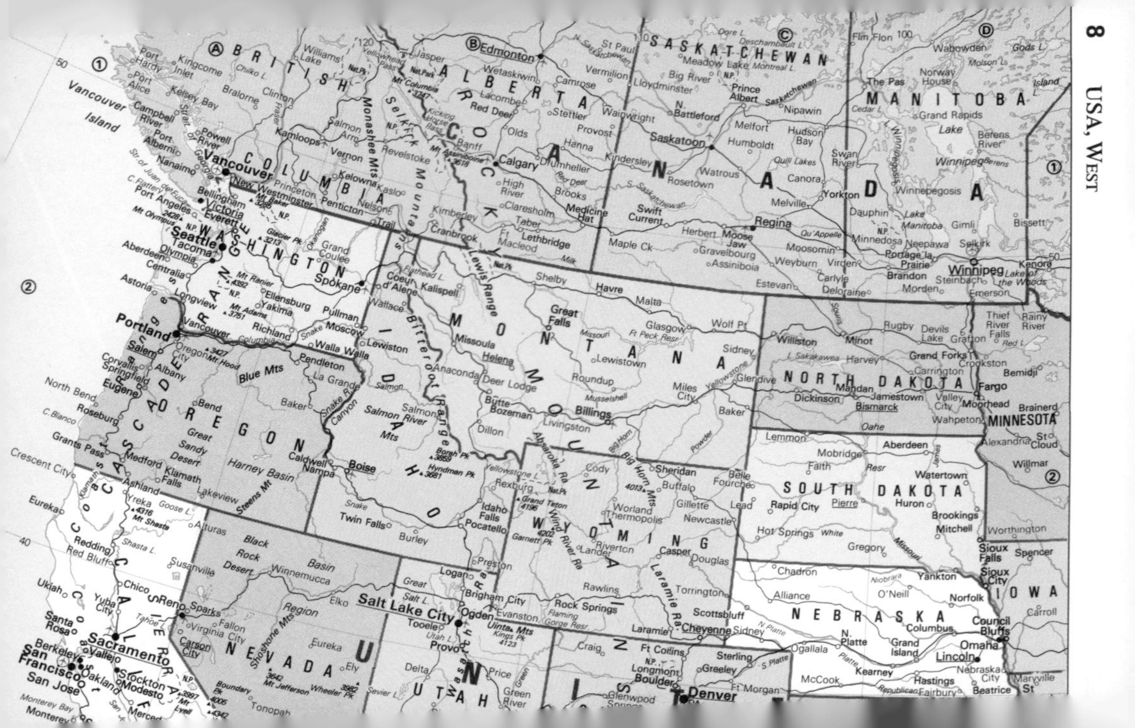
BRITISH COLUMBIA
ALBERTA
SASKATCHEWAN
MANITOBA
CANADA
ROCKY MOUNTAINS
WASHINGTON
OREGON
IDAHO
MONTANA
WYOMING
NORTH DAKOTA
SOUTH DAKOTA
NEBRASKA
MINNESOTA
IOWA
NEVADA
UTAH
CALIFORNIA
CASCADE RANGE
COAST RANGES
Vancouver Island
Vancouver
Victoria
Seattle
Tacoma
Olympia
Spokane
Portland
Salem
Eugene
Boise
Helena
Great Falls
Billings
Bismarck
Pierre
Cheyenne
Denver
Salt Lake City
Ogden
Provo
Carson City
Reno
Sacramento
San Francisco
Oakland
San Jose
Edmonton
Calgary
Saskatoon
Regina
Winnipeg
Lake Winnipeg
Lake Manitoba
Lewis Range
Bitterroot Range
Selkirk Mountains
Monashee Mts
Big Horn Mts
Wind River Ra
Laramie Ra
Uinta Mts
Salmon River Mts
Blue Mts
Great Basin
Black Rock Desert
Great Sandy Desert
Harney Basin
Great Salt L.
Str. of Juan de Fuca

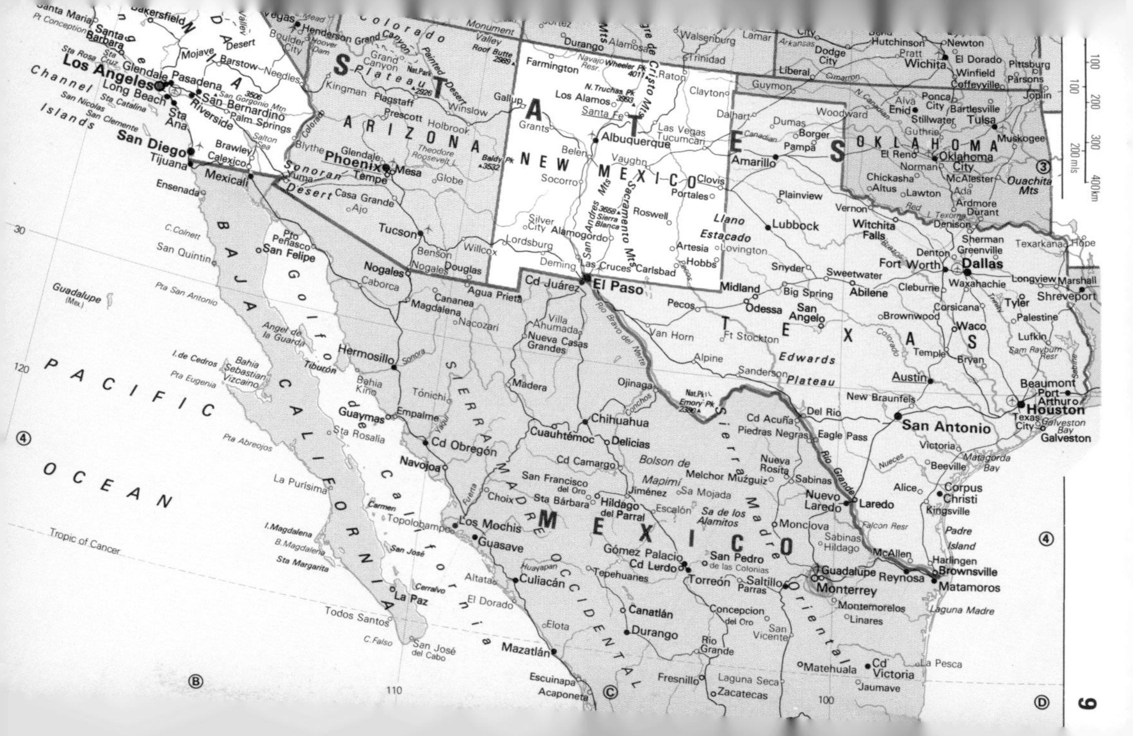

100 200 300 400km
100 200 mls
UNITED STATES
ARIZONA
NEW MEXICO
OKLAHOMA
TEXAS
MEXICO
BAJA CALIFORNIA
Golfo de California
PACIFIC OCEAN
SIERRA MADRE OCCIDENTAL
Sierra Madre Oriental
Colorado Plateau
Painted Desert
Sonoran Desert
Sacramento Mts
San Andres Mts
Llano Estacado
Edwards Plateau
Bolson de Mapimí
Rio Grande
Rio Bravo del Norte
Tropic of Cancer
Channel Islands
Los Angeles
Long Beach
Glendale
Pasadena
San Bernardino
Riverside
Palm Springs
San Diego
Tijuana
Mexicali
Calexico
Ensenada
Phoenix
Mesa
Tempe
Tucson
Nogales
Flagstaff
Albuquerque
Santa Fe
Los Alamos
Roswell
Carlsbad
El Paso
Cd Juárez
Amarillo
Lubbock
Midland
Odessa
Abilene
Fort Worth
Dallas
Waco
Austin
San Antonio
Houston
Galveston
Beaumont
Corpus Christi
Laredo
Nuevo Laredo
McAllen
Reynosa
Brownsville
Matamoros
Oklahoma City
Tulsa
Wichita
Shreveport
Chihuahua
Hermosillo
Guaymas
Cd Obregón
Los Mochis
Culiacán
Mazatlán
La Paz
Durango
Torreón
Saltillo
Monterrey
Cd Victoria
Zacatecas
Tiburón
30
120
110
100

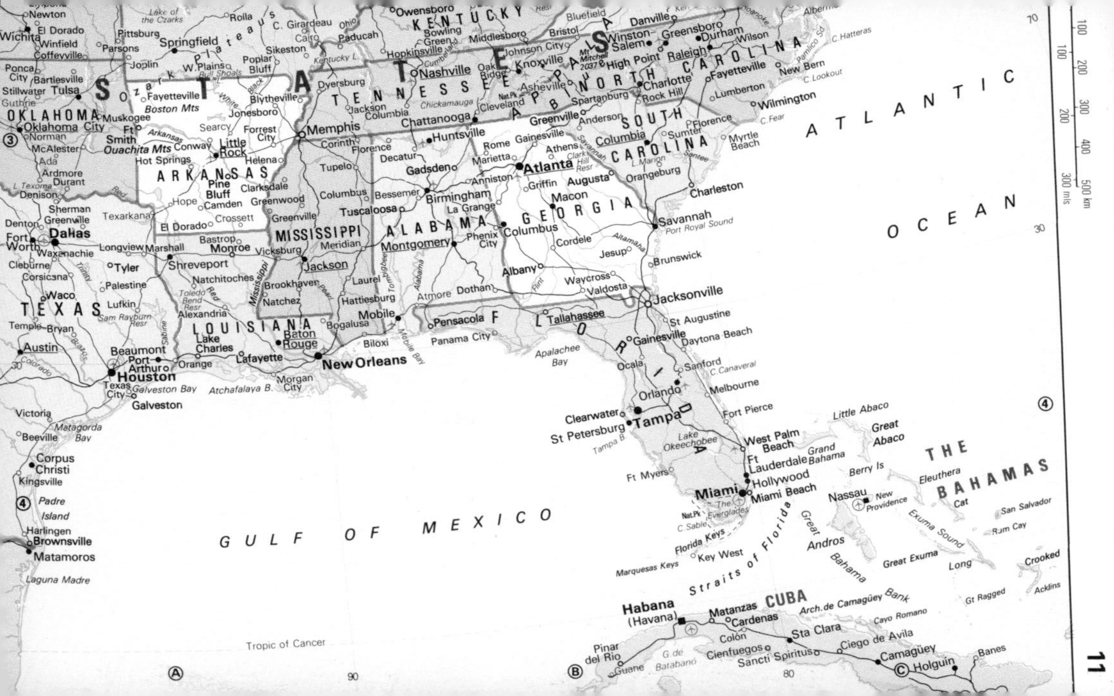
100 200 300 400 500 km
100 200 300 mls
ATLANTIC
OCEAN
GULF OF MEXICO
THE BAHAMAS
CUBA
Straits of Florida
Tropic of Cancer
KENTUCKY
TENNESSEE
NORTH CAROLINA
SOUTH CAROLINA
GEORGIA
ALABAMA
MISSISSIPPI
LOUISIANA
ARKANSAS
OKLAHOMA
TEXAS
Boston Mts
Ouachita Mts
Atlanta
New Orleans
Houston
Dallas
Fort Worth
Memphis
Nashville
Jacksonville
Tampa
Miami
Charleston
Savannah
Charlotte
Raleigh
Durham
Greensboro
Winston-Salem
Knoxville
Chattanooga
Birmingham
Montgomery
Mobile
Jackson
Baton Rouge
Shreveport
Little Rock
Tulsa
Oklahoma City
Wichita
Springfield
Austin
Waco
Corpus Christi
Brownsville
Matamoros
Galveston
Beaumont
Port Arthur
Lake Charles
Lafayette
Pensacola
Tallahassee
Gainesville
Orlando
St Petersburg
Clearwater
Ft Myers
Daytona Beach
St Augustine
West Palm Beach
Ft Lauderdale
Hollywood
Miami Beach
Key West
Florida Keys
Marquesas Keys
Lake Okeechobee
Habana (Havana)
Matanzas
Cardenas
Cienfuegos
Sta Clara
Sancti Spiritus
Ciego de Avila
Camagüey
Holguín
Pinar del Rio
Nassau
New Providence
Grand Bahama
Great Abaco
Little Abaco
Berry Is
Andros
Eleuthera
Cat
Exuma Sound
Great Exuma
Long
San Salvador
Rum Cay
Crooked
Acklins
Gt Ragged
Apalachee Bay
Mobile Bay
Galveston Bay
Matagorda Bay
Laguna Madre
Padre Island
C. Hatteras
C. Lookout
C. Fear
C. Canaveral
Mississippi
Red
Arkansas
Tombigbee
Alabama
Pearl
Sabine
Trinity
Brazos
Colorado
Savannah
Altamaha
Flint
90
80
30
70

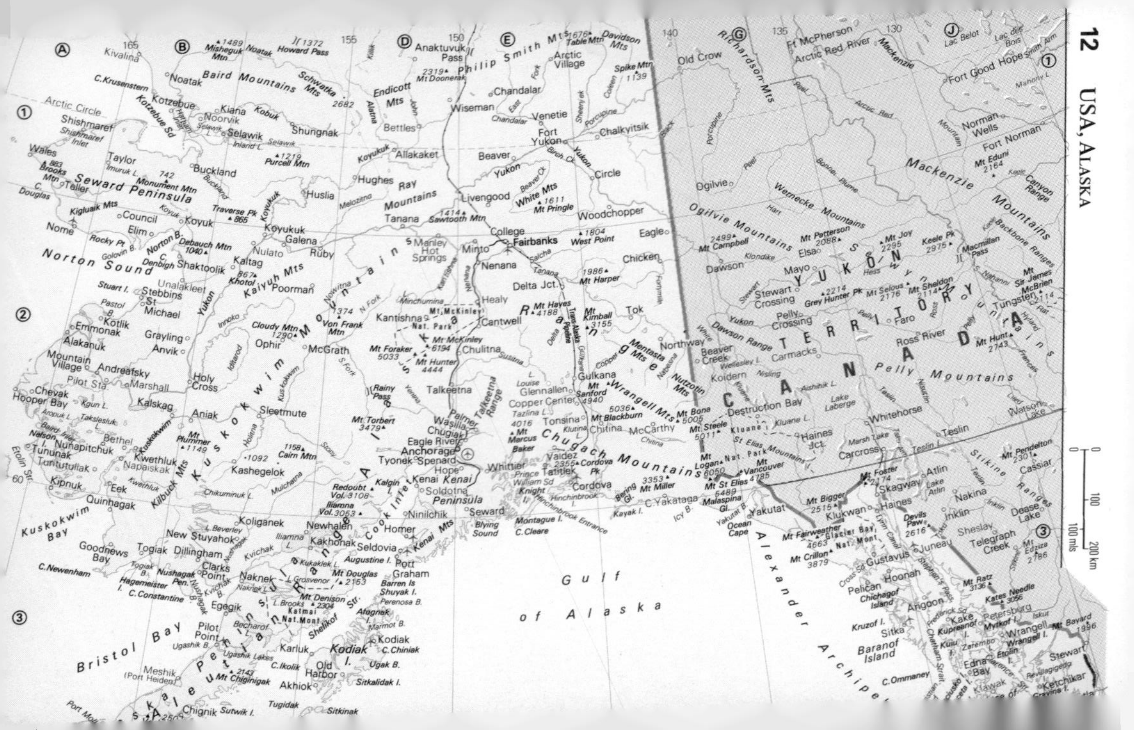

0 100 200 km
0 100 mls
Gulf of Alaska
Bristol Bay
Norton Sound
Kotzebue Sd
Kuskokwim Bay
Alexander Archipelago
Seward Peninsula
Kenai Peninsula
Baird Mountains
Endicott Mts
Philip Smith Mts
Richardson Mts
Ogilvie Mountains
Wernecke Mountains
Mackenzie Mountains
Pelly Mountains
Stikine Ranges
Kuskokwim Mountains
Kaiyuh Mts
Ray Mountains
Chugach Mountains
Wrangell Mts
St Elias Mountains
Talkeetna Range
Dawson Range
Mentasta Mts
Nutzotin Mts
Kilbuck Mts
YUKON TERRITORY
CANADA
Mt McKinley 6194
Mt Foraker 5033
Mt Hunter 4444
Mt Logan 6050
Mt St Elias 5489
Mt Vancouver 4785
Mt Steele 5011
Mt Bona 5005
Mt Blackburn 5036
Mt Sanford 4940
Mt Hayes 4188
Mt Fairweather 4663
Mt Crillon 3879
Mt Marcus Baker 4016
Redoubt Vol. 3108
Iliamna Vol. 3053
Trans-Alaska Pipeline
Arctic Circle
Anchorage
Fairbanks
College
Nome
Kotzebue
Juneau
Whitehorse
Dawson
Skagway
Haines
Sitka
Valdez
Cordova
Seward
Homer
Kodiak
Bethel
Tok
Delta Jct.
Fort Yukon
Circle
Eagle
Old Crow
Ft McPherson
Arctic Red River
Fort Good Hope
Norman Wells
Fort Norman
Yakutat
Glacier Bay Nat. Mon.
Katmai Nat. Mon.
Mt McKinley Nat. Park

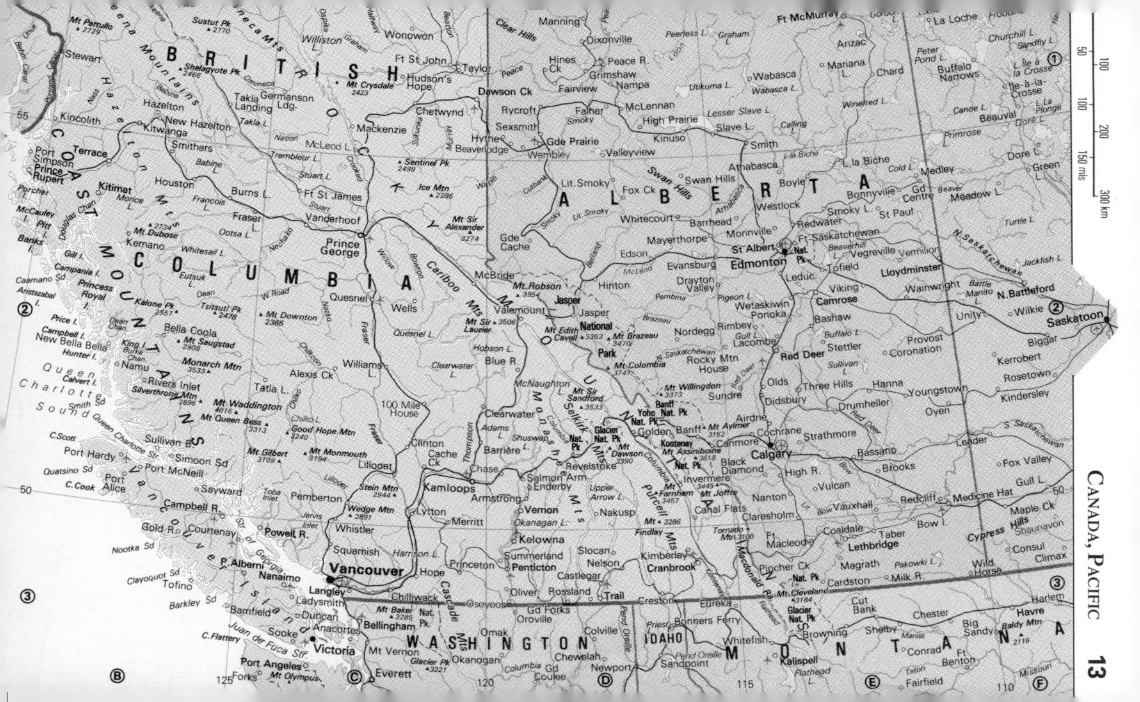
100
200
300 km
50
100
150 mls
BRITISH COLUMBIA
ALBERTA
MONTANA
WASHINGTON
IDAHO
COAST MOUNTAINS
Cariboo Mts
Monashee Mts
Selkirk Mts
Purcell Mts
Rocky Mts
Cascade Mts
Vancouver
Victoria
Calgary
Edmonton
Saskatoon
Prince George
Prince Rupert
Kamloops
Kelowna
Penticton
Vernon
Nanaimo
Lethbridge
Medicine Hat
Red Deer
Lloydminster
N. Battleford
Kitimat
Terrace
Quesnel
Williams L.
Jasper
Banff
Revelstoke
Nelson
Trail
Cranbrook
Dawson Ck
Ft St John
Ft McMurray
Bella Coola
Port Hardy
Campbell R.
Courtenay
Port Alberni
Bellingham
Everett
Port Angeles
Kalispell
Havre
Str. of Georgia
Juan de Fuca Str.
55
50
125
120
115
110

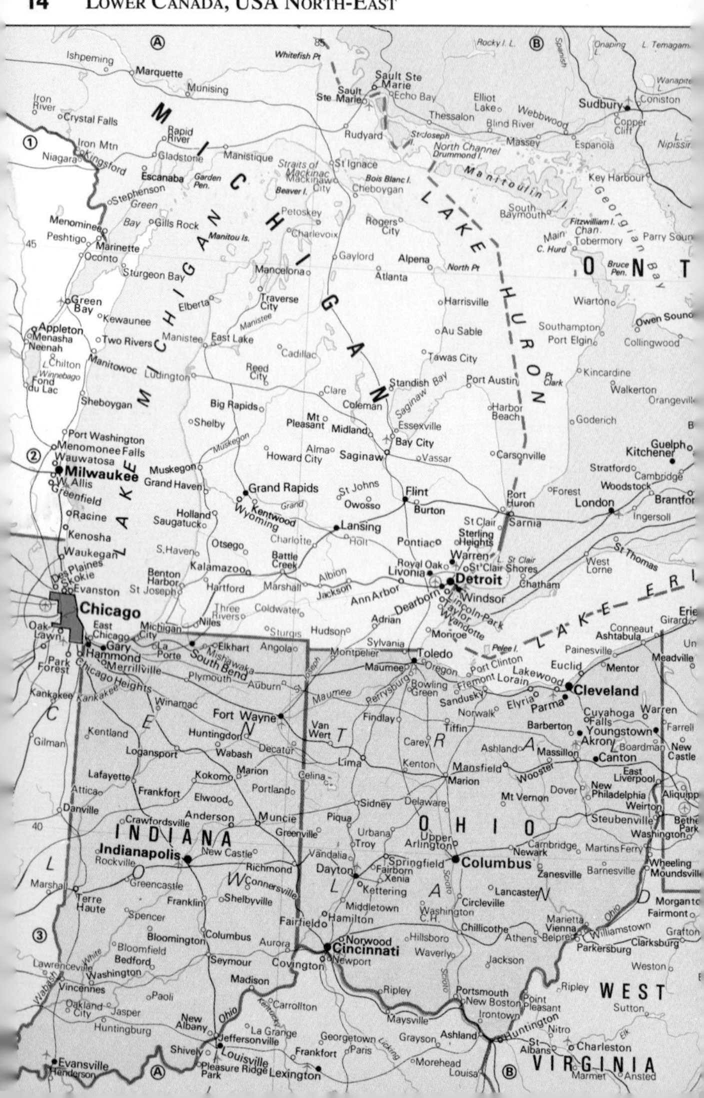

MICHIGAN
LAKE HURON
LAKE MICHIGAN
LAKE ERIE
ONT
INDIANA
OHIO
CENTRAL
WEST VIRGINIA
Manitoulin I.
Georgian Bay
North Channel
Straits of Mackinac
Saginaw Bay
Green Bay
Ishpeming
Marquette
Munising
Iron River
Crystal Falls
Iron Mtn
Niagara
Kingsford
Rapid River
Gladstone
Manistique
Escanaba
Garden Pen.
Stephenson
Menominee
Peshtigo
Marinette
Oconto
Sturgeon Bay
Gills Rock
Manitou Is.
Green Bay
Kewaunee
Appleton
Menasha
Neenah
Chilton
Winnebago
Fond du Lac
Two Rivers
Manitowoc
Sheboygan
Port Washington
Menomonee Falls
Wauwatosa
Milwaukee
W. Allis
Greenfield
Racine
Kenosha
Waukegan
Des Plaines
Skokie
Evanston
Chicago
Oak Lawn
Park Forest
East Chicago
Gary
Hammond
Merrillville
Chicago Heights
Kankakee
Gilman
Whitefish Pt
Sault Ste Marie
Echo Bay
Rudyard
St Joseph I.
Drummond I.
St Ignace
Mackinaw City
Bois Blanc I.
Beaver I.
Cheboygan
Petoskey
Charlevoix
Rogers City
Gaylord
Alpena
Atlanta
Mancelona
North Pt
Traverse City
Elberta
Manistee
East Lake
Harrisville
Au Sable
Cadillac
Tawas City
Reed City
Ludington
Clare
Standish
Port Austin
Coleman
Big Rapids
Shelby
Mt Pleasant
Midland
Essexville
Bay City
Harbor Beach
Muskegon
Alma
Howard City
Saginaw
Vassar
Carsonville
Grand Haven
Grand Rapids
St Johns
Owosso
Flint
Burton
Port Huron
Sarnia
Holland
Saugatuck
Kentwood
Wyoming
Lansing
Charlotte
Holt
Pontiac
St Clair
Sterling Heights
Otsego
S.Haven
Battle Creek
Warren
Royal Oak
St Clair Shores
Livonia
Detroit
Windsor
Kalamazoo
Benton Harbor
St Joseph
Hartford
Marshall
Albion
Jackson
Ann Arbor
Dearborn
Lincoln Park
Taylor
Wyandotte
Three Rivers
Coldwater
Niles
Adrian
Monroe
Sturgis
Hudson
Michigan City
La Porte
Elkhart
South Bend
Mishawaka
Angola
Sylvania
Montpelier
Toledo
Maumee
Oregon
Plymouth
Auburn
Bowling Green
Fremont
Port Clinton
Pelee I.
Sandusky
Lorain
Lakewood
Cleveland
Euclid
Mentor
Painesville
Ashtabula
Conneaut
Erie
Girard
Meadville
Winamac
Fort Wayne
Van Wert
Findlay
Tiffin
Norwalk
Elyria
Parma
Cuyahoga Falls
Warren
Farrell
Barberton
Youngstown
Akron
Boardman
New Castle
Kentland
Huntingdon
Wabash
Decatur
Carey
Ashland
Massillon
Canton
Logansport
Lima
Kenton
Mansfield
Wooster
Marion
East Liverpool
Lafayette
Kokomo
Marion
Celina
Attica
Frankfort
Elwood
Portland
Dover
New Philadelphia
Mt Vernon
Aliquippa
Weirton
Steubenville
Danville
Sidney
Delaware
Crawfordsville
Anderson
Muncie
Piqua
Greenville
Urbana
Troy
Upper Arlington
Washington
Cambridge
Newark
Martins Ferry
Indianapolis
Rockville
New Castle
Vandalia
Richmond
Springfield
Columbus
Dayton
Fairborn
Xenia
Kettering
Connersville
Zanesville
Barnesville
Wheeling
Moundsville
Marshall
Terre Haute
Greencastle
Franklin
Shelbyville
Lancaster
Circleville
Middletown
Hamilton
Washington C.H.
Morgantown
Fairmont
Spencer
Bloomington
Columbus
Fairfield
Chillicothe
Marietta
Vienna
Belpre
Athens
Williamstown
Grafton
Parkersburg
Clarksburg
Bloomfield
Bedford
Aurora
Norwood
Cincinnati
Hillsboro
Waverly
Newport
Covington
Seymour
Jackson
Weston
Lawrenceville
Washington
Vincennes
Madison
Ripley
Portsmouth
New Boston
Point Pleasant
Ripley
Sutton
Paoli
Carrollton
Maysville
Ironton
Oakland City
Jasper
Huntingburg
New Albany
Jeffersonville
La Grange
Georgetown
Grayson
Ashland
Huntington
Nitro
St Albans
Charleston
Shively
Louisville
Frankfort
Paris
Morehead
Louisa
Marmet
Ansted
Evansville
Henderson
Pleasure Ridge Park
Lexington
Sudbury
Coniston
Onaping L.
L. Temagami
Wanapitei L.
Rocky L. L.
Spanish
Elliot Lake
Thessalon
Webbwood
Blind River
Massey
Copper Cliff
Espanola
L. Nipissing
Key Harbour
South Baymouth
Fitzwilliam I.
Main Chan.
C. Hurd
Tobermory
Parry Sound
Bruce Pen.
Wiarton
Owen Sound
Southampton
Port Elgin
Collingwood
Pt Clark
Kincardine
Walkerton
Orangeville
Goderich
Guelph
Kitchener
Stratford
Cambridge
Woodstock
Brantford
Forest
London
Ingersoll
St Thomas
West Lorne
Chatham
L. St Clair
Ohio
Wabash
Kentucky
Scioto
Muskegon
Grand
Maumee
Kankakee
Licking
Elk
White
St Joseph

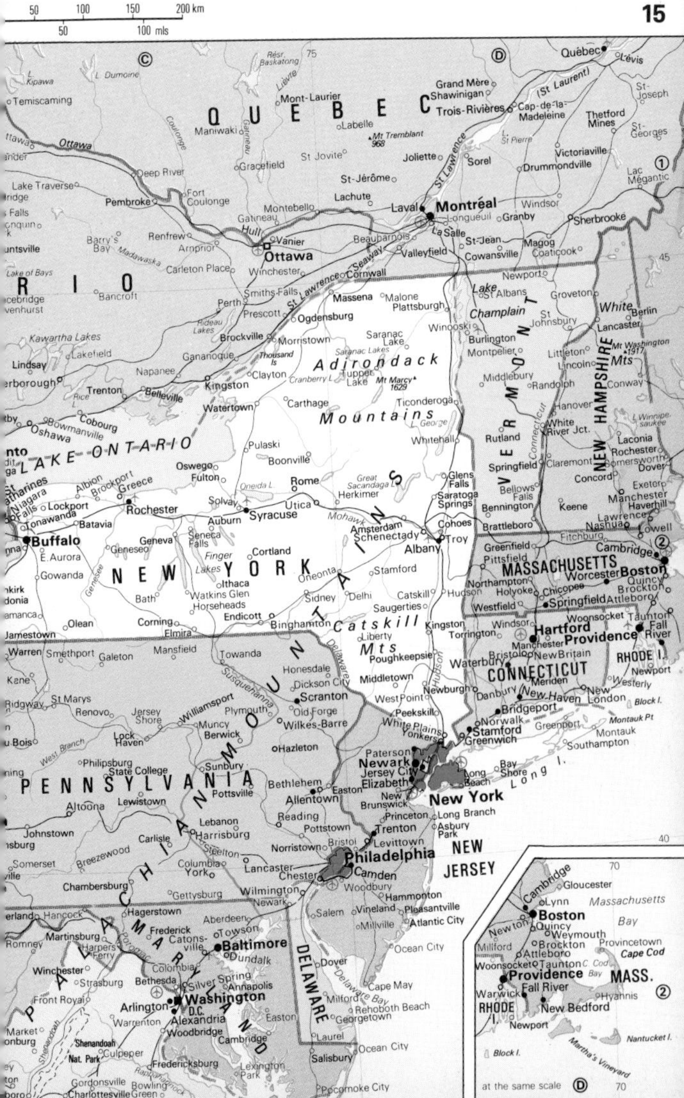

50   100   150   200 km

50   100 mls

L. Kipawa

Temiscaming

Résr. Baskatong

L. Dumoine

Québec

Lévis

Grand Mère

Mont-Laurier

Shawinigan

(St Laurent)

Cap-de-la-Madeleine

St-Joseph

Thetford Mines

St Georges

Maniwaki

Q U E B E C

Labelle

Trois-Rivières

Mt Tremblant

968

St Jovite

Joliette

St Pierre

Sorel

Victoriaville

Deep River

Gracefield

Montebello

Lachute

St-Jérôme

Sherbrooke

Drummondville

Pembroke

Fort Coulonge

Gatineau

Laval

Montréal

Longueuil

St-Jean

Granby

Windsor

Magog

Lac Mégantic

①

Renfrew

Arnprior

Hull

Vanier

Beauharnois

La Salle

Valleyfield

Cowansville

Coaticook

Barry's Bay

Carleton Place

Ottawa

Winchester

Cornwall

Newport

45

Perth

Smiths Falls

Massena

Malone

Plattsburgh

St Albans

Groveton

White

Berlin

Lake of Bays

Bancroft

Rideau Lakes

Prescott

Ogdensburg

Winooski

St Johnsbury

Lancaster

Mt Washington 1917

bridge

Kawartha Lakes

Brockville

Morristown

Saranac Lakes

Burlington

Montpelier

Littleton

Mts

Lindsay

Lakefield

Napanee

Gananoque

Thousand Is

Saranac Lake

Adirondack

Cranberry L

Lake

Middlebury

Randolph

Lincoln

Laconia

L Winnipesaukee

rborough

Kingston

Clayton

Mt Marcy 1629

Hanover

Rochester

Dover

Cobourg

Trenton

Belleville

Watertown

Carthage

Ticonderoga

L George

Rutland

White River Jct.

Concord

Manchester

Oshawa

Pulaski

Boonville

Whitehall

Springfield

Claremont

Keene

Nashua

Lowell

LAKE ONTARIO

Oswego

Fulton

Rome

Great Sacandaga L

Glens Falls

Saratoga Springs

Bennington

Brattleboro

Fitchburg

Lawrence

Cambridge

②

Niagara

Lockport

Greece

Solvay

Oneida L

Herkimer

Amsterdam

Cohoes

Greenfield

Pittsfield

Northampton

MASSACHUSETTS

Worcester

Boston

Buffalo

Tonawanda

Batavia

Rochester

Auburn

Syracuse

Utica

Schenectady

Troy

Albany

Hudson

Holyoke

Chicopee

Springfield

Quincy

Brockton

E. Aurora

Geneva

Seneca Falls

Cortland

Hadley

Westfield

Hartford

Attleboro

Gowanda

Geneseo

Finger Lakes

Ithaca

NEW YORK

Oneonta

Stamford

Catskill

Kingston

Windsor

New Britain

Providence

RHODE I.

Taunton

Fall River

nkirk

Bath

Watkins Glen

Horseheads

Sidney

Delhi

Saugerties

Torrington

Bristol

Newport

donia

Jamestown

Olean

Corning

Elmira

Endicott

Binghamton

Catskill Mts

Liberty

Poughkeepsie

Waterbury

Meriden

CONNECTICUT

New Haven

New London

Westerly

Warren

Smethport

Galeton

Mansfield

Towanda

Honesdale

Middletown

Newburgh

Danbury

Bridgeport

Norwalk

New

Montauk Pt

Kane

Ridgway

St Marys

Renovo

Williamsport

Jersey Shore

Plymouth

Dickson City

Scranton

West Point

Peekskill

White Plains

Stamford

Greenwich

Long I.

Montauk

u Bois

Lock Haven

Muncy

Berwick

Wilkes-Barre

Paterson

Jersey City

Bay Shore

Southampton

ning

Philipsburg

Sunbury

Hazleton

Newark

Elizabeth

Long I.

State College

Bethlehem

Easton

New

Brunswick

New York

Long Branch

Altoona

Lewistown

Allentown

Reading

Princeton

Asbury Park

Johnstown

sburg

PENNSYLVANIA

Lebanon

Harrisburg

Pottsville

Pottstown

Trenton

NEW

Somerset

Breezewood

Carlisle

Columbia

Lancaster

Norristown

Bristol

Levittown

JERSEY

②

erland

Hancock

Chambersburg

York

Philadelphia

Camden

Hammonton

40

Romney

Martinsburg

Harpers Ferry

Gettysburg

Hagerstown

Wilmington

Chester

Newark

Woodbury

Vineland

Pleasantville

Cambridge

Gloucester

Massachusetts

onburg

Winchester

Strasburg

Frederick

Catonsville

Towson

Columbia

DELAWARE

Salem

Millville

Atlantic City

70

Lynn

Boston

Bay

Front Royal

Market

Berryville

Bethesda

Silver Spring

D.C.

Baltimore

Dundalk

Annapolis

Dover

Ocean City

Newton

Quincy

Weymouth

Provincetown

arket

onburg

Shenandoah Nat. Park

Arlington

Washington

Alexandria

Woodbridge

Milford

Rehoboth Beach

Georgetown

Milford

Attleboro

Brockton

Cape Cod

②

Culpeper

Warrenton

Fredericksburg

Laurel

Cape May

Woonsocket

Taunton

Hyannis

Gordonsville

Bowling Green

Lexington Park

Salisbury

Ocean City

Pocomoke City

Providence

Warwick

RHODE

Fall River

New Bedford

MASS.

Charlottesville

Green

at the same scale

Newport

Block I.

Martha's Vineyard

Nantucket I.

Ⓓ

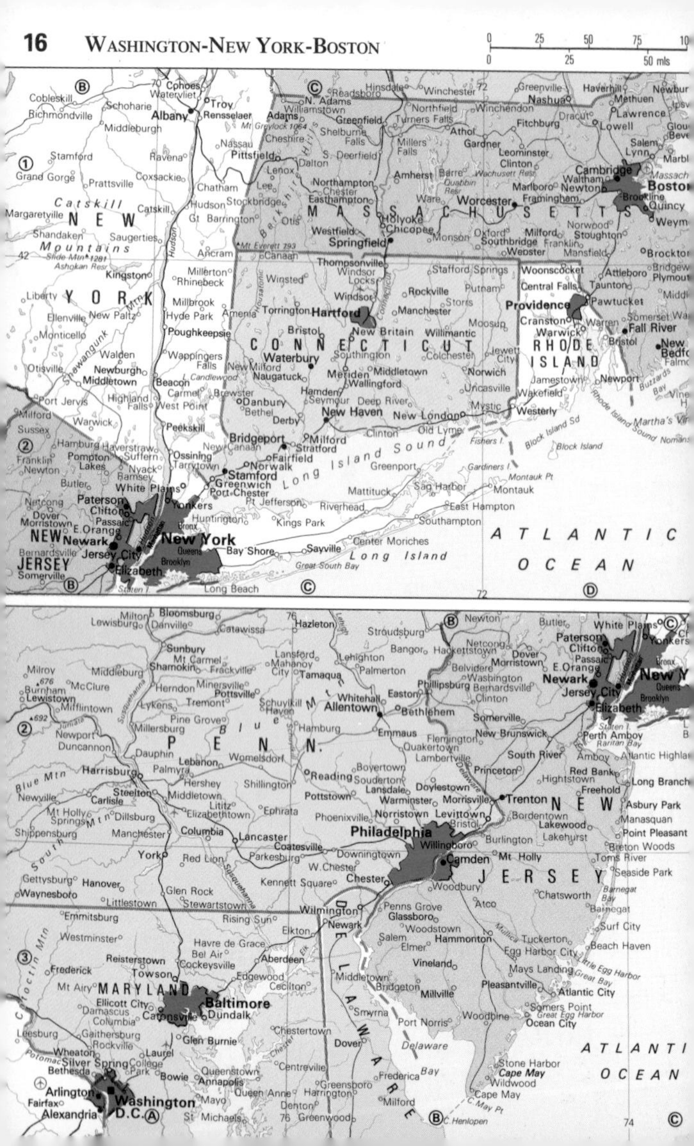
0 25 50 75 100 km
0 25 50 mls
NEW YORK
Catskill Mountains
MASSACHUSETTS
CONNECTICUT
RHODE ISLAND
NEW JERSEY
ATLANTIC OCEAN
Long Island Sound
Long Island
Block Island Sd
Rhode Island Sound
Great South Bay
Buzzards Bay
Martha's Vineyard
Block Island
Fishers I.
Gardiners I.
Montauk Pt
Staten I.
Cohoes
Watervliet
Troy
Albany
Rensselaer
Cobleskill
Schoharie
Richmondville
Middleburgh
Stamford
Grand Gorge
Prattsville
Coxsackie
Ravena
Nassau
Chatham
Hudson
Catskill
Margaretville
Shandaken
Saugerties
Slide Mtn 1281
Ashokan Resr
Kingston
Liberty
Ellenville
New Paltz
Monticello
Walden
Newburgh
Middletown
Otisville
Port Jervis
Highland Falls
West Point
Milford
Sussex
Warwick
Hamburg
Haverstraw
Suffern
Franklin
Newton
Pompton Lakes
Nyack
Ramsey
Butler
Netcong
Dover
Morristown
Paterson
Clifton
Passaic
E. Orange
Newark
Bernardsville
Jersey City
Elizabeth
Somerville
Yonkers
White Plains
Bronx
Manhattan
Queens
Brooklyn
New York
Long Beach
Huntington
Kings Park
Bay Shore
Sayville
Center Moriches
Riverhead
Southampton
East Hampton
Montauk
Sag Harbor
Mattituck
Greenport
Pt Jefferson
Port Chester
Greenwich
Stamford
Norwalk
Fairfield
Stratford
Bridgeport
Milford
New Canaan
Ossining
Tarrytown
Peekskill
Carmel
Brewster
Beacon
L. Candlewood
Wappingers Falls
Poughkeepsie
Hyde Park
Millbrook
Amenia
Rhinebeck
Millerton
Ancram
Gt Barrington
Stockbridge
Lee
Lenox
Pittsfield
Dalton
Cheshire
Adams
Mt Greylock 1064
N. Adams
Williamstown
Readsboro
Hinsdale
Winchester
Greenfield
Shelburne Falls
S. Deerfield
Turners Falls
Northfield
Millers Falls
Athol
Winchendon
Fitchburg
Gardner
Leominster
Clinton
Wachusett Resr
Quabbin Resr
Barre
Amherst
Northampton
Chester
Easthampton
Ware
Worcester
Westfield
Holyoke
Chicopee
Springfield
Monson
Otis
Mt Everett 793
Canaan
Berkshire Hills
Housatonic
Hudson
Connecticut
Greenville
Nashua
Haverhill
Methuen
Lawrence
Lowell
Dracut
Salem
Lynn
Marblehead
Cambridge
Waltham
Newton
Marlboro
Framingham
Brookline
Boston
Quincy
Weymouth
Norwood
Stoughton
Milford
Oxford
Southbridge
Franklin
Webster
Mansfield
Brockton
Bridgewater
Plymouth
Attleboro
Taunton
Woonsocket
Central Falls
Pawtucket
Providence
Cranston
Warwick
Warren
Bristol
Somerset
Fall River
New Bedford
Jamestown
Newport
Wakefield
Westerly
Stafford Springs
Putnam
Thompsonville
Windsor Locks
Windsor
Rockville
Storrs
Manchester
Hartford
Torrington
Winsted
Bristol
New Britain
Willimantic
Moosup
Waterbury
Southington
Colchester
Jewett City
New Milford
Naugatuck
Meriden
Middletown
Wallingford
Norwich
Hamden
Uncasville
Danbury
Bethel
Seymour
Deep River
Derby
New Haven
New London
Mystic
Clinton
Old Lyme
Milton
Bloomsburg
Lewisburg
Danville
Catawissa
Hazleton
Stroudsburg
Newton
Butler
Sunbury
Mt Carmel
Shamokin
Frackville
Lansford
Mahanoy City
Tamaqua
Lehighton
Palmerton
Bangor
Hackettstown
Netcong
Dover
Morristown
Belvidere
Washington
Phillipsburg
Bernardsville
Clinton
Easton
Whitehall
Allentown
Bethlehem
Milroy
Middleburg
McClure
Burnham
Lewistown
Mifflintown
Herndon
Minersville
Pottsville
Schuylkill Haven
Lykens
Tremont
Pine Grove
Millersburg
Newport
Duncannon
Hamburg
Emmaus
Somerville
New Brunswick
Flemington
Quakertown
Lambertville
Dauphin
Lebanon
Palmyra
Womelsdorf
Harrisburg
Hershey
Reading
Boyertown
Souderton
Lansdale
Doylestown
Princeton
South River
Amboy
Perth Amboy
Raritan Bay
Atlantic Highlands
Red Bank
Hightstown
Long Branch
Freehold
Blue Mtn
Newville
Carlisle
Steelton
Middletown
Lititz
Shillington
Ephrata
Pottstown
Warminster
Morrisville
Trenton
Mt Holly Springs
Dillsburg
Elizabethtown
Phoenixville
Norristown
Levittown
Bristol
Bordentown
Lakewood
Asbury Park
Manasquan
Shippensburg
Manchester
Columbia
Lancaster
Philadelphia
Burlington
Lakehurst
Point Pleasant
Brielle
Coatesville
Willingboro
Camden
Mt Holly
Toms River
York
Red Lion
Parkesburg
Downingtown
W. Chester
Chester
Kennett Square
Seaside Park
Gettysburg
Hanover
Waynesboro
Glen Rock
Littlestown
Stewartstown
Woodbury
Chatsworth
Barnegat Bay
Barnegat
Emmitsburg
Rising Sun
Wilmington
Penns Grove
Glassboro
Atco
Westminster
Elkton
Newark
Woodstown
Salem
Elmer
Hammonton
Tuckerton
Surf City
Beach Haven
Havre de Grace
Bel Air
Aberdeen
Reisterstown
Cockeysville
Towson
Frederick
Edgewood
Middletown
Vineland
Egg Harbor City
Little Egg Harbor
Great Bay
Mays Landing
Mt Airy
MARYLAND
Baltimore
Dundalk
Catonsville
Ellicott City
Damascus
Columbia
Cecilton
Bridgeton
Millville
Pleasantville
Atlantic City
Somers Point
Great Egg Harbor
Ocean City
Smyrna
Port Norris
Woodbine
Leesburg
Gaithersburg
Rockville
Chestertown
Glen Burnie
Dover
Delaware Bay
Wheaton
Silver Spring
College Park
Laurel
Bethesda
Potomac
Bowie
Centreville
Queenstown
Annapolis
Greensboro
Frederica
Stone Harbor
Cape May
Wildwood
Arlington
Fairfax
Alexandria
Washington D.C.
Mayo
Queen Anne
Harrington
Denton
St Michaels
Greenwood
Milford
C. May Pt
C. Henlopen
DELAWARE
PENN.
NEW JERSEY
Blue Mt
South Mtn
Catoctin Mtn
Susquehanna
Delaware
Lehigh
Schuylkill
Juniata
Chester
Elk
Mullica

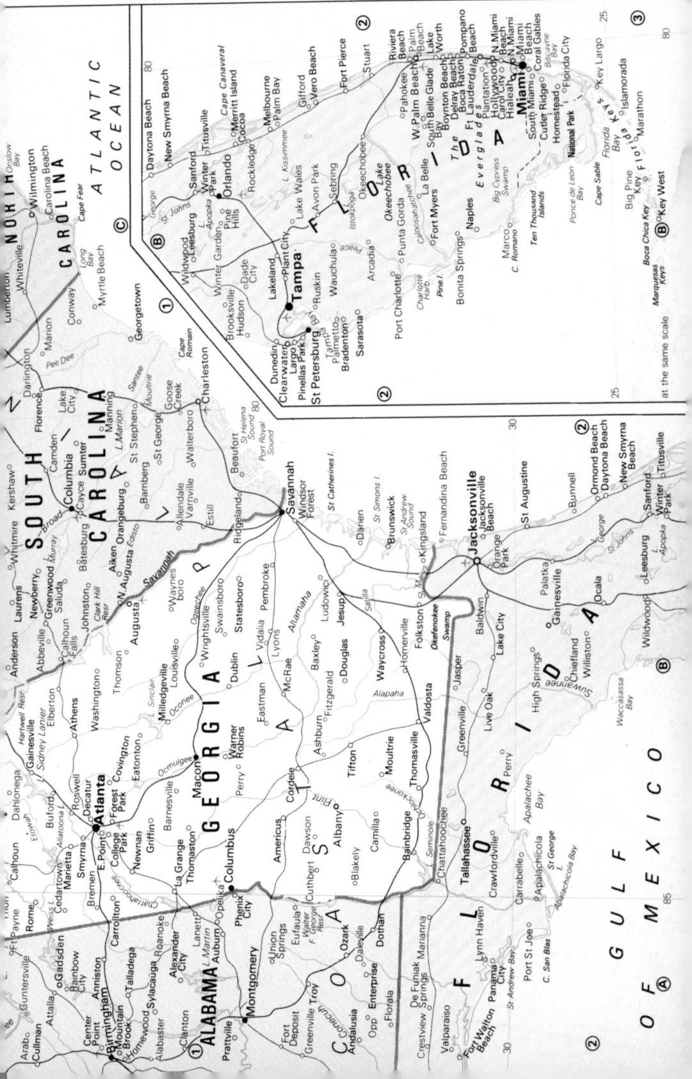

50 100 150 200 km
50 100 mils

at the same scale

NORTH CAROLINA

Onslow Bay · Wilmington · Carolina Beach · Long Bay · Myrtle Beach · Georgetown · Cape Romain · Charleston

SOUTH CAROLINA

Lumberton · Marion · Conway · Florence · Lake City · Darlington · Camden · Columbia · Sumter · L. Marion · St Stephens · Moncks Corner · Goose Creek · Pee Dee

Hartsville · Kershaw · Lancaster · Chester · Winnsboro · Newberry · Lexington · Orangeburg · Bamberg · Allendale · Hardeeville · Walterboro · Ridgeland · Beaufort · Port Royal Sound · St Helena Sound · Edisto I.

Laurens · Anderson · Abbeville · Greenwood · Saluda · Aiken · Barnwell · Estill

GEORGIA

Athens · Washington · Thomson · Augusta · Waynesboro · Statesboro · Swainsboro · Millen · Sylvania

Savannah · Ossabaw Sound · St Catherines I. · St Simons I. · Brunswick · Jekyll I. · St Andrew Sound · Cumberland I. · Kingsland · Fernandina Beach

Gainesville · Buford · Roswell · Marietta · Smyrna · Decatur · **Atlanta** · East Point · College Park · Forest Park · Newnan · Griffin · Barnesville · Thomaston · Macon · Milledgeville · Louisville · Dublin · Wrightsville · Eastman · McRae · Vidalia · Lyons · Jesup · Ludowici · Darien

La Grange · Thomaston · Warner Robins · Perry · Cordele · Fitzgerald · Douglas · Waycross · Homerville · Folkston · Okefenokee Swamp

Columbus · Phenix City · Americus · Dawson · Albany · Camilla · Moultrie · Tifton · Ashburn · Baxley · Hazlehurst · Alapaha

ALABAMA

Alexander City · Auburn · Opelika · Union Springs · Eufaula · Ozark · Enterprise · Dothan · Troy · Montgomery · Prattville · Greenville · Andalusia · Florala · Samson

Birmingham · Talladega · Sylacauga · Clanton · Calera

FLORIDA

Tallahassee · Crawfordville · Quincy · Bainbridge · Chattahoochee · Marianna · Panama City · Lynn Haven · Apalachicola · Carrabelle · St George I. · Port St Joe · C. San Blas · St Andrew Bay · Apalachee Bay · De Funiak Springs · Crestview · Valparaiso · Fort Walton Beach

GULF OF MEXICO

Jacksonville · Jacksonville Beach · Orange Park · Baldwin · Lake City · Jasper · Live Oak · Perry · Greenville · Madison · High Springs · Gainesville · Ocala · Palatka · St Augustine · Bunnell · Starke · Williston · Chiefland · Cedar Key · Suwannee · Waccasassa Bay

St Marys R. · Osceola Nat. Forest · Olustee · Suwannee R. · Withlacoochee R. · Aucilla R.

Ormond Beach · Daytona Beach · New Smyrna Beach · Titusville · Sanford · Winter Park · Orlando · Rockledge · Cocoa · Melbourne · Palm Bay · Vero Beach · Gifford · Fort Pierce · Stuart

Ocala · Leesburg · Wildwood · Dade City · Brooksville · Hudson · Dunedin · Clearwater · Largo · Pinellas Park · St Petersburg · **Tampa** · Plant City · Lakeland · Winter Haven · Auburndale · Bartow · Ruskin · Bradenton · Sarasota · Palmetto

Winter Garden · Kissimmee · L. Kissimmee · Lake Wales · Avon Park · Sebring · Wauchula · Arcadia · Lake Okeechobee

Venice · Port Charlotte · Punta Gorda · Fort Myers · Bonita Springs · Naples · Marco I. · C. Romano · Big Cypress Swamp · Ten Thousand Islands

Miami · Miami Beach · N. Miami · N. Miami Beach · Coral Gables · Hialeah · South Miami · Cutler Ridge · Homestead · Everglades National Park · Cape Sable · Flamingo · Ponce de Leon Bay · Whitewater Bay

Riviera Beach · Palm Beach · W. Palm Beach · Lake Worth · Boynton Beach · Delray Beach · Boca Raton · Deerfield Beach · Pompano Beach · Fort Lauderdale · Hollywood · Pahokee · Belle Glade · South Bay · La Belle · Ponte Vedra Beach

Florida City · Key Largo · Islamorada · Marathon · Big Pine Key · Boca Chica Key · Key West · Marquesas Keys · **FLORIDA KEYS**

The Everglades

ATLANTIC OCEAN

Cape Fear · Cape Canaveral · Merritt Island · Cape Romain

INDIANA

KENTUCKY

TENNESSEE

ILLINOIS

MISSOURI

IOWA

KANSAS

NEBRASKA

OKLAHOMA

Indianapolis

Nashville

Evansville

St. Louis

Des Moines

Kansas City

Independence

Omaha

Lincoln

Wichita

Topeka

Springfield

Columbia

Jefferson City

Boston Mts.

L. of the Ozarks

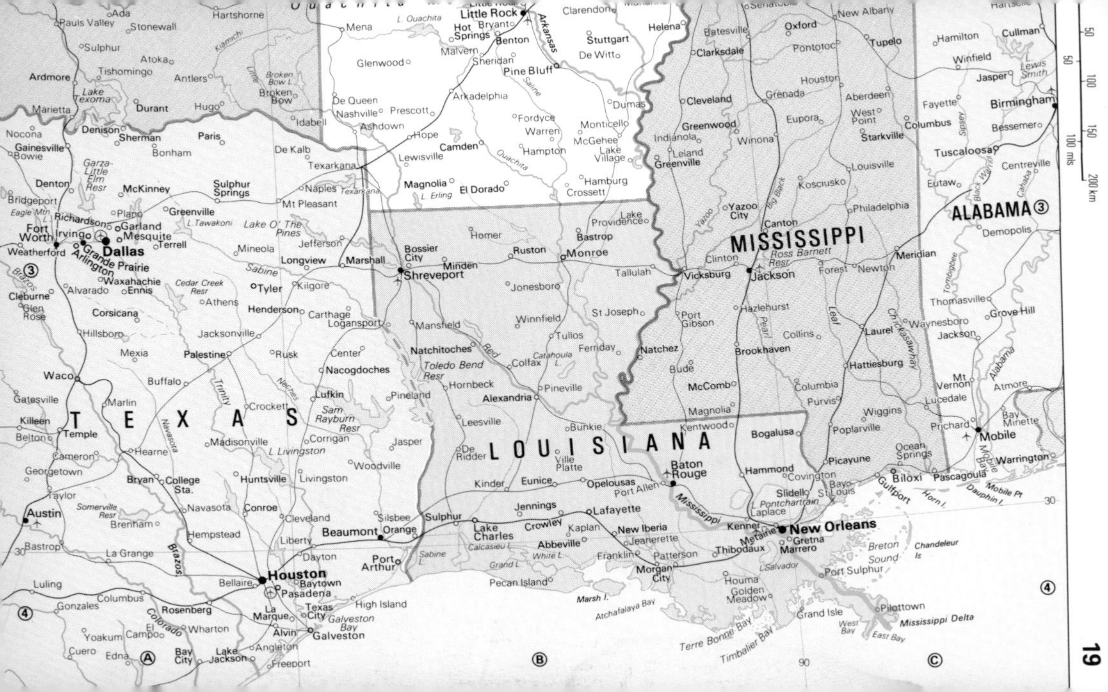

50
100
150
200 km
50
100 mls
ALABAMA
MISSISSIPPI
LOUISIANA
TEXAS
Birmingham
Tuscaloosa
Mobile
Jackson
Meridian
Hattiesburg
Vicksburg
Natchez
Gulfport
Biloxi
Pascagoula
Baton Rouge
New Orleans
Lafayette
Lake Charles
Alexandria
Monroe
Shreveport
Little Rock
Pine Bluff
Texarkana
Dallas
Fort Worth
Waco
Austin
Houston
Galveston
Beaumont
Port Arthur
Tyler
Longview
Mississippi Delta
Chandeleur Is
Breton Sound
Galveston Bay
Lake Texoma
Toledo Bend Resr
Sam Rayburn Resr
Arkansas
Red
Pearl
Brazos
Colorado
Trinity
Sabine
Neches
Tombigbee
Chickasawhay
Yazoo
Ouachita
Mississippi

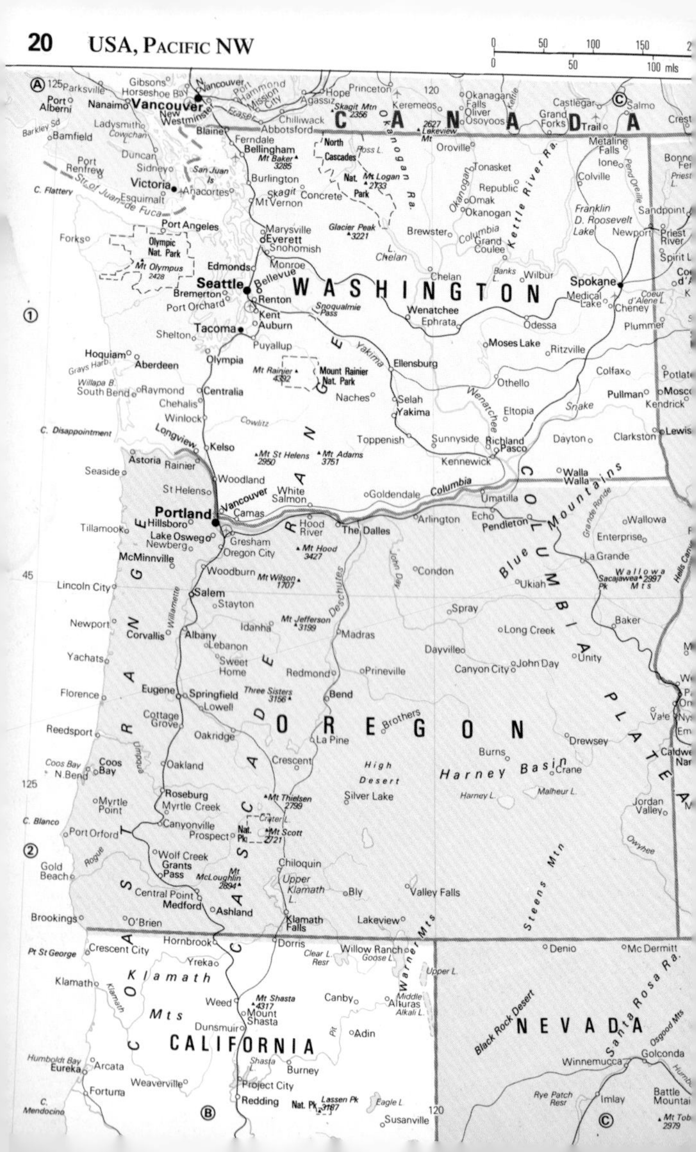
0 50 100 150
0 50 100 mls
CANADA
WASHINGTON
OREGON
CALIFORNIA
NEVADA
Vancouver
Victoria
Seattle
Tacoma
Olympia
Spokane
Portland
Salem
Eugene
Medford
Klamath Falls
Bend
Yakima
Ellensburg
Wenatchee
Pasco
Walla Walla
Pendleton
The Dalles
Astoria
Longview
Bellingham
Everett
Olympic Nat. Park
Mt Olympus 2428
Mt Rainier 4392
Mount Rainier Nat. Park
Mt St Helens 2950
Mt Adams 3751
Mt Hood 3427
Mt Baker 3285
Glacier Peak 3221
North Cascades Nat. Park
Mt Jefferson 3199
Three Sisters 3156
Mt Thielsen 2799
Mt Scott 2721
Mt McLoughlin 2894
Mt Shasta 4317
Lassen Pk 3187
Columbia
Snake
Blue Mountains
Wallowa Mts
High Desert
Harney Basin
Steens Mtn
Black Rock Desert
Santa Rosa Ra.
Klamath Mts
Str. of Juan de Fuca
C. Flattery
C. Disappointment
C. Blanco
C. Mendocino
Pt St George
Eureka
Redding
Winnemucca
Lakeview
Coos Bay
Roseburg
Grants Pass
Crescent City
Yreka
45
125
120

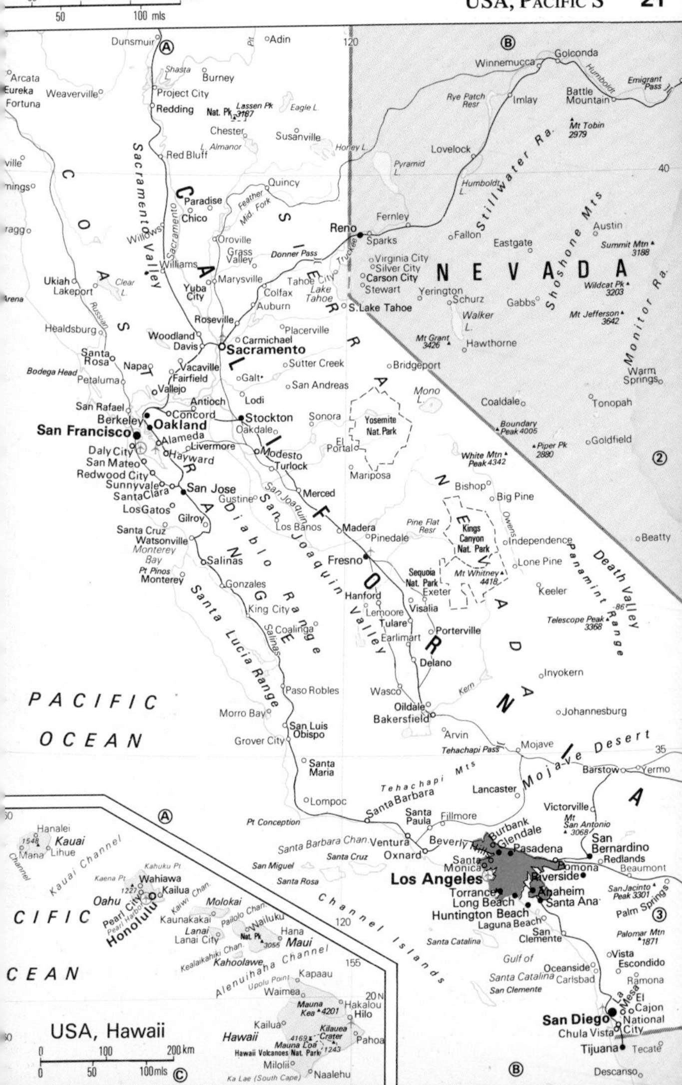
50 100 150 200 km
50 100 mls
PACIFIC OCEAN
NEVADA
COAST RANGES
SIERRA NEVADA
CALIFORNIA
Sacramento Valley
San Joaquin Valley
Diablo Range
Santa Lucia Range
Mojave Desert
Tehachapi Mts
Stillwater Ra.
Shoshone Mts
Monitor Ra.
Panamint Range
Death Valley
Channel Islands
Dunsmuir
Adin
Arcata
Eureka
Fortuna
Weaverville
Shasta L.
Burney
Project City
Redding
Lassen Pk 3187
Nat. Pk
Eagle L.
Chester
Susanville
L. Almanor
Honey L.
Red Bluff
Quincy
Paradise
Chico
Feather
Mid. Fork
Willows
Oroville
Grass Valley
Donner Pass
Truckee
Williams
Marysville
Yuba City
Tahoe City
Lake Tahoe
Colfax
Auburn
Ukiah
Lakeport
Clear L.
Russian
Healdsburg
Roseville
Placerville
Woodland
Davis
Carmichael
Sacramento
Santa Rosa
Bodega Head
Petaluma
Napa
Vacaville
Fairfield
Vallejo
Sutter Creek
Galt
San Andreas
Lodi
Antioch
Concord
San Rafael
Berkeley
Oakland
San Francisco
Stockton
Sonora
Oakdale
Alameda
Livermore
Daly City
San Mateo
Hayward
Modesto
Redwood City
Turlock
Sunnyvale
Santa Clara
San Jose
Los Gatos
Gustine
Merced
Gilroy
Los Banos
Santa Cruz
Watsonville
Monterey Bay
Pt Pinos
Monterey
Salinas
Gonzales
King City
Coalinga
Paso Robles
Morro Bay
San Luis Obispo
Grover City
Santa Maria
Lompoc
Pt Conception
Santa Barbara
Santa Paula
Fillmore
Ventura
Oxnard
Santa Barbara Chan.
San Miguel
Santa Cruz
Santa Rosa
Yosemite Nat. Park
El Portal
Mariposa
Madera
Pinedale
Fresno
Pine Flat Resr
Kings Canyon Nat. Park
Sequoia Nat. Park
Mt Whitney 4418
Hanford
Lemoore
Exeter
Visalia
Tulare
Earlimart
Porterville
Delano
Wasco
Kern
Oildale
Bakersfield
Arvin
Tehachapi Pass
Mojave
Lancaster
Victorville
Barstow
Yermo
Mt San Antonio 3068
San Bernardino
Redlands
Beaumont
Burbank
Glendale
Pasadena
Beverly Hills
Santa Monica
Los Angeles
Pomona
Riverside
Torrance
Long Beach
Anaheim
Santa Ana
Huntington Beach
Laguna Beach
San Clemente
Santa Catalina
Gulf of Santa Catalina
San Jacinto Peak 3301
Palm Springs
Palomar Mtn 1871
Vista
Escondido
Oceanside
Carlsbad
Ramona
La Mesa
El Cajon
San Diego
National City
Chula Vista
Tijuana
Tecate
Descanso
Winnemucca
Golconda
Humboldt
Emigrant Pass
Rye Patch Resr
Imlay
Battle Mountain
Mt Tobin 2979
Lovelock
Pyramid L.
Humboldt L.
Fernley
Reno
Sparks
Fallon
Eastgate
Austin
Summit Mtn 3188
Virginia City
Silver City
Carson City
Stewart
Yerington
Schurz
Gabbs
Wildcat Pk 3203
S.Lake Tahoe
Walker L.
Mt Jefferson 3642
Mt Grant 3426
Hawthorne
Bridgeport
Mono L.
Warm Springs
Coaldale
Tonopah
Boundary Peak 4005
Piper Pk 2880
Goldfield
White Mtn Peak 4342
Bishop
Big Pine
Owens
Independence
Lone Pine
Keeler
Beatty
Telescope Peak 3368
-86
Inyokern
Johannesburg
120
40
35
A
B
2
3
USA, Hawaii
Hanalei
Kauai
1548
Mana
Lihue
Kauai Channel
Kahuku Pt
Kaena Pt
Wahiawa
1227
Oahu
Kailua
Pearl City
Pearl Harbor
Honolulu
Kaiwi Chan.
Molokai
Kaunakakai
Pailolo Chan.
Lanai
Lanai City
Wailuku
Nat. Pk
3055
Hana
Maui
Kealaikahiki Chan.
Kahoolawe
Alenuihaha Channel
Upolu Point
Kapaau
Waimea
Mauna Kea 4201
Hakalau
Hilo
Kailua
Hawaii
Kilauea Crater
4169
Mauna Loa
1243
Hawaii Volcanoes Nat. Park
Pahoa
Milolii
Naalehu
Ka Lae (South Cape)
155
20 N
0 100 200 km
0 50 100mls
C
CIFIC
CEAN

0   25   50   75   100
0   25   50 mls

Lytton   Calistoga   L. Berryessa   Woodland   Folsom   Placerville   Camino
Healdsburg   St Helena   Winters   Davis   Folsom   Diamond Springs
Forestville   Yountville   Dixon   **Sacramento**   Plymouth   Markleeville
Sebastopol   Santa Rosa   Napa   Vacaville   Elmira   Elk Grove   Sutter Ck   West Pt   Dardanelle   Sonora Pass
Petaluma   Sonoma   Fairfield   Galt   Jackson   Mokelumne   Arnold   Bridgeport
Novato   Vallejo   Pittsburg   Lodi   Clements   San Andreas   Murphys   Pinecrest
San Rafael   Richmond   Concord   Antioch   Oakley   Angels Camp   Sonora   Groveland   Mather
Mill Valley   Berkeley   Oakland   Brentwood   Bellota   **Yosemite**
Golden Gate   Alameda   San Leandro   Byron   Tracy   **Stockton**   Farmington   Coulterville   El Portal
San Francisco   Hayward   Pleasanton   Ripon   Manteca   Oakdale   **National Park**
Daly City   S.San Francisco   San Mateo   Fremont   Livermore   Modesto   Ceres   Wawona   Fish Camp
Redwood City   Palo Alto   Mountain View   Patterson   Turlock   Snelling   Mariposa   Bass Lake
San Gregorio   Sunnyvale   Santa Clara   San Jose   Newman   Merced   Planada   Lakeshore
Pescadero   Los Gatos   Coyote   Mt Hamilton   Gustine   Atwater   Raymond
Boulder Creek   Morgan Hill   Los Banos   Chowchilla   Madera   Friant   Humphreys
Davenport   Soquel   Gilroy   San Luis Resr   Dos Palos   Berenda   Pinedale   Clovis   Piedra
Santa Cruz   Watsonville   San Juan Bautista   Firebaugh   Herndon   Minkler
Monterey Bay   Castroville   Hollister   Tres Pinos   Mendota   Kerman   **Fresno**   Sanger   Reedley
Pacific Grove   Salinas   Alisal   Helm   Selma   Kingsburg   Dinuba
Monterey   Seaside   Gabilan Ra   Pinnacles N.M.   Gonzales
Carmel   Carmel Valley

Los Alamos   Big Pine Mtn   Gorman   Lake Hughes   Rosamond   Helendale
Lompoc   Buellton   Los Olivos   Piru Ck   Lancaster
Pt Arguello   Solvang   Santa Ynez Mts   Ojai   Castaic   Palmdale   Adelanto   Victorville
Pt Conception   Gaviota   Goleta   Carpinteria   Fillmore   Acton   Littlerock   Hesperia
Santa Barbara Channel   Santa Barbara   Ventura   Santa Paula   Newhall   San Gabriel Mts   Wrightwood
San Miguel   Oxnard   Camarillo   Moorpark   San Fernando   Mt Wilson   Mt San Antonio   San Bernardino
Santa Rosa   Port Hueneme   Burbank   Pasadena   Upland   Colton
Anacapa Is   **Los Angeles**   Glendale   Hollywood   Monrovia   Riverside
Santa Cruz   Santa Monica   Beverly Hills   Inglewood   Whittier   Fullerton   Corona
Santa Monica Bay   Torrance   Lakewood   Anaheim   Santa Ana   Perris
C h a n n e l   Redondo Beach   Long Beach   Garden Grove   Orange   Elsinore
I s l a n d s   Huntington Beach   Newport Beach   Costa Mesa
Santa Barbara   San Pedro Channel   Laguna Beach   San Clemente   S Onofre
San Nicolas   Santa Catalina   Avalon   **Gulf of Santa Catalina**   Oceanside
P A C I F I C   Outer Santa Barbara Channel   Carlsbad   Encinitas
O C E A N   San Clemente   Del Mar   La Jolla   **San Diego**

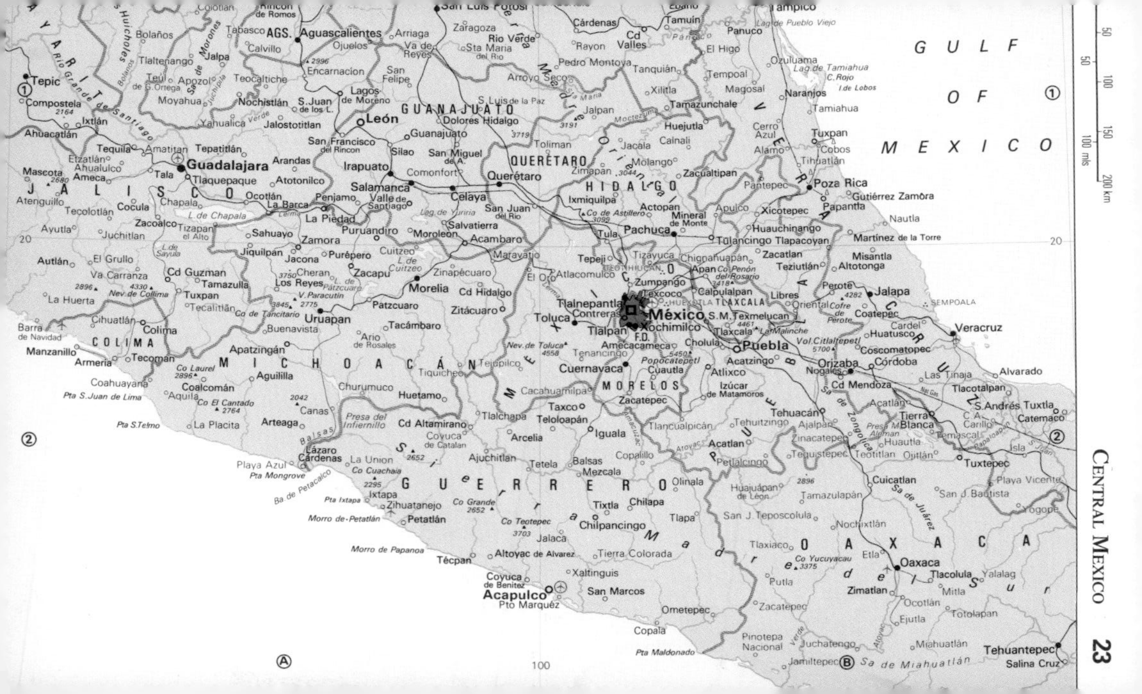
50 100 150 200 km
50 100 mls
GULF OF MEXICO
NAYARIT
JALISCO
COLIMA
MICHOACÁN
GUANAJUATO
QUERÉTARO
HIDALGO
MÉXICO
MORELOS
TLAXCALA
PUEBLA
VERACRUZ
GUERRERO
OAXACA
F.D.
Sierra Madre Oriental
Sierra Madre del Sur
Tepic
Compostela
Rio Grande de Santiago
Guadalajara
Tlaquepaque
Chapala
L. de Chapala
Colima
Manzanillo
Tecomán
Aguascalientes
AGS.
León
Irapuato
Salamanca
Celaya
Guanajuato
Dolores Hidalgo
San Miguel de A.
Querétaro
San Juan del Rio
Morelia
Uruapan
Patzcuaro
Zamora
Lázaro Cárdenas
Toluca
México
Xochimilco
Tlalpan
Tlalnepantla
Pachuca
Tula
Tlaxcala
Puebla
Cholula
Cuernavaca
Taxco
Iguala
Chilpancingo
Acapulco
Pto Marquéz
Zihuatanejo
Tehuacán
Orizaba
Córdoba
Jalapa
Veracruz
Alvarado
Poza Rica
Tuxpan
Papantla
Oaxaca
Tehuantepec
Salina Cruz
Popocatepetl 5450
Nev. de Toluca 4558
Vol. Citlaltepetl 5700
Panuco
Cd Valles
San Luis Potosí
Balsas
Morro de Papanoa
Pta Maldonado

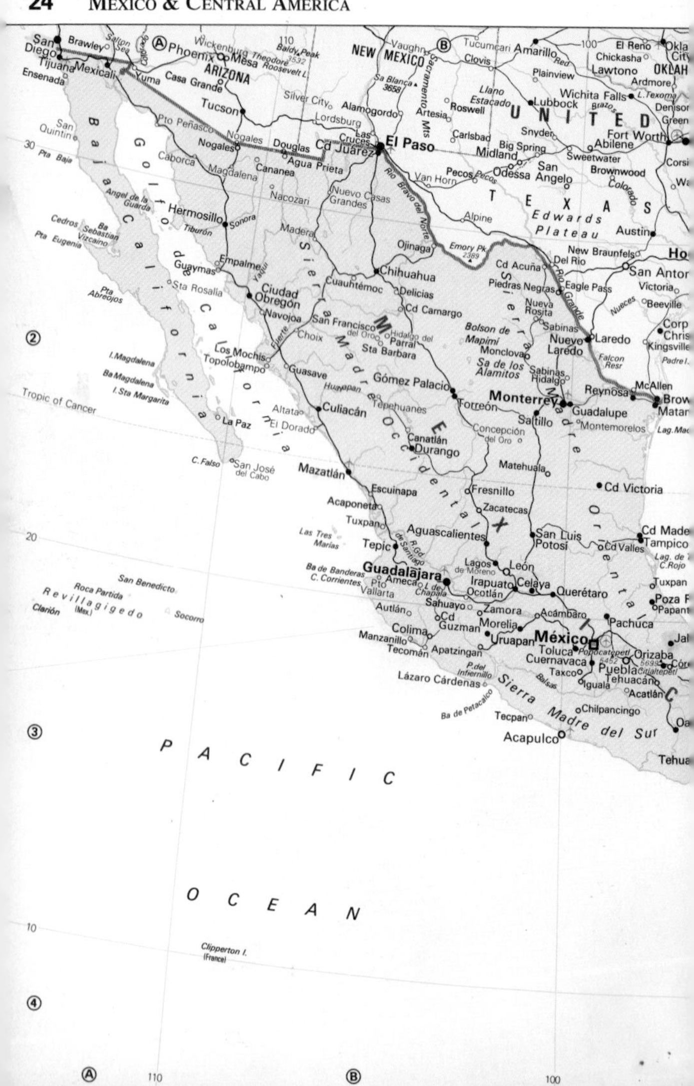

San Diego
Tijuana
Ensenada
Brawley
Salton Sea
Mexicali
Yuma
Phoenix
Mesa
Wickenburg
ARIZONA
Casa Grande
Tucson
Nogales
Douglas
Agua Prieta
Cananea
Nacozari
Lordsburg
Silver City
Alamogordo
Las Cruces
Cd Juárez
El Paso
NEW MEXICO
Vaughn
Sacramento Mts
Sa Blanca 3658
Artesia
Roswell
Clovis
Tucumcari
Amarillo
Plainview
Llano Estacado
Lubbock
Carlsbad
Big Spring
Midland
Odessa
San Angelo
Snyder
Sweetwater
Abilene
Brownwood
Fort Worth
Wichita Falls
Lawtono
Chickasha
El Reno
Ardmore
L. Texoma
Denison
Pecos
Van Horn
Alpine
TEXAS
UNITED
Edwards Plateau
Austin
New Braunfels
San Antonio
Del Rio
Eagle Pass
Cd Acuña
Piedras Negras
Nueva Rosita
Sabinas
Nuevo Laredo
Laredo
Falcon Resr
Victoria
Beeville
Kingsville
Padre I.
McAllen
Reynosa
Rio Bravo del Norte
Rio Grande
Emory Pk 2389
Ojinaga
Chihuahua
Delicias
Cd Camargo
Cuauhtémoc
Madera
Nuevo Casas Grandes
Hermosillo
Sonora
Tiburón
Guaymas
Empalme
Sta Rosalía
Ciudad Obregón
Navojoa
Los Mochis
Topolobampo
Choix
San Francisco del Oro
Hidalgo del Parral
Sta Barbara
Gómez Palacio
Torreón
Bolson de Mapimí
Monclova
Sa de los Alamitos
Sabinas Hidalgo
Monterrey
Guadalupe
Saltillo
Montemorelos
Concepción del Oro
Matehuala
Cd Victoria
Guasave
Culiacán
Tepehuanes
Canatlán
Durango
Altata
El Dorado
La Paz
C. Falso
San José del Cabo
Mazatlán
Escuinapa
Acaponeta
Tuxpan
Tepic
Fresnillo
Zacatecas
Aguascalientes
San Luis Potosí
Cd Valles
Tampico
Cd Madero
Lagos de Moreno
León
Guadalajara
Irapuato
Celaya
Querétaro
Ocotlán
Zamora
Sahuayo
Pto Vallarta
Ameca
Ba de Banderas
C. Corrientes
Autlán
Cd Guzman
Colima
Manzanillo
Tecomán
Apatzingan
Uruapan
Morelia
Acámbaro
Pachuca
México
Toluca
Cuernavaca
Taxco
Puebla
Tehuacán
Orizaba
Acatlán
Iguala
Lázaro Cárdenas
Ba de Petacalco
Tecpan
Acapulco
Chilpancingo
Sierra Madre del Sur
Sierra Madre Occidental
Sierra Madre Oriental
MEXICO
Golfo de California
Baja California
San Quintín
Pta Baja
Cedros
Ba Sebastián Vizcaíno
Pta Eugenia
Pta Abreojos
Angel de la Guarda
I. Magdalena
Ba Magdalena
I. Sta Margarita
Tropic of Cancer
Las Tres Marías
San Benedicto
Roca Partida
Revillagigedo (Mex.)
Clarión
Socorro
PACIFIC OCEAN
Clipperton I. (France)
110
100
30
20
10
A
B
2
3
4

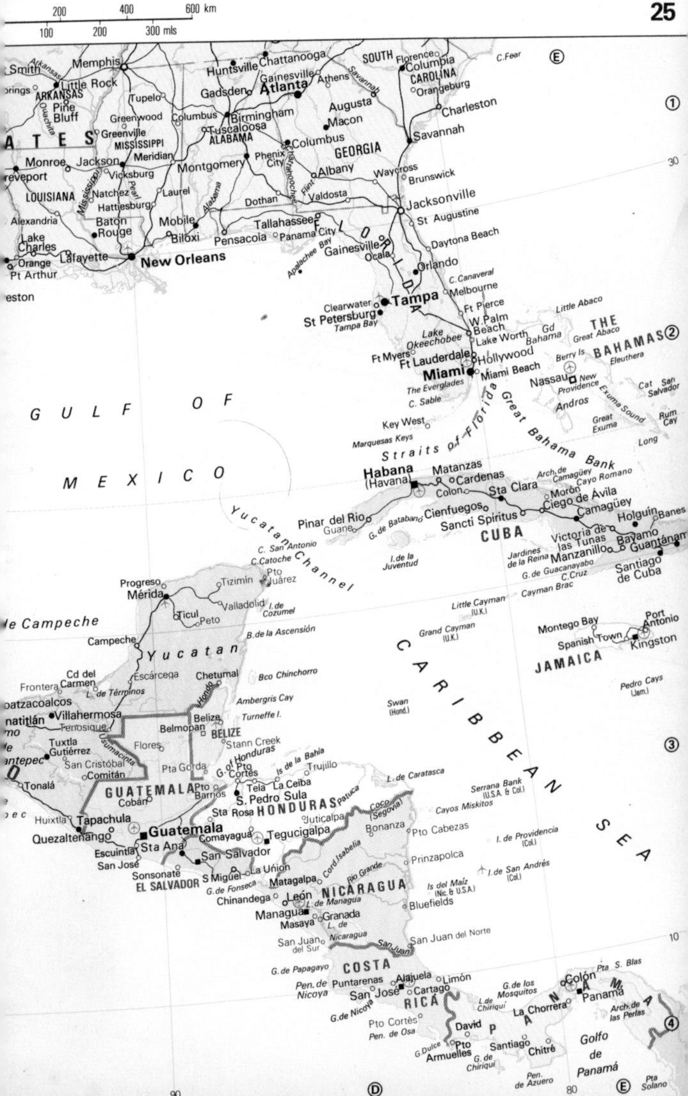

200 400 600 km
100 200 300 mls
GULF OF MEXICO
CARIBBEAN SEA
Straits of Florida
Great Bahama Bank
Yucatan Channel
THE BAHAMAS
CUBA
JAMAICA
GEORGIA
FLORIDA
ALABAMA
MISSISSIPPI
LOUISIANA
ARKANSAS
SOUTH CAROLINA
Memphis
Little Rock
Chattanooga
Huntsville
Atlanta
Birmingham
Montgomery
Jackson
New Orleans
Mobile
Tallahassee
Jacksonville
Savannah
Charleston
Columbia
Tampa
St Petersburg
Orlando
Miami
Ft Lauderdale
Key West
Nassau
Habana (Havana)
Matanzas
Cienfuegos
Camagüey
Holguín
Santiago de Cuba
Kingston
Mérida
Progreso
Campeche
Yucatan
Villahermosa
Belize
Belmopan
BELIZE
GUATEMALA
Guatemala
HONDURAS
Tegucigalpa
S. Pedro Sula
EL SALVADOR
San Salvador
NICARAGUA
Managua
León
COSTA RICA
San José
PANAMA
Panamá
Colón
Golfo de Panamá

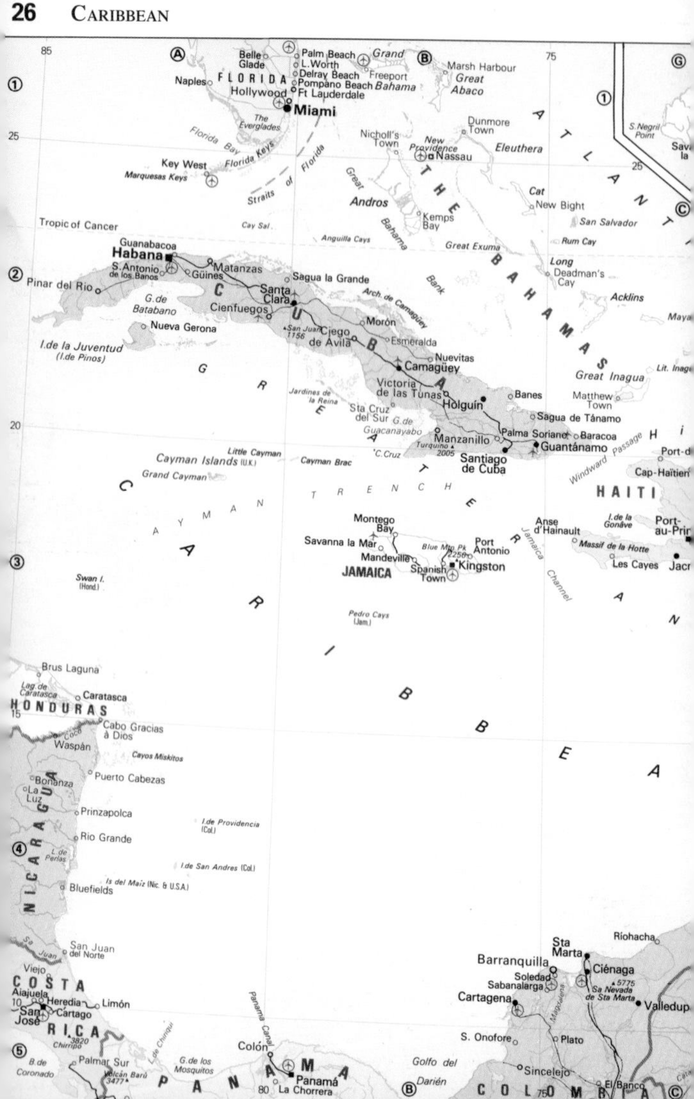

85

75

G

① A Belle B Marsh Harbour ①
Naples Glade Palm Beach *Grand*
FLORIDA L. Worth Freeport *Great* S. Negril
Hollywood Delray Beach *Bahama* *Abaco* Point
Pompano Beach Dunmore
Ft Lauderdale Town
Miami

25 Nicholl's New *Eleuthera* C
Town Providence *Nassau*
Key West *Florida Keys* °Nassau
Marquesas Keys Cat
Straits *Andros* Kemps New Bight
of Bay San Salvador A
Tropic of Cancer Florida Great Exuma Rum Cay T
Guanabacoa Cay Sal *Bank* Deadman's L
Habana Anguilla Cays Long Cay A
S. Antonio Matanzas Cay N
② de los Baños Güines Sagua la Grande Acklins T
Pinar del Río C Santa *Arch. de Camagüey* Mayag I
G. de Clara *Bank* C
Batabanó Cienfuegos U *San Juan* Morón
Nueva Gerona 1756 Ciego *Esmeralda* Lit. Inagua
I. de la Juventud de Ávila B Nuevitas M A
(I. de Pinos) G *Great Inagua* S
Victoria Camagüey Banes Matthew
U de las Tunas *Town*
R Sta Cruz Holguín Sagua de Tánamo 20
20 *Jardines de la Reina* del Sur G. de Palma Soriano Baracoa H
E Guacanayabo Manzanillo Guantánamo I
Little Cayman Santiago Cap-Haïtien
Cayman Islands (U.K.) C. Cruz *Turquino* de Cuba Windward Passage
Grand Cayman Cayman Brac T *2005*
C R *TRENCHE* Montego HAITI
A Port-
Y Bay Anse *I. de la Gonâve* au-Pri
M Savanna la Mar *Blue Mtn Pk* Port d'Hainault *Massif de la Hotte* Port-d
③ A Mandeville *2250m* Antonio Jacm ③
N JAMAICA Spanish **Kingston** Les Cayes
Swan I. Town
(Hond.) C
A *Pedro Cays*
Brus Laguna R *(Jam.)*
Lag. de I
Caratasca Caratasca B
HONDURAS Cabo Gracias B
15 Waspán á Dios E 15
Cayos Miskitos A
Puerto Cabezas N
La Bonanza
Luz Prinzapolca I. de Providencia
(Col.)
Río Grande
④ G. de I. de San Andrés (Col.) ④
NICARAGUA Perlas
Bluefields Is. del Maíz (Nic. & U.S.A.)
San Juan Riohacha
del Norte Sta
Viejo Marta
COSTA Barranquilla Ciénaga S 5775
Alajuela Heredia Soledad Sa Nevada
San Limón Sabanalarga de Sta Marta Valledup
José Cartagena COLOMB
RICA *5820* S. Onofre A
Chirripó Sincelejo El Banco
⑤ B. de Palmar Sur Colón Plato ⑤
Coronado *Volcán Barú* Panamá *Golfo del*
3477 La Chorrera *Darién*
PANAMÁ 80 COLOM B

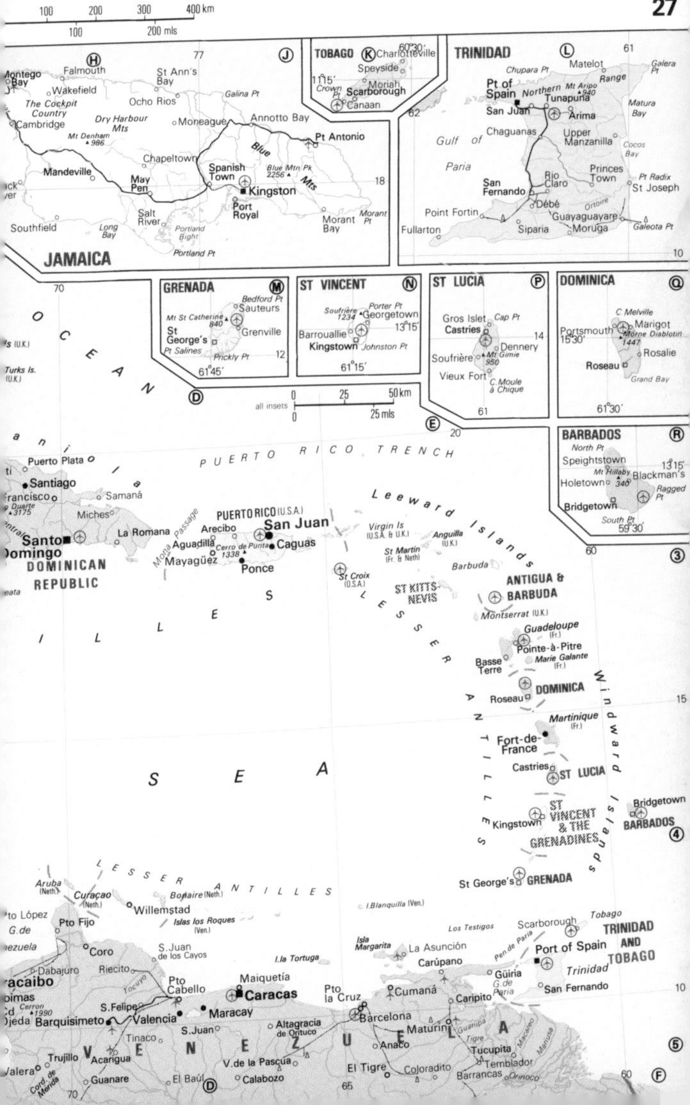

100   200   300   400 km
100   200 mls

TOBAGO
St Ann's Bay
Crown Pt
Moriah
Scarborough
Speyside
Charlotteville
Canaan

TRINIDAD
Chupara Pt   Matelot   Galera Pt
Pt of Spain   Northern   Mt Aripo   Range
San Juan   Tunapuna   Arima
Chaguanas   Upper   Manzanilla
Gulf of   Paria   Cocos
Rio   Princes   Bay
San   Claro   Town
Fernando   Débé   St Radix   St Joseph
Point Fortin   Siparia   Moruga   Guayaguayare
Fullarton   Galeota Pt

JAMAICA
Montego   Falmouth
Bay   Wakefield
St Ann's   Bay   Ocho Rios
The Cockpit   Galina Pt
Country   Dry Harbour   Moneague   Annotto Bay
Cambridge   Mts   Chapeltown   Pt Antonio
Mt Denham   986   Blue
Mandeville   Spanish   Mtn   Mts
May   Town   2256   Port Antonio
Pen   Kingston   Morant
Salt   River   Port   Bay
Southfield   Royal   Morant
Long Bay   Bay
Portland   Bight
Portland Pt

GRENADA
Bedford Pt
Mt St Catherine   Sauteurs
840   Grenville
St   George's
St Salines   Prickly Pt
61°45'   12

ST VINCENT
Porter Pt
Soufrière   Georgetown
1234   13°15'
Barrouallie   Johnston Pt
Kingstown
61°15'

ST LUCIA
Gros Islet   Cap Pt
Castries   14
Dennery
Soufrière   Mt Gimie
950   Vieux Fort
C. Moule   à   Chique
61   20

DOMINICA
C. Melville
Portsmouth   Marigot
1530   Morne Diablotin
1447   Rosalie
Roseau   Grand Bay
61°30'

BARBADOS
North Pt
Speightstown   13°15'
Holetown   340   Blackman's
Ragged
Bridgetown   Pt
South Pt
59°30'

all insets   0   25   50 km
0   25 mls

OCEAN

Turks Is.
(U.K.)

PUERTO RICO TRENCH

Puerto Plata
Santiago   Samaná
Francisco   Miches
3175   La Romana   Cerro de Punta   Caguas
Santo   DOMINICAN   PUERTORICO (U.S.A.)   Virgin Is
Domingo   REPUBLIC   Arecibo   San Juan   (U.S.A. & U.K.)   Anguilla
Mona   1338   (U.K.)
Passage   Aguadilla   Ponce   St Martin
Mayagüez   St Croix   (Fr. & Neth.)
(U.S.A.)   Barbuda

Leeward Islands

ANTIGUA &
BARBUDA
Montserrat (U.K.)
Guadeloupe
(Fr.)
Pointe-à-Pitre
Basse   Marie Galante
Terre   (Fr.)
DOMINICA
Roseau   Martinique
(Fr.)
Fort-de-
France
Castries   ST LUCIA
ST
VINCENT
Kingstown   & THE
GRENADINES
BARBADOS
Bridgetown

ST KITTS
NEVIS

LESSER   ANTILLES

Windward Islands

SEA

St George's   GRENADA

Aruba   Curaçao   Bonaire (Neth.)
(Neth.)   (Neth.)   I.Blanquilla (Ven.)
to López   Willemstad   Los Testigos
G.de   Pto Fijo   Islas los Roques
ezuela   Coro   (Ven.)   Isla
Dabajuro   S. Juan de los Cayos   Margarita   La Asunción
acaibo   Riecito   Pto   Margarita   Carúpano
S.Felipe   Cabello   Pto
aibo   1980   Maiquetía   la Cruz   Cumaná   Güiria
jeda   Barquisimeto   Valencia   Caracas   Carúpano
Valera   Trujillo   Maracay   Barcelona   Maturín   Caripito
Acarigua   S. Juan   Altagracia   Anaco   Tucupita
Coro   Guanare   Tinaco   de Orituco   El Tigre   Temblador
Maras   El Baúl   V.de la Pascua   Calabozo   Coloradito   Barrancas

TRINIDAD
AND
TOBAGO
Scarborough   Tobago
Golfo de Paria
Port of Spain
San Fernando

VENEZUELA

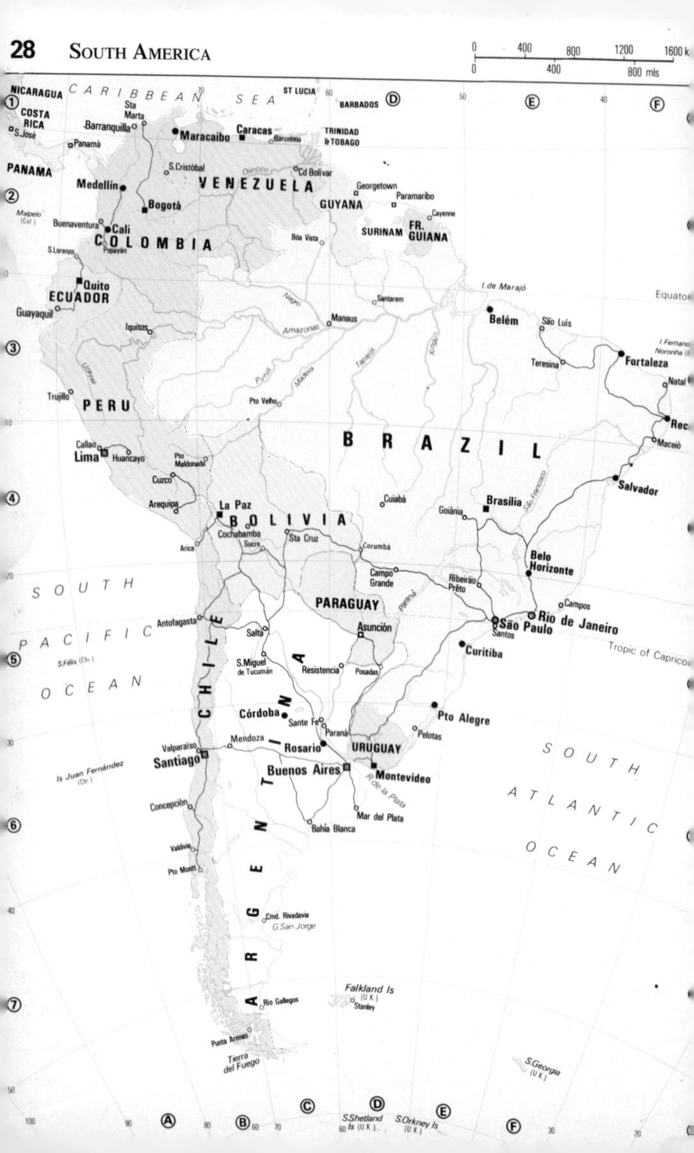

NICARAGUA
COSTA RICA
S.José
PANAMA
Panamá
Maracaibo
Sta Marta
Barranquilla
Caracas
Barcelona
CARIBBEAN SEA
ST LUCIA
BARBADOS
TRINIDAD & TOBAGO

Buenaventura
S.Cristóbal
VENEZUELA
Cd Bolívar
Georgetown
Paramaribo
GUYANA
Cayenne
FR. GUIANA
SURINAM

Medellín
Bogotá
COLOMBIA
Cali
Popayán
S.Lorenzo
Bda Vista

Quito
ECUADOR
Guayaquil
Iquitos
Manaus
Santarém
I. de Marajó
Belém
São Luís
Equato
Teresina
I. Fernando Noronha (I)
Fortaleza
Natal

PERU
Trujillo
Pto Velho
BRAZIL
Rec.
Maceió

Callao
Lima
Huancayo
Cuzco
Pto Maldonado
Salvador

Arequipa
La Paz
BOLIVIA
Cochabamba
Sucre
Sta Cruz
Cuiabá
Brasília
Goiânia
Belo Horizonte

Arica
Corumbá
Campo Grande
Ribeirão Prêto
Campos
Rio de Janeiro

SOUTH
PACIFIC
OCEAN
Antofagasta
PARAGUAY
Asunción
São Paulo
Santos
Tropic of Capricorn

S.Félix (Chi.)
Salta
CHILE
S.Miguel de Tucumán
Resistencia
Posadas
Curitiba

Córdoba
Santa Fe
Paraná
Pto Alegre
Pelotas

Is Juan Fernández (Chi.)
Valparaíso
Mendoza
Rosario
URUGUAY
SOUTH

Santiago
Concepción
A
R
G
E
N
T
I
N
A
Buenos Aires
Montevideo
Mar del Plata
ATLANTIC

Valdivia
Bahía Blanca
OCEAN

Pto Montt

Cmd. Rivadavia
G.San Jorge
Falkland Is
(U.K.)
Stanley

Río Gallegos
S.Georgia
(U.K.)

Punta Arenas
Tierra del Fuego
S.Shetland Is (U.K.)
S.Orkney Is (U.K.)

200 400 600 km
100 200 300 mls

Grl Manuel
Belgrano
6250 6380
Cru Alta
BRAZIL

La Serena
Coquimbo
Rivadavia
La Rioja
Sumampa
Reconquista
Vera
Goya
Corrientes
Paso de los Libres
Uruguaiana
Ibicui
Itaqui
Sta Maria

Punitaqui
Illapel
S. Agustín
Jáchal
Cruz del Eje
L. Mar
Chiquita
Rafaela
S. Francisco
Santa Fe
Paraná
Concepción
La Paz
Concordia
Paysandú
Salto
Tacuarembó
Rivera
do Livramento
Bagé

Los Vilos
S. Juan
Mendoza
6282
Olivares
6800
Tupungato
Salinas
Va Dolores
Villa María
Bell Ville
Rosario
San
Nicolás
Mercedes
Trinidad
Durazno
Florida
Minas
URUGUAY
Melo
Chuy

Viña del Mar
Valparaíso
S.Antonio
S.
Felipe
Aconcagua
6960
Santiago
Vol.Maipo
5290
San
Luis
Córdoba
Río Cuarto
Venado
Tuerto
Pergamino
Junín
Canelones
Colonia
La Plata
Avellaneda
Montevideo
Punta del Este
Rocha

Rancagua
Pichilemu
S. Fernando
Vol. Tupungato
6800
S. Rafael
Mercedes
Va Huidobro
Lincoln
Chivilcoy
Buenos
Aires
Chascomús
Maldonado

Curicó
Constitución
Talca
Mendoza
Vol Maipo
4090
Grl Alvear
Grl Pico
Trenque
Lauquen
Las Flores
Dolores

Cauquenes
Tomé
Concepción
Chillán
Linares
S. Carlos
Vol Domuyo
4800
Bardas Blancas
La Pampa
Sta Rosa
Carhué
Guaminí
Olavarría
Azul
Tandil
Ayacucho
Va Gesell

Los Ángeles
Coronel
Lebu
Angol
Colorado
Neuquén
Grl Roca
Choele Choel
Tres Arroyos
Cnl
Pringles
Balcarce
Miramar
Necochea
Mar del Plata

Carahue
Temuco
Toltén
Loncoche
Lonquimay
Zapala
Río
Negro
S. Antonio
Oeste
Bahía Blanca
Punta Alta
Claromeco
Bahía Blanca

Valdivia
La Unión
Osorno
Pto Varas
Pto Montt
Vol Lanín
3740
Emb
El Chocón
Valcheta
Carmen de Patagones

Ancud
Chiloé
Castro
Achao
S. Carlos de
Bariloche
El Bolsón
Nahuel Huapi
Maquinchao
Golfo
San Matías

G. Corcovado
Esquel
Chubut
Pto Pirámides
Pto Madryn
Trelew
Gaimán
Rawson

Las Plumas
Emb F.
Ameghino

ATLANTIC

OCEAN

Pto Aisén
Coihaique
L. Musters
L.C.Huapi
Sarmiento
Golfo
Camarones
C. Dos Bahías

San Valentín
4058
Caleta Olivia
Comodoro Rivadavia
San Jorge

Chubut

Colonia
Las Heras
Deseado
C.Tres Puntas

L. Buenos
Aires
L. Gral Carrera
Lautaro
3380
L. Cochrane
S. Martín
L. Viedma
Deseado
Pta Médanosa

Santa Cruz

S. Julián

L. Argentino
Sta Cruz
Río Gallegos
Bahía Grande
FALKLAND ISLANDS
(ISLAS MALVINAS)
(U.K.)
Jason Is
C. Dolphin
West Falkland
Stanley
East Falkland
Weddell
Beauchene Is

Calafate
Pto
Turbio
Río Turbio

Pto Natales
Arch. de la
Reina Adelaida
Punta Arenas
Río Grande
Isla Grande
de Tierra
del Fuego
Tierra del Fuego
Ushuaia
I. de los Estados

at the same scale
Shag Rocks
South Georgia
(U.K.)
C. Alexandra
Grytviken
C. Disappointment

Londonderry
Hoste
Navarino
C. de Hornos
(C Horn)
Is Wollaston
Is Diego Ramírez

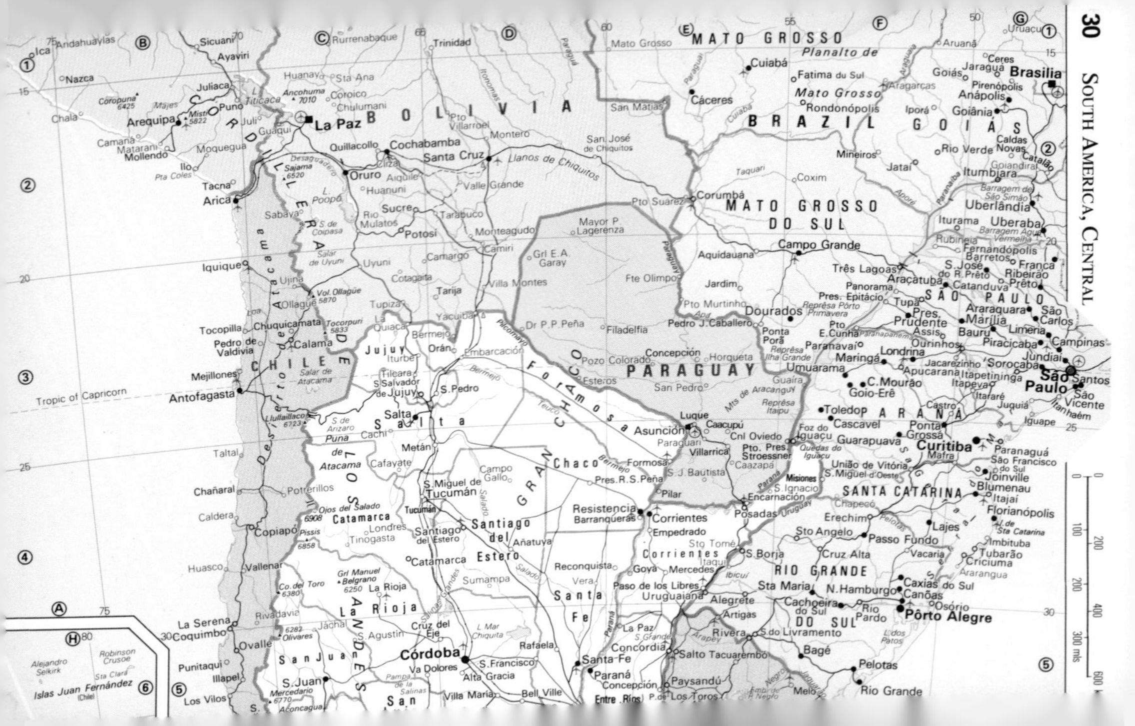

0
200
400
600
0
100
200
300 mls
MATO GROSSO
Planalto de Mato Grosso
BRAZIL
GOIÁS
MATO GROSSO DO SUL
SÃO PAULO
PARANÁ
SANTA CATARINA
RIO GRANDE DO SUL
BOLIVIA
PARAGUAY
CHILE
GRAN CHACO
Formosa
Chaco
Santiago del Estero
Santa Fe
Corrientes
Entre Rios
La Rioja
Catamarca
Jujuy
Salta
San Juan
LOS ANDES
CORDILLERA
Desierto de Atacama
Tropic of Capricorn
Brasília
Goiânia
Anápolis
Uberlândia
Uberaba
Campinas
Santos
São Paulo
Sorocaba
Curitiba
Florianópolis
Blumenau
Joinville
Pôrto Alegre
Pelotas
Rio Grande
Londrina
Maringá
Campo Grande
Dourados
Corumbá
Cuiabá
Cáceres
Asunción
Encarnación
Posadas
Resistencia
Corrientes
Santa Fe
Paraná
Córdoba
Tucumán
Santiago del Estero
Salta
La Paz
Cochabamba
Santa Cruz
Sucre
Potosí
Oruro
Arica
Iquique
Antofagasta
Calama
Copiapó
La Serena
Coquimbo
Arequipa
Puno
Tacna
Islas Juan Fernández (Chile)
Robinson Crusoe
Alejandro Selkirk

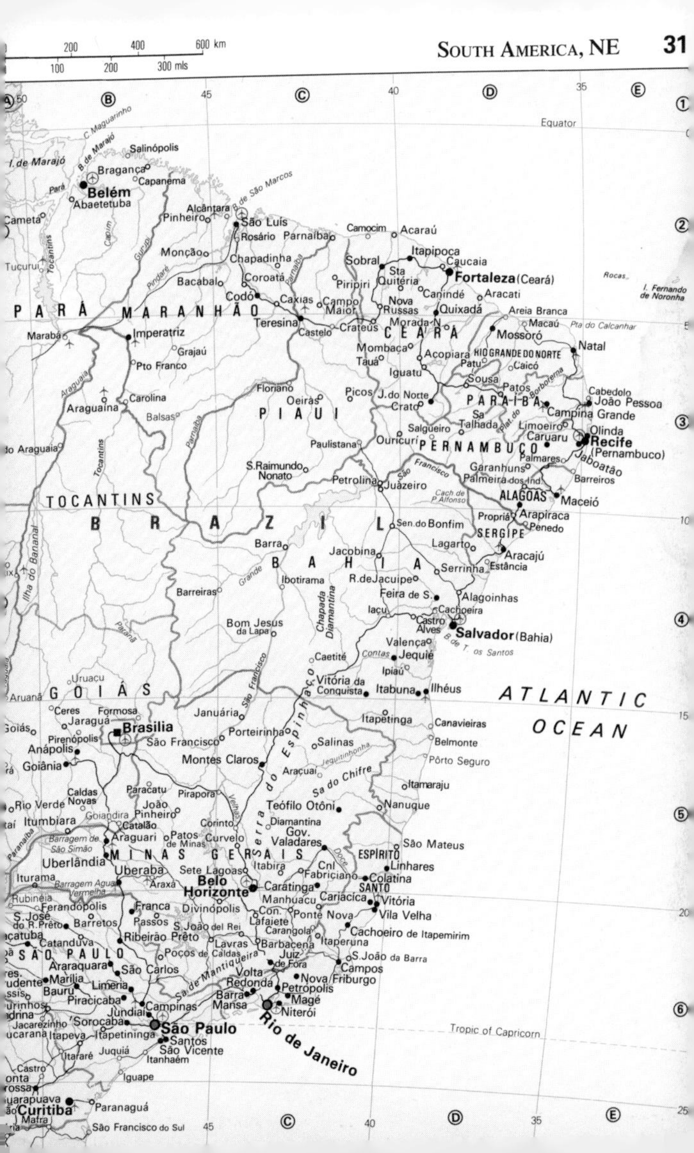

200   400   600 km
100   200   300 mls

Equator

I. de Marajó
C. Maguariho
B. de Marajó
Salinópolis
Bragança
Cameta
Pará **Belém**
Abaetetuba
Capanema
Pinheiro
Monção
Alcântara
São Luís
Rosário
Parnaíba
Camocim
Acaraú
Itapipoca
Caucaia
Chapadinha
Coroatá
Piripiri
Sta
Quitéria
Fortaleza (Ceará)
Bacabal
Codó
Caxias
Campo Maior
Nova
Russas
Quixadá
Canindé
Aracati
Areia Branca
Macau Pta do Calcanhar
Tucuruí
Marabá
Teresina
Castelo
Crateús
Mombaça
Tauá
Acopiara
Patu
RIO GRANDE DO NORTE
Natal
Rocas
I. Fernando
de Noronha

PARÁ   MARANHÃO   C E A R Á

Imperatriz
Pto Franco
Grajaú
Carolina
Balsas
Floriano
Oeiras
Picos
J.do Norte
Iguatu
Sa
Talhada
Pousa
Caicó
Cabedelo
João Pessoa

P I A U I

Araguaína
do Araguaia

T O C A N T I N S

S.Raimundo
Nonato
Paulistana
Ouricuri
Crato
Salgueiro

PARAÍBA
Campina Grande
Limoeiro
Caruaru
Recife (Pernambuco)
Olinda
Jaboatão

P E R N A M B U C O

B R A Z I L

Petrolina
Juazeiro
Cach. do
Afonso
Garanhuns
Palmares
Palmeira dos Ind.
Barreiros

ALAGOAS
Arapiraca
Penedo
Maceió

B A H I A

Barra
Jacobina
Lagarto
Serrinha
SERGIPE
Aracaju
Estância

Barreiras
Ibotirama
Iaçu
R.de Jacuípe
Feira de S.
Cachoeira
Alagoinhas

Bom Jesus
da Lapa
Chapada
Diamantina
Caetité
Vitória da
Conquista
Castro
Alves
Salvador (Bahia)
Valença
Jequié
Ipiaú
Itabuna
Ilhéus
B. de T. os Santos

A T L A N T I C
O C E A N

Aruanã
G O I Á S
Ceres
Jaraguá
Pirenópolis
Anápolis
Brasília
Goiânia

Januária
Porteirinha
Salinas
Araçuaí
Belmonte
Pôrto Seguro
Canavieiras
Itapetinga

São Francisco
Montes Claros
Sa do Chifre
Itamaraju
Nanuque

Caldas
Novas
Rio Verde
Itumbiara
Formosa
João
Pinheiro
Paracatu
Patos
de Minas
Pirapora
Corinto
Teófilo Otôni
São Mateus
Linhares
ESPÍRITO
SANTO

Barragem de
São Simão
Goiandira
Catalão
Curvelo
Itabira
Araguari
Cnl
Fabriciano
Colatina

Ituama
Uberlândia
Barragem Água
Vermelha
Uberaba
Araxá
M I N A S   G E R A I S
Sete Lagoas
**Belo
Horizonte**
Divinópolis
Carangola
Manhuaçu
Ponte Nova
Cariacica
Vitória
Vila Velha

Rubinéia
S.José
do R.Prêto
Franca
Passos
Barretos
Ribeirão Prêto
Poços de Caldas
Lavras
S.João del Rei
Lafaiete
Barbacena
Carangola
Itaperuna
Cachoeiro de Itapemirim

Catanduva
Araraquara
São Carlos
Limeira
Piracicaba
Jundiaí
Campinas
Volta
Redonda
Barra
Marisa
Nova
Friburgo
Magé
Petrópolis
Niterói
Juiz de
Fora
S.João da Barra
Campos

S Ã O   P A U L O
Marília
Bauru
Sorocaba
Itapetininga
São Paulo
Santos
São Vicente
Itanhaém
Rio de Janeiro

Tropic of Capricorn

Jacareí
Jacareí
Tatuí
Juquiá
Iguape

Itararé
Curitiba
Mafra
Paranaguá
São Francisco do Sul

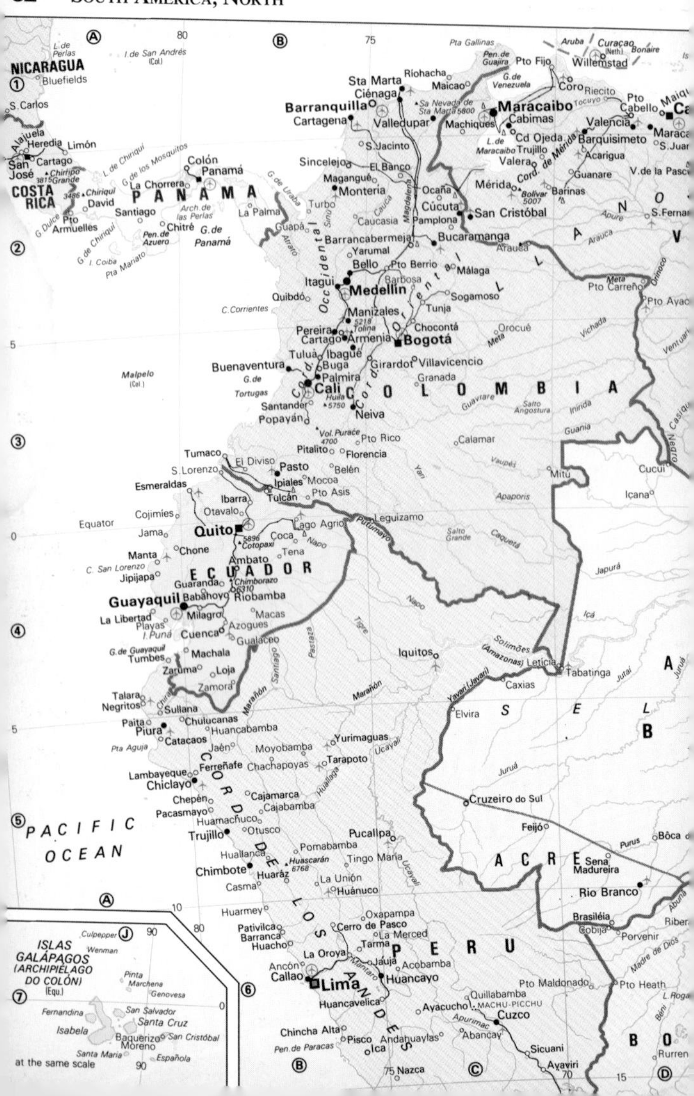

NICARAGUA
Bluefields
S. Carlos
Alajuela
Heredia
Limón
Cartago
San José
Chirripo Grande
COSTA RICA
Chiriquí
David
Pto Armuelles
G. Dulce
G. de Chiriquí
I. Coiba
Pta Mariato
L. de Chiriquí
G. de los Mosquitos
Colón
Panamá
La Chorrera
PANAMA
Santiago
Arch. de las Perlas
Chitré
Pen. de Azuero
G. de Panamá
G. de Urabá
La Palma
Turbo
I. de San Andrés (Col.)
L. de Perlas
Pta Gallinas
Pen. de Guajira
Pto Fijo
Aruba
Curaçao (Neth.)
Bonaire
Willemstad
Ríohacha
Sta Marta
Ciénaga
Maicao
G. de Venezuela
Barranquilla
Cartagena
Sa Nevada de Sta Marta 5800
Valledupar
Machiques
Maracaibo
Cabimas
L. de Maracaibo
Cd Ojeda
Trujillo
Valera
Coro
Riecito
Tocuyo
Pto Cabello
Valencia
Maracay
Barquisimeto
Acarigua
Guanare
V. de la Pascua
S. Juan
Cord. de Mérida
Mérida
Bolívar 5007
Barinas
Apure
S. Fernando
S. Jacinto
Sincelejo
El Banco
Magangué
Montería
Ocaña
Cúcuta
San Cristóbal
Pamplona
Caucasia
Cauca
Sinú
Magdalena
Guapi
Atrato
Barrancabermeja
Bucaramanga
Arauca
Yarumal
Bello
Pto Berrio
Málaga
Itaguí
Medellín
Barbosa
Quibdó
Sogamoso
Tunja
Cord. Occidental
Cord. Oriental
Pto Carreño
Meta
Orinoco
Pto Ayacucho
C. Corrientes
Manizales
5218 Tolima
Pereira
Cartago
Armenia
Chocontá
Bogotá
Orocué
Vichada
Ventuari
Tuluá
Ibagué
Buenaventura
Buga
Girardot
Villavicencio
Granada
Palmira
Cali
Huila 5750
Neiva
Santander
Popayán
G. de Tortugas
Malpelo (Col.)
COLOMBIA
Guaviare
Salto Angostura
Inírida
Guainía
Casiquiare
Negro
Vol. Puracé 4700
Pto Rico
Pitalito
Florencia
Calamar
Tumaco
El Diviso
Pasto
Belén
Vaupés
Mitú
Cucuí
S. Lorenzo
Esmeraldas
Ipiales
Mocoa
Tulcán
Pto Asís
Icana
Ibarra
Otavalo
Apaporis
Cojimíes
Equator
Quito
Jama
Lago Agrio
Putumayo
Leguízamo
5896 Cotopaxi
Coca
Napo
Tena
Salto Grande
Caquetá
Manta
Chone
Ambato
C. San Lorenzo
Jipijapa
ECUADOR
Guaranda
Chimborazo 6310
Riobamba
Japurá
Guayaquil
Babahoyo
La Libertad
Milagro
Macas
Playas
I. Puná
Cuenca
Azogues
Tigre
Içá
Gualaceo
Pastaza
G. de Guayaquil
Tumbes
Machala
Santiago
Iquitos
Solimões (Amazonas)
Letícia
Tabatinga
Jutaí
Juruá
Zaruma
Loja
Zamora
Marañón
Yavari (Javari)
Caxias
Talara
Negritos
Chira
Sullana
Elvira
Paita
Piura
Chulucanas
Huancabamba
Catacaos
Pta Aguja
Jaén
Moyobamba
Yurimaguas
Ucayali
Tarapoto
Lambayeque
Ferreñafe
Chachapoyas
Huallaga
Chiclayo
Chepén
Cajamarca
Cajabamba
Cruzeiro do Sul
Pacasmayo
Huamachuco
Otusco
Feijó
PACIFIC OCEAN
Trujillo
Pucallpa
Purus
Bôca do Acre
Pomabamba
Huallanca
Huascarán 6768
Tingo María
ACRE
Sena Madureira
Chimbote
Huaráz
La Unión
Casma
Huánuco
Rio Branco
Huarmey
Oxapampa
Abunã
Brasiléia
Cobija
Porvenir
Riberalta
Pativilca
Barranca
Huacho
Cerro de Pasco
La Merced
Tarma
La Oroya
Jauja
PERU
Madre de Dios
Ancón
Callao
Lima
Mantaro
Huancayo
Acobamba
Pto Maldonado
Pto Heath
L. Rogagua
Beni
Huancavelica
Ayacucho
Quillabamba
MACHU-PICCHU
Cuzco
Apurímac
Abancay
Chincha Alta
Pisco
Andahuaylas
Sicuani
Pen. de Paracas
Ica
Nazca
Ayaviri
Rurrenabaque
CORD. DE LOS ANDES
LLANOS
SELVAS
ISLAS GALÁPAGOS (ARCHIPIÉLAGO DO COLÓN) (Equ.)
Culpepper
Wenman
Pinta
Marchena
Genovesa
Fernandina
San Salvador
Santa Cruz
Isabela
Baquerizo Moreno
San Cristóbal
Santa María
Española
at the same scale

200   400   600 km
100   200   300 mls

The Grenadines
GRENADA °St George's
I.de Margarita
La Asunción Pen.de Paria °Tobago
Carúpano °Güiria G.of Paria **TRINIDAD AND TOBAGO**
Caripito Trinidad San Fernando Port of Spain
°Maturín
Tucupita
Barrancas
Cd Guayana Orinoco
I Bolívar °Upata
Cd Piar **Mabaruma**
Paragua
UELA Charity
Suddie
El Dorado Roraima **V.en Hoop** **Georgetown**
Salto 2180 Bartica **New Amsterdam**
del Angel **Linden** **Paramaribo**
La Gran Kaieteur Nieuw **Marienburg**
Sabana Fall **Nickerie** Totness Sinnamary
Sta Elena Apoera Witagron Albina I.du Diable (Devil's I.)
Sa Pacaraima **GUYANA** Blommesteinmeer Kourou °Cayenne
SURINAM **FRENCH** Cabo Orange
Bonfim °Lethem Julianatop **GUIANA** Oiapoque
1280
Boa Vista **RORAIMA** Serra Tumucumaque Amapá Ilha de Maracá
°Caracaraí **AMAPÁ**
Sa do Navio
Macapá
C Maguarinho
Pto Santana Salinópolis
I. de Marajó Bragança
Capanema
Oriximiná °Óbidos Amazonas Pará °Belém
Manaus Santarém Monte Abaetetuba
Manacapuru Careiro Itacoatiara Alegre Cametá
Tefé Altamira °
ZONAS Aveiro Tucuruí
Itaituba °
AS Madeira **PARÁ**
Pimenta
AZIL Marabá °Imperatriz
Jacareacanga
Humaitá °Prainha Pto
Franco
S.Félix Carolina
Pôrto Velho Aripuanã Araguaína
Serra do Cachimbó C.do Araguaia
Cachimbo
TOCANTINS
pará-Mirim °Rondônia Serra dos
RONDÔNIA Parecis
Vilhena São Félix
MATO GROSSO **GOIÁS**
VIA Trinidad
Mato Grosso Pto Artur Uruaçu
Aruanã

ATLANTIC OCEAN

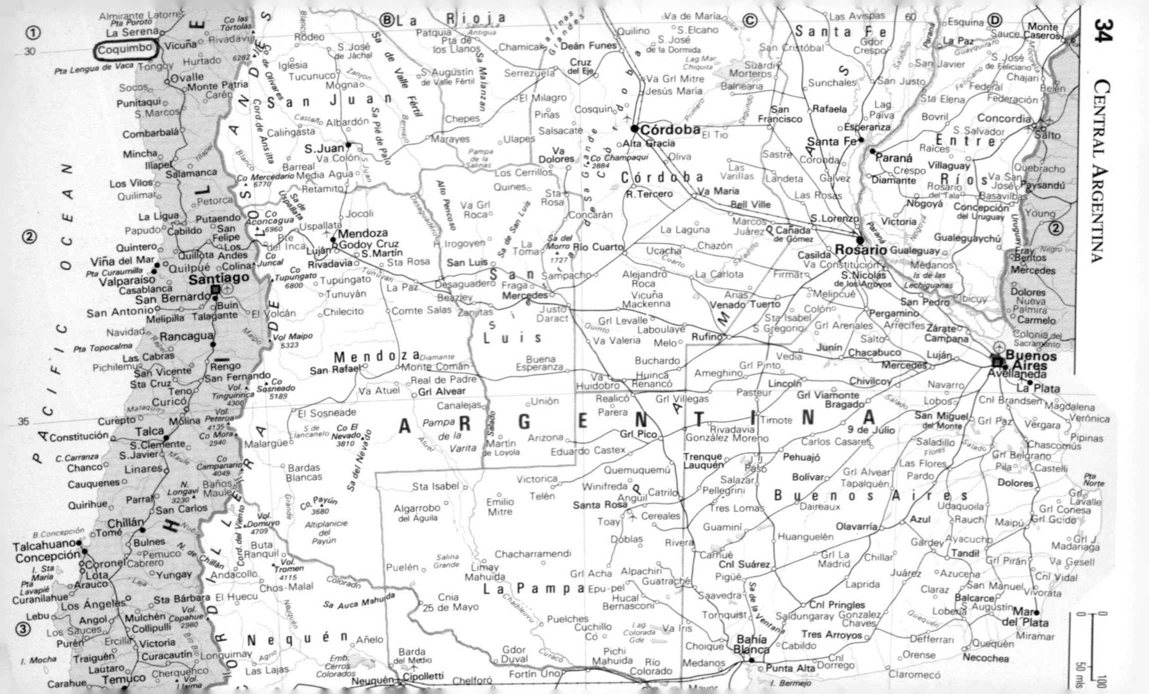
0
100
50 mls
Buenos Aires
La Plata
Avellaneda
Mar del Plata
Bahía Blanca
Punta Alta
Necochea
Tandil
Olavarría
Azul
Rosario
Santa Fe
Paraná
Córdoba
Río Cuarto
Va María
San Luis
Mendoza
San Juan
San Rafael
Santa Rosa
Neuquén
Santiago
Valparaíso
Viña del Mar
Rancagua
Talca
Chillán
Concepción
Talcahuano
Temuco
La Serena
Coquimbo
Salto
Paysandú
Concordia
Gualeguaychú
Entre Ríos
Santa Fe
Córdoba
San Luis
Mendoza
San Juan
La Pampa
Buenos Aires
Neuquén
La Rioja
ARGENTINA
CHILE
URUGUAY
Co Aconcagua 6960
Co Tupungato 6800
Co Mercedario 6770
Vol Maipo 5323
Sa de Valle Fértil
Sa de San Luis
Sa de la Ventana
Pampa de la Varita
OCEANO PACIFICO

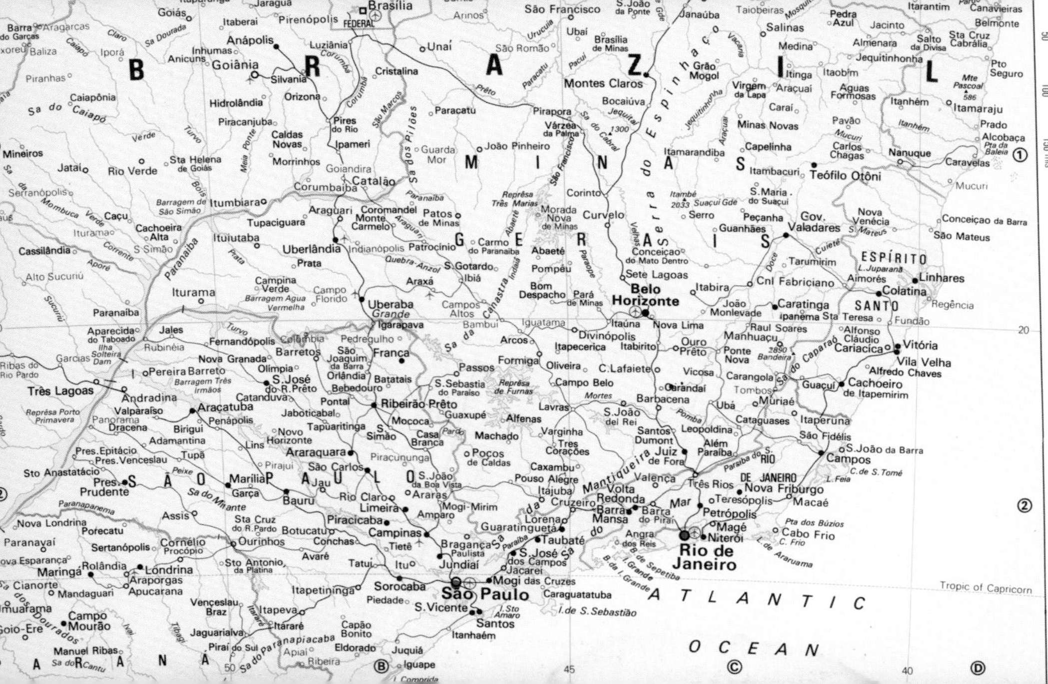
50 100 150 mls
100 200 300 km
ATLANTIC OCEAN
Tropic of Capricorn
BRAZIL
MINAS GERAIS
ESPÍRITO SANTO
RIO DE JANEIRO
SÃO PAULO
PARANÁ
FEDERAL
Brasília
Belo Horizonte
Rio de Janeiro
São Paulo
Vitória
Goiânia
Anápolis
Santos
Campinas
Niterói
Petrópolis
Juiz de Fora
Uberaba
Uberlândia
Ribeirão Prêto
Montes Claros
Gov. Valadares
Londrina
Maringá
Campos
Paranaíba
São Francisco
Serra do Espinhaço
Serra da Mantiqueira
Serra da Canastra
Cabo Frio
I. de S. Sebastião
I. Grande

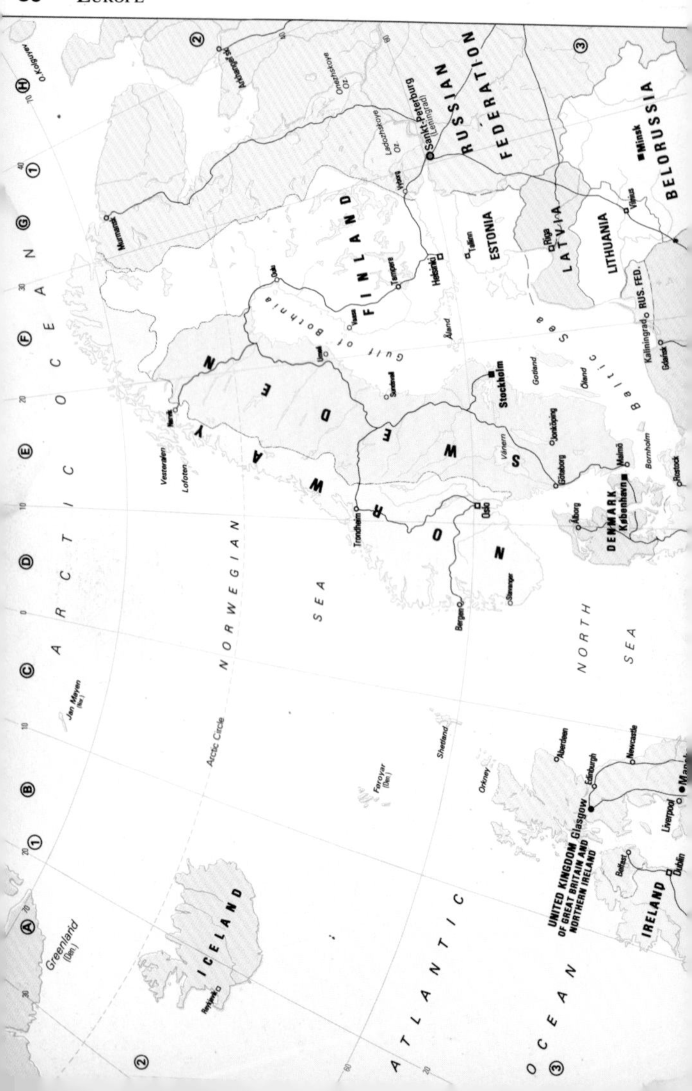
ARCTIC OCEAN
NORWEGIAN SEA
NORTH SEA
ATLANTIC OCEAN
Baltic Sea
Gulf of Bothnia
ICELAND
Reykjavik
Greenland (Den.)
Jan Mayen (Nor.)
Føroyar (Den.)
Shetland
Orkney
UNITED KINGDOM OF GREAT BRITAIN AND NORTHERN IRELAND
Glasgow
Edinburgh
Aberdeen
Newcastle
Liverpool
Belfast
Dublin
IRELAND
NORWAY
Bergen
Stavanger
Oslo
Trondheim
Narvik
Vesterålen
Lofoten
SWEDEN
Stockholm
Göteborg
Jönköping
Vänern
Sundsvall
Umeå
Malmö
Gotland
Öland
Bornholm
DENMARK
København
Ålborg
FINLAND
Helsinki
Tampere
Vaasa
Oulu
Åland
Vyborg
ESTONIA
Tallinn
LATVIA
Riga
LITHUANIA
Vilnius
RUS. FED.
Kaliningrad
Gdańsk
Rostock
BELORUSSIA
Minsk
RUSSIAN FEDERATION
Sankt-Peterburg (Leningrad)
Ladozhskoye Oz.
Onezhskoye Oz.
Arkhangel'sk
Murmansk
o. Kolguyev
Arctic Circle

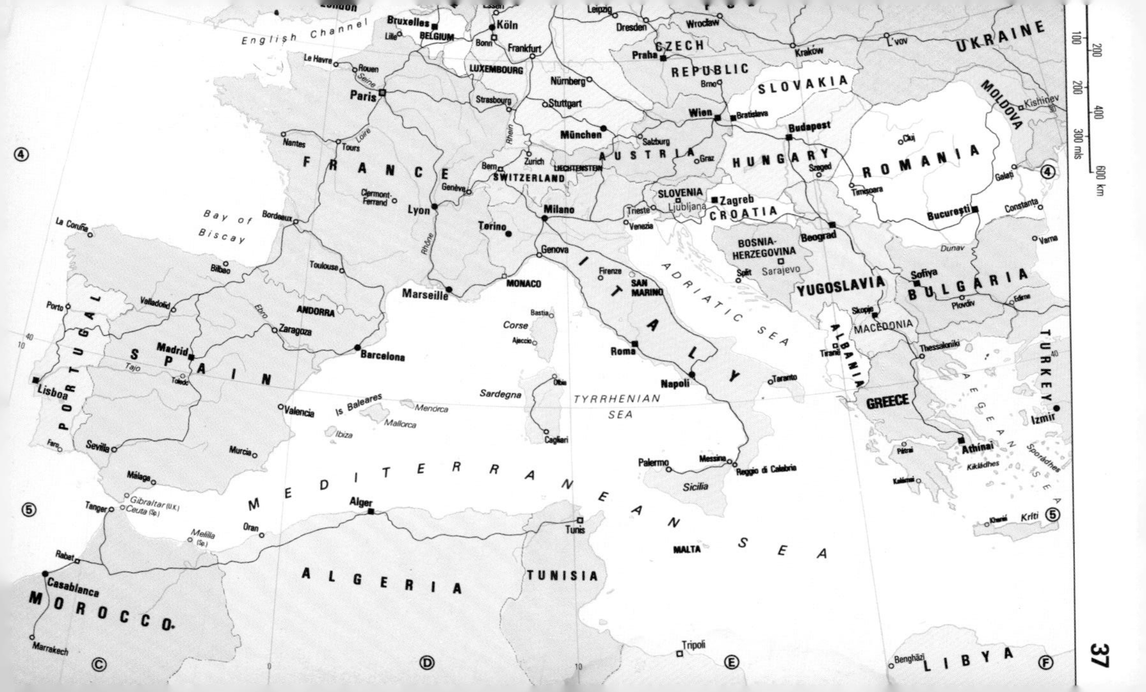
200
400
600 km
100
200
300 mls
English Channel
Bay of Biscay
Bruxelles
BELGIUM
Lille
Köln
Bonn
Frankfurt
LUXEMBOURG
Leipzig
Dresden
Wrocław
Kraków
L'vov
UKRAINE
MOLDOVA
Kishinev
CZECH REPUBLIC
Praha
Brno
SLOVAKIA
Le Havre
Rouen
Seine
Paris
Nürnberg
Stuttgart
Strasbourg
Wien
Bratislava
Budapest
HUNGARY
Szeged
Cluj
ROMANIA
Galați
Timișoara
București
Constanța
Varna
Dunav
Nantes
Tours
Loire
FRANCE
Rhein
München
Salzburg
AUSTRIA
Graz
Zurich
Bern
SWITZERLAND
LIECHTENSTEIN
Genève
Clermont-Ferrand
Lyon
Rhône
SLOVENIA
Ljubljana
Zagreb
CROATIA
Trieste
Venezia
Milano
Torino
Genova
MONACO
Marseille
Bordeaux
Toulouse
La Coruña
Bilbao
Beograd
BOSNIA-HERZEGOVINA
Sarajevo
Split
YUGOSLAVIA
Sofiya
BULGARIA
Plovdiv
Edirne
Skopje
MACEDONIA
ALBANIA
Tiranë
Thessaloníki
TURKEY
Izmir
GREECE
Athínai
Pátrai
Kalámai
AEGEAN SEA
Sporádhes
Kikládhes
Kríti
Khaniá
Firenze
SAN MARINO
ITALY
ADRIATIC SEA
Roma
Napoli
Taranto
Corse
Bastia
Ajaccio
Sardegna
Olbia
Cagliari
TYRRHENIAN SEA
Palermo
Messina
Reggio di Calabria
Sicilia
MALTA
Porto
PORTUGAL
Lisboa
Faro
Valladolid
Ebro
ANDORRA
Zaragoza
Madrid
SPAIN
Tajo
Toledo
Barcelona
Valencia
Is Baleares
Menorca
Mallorca
Ibiza
Murcia
Sevilla
Málaga
Gibraltar (U.K.)
Ceuta (Sp.)
Tanger
Melilla (Sp.)
Oran
Alger
MEDITERRANEAN SEA
Tunis
TUNISIA
ALGERIA
Rabat
Casablanca
MOROCCO
Marrakech
Tripoli
Benghāzī
LIBYA
40
10
0
④
⑤
Ⓒ
Ⓓ
Ⓔ
Ⓕ

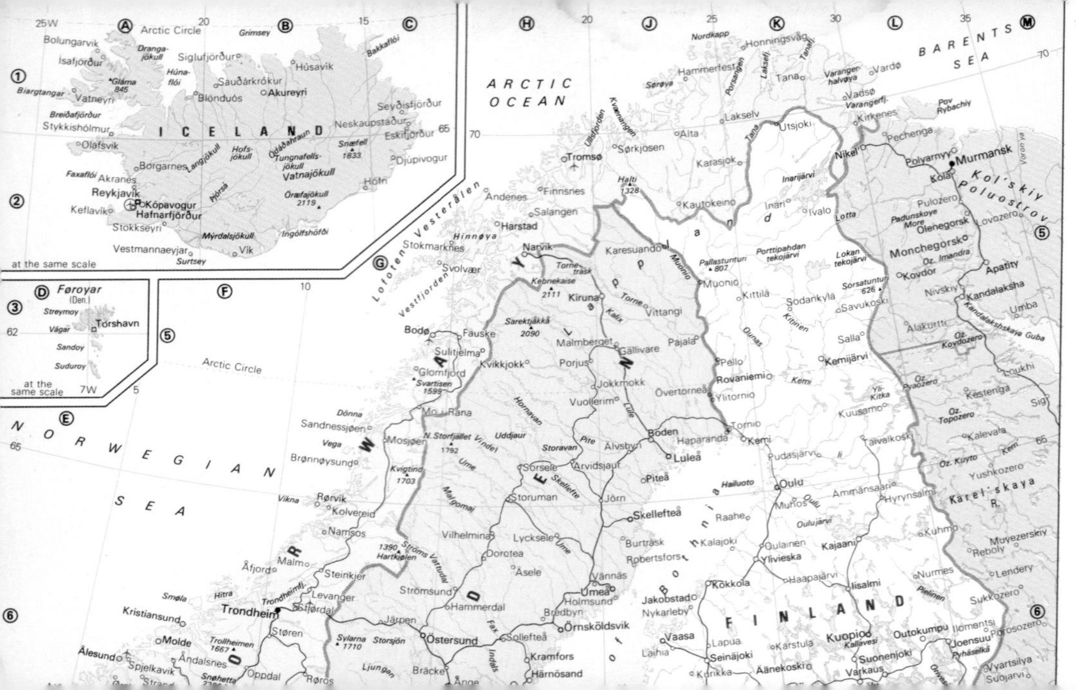
BARENTS SEA
ARCTIC OCEAN
NORWEGIAN SEA
Kol'skiy Poluostrov
Murmansk
Kola
Polyarnyy
Pechenga
Pov Rybachiy
Nikel'
Kirkenes
Vardø
Vadsø
Varangerfj.
Varangerhalvøya
Tana
Tanafj.
Honningsvåg
Nordkapp
Hammerfest
Porsangen
Lakselv
Laksefj.
Alta
Karasjok
Kautokeino
Sørøya
Kvænangen
Tromsø
Ullsfjorden
Finnsnes
Halti 1328
Utsjoki
Inarijärvi
Inari
Ivalo
Lotta
Pulozero
Padunskoye More
Olenegorsk
Lovozero
Monchegorsk
Oz. Imandra
Kovdor
Apatity
Nivskiy
Kandalaksha
Kandalakshskaya Guba
Umba
Oz. Kovdozero
Alakurtti
Loukhi
Oz. Pyaozero
Kestenga
Sig
Oz. Topozero
Kalevala
Kem'
Oz. Kuyto
Yushkozero
Karel'skaya R.
Muyezerskiy
Reboly
Lendery
Sukkozero
Porosozero
Vyartsilya
Suojärvi
Joensuu
Ilomantsi
Pyhäselkä
Orivesi
Outokumpu
Nurmes
Pielinen
Kuhmo
Hyrynsalmi
Yli-Kitka
Kuusamo
Taivalkoski
Sorsatunturi 626
Savukoski
Salla
Kemijärvi
Lokan tekojärvi
Sodankylä
Kitinen
Porttipahdan tekojärvi
Kittilä
Ounas
Pallastunturi 807
Muonio
Pello
Rovaniemi
Ylitornio
Tornio
Kemi
Oulu
Pudasjärvi
Ii
Oulujärvi
Muhos
Kajaani
Ämmänsaari
Iisalmi
Kuopio
Kallavesi
Suonenjoki
Varkaus
Haapajärvi
Ylivieska
Oulainen
Raahe
Hailuoto
Kalajoki
Kokkola
Jakobstad
Nykarleby
Vaasa
Laihia
Seinäjoki
Lapua
Kurikka
Karstula
Äänekoski
FINLAND
Haparanda
Luleå
Boden
Piteå
Skellefteå
Burträsk
Robertsfors
Övertorneå
Pajala
Vittangi
Karesuando
Torne
Kalix
Kiruna
Torneträsk
Kebnekaise 2111
Sarektjåkkå 2090
Gällivare
Malmberget
Jokkmokk
Porjus
Vuollerim
Lule
Älvsbyn
Arvidsjaur
Jörn
Pite
Storavan
Skellefte
Sorsele
Storuman
Hornavan
Uddjaur
Lycksele
Ume
Vindel
Vännäs
Umeå
Holmsund
Bredbyn
Örnsköldsvik
Åsele
Dorotea
Vilhelmina
Malgomaj
Kramfors
Härnösand
Sollefteå
Fax
Indals
Hammerdal
Strömsund
Ströms Vattudal
Östersund
Bräcke
Ånge
Järpen
Storsjön
Ljungan
Sylarna 1710
Røros
Narvik
Harstad
Salangen
Andenes
Hinnøya
Stokmarknes
Svolvær
Vesterålen
Lofoten
Vestfjorden
Kvikkjokk
Fauske
Sulitjelma
Bodø
Glomfjord
Svartisen 1599
Mo i Rana
N. Storfjället 1792
Mosjøen
Kvigtind 1703
Hartkjølen 1390
Dønna
Sandnessjøen
Vega
Brønnøysund
Rørvik
Kolvereid
Namsos
Vikna
Steinkjer
Levanger
Stjørdal
Malmo
Åfjord
Trondheimfj.
Trondheim
Hitra
Støren
Oppdal
Trollheimen 1667
Snøhetta
Smøla
Kristiansund
Molde
Åndalsnes
Ålesund
Spjelkavik
ICELAND
Arctic Circle
Drangajökull
Húnaflói
Siglufjörður
Grímsey
Sauðárkrókur
Blönduós
Akureyri
Húsavík
Bakkaflói
Seyðisfjörður
Neskaupstaður
Eskifjörður
Djúpivogur
Höfn
Snæfell 1833
Vatnajökull
Öræfajökull 2119
Ingólfshöfði
Ódáðahraun
Tungnafellsjökull
Hofsjökull
Langjökull
Þjórsá
Mýrdalsjökull
Vík
Surtsey
Vestmannaeyjar
Stokkseyri
Hafnarfjörður
Kópavogur
Reykjavík
Keflavík
Akranes
Faxaflói
Borgarnes
Ólafsvík
Stykkishólmur
Breiðafjörður
Biargtangar
Vatneyri
Ísafjörður
Bolungarvík
Gláma 845
at the same scale
Føroyar (Den.)
Streymoy
Vágar
Tórshavn
Sandoy
Suðuroy
at the same scale

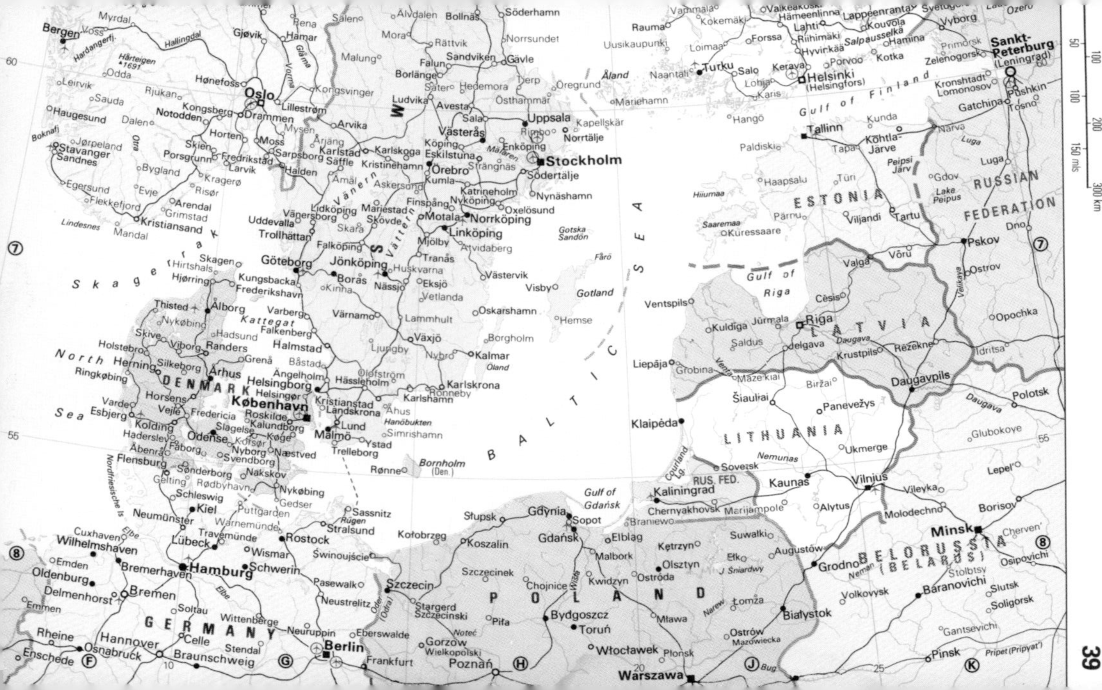

50 100 150 mls
100 200 300 km
Bergen
Voss
Myrdal
Hardangerfj.
Hallingdal
Hårteigen 1691
Odda
Leirvik
Sauda
Haugesund
Boknafj
Stavanger
Sandnes
Jørpeland
Egersund
Flekkefjord
Lindesnes
Mandal
Kristiansand
Grimstad
Arendal
Risør
Kragerø
Larvik
Skien
Porsgrunn
Horten
Kongsberg
Notodden
Rjukan
Hønefoss
Gjøvik
Hamar
Rena
Glåma
Vorma
Oslo
Drammen
Moss
Fredrikstad
Sarpsborg
Halden
Lillestrøm
Kongsvinger
Skagen
Hirtshals
Hjørring
Ålborg
Thisted
Skive
Viborg
Randers
Århus
Silkeborg
Herning
Holstebro
Ringkøbing
Horsens
Vejle
Fredericia
Kolding
Esbjerg
Varde
Haderslev
Åbenrå
Flensburg
Odense
Svendborg
Nyborg
Slagelse
Roskilde
København
Helsingør
Helsingborg
DENMARK
Skagerrak
Kattegat
North Sea
Göteborg
Kungsbacka
Varberg
Falkenberg
Halmstad
Uddevalla
Trollhättan
Vänersborg
Borås
Jönköping
Vänern
Vättern
Karlstad
Säffle
Arvika
Kristinehamn
Karlskoga
Örebro
Västerås
Uppsala
Stockholm
Södertälje
Nynäshamn
Norrtälje
Norrköping
Linköping
Motala
Nyköping
Eskilstuna
Gävle
Söderhamn
Sandviken
Falun
Borlänge
Mora
Malung
Ludvika
Avesta
Sala
Växjö
Kalmar
Karlskrona
Karlshamn
Kristianstad
Landskrona
Malmö
Lund
Ystad
Trelleborg
Öland
Gotland
Visby
Hemse
Fårö
Bornholm (Den.)
Rønne
Åland
Mariehamn
Turku
Salo
Naantali
Rauma
Forssa
Lahti
Kouvola
Kotka
Hamina
Porvoo
Helsinki (Helsingfors)
Lappeenranta
Vyborg
Hangö
Gulf of Finland
Tallinn
Paldiski
Haapsalu
Pärnu
Kuressaare
Saaremaa
Hiiumaa
Tartu
Viljandi
Narva
Kohtla-Järve
ESTONIA
Lake Peipus
Sankt-Peterburg (Leningrad)
Kronshtadt
Lomonosov
Gatchina
Pushkin
Tosno
Luga
Pskov
Ostrov
Dno
RUSSIAN FEDERATION
Velikaya
Opochka
Valga
Cēsis
Riga
Jūrmala
Jelgava
Gulf of Riga
Ventspils
Kuldīga
Liepāja
Daugavpils
Rēzekne
Krustpils
Daugava
LATVIA
Šiauliai
Panevėžys
Kaunas
Vilnius
Alytus
Ukmerge
Klaipėda
LITHUANIA
Nemunas
Sovetsk
Kaliningrad
RUS. FED.
Polotsk
Lepel'
Borisov
Minsk
Molodechno
Vileyka
Grodno
Baranovichi
Slutsk
Soligorsk
Pinsk
BELORUSSIA (BELARUS)
Gdańsk
Gdynia
Sopot
Gulf of Gdańsk
Elbląg
Olsztyn
Słupsk
Koszalin
Szczecin
Bydgoszcz
Toruń
Włocławek
Warszawa
Białystok
Augustów
Suwałki
Łomża
Poznań
Gorzów Wielkopolski
POLAND
BALTIC SEA
Kiel
Lübeck
Hamburg
Rostock
Stralsund
Wismar
Schwerin
Bremen
Bremerhaven
Wilhelmshaven
Oldenburg
Hannover
Osnabrück
Braunschweig
Celle
Berlin
Frankfurt
Elbe
GERMANY
Nordfriesische Is

NORWAY

Nordhordland
Dale
Bergen
Sotra
Sunnhordland
Stord
Bömlo
Skålöo
Lervik
Haugesund
Karmöy

Shetland
Herma Ness
Unst
Yell
Isbister
Whalsay
St Magnus B.
Lerwick
Foula
Sumburgh Hd

Fair Isle

Orkney
Westray
Sanday
Stronsay
Rousay
Kirkwall
Stromness
Hoy
Scapa Flow
Duncansby Hd

Sule Skerry
Stack Skerry

N O R T H   S E A

Thurso
Wick
Helmsdale
Ben Hope 927
C. Wrath
Ben More Assynt 998
Dornoch
Dornoch Firth
Dingwall
Ullapool
Inverness
Fort Augustus
L. Ness
Elgin
Banff
Fraserburgh
Peterhead
Buchan Ness
Aberdeen
Stonehaven
Montrose
Arbroath
F. of Tay
St Andrews
Pitlochry
Braemar
Ben Macdui 1309
Perth
Dee
Don
Spey
Deveron

N. Rona
Sule Sgeir
Butt of Lewis
Flannan Is
Stornoway
Lewis
Harris
N. Uist
S. Uist
Barra
St Kilda

Outer Hebrides

The Minch

Skye
Portree
Kyle of Lochalsh
Mallaig
Fort William
Ben Nevis 1343
Rum
Eigg
Coll
Tiree
Mull
Oban
F. of Lorn
Colonsay
Jura
Islay
Campbeltown
Rathlin

SCOTLAND

Grampian Mts
Stirling
Loch Lomond
Greenock
Paisley
Glasgow
Motherwell
Arran
F. of Clyde
Kilmarnock
Irvine
Ayr
Girvan
Merrick 843
Moffat
Dumfries
Nith
Edinburgh
F. of Forth
Kirkcaldy
White Coomb 822
Hawick
Galashiels
Berwick-upon-Tweed
St Abbs Hd
Tweed
Cheviot Hills
Alnwick
Morpeth
Blyth
Newcastle upon Tyne

N. IRELAND
Coleraine
Londonderry
Lough Foyle
Main Hd
Errigal
Aran I.
Tory I.

50 100 150 200 km
50 100 mls

③

NETHERLANDS
's-Gravenhage (Den Haag)
Rotterdam
Vlissingen
Zeebrugge
Oostende
Brugge
Gent
Antwerpen
Mechelen
Bruxelles (Brussel)
BELGIUM
Roubaix
Tourcoing
Lille
Kortrijk
Dunkerque
Calais
Douai
Valenciennes
Denain
St-Quentin
PICARDIE
Béthune
Arras
Cambrai
Dover
Boulogne
St-Omer
Montreuil
Abbeville
Amiens
Beauvais
Compiègne
Senlis
Soissons
Château-Thierry
Provins
Meaux
PARIS
④
Sézanne
Seine
Montdidier
Noyon
Cergy
Versailles
FRANCE
Rambouillet
Étampes
Fontainebleau
Chartres
Dreux
Évreux
Mantes
Neufchâtel
Rouen
Dieppe
Le Tréport
Bolbec
Fécamp
Le Havre
Elbeuf
Lisieux
Louviers
Argentan
Alençon
Mayenne
Domfront
Deauville
Bayeux
Caen
St-Lô
NORMANDIE
Coutances
C. de Barfleur
Cherbourg
C. de la Hague
Valognes
St-Hélier
Jersey
Guernsey
Sark
Alderney
Channel Is.
(U.K.)
Golfe de St-Malo
Granville
St-Michel
Mont St-Michel
Avranches
Fougères
Dinan
Dinard
St-Malo
St-Brieuc
Cahaix
Plouha
Morlaix
Roscoff
Brest
L'Ouessant

② ③ ④

Flamborough Hd
Scarborough
Bridlington
Hull
Spurn Hd
Grimsby
Humber
Great Yarmouth
Lowestoft
Scunthorpe
Doncaster
York
Selby
Ouse
Trent
Leeds
Harrogate
Bradford
Huddersfield
Lancaster
Morecambe
Blackpool
Preston
Bolton
Manchester
Warrington
Liverpool
Birkenhead
Chester
Crewe
Stoke-on-Trent
Sheffield
Lincoln
Newark
King's Lynn
Norwich
The Wash
Peterborough
Nottingham
Derby
Leicester
Newmarket
Cambridge
Ipswich
Felixstowe
Harwich
Colchester
Bedford
Northampton
Coventry
Birmingham
Wolverhampton
Shrewsbury
ENGLAND
Stratford
Gloucester
Oxford
Luton
Chelmsford
Southend-on-Sea
London
Thames
Maidstone
Canterbury
Dover
Folkestone
Crawley
Guildford
Reading
Windsor
Swindon
Bristol
Bath
Salisbury
Winchester
Southampton
Portsmouth
Isle of Wight
Brighton
Hastings
Eastbourne
Bournemouth
Weymouth
Barrow-in-Furness
Kendal
Douglas
Isle of Man
Holyhead (Caergybi)
Anglesey
Bangor
Caernarfon
Snowdon
Pwllheli
Aberystwyth
Cardigan Bay
WALES
Builth Wells
Brecon
Newport
Cardiff
Bristol Chan.
Weston-super-Mare
Taunton
Exeter
Barnstaple
Bideford
Bude
Newquay
Padstow
Truro
Falmouth
Penzance
Land's End
Lizard Pt
Isles of Scilly
Plymouth
Torquay
Dartmoor
Tavistock
Prawle Pt
Exmoor
Fishguard
Carmarthen
Swansea
Pembroke
St David's Hd
Cardigan
Lundy I.
Bristol Channel
English Channel

IRISH SEA

Newry
Dundalk
Drogheda
Dublin (Baile Átha Cliath)
Dún Laoghaire
Bray
Wicklow
Arklow
Wexford
Rosslare
Wicklow Mts
REP. OF IRELAND
Cavan
Longford
Mullingar
Port Laoise
Athlone
Shannon
Roscommon
Boyle
Castlebar
Ballina
Castlerea
L. Conn
L. Mask
L. Corrib
Galway
Ennis
Limerick
Tipperary
Kilkenny
Clonmel
Waterford
Carlow
Monasterevin
Thurles
Nenagh
Dungarvan
Youghal
Cork
Old Hd of Kinsale
Mallow
Killarney
Tralee
Dingle
Dingle Bay
Kenmare
Bantry
Bantry B.
C. Clear
Aran Is.
Clew B.
Achill Hd
Slyne Hd
Galway B.
L. Derg
L. Ree
Mizen Hd

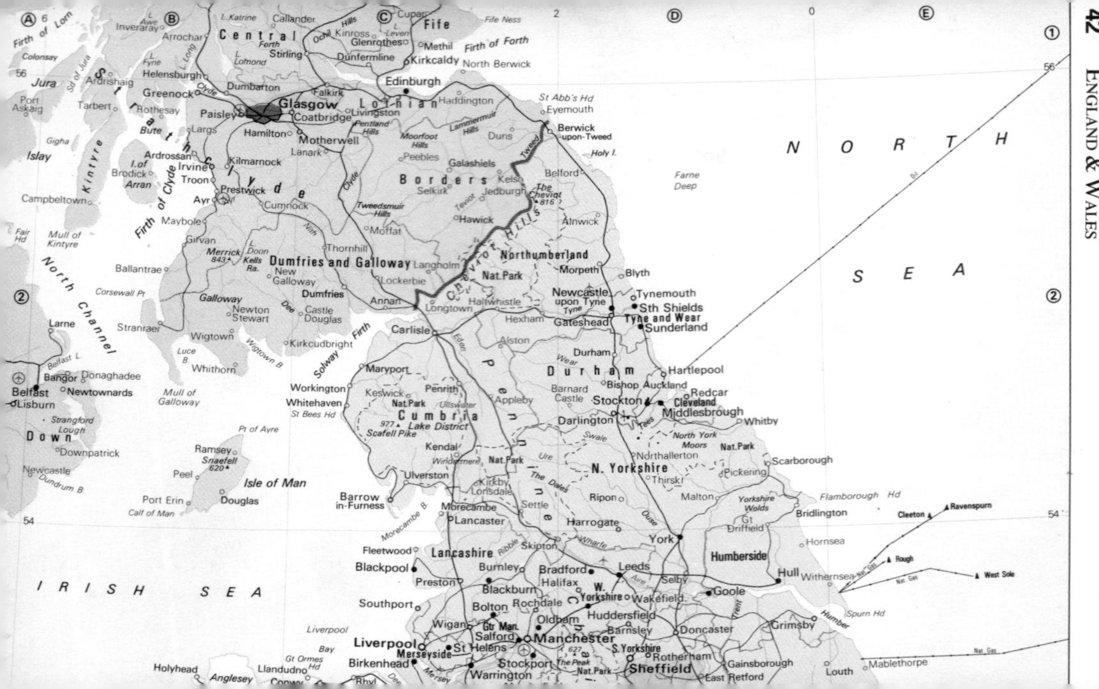
N O R T H
S E A
I R I S H
S E A
North Channel
Firth of Forth
Firth of Clyde
Solway Firth
Central
Fife
Lothian
Strathclyde
Borders
Dumfries and Galloway
Northumberland
Tyne and Wear
Durham
Cleveland
Cumbria
N. Yorkshire
Humberside
Lancashire
Merseyside
Gtr Man.
W. Yorkshire
S. Yorkshire
Isle of Man
Down
Edinburgh
Glasgow
Coatbridge
Motherwell
Hamilton
Paisley
Greenock
Dumbarton
Stirling
Falkirk
Livingston
Dunfermline
Kirkcaldy
Glenrothes
Kinross
Cupar
Methil
North Berwick
Haddington
Kilmarnock
Irvine
Troon
Ayr
Prestwick
Cumnock
Lanark
Peebles
Galashiels
Selkirk
Kelso
Jedburgh
Hawick
Moffat
Langholm
Lockerbie
Annan
Dumfries
Castle Douglas
Kirkcudbright
Newton Stewart
Wigtown
Whithorn
Stranraer
Ballantrae
Girvan
Maybole
Berwick-upon-Tweed
Eyemouth
Duns
Belford
Alnwick
Morpeth
Blyth
Newcastle upon Tyne
Tynemouth
Sth Shields
Gateshead
Sunderland
Hexham
Haltwhistle
Alston
Durham
Hartlepool
Bishop Auckland
Barnard Castle
Stockton
Middlesbrough
Redcar
Darlington
Whitby
Scarborough
Pickering
Northallerton
Thirsk
Malton
Ripon
Harrogate
York
Bridlington
Driffield
Hornsea
Hull
Withernsea
Carlisle
Longtown
Penrith
Appleby
Keswick
Maryport
Workington
Whitehaven
Kendal
Ulverston
Barrow in-Furness
Kirkby Lonsdale
Settle
Morecambe
Lancaster
Fleetwood
Blackpool
Preston
Southport
Liverpool
Birkenhead
St Helens
Warrington
Wigan
Bolton
Blackburn
Burnley
Rochdale
Oldham
Salford
Manchester
Stockport
Skipton
Bradford
Halifax
Leeds
Huddersfield
Wakefield
Barnsley
Selby
Goole
Doncaster
Rotherham
Sheffield
Gainsborough
East Retford
Grimsby
Louth
Mablethorpe
Holyhead
Llandudno
Rhyl
Conwy
Anglesey
Douglas
Ramsey
Peel
Port Erin
Snaefell 620
Calf of Man
Pt of Ayre
Belfast
Lisburn
Bangor
Donaghadee
Newtownards
Larne
Downpatrick
Newcastle
Strangford Lough
Dundrum B.
Belfast L.
Islay
Jura
Colonsay
Port Askaig
Gigha
Kintyre
Campbeltown
Mull of Kintyre
Fair Hd
Tarbert
Ardrishaig
Rothesay
Bute
Largs
Ardrossan
Brodick
I. of Arran
Inveraray
Arrochar
Helensburgh
Callander
Firth of Lorn
Sd of Jura
L. Katrine
L. Lomond
L. Fyne
L. Awe
L. Long
L. Leven
Ochil Hills
Pentland Hills
Moorfoot Hills
Lammermuir Hills
Tweedsmuir Hills
Cheviot Hills
The Cheviot 816
Merrick 843
Kells Ra.
Galloway
Lake District
Scafell Pike 977
Nat. Park
North York Moors
Yorkshire Wolds
The Dales
The Peak 627
Pennines
Fife Ness
St Abb's Hd
Holy I.
Farne Deep
Flamborough Hd
Spurn Hd
Humber
St Bees Hd
Morecambe B.
Liverpool Bay
Gt Ormes Hd
Mull of Galloway
Luce B.
Wigtown B.
Corsewall Pt
Clyde
Tweed
Teviot
Nith
Dee
Eden
Wear
Tees
Swale
Ure
Ouse
Wharfe
Aire
Ribble
Trent
Mersey
Cleeton
Ravenspurn
Rough
West Sole
Nat. Gas
Oil

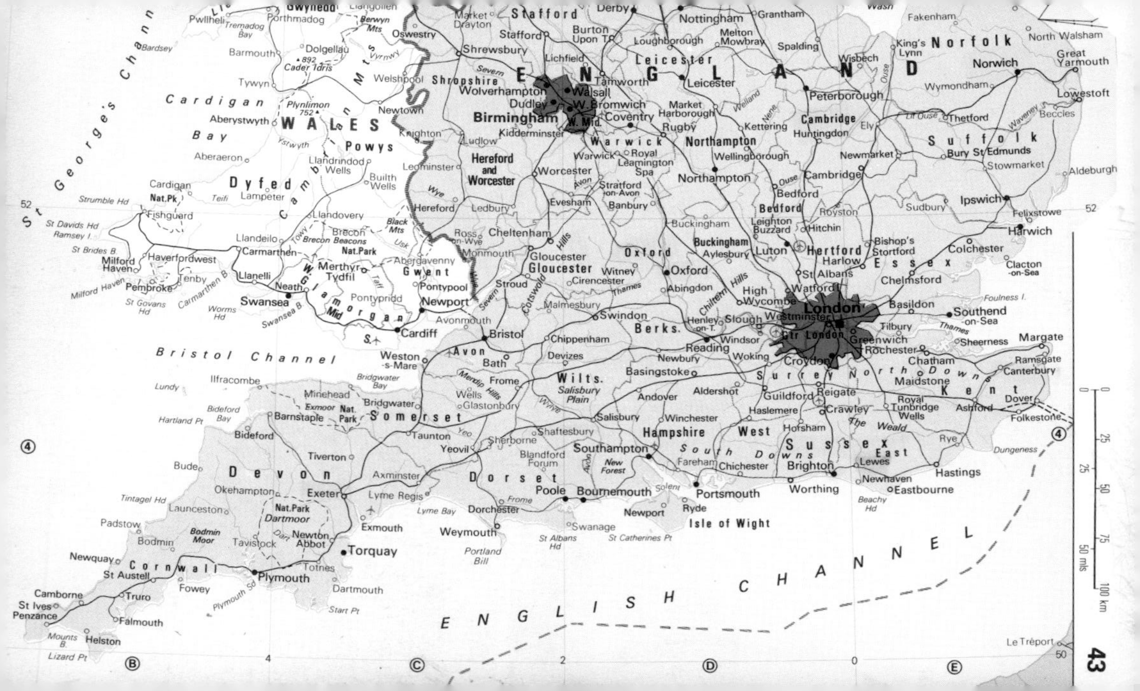

ENGLAND
WALES
Norfolk
Suffolk
Essex
Kent
East Sussex
West Sussex
Surrey
Hampshire
Dorset
Devon
Cornwall
Somerset
Avon
Wilts.
Berks.
Oxford
Buckingham
Hertford
Bedford
Cambridge
Northampton
Leicester
Warwick
Stafford
Shropshire
Hereford and Worcester
Gloucester
Gwent
W. Glamorgan
Mid Glamorgan
S. Glamorgan
Dyfed
Powys
Gwynedd
W. Mid.
Gtr London
London
Westminster
Birmingham
Wolverhampton
Walsall
Dudley
W. Bromwich
Coventry
Norwich
Great Yarmouth
Lowestoft
Ipswich
Colchester
Chelmsford
Southend-on-Sea
Oxford
Reading
Bristol
Cardiff
Newport
Swansea
Southampton
Portsmouth
Brighton
Bournemouth
Poole
Plymouth
Exeter
Torquay
Peterborough
Cambridge
Northampton
Leicester
Nottingham
Derby
Gloucester
Worcester
Hereford
Bath
Salisbury
Winchester
Dover
Canterbury
Margate
Hastings
Eastbourne
Isle of Wight
Bristol Channel
ENGLISH CHANNEL
Cardigan Bay
St George's Channel
Salisbury Plain
New Forest
North Downs
South Downs
The Weald
Nat. Park Dartmoor
Exmoor Nat. Park
Bodmin Moor
Brecon Beacons Nat. Park
Le Tréport
0 25 50 75 100 km
0 25 50 mls
43

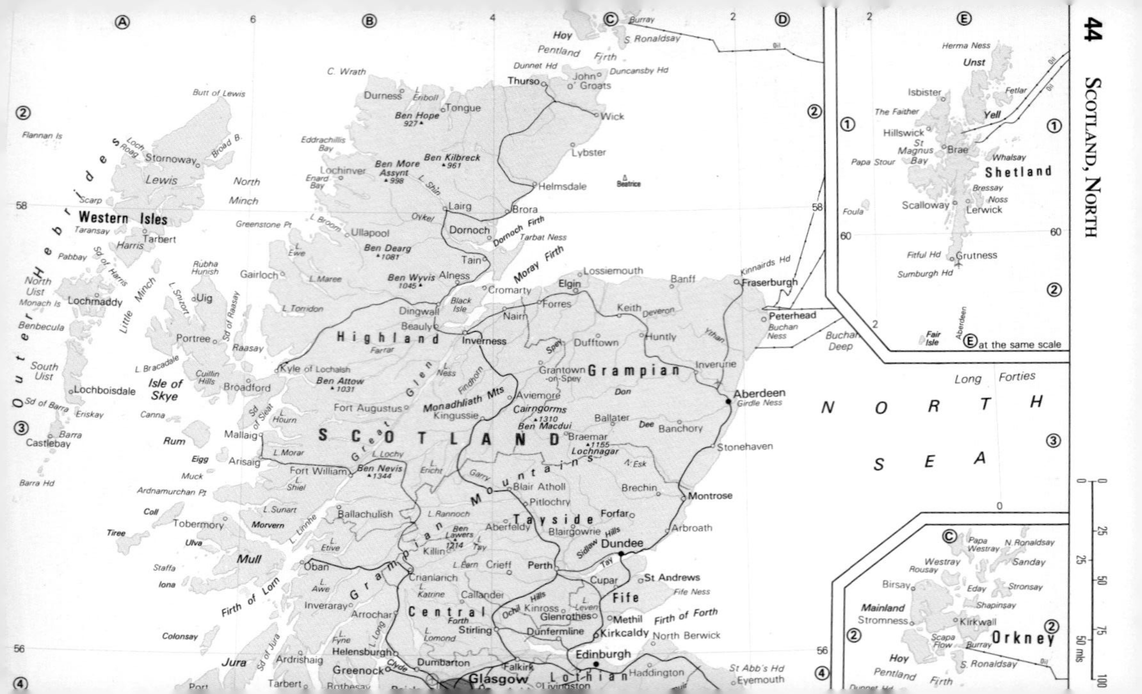
0 25 50 75 100
0 25 50 mls
Shetland
Unst
Yell
Fetlar
Whalsay
Herma Ness
Isbister
The Faither
Hillswick
St Magnus Bay
Papa Stour
Brae
Bressay
Noss
Lerwick
Scalloway
Foula
Fitful Hd
Sumburgh Hd
Grutness
Fair Isle
Aberdeen
at the same scale
Orkney
Papa Westray
N. Ronaldsay
Sanday
Westray
Rousay
Stronsay
Eday
Shapinsay
Kirkwall
Birsay
Mainland
Stromness
Scapa Flow
Burray
S. Ronaldsay
Hoy
Pentland Firth
NORTH SEA
Long Forties
Buchan Deep
Outer Hebrides
Western Isles
Lewis
Butt of Lewis
Broad B.
Stornoway
Loch Roag
Harris
Tarbert
Scarp
Taransay
Sd of Harris
Pabbay
Lochmaddy
North Uist
Monach Is
Benbecula
South Uist
Lochboisdale
Eriskay
Sd of Barra
Barra
Castlebay
Barra Hd
Flannan Is
Little Minch
North Minch
Isle of Skye
Uig
Portree
Broadford
Cuillin Hills
L. Snizort
L. Bracadale
Rubha Hunish
Raasay
Sd of Raasay
Canna
Rum
Egg
Muck
Ardnamurchan Pt
Coll
Tiree
Tobermory
Mull
Ulva
Staffa
Iona
Colonsay
Jura
Sd of Jura
Firth of Lorn
Morvern
Mallaig
Arisaig
Sd of Sleat
L. Hourn
L. Morar
L. Shiel
L. Sunart
Fort William
Ben Nevis 1344
Ballachulish
L. Etive
L. Linnhe
Oban
L. Awe
Inveraray
L. Fyne
Ardrishaig
Tarbert
C. Wrath
Durness
L. Eriboll
Tongue
Ben Hope 927
Ben Kilbreck 961
Ben More Assynt 998
L. Shin
Lairg
Eddrachillis Bay
Lochinver
Enard Bay
Ullapool
L. Broom
Ben Dearg 1081
Oykel
Greenstone Pt
L. Ewe
L. Maree
Gairloch
L. Torridon
Kyle of Lochalsh
Ben Attow 1031
Ben Wyvis 1045
Alness
Dingwall
Beauly
Farrar
Highland
Thurso
Dunnet Hd
John o' Groats
Duncansby Hd
Wick
Lybster
Helmsdale
Beatrice
Brora
Dornoch
Dornoch Firth
Tain
Tarbat Ness
Moray Firth
Cromarty
Black Isle
Inverness
Nairn
Forres
Elgin
Lossiemouth
Banff
Fraserburgh
Kinnairds Hd
Peterhead
Buchan Ness
Keith
Deveron
Huntly
Ythan
Inverurie
Aberdeen
Girdle Ness
Stonehaven
Banchory
Dee
Don
Dufftown
Grampian
Spey
Grantown-on-Spey
Aviemore
Cairngorms 1310
Ben Macdui
Braemar
Lochnagar 1155
Ballater
Monadhliath Mts
Findhorn
Kingussie
L. Ness
Great Glen
Fort Augustus
L. Lochy
SCOTLAND
Grampian Mountains
L. Ericht
Garry
Blair Atholl
Pitlochry
L. Rannoch
Ben Lawers 1214
L. Tay
Killin
Aberfeldy
Tayside
Blairgowrie
Sidlaw Hills
Forfar
Brechin
N. Esk
Montrose
Arbroath
Dundee
Tay
Perth
Crieff
L. Earn
Ochil Hills
Cupar
St Andrews
Fife Ness
Fife
Firth of Forth
L. Leven
Glenrothes
Methil
Kirkcaldy
Kinross
Dunfermline
North Berwick
Haddington
St Abb's Hd
Eyemouth
Edinburgh
Lothian
Livingston
Falkirk
Stirling
Callander
Forth
Central
L. Katrine
L. Lomond
Crianlarich
Arrochar
L. Long
Dumbarton
Helensburgh
Greenock
Clyde
Glasgow
Rothesay

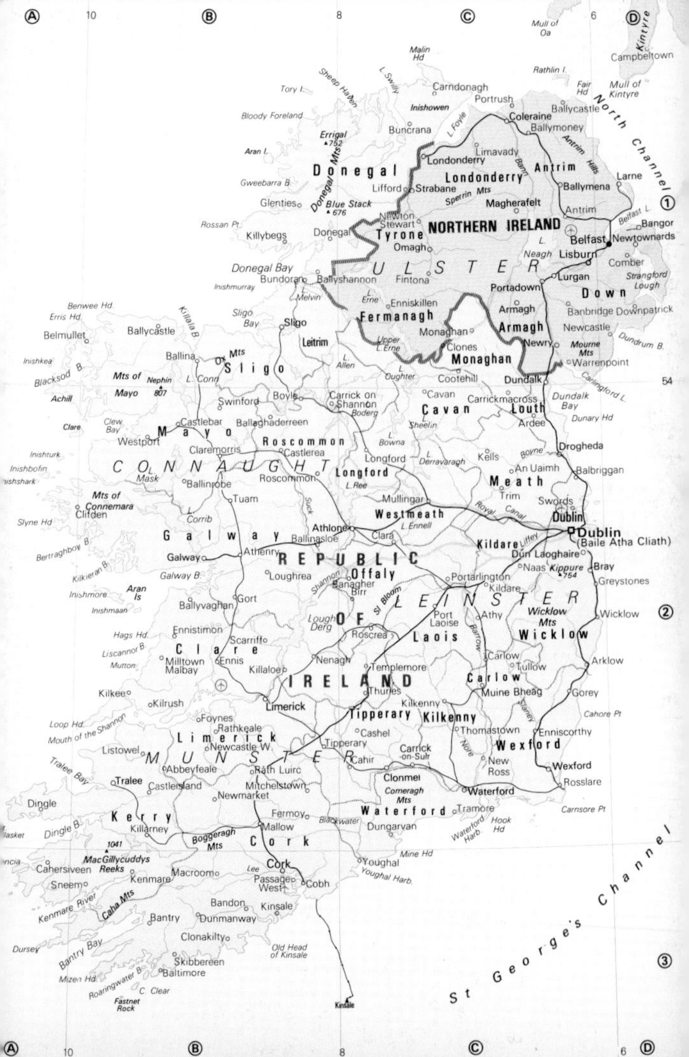

25   50   75   100 km

25   50 mls

Mull of Oa

Kintyre

Tory I.   Sheep Ha. Hd.   Malin Hd.   Campbeltown

Carndonagh   Fair Hd.   Mull of Kintyre

Bloody Foreland   Inishowen   Portrush   Rathlin I.

Errigal ▲752   Buncrana   Coleraine   Ballycastle   North Channel

Aran I.   Limavady   Ballymoney

Gweebarra B.   Londonderry   Antrim   Larne

Glenties   Donegal   Strabane   Sperrin Mts   Magherafelt   Antrim Hills   Ballymena   ①

Rossan Pt.   Blue Stack ▲676   Newton Stewart   Antrim   54

Killybegs   Omagh   NORTHERN IRELAND   L. Neagh   Belfast   Bangor

Donegal   Tyrone   U L S T E R   Lisburn   Newtownards

Donegal Bay   Ballyshannon   Fintona   Portadown   Down   Comber   Strangford Lough

Inishmurray   Bundoran   Lurgan   Banbridge   Downpatrick

Benwee Hd.   Melvin   Enniskillen   Monaghan   Armagh   Newry   Dundrum B.

Erris Hd.   Ballycastle   L. Erne   Fermanagh   Clones   Armagh   Mourne Mts   Warrenpoint

Belmullet   Sligo B.   Sligo   Upper L. Erne   Monaghan   Newcastle   Carlingford L.

Blacksod B.   Mts of   Leitrim   L. Allen   Cootehill   Dundalk   54

Achill   Mayo   Nephin ▲807   Ballina   Carrick on Shannon Boderg   Cavan   Carrickmacross   Louth   Dundalk Bay

Inishkea   Clare   Swinford   Boyle   L. Sheelin   Ardee   Dunany Hd.

Inishturk   Clew Bay   Castlebar   Ballaghaderreen   Kells   Drogheda

Westport   Roscommon   Castlerea   Longford   L. Derravaragh   Na Uaimh   Balbriggan

Inishbofin   Mask   Claremorris   Castlerea   Meath

Inishshark   Mts of   C O N N A U G H T   Roscommon   Longford   Mullingar   Swords   Dublin

Slyne Hd.   Connemara   Ballinrobe   L. Corrib   Tuam   Westmeath   L. Ree   Royal Canal   Dublin (Baile Átha Cliath)

Clifden   Galway   Athenry   Athlone   Ballinasloe   Clara   L. Ennel   Liffey   Dún Laoghaire

Bertraghboy B.   G A L W A Y   R E P U B L I C   Offaly   Kildare   Kippure ▲754   Bray

Kilkieran B.   Galway   Galway B.   Loughrea   Shannon   Banagher   L. Ennell   Naas   Greystones

Aran Is.   Gort   L. Derg   O F   Birr   Bloom   Port Laoise   Athy   Wicklow Mts   Wicklow   ②

Inishmore   Ballyvaughan   I R E L A N D   L E I N S T E R   Portarlington

Inishmaan   Hags Hd.   Ennistimon   Scariff   Roscrea   Laois   Carlow   Arklow

Liscannor B.   C L A R E   Killaloe   Nenagh   Wicklow   Gorey

Mutton I.   Milltown Malbay   Ennis   Templemore   Muine Bheagh   Carlow

Kilkee   Thurles   Kilkenny   Wexford

Loop Hd.   Kilrush   Limerick   Tipperary   Kilkenny   Enniscorthy

Mouth of the Shannon   Rathkeale   Cashel   Thomastown   New Ross

Foynes   L I M E R I C K   Tipperary   Carrick on Suir   Wexford   Wexford

Listowel   Newcastle W.   M U N S T E R   Cahir   Clonmel   Waterford   Rosslare

Tralee Bay   Abbeyfeale   Rath Luirc   Comeragh Mts   Waterford   Carnsore Pt.

Tralee   Castleisland   Mitchelstown   Dungarvan   Tramore   Hook Hd.

Dingle   Newmarket   Fermoy   Blackwater   Waterford Harb.   Mine Hd.

Dingle B.   Kerry   Killarney   Boggeragh Mts   Mallow   Lee   Youghal Harb.

Blasket   MacGillycuddys   ▲1041   Macroom   Cork   Cobh

Reeks   K E R R Y   Caha Mts   Bandon   Passage West   Cork

Cahersiveen   Sneem   Kenmare River   C O R K   Kinsale   Old Head of Kinsale   ③

Dursey   Bantry   Dunmanway   Clonakilty

Bantry Bay   Mizen Hd.   Skibbereen   Baltimore

Roaringwater B.   C. Clear

Fastnet Rock   Kenale   St George's Channel

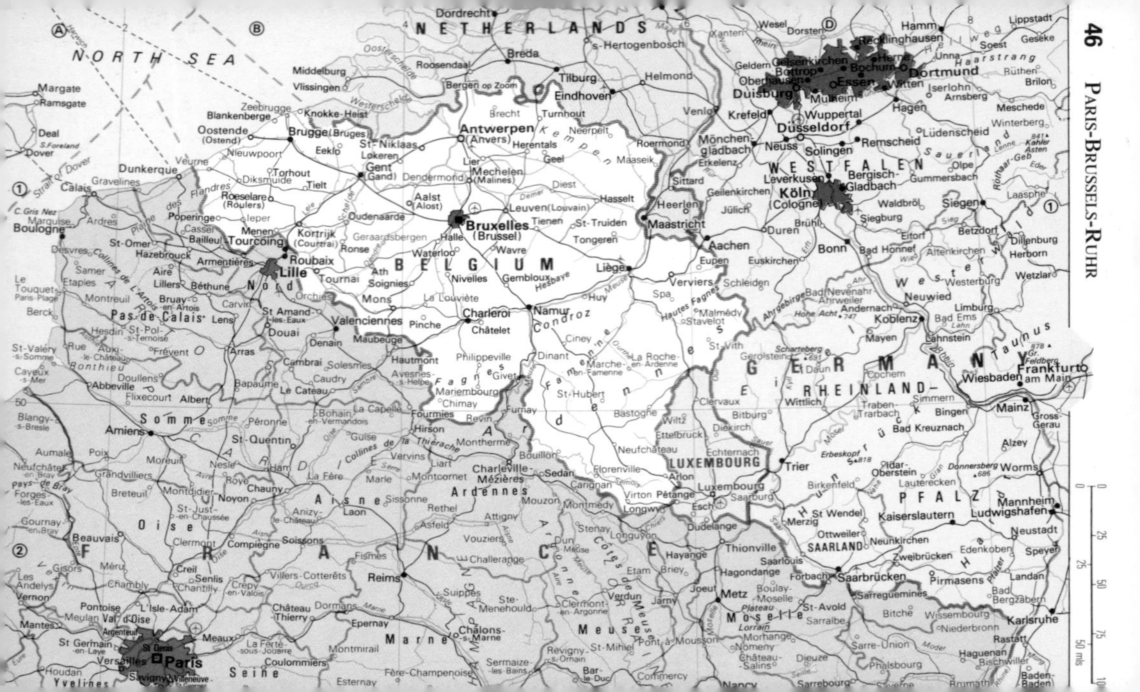

0 25 50 75 100
0 25 50 mls
NORTH SEA
NETHERLANDS
BELGIUM
LUXEMBOURG
FRANCE
GERMANY
NORDRHEIN-WESTFALEN
RHEINLAND-PFALZ
SAARLAND
Dordrecht
Breda
Tilburg
Eindhoven
's-Hertogenbosch
Helmond
Venlo
Roermond
Maastricht
Middelburg
Vlissingen
Roosendaal
Bergen op Zoom
Antwerpen (Anvers)
Brugge (Bruges)
Oostende (Ostend)
Gent (Gand)
Bruxelles (Brussel)
Leuven (Louvain)
Mechelen (Malines)
Liège
Namur
Charleroi
Mons
Tournai
Kortrijk (Courtrai)
Hasselt
Verviers
Aachen
Köln (Cologne)
Düsseldorf
Duisburg
Essen
Bochum
Dortmund
Wuppertal
Bonn
Koblenz
Siegen
Wiesbaden
Mainz
Frankfurt am Main
Mannheim
Ludwigshafen
Karlsruhe
Kaiserslautern
Saarbrücken
Trier
Luxembourg
Metz
Nancy
Thionville
Verdun
Sedan
Charleville-Mézières
Reims
Châlons-s-Marne
Épernay
Soissons
Laon
St-Quentin
Amiens
Arras
Lille
Roubaix
Tourcoing
Valenciennes
Douai
Cambrai
Calais
Dunkerque
Boulogne
Abbeville
Beauvais
Compiègne
Paris
Versailles
Meaux
Dover
Deal
Margate
Ramsgate
Ardennes
Somme
Oise
Aisne
Marne
Seine
Meuse
Moselle
Rhein

25 50 75 100 km
25 50 mls
AUSTRIA
SWITZERLAND
FRANCE
ITALY
LIECHTENSTEIN
VORALBERG
TIROL
TRENTINO
VENETO
LOMBARDIA
PIEMONTE
VALLE D'AOSTA
EMILIA ROMAGNA
FRANCHE COMTÉ
JURA
Innsbruck
Bolzano (Bozen)
Trento
Verona
Vicenza
Padova (Padua)
Venezia (Venice)
Treviso
Brescia
Bergamo
Milano (Milan)
Pavia
Piacenza
Parma
Modena
Bologna
Ferrara
Mantova (Mantua)
Cremona
Novara
Vercelli
Alessandria
Asti
Torino (Turin)
Aosta
Zürich
Bern (Berne)
Luzern (Lucerne)
Lausanne
Genève (Geneva)
Annecy
Chambéry
Besançon
Chur
Davos
St Moritz
Lugano
Como
Locarno
Bellinzona
Lago Maggiore
Lago di Garda
L. Léman (L. of Geneva)
Mt Blanc 4808
Matterhorn 4478
Jungfrau
Gran Paradiso 4061
Alpi Pennine
Berner Oberland
Ortles
Dolomiti
Engadin
Rhein
Po
Adige
Adda
Ticino

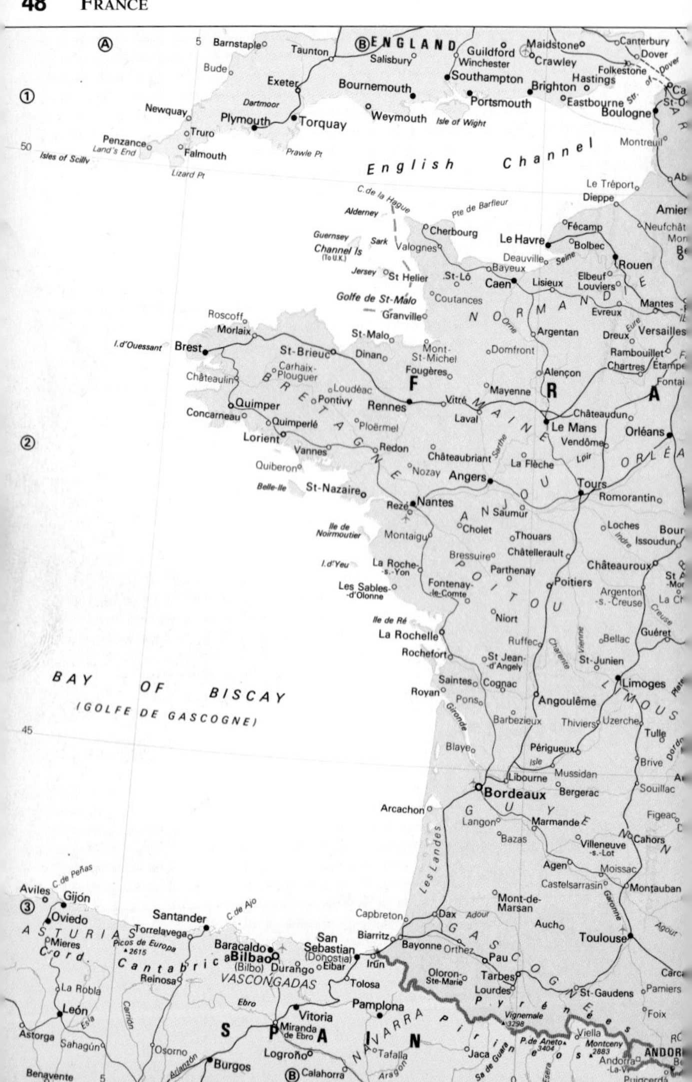
A
B
1
2
3
5
50
45
ENGLAND
Barnstaple
Taunton
Salisbury
Guildford
Winchester
Maidstone
Crawley
Canterbury
Dover
Folkestone
Str. of Dover
Bude
Exeter
Bournemouth
Southampton
Hastings
Brighton
Portsmouth
Eastbourne
Boulogne
Newquay
Dartmoor
Plymouth
Torquay
Weymouth
Isle of Wight
Truro
Penzance
Land's End
Falmouth
Isles of Scilly
Lizard Pt
Prawle Pt
English Channel
Montreuil
Le Tréport
Dieppe
C.de la Hague
Alderney
Pte de Barfleur
Cherbourg
Guernsey
Sark
Channel Is
(To U.K.)
Valognes
Fécamp
Le Havre
Bolbec
Deauville
Seine
Bayeux
Rouen
Jersey
St Helier
St-Lô
Caen
Lisieux
Elbeuf
Louviers
Golfe de St-Malo
Coutances
Mantes
Evreux
Granville
Roscoff
NORMANDIE
Morlaix
Orne
Argentan
Dreux
Eure
Versailles
St-Malo
I.d'Ouessant
Brest
St-Brieuc
Dinan
Mont-St-Michel
Domfront
Rambouillet
Chartres
Carhaix-Plouguer
Fougères
Alençon
Châteaulin
BRETAGNE
F
Mayenne
R
A
Loudéac
Pontivy
Rennes
Vitré
MAINE
Quimper
Laval
Châteaudun
Concarneau
Quimperlé
Ploërmel
Le Mans
Orléans
Lorient
Vendôme
Vannes
Redon
Châteaubriant
Sarthe
La Flèche
Loir
ORLÉANS
Quiberon
Nozay
Angers
ANJOU
Belle-Ile
St-Nazaire
Tours
Rezé
Nantes
Saumur
Romorantin
Ile de Noirmoutier
Montaigu
Cholet
Loches
Thouars
Indre
Issoudun
Bressuire
Châtellerault
I.d'Yeu
La Roche-s.-Yon
Parthenay
Châteauroux
Les Sables-d'Olonne
Fontenay-le-Comte
POITOU
Poitiers
Argenton-s.-Creuse
Creuse
Niort
Ile de Ré
La Rochelle
Ruffec
Charente
Vienne
Bellac
Guéret
Rochefort
St Jean-d'Angely
St-Junien
Limoges
BAY OF BISCAY
(GOLFE DE GASCOGNE)
Saintes
Cognac
LIMOUSIN
Royan
Pons
Gironde
Angoulême
Barbezieux
Thiviers
Uzerche
Tulle
Blaye
Périgueux
Isle
Brive
Mussidan
Libourne
Bordeaux
Bergerac
Souillac
Arcachon
GUYENNE
Langon
Marmande
Figeac
Bazas
Villeneuve-s.-Lot
Cahors
Les Landes
Agen
Moissac
Castelsarrasin
Montauban
Mont-de-Marsan
Garonne
C. de Peñas
Aviles
Gijón
C. de Ajo
Capbreton
Dax
Adour
Auch
Agout
Oviedo
Santander
Torrelavega
ASTURIAS
Mieres
Picos de Europa
2615
Biarritz
San Sebastian
(Donostia)
Bayonne
Orthez
GASCOGNE
Pau
Toulouse
Baracaldo
Bilbao
(Bilbo)
Durango
Eibar
Irún
Cord. Cantabrica
Reinosa
VASCONGADAS
Tolosa
Oloron-Ste-Marie
Tarbes
Lourdes
St-Gaudens
Pamiers
La Robla
Ebro
Pamplona
Pyrénées
Vignemale
3298
Foix
León
Carrión
Esla
Vitoria
NAVARRA
Astorga
Sahagún
SPAIN
Miranda de Ebro
Viella
P. de Aneto
3404
Montceny
2883
Osorno
Logroño
Tafalla
Jaca
Andorra
-La-V
ANDORRA
Burgos
Arlanzón
Sa de Guara
Esera
Benavente
Calahorra
Aragon
Puigcerdà

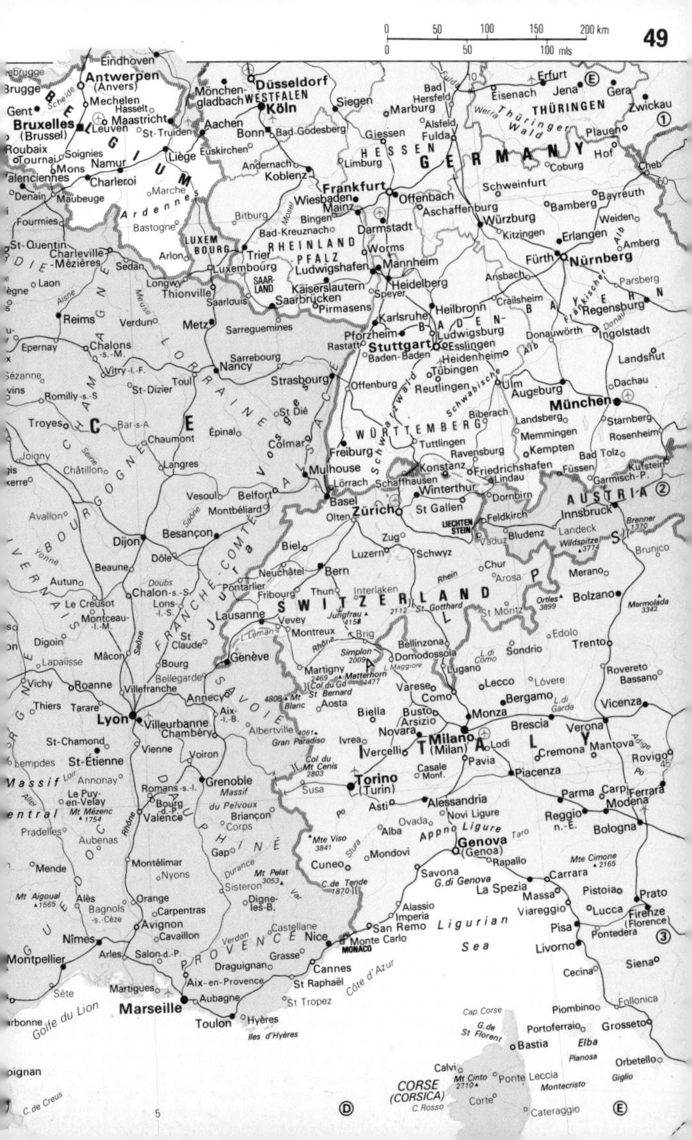
0 50 100 150 200 km
0 50 100 mls
Eindhoven
Brugge
Antwerpen
(Anvers)
Schelde
Mechelen
Hasselt
Gent
Maastricht
Bruxelles
(Brussel)
Leuven
St-Truiden
BELGIUM
Roubaix
Soignies
Tournai
Mons
Namur
Liège
Valenciennes
Charleroi
Denain
Maubeuge
Marche
Ardennes
Fourmies
Bastogne
St-Quentin
Charleville
-Mézières
Sedan
Arlon
LUXEMBOURG
Luxembourg
Laon
Aisne
Meuse
Longwy
Thionville
Reims
Verdun
Metz
Epernay
Chalons
-s.-M.
Vitry-l.-F.
Sézanne
St-Dizier
Toul
Nancy
Romilly-s.-S.
Troyes
Bar-s-A.
Chaumont
Épinal
St Dié
Colmar
Joigny
Seine
Châtillon
Langres
Mulhouse
Vesoul
Belfort
Montbéliard
Avallon
Dijon
Besançon
Saône
Dôle
Beaune
Autun
Le Creusot
Chalon-s.-S.
Lons-l.-S.
Montceau-l.-M.
Doubs
Pontarlier
Digoin
Mâcon
St Claude
Lapalisse
Bourg
Bellegarde
Vichy
Roanne
Villefranche
Thiers
Tarare
Lyon
Villeurbanne
St-Chamond
St-Étienne
Vienne
Lempdes
Annonay
Le Puy-en-Velay
Mt Mézenc 1754
Pradelles
Aubenas
Mende
Mt Aigoual 1565
Alès
Bagnols-s.-Cèze
Nîmes
Arles
Montpellier
Sète
Golfe du Lion
C. de Creus
Massif Central
CHAMPAGNE
LORRAINE
BOURGOGNE
FRANCHE-COMTÉ
Jura
NIVERNAIS
SAVOIE
DAUPHINÉ
PROVENCE
LANGUEDOC
Vosges
ALSACE
Sarrebourg
Sarreguemines
Strasbourg
Mönchen-gladbach
Düsseldorf
WESTFALEN
Köln
Aachen
Bonn
Bad Godesberg
Euskirchen
Andernach
Koblenz
Siegen
Marburg
Giessen
Limburg
Frankfurt
Offenbach
Wiesbaden
Mainz
Bingen
Mosel
Bitburg
Bad-Kreuznach
Darmstadt
Trier
RHEINLAND-PFALZ
Worms
Mannheim
Ludwigshafen
SAAR-LAND
Saarlouis
Saarbrücken
Kaiserslautern
Pirmasens
Speyer
Heidelberg
Karlsruhe
Pforzheim
Rastatt
Baden-Baden
Stuttgart
Esslingen
Offenburg
Tübingen
Reutlingen
Freiburg
Schwarzwald
Lörrach
Basel
Schaffhausen
Konstanz
Tuttlingen
WÜRTTEMBERG
BADEN-
Ludwigsburg
Heilbronn
Heidenheim
Ulm
Schwäbische Alb
Biberach
Ravensburg
Friedrichshafen
Lindau
Bad
Hersfeld
Fulda
Alsfeld
HESSEN
GERMANY
Erfurt
Eisenach
Jena
Gera
Zwickau
THÜRINGEN
Thüringer Wald
Werra
Plauen
Hof
Coburg
Cheb
Schweinfurt
Bayreuth
Bamberg
Aschaffenburg
Würzburg
Kitzingen
Weiden
Erlangen
Amberg
Fürth
Nürnberg
Ansbach
Crailsheim
Parsberg
Regensburg
Fränkische Alb
BAYERN
Donauwörth
Ingolstadt
Donau
Landshut
Augsburg
Dachau
München
Landsberg
Memmingen
Starnberg
Rosenheim
Kempten
Bad Tolz
Füssen
Kufstein
Garmisch-P.
AUSTRIA
Innsbruck
Brenner 1370
Dornbirn
Feldkirch
LIECHTENSTEIN
Vaduz
Bludenz
Landeck
Wildspitze 3774
Winterthur
St Gallen
Olten
Zürich
Zug
Biel
Luzern
Schwyz
Neuchâtel
Bern
Chur
Arosa
Rhein
Thun
Interlaken
Fribourg
SWITZERLAND
Jungfrau 4158
2112
St Gotthard
St Moritz
Ortles 3899
Lausanne
Vevey
Montreux
L. Léman
Rhône
Brig
Genève
Simplon 2009
Martigny
Matterhorn 4477
Col du Gd St Bernard 2469
Mt Blanc 4808
Annecy
Aix-l.-B.
Chambéry
Albertville
Aosta
Gran Paradiso 4061
Col du Mt Cenis 2803
Voiron
Grenoble
Romans-s.-I.
Bourg-d.-P.
Valence
Massif du Pelvoux
Briançon
Corps
Gap
Susa
Durance
Montélimar
Nyons
Sisteron
Mt Pelat 3053
Orange
Carpentras
Digne-les-B.
Avignon
Cavaillon
Verdon
Castellane
Var
Salon-d.-P.
Aix-en-Provence
Draguignan
Grasse
Martigues
Marseille
Aubagne
Toulon
Hyères
Iles d'Hyères
St Tropez
St Raphaël
Cannes
Côte d'Azur
Nice
MONACO
Monte Carlo
San Remo
Imperia
Alassio
C. de Tende 1870
Cuneo
Stura
Mte Viso 3841
Mondovi
Bellinzona
Domodossola
L. Maggiore
Lugano
L. di Como
Sondrio
Edolo
Bolzano
Merano
Brunico
Marmolada 3342
Trento
Rovereto
Bassano
Lecco
Lóvere
Varese
Como
Bergamo
L. di Garda
Biella
Busto Arsizio
Monza
Brescia
Verona
Vicenza
Novara
Milano
(Milan)
Lodi
Cremona
Mantova
Adige
Rovigo
Ivrea
Vercelli
Pavia
Piacenza
Po
Casale Monf.
Torino
(Turin)
Asti
Alessandria
Parma
Carpi
Ferrara
Modena
Reggio n.-E.
Bologna
Novi Ligure
Ovada
Alba
Appno Ligure
Genova
(Genoa)
Taro
Rapallo
Mte Cimone 2165
Savona
G. di Genova
La Spezia
Carrara
Massa
Pistoia
Prato
Viareggio
Lucca
Firenze
(Florence)
Ligurian Sea
Pisa
Pontedera
Livorno
Siena
Cecina
Piombino
Follonica
Cap Corse
G. de St Florent
Portoferraio
Grosseto
Bastia
Elba
Pianosa
Orbetello
Giglio
Calvi
Mt Cinto 2710
Ponte Leccia
Montecristo
CORSE
(CORSICA)
Corte
C. Rosso
Cateraggio
ITALY
ALPS
Narbonne
Perpignan
1
2
3
D
E
5
45
10

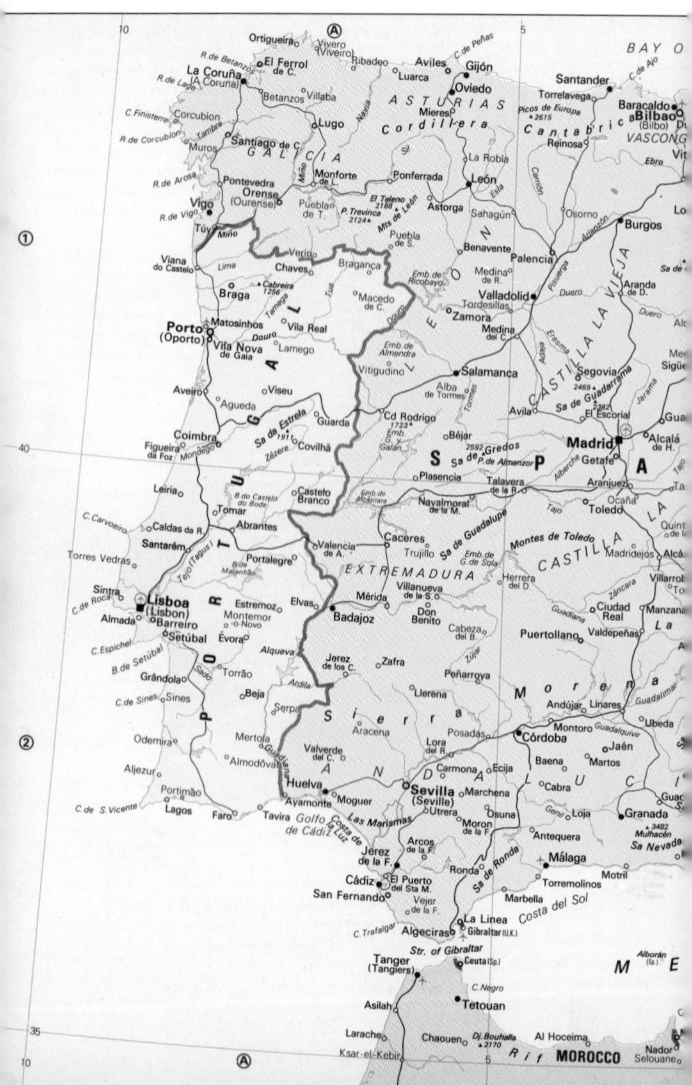

Ortigueira
Vivero (Viveiro)
Ribadeo
Aviles
C. de Peñas
Gijón
BAY O
R. de Betanzos
El Ferrol de C.
La Coruña (A Coruña)
R. de Lage
Luarca
Santander
C. de Ajo
Betanzos
Villaba
Oviedo
Torrelavega
Baracaldo
Bilbao (Bilbo)
C. Finisterre
Corcubion
Tambre
A S T U R I A S
Picos de Europa 2615
Lugo
Mieres
Navia
R. de Corcubion
Muros
Santiago de C.
C o r d i l l e r a
C a n t a b r i c a
VASCONG
G A L I C I A
Reinosa
Sil
La Robla
Ebro
Miño
Monforte de L.
Ponferrada
León
Carrión
R. de Arosa
Pontevedra
Orense (Ourense)
Esla
El Teleno 2188
Astorga
Vigo
Puebla de T.
P. Trevinca 2124
Mts de León
Sahagún
Osorno
Burgos
R. de Vigo
Túy
Miño
Arlanzón
Puebla de S.
Benavente
Verín
Viana do Castelo
Lima
Chaves
Bragança
Palencia
Emb. de Ricobayo
Medina de R.
Pisuerga
Cabreira 1256
Braga
Tua
Macedo de C.
Duero
Valladolid
Aranda de D.
Tamega
Tordesillas
Zamora
Duero
Matosinhos
Douro
Porto (Oporto)
Vila Real
Medina del C.
Douro
Vila Nova de Gaia
Lamego
Emb. de Almendra
Eresma
Adaja
Vitigudino
Salamanca
Segovia
Aveiro
Viseu
2469
Sa de Guadarrama
Jarama
Agueda
Alba de Tormes
Tormes
C A S T I L L A L A V I E J A
Avila
2382
El Escorial
Guarda
Sa da Estrela
Cd Rodrigo 1723
Coimbra
1911
Emb. G. y Galán
Béjar
Madrid
Alcalá de H.
Figueira da Foz
Mondego
Covilhã
Zêzere
2592 Gredos
Sa de P. de Almanzor
Alberche
Getafe
S
P
A
Tajo
Plasencia
Talavera de la R.
Aranjuez
Leiria
Castelo Branco
B. do Castelo do Bode
Emb. de Alcántara
Navalmoral de la M.
Ocaña
Tomar
Tajo
Toledo
C. Carvoeiro
Caldas da R.
Abrantes
Montes de Toledo
Valencia de A.
Cáceres
Sa de Guadalupe
Santarém
Tejo (Tagus)
Trujillo
Emb. de G. de Sola
C A S T I L L A
Madridejos
Torres Vedras
Portalegre
B. de Maranhão
E X T R E M A D U R A
Herrera del D.
Záncara
Villarrob
Sintra
C. de Roca
Lisboa (Lisbon)
Estremoz
Elvas
Mérida
Villanueva de la S.
Guadiana
Ciudad Real
Manzana
Almada
Barreiro
Montemor -o-Novo
Badajoz
Don Benito
Setúbal
Évora
Cabeza del B.
Puertollano
Valdepeñas
C. Espichel
B. de Setúbal
Alqueva
Jerez de los C.
Zafra
Zújar
Sado
Torrão
Grândola
Ardila
Peñarroya
M o r e n a
C. de Sines
Sines
Beja
Llerena
Andújar
Linares
Guadalimar
Serpa
S i e r r a
Montoro
Guadalquivir
Ubeda
Aracena
Posadas
Córdoba
Odemira
Mertola
Guadiana
Lora del R.
Jaén
Valverde del C.
Almodôvar
Carmona
Ecija
Baena
Martos
Aljezur
A N D A L U C I
Huelva
Sevilla (Seville)
Marchena
Cabra
Portimão
Moguer
Genil
Loja
Granada
C. de S. Vicente
Lagos
Faro
Ayamonte
Tavira
Golfo de Cádiz
Costa de la Luz
Las Marismas
Utrera
Osuna
Moron de la F.
Antequera
3482 Mulhacén
Sa Nevada
Arcos de la F.
Jerez de la F.
Málaga
Ronda
Sa de Ronda
Motril
Cádiz
El Puerto del Sta M.
Torremolinos
San Fernando
Vejer de la F.
Marbella
Costa del Sol
La Linea
C. Trafalgar
Algeciras
Gibraltar (U.K.)
Str. of Gibraltar
Tanger (Tangiers)
Ceuta (Sp.)
Alborán (Sp.)
M E
C. Negro
Tetouan
Asilah
Larache
Chaouen
Dj. Bouhalla 2170
Al Hoceima
Nador
Selouane
Ksar-el-Kebir
R i f
MOROCCO

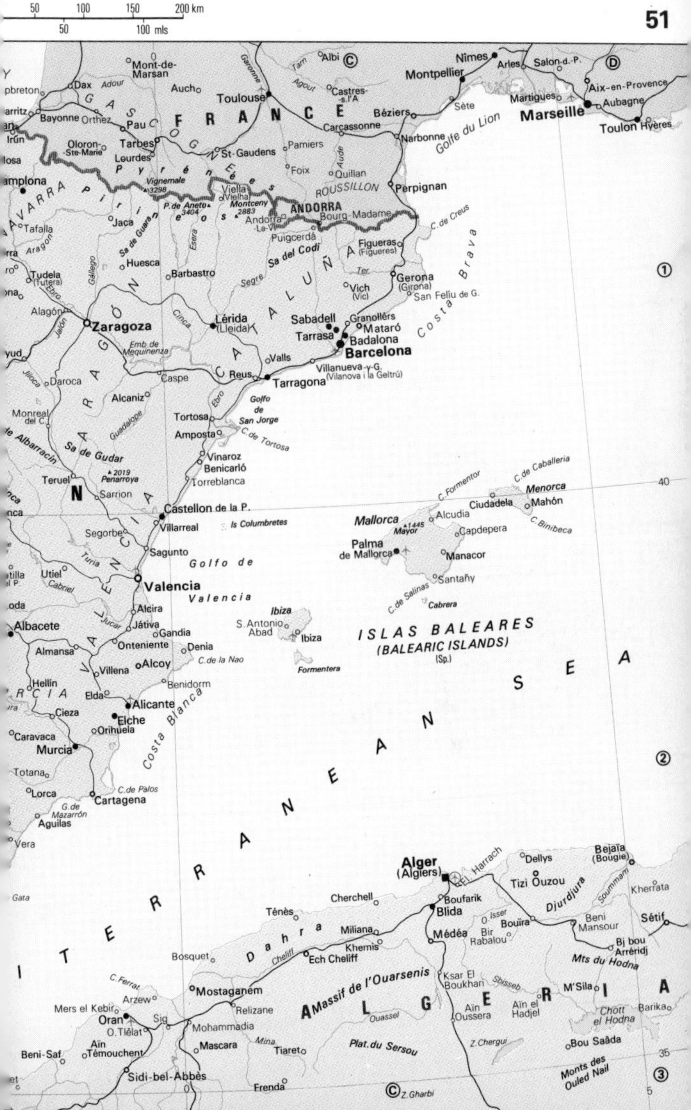
50 100 150 200 km
50 100 mls
FRANCE
Mont-de-Marsan
Albi
Nîmes
Arles
Salon-d.-P.
Dax
Adour
Montpellier
Aix-en-Provence
Auch
Castres-s.l'A
Toulouse
Garonne
Tarn
Agout
Martigues
Aubagne
Marseille
Toulon
Hyères
Sète
Béziers
Carcassonne
Bayonne
Orthez
Pau
GASCOGNE
Golfe du Lion
Narbonne
Irún
Oloron-Ste-Marie
Tarbes
Lourdes
St-Gaudens
Pamiers
Aude
Foix
Quillan
ROUSSILLON
Perpignan
Pamplona
NAVARRA
Pyrénées
Vignemale 3298
Viella (Vielha)
Montceny 2883
P. de Aneto 3404
ANDORRA
Andorra-La-V.
Bourg-Madame
Puigcerdá
C. de Creus
Tafalla
Jaca
Aragón
Sa de Guara
Esera
Sa del Codi
Figueras (Figueres)
Huesca
Gállego
CATALUÑA
Ter
Tudela (Tutera)
Ebro
Barbastro
Segre
Gerona (Girona)
Vich (Vic)
San Feliu de G.
Costa Brava
Alagón
Zaragoza
Cinca
Lérida (Lleida)
Sabadell
Granollérs
Mataró
Tarrasa
Badalona
Barcelona
Jalón
Emb. de Mequinenza
ARAGÓN
Valls
Villanueva-y-G. (Vilanova i la Geltrú)
Daroca
Caspe
Reus
Tarragona
Jiloca
Alcaniz
Golfo de San Jorge
Monreal del C.
Guadalope
Tortosa
Amposta
C. de Tortosa
Sa de Albarracín
Sa de Gudar
Vinaroz
Benicarló
2019 Peñarroya
Torreblanca
Teruel
Sarrion
C. Formentor
C. de Caballeria
Menorca
Castellon de la P.
Ciudadela
Mahón
Is Columbretes
Mallorca
Alcudia
Villarreal
1445 Mayor
Capdepera
C. Binibeca
Segorbe
Palma de Mallorca
Sagunto
Manacor
Turia
Golfo de Valencia
Utiel
Cabriel
Santañy
Valencia
VALENCIA
C. de Salinas
Cabrera
Alcira
Ibiza
Albacete
Júcar
Játiva
Gandia
S. Antonio Abad
ISLAS BALEARES (BALEARIC ISLANDS) (Sp.)
Onteniente
Denia
Almansa
C. de la Nao
Alcoy
Formentera
Villena
Benidorm
Hellín
MURCIA
Elda
Alicante
Costa Blanca
Cieza
Elche
Orihuela
Caravaca
Murcia
Totana
C. de Palos
Lorca
Cartagena
G. de Mazarrón
Aguilas
Vera
MEDITERRANEAN SEA
Gata
Bejaïa (Bougie)
Dellys
Alger (Algiers)
El Harrach
Tizi Ouzou
Kherrata
Cherchell
Djurdjura
Soummam
Boufarik
Ténès
Blida
Isser
Bouïra
Beni Mansour
Sétif
Dahra
Miliana
Médéa
Bir Rabalou
Khemis
Bj bou Arréridj
Bosquet
Cheliff
Ech Cheliff
Mts du Hodna
C. Ferrat
Massif de l'Ouarsenis
Ksar El Boukhari
Sbisseb
M'Sila
Arzew
Mostaganem
ALGERIA
Mers el Kebir
Oran
Sig
Relizane
Aïn Oussera
Aïn el Hadjel
Chott el Hodna
Barika
Ouassel
O. Tlélat
Mohammadia
Mina
Plat. du Sersou
Z. Chergui
Beni-Saf
Aïn Témouchent
Mascara
Tiaret
Bou Saâda
Sidi-bel-Abbès
Monts des Ouled Nail
Frenda
40
35
5
0
© Z. Gharbi
①
②
③
Ⓒ
Ⓓ

AUSTRIA
SWITZERLAND
LIECHTENSTEIN
GER.
FRANCE
HUNGARY
SLOVENIA
CROATIA
BOSNIA-HERZEGOVINA
SAN MARINO
MONACO
ADRIATIC
DALMATIA
SAVOIE
Ligurian Sea
Alpi Dolomitiche
Appno Tosco-Emilliano
Appno Ligure
Appno Umbro-Marchigiano
Velebit
Istra
G. di Venezia
G. di Genova
Côte d'Azur

Wien
Bratislava
Budapest
München
Zürich
Basel
Bern
Genève
Lausanne
Torino (Turin)
Milano (Milan)
Genova (Genoa)
Venezia (Venice)
Firenze (Florence)
Bologna
Verona
Padova
Trieste
Ljubljana
Zagreb
Sarajevo
Innsbruck
Salzburg
Graz
Klagenfurt
Villach
Bolzano
Trento
Udine
Rijeka (Fiume)
Split (Spalato)
Mostar
Pécs
Győr
Sopron
Maribor
Linz
Vöcklabruck
Wels
Steyr
St Pölten
Mödling
Wr. Neustadt
Neunkirchen
Bruck an der Mur
Leoben
Judenburg
Eisenerz
Mariazell
Hainfeld
Gmunden
Bad Ischl
Liezen
Radstad
Badgastein
Dachstein 2996
Hochkönig 2938
Grossglockner 3798
Lienz
Spittal
Wolfsberg
Kitzbühel
Kufstein
Rosenheim
Starnberg
Garmisch-P.
Bad Tolz
Füssen
Kempten
Memmingen
Landsberg
Biberach
Ravensburg
Friedrichshafen
Lindau
Konstanz
Tuttlingen
Schaffhausen
Winterthur
St Gallen
Dornbirn
Feldkirch
Bludenz
Vaduz
Landeck
Wildspitze 3774
Brenner 1370
Chur
Arosa
St Moritz
Merano
Ortles 3899
Edolo
Sondrio
Lovere
Brunico
Cortina d'A.
Marmolada 3342
Belluno
Gemona
Tarvisio
Jesenice
Kranj
Postojna
Koper
Gorizia
Monfalcone
Novo Mesto
Celje
Velenje
Leibnitz
Brežice
Karlovac
Ogulin
Vrbovsko
Senj
Krk
Cres
Rab
Lošinj
Pag
Karlobag
Gospić
Perušić
Zadar
Dugi O.
Kornat
Šibenik
Knin
Vrtoče
Bihać
Banja Luka
Ključ
Jajce
Donji Vakuf
Zenica
Doboj
Tuzla
Livno
Čincer 2004
Makarska
Ploče
Pelješac
Dubrovnik
Mljet
Hvar
Brač
Vis
Korčula
Lastovo
Palagruža
Bileća
Trebinje
Nikšić
Kotor
Budva
Konjic
Lelija 2032
Goražde
Avtovac
Vinkovci
Vukovar
Osijek
Apatin
Dakovo
Bosanki Brod
Našice
Pakrac
Daruva
Virovitica
Bjelovar
Koprivnica
Sisak
Varazdin
Nagykanizsa
Zalaegerszeg
Szombathely
Veszprém
Papa
Talabanya
Komárno
Nové Zámky
Esztergom
Vác
Székesfehérvár
Siófok
Paks
Szekszard
Baja
Dombóvár
Kaposvár
Fonyód
Balaton
Gleisdorf
M'óvár
Raba
Mulhouse
Freiburg
Lörrach
Olten
Luzern
Zug
Schwyz
Thun
Interlaken
Jungfrau 4158
Biel
Neuchâtel
Fribourg
Vevey
Montreux
Martigny
Brig
Simplon 2009
Matterhorn 4477
Col du Gd St Bernard 2469
Aosta
St Gotthard 2112
Bellinzona
Domodossola
L. Maggiore
Lugano
L. di Como
Como
Varese
Lecco
Bergamo
Monza
Brescia
L. di Garda
Busto Arsizio
Novara
Vercelli
Biella
Ivrea
Casale Monf.
Alessandria
Pavia
Lodi
Piacenza
Cremona
Mantova
Parma
Reggio n.-E.
Modena
Carpi
Rovigo
Ferrara
Vicenza
Bassano
Rovereto
Treviso
Mestre
Chioggia
Poreč
Rovinj
Pula
Argenta
Ravenna
Imola
Faenza
Forlì
Cesena
Rimini
Pesaro
Fano
Senigallia
Ancona
Macerata
Fabriano
Ascoli Piceno
Teramo
Pescara
Chieti
Mte Corno 2914
L'Aquila
Urbino
Città di Castello
Perugia
Foligno
Terni
Rieti
Viterbo
L. di Bracciano
Tevere (Tiber)
L. di Bolsena
Mte Amiata 1738
Arezzo
Siena
Grosseto
Orbetello
Giglio
Follonica
Piombino
Elba
Portoferraio
Pianosa
Montecristo
Cecina
Livorno
Pisa
Pontedera
Lucca
Pistoia
Prato
Mte Cimone 2165
Carrara
Massa
Viareggio
La Spezia
Rapallo
Novi Ligure
Ovada
Savona
Alassio
Imperia
San Remo
Monte Carlo
Nice
Cannes
St Raphaël
St Tropez
Grasse
Castellane
Mt. Pelat 3053
Var
Durance
Briançon
Massif du Pelvoux
Susa
Col du Mt Cenis 2803
Gran Paradiso 4061
Albertville
Mt Blanc 4808
Mte Viso 3841
Cuneo
C. de Tende 1870
Mondovi
Alba
Asti
Po
Stura
Taro
Reno
Adige
Pave
Drava
Sava
Mur
Enns
Kupa
Una
Vrbas
Bosna
Neretva
Cetina
Rhône
Rhein
L. Léman
Besançon
Montbéliard
Belfort
Vesoul
Saône
Pontarlier
Bastia
Ponte Leccia
Corte
Calvi
Mt Cinto 2710
C. Rosso
Cap Corse
G. de St Florent

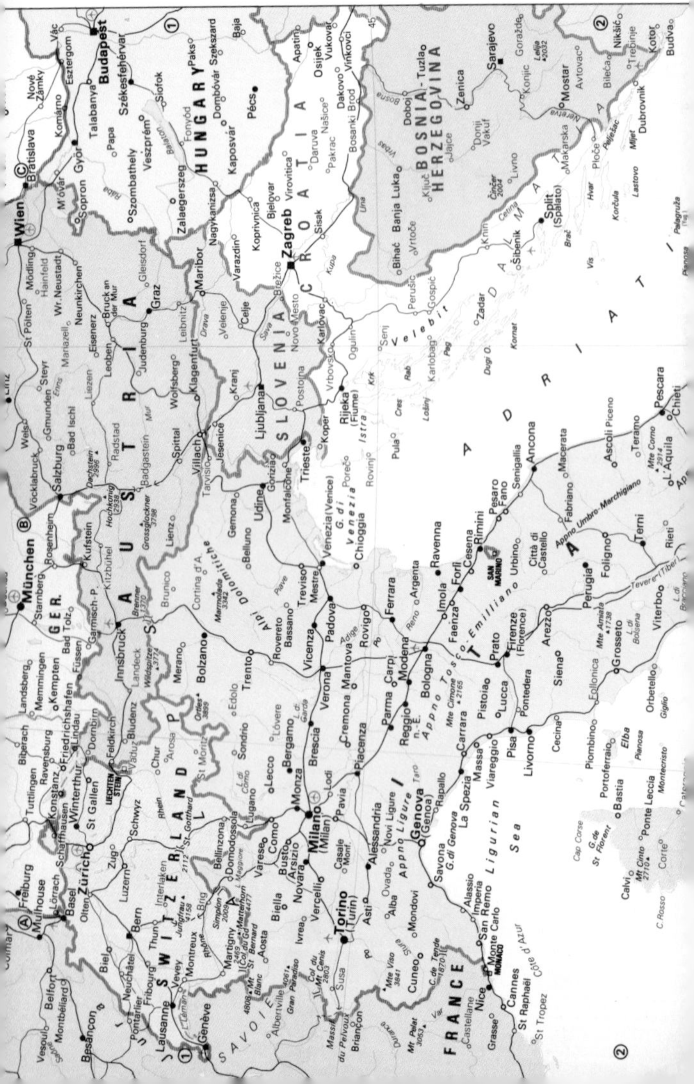

0 50 100 150 200 km
0 50 100 mls

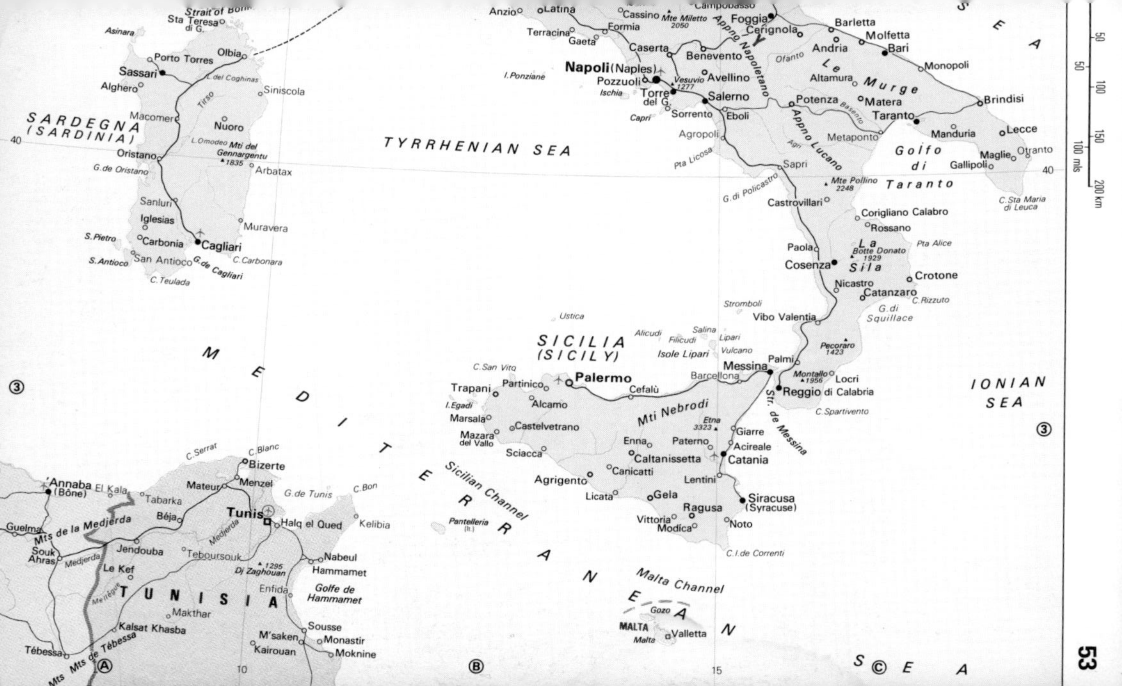

TYRRHENIAN SEA
IONIAN SEA
M E D I T E R R A N E A N S E A
Golfo di Taranto
SARDEGNA (SARDINIA)
SICILIA (SICILY)
TUNISIA
Strait of Bonif.
Sta Teresa di G.
Asinara
Porto Torres
Sassari
Alghero
Olbia
L. del Coghinas
Siniscola
Tirso
Macomer
Nuoro
L. Omodeo
Mti del Gennargentu
1835
Oristano
G. de Oristano
Arbatax
Sanluri
Iglesias
Muravera
S. Pietro
Carbonia
Cagliari
S. Antioco
San Antioco
G. de Cagliari
C. Carbonara
C. Teulada
Anzio
Latina
Cassino
Mte Miletto 2050
Foggia
Terracina
Formia
Gaeta
Appno Napoletano
Cerignola
Barletta
Molfetta
Bari
Caserta
Benevento
Ofanto
Andria
Le Murge
Monopoli
Napoli (Naples)
I. Ponziane
Pozzuoli
Vesuvio 1277
Avellino
Altamura
Ischia
Torre del G.
Salerno
Potenza
Matera
Brindisi
Capri
Sorrento
Eboli
Basento
Taranto
Appno Lucano
Agropoli
Metaponto
Manduria
Lecce
Agri
Maglie
Otranto
Pta Licosa
Sapri
Gallipoli
G. di Policastro
Mte Pollino 2248
Castrovillari
C. Sta Maria di Leuca
Corigliano Calabro
Rossano
Pta Alice
Paola
La Sila
Botte Donato 1929
Cosenza
Crotone
Nicastro
Catanzaro
C. Rizzuto
G. di Squillace
Stromboli
Ustica
Vibo Valentia
Alicudi
Salina
Filicudi
Lipari
Isole Lipari
Vulcano
Pecoraro 1423
Palmi
Messina
C. San Vito
Barcellona
Montalto 1956
Locri
Trapani
Partinico
Palermo
Cefalù
Reggio di Calabria
I. Egadi
Alcamo
C. Spartivento
Marsala
Mti Nebrodi
Castelvetrano
Etna 3323
Giarre
Str. de Messina
Mazara del Vallo
Enna
Paternò
Acireale
Sciacca
Caltanissetta
Catania
Canicatti
Agrigento
Lentini
Licata
Gela
Siracusa (Syracuse)
Ragusa
Vittoria
Modica
Noto
C. I. de Correnti
C. Serrat
C. Blanc
Bizerte
'Annaba (Bône)
El Kala
Mateur
Menzel
G. de Tunis
C. Bon
Tabarka
Sicilian Channel
Tunis
Béja
Halq el Qued
Kelibia
Pantelleria (It.)
Guelma
Mts de la Medjerda
Medjerda
Souk Ahras
Jendouba
Tebourzouk
Nabeul
Le Kef
Dj Zaghouan 1295
Hammamet
Enfida
Golfe de Hammamet
Malta Channel
Gozo
Makthar
Kalsat Khasba
Sousse
MALTA
Malta
Valletta
M'saken
Monastir
Tébessa
Mts de Tébessa
Kairouan
Moknine
40
10
15
A
B
C
3

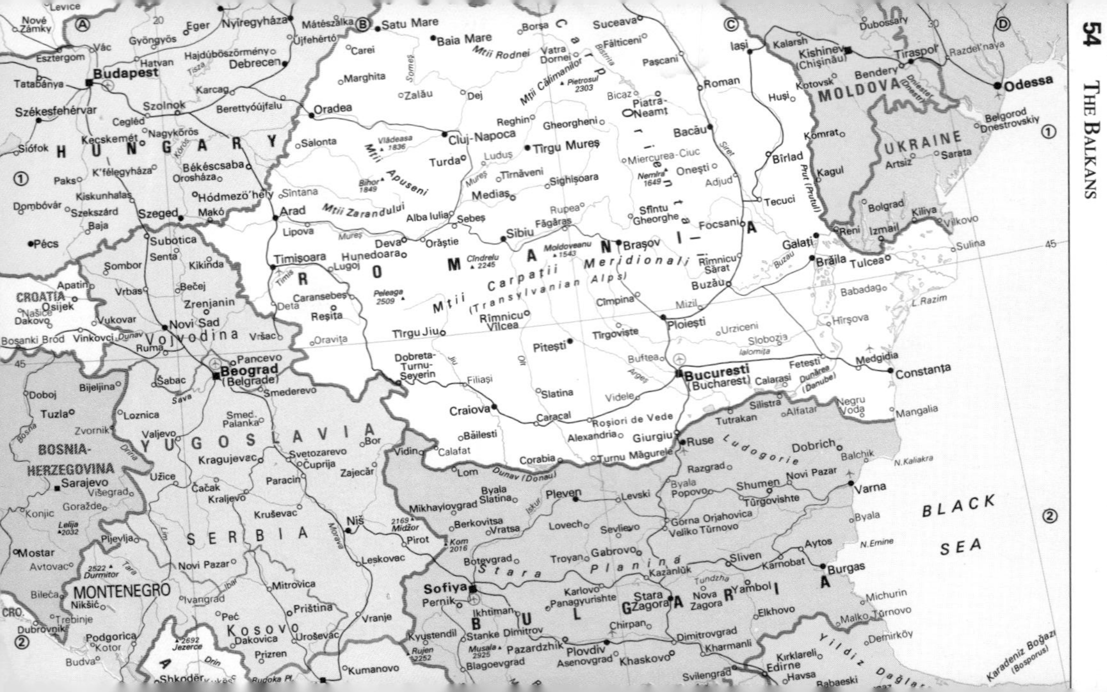
BLACK SEA
UKRAINE
MOLDOVA
ROMANIA
HUNGARY
YUGOSLAVIA
SERBIA
BULGARIA
MONTENEGRO
BOSNIA-HERZEGOVINA
CROATIA
KOSOVO
Vojvodina
Odessa
Kishinev (Chişinău)
Tiraspol
Bendery
Belgorod Dnestrovskiy
Izmail
Reni
Galaţi
Brăila
Tulcea
Constanţa
Mangalia
Iaşi
Bacău
Suceava
Piatra-Neamţ
Focsani
Buzău
Ploieşti
Bucuresti (Bucharest)
Giurgiu
Ruse
Varna
Burgas
Dobrich
Shumen
Sliven
Stara Zagora
Plovdiv
Sofiya
Pernik
Pleven
Vidin
Craiova
Piteşti
Braşov
Sibiu
Cluj-Napoca
Tîrgu Mureş
Baia Mare
Satu Mare
Oradea
Arad
Timişoara
Deva
Hunedoara
Reşiţa
Beograd (Belgrade)
Novi Sad
Subotica
Niš
Kragujevac
Priština
Prizren
Podgorica
Sarajevo
Tuzla
Mostar
Dubrovnik
Budapest
Debrecen
Szeged
Pécs
Kecskemét
Szolnok
Nyíregyháza
Edirne
Kırklareli
Carpaţii Meridionali (Transylvanian Alps)
Stara Planina
Dunav (Donau)
Prut (Prutul)
Dniester (Dnestr)
Siret
Mureş
Olt
Jiu
Morava
Drina
Sava
Tisza
Ludogorie
Yildiz Dağlar
Karadeniz Boğazı (Bosporus)
Musala 2925
Moldoveanu 1543
Cîndrelu 2245
Pietrosul 2303
Nemira 1649
Vlădeasa 1836
Bihor 1849
Peleaga 2509
Durmitor 2522
Jezerce 2692
Midžor 2169
Kom 2016
Rujen 2252
Lelija 2032

50   100   150   200 km
50   100 mls

③ ④

Bursa
Gemlik
Karacabey° °Kemalpaşa
Mustafa Kemalpaşa
Akdağ 2089
Sinav
Tavşanlı
Susurluk Buldano
Denizli
Bandırma
Marmara Adi
Balıkesir
Sirdirği °Kütahya
Manisa Salihli
Kula
Nazilli
Gönen Biga
Edremit K.
Buharkent
Uşak
Menemen Turgutlu
İzmir
Aydın
Çanakkale
Ezine Bayramiç
Ayvalık
Bergama
Torbalı
Selçuk
Söke
Milas
Bodrum
Çeşme
Ödemiş
TURKEY
Gallipoli (Gelibolu)
Mitilini
Kuşadası K.
Güllük K.
Bozburun
Marmaris
Ova
Saros Körfezi
Eceabat Bozca Ada
Ayvacık
Kuşadası
Pağondhiki
Samos
İkaria
Kalimnos
Rodhos
Ródhos
Lindos
Alexandroúpolis
Kástron
Ayios Evstratios
Límnos
Lésvos
Khíos
Psará
Ándros
Lévos
SPORÁDHES (DHODHEKANISOS)
Léros
Kós
Astrapalaia
Níssiros
Tílos
Sími
Alimnia
Karpathos
Akr. Sídheros
Akr. Kríou
Sitía
Samothráki
Thásos
K.Strimonikós
Áthos 2033
Ierápetra
AEGEAN SEA
Skíros
Límnos
Makronisos
Khálki
Náxos
Páros
Íos
Thíra
Sea of Crete
Kríti
Khaniá
Réthimnon
Iráklion
Ídhi Óri 2456
Psilorítis
Lefká Óri 2452
Kastélli
Timbákion
Kaválla
Kýknos
Nigríta
Sérrai
Polígiros
Khalkidhikí
Sithonía
KírraC
Thessaloníki (Salónica)
Kilkís
Sárron
Thermaïkós Kólpos
Véroia
Édhessa
Náousa
Katerini
Kozáni
Ólimbos (Olympus) 2917
Lárisa
Kardhítsa
Tríkala
Tírnavos
Vólos
Pagasitic G.
Istiaia
Evvoia
Skópelos
Skiáthos
Skyros
Pílion 1551
Khalkís
Khíos
Kími
Kárystos
Kikládhes (Cyclades)
Sífnos
Sérifos
Kíthnos
Kéa
Mílos
Kímolos
Andíkithira
Akr. Spátha
Kýthira
Akr. Maléa
Neápolis
Monemvasía
MACEDONIA
Ohrid
Bitola
Florina
Ptolemaïs
Kastoría
Grevená
Smólikas 2637
Kalabáka
Dhomokós
Farsala
Almirós
Lamía
Anfíklia
Lévadhia
Thívai
Athínai (Athens)
Piraiévs (Piraeus)
Akhárnai
Mégara
Eleusis K.
Elevsís
Korinthos
Korinthiakós K.
Sikionías K.
Aíyina
Saronikós K.
Ándros
Nigrítca
Albania
ALBANIA
Durrës
Kavajë
Elbasan
Lushnjë
Fier
Berat
Ballsh
Vlorë
Sarandë
Gjirokastër
Tomorrit 2486
Devoll
Vijosë
Konitsa
Ioánnina
Igoumenítsa
Paramithiá
Préveza
Ártha
Agrínion
Amfilokhía
Mesolóngion
Aíyion
Navpaktos
Patra
Pírgos
Amaliás
Argostóli
Kefallinía
Zákinthos
Zákinthos
Levkás
Levkás
Kérkira (Corfu)
Kérkyra
IÓNIOI NÍSOI (Ionian Islands)
Tripolis
Argos
Spárti
Megalópolis
Kalámai
Kiparissía
Filiatrá
Pírgos
Kalámai
Pilos
Kóroni
Kiparissiakós Kólpos
Messiniakós Kólpos
Parnon 1935
Taíyetos 2407
Yíthion
Akr. Taínaron
Lakonikós Kólpos
GREECE
Mittoan Sea
Mírtoan Sea
Argolikós K.
Návplion
Tríkeri
Kíthnos
Brindisi
Lecce
Maglie
Gallipoli
C. Sta Maria di Leuca
Strait of Otranto
Otranto
IONIAN SEA

③ ④

20

Ⓐ Ⓑ Ⓒ

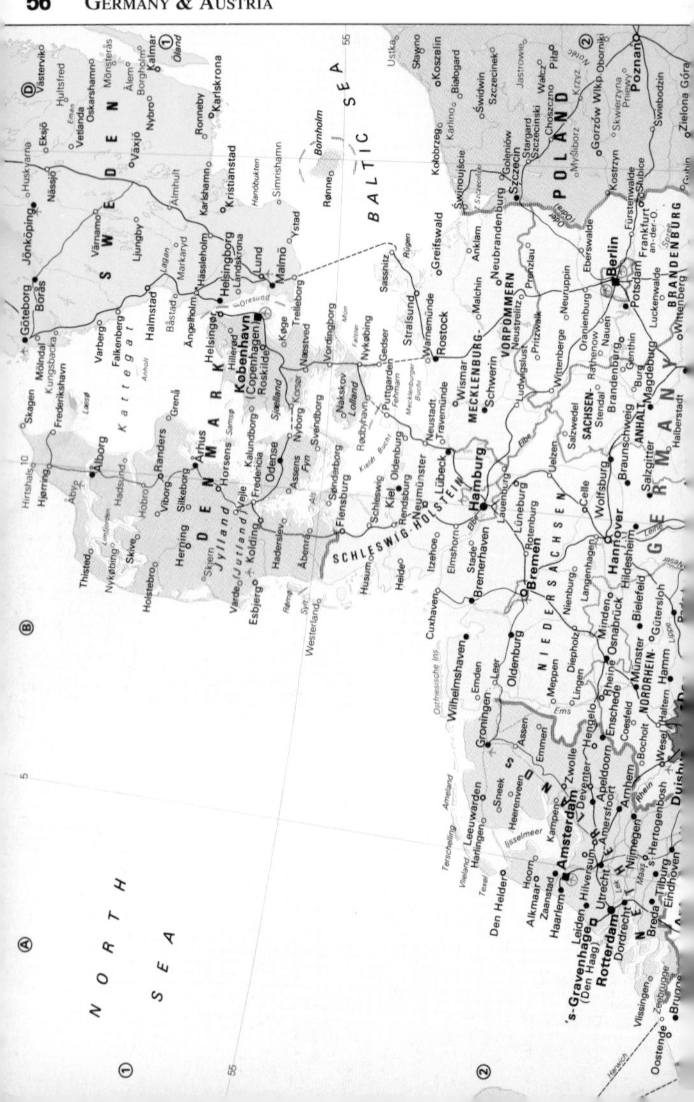
NORTH SEA
BALTIC SEA
SWEDEN
DENMARK
POLAND
GERMANY
Kattegat
Jylland (Jutland)
SCHLESWIG-HOLSTEIN
MECKLENBURG-VORPOMMERN
NIEDERSACHSEN
SACHSEN-ANHALT
BRANDENBURG
NORDRHEIN-
Göteborg
Jönköping
Malmö
Helsingborg
Kristianstad
Karlskrona
København (Copenhagen)
Odense
Århus
Ålborg
Esbjerg
Flensburg
Kiel
Lübeck
Hamburg
Bremen
Bremerhaven
Rostock
Stralsund
Greifswald
Schwerin
Berlin
Potsdam
Frankfurt an-der-O.
Szczecin
Poznań
Hannover
Braunschweig
Magdeburg
Wolfsburg
Osnabrück
Münster
Bielefeld
Oldenburg
Wilhelmshaven
Emden
Groningen
Leeuwarden
Amsterdam
's-Gravenhage (Den Haag)
Rotterdam
Utrecht
Arnhem
Nijmegen
Eindhoven
Tilburg
Breda
Duisburg
Bornholm
Rügen
IJsselmeer
Harwich

50 100 150 200 km

50 100 mls

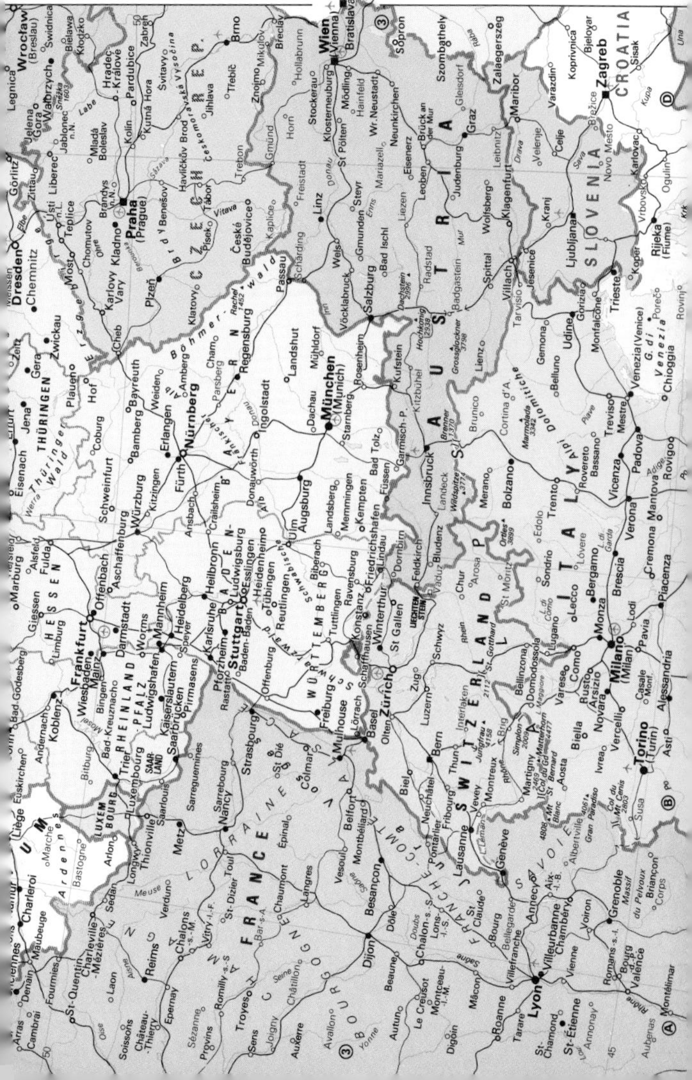

Wrocław (Breslau)
Legnica
Świdnica
Kłodzko
Zábřeh
Brno
Wien
Bratislava
Sopron
Szombathely
CROATIA
Zagreb

Görlitz
Jelenia Góra
Wałbrzych
Hradec Králové
Pardubice
Zábřeh
Znojmo
Hollabrunn
Stockerau
Korneuburg
Gänserndorf
Neusiedl
Zalaegerszeg
Nagykanizsa
Varaždin
Koprivnica
Sisak

Dresden
Chemnitz
Zwickau
Gera
Jena
Ústí n.L.
Teplice
Mladá Boleslav
Kolín
Kutná Hora
Havlíčkův Brod
Jihlava
Třebíč
Mikulov
Wr. Neustadt
Gleisdorf
Maribor
Celje
Novo Mesto
Krk

THÜRINGEN
Eisenach
Coburg
Bamberg
Bayreuth
Plauen
Hof
Weiden
Cheb
Karlovy Vary
Plzeň
Praha (Prague)
Kladno
Beroun
Příbram
Tábor
Benešov
Písek
České Budějovice
Linz
Wels
Steyr
Amstetten
St. Pölten
Gmünd
Freistadt
Krems
Mödling
Wiener Neustadt
Bruck a.d.M.
Leoben
Graz
Wolfsberg
Klagenfurt
Villach
Ljubljana
SLOVENIA
Trieste
Rijeka (Fiume)

BAYERN
Nürnberg
Fürth
Erlangen
Regensburg
Ingolstadt
Landshut
Passau
Straubing
München (Munich)
Rosenheim
Salzburg
Bad Ischl
Vöcklabruck
Gmunden
Ried
Bad Reichenhall
Kufstein
Innsbruck
Landeck
AUSTRIA
Lienz
Spittal
Cortina d'Ampezzo
Bolzano
Merano
Brunico
Belluno

Würzburg
Schweinfurt
Kitzingen
Ansbach
Donauwörth
Augsburg
Dachau
Memmingen
Kempten
Füssen
Garmisch-P.
Mittenwald
Bludenz
Trento
Rovereto
Trento
Bassano
Treviso
Venezia (Venice)
Mestre
Padova
Vicenza
Rovigo
Chioggia

HESSEN
Fulda
Marburg
Gießen
Frankfurt
Offenbach
Aschaffenburg
Darmstadt
Worms
Mannheim
Heidelberg
Heilbronn
Crailsheim
Schwäbisch Hall
Aalen
Ulm
Günzburg
Biberach
Ravensburg
Kempten
Lindau
Bregenz
Dornbirn
Feldkirch
Chur
Arosa
St. Moritz
Sondrio
Lecco
Como
Bergamo
Brescia
Verona
Mantova
Cremona
Piacenza

RHEINLAND-PFALZ
Koblenz
Bad Kreuznach
Bingen
Bad Godesberg
Andernach
Bitburg
Trier
Kaiserslautern
Saarbrücken
SAARLAND
Pirmasens
Landau
Karlsruhe
Pforzheim
Rastatt
Baden-Baden
Stuttgart
Ludwigsburg
Esslingen
Böblingen
Tübingen
Reutlingen
WÜRTTEMBERG
Sigmaringen
Tuttlingen
Konstanz
Singen
St. Gallen
Winterthur
Zürich
Rapperswil
Schwyz
Glarus
Bellinzona
Lugano
Varese
Novara
Milano (Milan)
Monza
Lodi
Pavia
Alessandria

Offenburg
Freiburg
Lörrach
Basel
Mulhouse
Belfort
Montbéliard
Olten
Solothurn
Biel
Bern
Thun
Interlaken
Luzern
Brig
Domodossola
Locarno
Aosta
Ivrea
Biella
Vercelli
Torino (Turin)

Liège
Charleroi
Luxembourg
LUXEMBOURG
Thionville
Longwy
Metz
Nancy
Lunéville
Saarbourg
Sarreguemines
Strasbourg
Sélestat
St. Dié
Épinal
Remiremont
Vesoul
Besançon
Pontarlier
Neuchâtel
Lausanne
Montreux
Martigny
Grand St. Bernard
Gran Paradiso
Susa
Briançon

Charleville-Mézières
Sedan
Bastogne
Ardennes
Verdun
Bar-le-Duc
St. Dizier
Toul
Chaumont
Langres
Dijon
Dole
Lons-le-Saunier
Bourg
Bourg-en-Bresse
Ambérieu
Bellegarde
Genève
Annecy
Chambéry
Albertville
SAVOIE
Grenoble
Le Pellerin

St. Quentin
Cambrai
Laon
Soissons
Château-Thierry
Reims
Épernay
Romilly
Troyes
Chaumont
Châtillon
Auxerre
Avallon
Autun
Le Creusot
Chalon-s.-S.
Mâcon
Villefranche
Tarare
Roanne
Lyon
Vienne
St. Étienne
Annonay
Romans-s.-I.
Valence
Montélimar

FRANCE
BOURGOGNE
Nevers
LORRAINE
FRANCHE-COMTÉ
SWITZERLAND
ITALY
DOLOMITI

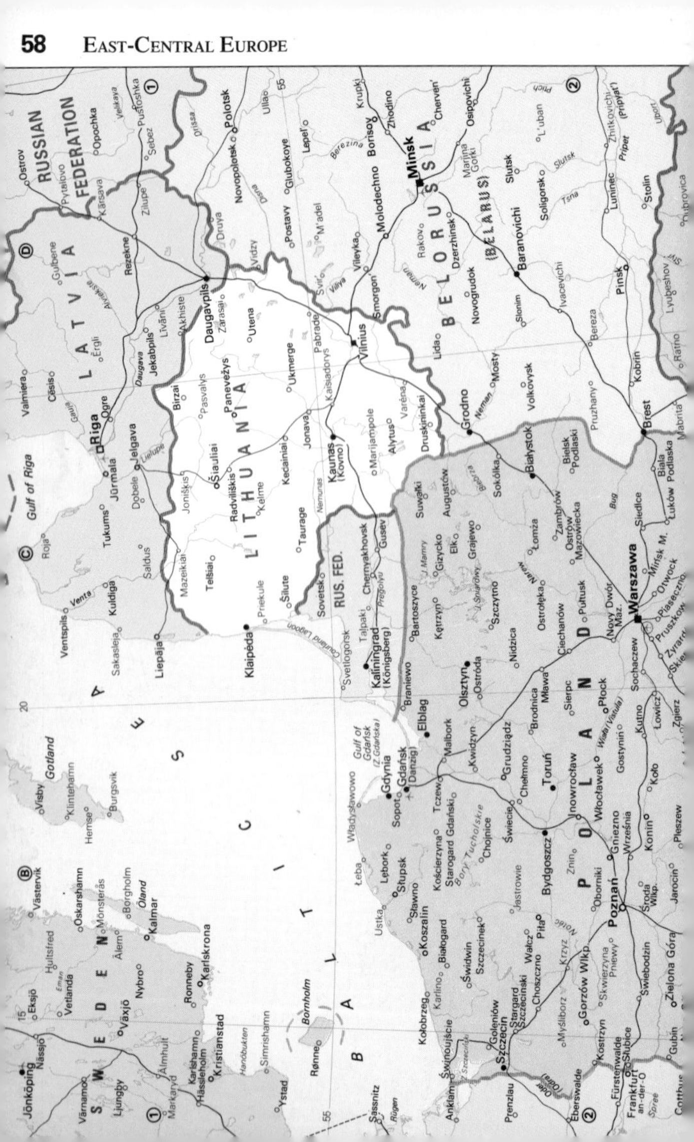
RUSSIAN FEDERATION
LATVIA
LITHUANIA
BELORUSSIA (BELARUS)
POLAND
SWEDEN
BALTIC SEA
RUS. FED.
Gulf of Riga
Gulf of Gdańsk (Z. Gdańska)
Gotland
Öland
Bornholm
Rügen
Courland Lagoon
Riga
Daugavpils
Jelgava
Jūrmala
Liepāja
Ventspils
Rezekne
Vilnius
Kaunas (Kovno)
Klaipėda
Šiauliai
Panevėžys
Kaliningrad (Königsberg)
Sovetsk
Chernyakhovsk
Minsk
Grodno
Brest
Pinsk
Baranovichi
Molodechno
Borisov
Polotsk
Novopolotsk
Warszawa
Gdańsk (Danzig)
Gdynia
Sopot
Elbląg
Olsztyn
Białystok
Toruń
Bydgoszcz
Poznań
Szczecin
Płock
Włocławek
Koszalin
Słupsk
Gorzów Wlkp.
Zielona Góra
Frankfurt an-der-O
Kalmar
Karlskrona
Kristianstad
Växjö
Jönköping
Visby
Ystad
Nemunas
Neman
Daugava
Narew
Bug
Wisła (Vistula)
Odra (Oder)
Noteć
Pripet
Berezina
15
20
55
B
C
D
1
2

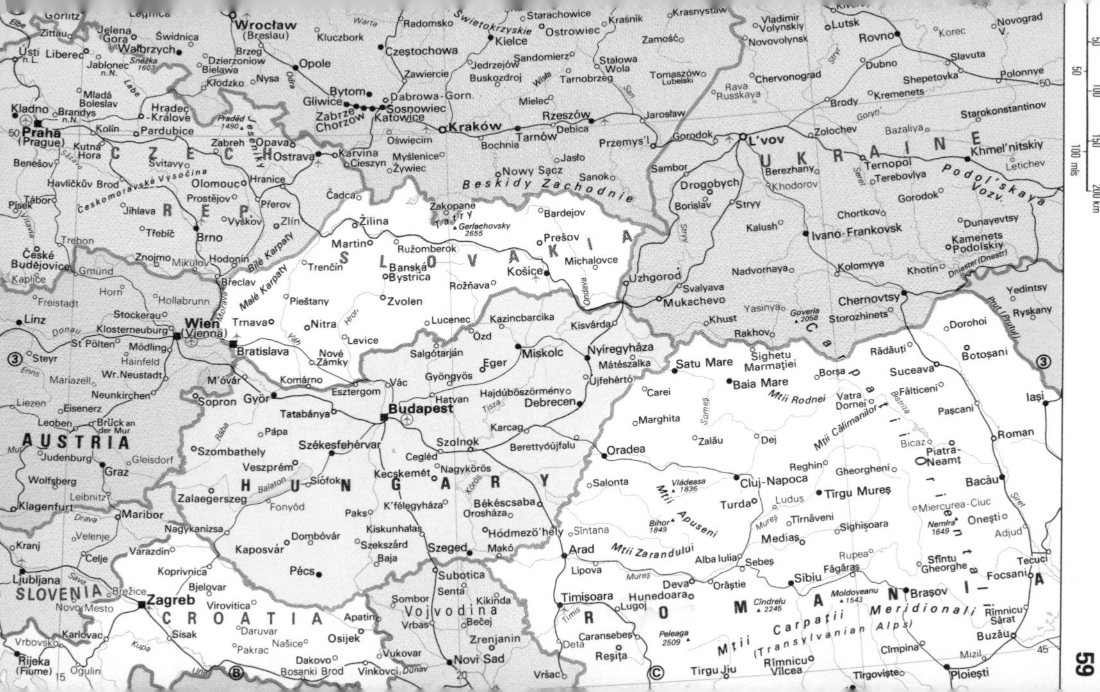

50
100
150
200 km
50
100 mls
Görlitz
Elbe
Zittau
Ústí n.L.
Liberec
Jablonec n.N.
Sněžka 1603
Jelena Góra
Wałbrzych
Świdnica
Legnica
Wrocław (Breslau)
Warta
Brzeg
Dzierżoniów
Bielawa
Kłodzko
Nysa
Odra
Opole
Kluczbork
Radomsko
Częstochowa
Zawiercie
Bytom
Gliwice
Zabrze
Chorzów
Katowice
Sosnowiec
Dąbrowa-Gorn.
Świętokrzyskie
Kielce
Jędrzejów
Buskozdrój
Sandomierz
Starachowice
Ostrowiec
Kraśnik
Stalowa Wola
Tarnobrzeg
Wisła
San
Mielec
Zamość
Krasnystaw
Tomaszów Lubelski
Rava Russkaya
Vladimir Volynskiy
Novovolynsk
Chervonograd
Lutsk
Rovno
Korec
Novograd V.
Dubno
Slavuta
Shepetovka
Polonnye
Kremenets
Brody
Starokonstantinov
Goryn'
Bazaliya
Zolochev
Khmel'nitskiy
Letichev
UKRAINE
Ternopol
Terebovlya
Seret
Podol'skaya Vozv.
Gorodok
Chortkov
Dunayevtsy
Kamenets Podolskiy
Khotin
Dniester (Dnestr)
Kalush
Ivano-Frankovsk
Kolomyya
Nadvornaya
Yasinya
Goverla 2058
Storozhinets
Chernovtsy
Yedintsy
Ryskany
Prut (Prutul)
L'vov
Gorodok
Berezhany
Khodorov
Sambor
Drogobych
Borislav
Stryy
Mladá Boleslav
Brandys n.N.
Hradec Králové
Labe
Kladno
Praha (Prague)
Kolín
Pardubice
Praděd 1490
Jeseníky
Kutná Hora
Sázava
Benešov
Svitavy
Zábřeh
Opava
Ostrava
Karviná
Cieszyn
Oświęcim
Kraków
Bochnia
Tarnów
Dębica
Rzeszów
Jarosław
Przemyśl
Jasło
Sanok
Nowy Sącz
Myślenice
Żywiec
Beskidy Zachodnie
CZECH REP.
Havlíčkův Brod
Českomoravská Vysočina
Olomouc
Hranice
Prostějov
Přerov
Tábor
Písek
Vltava
Jihlava
Vyškov
Zlín
Třebíč
Brno
Čadca
Trebon
České Budějovice
Kaplice
Gmünd
Znojmo
Mikulov
Hodonín
Bílé Karpaty
Břeclav
Morava
Zakopane
Tatry
Gerlachovský 2655
Žilina
Bardejov
Martin
Ružomberok
Prešov
SLOVAKIA
Trenčín
Banská Bystrica
Košice
Michalovce
Malé Karpaty
Piešťany
Zvolen
Rožňava
Ondava
Uzhgorod
Svalyava
Mukachevo
Khust
Rakhov
Horn
Hollabrunn
Freistadt
Linz
Stockerau
Donau
Klosterneuburg
Wien (Vienna)
Trnava
Nitra
Hron
Lučenec
Kazincbarcika
Kisvárda
Váh
Levice
Ózd
St Pölten
Mödling
Bratislava
Nové Zámky
Salgótarján
Miskolc
Nyíregyháza
Steyr
Hainfeld
Eger
Mátészalka
Enns
Mariazell
Wr. Neustadt
Komárno
Gyöngyös
Satu Mare
Sighetu Marmaţiei
Rădăuţi
Botoşani
Dorohoi
M'óvár
Vác
Újfehértó
Baia Mare
Borşa
Suceava
Neunkirchen
Esztergom
Hajdúböszörmény
Carei
Mţii Rodnei
Vatra Dornei
Fălticeni
Liezen
Sopron
Győr
Hatvan
Debrecen
Bistriţa
Iaşi
Eisenerz
Tatabánya
Budapest
Tisza
Someş
Paşcani
Leoben
Brück an der Mur
Rába
Pápa
Karcag
Marghita
Mţii Călimanilor
Roman
AUSTRIA
Székesfehérvár
Szolnok
Zalău
Dej
Bicaz
Mur
Szombathely
Cegléd
Berettyóújfalu
Oradea
Piatra-Neamţ
Judenburg
Gleisdorf
Graz
Veszprém
Nagykőrös
Reghin
Gheorgheni
Wolfsberg
Siófok
Kecskemét
Salonta
Vlădeasa 1836
Cluj-Napoca
Bacău
Balaton
HUNGARY
Körös
Mţii Apuseni
Tîrgu Mureş
Leibnitz
Zalaegerszeg
Békéscsaba
Turda
Luduş
Miercurea-Ciuc
Klagenfurt
K'félegyháza
Orosháza
Siret
Fonyód
Paks
Maribor
Mureş
Tîrnăveni
Oneşti
Drava
Bihor 1849
Nemira 1649
Kiskunhalas
Hódmezővásárhely
Sîntana
Sighişoara
Nagykanizsa
Adjud
Velenje
Dombóvár
Mediaş
Szekszárd
Kranj
Kaposvár
Varaždin
Szeged
Makó
Arad
Mţii Zarandului
Rupea
Celje
Tecuci
Baja
Alba Iulia
Sebeş
Sfîntu Gheorghe
Ljubljana
Koprivnica
Pécs
Subotica
Lipova
Făgăraş
Sava
Focşani
Brežice
Deva
Orăştie
Sibiu
SLOVENIA
Bjelovar
Senta
Hunedoara
Braşov
Zagreb
Sombor
Kikinda
Timişoara
Cindrelu 2245
Moldoveanu 2543
Novo Mesto
Virovitica
Vojvodina
Lugoj
ROMANIA
Munţii Meridionali
Rîmnicu Sărat
CROATIA
Apatin
Vrbas
Bečej
Timiş
Daruvar
Carpaţii
Karlovac
Sisak
Zrenjanin
Caransebeş
Peleaga 2509
Buzău
Vrbovsko
Osijek
Deta
(Transylvanian Alps)
Kupa
Našice
Pakrac
Reşiţa
Mţii
Cîmpina
Rijeka (Fiume)
Dakovo
Vukovar
Novi Sad
Rîmnicu Vîlcea
Mizil
15
Ogulin
Una
Bosanski Brod
Vinkovci
Dunav
20
Vršac
Tîrgu Jiu
Tîrgovişte
45
Ploieşti

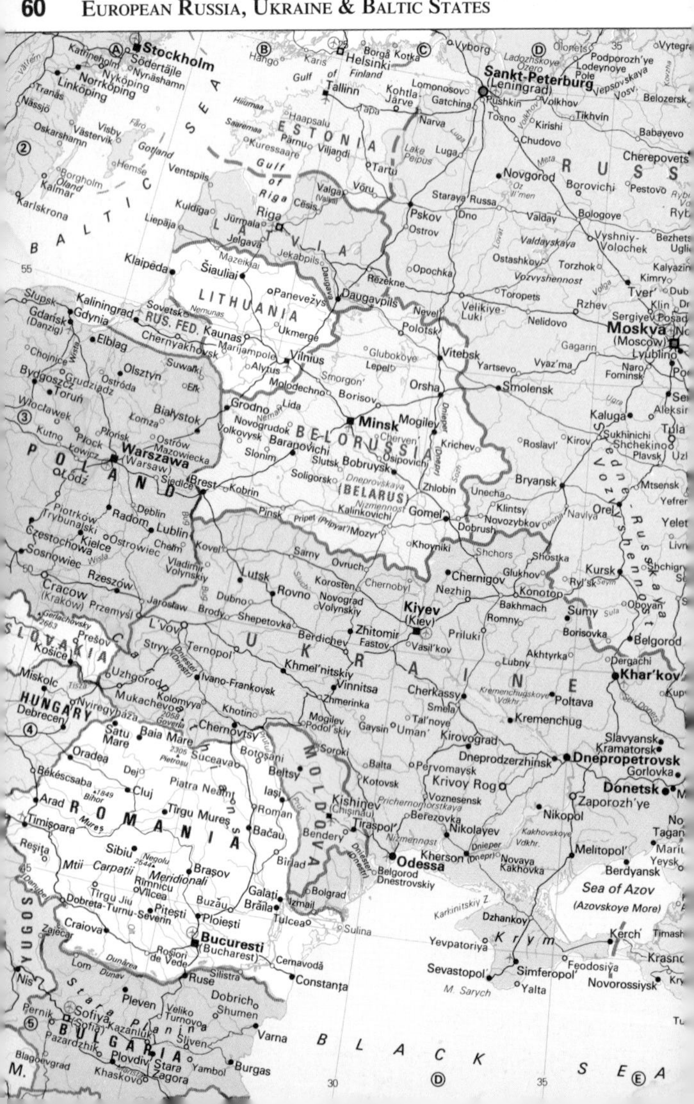

Stockholm
Södertälje
Nynäshamn
Nyköping
Norrköping
Linköping
Tranås
Nässjö
Oskarshamn
Västervik
Visby
Gotland
Hemse
Borgholm
Öland
Kalmar
Karlskrona
BALTIC SEA
Hango
Karis
Borgå
Kotka
Helsinki
Gulf of Finland
Tallinn
Kohtla-Järve
Hiiumaa
Saaremaa
Haapsalu
Pärnu
Viljandi
Kuressaare
ESTONIA
Tapa
Narva
Tartu
Lake Peipus
Võru
Valga
Cēsis
Gulf of Riga
Riga
Jūrmala
Ventspils
Kuldīga
Liepāja
LATVIA
Jelgava
Jekabpils
Daugava
Rēzekne
Daugavpils
Mazeikiai
Klaipėda
Šiauliai
Panevežys
LITHUANIA
Ukmerge
Kaunas
Marijampole
Alytus
Vilnius
Vyborg
Ladozhskoye Ozero
Olonets
Podporozh'ye
Lodeynoye Pole
Vytegra
Sankt-Peterburg
(Leningrad)
Pushkin
Lomonosov
Gatchina
Volkhov
Tikhvin
Belozersk
Tosno
Kirishi
Chudovo
Babayevo
Luga
Novgorod
Cherepovets
RUSSIA
Borovichi
Pestovo
Staraya Russa
Pskov
Dno
Valday
Bologoye
Ostrov
Valdayskaya
Vyshniy-Volochek
Bezhetsk
Ostashkov
Torzhok
Kalyazin
Vozvyshennost
Opochka
Toropets
Kimry
Tver'
Rzhev
Klin
Sergiyev Posad
Velikiye-Luki
Nelidovo
Nevel
Polotsk
Moskva
(Moscow)
Lyublino
Gagarin
Glubokoye
Lepel
Vitebsk
Yartsevo
Vyaz'ma
Naro Fominsk
Orsha
Smolensk
Kaluga
Aleksin
Tula
Słupsk
Kaliningrad
Gdańsk
(Danzig)
Gdynia
Sovetsk
RUS. FED.
Nemunas
Elbląg
Chernyakhovsk
Chojnice
Suwałki
Olsztyn
Bydgoszcz
Grudziądz
Ostróda
Ełk
Toruń
Włocławek
Białystok
Łomża
Kutno
Płock
Płońsk
Ostrów Mazowiecka
Łowicz
Warszawa
(Warsaw)
POLAND
Łódź
Siedlce
Brest
Kobrin
Grodno
Lida
Novogrudok
Volkovysk
Baranovichi
Slonim
Smorgon'
Molodechno
Borisov
Minsk
Mogilev
Cherven'
BELORUSSIA
(BELARUS)
Osipovichi
Bobruysk
Slutsk
Soligorsk
Dneprovskaya Nizmennost
Krichev
Roslavl'
Kirov
Sukhinichi
Shchekino
Plavsk
Bryansk
Zhlobin
Unecha
Mtsensk
Kalinkovichi
Gomel'
Klintsy
Novozybkov
Navlya
Orel
Pinsk
Pripet (Pripyat')
Mozyr'
Dobrush
Desna
Khoyniki
Shchors
Shostka
Kursk
Dęblin
Radom
Lublin
Piotrków Trybunalski
Kielce
Ostrowiec
Chełm
Częstochowa
Sosnowiec
Wisła
Kovel'
Vladimir Volynskiy
Lutsk
Sarny
Ovruch
Korosten'
Chernobyl
Chernigov
Nezhin
Glukhov
Ryl'sk
Rovno
Novograd Volynskiy
Konotop
Bakhmach
Sumy
Oboyan'
Rzeszów
Cracow
(Kraków)
Przemyśl
Jarosław
Dubno
Brody
Shepetovka
Kiyev
(Kiev)
Romny
Priluki
Borisovka
Belgorod
L'vov
Zhitomir
Berdichev
Fastov
Vasil'kov
Stryy
Ternopol'
UKRAINE
Lubny
Akhtyrka
Dergachi
Khar'kov
Gerlachovsky
2663
Prešov
Košice
SLOVAKIA
Khmel'nitskiy
Vinnitsa
Zhmerinka
Cherkassy
Smela
Kremenchugskoye Vdkhr.
Poltava
Kremenchug
Miskolc
Tisza
Uzhgorod
Ivano-Frankovsk
Mukachevo
Kolomyya
Nyíregyháza
HUNGARY
Debrecen
Goverla
2058
Khotin
Chernovtsy
Mogilev Podol'skiy
Gaysin
Tal'noye
Uman'
Kirovograd
Slavyansk
Kramatorsk
Satu Mare
Baia Mare
Suceava
Botoşani
Soroki
Dneprodzerzhinsk
Dnepropetrovsk
Gorlovka
Oradea
Dej
Beltsy
MOLDOVA
Balta
Pervomaysk
Krivoy Rog
Donetsk
Békéscsaba
Bihor
1849
Cluj
Piatra Neamţ
Iaşi
Kotovsk
Zaporozh'ye
Arad
ROMANIA
Tîrgu Mureş
Roman
Kishinev
(Chişinău)
Prichernomorstkaya
Voznesensk
Nikopol
Timişoara
Mureş
Bacău
Berezovka
Tiraspol'
Bendery
Nizmennost
Nikolayev
Kakhovskoye Vdkhr.
Reşiţa
Sibiu
Negolu
2544
Braşov
Bîrlad
Odessa
Kherson
Dnieper (Dnepr)
Novaya Kakhovka
Melitopol'
Berdyansk
Mtii Carpaţii Meridionali
Rîmnicu Vîlcea
Belgorod Dnestrovskiy
Sea of Azov
(Azovskoye More)
Tîrgu Jiu
Dobreta-Turnu-Severin
Piteşti
Buzău
Galaţi
Brăila
Izmail
Bolgrad
Karkinitskiy Z.
Dzhankoy
Craiova
Ploieşti
Tulcea
Sulina
Krym
Kerch'
Bucuresti
(Bucharest)
Yevpatoriya
Roşiori de Vede
Cernavodă
Feodosiya
Lom
Dunărea
Dunav
Ruse
Silistra
Constanţa
Sevastopol'
Simferopol'
Yalta
Novorossiysk
M. Sarych
Niš
Pleven
Dobrich
Shumen
Veliko Turnovo
Stara Planina
Pernik
Sofiya
(Sofia)
Kazanlŭk
Sliven
Varna
BLACK SEA
BULGARIA
Pazardzhik
Plovdiv
Stara Zagora
Yambol
Burgas
Blagoevgrad
Khaskovo
55
50
45
30
35

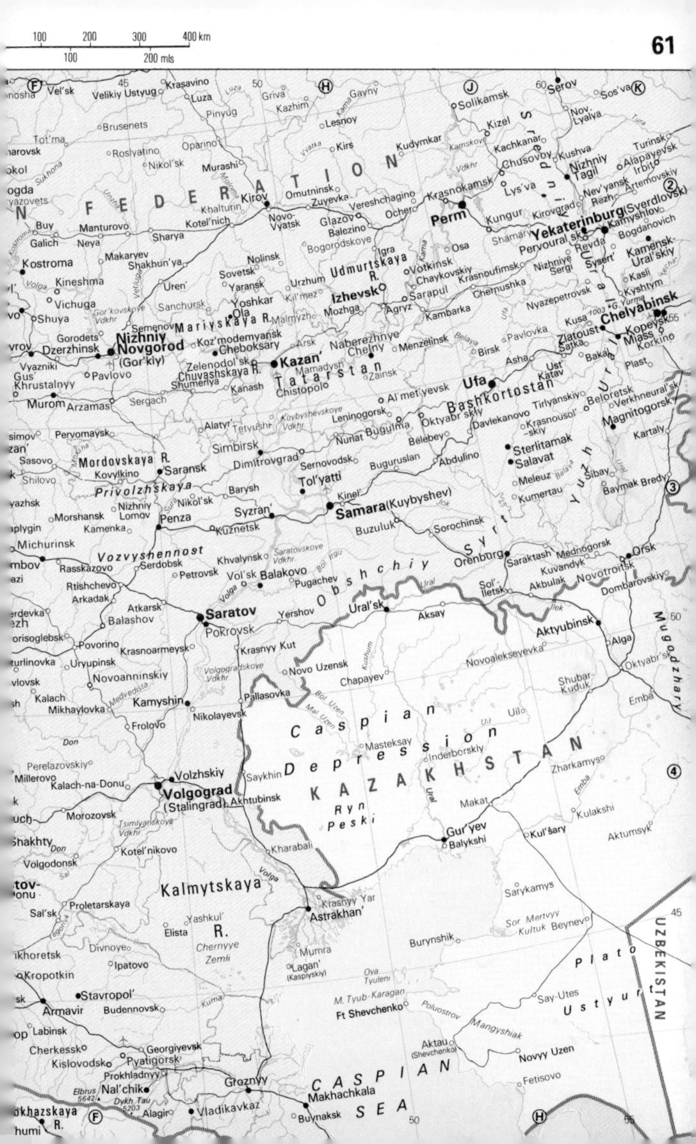

100 200 300 400 km
100 200 mls
F
H
J
K
Vel'sk
Velikiy Ustyug
Krasavino
Luza
Griva
Gayny
Kazhim
Lesnoy
Pinyug
Brusenets
Serov
Sos'va
Solikamsk
Nov. Lyalya
Kizel
Tot'ma
Roslyatino
Oparino
Kirs
Kudymkar
Kachkanar
Kushva
Turinsk
Nikol'sk
Murashi
Nizhniy Tagil
Alapayevsk
Irbit
Artemovskiy
FEDERATION
Omutninsk
Zuyevka
Vereshchagino
Krasnokamsk
Chusovoy
Lys'va
Nev'yansk
Rezh
Kirov
Khalturin
Kotel'nich
Novo-Vyatsk
Glazov
Ocher
Perm
Kungur
Kirovgrad
Yekaterinburg (Sverdlovsk)
Kamyshlov
Buy
Manturovo
Sharya
Balezino
Bogorodskoye
Shamary
Pervouralsk
Revda
Bogdanovich
Galich
Neya
Igra
Osa
Sysert'
Kamensk-Ural'skiy
Kostroma
Makaryev
Shakhun'ya
Nolinsk
Udmurtskaya R.
Votkinsk
Chaykovskiy
Krasnoufimsk
Nizhniye Sergi
Kasli
Kineshma
Sovetsk
Yaransk
Urzhum
Kil'mez
Izhevsk
Sarapul
Chernushka
Kyshtym
Vichuga
Uren'
Sanchursk
Yoshkar Ola
Mozhga
Agryz
Kambarka
Nyazepetrovsk
Shuya
Semenov
Mariyskaya R.
Malmyzh
Kusa
Chelyabinsk
Gorodets
Nizhniy Novgorod (Gor'kiy)
Koz'modemyansk
Cheboksary
Arsk
Naberezhnye Chelny
Menzelinsk
Pavlovka
Zlatoust
Satka
Kopeysk
Miass
Korkino
Dzerzhinsk
Zelenodol'sk
Chuvashskaya R.
Kazan'
Mamadysh
Tatarstan
Zainsk
Birsk
Asha
Ust' Katav
Bakal
Plast
Vyazniki
Pavlovo
Gus' Khrustalnyy
Shumerlya
Kanash
Chistopolo
Ufa
Bashkortostan
Murom
Arzamas
Sergach
Al'met'yevsk
Tirlyanskiy
Beloretsk
Verkhneural'sk
Magnitogorsk
Alatyr'
Tetyushi
Kuybyshevskoye Vdkhr.
Leninogorsk
Bugul'ma
Oktyabr'skiy
Davlekanovo
Krasnousol'-skiy
Pervomaysk
Nurlat
Belebey
Kartaly
Simbirsk
Sasovo
Mordovskaya R.
Sterlitamak
Salavat
Kovylkino
Saransk
Dimitrovgrad
Sernovodsk
Bugurusian
Abdulino
Shilovo
Privolzhskaya
Tol'yatti
Meleuz
Sibay
Baymak
Bredy
Nikol'sk
Barysh
Kinel'
Kumertau
Nizhniy Lomov
Morshansk
Samara (Kuybyshev)
Syzran'
Penza
Kamenka
Kuznetsk
Buzuluk
Sorochinsk
Michurinsk
Vozvyshennost
Khvalynsk
Saratovskoye Vdkhr.
Syrt
Orenburg
Saraktash
Mednogorsk
Orsk
Rasskazovo
Serdobsk
Petrovsk
Vol'sk
Balakovo
Obshchiy
Kuvandyk
Novotroitsk
Rtishchevo
Pugachev
Sol'-Iletsk
Akbulak
Dombarovskiy
Arkadak
Atkarsk
Ural
Ural'sk
Aksay
Balashov
Saratov
Yershov
Aktyubinsk
Pokrovsk
Mugodzhary
Borisoglebsk
Povorino
Krasnoarmeysk
Krasnyy Kut
Alga
Uryupinsk
Volgogradskoye Vdkhr.
Novo Uzensk
Novoalekseyevka
Oktyabr'sk
Novoanninskiy
Chapayev
Shubar-Kuduk
Kalach
Pallasovka
Mikhaylovka
Medvedista
Kamyshin
Nikolayevsk
Emba
Uilo
Frolovo
Caspian
Depression
KAZAKHSTAN
Don
Masteksay
Inderborskiy
Perelazovskiy
Zharkamys
Millerovo
Volzhskiy
Saykhin
Kalach-na-Donu
Volgograd (Stalingrad)
Akhtubinsk
Makat
Morozovsk
Ryn Peski
Kulakshi
Tsimlyanskoye Vdkhr.
Gur'yev
Balykshi
Kul'sary
Aktumsyk
Shakhty
Kotel'nikovo
Kharabali
Volgodonsk
Kalmytskaya R.
Sarykamys
Proletarskaya
Krasnyy Yar
Astrakhan'
Sal'sk
Yashkul'
Elista
Sor Mertvyy Kultuk
Beyneu
UZBEKISTAN
Chernyye Zemli
Divnoye
Burynshik
Tikhoretsk
Ipatovo
Mumra
Plato
Kropotkin
Lagan' (Kaspiyskiy)
Ova Tyuleni
Stavropol'
Say-Utes
Armavir
Budennovsk
Kuma
M. Tyub-Karagan
Ft Shevchenko
Poluostrov
Ustyurt
Labinsk
Mangyshlak
Cherkessk
Georgiyevsk
Aktau (Shevchenko)
Novyy Uzen
Kislovodsk
Pyatigorsk
Prokhladnyy
Fetisovo
Elbrus 5642
Nal'chik
Groznyy
CASPIAN SEA
Dykh Tau 5203
Makhachkala
Alagir
Vladikavkaz
Buynaksk

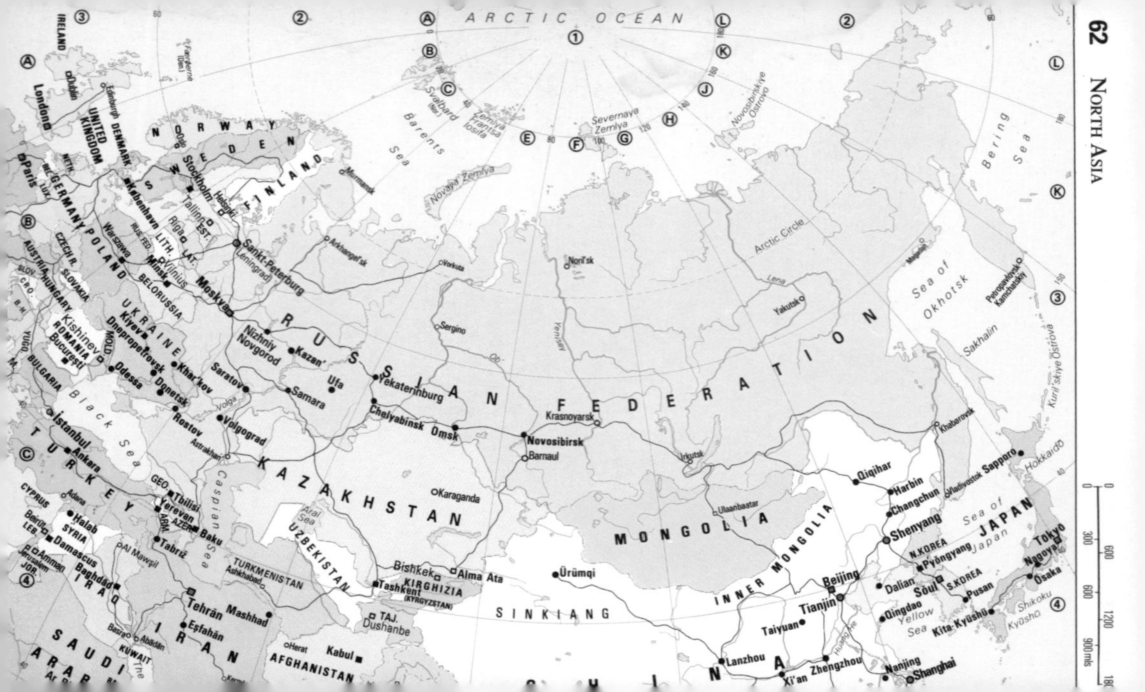
0
600
1200
0
300
600
900 mls
ARCTIC OCEAN
Svalbard (Nor.)
Zemlya Frantsa Iosifa
Novaya Zemlya
Severnaya Zemlya
Novosibirskiye Ostrova
Barents Sea
Arctic Circle
Bering Sea
Sea of Okhotsk
Sakhalin
Kuril'skiye Ostrova
Hokkaido
Sea of Japan
Yellow Sea
Shikoku
Kyūshū
RUSSIAN FEDERATION
MONGOLIA
INNER MONGOLIA
SINKIANG
KAZAKHSTAN
UZBEKISTAN
TURKMENISTAN
KIRGHIZIA (KYRGYZSTAN)
TAJ.
AFGHANISTAN
IRAN
IRAQ
SYRIA
TURKEY
JAPAN
N.KOREA
S.KOREA
FINLAND
SWEDEN
NORWAY
DENMARK
UNITED KINGDOM
IRELAND
GERMANY
POLAND
UKRAINE
BELORUSSIA
ROMANIA
BULGARIA
HUNGARY
SLOVAKIA
CZECH R.
AUSTRIA
NETH.
BEL.
LUX.
SLOV.
CRO.
B.H.
YUGO.
MOLD.
LITH.
LAT.
EST.
RUS. FED.
GEO.
ARM.
AZER.
CYPRUS
LEB.
JOR.
KUWAIT
SAUDI ARAB
Færøerne (Den.)
Caspian Sea
Aral Sea
Black Sea
Yenisey
Ob
Lena
Volga
Huang He
Murmansk
Arkhangel'sk
Vorkuta
Sergino
Noril'sk
Yakutsk
Magadan
Petropavlovsk-Kamchatskiy
Khabarovsk
Vladivostok
Sapporo
Tokyo
Nagoya
Ōsaka
Kita-Kyūshū
Pusan
Sŏul
P'yŏngyang
Dalian
Qingdao
Shenyang
Changchun
Harbin
Qiqihar
Beijing
Tianjin
Shanghai
Nanjing
Zhengzhou
Xi'an
Taiyuan
Lanzhou
Ürümqi
Ulaanbaatar
Irkutsk
Krasnoyarsk
Novosibirsk
Barnaul
Omsk
Karaganda
Alma Ata
Bishkek
Tashkent
Dushanbe
Kabul
Herat
Mashhad
Ashkhabad
Tehrān
Eşfahān
Tabrīz
Baku
Tbilisi
Yerevan
Astrakhan'
Volgograd
Saratov
Samara
Ufa
Kazan'
Chelyabinsk
Yekaterinburg
Nizhniy Novgorod
Moskva
Sankt-Peterburg (Leningrad)
Helsinki
Tallinn
Riga
Vilnius
Minsk
Stockholm
Oslo
København
Edinburgh
Dublin
London
Paris
Warszawa
Kiyev
Khar'kov
Donetsk
Dnepropetrovsk
Odessa
Rostov
Kishinev
Bucureşti
İstanbul
Ankara
Adana
Halab
Damascus
Beirut
Amman
Jerusalem
Baghdād
Al Mawşil
Basra
Ābādān

200 400 600 800 km
200 400 mls

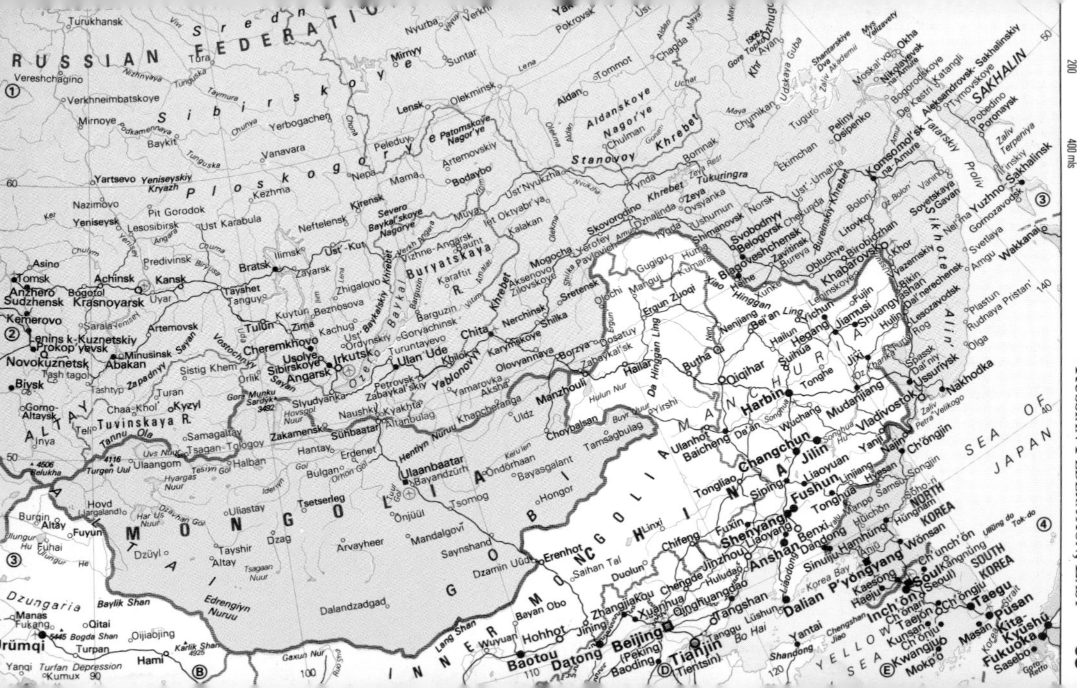
RUSSIAN FEDERATION
Sredne Sibirskoye Ploskogorye
MONGOLIA
INNER MONGOLIA
MANCHURIA
SEA OF JAPAN
YELLOW SEA
NORTH KOREA
SOUTH KOREA
SAKHALIN
ALTAY
Tuvinskaya R.
Buryatskaya R.
Sikhote Alin'
Stanovoy Khrebet
Aldanskoye Nagor'ye
Yablonovyy Khrebet
Da Hinggan Ling
Xiao Hinggan
Tatarskiy Proliv
Dzungaria
Turfan Depression
Ozero Baykal
Vladivostok
Khabarovsk
Komsomol'sk-na-Amure
Yuzhno-Sakhalinsk
Aleksandrovsk-Sakhalinskiy
Nakhodka
Ussuriysk
Blagoveshchensk
Svobodnyy
Harbin
Qiqihar
Changchun
Jilin
Mudanjiang
Shenyang
Fushun
Anshan
Dalian
P'yongyang
Seoul
Inch'ŏn
Taegu
Pusan
Kita-Kyushu
Fukuoka
Beijing (Peking)
Tianjin (Tientsin)
Baotou
Datong
Hohhot
Erenhot
Ulaanbaatar
Choybalsan
Manzhouli
Hailar
Ulan Ude
Chita
Irkutsk
Angarsk
Bratsk
Krasnoyarsk
Kansk
Achinsk
Tomsk
Kemerovo
Novokuznetsk
Abakan
Kyzyl
Biysk
Lensk
Mirnyy
Kirensk
Aldan
Tynda
Ürümqi
Turpan
Hami

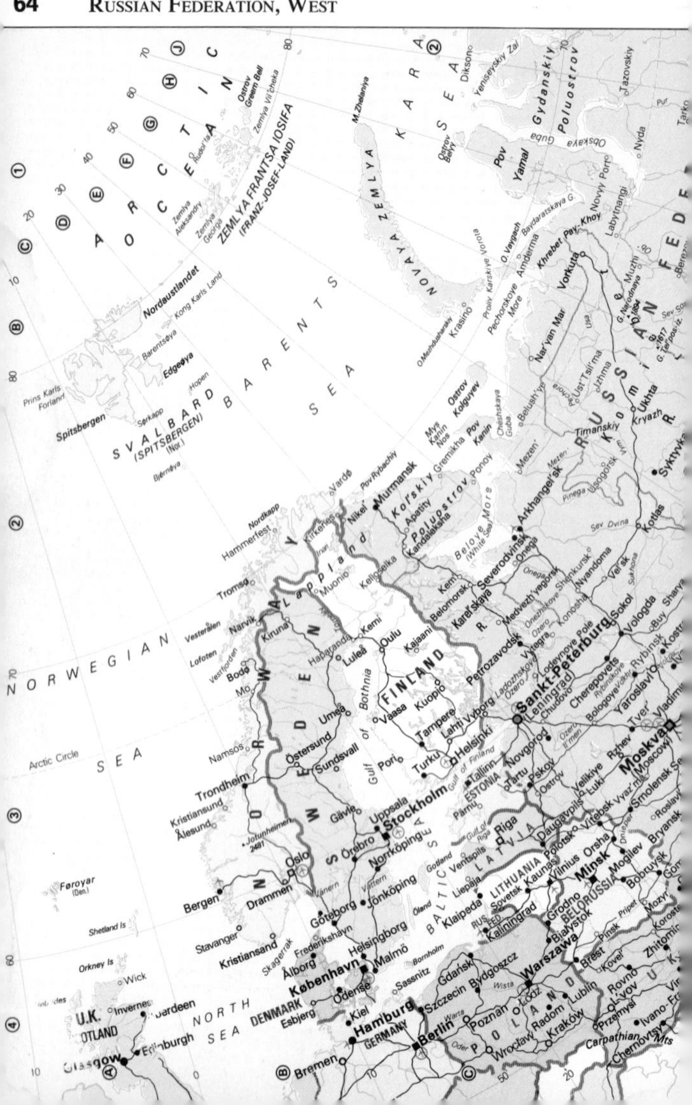
ARCTIC OCEAN
KARA SEA
BARENTS SEA
NORWEGIAN SEA
NORTH SEA
BALTIC SEA
Beloye More (White Sea)
Pechorskoye More
Gulf of Bothnia
Gulf of Finland
Gulf of Riga
Skagerrak
ZEMLYA FRANTSA IOSIFA (FRANZ-JOSEF-LAND)
Zemlya Aleksandry
Zemlya Georga
Zemlya Vil'cheka
Ostrov Greem Bell
Rudol'fa
NOVAYA ZEMLYA
M. Zhelaniya
Ostrov Belyy
Dikson
Yeniseyskiy Zal
Gydanskiy Poluostrov
Obskaya Guba
Pov Yamal
Tazovskiy
Pur
Tarko
Nyda
Novyy Port
Labytnangi
Baydaratskaya G.
O. Vaygach
Amderma
Proliv Karskiye Vorota
Khrebet Pay-Khoy
Vorkuta
Muzhi
G. Narodnaya 1894
G. Tel'pos-iz 1617
Berezovo
Krasino
O. Mezhdusharskiy
Nar'yan Mar
Usa
Pechora
Ust'Tsil'ma
Izhma
Ukhta
Kryazh
Timanskiy
Komi
RUSSIAN FEDERATION
Belush'ye
Ostrov Kolguyev
Cheshskaya Guba
Mys Kanin Nos
Pov Kanin
Mezen'
Pinega
Usogorsk
Syktyvkar
Kotlas
Sev. Dvina
Arkhangel'sk
Severodvinsk
Onega
Nyandoma
Shenkursk
Vel'sk
Sukhona
Sokol
Vologda
Buy
Sharya
Kostroma
Rybinsk
Yaroslavl'
Rybinskoye Vdkhr.
Cherepovets
Vladimir
Tver'
Moskva (Moscow)
Rzhev
Velikiye Luki
Smolensk
Vyaz'ma
Roslavl'
Bryansk
Gremikha
Ponoy
Kol'skiy Poluostrov
Murmansk
Pov Rybachiy
Apatity
Kandalaksha
Nikel
Vardø
Kirkenes
Inari
Nordkapp
Hammerfest
Tromsø
Narvik
Vesterålen
Lofoten
Vestfjorden
Bodø
Mo
Lappland
Kiruna
Muonio
Kemijärvi
Kem'
Belomorsk
Karel'skaya R.
Medvezh'yegorsk
Onezhskoye Ozero
Konosha
Petrozavodsk
Vytegra
Lodeynoye Pole
Ladozhskoye Ozero
Sankt-Peterburg (Leningrad)
Chudovo
Bologoye
Novgorod
Ozero Il'men
Pskov
Ostrov
Tartu
Tallinn
ESTONIA
Pärnu
Riga
LATVIA
Ventspils
Liepāja
Daugavpils
Polotsk
Vitebsk
Orsha
Mogilev
Minsk
BELORUSSIA
Bobruysk
Gomel
Mozyr
Korosten
Zhitomir
Dnieper
Pripet
Pinsk
Brest
Kovel
Rovno
L'vov
Przemysl
Ivano-Frankovsk
Chernovtsy
Carpathian Mts
Vilnius
Kaunas
LITHUANIA
Sovetsk
Klaipeda
RUS. FED.
Kaliningrad
Grodno
Białystok
Warszawa
Lublin
Radom
Łódź
Kraków
POLAND
Wista
Gdańsk
Bydgoszcz
Szczecin
Poznań
Warta
Oder
Wrocław
Berlin
GERMANY
Hamburg
Kiel
Bremen
Sassnitz
Bornholm
DENMARK
København
Odense
Esbjerg
Ålborg
Frederikshavn
Helsingborg
Malmö
Öland
Gotland
Norrköping
Stockholm
Uppsala
Örebro
Vänern
Vättern
Jönköping
Göteborg
Gävle
Sundsvall
Östersund
Umeå
Luleå
Haparanda
Kemi
Oulu
Kajaani
FINLAND
Vaasa
Kuopio
Tampere
Lahti
Vyborg
Helsinki
Turku
Pori
SWEDEN
NORWAY
Namsos
Trondheim
Kristiansund
Ålesund
Jotunheimen 2481
Oslo
Drammen
Bergen
Stavanger
Kristiansand
Føroyar (Den.)
Shetland Is
Orkney Is
Wick
Hebrides
Inverness
Aberdeen
U.K.
SCOTLAND
Edinburgh
Glasgow
SVALBARD (SPITSBERGEN) (Nor.)
Spitsbergen
Nordaustlandet
Kong Karls Land
Barentsøya
Edgeøya
Hopen
Sørkapp
Prins Karls Forland
Bjørnøya
Arctic Circle

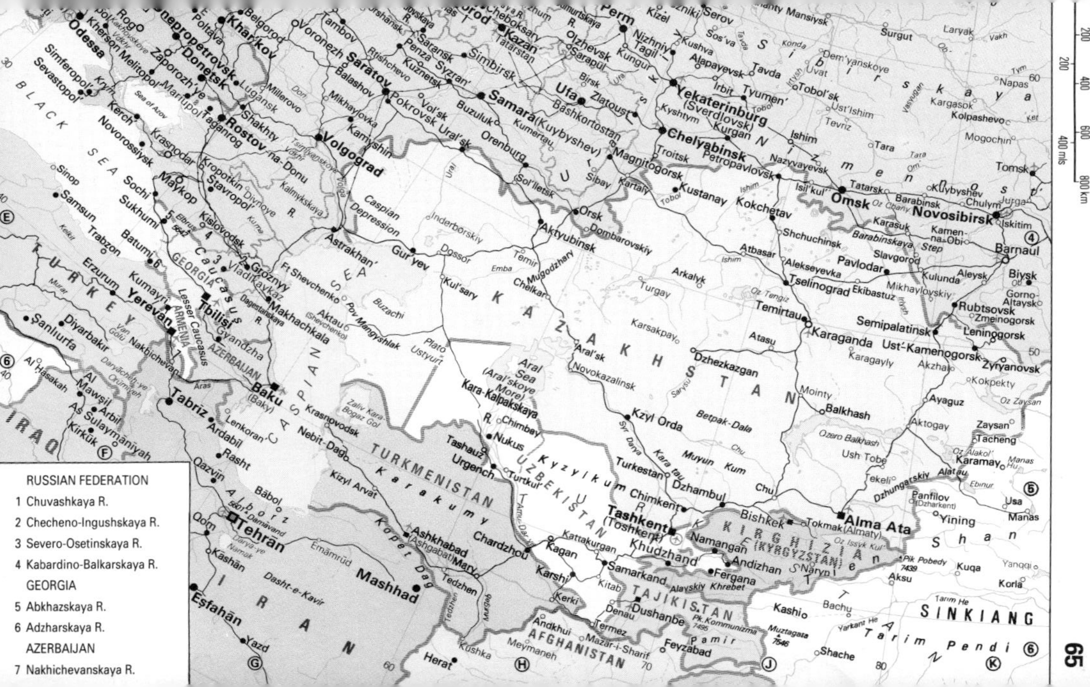

200   400   600   800 km

200   400 mils

RUSSIAN FEDERATION
1 Chuvashskaya R.
2 Checheno-Ingushskaya R.
3 Severo-Osetinskaya R.
4 Kabardino-Balkarskaya R.

GEORGIA
5 Abkhazskaya R.
6 Adzharskaya R.

AZERBAIJAN
7 Nakhichevanskaya R.

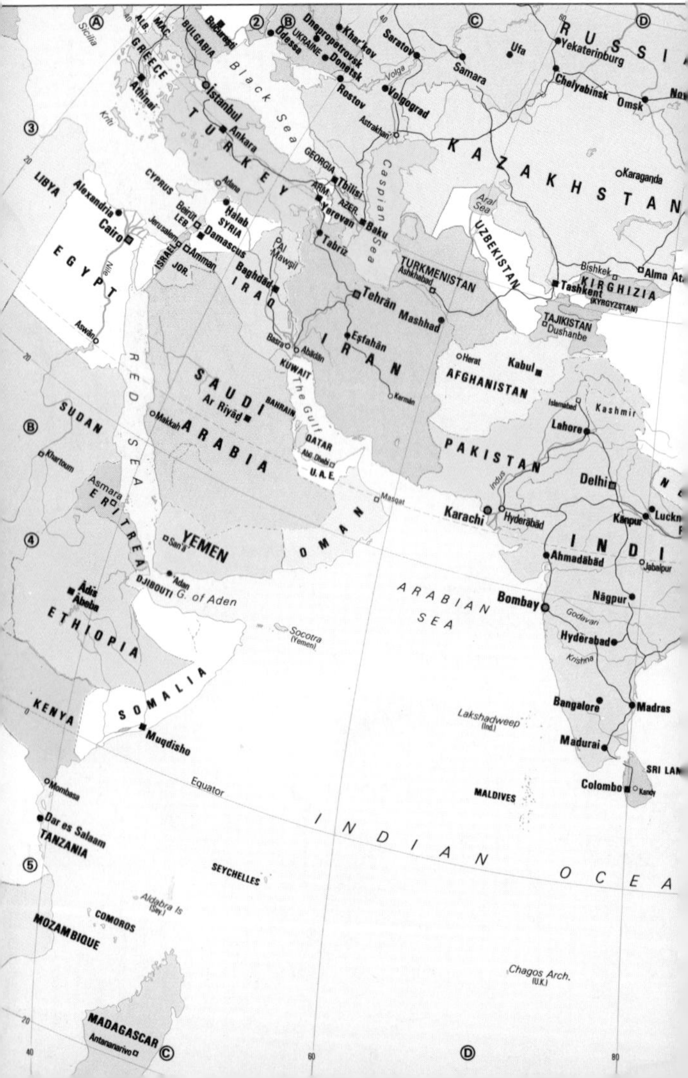

Sicily

ⒶⒷⒸⒹ

RUSSIA

GREECE
ALB.
MAC.
BULGARIA
Beograd
②
Odessa
Dnepropetrovsk
UKRAINE
Khar'kov
Saratov
Ufa
Yekaterinburg
Omsk
Nos

Athinai
Kriti
Istanbul
Black Sea
Rostov
Donetsk
Volga
Samara
Chelyabinsk

Ankara
TURKEY
GEORGIA
Tbilisi
ARM.
Astrakhan'
KAZAKHSTAN
Karaganda

③

LIBYA
Alexandria
CYPRUS
Beirut
SYRIA
Halab
Adana
Yerevan
AZER.
Baku
Caspian Sea
Aral Sea

EGYPT
Cairo
LEB.
ISRAEL
Damascus
Jerusalem
JOR.
Amman
IRAQ
Baghdad
Basra
Mawsil
Tabriz
TURKMENISTAN
Ashkhabad
UZBEKISTAN
Bishkek
Tashkent
Alma Ata
KIRGHIZIA
(KYRGYZSTAN)

Aswan
Nile
SAUDI
Abadan
Esfahan
IRAN
Tehran
Mashhad
TAJIKISTAN
Dushanbe

SUDAN
RED SEA
Makkah
Ar Riyad
ARABIA
KUWAIT
BAHRAIN
The Gulf
QATAR
Abu Dhabi
U.A.E.
Herat
Kerman
Kabul
AFGHANISTAN
Islamabad
Kashmir
Lahore
PAKISTAN
Delhi
N

Ⓑ
Khartoum
ERITREA
Asmara
YEMEN
Sana
OMAN
Muscat
Karachi
Hyderabad
INDI
Kanpur
Luckn
Jabalpur

Adis Abeba
DJIBOUTI
G. of Aden
Aden
Ahmadabad
Bombay
Nagpur
Godavari

ETHIOPIA
Socotra
(Yemen)
ARABIAN
SEA
Hyderabad
Krishna

KENYA
SOMALIA
Muqdisho
Bangalore
Madras

Lakshadweep
(India)
Madurai
SRI LAN
Mombasa
Equator
Colombo
Kandy

Dar es Salaam
TANZANIA
MALDIVES
INDIAN OCEA

④

Aldabra Is.
(Sey.)
SEYCHELLES

⑤

MOZAMBIQUE
COMOROS
Chagos Arch.
(U.K.)

MADAGASCAR
Antananarivo

20

40
Ⓒ
60
Ⓓ
80

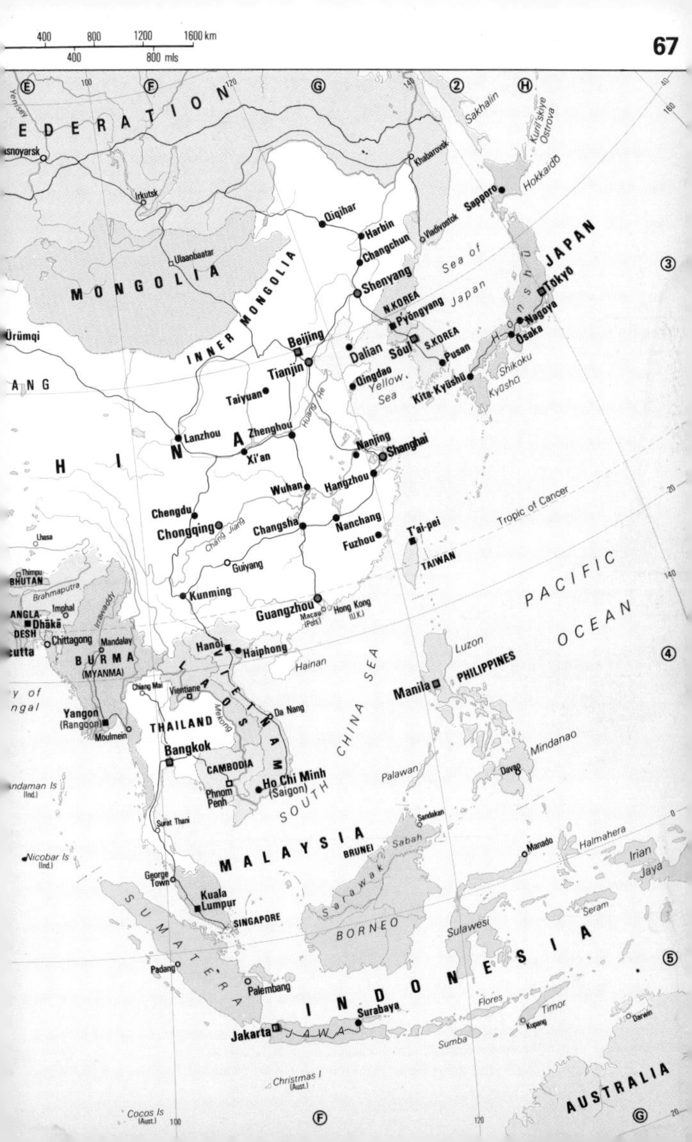
400 800 1200 1600 km
400 800 mls
FEDERATION
MONGOLIA
INNER MONGOLIA
CHINA
JAPAN
N.KOREA
S.KOREA
TAIWAN
PHILIPPINES
BURMA (MYANMA)
THAILAND
LAOS
VIETNAM
CAMBODIA
MALAYSIA
BRUNEI
SINGAPORE
INDONESIA
AUSTRALIA
BHUTAN
PACIFIC OCEAN
SOUTH CHINA SEA
Sea of Japan
Yellow Sea
Tropic of Cancer
Beijing
Tianjin
Shanghai
Shenyang
Harbin
Changchun
Qiqihar
Dalian
Qingdao
Taiyuan
Zhenghou
Nanjing
Hangzhou
Wuhan
Xi'an
Lanzhou
Chengdu
Chongqing
Changsha
Nanchang
Fuzhou
Guiyang
Kunming
Guangzhou
Hong Kong (U.K.)
Macau (Port.)
T'ai-pei
Pyŏngyang
Sŏul
Pusan
Tōkyō
Nagoya
Ōsaka
Kita-Kyūshū
Sapporo
Hokkaidō
Honshu
Shikoku
Kyūshū
Sakhalin
Kuril'skiye Ostrova
Khabarovsk
Vladivostok
Irkutsk
Ulaanbaatar
Ürümqi
Lhasa
Thimpu
Dhākā
Chittagong
Imphal
Mandalay
Yangon (Rangoon)
Moulmein
Chiang Mai
Vientiane
Hanoi
Haiphong
Hainan
Da Nang
Bangkok
Phnom Penh
Ho Chi Minh (Saigon)
Manila
Luzon
Mindanao
Davao
Palawan
Sandakan
Sabah
Sarawak
Borneo
Surat Thani
George Town
Kuala Lumpur
Sumatera
Padang
Palembang
Jakarta
Jawa
Surabaya
Sulawesi
Manado
Halmahera
Seram
Irian Jaya
Flores
Sumba
Timor
Kupang
Darwin
Christmas I (Aust.)
Cocos Is (Aust.)
Nicobar Is (Ind.)
Andaman Is (Ind.)
Yenisey
Brahmaputra
Irrawaddy
Mekong
Chang Jiang
Huang He
E F G H
2 3 4 5
100 120 140 160
40 20 0 20

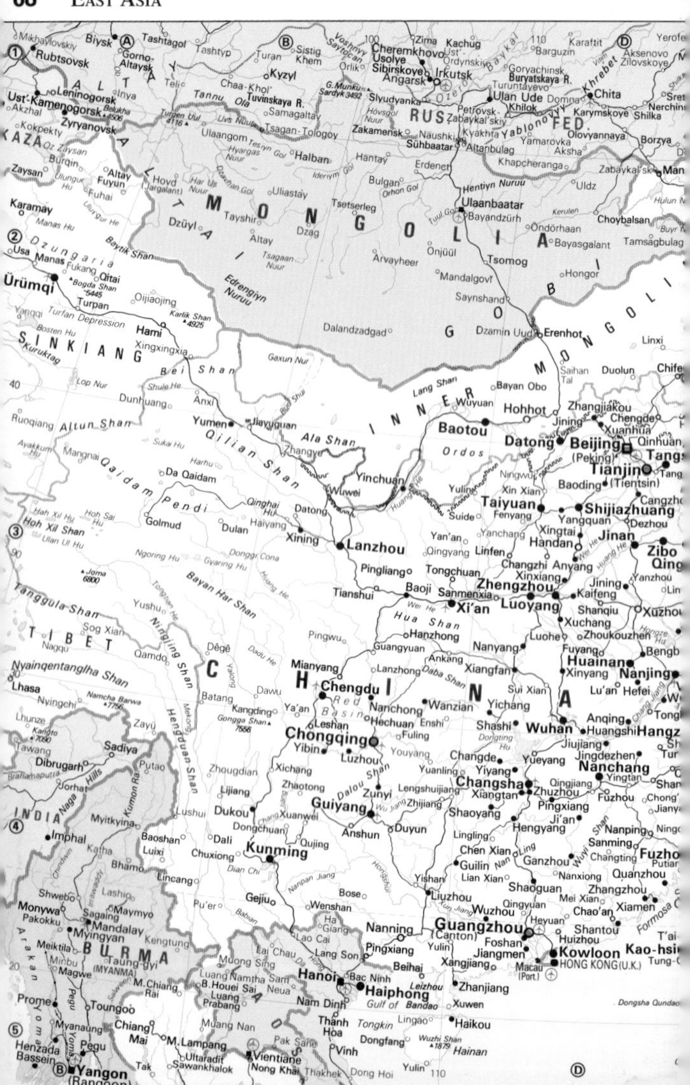

MONGOLIA
RUS. FED.
KAZA
SINKIANG
INNER MONGOLIA
TIBET
CHINA
INDIA
BURMA
(MYANMA)
LAOS
GOBI
Altai
Dzungaria
Rubtsovsk
Biysk
Tashtagol
Gorno-Altaysk
Leninogorsk
Ust'-Kamenogorsk
Zyryanovsk
Zaysan
Karamay
Ürümqi
Turpan
Hami
Turfan Depression
Kyzyl
Tuvinskaya R.
Ulaangom
Halban
Hovd
Uliastay
Tsetserleg
Bulgan
Ulaanbaatar
Bayandzürh
Öndörhaan
Choybalsan
Bayasgalant
Tamsagbulag
Tsomog
Mandalgovĭ
Saynshand
Dalandzadgad
Dzamin Uud
Erenhot
Arvayheer
Onjüül
Altay
Tayshir
Dzüyl
Dzag
Cheremkhovo
Usolye Sibirskoye
Irkutsk
Angarsk
Ozero Baykal
Ulan Ude
Buryatskaya R.
Chita
Petrovsk-Zabaykal'skiy
Khilok
Kyakhta
Sühbaatar
Altanbulag
Naushki
Zakamensk
Slyudyanka
Yablonovyy Khrebet
Karymskoye
Shilka
Nerchinsk
Borzya
Aksha
Olovyannaya
Yamarovka
Khapcheranga
Zabaykal'sk
Hentiyn Nuruu
Kerulen
Hongor
Edrengiyn Nuruu
Baytik Shan
Bogda Shan 5445
Karlik Shan 4925
Bei Shan
Lop Nur
Dunhuang
Anxi
Altun Shan
Ruoqiang
Qilian Shan
Qaidam Pendi
Da Qaidam
Golmud
Dulan
Yumen
Jiayuguan
Ala Shan
Zhangye
Wuwei
Yinchuan
Baotou
Hohhot
Ordos
Datong
Zhangjiakou
Beijing (Peking)
Tianjin (Tientsin)
Chengde
Baoding
Shijiazhuang
Taiyuan
Jinan
Zibo
Xining
Lanzhou
Qinghai Hu
Hoh Xil Shan
Tanggula Shan
Bayan Har Shan
Yushu
Qamdo
Nyainqentanglha Shan
Lhasa
Nyingchi
Namcha Barwa 7756
Hengduan Shan
Ningjing Shan
Gongga Shan 7556
Chengdu
Red Basin
Chongqing
Mianyang
Nanchong
Leshan
Yibin
Luzhou
Guiyang
Kunming
Dali
Gejiu
Baoji
Xi'an
Tianshui
Hua Shan
Hanzhong
Zhengzhou
Luoyang
Kaifeng
Xuzhou
Nanyang
Xiangfan
Huainan
Nanjing
Hefei
Wuhan
Yichang
Shashi
Changde
Changsha
Xiangtan
Zhuzhou
Hengyang
Nanchang
Jiujiang
Jingdezhen
Guilin
Liuzhou
Nanning
Wuzhou
Guangzhou (Canton)
Foshan
Jiangmen
Kowloon
HONG KONG (U.K.)
Macau (Port.)
Shantou
Xiamen
Zhangzhou
Quanzhou
Fuzhou
Zhanjiang
Haikou
Hainan
Gulf of Tonkin
Hanoi
Haiphong
Nam Dinh
Thanh Hoa
Vinh
Vientiane
Nong Khai
Luang Prabang
Lao Cai
Lang Son
Imphal
Mandalay
Myitkyina
Lashio
Bhamo
Sagaing
Monywa
Meiktila
Magwe
Prome
Toungoo
Pegu
Yangon (Rangoon)
Bassein
Henzada
Chiang Mai
Chiang Rai
Sadiya
Dibrugarh
Brahmaputra
Naga Hills
Kumon Ra
Dongsha Qundao
Wuzhi Shan 1879

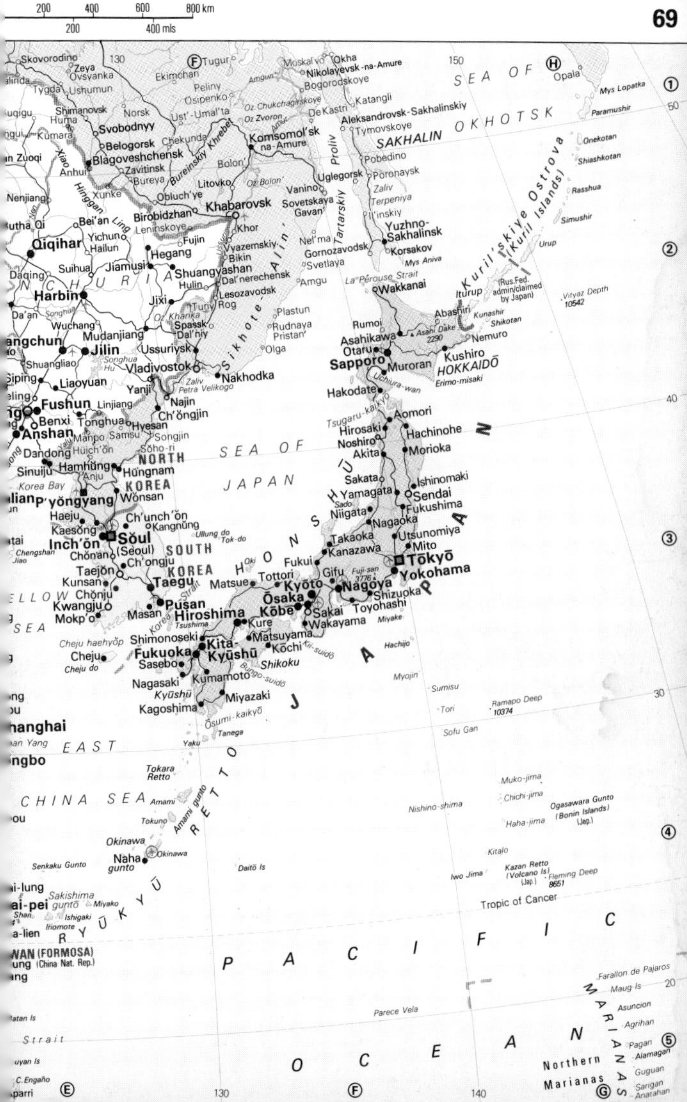
200 400 600 800 km
200 400 mls
SEA OF OKHOTSK
SAKHALIN
SEA OF JAPAN
NORTH KOREA
SOUTH KOREA
HONSHŪ
HOKKAIDŌ
JAPAN
Kyūshū
Shikoku
EAST CHINA SEA
RYŪKYŪ RETTO
PACIFIC OCEAN
Kuril'skiye Ostrova (Kuril Islands)
(Rus.Fed. admin/claimed by Japan)
Ogasawara Gunto (Bonin Islands) (Jap.)
Kazan Retto (Volcano Is) (Jap.)
Tropic of Cancer
Vityaz Depth 10542
Ramapo Deep 10374
Fleming Deep 8651
Northern Marianas
MARIANAS
Harbin
Qiqihar
Jilin
Khabarovsk
Vladivostok
Nakhodka
Blagoveshchensk
Komsomol'sk na-Amure
Yuzhno-Sakhalinsk
Wakkanai
Sapporo
Hakodate
Aomori
Sendai
Niigata
Tōkyō
Yokohama
Nagoya
Kyōto
Ōsaka
Kōbe
Hiroshima
Kita-Kyūshū
Fukuoka
Nagasaki
Kumamoto
Kagoshima
P'yŏngyang
Sŏul (Seoul)
Inch'ŏn
Taegu
Pusan
Okinawa
Naha
La Pérouse Strait
Tsugaru-kaikyō
Fuji-san 3776
Asahi Dake 2290
Daitō Is
Iwo Jima
Parece Vela
130
140
150
50
40
30
20

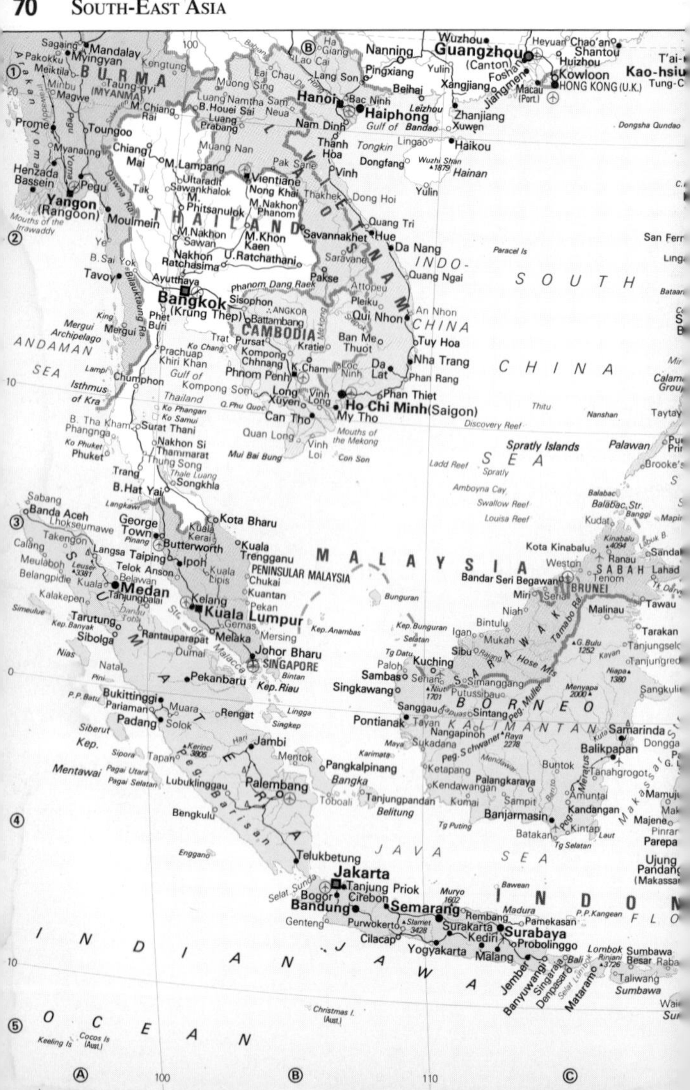

BURMA (MYANMA)
Sagaing
Mandalay
Myingyan
Pakokku
Meiktila
Taunggyi
Minbu
Magwe
Kengtung
Prome
Toungoo
Myanaung
Henzada
Bassein
Pegu
Yangon (Rangoon)
Moulmein
Mouths of the Irrawaddy
Ye
Tavoy
Mergui
Mergui Archipelago
ANDAMAN SEA
Isthmus of Kra
THAILAND
Chiang Mai
M. Chiang Rai
M. Lampang
Uttaradit
Sawankhalok
Tak
M. Phitsanulok
M. Nakhon Sawan
Nakhon Ratchasima
U. Ratchathani
Ayutthaya
Bangkok (Krung Thep)
Phet Buri
Prachuap Khiri Khan
Chumphon
Gulf of Thailand
Ko Phangan
Ko Samui
B. Tha Kham
Surat Thani
Phangnga
Ko Phuket
Phuket
Nakhon Si Thammarat
Thung Song
Thale Luang
Trang
Songkhla
B. Hat Yai
LAOS
Luang Namtha
B. Houei Sai
Sam Neua
Luang Prabang
Muang Nan
Vientiane
Nong Khai
M. Nakhon Phanom
Thakhek
Savannakhet
Saravane
Pakse
Attopeu
Phanom Dang Raek
CAMBODIA
Sisophon
ANGKOR
Battambang
Pursat
Trat
Ko Chang
Kompong Chhnang
Kratie
K. Cham
Phnom Penh
Kompong Som
Q. Phu Quoc
VIETNAM
Ha Giang
Lao Cai
Lai Chau
Lang Son
Bac Ninh
Hanoi
Haiphong
Nam Dinh
Thanh Hoa
Vinh
Dong Hoi
Quang Tri
Hue
Da Nang
Quang Ngai
Pleiku
Qui Nhon
An Nhon
Ban Me Thuot
Tuy Hoa
Nha Trang
Da Lat
Loc Ninh
Phan Rang
Phan Thiet
Ho Chi Minh (Saigon)
My Tho
Long Xuyen
Vinh Long
Can Tho
Quan Long
Vinh Loi
Mouths of the Mekong
Con Son
Mui Bai Bung
Nanning
Pingxiang
Beihai
Wuzhou
Guangzhou (Canton)
Foshan
Jiangmen
Yulin
Xangjiang
Macau (Port.)
Kowloon
HONG KONG (U.K.)
Heyuan
Chao'an
Shantou
Huizhou
Leizhou
Zhanjiang
Xuwen
Gulf of Tongkin
Lingao
Haikou
Dongfang
Wuzhi Shan 1879
Hainan
Yulin
Dongsha Qundao
Paracel Is
SOUTH CHINA SEA
Discovery Reef
Thitu
Nanshan
Spratly Islands
Spratly
Ladd Reef
Amboyna Cay
Swallow Reef
Louisa Reef
Palawan
Balabac
Balabac Str.
MALAYSIA
PENINSULAR MALAYSIA
Langkawi
George Town
Pinang
Butterworth
Kota Bharu
Kuala Kerai
Kuala Trengganu
Taiping
Ipoh
Telok Anson
Kuala Lipis
Chukai
Kuantan
Pekan
Kelang
Kuala Lumpur
Gemas
Melaka
Mersing
Johor Bharu
SINGAPORE
Str. of Malacca
Kep. Anambas
Bunguran
Kep. Bunguran Selatan
Kota Kinabalu
Kinabalu 4094
Ranau
Kudat
Sandakan
SABAH
Lahad
Tenom
Weston
Bandar Seri Begawan
BRUNEI
Seria
Miri
Niah
Bintulu
Mukah
Sibu
SARAWAK
Hose Mts
Kuching
Malinau
Tawau
Tarakan
Tanjungselor
Tanjungredeb
Sabang
Banda Aceh
Lhokseumawe
Takengon
Calang
Langsa
Meulaboh
Leuser 3381
Belangpidie
Kuala
Medan
Belawan
Tanjungbalai
Kalakepen
Simeulue
Danau Toba
Tarutung
Kep. Banyak
Sibolga
Rantauparapat
Nias
Dumai
Natal
Pekanbaru
Kep. Riau
Bintan
SUMATERA
Bukittinggi
Pariaman
Padang
Solok
Muara
Rengat
Lingga
Singkep
Siberut
Kep. Mentawai
Sipora
Pagai Utara
Pagai Selatan
Tapan
Kerinci 3805
Jambi
Mentok
Pangkalpinang
Bangka
Lubuklinggau
Palembang
Toboali
Tanjungpandan
Belitung
Bengkulu
Peg. Barisan
Enggano
Telukbetung
Selat Sunda
BORNEO
KALIMANTAN
Singkawang
Sambas
Paloh
Serian
Simanggang
Putussibau
Sanggau
Sintang
Pontianak
Tayan
Nangapinoh
Sukadana
Peg. Schwaner
Raya 2278
Karimata
Ketapang
Kendawangan
Palangkaraya
Kumai
Sampit
Tg Puting
Banjarmasin
Batakan
Tg Selatan
Kintap
Kandangan
Amuntai
Peg. Meratus
Buntok
Samarinda
Balikpapan
Tanahgrogot
Sangkulirang
Menyapa 2000
Niapa 1380
G. Bulu 1252
Kayan
Laut
Mamuju
Majene
Pinrang
Parepare
Ujung Pandang (Makassar)
JAVA SEA
Jakarta
Tanjung Priok
Bogor
Cirebon
Bandung
Semarang
Muryo 1602
Slamet 3428
Purwokerto
Genteng
Cilacap
Yogyakarta
Surakarta
Rembang
Madura
Pamekasan
Bawean
Surabaya
Kediri
Probolinggo
Malang
Jember
Banyuwangi
Singaraja
Denpasar
Bali
Lombok
Rinjani 3726
Mataram
Sumbawa Besar
Taliwang
Sumbawa
P.P. Kangean
INDONESIA
JAWA
INDIAN OCEAN
Christmas I. (Aust.)
Cocos Is (Aust.)
Keeling Is
100
110
10
20
0

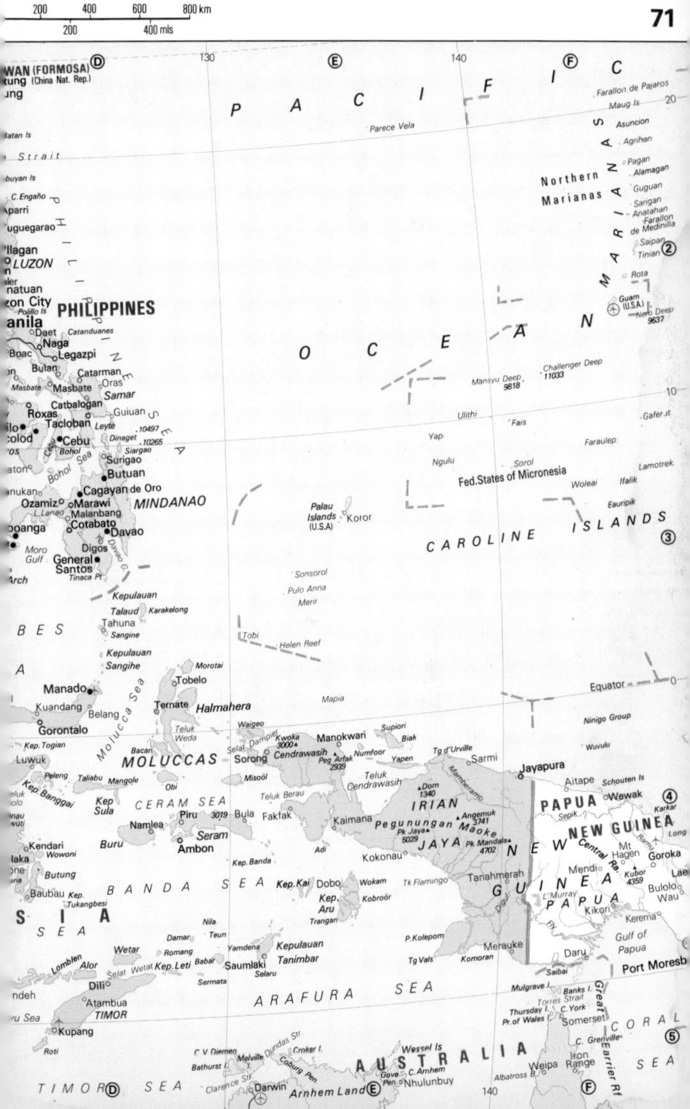

200   400   600   800 km
200   400 mls

TAIWAN (FORMOSA) D
ung (China Nat. Rep.)
ung

PACIFIC

E   130   140   F

Farallon de Pajaros
Maug Is   20
Asuncion

Parece Vela

Agrihan

atan Is

Pagan
Alamagan

uyan Is

Northern
Marianas

Guguan
Sarigan

Strait

Anatahan
Farallon
de Medinilla
Saipan   2
Tinian

C. Engaño
Aparri
uguegarao

Rota

PHILIPPINES

OCEAN

Guam
(U.S.A.) +
Nati Pt.
9637

llagan
on City
natuan
anila

LUZON

Daet   Catanduanes
Naga   Legazpi
Boac   Bulan

Mariveles Deep
9818

Challenger Deep
11033   10

Masbate   Catarman
Oras
Masbate   Samar
Catbalogan
Roxas   Tacloban   Guiuan
olod   Cebu   Leyte
os   Bohol   Surigao
aton   Butuan

10497

Ulithi   Fais

Gafer I.

Yap

Faraulep

Ngulu

12265
Dinagat
Siargao

Sorol
Fed.States of Micronesia

Woleai

Lamotrek
Ifalik

Eauripik

Ozamiz   Marawi   MINDANAO
oanga   Malanbang
Cotabato   Davao
Digos
General
Santos
arch   Moro
Gulf   Tinaca Pt.

Palau
Islands
(U.S.A)   Koror

CAROLINE   ISLANDS   3

Sonsorol

Kepulauan
Talaud   Karakelong
Tahuna
Sangihe

Pulo Anna
Merir

BES

I.Tobi

Helen Reef

Kepulauan
Sangihe   Morotai

Manado
Kuandang   Belang
Gorontalo
Luwuk   Kep. Togian

Tobelo
Ternate   Halmahera

Mapia

Equator

Ninigo Group

Wuvulu

Waigeo   Supiori
Selat Dampir   Biak
Sorong   Manokwari
Kep. Sula   Cendrawasih   Numfoor
Misool   Yapen

Aitape   Schouten Is
Sarmi   Jayapura   Karkar

Kwoka
3000+
Peg Arfak
2939
Teluk
Cendrawasih

PAPUA   4

NEW GUINEA

Kep.Togian
Peleng   Taliabu
Mangoli
Banggai
Kep.
Sula
Namlea   Piru   Bula
Buru   Seram
Ambon
Kendari   Wowoni

Teluk
Berau
Faklak

MOLUCCAS
CERAM SEA
3019

Dom
1340

Mt Hagen
Mendi   Kubor   Goroka
4359
Murray   Bulolo
Kikori   Wau

Kaimana
Pegunungan Maoke
Mandala
4702

IRIAN
JAYA   Anggemuk
5029   3741

Baubau   Wowoni

BANDA   SEA
Kep.Banda
Kep.Kai   Dobo
Kep.
Aru
Kokonau   Tanahmerah
GUINEA
Trangan
PAPUA
Kerema

SIA
SEA
Nila
Damar   Teun
Wetar   Romang   Yamdena
Lomblen   Selat
Alor   Kep.Leti   Babar   Saumlaki
Selaru
Dili
ndeh   TIMOR   Kupang
Atambua
Roti

P.Kolepom
Tk Flamingo
Merauke

Gulf of
Papua
Daru   Saibai   Port Moresby

Kepulauan
Tanimbar

Tg Vals   Komoran

Mulgrave I.   Banks I.
C. York
Thursday I.   Central
Pr. of Wales   Somerset
Torres Strait

Nhulunbuy

ARAFURA   SEA
140

C.V.Diemen   Smith Str.
Bathurst I.   Melville I.   Croker I.   Wessel Is
Coburg Pen.   Gove
Darwin   C.Arnhem
Pen
Arnhem Land
Clarence Str.

CORAL   5

R.Grenville
Iron
Range   F

Weipa
AUSTRALIA
Albatross B.

TIMOR   SEA   D   Alligator R.   Nhulunbuy   E

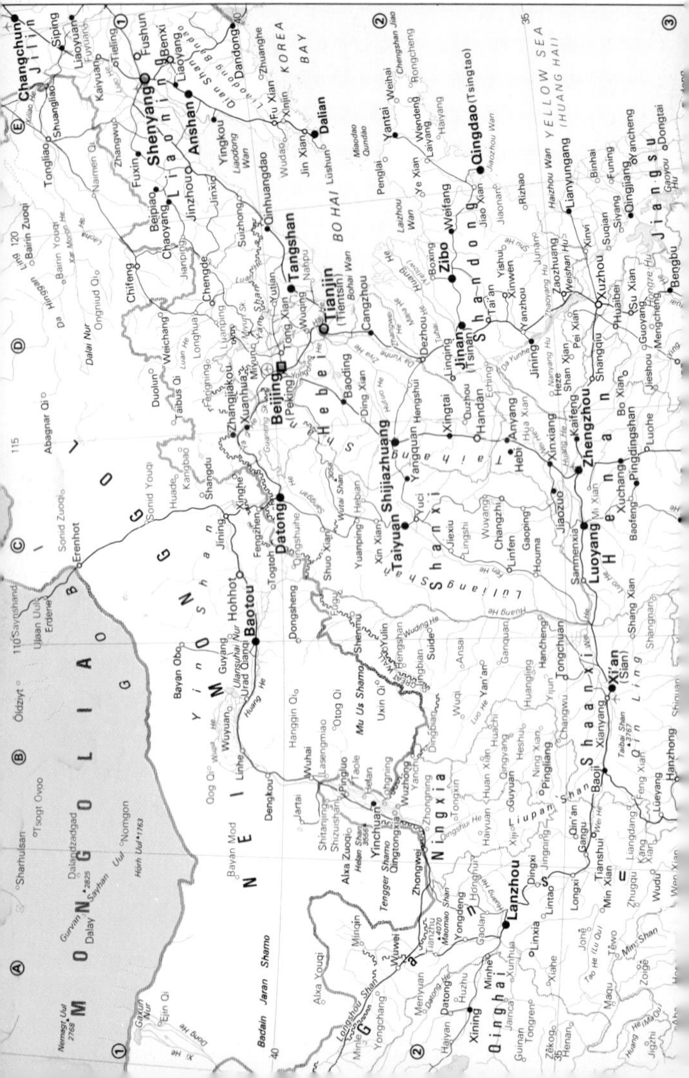

MONGOLIA

NEI MONGOL

YELLOW SEA (HUANG HAI)

KOREA BAY

BO HAI

Bohai Wan

Changchun Jilin

Shenyang Anshan Liaoning

Dandong Dalian Lüshun

Qinhuangdao Tangshan Tianjin (Tientsin)

Beijing (Peking)

Hebei

Shanxi Taiyuan Datong Baotou Hohhot

Shijiazhuang Baoding

Shandong Jinan (Tsinan) Zibo Weifang Qingdao (Tsingtao) Yantai Weihai

Henan Zhengzhou Luoyang Kaifeng Anyang Handan

Shaanxi Xi'an Xianyang Baoji

Ningxia Yinchuan

Gansu Lanzhou

Qinghai Xining

Jiangsu Lianyungang Xuzhou

Qin Ling

Yin Shan

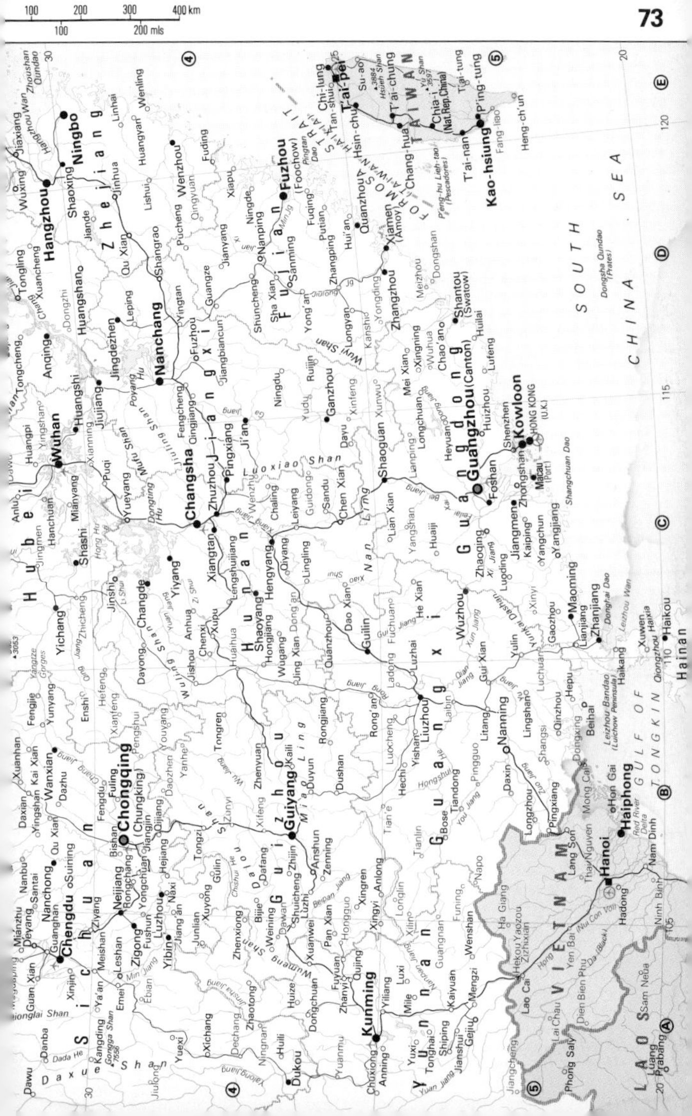

100   200   300   400 km
100   200 mils

100 200 mls
Hubei
Hunan
Jiangxi
Zhejiang
Fujian
Guangdong
Guangxi
Guizhou
Sichuan
Yunnan
TAIWAN
VIETNAM
LAOS
Hainan
SOUTH CHINA SEA
GULF OF TONGKIN
FORMOSA STRAIT
TAIWAN HAIXIA
Wuhan
Changsha
Nanchang
Hangzhou
Ningbo
Fuzhou (Foochow)
T'ai-pei
Chi-lung
Hsin-chu
T'ai-chung
Chang-hua
Chia-i (Nat.Rep.China)
T'ai-nan
Kao-hsiung
P'ing-tung
T'ai-tung
Su-ao
Guangzhou (Canton)
Kowloon
HONG KONG (U.K.)
Macau (Port.)
Shantou (Swatow)
Xiamen (Amoy)
Zhangzhou
Quanzhou
Shaoguan
Guilin
Liuzhou
Nanning
Wuzhou
Zhanjiang
Maoming
Haikou
Guiyang
Kunming
Chongqing (Chungking)
Chengdu
Zigong
Yibin
Luzhou
Neijiang
Nanchong
Wanxian
Yichang
Shashi
Hengyang
Xiangtan
Zhuzhou
Yiyang
Changde
Huangshi
Jiujiang
Jingdezhen
Anqing
Wenzhou
Shaoxing
Ganzhou
Haiphong
Hanoi
Lao Cai
Nam Dinh
Luang Prabang
Phong Saly
Dukou
Xichang
Yangtze Gorges
Dongting Hu
Poyang Hu
Xi Jiang
Nan Ling
Wuyi Shan
Miao Ling
Daxue Shan
Luoxiao Shan
Dongsha Qundao (Prates)
P'eng-hu Lieh-tao (Pescadores)
Leizhou Bandao (Luichow Peninsula)
Red River Delta

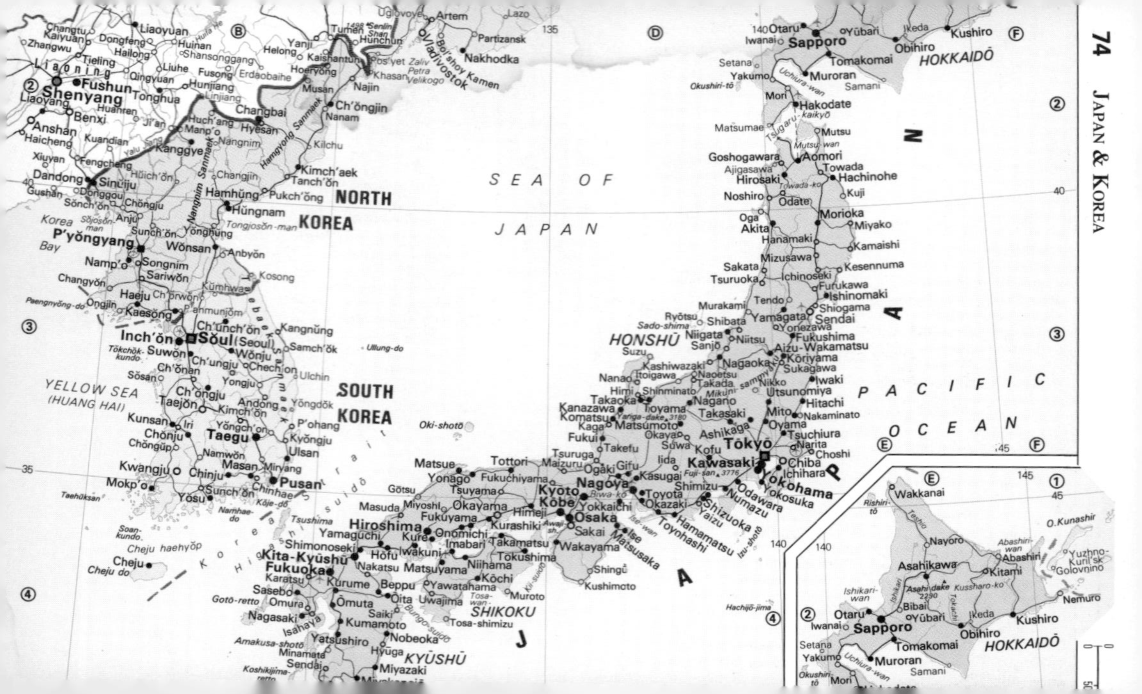
SEA OF JAPAN
PACIFIC OCEAN
NORTH KOREA
SOUTH KOREA
YELLOW SEA
(HUANG HAI)
Korea Bay
HONSHŪ
HOKKAIDŌ
SHIKOKU
KYŪSHŪ
JAPAN
Tōkyō
Yokohama
Kawasaki
Nagoya
Kyoto
Kōbe
Ōsaka
Sapporo
Hakodate
Aomori
Sendai
Niigata
Hiroshima
Fukuoka
Kita-Kyūshū
Nagasaki
Kumamoto
Sŏul (Seoul)
Inch'ŏn
P'yŏngyang
Pusan
Taegu
Kwangju
Taejŏn
Hamhŭng
Wŏnsan
Ch'ŏngjin
Sinŭiju
Cheju
Cheju do
Vladivostok
Nakhodka
Shenyang
Fushun
Dandong
Anshan
Oki-shotō
Sado-shima
Tsushima
Ullung-do
Hachijō-jima
Fuji-san 3776
Korea Strait
Tsugaru-kaikyō

50   100   150   200km
50   100 mls

① ② ©

Sendai Ishinomaki
Natori Shiogama
Murakami Yamagata Tendo Okada Onagawa
Niigata Shibata Aizu Kaminoyama Fukushima Soma
Nagaoka Sanjo Koriyama Haranomachi
Wakamatsu Shirakawa Hitachi-Ota Nakaminato
Kashiwazaki Nagaoka Nikko Utsunomiya Mito Katsuta Tokai
Teradomari Tokamachi Ashikaga Oyama Kasama Ishioka
Ryotsu Itoigawa Takada Numata Maebashi Sawara Choshi
Sado-shima Joetsu Nagano Suzaka Kiryu Urawa **Tokyo** Chiba
Aikawa Matsumoto Karuizawa Kumagaya **Kawasaki** Bōsō
Naoetsu Ueda Chichibu Kawaguchi **Yokohama** Mobara
Wajima Suzu Komoro Suwa Hachioji Atsugi Yokosuka Katsuura
Nanao Toyama Shimosuwa Kofu Fujisawa Tateyama
Noto hanto Takaoka Matsumoto Enzan Odawara Hamamatsu
Himi Kamikochi Ina Fujiyoshida Numazu Ito
Kanazawa Komatsu Takayama Yatsu Fuji Shimoda
Kaga Ono Gujo-Hachiman Shizuoka Shimizu
Fukui Shintoro Nakatsugawa Fujinomiya Omae-zaki
Sabae Gifu Seto **Nagoya** Hamamatsu
Wakasa-wan Maizuru Ogaki Kasugai Okazaki Toyohashi
Obama Hikone Ichinomiya Handa Toba
Kasumi Ayabe Kameoka Kuwana Ise Matsuzaka
Miyazu Sasayama **Kyoto** Yokkaichi Tsu
Tottori Fukuchiyama Otsu Suzuka Ueno
Toyooka Takarazuka **Osaka** Owase
Sakaiminato Toyooka **Kobe** **Sakai** Kishiwada Owase
Matsue Yonago Himeji Akashi Izumi-Sano Kainan Kumano
Kurayoshi Takahashi Kakogawa Naruto Wakayama Gobo
Okayama Kishiwada Tokushima Anan Tanabe
Shobara Kurashiki Marugame Komatsushima Hikigawa
Miyoshi Onomichi Sakaide Takamatsu Kushimoto
Hiroshima Mihara Imabari Matsuyama Kochi Muroto
Kure Niihama Ino Susaki Muroto-zaki
Iwakuni Ozu Ozu Iyo Tosa Nakamura
Tokuyama Yawatahama Uwajima Sukumo
Shimonoseki Ube Oita Beppu Saiki
Kita-Kyushu Nakatsu Taketa Nobeoka

SEA OF JAPAN

PACIFIC OCEAN

SHIKOKU

KYUSHU

140 135
35

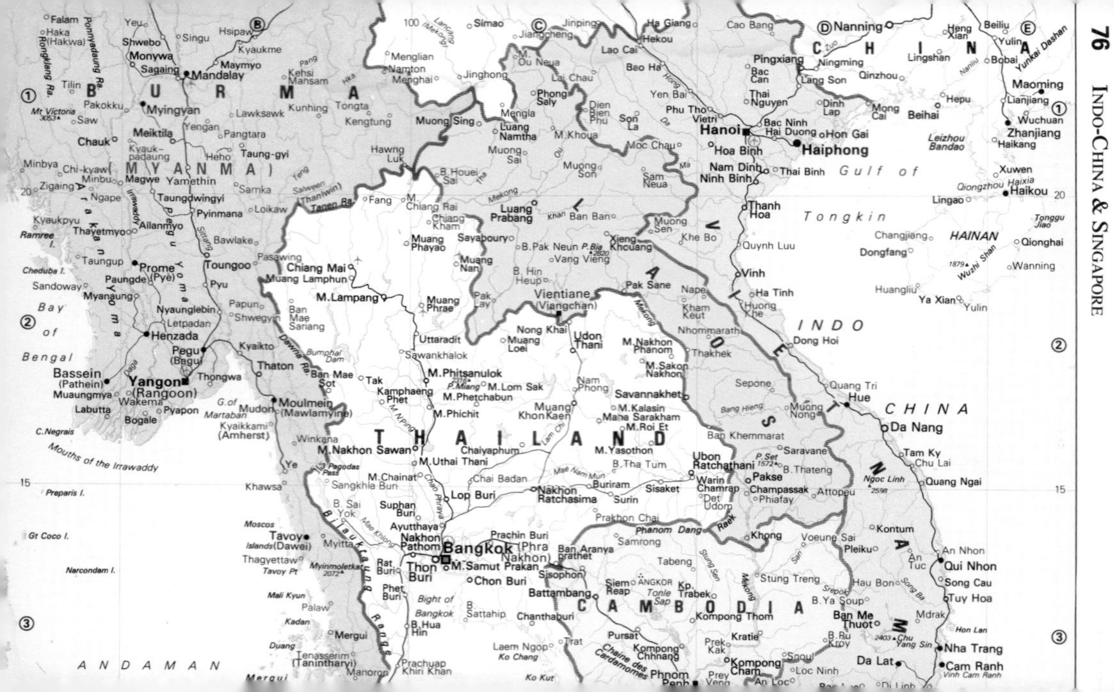

BURMA
MYANMAR
CHINA
THAILAND
CAMBODIA
VIETNAM
LAOS
HAINAN
INDO CHINA
Gulf of Tongkin
Bay of Bengal
ANDAMAN
Mouths of the Irrawaddy
G. of Martaban
Bight of Bangkok
Mandalay
Yangon (Rangoon)
Bassein (Pathein)
Pegu (Bagu)
Moulmein (Mawlamyine)
Toungoo
Prome (Pye)
Henzada
Tavoy (Dawei)
Mergui
Chiang Mai
M.Lampang
Bangkok (Phra Nakhon)
Thon Buri
Nakhon Ratchasima
Ubon Ratchathani
Udon Thani
Vientiane (Viangchan)
Luang Prabang
Pakse
Savannakhet
Battambang
Kompong Thom
Kompong Cham
Hanoi
Haiphong
Nanning
Zhanjiang
Haikou
Vinh
Hue
Da Nang
Qui Nhon
Nha Trang
Cam Ranh
Da Lat
Mekong
Irrawaddy

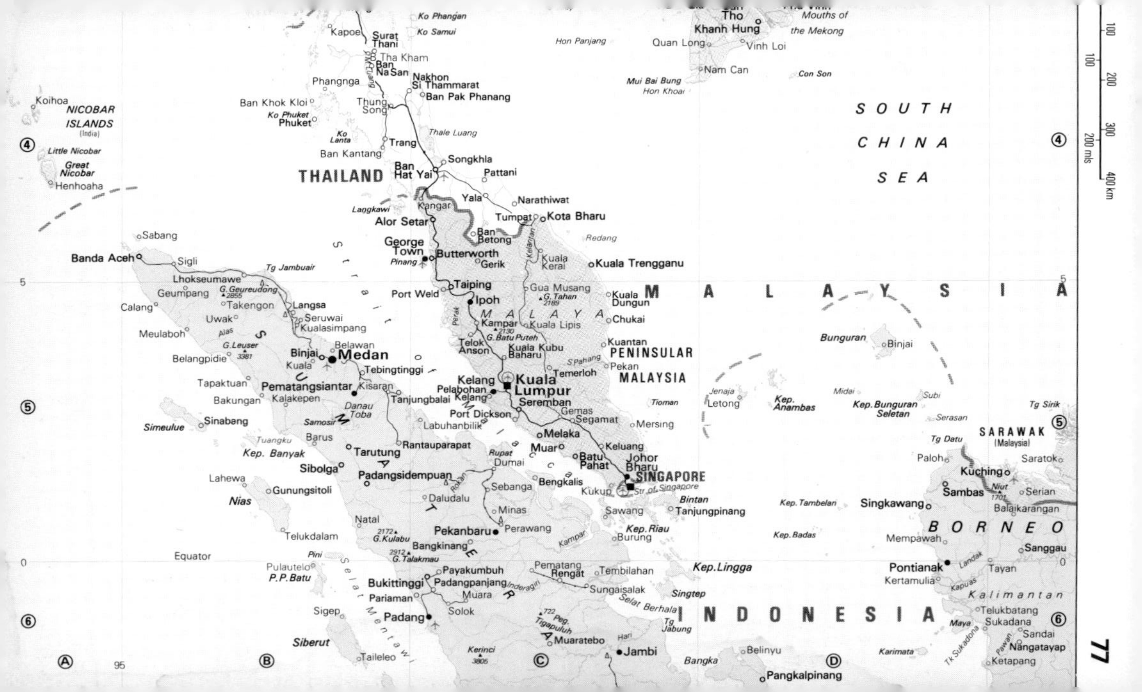
100
200
300
400 km
100
200 mls
SOUTH
CHINA
SEA
M A L A Y S I A
I N D O N E S I A
THAILAND
PENINSULAR
MALAYSIA
M A L A Y A
SARAWAK
(Malaysia)
B O R N E O
K a l i m a n t a n
S U M A T E R A
S t r a i t o f M a l a c c a
Selat Mentawi
NICOBAR
ISLANDS
(India)
Koihoa
Little Nicobar
Great
Nicobar
Henhoaha
Sabang
Banda Aceh
Sigli
Lhokseumawe
Geumpang
G. Geureudong
2855
Takengon
Calang
Uwak
Meulaboh
Alas
G. Leuser
3381
Belangpidie
Tapaktuan
Bakungan
Simeulue
Sinabang
Tuangku
Kep. Banyak
Lahewa
Nias
Gunungsitoli
Telukdalam
Equator
Pini
Pulautelo
P.P. Batu
Sigep
Siberut
Taileleo
Tg Jambuair
Langsa
Seruwai
Kualasimpang
Binjai
Kuala
Belawan
Medan
Tebingtinggi
Pematangsiantar
Kisaran
Kalakepen
Danau
Toba
Samosir
Barus
Tarutung
Sibolga
Padangsidempuan
Tanjungbalai
Labuhanbilik
Rantauparapat
Daludalu
Natal
2172
G. Kulabu
2912
G. Talakmau
Bangkinang
Pekanbaru
Perawang
Minas
Sebanga
Rokan
Rupat
Dumai
Bengkalis
Payakumbuh
Bukittinggi
Padangpanjang
Pariaman
Muara
Solok
Padang
Kerinci
3805
Indragiri
Pematang
Rengat
Tembilahan
Sungaisalak
722
Peg. Tigapuluh
Muaratebo
Hari
Jambi
Kampar
Kapoe
Surat
Thani
M. Luang
Tha Kham
Ban
Na San
Nakhon
Si Thammarat
Ban Pak Phanang
Phangnga
Ban Khok Kloi
Ko Phuket
Phuket
Thung
Song
Ko
Lanta
Trang
Ban Kantang
Thale Luang
Ko Phangan
Ko Samui
Songkhla
Ban
Hat Yai
Pattani
Yala
Narathiwat
Langkawi
Kangar
Alor Setar
Tumpat
Kota Bharu
Ban
Betong
George
Town
Pinang
Butterworth
Gerik
Kelantan
Kuala
Kerai
Redang
Kuala Trengganu
Taiping
Port Weld
Ipoh
Perak
Gua Musang
G. Tahan
2189
Kuala
Dungun
Kampar
2130
G. Batu Puteh
Kuala Lipis
Chukai
Telok
Anson
Kuala Kubu
Baharu
Kuantan
S. Pahang
Pekan
Temerloh
Kelang
Pelabohan
Kelang
Kuala
Lumpur
Seremban
Port Dickson
Gemas
Segamat
Mersing
Tioman
Melaka
Muar
Batu
Pahat
Keluang
Johor
Bharu
SINGAPORE
Kukup
Str. of Singapore
Bintan
Tanjungpinang
Sawang
Kep. Riau
Burung
Kep. Lingga
Singtep
Selat Berhala
Tg
Jabung
Bangka
Belinyu
Pangkalpinang
Tho
Khanh Hung
Mouths of
the Mekong
Quan Long
Vinh Loi
Nam Can
Con Son
Hon Panjang
Mui Bai Bung
Hon Khoai
Bunguran
Binjai
Jenaja
Letong
Kep.
Anambas
Midai
Kep. Bunguran
Seletan
Subi
Serasan
Tg Sirik
Tg Datu
Paloh
Kuching
Saratok
Sambas
Niut
1701
Serian
Balaikarangan
Singkawang
Kep. Tambelan
Kep. Badas
Mempawah
Sanggau
Pontianak
Landak
Tayan
Kertamulia
Kapuas
Telukbatang
Sukadana
Maya
Sandai
Nangatayap
Pawan
Tk Sukadona
Ketapang
Karimata
A
B
C
D
95
5
0
4
5
6

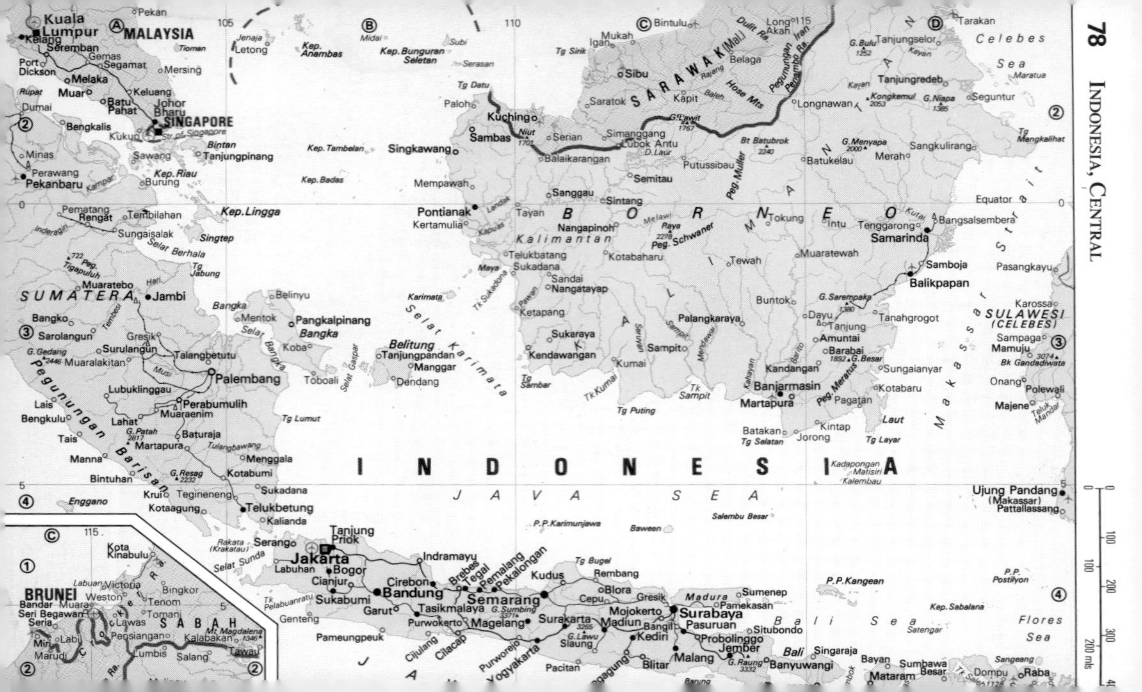
MALAYSIA
SINGAPORE
SARAWAK (Mal.)
SABAH
BRUNEI
SUMATERA
BORNEO
Kalimantan
SULAWESI (CELEBES)
INDONESIA
JAVA SEA
Celebes Sea
Makassar Strait
Bali Sea
Flores Sea
Selat Karimata
Selat Gaspar
Selat Bangka
Selat Berhala
Selat Sunda
Equator
Kuala Lumpur
Kelang
Seremban
Port Dickson
Melaka
Muar
Batu Pahat
Keluang
Segamat
Gemas
Mersing
Johor Bharu
Pekan
Tioman
Bengkalis
Dumai
Rupat
Pekanbaru
Perawang
Minas
Kukup
Sawang
Pematang
Rengat
Tembilahan
Sungaisalak
Jambi
Muaratebo
Bangko
Sarolangun
Surulangun
Muaralakitan
Gresik
Talangbetutu
Palembang
Pangkalpinang
Bangka
Belitung
Tanjungpandan
Manggar
Dendang
Toboali
Mentok
Belinyu
Koba
Perabumulih
Muaraenim
Lahat
Baturaja
Martapura
Lubuklinggau
Lais
Bengkulu
Tais
Manna
Bintuhan
Krui
Kotaagung
Tegineneng
Telukbetung
Kalianda
Menggala
Kotabumi
Sukadana
Enggano
Pegunungan Barisan
Kep. Lingga
Singtep
Kep. Riau
Burung
Bintan
Tanjungpinang
Letong
Kep. Anambas
Kep. Bunguran Seletan
Kep. Tambelan
Kep. Badas
Kuching
Sambas
Singkawang
Paloh
Pontianak
Kertamulia
Mempawah
Tayan
Sanggau
Sintang
Semitau
Putussibau
Nangapinoh
Kotabaharu
Telukbatang
Sukadana
Sandai
Nangatayap
Ketapang
Kendawangan
Sukaraya
Kumai
Sampit
Palangkaraya
Tewah
Buntok
Muaratewah
Tokung
Banjarmasin
Martapura
Kandangan
Barabai
Amuntai
Tanjung
Dayu
Balikpapan
Samarinda
Tenggarong
Intu
Samboja
Tanahgrogot
Sungaianyar
Kotabaru
Pagatan
Batakan
Jorong
Kintap
Bangsalsembera
Tarakan
Tanjungselor
Tanjungredeb
Seguntur
Sangkulirang
Merah
Batukelau
Longnawan
Long Akah
Belaga
Kapit
Sibu
Mukah
Igan
Bintulu
Saratok
Simanggang
Serian
Balaikarangan
Lubok Antu
Hose Mts
Peg. Muller
Peg. Schwaner
Peg. Meratus
Pasangkayu
Karossa
Sampaga
Mamuju
Onang
Majene
Polewali
Ujung Pandang (Makassar)
Pattallassang
Jakarta
Tanjung Priok
Serang
Labuhan
Bogor
Sukabumi
Cianjur
Bandung
Cirebon
Indramayu
Garut
Tasikmalaya
Pameungpeuk
Genteng
Purwokerto
Cijulang
Cilacap
Brebes
Tegal
Pemalang
Pekalongan
Semarang
Magelang
Yogyakarta
Purworejo
Kudus
Rembang
Blora
Cepu
Surakarta
Madiun
Slaung
Pacitan
Mojokerto
Gresik
Kediri
Blitar
Malang
Surabaya
Pasuruan
Probolinggo
Jember
Situbondo
Banyuwangi
Madura
Sumenep
Pamekasan
Bali
Singaraja
Bayan
Mataram
Sumbawa Besar
Dompu
Raba
Kota Kinabulu
Bingkor
Tenom
Tomani
Kalabakan
Tawau
Salang
Lumbis
Pensiangan
Labuan
Victoria
Weston
Muara
Bandar Seri Begawan
Seria
Lawas
Miri
Labi
Marudi
0
100
200
300
100
200 mls

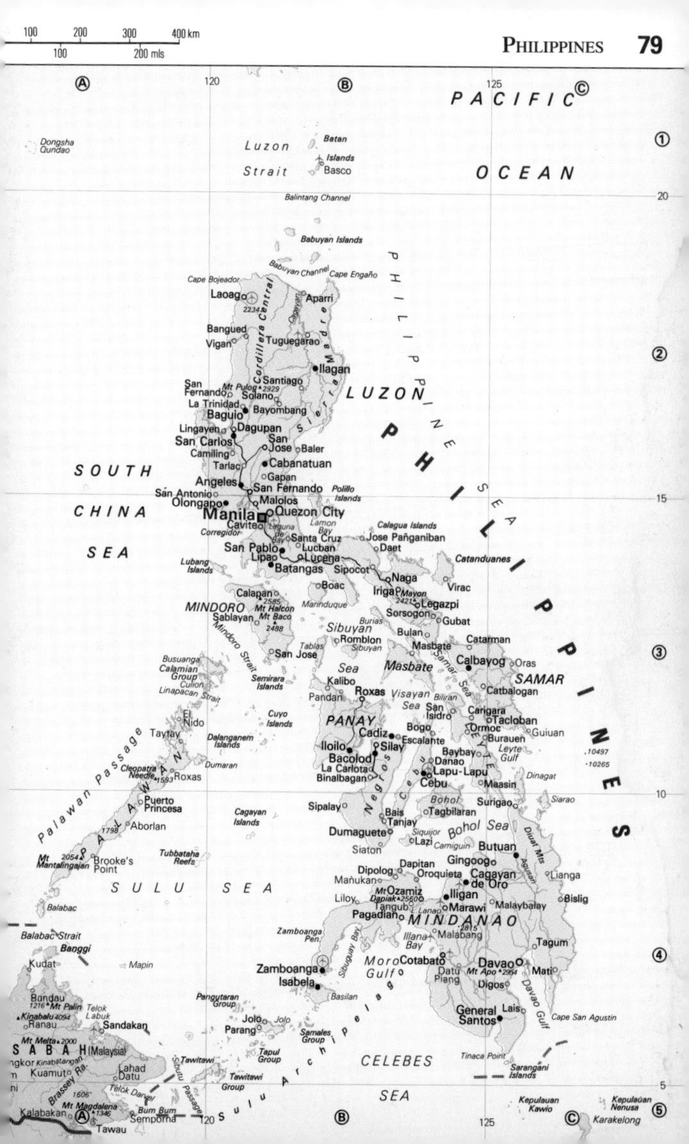

Map labels

100 200 300 400 km
100 200 mls

PACIFIC

①

Luzon Batan
Strait Islands
Basco

OCEAN

Balintang Channel

20

Babuyan Islands

Cape Bojeador Babuyan Channel Cape Engaño

Laoag Aparri

②

Bangued Tuguegarao

Vigan Ilagan

San Fernando Santiago

La Trinidad Solano

Baguio Bayombang

Lingayen Mt Pulog 2234▲ Dagupan

San Carlos San

Camiling Jose Baler

Tarlac Cabanatuan

Gapan

San Antonio San Fernando Polillo

Angeles Malolos Islands

Olongapo Quezon City

Manila Lamon

Corregidor Cavite Laguna Calagua Islands

Lubang San Pablo Santa Cruz Jose Pañganiban Daet

Islands Lipa Lucban

Batangas Lucena Naga Virac

Boac Iriga Catanduanes

Calapan Mt Baco Legazpi

MINDORO Mt Halcon Marinduque Sorsogon

Sablayan Bulan

San Jose Romblon Masbate

Sibuyan Catarman

Busuanga *Sea* Calbayog Oras

Calamian Masbate *SAMAR*

Group Pandan Catbalogan

Culion Roxas Biliran

El Nido Cuyo Kalibo San Isidro

Taytay Islands *PANAY* Carigara Tacloban

Cleopatra Dalanganan Cadiz Bogo Burauen

Needle 1798 Islands Iloilo Silay Baybay *Leyte*

Roxas Dumaran Bacolod Danao Maasin Gulf

Puerto La Carlota Lapu-Lapu Dinagat

Princesa Binalbagan Cebu

Aborlan Sipalay Bais Surigao Siargao

Mt Cagayan Tanjay *Bohol*

Mantalingajan 2054 Islands Dumaguete Siquijor Butuan

Brooke's Siaton *Bohol Sea* Gingoog

Point Dipolog Dapitan Camiguin Cagayan

SULU SEA Mañukan Oroquieta de Oro Lianga

Liloy Mt Ozamiz Iligan Malaybalay

Balabac Pagadian Marawi Bislig

Balabac Strait *Zamboanga* Tangub *MINDANAO*

Banggi Pen. Malabang Davao Tagum

Kudat **Zamboanga** Moro Cotabato

Isabela Gulf Datu Mati

Basilan Piang Mt Apo 2954▲ Digos

Mapin *Illana Bay*

General Lais

Santos

Sandakan Jolo Jolo *Samales* Cape San Agustin

Parang *Group*

Pangutaran

Group

Tapul Group

Tawitawi *Sulu Archipelago*

CELEBES

Tawitawi *SEA*

Bum Bum Sarangani

Group Islands

125

Kepulauan

Kawio

Karakelong

⑤

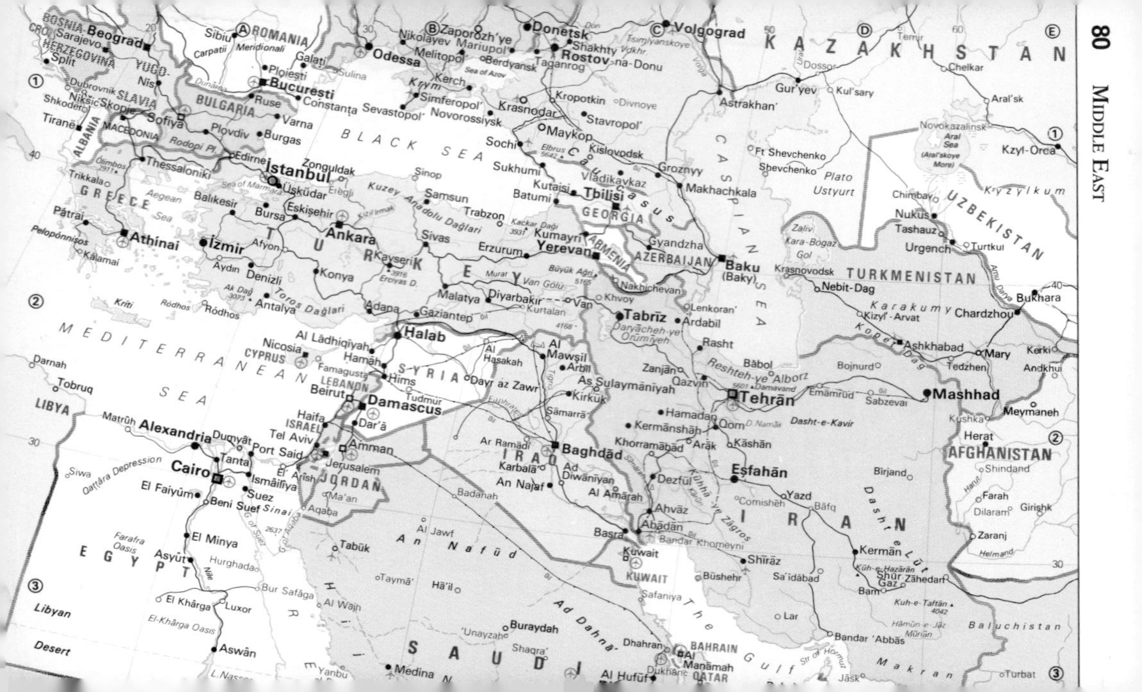
KAZAKHSTAN
UZBEKISTAN
TURKMENISTAN
AFGHANISTAN
IRAN
IRAQ
SAUDI
KUWAIT
BAHRAIN
QATAR
SYRIA
LEBANON
ISRAEL
JORDAN
TURKEY
GEORGIA
ARMENIA
AZERBAIJAN
CYPRUS
EGYPT
LIBYA
GREECE
ALBANIA
MACEDONIA
BULGARIA
ROMANIA
YUGO.
SLAVIA
BOSNIA-HERZEGOVINA
BLACK SEA
CASPIAN SEA
MEDITERRANEAN SEA
Aegean Sea
Aral Sea
The Gulf
Caucasus
Dasht-e-Kavir
Dasht-e Lūt
Plato Ustyurt
Karakumy
Kyzylkum
An Nafūd
Ad Dahnā'
Libyan Desert
Volgograd
Astrakhan'
Gur'yev
Rostov-na-Donu
Donetsk
Odessa
Bucuresti
Beograd
Sofiya
Istanbul
Ankara
Izmir
Athinai
Thessaloniki
Tbilisi
Yerevan
Baku
Tehrān
Mashhad
Esfahān
Shīrāz
Tabrīz
Baghdād
Basra
Kuwait
Damascus
Halab
Beirut
Amman
Jerusalem
Tel Aviv
Cairo
Alexandria
Port Said
Suez
Aswân
Medina
Buraydah
Herat
Ashkhabad
Chardzhou
Bukhara
Nukus
Kermān
Bandar 'Abbās
Nicosia
Antalya
Konya
Adana
Trabzon
Erzurum
Diyarbakir
Al Mawsil
Kirkūk
Tigris
Euphrates
Nile

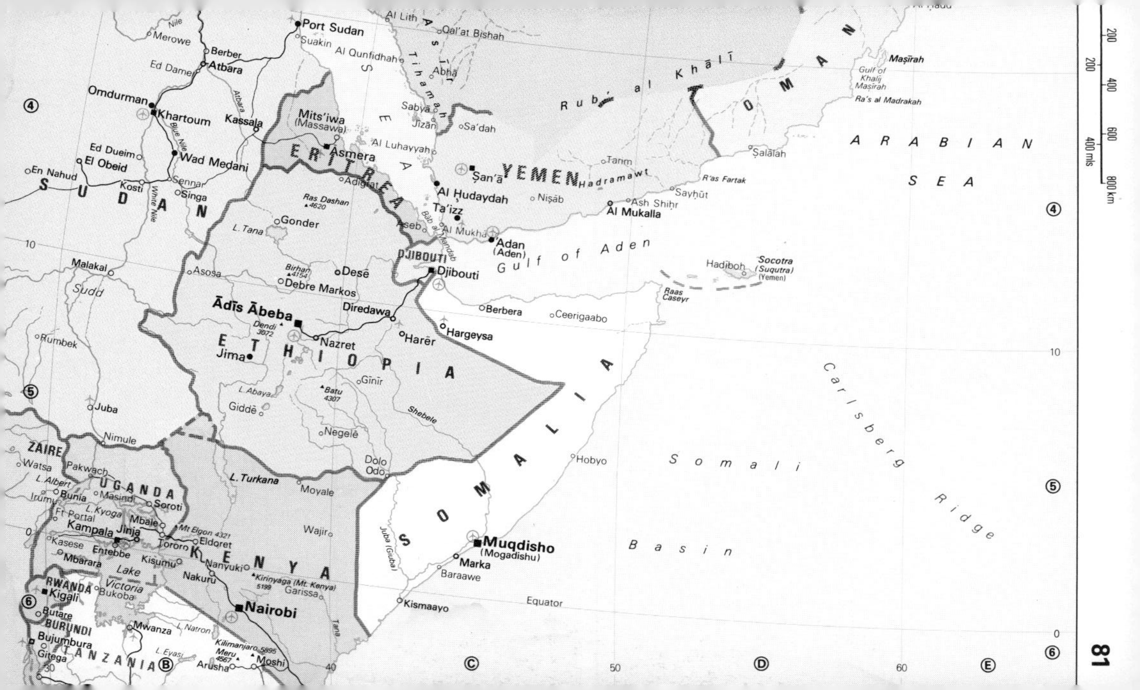

200
400
600
800 km
200
400 mls
ARABIAN SEA
OMAN
Maşīrah
Gulf of Khalīj Maşīrah
Ra's al Madrakah
Rub' al Khālī
Şalālah
R'as Fartak
Sayḩūt
Ash Shiḩr
Al Mukalla
Tarīm
Hadramawt
YEMEN
Nişāb
Adan (Aden)
Şan'ā
Sa'dah
Al Ḩudaydah
Ta'izz
Al Mukhā
Bāb al Mandab
Socotra (Suqutra) (Yemen)
Hadiboh
Raas Caseyr
Gulf of Aden
Carlsberg Ridge
Somali Basin
SOMALIA
Ceerigaabo
Berbera
Hargeysa
Hobyo
Muqdisho (Mogadishu)
Marka
Baraawe
Kismaayo
Juba (Giuba)
Shebele
Equator
DJIBOUTI
Djibouti
Qal'at Bīshah
Abhā
Tihāmah
Jīzān
Şabyā
Al Lith
Al Qunfidhah
Al Luhayyah
RED SEA
Port Sudan
Suakin
Mits'iwa (Massawa)
Asmera
ERITREA
Adigrat
Aseb
ETHIOPIA
Ādīs Ābeba
Harēr
Diredawa
Gīnīr
Desē
Nazret
Debre Markos
Gonder
Ras Dashan 4620
Birhan 4154
Dendi 3072
Batu 4307
Jīma
L. Tana
L. Abaya
Giddē
Negelē
Dolo Odo
Asosa
SUDAN
Atbara
Berber
Merowe
Ed Damer
Nile
Kassala
Khartoum
Omdurman
Wad Medani
Blue Nile
Sennar
Singa
White Nile
Kosti
Ed Dueim
El Obeid
En Nahud
Malakal
Sudd
Rumbek
Juba
Nimule
KENYA
L. Turkana
Moyale
Wajir
Tana
Garissa
Kirinyaga (Mt. Kenya) 5199
Nairobi
Nanyuki
Nakuru
Eldoret
Mt Elgon 4321
Kisumu
Kilimanjaro 5895
Meru 4567
Moshi
Arusha
L. Natron
L. Eyasi
TANZANIA
Mwanza
Bukoba
Lake Victoria
UGANDA
Soroti
Tororo
Mbale
Jinja
Kampala
Entebbe
L. Kyoga
Masindi
Pakwach
Bunia
L. Albert
Ft Portal
Kasese
Mbarara
Irumu
ZAIRE
Watsa
RWANDA
Kigali
Butare
BURUNDI
Bujumbura
Gitega
10
0
30
40
50
60
B
C
D
E
4
5
6

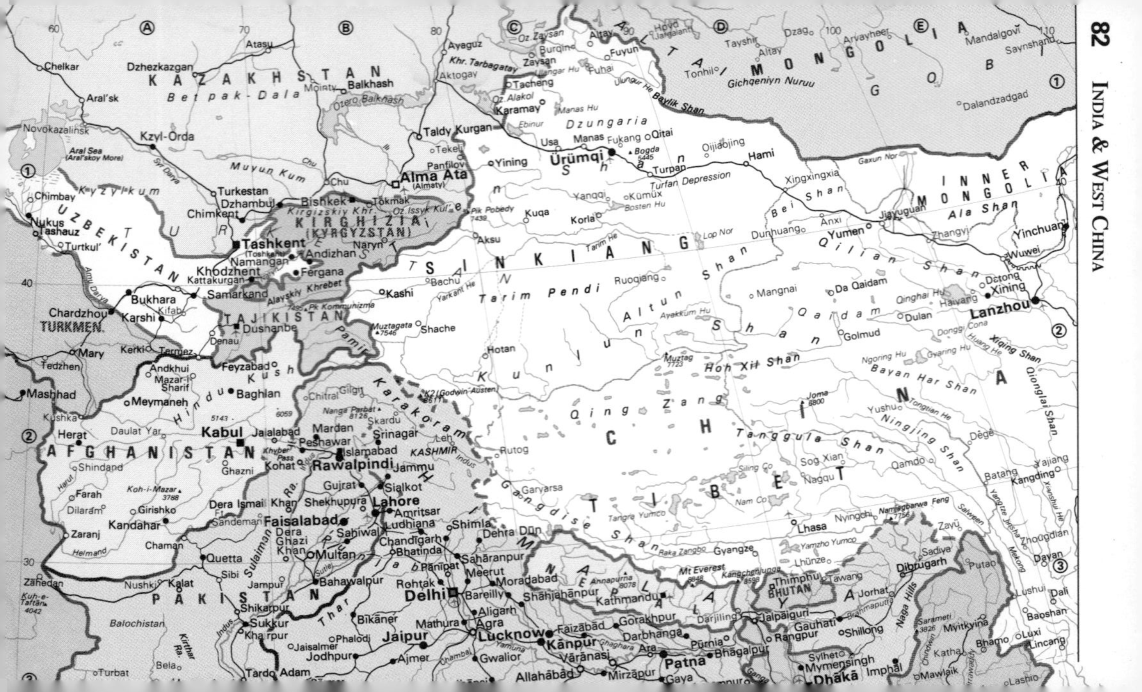
KAZAKHSTAN
UZBEKISTAN
TURKMEN.
KIRGHIZIA (KYRGYZSTAN)
TAJIKISTAN
AFGHANISTAN
PAKISTAN
INDIA
NEPAL
BHUTAN
MONGOLIA
INNER MONGOLIA
XINJIANG
TIBET
QINGHAI
KASHMIR
Tashkent
Alma Ata (Almaty)
Bishkek
Dushanbe
Samarkand
Bukhara
Kabul
Herat
Kandahar
Islamabad
Rawalpindi
Lahore
Faisalabad
Multan
Quetta
Peshawar
Delhi
Jaipur
Agra
Lucknow
Kanpur
Patna
Kathmandu
Thimphu
Lhasa
Ürümqi
Hami
Lanzhou
Xining
Kashi
Hotan
Aral Sea
Balkhash
Karakoram
Pamir
Tarim Pendi
Turfan Depression
Kunlun Shan
Tanggula Shan
Qilian Shan
Mt Everest 8848
Dhaka
Imphal
Mashhad

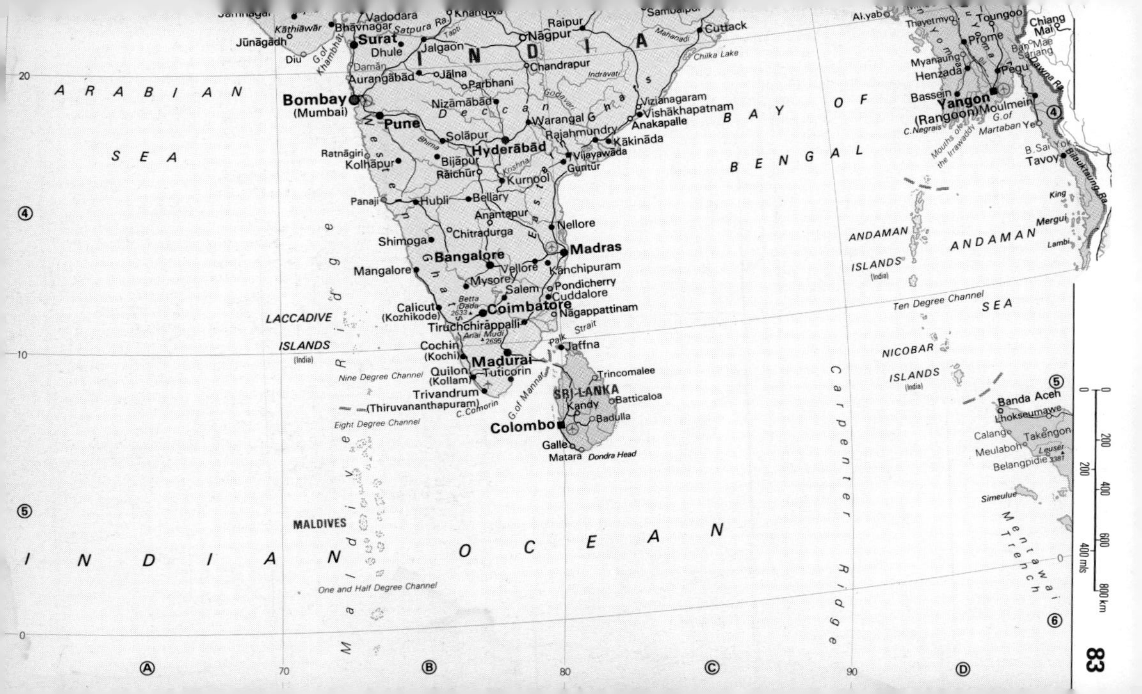
0 200 400 600 800 km
0 200 400 mls
ARABIAN SEA
BAY OF BENGAL
ANDAMAN SEA
INDIAN OCEAN
INDIA
SRI LANKA
MALDIVES
Carpenter Ridge
Mentawai Trench
Deccan
Eastern Ghats
Western Ghats
Maldive Ridge
LACCADIVE ISLANDS (India)
ANDAMAN ISLANDS (India)
NICOBAR ISLANDS (India)
Ten Degree Channel
Nine Degree Channel
Eight Degree Channel
One and Half Degree Channel
Palk Strait
G. of Mannar
G. of Khambhat
G. of Martaban
Mouths of the Irrawaddy
C. Negrais
C. Comorin
Dondra Head
Chilka Lake
Bilauktaung Ra.
Dawna Ra.
Satpura Ra.
Mahanadi
Godavari
Indravati
Krishna
Bhima
Tapti
Betta Dada 2633
Anai Mudi 2695
Leuser 3381
Kāthiāwār
Jūnāgadh
Diu
Bhāvnagar
Vadodara
Surat
Dhule
Jalgaon
Damān
Aurangābād
Jālna
Parbhani
Bombay (Mumbai)
Pune
Nizāmābād
Solāpur
Hyderābād
Bijāpur
Rāichūr
Ratnāgiri
Kolhāpur
Panaji
Hubli
Bellary
Kurnool
Anantapur
Chitradurga
Shimoga
Mangalore
Bangalore
Mysore
Vellore
Salem
Calicut (Kozhikode)
Coimbatore
Tiruchchirāppalli
Cochin (Kochi)
Madurai
Quilon (Kollam)
Tuticorin
Trivandrum (Thiruvananthapuram)
Nāgpur
Raipur
Chandrapur
Warangal
Rajahmundry
Kākināda
Vijayawada
Guntur
Nellore
Madras
Kānchipuram
Pondicherry
Cuddalore
Nāgappattinam
Vizianagaram
Vishākhapatnam
Anakapalle
Cuttack
Jaffna
Trincomalee
Batticaloa
Kandy
Badulla
Colombo
Galle
Matara
Akyab
Thayetmyo
Toungoo
Prome
Myanaung
Henzada
Bassein
Yangon (Rangoon)
Pegu
Moulmein
Ye
B. Sai Yok
Tavoy
King
Mergui
Lambi
Chiang Mai
Ban Mae Sariang
Banda Aceh
Lhokseumawe
Calang
Takengon
Meulaboh
Belangpidie
Simeulue
20
10
0
70
80
90
A
B
C
D
4
5
6

T I B E T

C H I N A

TAJIKISTAN

TAJIK.

UZBEK.

TURKMEN.

A F G H A N I S T A N

P A K I S T A N

KASHMIR

JAMMU

HIMACHAL PRADESH

PUNJAB

HARYANA

UTTAR PRADESH

BAHAWALPUR

KARAKORAM Range

HINDU KUSH

Pamir Mountains

Ladakh Range

Pir Panjal Range

Salt Range

New Delhi

Delhi

Kabul

Quetta

Kandahar

Rawalpindi

Islamabad

Lahore

Peshawar

Srinagar

Faisalabad

Multan

Bahawalpur

Amritsar

Ludhiana

Jalandhar

Chandigarh

Patiala

Meerut

Ghaziabad

Moradabad

Rampur

Bareilly

Pilibhit

Saharanpur

Roorkee

Dehra Dün

Muzaffarnagar

Ambala

Rohtak

Sonipat

Panipat

Karnal

Hisar

Bhiwani

Sirsa

Bhatinda

Ferozpur

Moga

Kasur

Okara

Sahiwal

Gujranwala

Sialkot

Jhelum

Gujrat

Guru

Chakwal

Sargodha

Mianwali

Bannu

Kohat

Mardan

Nowshera

Campbellpore

Charsadda

Dera Ismail Khan

Dera Ghazi Khan

Jacobabad

Khuzdar

Kalat

Chaman

Nushki

Ghazni

Gardez

Charikar

Kunduz

Baghlan

Mazar-i-Sharif

Taloqan

Feyzabad

Samangan

Pul-i-Khumri

Bamiyan

Maimana

Shibarghan

Andkhui

Termez

Khorog

Gilgit

Chilas

Skardu

Leh

Kargil

Chamba

Mandi

Shimla

Bilaspur

Nahan

Dharmshala

Pathankot

Jammu

Anantnag

Baramula

Muzaffarabad

Mirpur

Abbottabad

Rasul

Udhampur

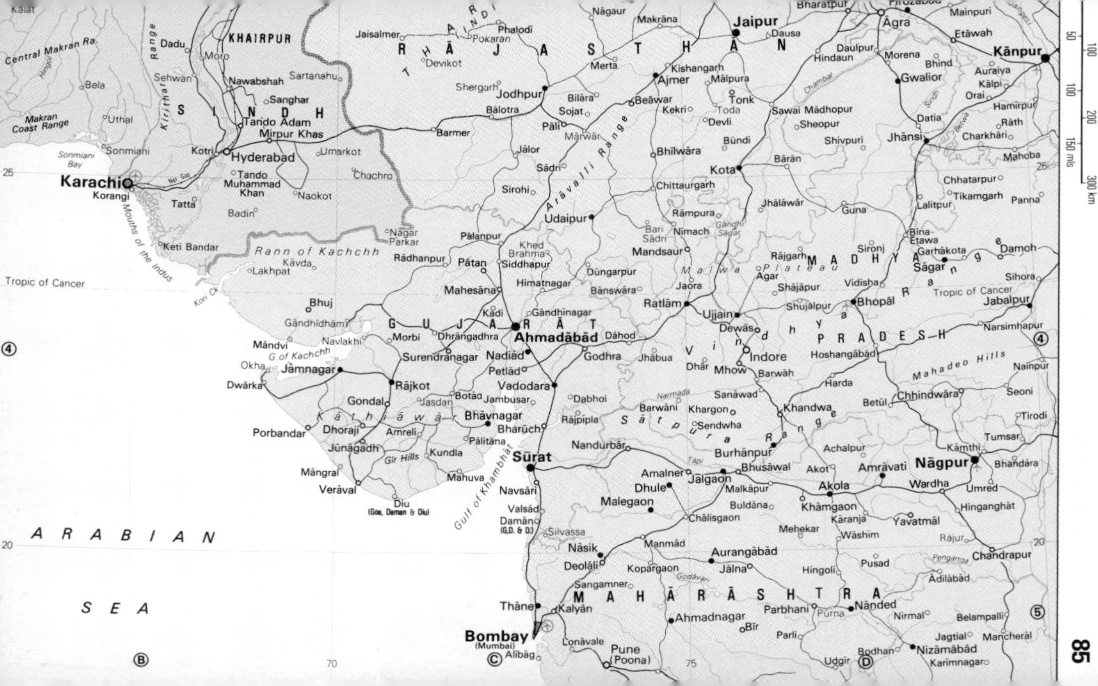
Kalat
Central Makran Ra.
Hingol
Makran Coast Range
Bela
Uthal
Sonmiani
Sonmiani Bay
Karachi
Korangi
Mouths of the Indus
Kirthar Range
Dadu
Moro
KHAIRPUR
Sehwan
Nawabshah
Sartanahu
Sanghar
SINDH
Tando Ādam
Mirpur Khas
Kotri
Hyderabad
Tando Muhammad Khan
Umarkot
Chachro
Naokot
Tatta
Badin
Keti Bandar
Kori Cr.
Tropic of Cancer
Rann of Kachchh
Kāvda
Lakhpat
Nagar Parkar
Jaisalmer
Pokaran
Phalodi
Devikot
RĀJASTHĀN
Nāgaur
Makrāna
Jaipur
Dausa
Bharatpur
Āgra
Mainpuri
Etāwah
Kānpur
Merta
Kishangarh
Ajmer
Mālpura
Tonk
Toda
Devli
Shergarh
Jodhpur
Bilāra
Beāwar
Kekri
Bālotra
Sojat
Pāli
Mārwār
Barmer
Jālor
Sādri
Sirohi
Arāvalli Range
Udaipur
Bhilwāra
Būndi
Kota
Chittaurgarh
Sawai Mādhopur
Sheopur
Shivpuri
Bārān
Jhālāwār
Rāmpura
Gāndhi Sāgar
Bari Sādri
Nimach
Mandsaur
Hindaun
Daulpur
Chambal
Morena
Bhind
Gwalior
Auraiya
Kālpi
Orai
Hamirpur
Sindh
Betwa
Datia
Rāth
Jhānsi
Charkhāri
Mahoba
Chhatarpur
Tikamgarh
Panna
Lalitpur
Guna
Bina-Etawa
Sironj
Garhākota
Damoh
Sāgar
Sihora
Tropic of Cancer
Jabalpur
Narsimhapur
MADHYA PRADESH
Vindhya Range
Mālwa Plateau
Rājgarh
Agar
Shājāpur
Vidisha
Shujālpur
Bhopāl
Ratlām
Ujjain
Dewās
Indore
Mhow
Dhār
Jhābua
Barwāh
Hoshangābād
Mahadeo Hills
Nainpur
Seoni
Harda
Chhindwāra
Betūl
Tirodi
Khandwa
Sātpura Range
Narmada
Sanāwad
Barwāni
Khargon
Sendwha
Burhānpur
Achalpur
Tumsar
Kāmthi
Nāgpur
Bhandāra
Umred
Wardha
Amrāvati
Akot
Akola
Bhusāwal
Tāpi
Pālanpur
Khed Brahma
Rādhanpur
Pātan
Siddhapur
Dūngarpur
Mahesāna
Himatnagar
Bānswāra
Jaora
Bhuj
Gāndhidhām
Kādi
Gāndhinagar
GUJARĀT
Morbi
Dhrāngadhra
Ahmadābād
Dāhod
Māndvi
Navlakhi
G. of Kachchh
Surendranagar
Nadiād
Godhra
Okha
Jāmnagar
Petlād
Rājkot
Dwārka
Vadodara
Botād
Jasdan
Jambusar
Dabhoi
Gondal
Kāthiāwār
Bhāvnagar
Rājpipla
Porbandar
Dhorāji
Amreli
Bharūch
Pālitāna
Jūnāgadh
Gīr Hills
Kundla
Nandurbār
Māngrol
Mahuva
Gulf of Khambhāt
Sūrat
Verāval
Diu (Goa, Daman & Diu)
Navsāri
Valsād
Damān (G.D. & D.)
Silvassa
Amalner
Jalgaon
Malkāpur
Dhule
Malegaon
Buldāna
Khāmgaon
Chālisgaon
Kāranja
Yavatmāl
Hinganghāt
Mehekar
Wāshim
Rājur
Manmād
Nāsik
Aurangābād
Pusad
Penganga
Chandrapur
Deolāli
Kopargaon
Jālna
Hingoli
Ādilābād
Godāvari
Sangamner
MAHĀRĀSHTRA
Thāne
Kalyān
Ahmadnagar
Parbhani
Pūrna
Nānded
Nirmal
Belampalli
Bīr
Parli
Jagtial
Mancherāl
Bombay (Mumbai)
Lonāvale
Pune (Poona)
Alībāg
Bodhan
Nizāmābād
Udgīr
Karimnagar
ARABIAN SEA
25
20
70
75
4
5
B
C
D
50
100
100
200
150 mls
300 km

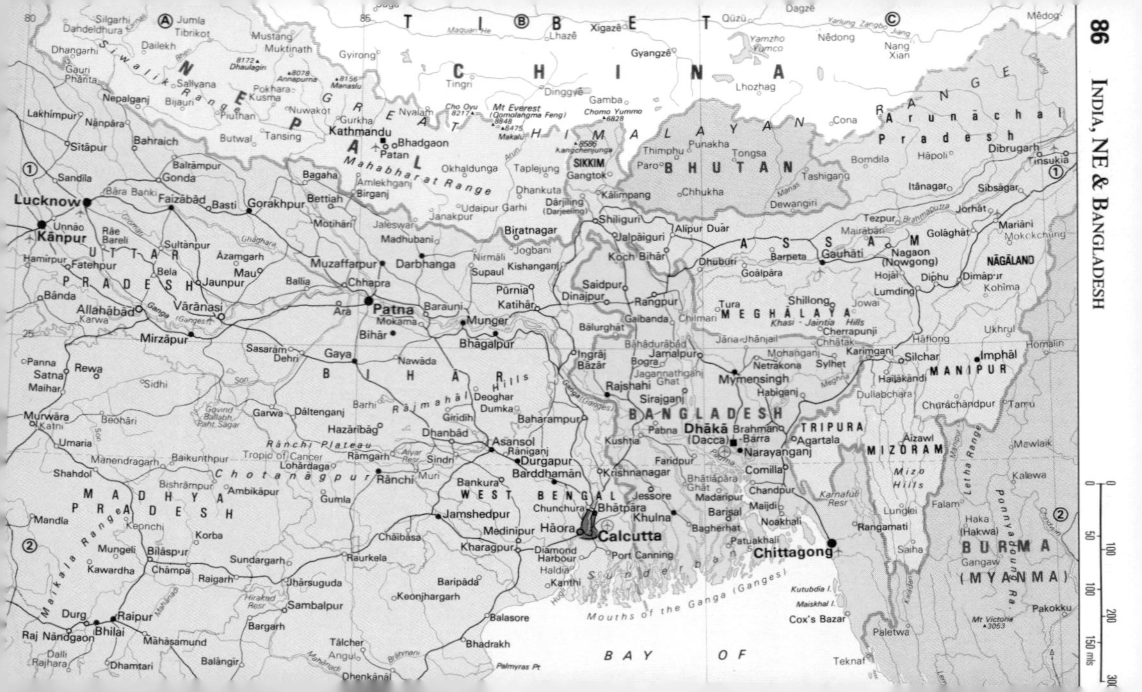
0 100 200 300
0 50 100 150 mls
TIBET
CHINA
NEPAL
GREAT HIMALAYAN RANGE
Arunāchal Pradesh
BHUTAN
SIKKIM
ASSAM
MEGHĀLAYA
NĀGĀLAND
MANIPUR
MIZORAM
TRIPURA
BANGLADESH
WEST BENGAL
BIHĀR
UTTAR PRADESH
MADHYA PRADESH
BURMA (MYANMA)
BAY OF
Mouths of the Ganga (Ganges)
Mt Everest (Qomolangma Feng) 8848
Kathmandu
Thimphu
Dhākā (Dacca)
Calcutta
Chittagong
Patna
Lucknow
Kānpur
Vārānasi
Allahābād
Gauhāti
Shillong
Imphāl
Agartala
Aizawl
Kohīma
Dibrugarh
Dārjiling (Darjeeling)
Gangtok
Rānchi
Jamshedpur
Raipur
Bhilai
Durg
Gorakhpur
Gaya
Bhāgalpur
Rājshahi
Khulna
Mymensingh
Sylhet
Comilla
Cox's Bazar
Tropic of Cancer
Chotanāgpur
Rājmahāl Hills
Mahabharat Range
Siwalik Range
Khasi - Jaintia Hills
Mizo Hills
Letha Range
Ponnyadaung Ra.
Chomo Yummo 6828
Kangchenjunga 8586
Makalu 8475
Cho Oyu 8217
Annapurna 8078
Dhaulagiri 8172
Manaslu 8156
Mt Victoria 3053

100 200 300 km
50 100 150 mls

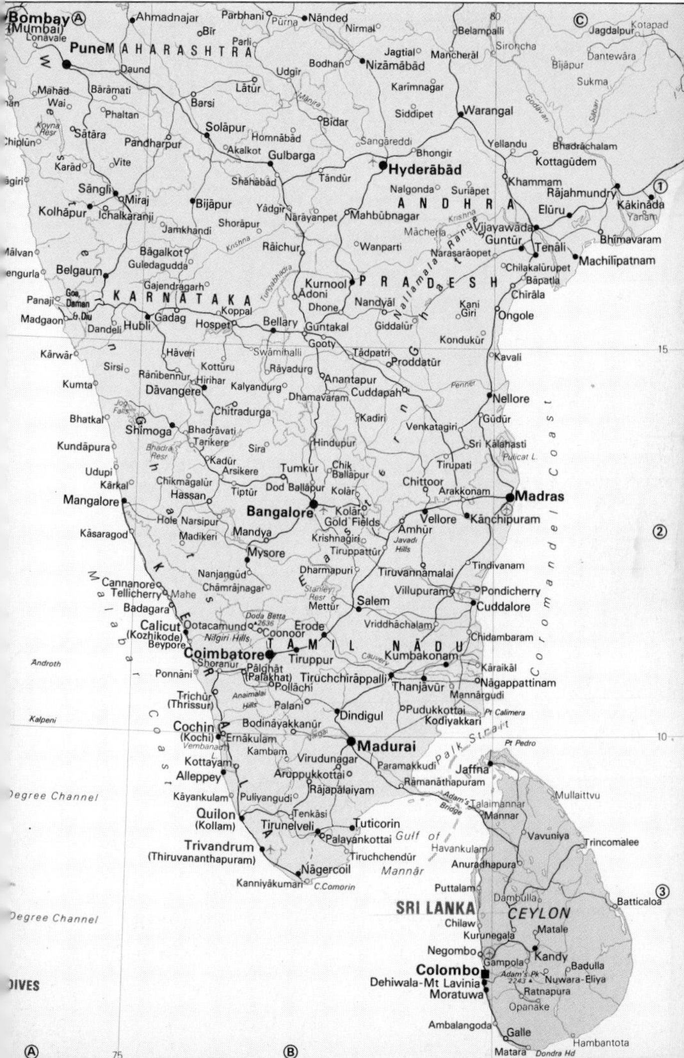

Bombay (Mumbai)
Lonavale
Ahmadnajar
Bīr
Parbhani
Pūrna
Nānded
Nirmal
Belampalli
Jagdalpur
Kotapad
Pune
MAHARASHTRA
Parli
Jagtial
Mancherāl
Sironcha
Dantewāra
Bījāpur
Daund
Udgīr
Bodhan
Nizāmābād
Sukma
Mahād
Bārāmati
Lātūr
Karīmnagar
Wai
Barsi
Mānjra
Siddipet
Warangal
Godāvari
Sabari
Phaltan
Koyna Resr
Sātāra
Solāpur
Bidar
Chiplūn
Pandharpur
Homnābād
Sangāreddi
Yellandu
Bhadrāchalam
Akalkot
Gulbarga
Bhongir
Kottagūdem
Karād
Vite
Hyderābād
Shāhābād
Tāndūr
Khammam
Sāngli
Nalgonda
Suriāpet
Rājahmundry
Miraj
Bijāpur
ANDHRA
Kākināda
Kolhāpur
Ichalkaranji
Yādgīr
Elūru
Yanam
Shorāpur
Nārāyanpet
Mahbūbnagar
Krishna
Vijayawāda
Jamkhandi
Mācherla
Guntūr
Bhīmavaram
Mālvan
Krishna
Rāichur
Wanparti
Nallamala Range
Tenāli
Bāgalkot
Narasarāopet
Machilīpatnam
Guledagudda
Chilakalūrupet
Vengurla
Belgaum
Tungabhadra
Kurnool
PRADESH
Bāpatla
Gajendragarh
Ādoni
Chīrāla
Panaji
Goa, Daman & Diu
KARNATAKA
Koppal
Dhone
Nandyāl
Kani Giri
Ongole
Madgaon
Dandeli
Hubli
Gadag
Hospet
Bellary
Guntakal
Giddalūr
Kondukūr
Gooty
Kārwār
Hāveri
Swāmihalli
Tādpatri
Proddatūr
Kavali
Sirsi
Kottūru
Rāyadurg
Rānibennur
Hirihar
Anantapur
Kumta
Dāvangere
Kalyandurg
Cuddapah
Pennar
Nellore
Dhamavaram
Jog Falls
Chitradurga
Bhatkal
Kadiri
Gūdūr
Shimoga
Bhadrāvati
Venkatagiri
Tarikere
Sri Kālahasti
Kundāpura
Bhadra Resr
Sira
Hindupur
Pulicat L.
Kadūr
Tirupati
Udupi
Arsikere
Tumkūr
Chik Ballāpur
Kārkal
Chikmagalūr
Chittoor
Hassan
Tiptūr
Dod Ballāpur
Kolār
Arakkonam
Madras
Mangalore
Bangalore
Kolār Gold Fields
Hole Narsipur
Vellore
Kānchipuram
Kāsaragod
Madikeri
Mandya
Krishnagiri
Amhūr
Javadi Hills
Mysore
Tiruppattūr
Tindivanam
Nanjangūd
Dharmapuri
Tiruvannāmalai
Cannanore
Chāmrājnagar
Stanley Resr
Villupuram
Pondicherry
Tellicherry
Mahe
Mettūr
Salem
Badagara
Cuddalore
Doda Betta 2636
Calicut (Kozhikode)
Ootacamund
Erode
Coonoor
Vriddhāchalam
Beypore
Nilgiri Hills
Chidambaram
Coimbatore
TAMIL NĀDU
Kumbakonam
Androth
Shoranur
Tiruppur
Cauvery
Kāraikāl
Ponnāni
Pālghāt (Palakhat)
Tiruchchirāppalli
Thanjāvūr
Nāgappattinam
Pollāchi
Mannārgudi
Trichūr (Thrissur)
Anaimalai Hills
Palani
Pudukkottai
Pt Calimera
Kalpeni
Dindigul
Kodiyakkari
Cochin (Kochi)
Bodināyakkanūr
Ernākulam
Vembanad L.
Madurai
Pt Pedro
Kambam
Palk Strait
Kottayam
Virudunagar
Paramakkudi
Jaffna
Alleppey
Aruppukkottai
Rāmanāthapuram
Mullaittivu
Rājapālaiyam
Degree Channel
Kāyankulam
Puliyangudi
Adam's Bridge
Talaimannar
Mannar
Tenkāsi
Quilon (Kollam)
Tirunelveli
Tuticorin
Vavuniya
Trincomalee
Palayankottai
Gulf of Mannār
Trivandrum (Thiruvananthapuram)
Havankulam
Tiruchchendūr
Anurādhapura
Nāgercoil
Kanniyākumari
C.Comorin
Puttalam
Dambulla
Batticaloa
SRI LANKA
CEYLON
Degree Channel
Chilaw
Matale
Kurunegala
Negombo
Kandy
Gampola
Colombo
Badulla
Adam's Pk 2243
Nuwara-Eliya
Dehiwala-Mt Lavinia
Moratuwa
Ratnapura
DIVES
Opanake
Ambalangoda
Galle
Hambantota
Matara
Dondra Hd
A
B
C
1
2
3
75
80
15
10

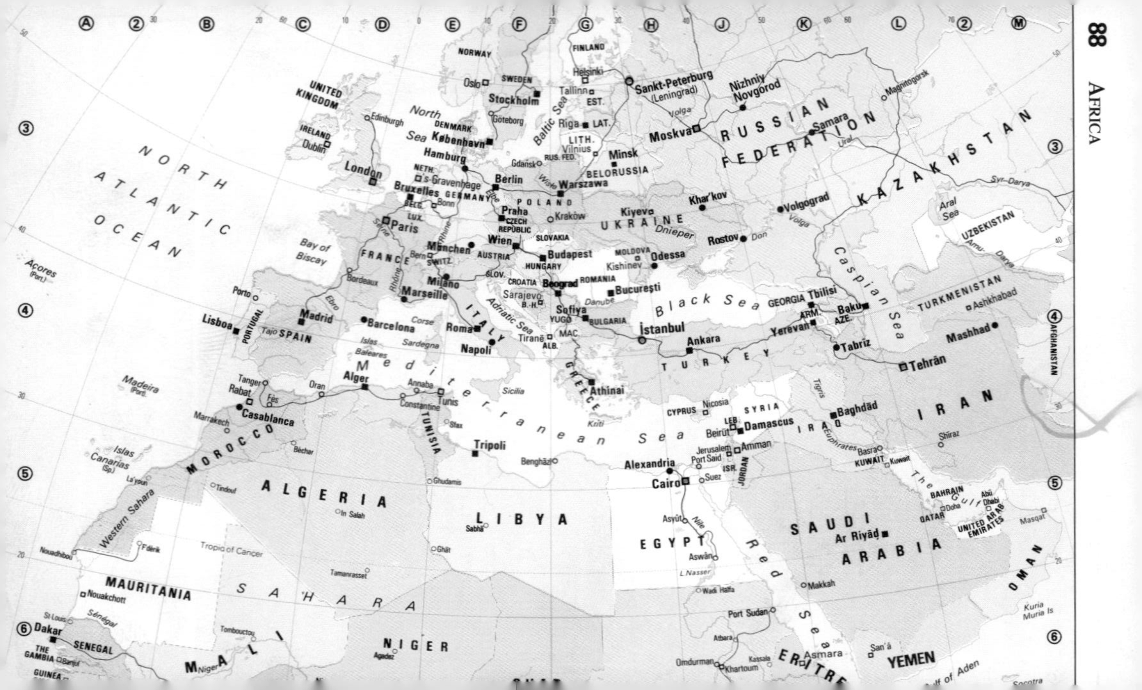
NORTH ATLANTIC OCEAN
Açores (Port.)
Madeira (Port.)
Islas Canarias (Sp.)
UNITED KINGDOM
IRELAND
Dublin
Edinburgh
London
North Sea
NORWAY
Oslo
SWEDEN
Stockholm
Göteborg
FINLAND
Helsinki
DENMARK
København
Baltic Sea
Tallinn
EST.
Riga
LAT.
LITH.
Vilnius
RUS. FED.
Gdańsk
Minsk
BELORUSSIA
Sankt-Peterburg
(Leningrad)
Moskva
Volga
Nizhniy Novgorod
RUSSIAN FEDERATION
Samara
Ural
Magnitogorsk
KAZAKHSTAN
Syr-Darya
Aral Sea
UZBEKISTAN
Amu-Darya
TURKMENISTAN
Ashkhabad
AFGHANISTAN
Caspian Sea
Hamburg
NETH.
's-Gravenhage
Bruxelles
BELG.
Bonn
GERMANY
LUX.
Berlin
Elbe
Warszawa
Wisła
POLAND
Praha
CZECH REPUBLIC
Kraków
Kiyev
Khar'kov
UKRAINE
Dnieper
Volgograd
Rostov
Don
Paris
Seine
Rhine
FRANCE
Bay of Biscay
Bordeaux
Rhône
München
Bern
SWITZ.
Wien
AUSTRIA
SLOVAKIA
Budapest
HUNGARY
SLOV.
MOLDOVA
Kishinev
Odessa
Milano
Marseille
CROATIA
Beograd
ROMANIA
București
Sarajevo
B.-H.
Danube
Black Sea
GEORGIA
Tbilisi
ARM.
Baku
AZE.
Porto
Ebro
Madrid
Lisboa
PORTUGAL
Tajo
SPAIN
Barcelona
Corse
Islas Baleares
Sardegna
Roma
ITALY
Napoli
Adriatic Sea
Tiranë
ALB.
MAC.
YUGO.
Sofiya
BULGARIA
İstanbul
Ankara
TURKEY
Yerevan
Tabrīz
Mashhad
Tehrān
Mediterranean Sea
Tanger
Rabat
Fès
Oran
Alger
Annaba
Constantine
Tunis
TUNISIA
Sfax
Sicilia
GREECE
Athinai
Kriti
CYPRUS
Nicosia
SYRIA
LEB.
Beirūt
Damascus
IRAQ
Baghdād
Tigris
Euphrates
IRAN
Shīrāz
Casablanca
Marrakech
MOROCCO
Béchar
Tripoli
Benghāzī
Jerusalem
Port Said
Amman
ISR.
JORDAN
Alexandria
Suez
Cairo
Basra
KUWAIT
Kuwait
The Gulf
BAHRAIN
Doha
QATAR
Abū Dhabi
UNITED ARAB EMIRATES
Masqat
La'youn
Tindouf
Ghudamis
ALGERIA
In Salah
LIBYA
Sabhā
Ghāt
EGYPT
Asyūt
Nile
Aswān
L. Nasser
Red Sea
SAUDI ARABIA
Ar Riyāḍ
Makkah
OMAN
Western Sahara
Nouadhibou
F'dérik
Tropic of Cancer
Tamanrasset
MAURITANIA
Nouakchott
SAHARA
Wadi Halfa
Port Sudan
Kuria Muria Is
St Louis
Sénégal
Dakar
SENEGAL
THE GAMBIA
Banjul
GUINEA
Tombouctou
MALI
Niger
NIGER
Agadez
Atbara
Omdurman
Khartoum
Kassala
ERITREA
Asmara
San'ā
YEMEN
Gulf of Aden
Socotra

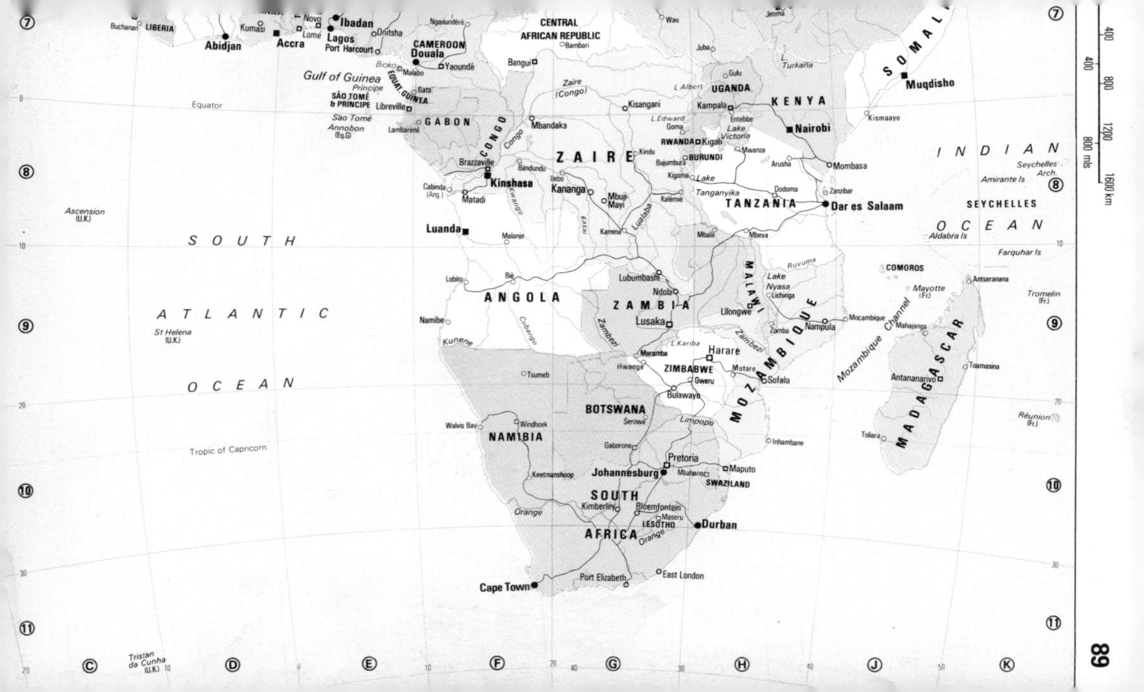
400
800
1200
1600 km
400
800 mls
Buchanan
LIBERIA
Abidjan
Kumasi
Accra
Lomé
Ibadan
Lagos
Port Harcourt
Onitsha
Ngaoundéré
CENTRAL AFRICAN REPUBLIC
Bambari
CAMEROON
Douala
Yaoundé
Bioko
Malabo
Gulf of Guinea
Príncipe
EQUAT. GUINEA
Bata
SÃO TOMÉ & PRINCIPE
Libreville
São Tomé
Annobon (Eq.G)
Lambaréné
GABON
Equator
Bangui
Zaire (Congo)
CONGO
Congo
Mbandaka
Brazzaville
Kinshasa
Bandundu
Cabinda (Ang.)
Matadi
Kwango
ZAIRE
Kisangani
Kindu
Ilebo
Kananga
Mbuji-Mayi
Kasai
Kamina
Lualaba
Kalemie
Wau
Juba
Jimma
Gulu
L. Turkana
L. Albert
UGANDA
KENYA
Kampala
Entebbe
Lake Victoria
L. Edward
Goma
RWANDA
Kigali
BURUNDI
Bujumbura
Mwanza
Nairobi
Arusha
Mombasa
Kigoma
Lake Tanganyika
Dodoma
TANZANIA
Zanzibar
Dar es Salaam
Kismaayo
SOMALIA
Muqdisho
INDIAN OCEAN
Seychelles Arch.
Amirante Is
SEYCHELLES
Aldabra Is
Farquhar Is
Ascension (U.K.)
SOUTH ATLANTIC OCEAN
Luanda
Malanje
Mbala
Mbeya
Lobito
Bié
ANGOLA
Lubumbashi
Ndola
ZAMBIA
Lusaka
Zambezi
Namibe
Cubango
Kunene
St Helena (U.K.)
MALAWI
Ruvuma
Lake Nyasa
Lichinga
Lilongwe
Zomba
Nampula
Moçambique
MOZAMBIQUE
COMOROS
Mayotte (Fr.)
Antseranana
Tromelin (Fr.)
Mozambique Channel
Mahajanga
MADAGASCAR
Toamasina
Antananarivo
Toliara
Réunion (Fr.)
L. Kariba
Maramba
Harare
Hwange
ZIMBABWE
Mutare
Gweru
Sofala
Bulawayo
Tsumeb
BOTSWANA
Serowe
Limpopo
Walvis Bay
Windhoek
NAMIBIA
Inhambane
Tropic of Capricorn
Gaborone
Pretoria
Maputo
Johannesburg
Mbabane
SWAZILAND
Keetmanshoop
SOUTH AFRICA
Kimberley
Bloemfontein
Maseru
LESOTHO
Durban
Orange
East London
Port Elizabeth
Cape Town
Tristan da Cunha (U.K.)
C
D
E
F
G
H
J
K
7
8
9
10
11

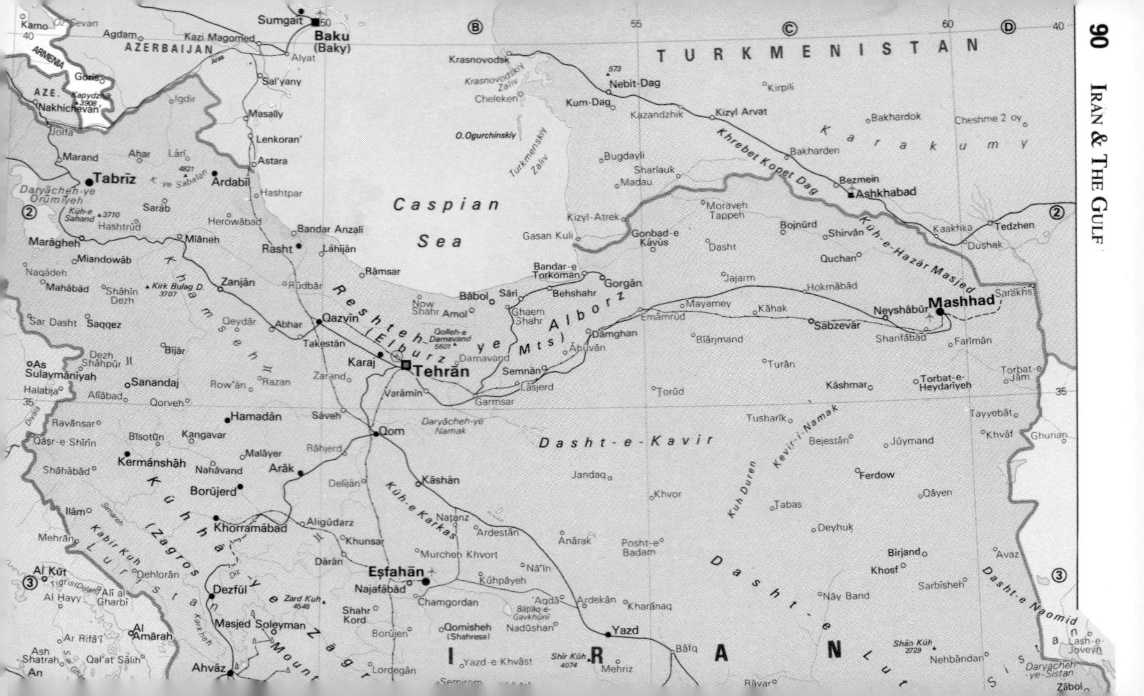
TURKMENISTAN
AZERBAIJAN
ARMENIA
AZE.
IRAN
Caspian Sea
Baku (Baky)
Sumgait
Alyat
Sal'yany
Kazi Magomed
Agdam
Kamo
Goris
Nakhichevan
Julfa
Masally
Lenkoran'
Astara
Ardabīl
Tabrīz
Marand
Ahar
Sarāb
Mīāneh
Marāgheh
Miandowāb
Mahābād
Naqādeh
Sar Dasht
Saqqez
Bījār
Zanjān
Qazvīn
Takestān
Abhar
Rasht
Bandar Anzalī
Lāhījān
Rūdbār
Rāmsar
Now Shahr
Āmol
Bābol
Sārī
Ghaem Shahr
Behshahr
Bandar-e Torkoman
Gorgān
Gonbad-e Kāvūs
Dāmghan
Semnān
Garmsar
Damavand
Tehrān
Karaj
Varāmīn
Qom
Sāveh
Zarand
Kāshān
Eşfahān
Najafābād
Shahr Kord
Yazd
Mehrīz
Bāfq
Ardestān
Nā'īn
Ardekān
Hamadān
Kermānshāh
Sanandaj
Arāk
Borūjerd
Malāyer
Nahāvand
Khorramābād
Dezfūl
Masjed Soleyman
Ahvāz
Al Amārah
Al Kūt
Ilām
Mehrān
Mashhad
Neyshābūr
Sabzevār
Torbat-e Heydarīyeh
Torbat-e Jām
Kāshmar
Bīrjand
Ferdow
Tabas
Qāyen
Nehbandān
Zābol
Quchan
Bojnūrd
Shīrvān
Ashkhabad
Bezmein
Bakharden
Kizyl Arvat
Kazandzhik
Nebit-Dag
Kum-Dag
Krasnovodsk
Cheleken
Gasan Kuli
Kizyl-Atrek
Tedzhen
Dushak
Kaakhka
Sarakhs
Karakumy
Khrebet Kopet Dag
Kūh-e Hazār Masjed
Reshteh-ye Alborz (Elburz Mts)
Dasht-e Kavir
Dasht-e Lut
Dasht-e Naomid
Kūh-e Karkas
Kūhhā-ye Zāgros
Daryācheh-ye Orūmīyeh
Daryācheh-ye Namak
Kevir-i-Namak
Kuh Duren
Qolleh-ye Damavand 5601
Shīr Kūh 4074
Zard Kuh 4548

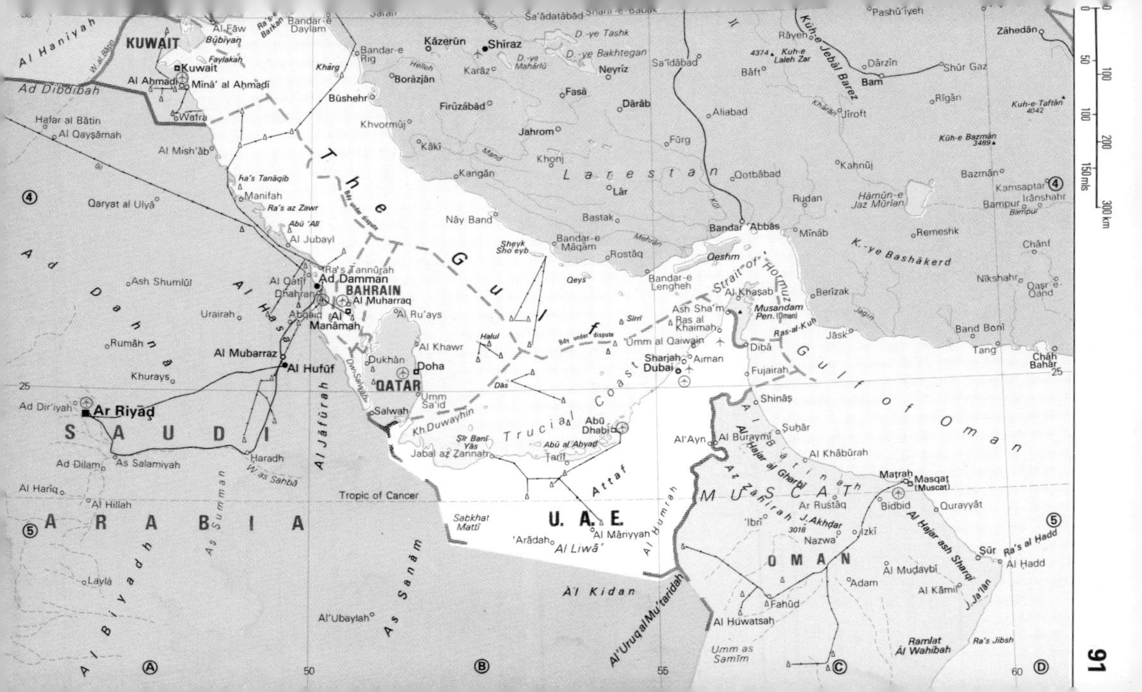
0
100
200
300 km
0
50
100
150 mls
The Gulf
Gulf of Oman
Strait of Hormuz
Trucial Coast
Bdy under dispute
KUWAIT
Kuwait
Al Ahmadi
Mīnā' al Ahmadī
Wafra
Al Fāw
Būbiyān
Faylakah
BAHRAIN
Al Manāmah
Al Muharraq
QATAR
Doha
Dukhān
Umm Sa'id
Al Khawr
Al Ru'ays
Salwah
Dw. Salwah
U. A. E.
Abū Dhabi
Dubai
Sharjah
Ajman
Umm al Qaiwain
Ras al Khaimah
Fujairah
Dibā
Al 'Ayn
Al Buraymi
OMAN
MUSCAT
Masqat (Muscat)
Matrah
Bidbid
Qurayyāt
Sūr
Ra's al Hadd
Al Hadd
Ja'lān
Al Kāmil
Al Mudaybī
Adam
Izkī
Nazwa
J. Akhdar
3018
Ar Rustāq
Al Khābūrah
Suhār
Shināş
Al Bāţinah
Hajar al Gharbī
Al Hajar ash Sharqī
Az Zāhirah
'Ibrī
Fahūd
Al Huwatsah
Umm as Samīm
Ramlat Āl Wahibah
Ra's Jibsh
Musandam Pen. (Oman)
Ras-al-Kuh
Al Khaşab
Ash Sha'm
SAUDI ARABIA
Ar Riyād
Ad Dir'iyah
Ad Dilam
Al Hariq
Al Hillah
Laylā
As Salamiyah
Khurays
Rumāh
Al Hufūf
Al Mubarraz
Al Qatīf
Ad Dammān
Dhahran
Abqaiq
Ra's Tannūrah
Al Jubayl
Abū 'Alī
Ra's az Zawr
Manīfah
Ra's Tanāqib
Al Mish'āb
Qaryat al Ulyā
Hafar al Bāţin
Al Qaysūmah
Ash Shumlūl
Urairah
Haradh
Al 'Ubaylah
Al Hasa
Ad Dahnā
Ad Dibdibah
Al Hanīyah
W. al Bāţin
Al Jāfūrah
As Summān
W. as Sahbā
As Sanām
Al Biyadh
Al Kidan
Al 'Urūq al Mu'tariḑah
Sabkhat Maţţī
Tropic of Cancer
Al Humrah
Al Liwā'
'Arādah
Al Māriyyah
Attaf
Ţarīf
Abū al Abyad
Jabal az Zannah
Şīr Banī Yās
Kh. Duwayhin
Das
Halul
Sirri
Qeys
Sheykh Sho'eyb
Bandar-e Lengeh
Qeshm
Bandar 'Abbās
Mīnāb
Rudan
Jāsk
Jagīn
Berīzak
Tang
Band Bonī
Chāh Bahār
Nīkshahr
Qasr-e Qand
Chānf
Bampur
Irānshahr
Kamsaptar
Bazmān
Kūh-e Bazmān 3489
Kūh-e Taftān 4042
Zāhedān
Shūr Gaz
Rīgān
Pashū'īyeh
Dārzīn
Bam
Kūh-e Jebāl Barez
Jīroft
Kahnūj
Hāmūn-e Jaz Mūrīān
Remeshk
K.-ye Bashākerd
Qotbābād
Kūl
Rāyen
Kūh-e Laleh Zār 4374
Bāft
Allābād
Sa'īdābād
Fūrg
Dārāb
Lārestān
Lār
Bastak
Rostāq
Mehrān
Bandar-e Māqām
Neyrīz
D.-ye Bakhtegān
D.-ye Tashk
D.-ye Mahārlū
Fasā
Jahrom
Khonj
Shīrāz
Kārāz
Fīrūzābād
Mand
Kangān
Nāy Band
Kāzerūn
Borāzjān
Heleh
Kākī
Khvormūj
Bandar-e Rīg
Būshehr
Khārg
Bandar-e Daylam
Ra's-e Barkan
25
50
55
60
A
B
C
D
4
5
91

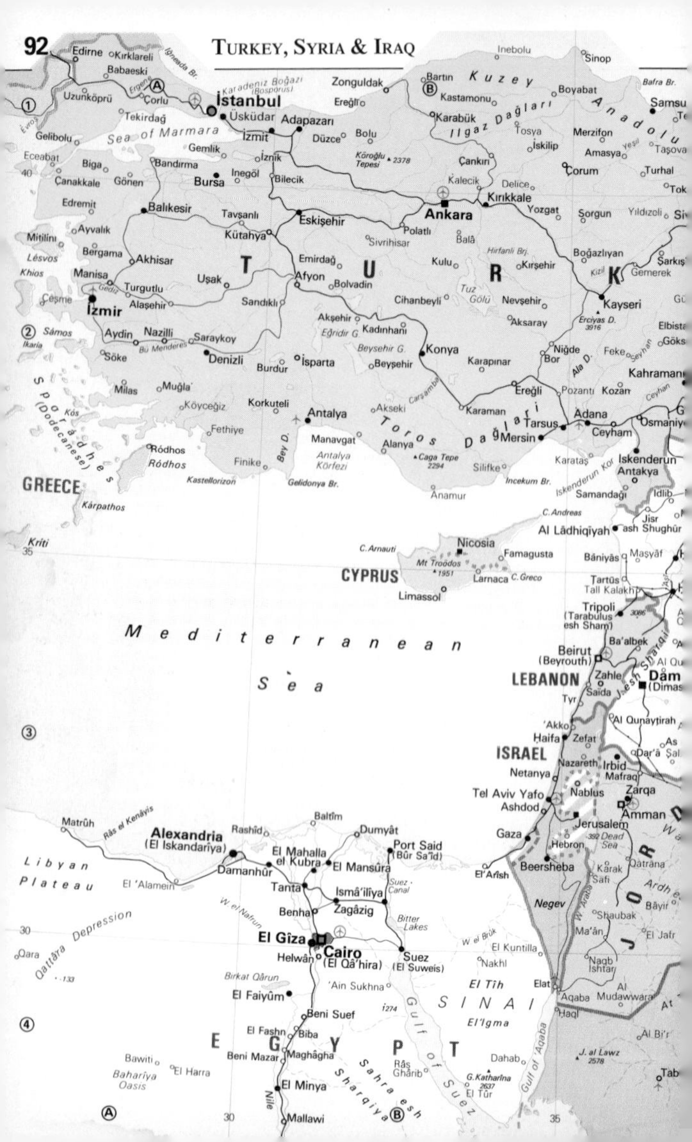

Edirne
Kırklareli
Babaeski
Uzunköprü
Çorlu
Karadeniz Boğazı (Bosporus)
İstanbul
Üsküdar
Tekirdağ
Gelibolu
Sea of Marmara
İzmit
Adapazarı
Zonguldak
Ereğli
Düzce
Bolu
Bartın
Kastamonu
Karabük
Ilgaz Dağları
Kuzey Anadolu
Inebolu
Sinop
Boyabat
Bafra Br.
Samsu
Tosya
İskilip
Merzifon
Amasya
Taşova
Turhal
Tok
Çorum
Çankırı
Kalecik
Delice
Kırıkkale
Yozgat
Sorgun
Yıldızoli
Ankara
Polatlı
Balâ
Köroğlu Tepesi 2378
Eceabat
Biga
Gemlik
İznik
Bandırma
Çanakkale
Gönen
Bursa
İnegöl
Bilecik
Edremit
Balıkesir
Tavşanlı
Eskişehir
Kütahya
Sivrihisar
Mitilini
Ayvalık
Lésvos
Bergama
Akhisar
Khios
Manisa
Turgutlu
Çeşme
İzmir
Alaşehir
Uşak
Sandıklı
Afyon
Bolvadin
Emirdağ
Kulu
Hirfanlı Brj.
Kırşehir
Tuz Gölü
Cihanbeyli
Nevşehir
Aksaray
Boğazlıyan
Şarkış
Gemerek
Kayseri
Erciyas D. 3916
Sámos
Ikaria
Aydin
Nazilli
Bü Menderes
Saraykoy
Denizli
Söke
Burdur
İsparta
Akşehir
Eğridir G.
Kadınhanı
Beyşehir G.
Beyşehir
Konya
Karapınar
Niğde
Bor
Ala D.
Feke
Kahraman
Elbista
Göks
Milas
Muğla
Köyceğiz
Kos
Korkuteli
Antalya
Akseki
Çarşamba
Karaman
Ereğli
Pozantı
Kozan
Ceyhan
Adana
Osmaniy
Sporádhes (Dodecanese)
Fethiye
Manavgat
Alanya
Toros Dağları
Tarsus
Mersin
Ceyham
Ródhos
Finike
Bey D.
Antalya Körfezi
Caga Tepe 2294
Silifke
Karataş
Iskenderun
Antakya
GREECE
Kastellorizon
Gelidonya Br.
Incekum Br.
Iskenderun Kor
Anamur
Samandağı
Idlib
Kárpathos
C. Andreas
Jisr ash Shughûr
Al Lâdhiqiyah
Kriti
C. Arnauti
Nicosia
Famagusta
Mt Troödos 1951
CYPRUS
Larnaca
C. Greco
Limassol
Bâniyâs
Maşyâf
Tartûs
Tall Kalakh
Tripoli (Tarabulus esh Sham)
Mediterranean Sea
Ba'albek
Beirut (Beyrouth)
LEBANON
Zahle
Saida
Dam (Dimas
Jesh Sharqi
Tyr
'Akko
Al Qunaytirah
Haifa
Zefat
ISRAEL
Dar'a
Nazareth
Irbid
Netanya
Mafraq
Tel Aviv Yafo
Nablus
Zarqa
Ashdod
Amman
Jerusalem
Gaza
Dead Sea
Hebron
Beersheba
Qatrana
Karak
Safi
Negev
W. Araba
Shaubak
Bâyir
Ma'ân
El Jafr
Matrûh
Râs el Kenâyis
Baltîm
Alexandria (El Iskandarîya)
Rashîd
Dumyât
Port Said (Bûr Sa'îd)
El Mahalla el Kubra
El Mansûra
Libyan Plateau
Damanhûr
El 'Alamein
Tanta
Ismâ'ilîya
Suez Canal
El 'Arîsh
Zagâzig
Benha
W. el Natrun
Bitter Lakes
Qattâra Depression
El Gîza
Cairo (El Qâ'hira)
Helwân
Suez (El Suweis)
W. el Brûk
El Kuntilla
Nakhl
Naqb Ishtar
Qara
Birkat Qârun
'Ain Sukhna
El Tîh
Elat
El Faiyûm
SINAI
Aqaba
Al Mudawwara
Beni Suef
Haql
El'Igma
El Fashn
Biba
EGYPT
Al Bi'r
Beni Mazar
Maghâgha
Dahab
Bawiti
El Harra
Bahariya Oasis
Râs Ghârib
G. Katharina 2637
El Tûr
J. al Lawz 2578
Tab
El Minya
Sahra esh Sharqiya
Gulf of Suez
Gulf of 'Aqaba
Nile
Mallawi
30
35
40

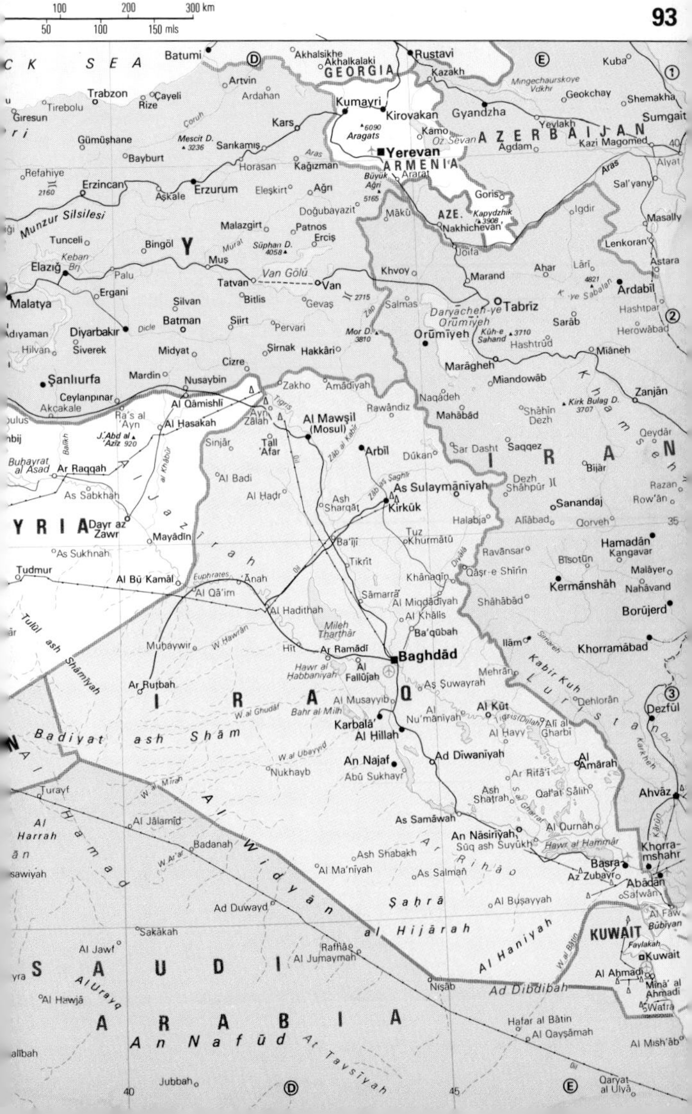
100 200 300 km
50 100 150 mls
BLACK SEA
Batumi
Akhalsikhe
Akhalkalaki
GEORGIA
Rustavi
Kazakh
Kuba
Mingechaurskoye Vdkhr
Geokchay
Shemakha
Sumgait
Trabzon
Çayeli
Rize
Tirebolu
Giresun
Artvin
Ardahan
Çoruh
Kumayri
Kirovakan
Gyandzha
Yevlakh
AZERBAIJAN
Kars
6090 Aragats
Kamo
Oz. Sevan
Agdam
Kazi Magomed
Alyat
Gümüşhane
Mescit D. 3236
Sarıkamış
Yerevan
ARMENIA
Bayburt
Horasan
Kağızman
Aras
Ararat
Büyük Ağrı 5165
Refahiye
2160
Erzincan
Aşkale
Erzurum
Eleşkirt
Ağrı
Goris
Sal'yany
Doğubayazit
Mākū
AZE.
Kapydzhik 3908
Nakhichevan'
Igdir
Masally
Munzur Silsilesi
Malazgirt
Patnos
Erciş
Tunceli
Bingöl
Murat
Süphan D. 4058
Jolfa
Lenkoran'
Astara
Keban Brj
Elazığ
Palu
Muş
Van Gölü
Khvoy
Marand
Ahar
Lārī
4821
Ardabīl
Tatvan
Van
Malatya
Ergani
Silvan
Bitlis
Gevaş
2715
Salmas
Kūh-e Sabalan
Hashtpar
Daryācheh-ye Orūmīyeh
Tabrīz
Sarāb
Batman
Siirt
Pervari
Zap
Adıyaman
Diyarbakır
Dicle
Mor D. 3810
Orūmīyeh
Kūh-e Sahand 3710
Herowābād
Hashtrūd
Hilvan
Siverek
Midyat
Şırnak
Hakkâri
Cizre
Marāgheh
Mīāneh
Şanlıurfa
Mardin
Nusaybin
Zakho
Amādīyah
Miandowāb
Khamseh
Ceylanpınar
Akçakale
Al Qāmishlī
Tigris
Naqādeh
Zanjān
Ra's al 'Ayn
Al Hasakah
'Ayn Zālah
Rawāndiz
Kirk Bulag D. 3707
Mahābād
Shāhīn Dezh
Al Mawşil (Mosul)
Qeydār
J. 'Abd al 'Azīz 920
Balīkh
Sinjār
Tall 'Afar
Zāb al Kabīr
Arbīl
Dūkān
Sar Dasht
Saqqez
IRAN
Buhayrat al Asad
Ar Raqqah
al Khābūr
Al Badī
Bījār
As Sabkhah
Al Ḥaḍr
Zāb aş Şaghīr
As Sulaymānīyah
Dezh Shāhpūr
Razan
Ash Sharqāt
Kirkūk
Sanandaj
Row'ān
SYRIA
Dayr az Zawr
Jazīrah
Halabja
Alīābād
Qorveh
Mayādīn
Tuz Khurmātū
Baʼījī
Hamadān
Kangavar
As Sukhnah
Ravānsar
Tikrīt
Bīsotūn
Malāyer
Tudmur
Al Bū Kamāl
Euphrates
'Ānah
Khānaqīn
Qaşr-e Shīrīn
Kermānshāh
Nahāvand
Al Qā'im
Sāmarrā'
Al Miqdādīyah
Shāhābād
Al Hadīthah
Al Khāliş
Borūjerd
Tulūl ash Shāmīyah
Mileh Tharthār
Ba'qūbah
Ilām
Saimareh
Khorramābād
Muḩaywir
W. Ḩawrān
Hīt
Ar Ramādī
Baghdād
Hawr al Ḩabbānīyah
Al Fallūjah
Mehrān
Kabīr Kūh
Luristan
Ar Ruţbah
IRAQ
Aş Şuwayrah
Dehlorān
W. al Ghudāf
Al Musayyib
Bahr al Milh
Al Kūt
Dezfūl
Nu'mānīyah
Tigris (Dijlah)
'Alī al Gharbī
Karbalā'
Al Ḩillah
Al Ḩayy
Badiyat ash Shām
W. al Ubayyid
Ad Dīwānīyah
Karkheh
An Najaf
Al 'Amārah
Nukhayb
Abū Şukhayr
Ar Rifā'ī
Ahvāz
Turayf
W. al Mirah
Ash Shaţrah
Qal'at Şāliḩ
Shaţţ al Gharrāf
Kārūn
Al Harrah
Al Jalāmīd
As Samāwah
Al Qurnah
Hamad
An Nāşirīyah
Badanah
Sūq ash Suyūkh
Hawr al Hammār
Khorramshahr
W. Ar'ar
Ash Shabakh
Al Widyān
Ar Rihāb
Basra
Al Ma'nīyah
As Salmān
Az Zubayr
Ābādān
Safwān
Ad Duwayd
Şahrā
Al Buşayyah
Al Fāw
Būbiyān
Sakākah
al Ḩijārah
KUWAIT
Faylakah
Al Jawf
Rafḩā
Al Jumaymah
Al Haniyah
W. al Bāţin
Kuwait
SAUDI ARABIA
Al Ahmadī
Al 'Urayq
Nişāb
Mīnā' al Ahmadī
Al Hawjā
Ad Dibdibah
Wafra
Ḩafar al Bāţin
An Nafūd
At Taysīyah
Al Qayşūmah
Al Mish'āb
Jubbah
Qaryat al Ulyā
40
45
35
D
E
1
2
3

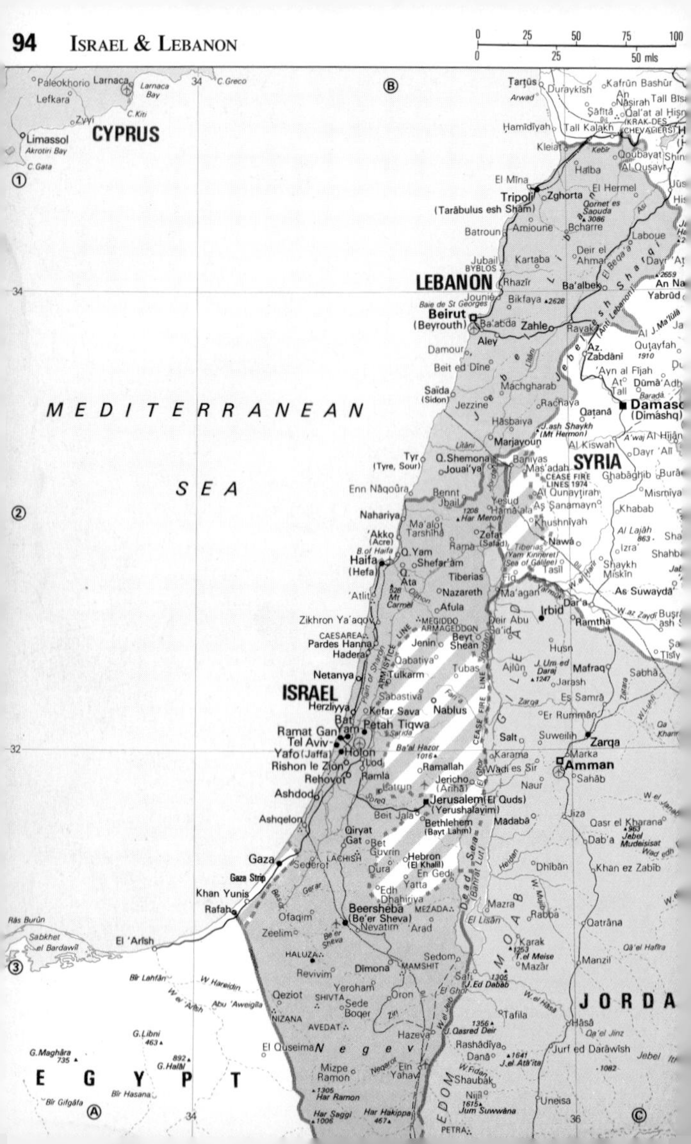
0 25 50 75 100
0 25 50 mls
Paleokhorio
Larnaca
Larnaca Bay
C.Greco
Lefkara
C.Kiti
Zyyi
Limassol
CYPRUS
Akrotiri Bay
C.Gata
Tartus
Arwad
Duraykish
Kafrûn Bashûr
An Nasirah
Tall Bisa
Safita
Qal'at al Hisn
(KRAK DES CHEVALIERS)
Hamidiyah
Tall Kalakh
Kleiat
Kebir
Qoubayat
Al Qusayr
Halba
El Mina
Tripoli
(Tarabulus esh Sham)
Zghorta
El Hermel
Qornet es Saouda
3086
Batroun
Amioune
Bcharre
Laboue
Deir el Ahmar
Jubail
BYBLOS
Kartaba
El Beqa'a
LEBANON
Rhazir
Ba'albek
2659
An Na
Yabrûd
Jounié
Baie de St Georges
Bikfaya
2628
Beirut
(Beyrouth)
Ba'abda
Zahle
Rayak
Anti Lebanon
Aley
Damour
Az. Zabdani
Qutayfah
1910
Beit ed Dine
'Ayn al Fijah
At Tall
Dûmâ
Machgharab
Saida
(Sidon)
Jezzine
Rachaya
Damascus
(Dimashq)
Qatana
MEDITERRANEAN
Hasbaiya
J.ash Shaykh
(Mt Hermon)
Litani
Marjayoun
Al Kiswah
Tyr
(Tyre, Sour)
Q.Shemona
Jouai'ya
Baniyas
Mas'adah
SYRIA
CEASE FIRE LINES 1974
Ghabaghib
Dayr 'Ali
SEA
Enn Naqoura
Bennt Jbail
Yesud Hama'ala
Al Qunaytirah
As Sanamayn
Mismiya
Nahariya
1208
Har Meron
Khushniyah
Khabab
Ma'alot Tarshiha
'Akko
(Acre)
Zefat
(Safad)
Nawa
Al Lajah
863
B.of Haifa
Haifa
(Hefa)
Q.Yam
Shefar'am
Rama
L.Tiberias
(Yam Kinneret)
(Sea of Galilee)
Tasil
Izra
Shaykh Miskin
Q.Ata
Tiberias
Fiq
'Atlit
528
Mt Carmel
Nazareth
Ma'agan
As Suwayda'
Dar'a
Afula
Irbid
Zikhron Ya'aqov
MEGIDDO
ARMAGEDDON
Deir Abu Sa'id
Ramtha
CAESAREA
Pardes Hanna
Jenin
Beyt Shean
Hadera
Husn
Qabatiya
ARMISTICE LINE
Plain of Sharon
Netanya
Tulkarm
Tubas
Ajlûn
J.Um ed Daraj
1247
Mafraq
Sabha
Jarash
ISRAEL
Sabastiya
CEASE FIRE LINE
Herzliyya
Kefar Sava
Nablus
Es Samra
Zarqa
Er Rumman
Bat Yam
Ramat Gan
Petah Tiqwa
Tel Aviv
Salt
Suweilih
Zarqa
Yafo (Jaffa)
Holon
Ba'al Hazor
1016
Karama
Marka
Rishon le Zion
Lod
Ramallah
Wadi es Sir
Amman
Rehovot
Ramla
Jericho
(Ariha)
Naur
Sahab
Latrun
Ashdod
Jerusalem (El Quds)
(Yerushalayim)
Soreq
Beit Jala
Jiza
Ashqelon
Bethlehem
(Bayt Lahm)
Madaba
Qasr el Kharana
963
Jebel Mudeisisat
Qiryat Gat
Bet Guvrin
Dab'a
LACHISH
Gaza
Sederot
Gaza Strip
Dura
Hebron
(El Khalil)
En Gedi
Dhiban
Khan ez Zabib
Heidan
Khan Yunis
Gerar
Yatta
Edh Dhahiriya
Dead Sea
(Bahret Lut)
Rafah
MEZADA
Mazra
Rabba
Ras Burûn
Ofaqim
Beersheba
(Be'er Sheva)
El Lisan
Qatrana
Nevatim
'Arad
Sabkhet el Bardawil
El 'Arish
Zeelim
Be'er Sheva
Karak
1253
T.el Meise
Mazar
Qa'el Hafira
HALUZA
Sedom
MAMSHIT
Manzil
Revivim
Dimona
Bir Lahfan
W.Hareidin
Safi
1305
J.Ed Dabab
El Ghor
W.el Arish
Abu 'Aweigila
Yeroham
Oron
Qeziot
SHIVTA
Sede Boqer
W.el Hasa
JORDAN
Tafila
NIZANA
Zin
1356
Hasa
AVEDAT
J.Qasred Deir
Qa'el Jinz
G.Libni
463
Hazeva
Rashadiya
G.Maghara
735
El Quseima
Negev
Jurf ed Darawish
892
G.Halal
Dana
1641
J.el Ata'ita
Jebel
1082
Mizpe Ramon
Negarot
Ein Yahav
W.Fidan
Shaubak
EGYPT
Bir Hasana
1305
Har Ramon
EDOM
Nijil
1615
Jum Suwwana
Uneisa
Bir Gifgafa
Har Saggi
1006
Har Hakippa
467
PETRA
34
36

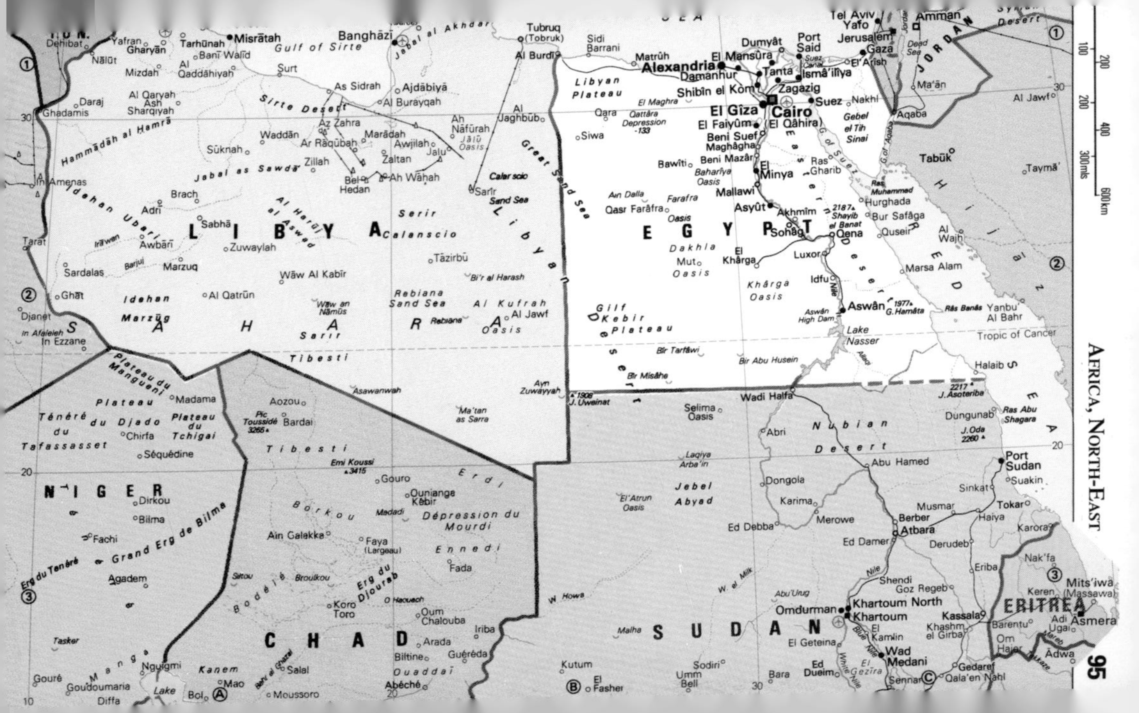

200   400   600 km
100   200   300 mls

①

Al Jawf

Tayma'

Ma'ān

Al Jawf

Syrian Desert

Amman

JORDAN

Tabūk

②

Tropic of Cancer

Halā'ib

③

Mits 'Iwā'
Adi Kayih
Adwa

ERITREA

Keren
Kerkebet
Barentu

Tel Aviv-Yafo
Jerusalem
Gaza

Suez
Port Said
El 'Arish
Gebel el Tih
Sinai
Ra's Gharib

Marsa Alam
Muhammad Qal
Ra's Safāga
Hurghada
Quseir

Port Sudan
Suakin

Nak'fa
Karora
Mits 'Iwā'
Massawa
Asmera

SEA

Banha
Dumyāt
El Manşūra
Zagazig
El Qāhira
Ismā'iliya

Būr Safāga

Dungunab
Ra's Abu Shagara

Sinkat
Derudeb

EGYPT

Alexandria
El Gîza
Tanta
Shibîn el Kôm
El Faiyûm
Beni Suef
Maghagha
Minya
Mallawi
Asyût
Akhmîm
Sôhâg
Qena
Luxor
Idfû
Aswân
Aswân High Dam

Gebel Shāyib
Shendi
Ra's Banâs
G. Hamāta

Khârga
Bahariya
Oasis
Farafra
Oasis
Dakhla
Oasis
Muṭ
Kharga
Oasis

Marawe
Lake Nasser

Berber
Atbara
Ed Damer

Khartoum North
Khartoum
Omdurman

Ed Debba
Dongola
Abu Hamed
Musmar

Ed Dueim
Ed Medani

Wad Medani

SUDAN

Marsa Matruh
El Daba
Qattara Depression
-133
Siwa

El Alamein
Ogra
Qara

Ain Dalla
Qasr Faráfra
Bîr Tarfâwi

Selima
Oasis

Abri
Wadi Halfa

Nubian Desert

Karima
El Obeid

Sodiri
Umm Badr

Bāra

Libyan
Plateau

Siwa

Gilf
Kebir
Plateau

Laqiya
Arba'in

Jebel
Abyad

Maiha
Kutum
Sodiri
El Fasher

El 'Atrun
Oasis

Tubruq
(Tobruk)
Al Burdi

Sarir
Calanscio
Sand Sea

Great Sand Sea

Libyan
Desert

'Ayn Zuwayyah

Al Kufrah
Al Jawf
Oasis

LIBYA

Banghāzī
Gulf of Sirte
Ajdabiyā
Al Burayqah

An Nafūrah
Awjilah
Jalu
Zaltan

Rebiana
Sand Sea

Serir Tibesti

Sarir
Calanscio

Ma'tan
as Sarra

Plateau
du
Mourdi
Erdi

Depression du
Mourdi

Misrātah
Tarhūnah
Banī Walid
Al Qaddāhiyah
As Sidrah
Az Zahrā
Marādah
Ar Rāqūbah
Waddān
Zillah

Bū Njēm
Hūn

Jabal as Sawdā

Al Haruj
al Aswad

Waw al Kabir

Hamada
Tibesti

Emi Koussi

Aozou
Bardaï

Pic
Toussidé
3265

TIBESTI

Borkou

Ain Galakka

Faya
(Largeau)

Ounianga
Kebir

Fada

Bir
Misaha

Iriba
Arada
Biltine
Guéréda
Oum
Chalouba

Ouaddaï
Abéché

CHAD

Ennedi

Kôro Toro

Oum
Hadjer

Maméa

N'Djamena area

Kelo
Moussoro

Qaryah
ash Sharqiyah
Mizdah
Gharyān
Naft

Brach
Sabhā
Adiri
Awbari
Marzuq
Al Qatrūn

Ubāri
Sand Sea

Idahan
Marzūq

Madama
Plateau
du
Tchigai

Séguédine

Dao Timmi

Plateau
Manguéni

Plateau du Djado

Madama

Chirfa

Enneri Blaka

NIGER

Dirkou
Bilma

Grand Erg de Bilma

Fachi

Agadem

Termit

Zinder area

Gashua

Nguru
Nguigmi

Lake
Chad

Kanem

Bol
Goudoumaria

Maïné-Soroa

Nālūt
Daraj
Ghadāmis

Tiaret
Djanet
In Ezzane
In Amguel
In Salah

Ghāt

Serdeles

Tassili-n-Ajjer

Ténéré du
Tafassasset

Ténéré

N.&H.
Dehibat

Remada

ALGERIA

TUNISIA

Tafasâsset

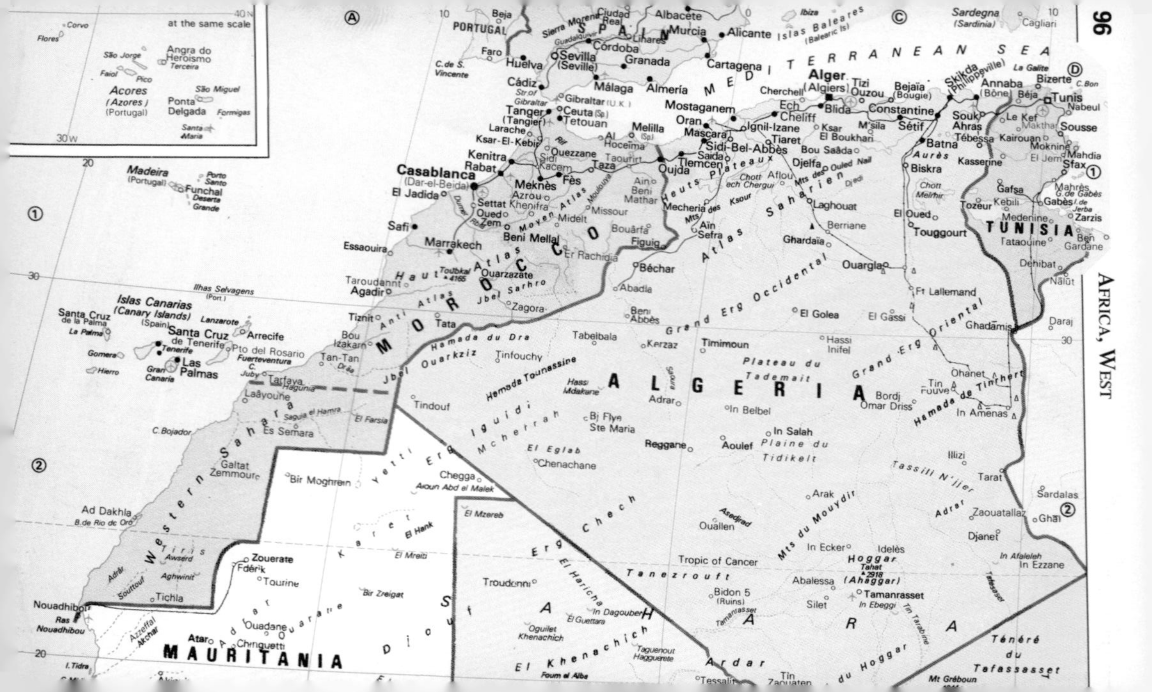

at the same scale
Açores (Azores) (Portugal)
Angra do Heroísmo
Ponta Delgada
Madeira (Portugal)
Funchal
Islas Canarias (Canary Islands) (Spain)
Santa Cruz de Tenerife
Las Palmas
Arrecife
Ilhas Selvagens (Port.)
PORTUGAL
SPAIN
Sevilla (Seville)
Córdoba
Granada
Málaga
Almería
Murcia
Cartagena
Alicante
Albacete
Huelva
Cádiz
Gibraltar (U.K.)
Ceuta (Sp.)
Melilla (Sp.)
Tanger (Tangier)
Tetouan
Rabat
Kenitra
Casablanca (Dar-el-Beida)
El Jadida
Safi
Essaouira
Marrakech
Agadir
Taroudannt
Tiznit
Fès
Meknès
Oujda
MOROCCO
Haut Atlas
Anti Atlas
Moyen Atlas
Western Sahara
Tarfaya
Laâyoune
Es Semara
Ad Dakhla
MAURITANIA
Nouadhibou
Zouerate
Atar
Ouadane
Chinguetti
ALGERIA
Alger (Algiers)
Oran
Constantine
Annaba (Bône)
Sétif
Biskra
Tlemcen
Béchar
Ghardaïa
Ouargla
Touggourt
Laghouat
El Golea
Timimoun
Adrar
Reggane
In Salah
Tamanrasset
Tindouf
Hoggar (Ahaggar)
Grand Erg Occidental
Grand Erg Oriental
Tanezrouft
Tropic of Cancer
TUNISIA
Tunis
Bizerte
Sousse
Sfax
Gabès
Kairouan
Tozeur
MEDITERRANEAN SEA
Sardegna (Sardinia)
Islas Baleares (Balearic Is)
Ghadāmis
Ghāt

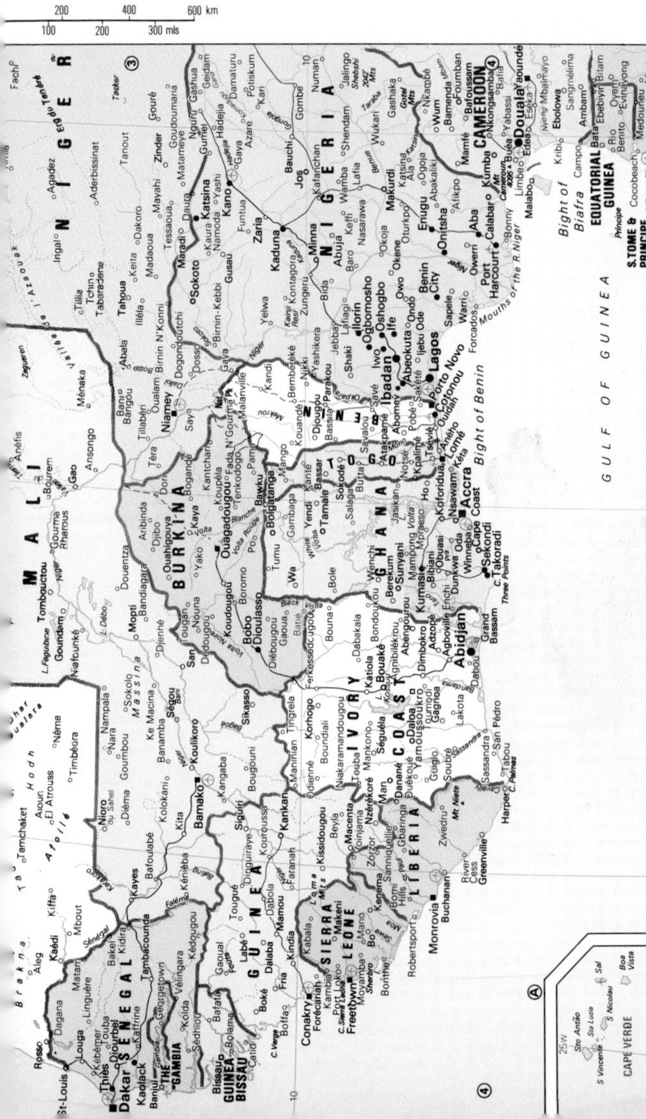

200 400 600 km
100 200 300 mils

NIGER

MALI

NIGERIA

BURKINA

GHANA

TOGO

BENIN

IVORY COAST

LIBERIA

GUINEA

SIERRA LEONE

SENEGAL

THE GAMBIA

GUINEA BISSAU

CAMEROON

EQUATORIAL GUINEA

S. TOME & PRINCIPE

GULF OF GUINEA

Bight of Benin

Bight of Biafra

Mouths of the R. Niger

CAPE VERDE

Agadez, Zinder, Tahoua, Niamey, Gao, Tombouctou, Mopti, Bamako, Kano, Kaduna, Zaria, Sokoto, Katsina, Maiduguri, Jos, Abuja, Minna, Ilorin, Ibadan, Lagos, Abeokuta, Ife, Benin City, Onitsha, Enugu, Port Harcourt, Calabar, Douala, Yaoundé, Libreville, Bouaké, Abidjan, Kumasi, Accra, Lomé, Cotonou, Porto Novo, Sekondi-Takoradi, Tamale, Ouagadougou, Bobo Dioulasso, Monrovia, Freetown, Conakry, Bissau, Banjul, Dakar, St-Louis, Kaolack, Nouakchott, Nioro, Kayes, Ségou, Sikasso, Korhogo, Yamoussoukro, São Tomé, Malabo

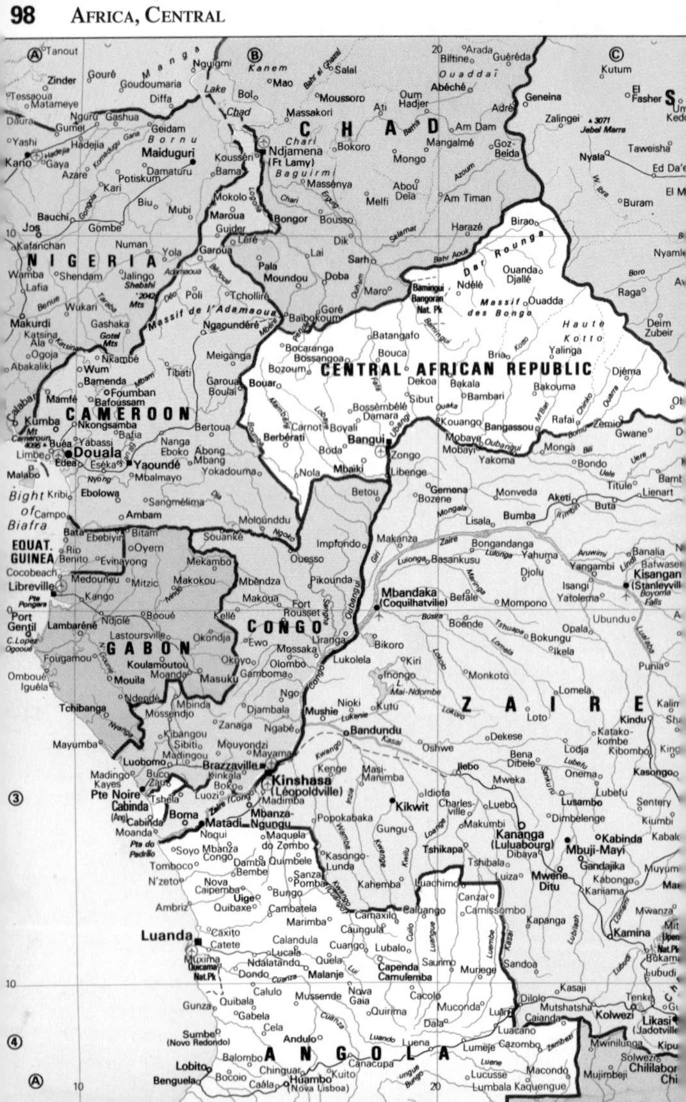
CHAD
NIGERIA
CAMEROON
CENTRAL AFRICAN REPUBLIC
EQUAT. GUINEA
GABON
CONGO
ZAIRE
ANGOLA
Tanout
Zinder
Gouré
Goudoumaria
Manga
Nguigmi
Kanem
Mao
Salal
Bahr el Ghazal
Arada
Biltine
Guéréda
Kutum
Ouaddaï
Abéché
Oum Hadjer
El Fasher
Tessaoua
Matameye
Diffa
Lake Chad
Bol
Moussoro
Ati
Adré
Geneina
Daura
Nguru
Gashua
Gumel
Massakori
Batha
Am Dam
Zalingei
3071 Jebel Marra
Yashi
Hadejia
Geidam
Bornu
Chari
Ndjamena (Ft Lamy)
Bokoro
Mangalmé
Goz-Beïda
Taweisha
Kano
Gaya
Azare
Maiduguri
Kousséri
Bama
Damaturu
Potiskum
Baguirmi
Massenya
Mongo
Nyala
Ed Da'ein
Kari
Abou Deïa
Melfi
Am Timan
Buram
Bauchi
Biu
Mubi
Mokolo
Maroua
Bongor
Bousso
Jos
Gombe
Guider
Léré
Dik
Harazé
Birao
Kafanchan
Numan
Yola
Garoua
Lai
Sarh
Salamat
Bahr Aouk
Dar Rounga
Wamba
Shendam
Jalingo
Shebshi Mts
2042
Pala
Moundou
Doba
Ouanda Djallé
Lafia
Poli
Tcholliré
Maro
Bamingui Bangoran Nat. Pk
Ndélé
Massif des Bongo
Ouadda
Raga
Wukari
Massif de l'Adamaoua
Goré
Baïbokoum
Makurdi
Gashaka
Gotel Mts
Ngaoundéré
Batangafo
Haute Kotto
Deim Zubeir
Katsina Ala
Ogoja
Nkambé
Meiganga
Bocaranga
Bossangoa
Bouca
Bria
Yalinga
Abakaliki
Wum
Tibati
Bozoum
Djéma
Bamenda
Foumban
Garoua Boulaï
Bouar
Dekoa
Bakala
Bakouma
Mamfé
Bafoussam
Sibut
Bambari
Kumba
Nkongsamba
Bertoua
Bossembélé
Damara
Kouango
Bangassou
Rafai
Zemio
Mt Cameroun 4095
Buéa
Bafia
Carnot
Boyali
Gwane
Yabassi
Berbérati
Bangui
Mobaye
Mobayi
Monga
Limbe
Douala
Nanga Eboko
Abong Mbang
Boda
Zongo
Yakoma
Bondo
Edea
Eséka
Yaoundé
Yokadouma
Mbaiki
Nola
Libenge
Uele
Malabo
Nyong
Mbalmayo
Betou
Titule
Bambili
Bight of Biafra
Kribi
Ebolowa
Sangmélima
Gemena
Bozene
Monveda
Aketi
Lienart
Campo
Ambam
Buta
Lisala
Bumba
Mongala
Moloundou
Bata
Ebebiyin
Bitam
Souanké
Makanza
Rio Benito
Oyem
Impfondo
Bongandanga
Banalia
Evinayong
Mekambo
Ouesso
Basankusu
Yahuma
Yangambi
Bafwasende
Cocobeach
Djolu
Kisangani (Stanleyville)
Libreville
Medouneu
Mitzic
Makokou
Mbendza
Pikounda
Isangi
Boyoma Falls
Mbandaka (Coquilhatville)
Befale
Mompono
Yatolema
Pte Pongara
Kango
Makoua
Fort Rousset
Port Gentil
Lambaréné
Ndjolé
Booué
Kellé
Busira
Boende
Tshuapa
Bokungu
Ubundu
Opala
C. Lopez
Lastoursville
Okondja
Ewo
Liranga
Ikela
Fougamou
Mossaka
Bikoro
Lukolela
Kiri
Punia
Koulamoutou
Mouila
Moanda
Masuku
Okoyo
Olombo
Gamboma
Inongo
Monkoto
Omboué
Iguéla
Lac Mai-Ndombe
Lomela
Ngo
Ndendé
Mbinda
Mossendjo
Djambala
Nioki
Kutu
Mushie
Loto
Kindu
Tchibanga
Zanaga
Ngabé
Bandundu
Katako-kombe
Mayumba
Kibangou
Sibiti
Madingou
Mouyondzi
Mayama
Oshwe
Dekese
Lodja
Kibombo
Bena Dibele
Onema
Kasongo
Luobomo
Brazzaville
Kinkala
Kinshasa (Léopoldville)
Kenge
Masi-Manimba
Ilebo
Mweka
Madingo-Kayes
Pte Noire
Cabinda
Tshela
Luozi
Boko
Madimba
Idiofa
Lubefu
Sentery
Kikwit
Charlesville
Luebo
Lusambo
Boma
Matadi
Mbanza-Ngungu
Popokabaka
Makumbi
Dimbelenge
Kiumbi
Moanda
Noqui
Maquela do Zombo
Gungu
Kananga (Luluabourg)
Mbuji-Mayi
Kabinda
Pta do Padrão
Soyo
Mbanza Congo
Damba
Quimbele
Kasongo-Lunda
Tshikapa
Dibaya
Gandajika
Tomboco
Bembe
Tshibala
Luiza
Mwene-Ditu
Kabongo
Kaniama
N'zeto
Nova Caipemba
Sanza Pomba
Bungo
Uige
Kahemba
Luachimo
Canzar
Ambriz
Quibaxe
Cambatela
Camaxilo
Caluango
Camissombo
Kapanga
Mwanza
Marimba
Caungula
Kamina
Luanda
Caxito
Catete
Calandula
Cuango
Lubalo
Muxima
Quiçama Nat. Pk
Lucala
Ndalatando
Quela
Capenda Camulemba
Saurimo
Muriege
Sandoa
Bukama
Dondo
Malanje
Lubudi
Calulo
Nova Gaia
Cacolo
Kasaji
Tenke
Mussende
Muconda
Dilolo
Mutshatsha
Kolwezi
Likasi (Jadotville)
Gunza
Quibala
Gabela
Quirima
Dala
Luau
Caianda
Cela
Luacano
Sumbe (Novo Redondo)
Andulo
Luena
Cazombo
Mwinilunga
Kipushi
Lumeje
Balombo
Canacupa
Lucusse
Macondo
Solwezi
Chililabombwe
Lobito
Chinguar
Kuito
Mujimbeji
Benguela
Bocoio
Caála
Huambo (Nova Lisboa)
Lumbala Kaquengue

200 400 600 km
100 200 300 mils

ERITREA

Kassala
Khashm
Girba
Barentu
Adi
Keren
Mits'iwa
(Massawa)
Asmera
Mersa
Fatma

Gedaref
Qala'en Nahl
Om
Adwa
Mek'ele
Ed
Ta'izz
Al
Mukhā
(Mocha)
Shaykh
'Uthman
Adan
(Aden)
Gulf of Aden

El Geteina
Wad
Medani
El Gezira
Sennar
Singa
El Hawata
Ras Dashan
4620
Dabat
Sek'ot'a
3657
Tendaho
Weldiya
Aseb
Obock
Tadjoura
Dikhil
DJIBOUTI
Djibouti
Str. of
Bab al Mandeb
Ras
Khanzira
Zeila
Karin
Ceerigaabo
Berbera

El Obeid
Bara
Ed
Dueim
Umm
Ruwaba
Kosti
Rashad
El Jebelein
Roseires
Er Rahad
Dunkur
Gonder
Tana
Bahir
Dar
Debre
Tabor
Lake Tana
Deshe
4150
Abuye
Meda
Biyo
Kaboba
Guban
Burao
Hargeysa
Caynabo
Laascaanood

Dilling
Nuba
Mts
Kadugli
Belfodiyo
Dangila
Burye
Debre
Markos
Fiche
Debre
Birhan
Diré Dawa
Hārer
Caynabo

ETHIOPIA
Nejo
Dembi Dolo
Sodo
Dendi
3286
Adis
Abeba
Nazret
Awash
Ahmar Mts
Degeh Bur
Aware
H A U D
Ogaden
Warder
Geladi
Gaalkacyo

Malakal
Abwong
Nasir
Akobo
Tor
Goré
Jima
Shashemene
Asela
Golocha
Ginir
Goba
Damot

Sudd
Fangak
Er Reto
Ayod
Duk
Faiwil
Pibor
Post
Mizan
Teferi
Maji
Abera
Yirga
Alem
Mendebo
Mts
Gughe
4200
Abaya
Hara
Fanna
Imi
Danan
Sina Dhaqa
El Goran

Shambe
Rumbek
Yirol
Bor
Kenamuke
Swamp
Bako
Gidolé
Arba Minch
Negelli
Melka
Guba
Dolo
Odo
Beled
Weyne
Tiyeglow
Buulo
Barde
Dirri
Meregh

Amadi
Mongalla
Juba
Torit
Lotikipi
Lokitaung
Lake
Turkana
Mega
Moyale
Mandera
Luuq
Xuddur
Baydhabo
Wanle
Weyne
Buur
Hakaba
Ceelbuur

Nimule
Kitgum
Gulu
Moroto
Lodwar
Mt Kulal
2293
Buna
Baardheere
Afgooye
Marka
Muqdisho
(Mogadishu)
Uarsciek

UGANDA
Soroti
Mt Elgon
4321
Mbale
Tororo
Mt Nyiru
2805
Marsabit
Wajir
Mado
Gashi
Baraawe
Giamame
Afmadu

Kampala
Jinja
Kakamega
Eldoret
Isiolo
Nanyuki
Embu
Garissa
Kismaayo

Lake
Victoria
Bukoba
Musoma
Kisii
Nakuru
Nyeri
Kiriniaga
(Mt Kenya)
5199
Thika
Nairobi
Machakos
Patta I.
Lamu

RWANDA
Kigali
BURUNDI
Mwanza
Geita
Shinyanga
KENYA
Arusha
Kilimanjaro
5895
Moshi
Same
Taveta
Malindi
Mombasa
Kwale
Pemba I.

TANZANIA
Nzega
Kahama
Tabora
Singida
Kondoa
Babati
Masai
Steppe
Lushoto
Korogwe
Tanga
Wete
Zanzibar

Kigoma
Ujiji
Uvinza
Kaliua
Manyoni
Dodoma
Handeni
Pangani
Bagamoyo
Dar es Salaam

Mpanda
Kitunda
Rungwa
Mpwapwa
Kilosa
Morogoro
Kisiju
Mafia

Sumbawanga
Chunya
Iringa
Mikumi
Mohoro
Kilwa Kivinje

Mbeya
Njombe
Ifakara
Matenge
Kilwa Kiswani

Tukuyu
Njombe
Liwale
Lindi
Mtwara

Songea
Tunduru
Masasi
Newala
Palma
Mocimboa da Praia

COMOROS
Moroni
Grande
Comore
Anjouan

SEYCHELLES

Equator

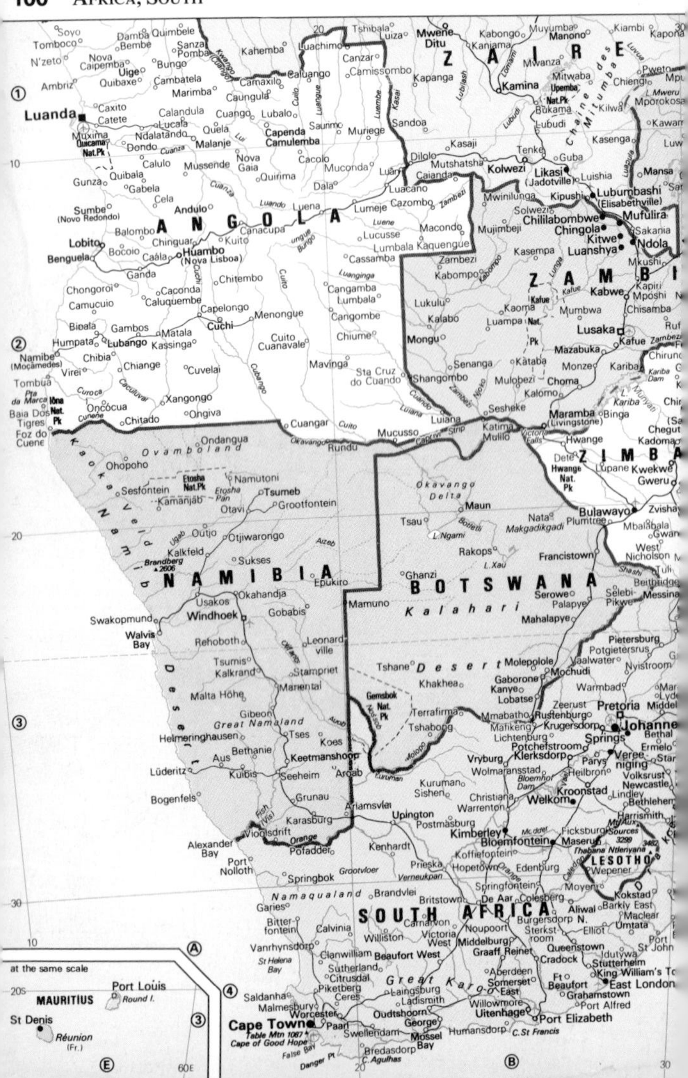

MAURITIUS
St Denis
Réunion
(Fr.)

at the same scale
Port Louis
Round I.

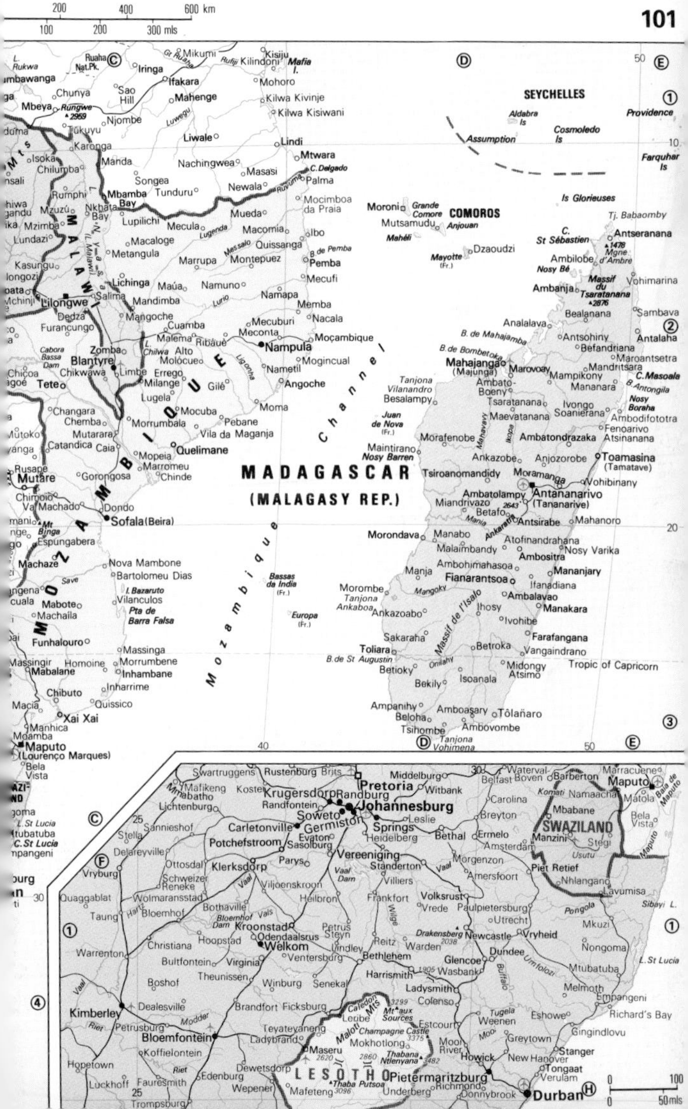

Map labels

Scale bars (top)
200 400 600 km
100 200 300 mls

Tanzania / northern area
L. Rukwa
mbawanga
Ruaha Nat.Pk. ©
Iringa
Mikumi
Kilindoni
Rufiji
Mafia I.
Kisiju
Mohoro
Kilwa Kivinje
Kilwa Kisiwani
Mbeya
Chunya
Sao Hill
Mahenge
Rungwe ▲2959
Njombe
Liwale
Lindi
Mtwara
Masasi
C.Delgado
Palma

SEYCHELLES / islands
SEYCHELLES
Aldabra Is
Assumption
Cosmoledo Is
Providence
Farquhar Is
Is Glorieuses
Tj. Babaomby

COMOROS
Grande Comore
Moroni
Mutsamudu
Mahéli
COMOROS
Anjouan
Mayotte (Fr.)
Dzaoudzi

Madagascar
MADAGASCAR
(MALAGASY REP.)

Antananarivo
(Tananarive)
Toamasina
(Tamatave)
Fianarantsoa
Toliara
Antseranana
Mahajanga
(Majunga)
Morondava
Tropic of Capricorn

Mozambique
MOZAMBIQUE
Nampula
Blantyre
Zomba
Quelimane
Sofala (Beira)
Inhambane
Maputo
(Lourenço Marques)

Mozambique Channel
Mozambique Channel
Juan de Nova (Fr.)
Bassas da India (Fr.)
Europa (Fr.)

Southern Africa inset
Pretoria
Johannesburg
Soweto
Krugersdorp
Randburg
Germiston
Vereeniging
SWAZILAND
Mbabane
Maputo
Kimberley
Bloemfontein
LESOTHO
Pietermaritzburg
Durban
Richard's Bay
St Lucia

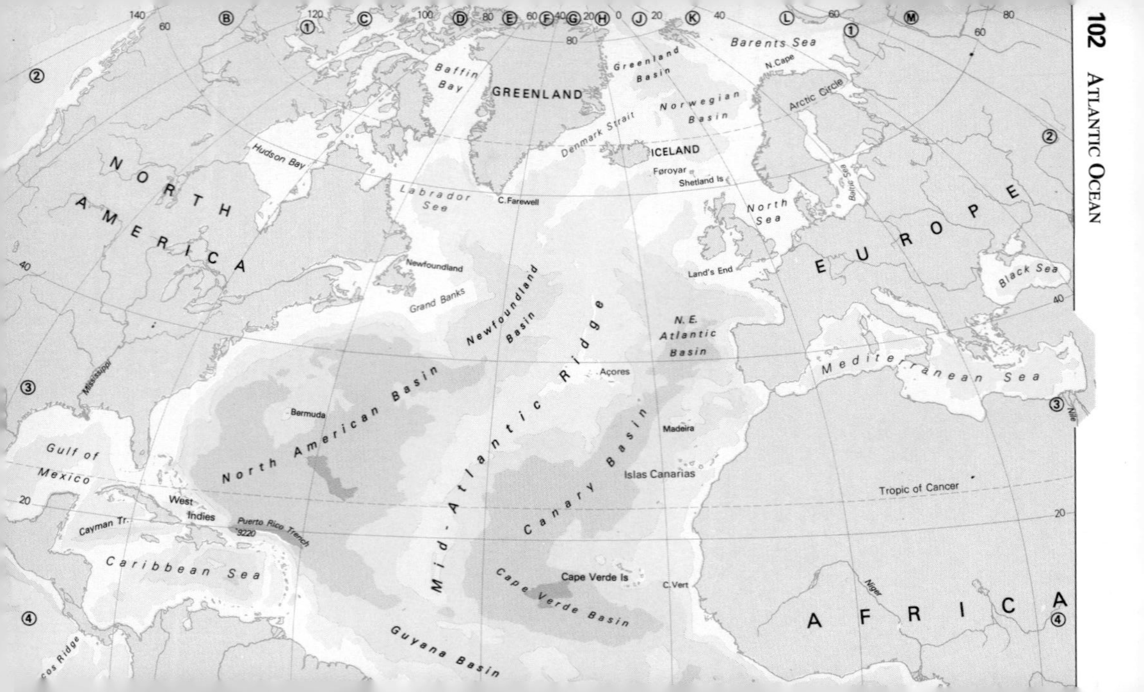
NORTH AMERICA
GREENLAND
ICELAND
EUROPE
AFRICA
Barents Sea
N.Cape
Arctic Circle
Greenland Basin
Norwegian Basin
Baffin Bay
Denmark Strait
Hudson Bay
Føroyar
Shetland Is
Baltic Sea
Labrador Sea
C.Farewell
North Sea
Newfoundland
Land's End
Black Sea
Grand Banks
Newfoundland Basin
N.E. Atlantic Basin
Açores
Mediterranean Sea
Nile
Mississippi
Bermuda
North American Basin
Mid-Atlantic Ridge
Madeira
Canary Basin
Islas Canarias
Gulf of Mexico
Tropic of Cancer
West Indies
Cayman Tr.
Puerto Rico Trench
9220
Caribbean Sea
Cape Verde Is
C.Vert
Cape Verde Basin
Niger
Guyana Basin

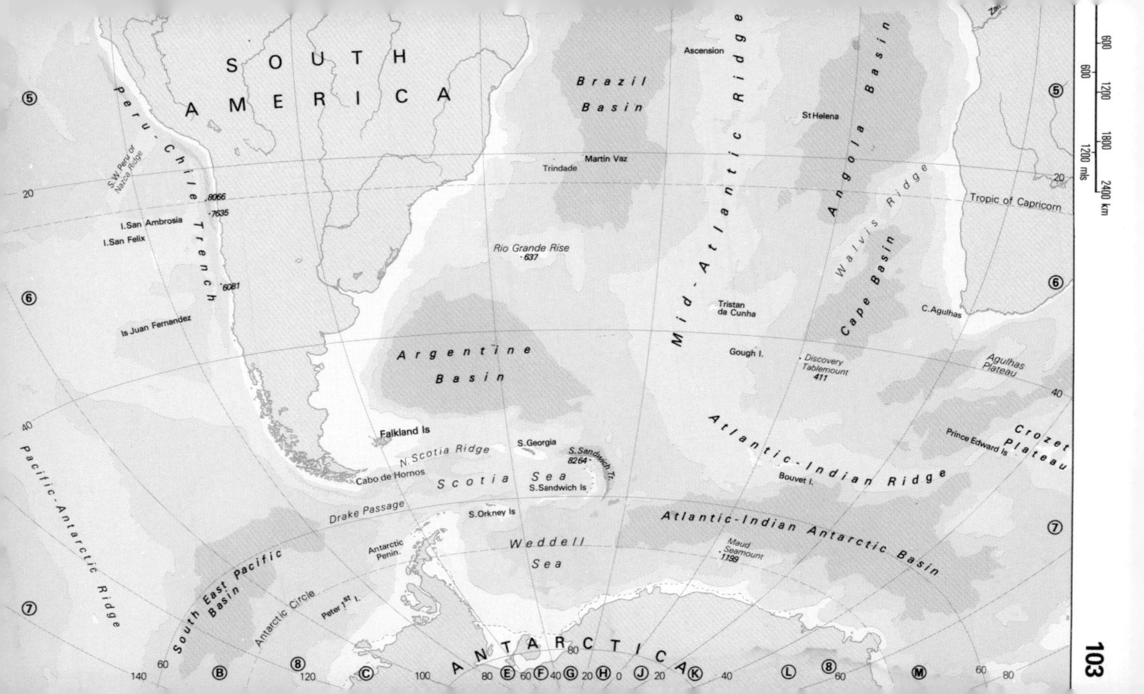

600   1200   1800   2400 km
600   1200 mls

Tropic of Capricorn

C. Agulhas

Agulhas Plateau

Crozet Plateau

Prince Edward Is

Atlantic-Indian Ridge

Bouvet I.

Atlantic-Indian Antarctic Basin

Maud Seamount 1788

Walvis Ridge

Cape Basin

Angola Basin

St Helena

Mid-Atlantic Ridge

Ascension

Tristan da Cunha

Gough I.

Discovery Tablemount 411

Brazil Basin

Martin Vaz

Trindade

Rio Grande Rise -637

Argentine Basin

S. Sandwich Tr. 8264

S. Sandwich Is

Scotia Sea

Weddell Sea

ANTARCTICA

SOUTH AMERICA

S. Georgia

N. Scotia Ridge

Falkland Is

S. Scotia Ridge

S. Orkney Is

Cabo de Hornos

Drake Passage

Antarctic Penin.

Peter I. I.

Antarctic Circle

Peru-Chile Trench

8066
7635
6687

I. San Ambrosia
I. San Felix
Is Juan Fernandez

abis. plain M.S.

South East Pacific Basin

Pacific-Antarctic Ridge

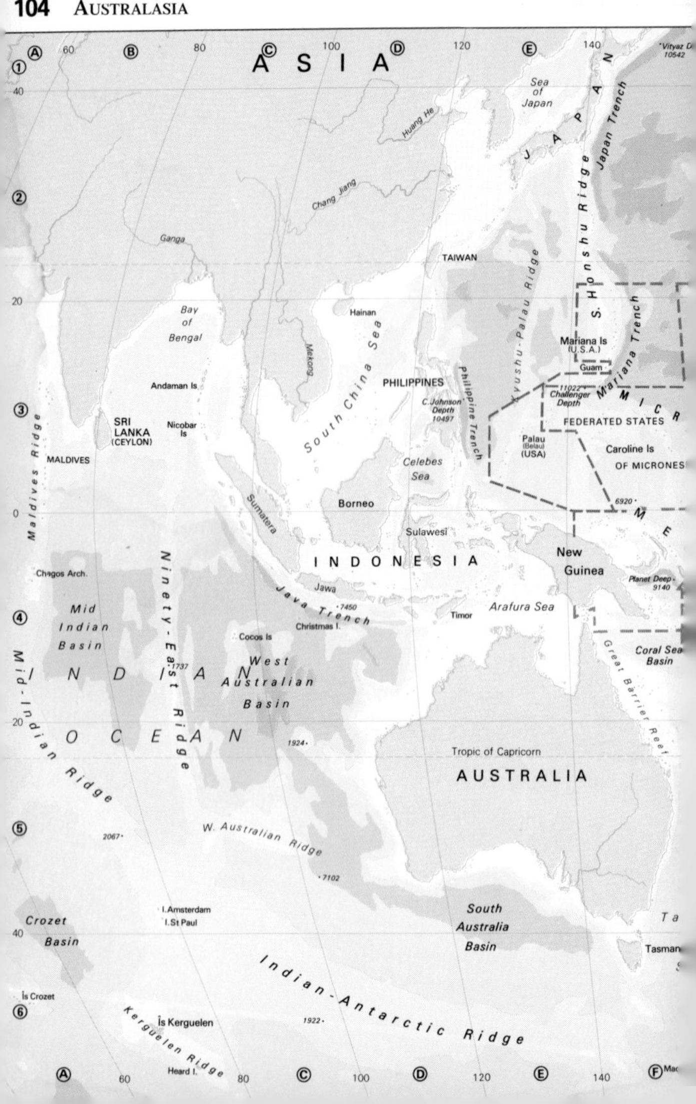

ASIA

Sea of Japan

Huang He

Chang Jiang

Ganga

TAIWAN

Bay of Bengal

Hainan

Maldives Ridge

Andaman Is

SRI LANKA (CEYLON)

Nicobar Is

MALDIVES

South China Sea

PHILIPPINES

C. Johnson Depth 10497

Philippine Trench

Yap-Palau Ridge

S. Honshu Ridge

Japan Trench

JAPAN

Mariana Is (U.S.A.)

Guam

Challenger Depth 11022

Mariana Trench

MICR

FEDERATED STATES

Palau (USA)

Caroline Is

OF MICRONES

6920

M E

Chagos Arch.

Mid Indian Basin

Ninety-East Ridge

Sumatra

Java Trench

Celebes Sea

Borneo

Sulawesi

INDONESIA

Jawa

7450

Christmas I.

Timor

Arafura Sea

New Guinea

Planet Deep 9140

Coral Sea Basin

Mid-Indian Ridge

I N D I A N

Cocos Is

West Australian Basin

1924

Tropic of Capricorn

AUSTRALIA

Great Barrier Reef

O C E A N

1737

2067

W. Australian Ridge

7102

South Australia Basin

Ta

Tasman

Crozet Basin

I. Amsterdam I. St Paul

Indian-Antarctic Ridge

Îs Crozet

Kerguelen Ridge

Îs Kerguelen

1922

Heard I.

Mac

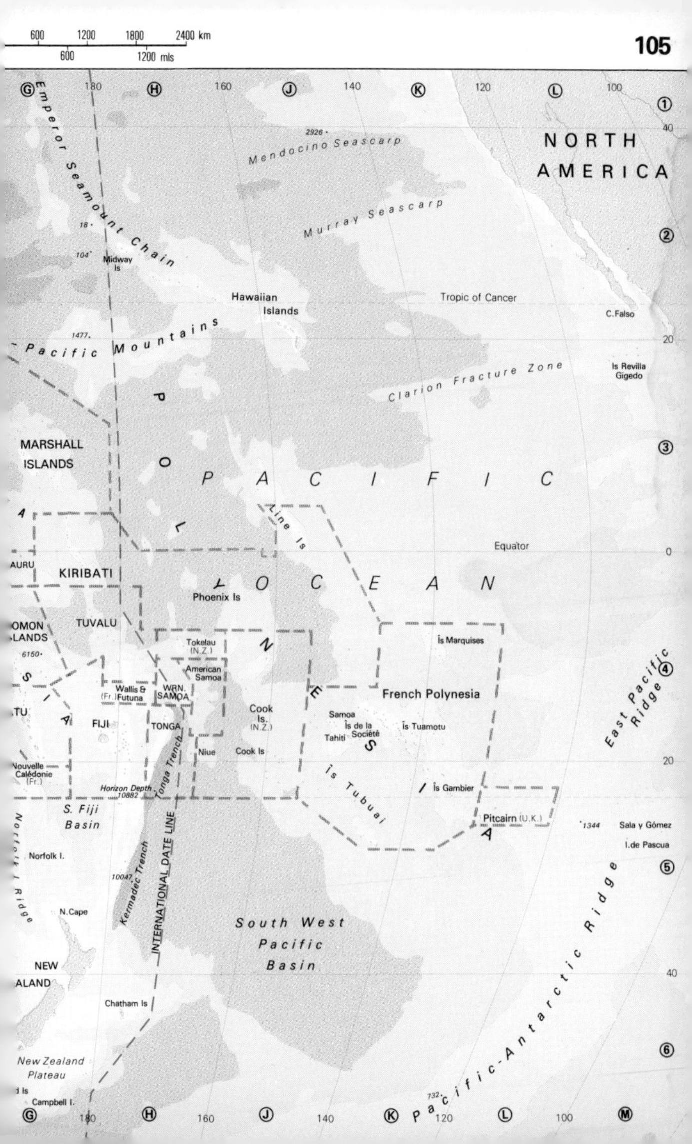

600   1200   1800   2400 km
600   1200 mls

G 180 **H** 160 **J** 140 **K** 120 **L** 100

①
40

Emperor Seamount Chain

2926

Mendocino Seascarp

NORTH AMERICA

②

18

104 Midway Is

Murray Seascarp

Tropic of Cancer

C.Falso

Hawaiian Islands

1477

Pacific Mountains

Clarion Fracture Zone

Is Revilla Gigedo

P

MARSHALL ISLANDS

O

L

Y

PACIFIC

③

A

Line Is

AURU

KIRIBATI

N

Equator
0

Phoenix Is

TUVALU

E

OMON LANDS

6150

I

S

Tokelau (N.Z.)

Is Marquises

East Pacific Ridge

④

TU

A

Wallis & Futuna (Fr.)

American Samoa

WRN SAMOA

French Polynesia

S

I

FIJI

TONGA

Cook Is (N.Z.)

Samoa
Is de la Société
Tahiti

Is Tuamotu

20

Niue

Cook Is

Nouvelle Calédonie (Fr.)

Is Tubuai

Is Gambier

Horizon Depth 10882

10047

Tonga Trench

INTERNATIONAL DATE LINE

A

Pitcairn (U.K.)

1344

Sala y Gómez

I.de Pascua

⑤

S. Fiji Basin

Norfolk I.

Norfolk I Ridge

Kermadec Trench

South West Pacific Basin

40

N. Cape

Pacific-Antarctic Ridge

NEW ALAND

Chatham Is

⑥

New Zealand Plateau

732

d Is

Campbell I.

G 180 **H** 160 **J** 140 **K** *Pacific-Antarctic Ridge* 120 **L** 100 **M**

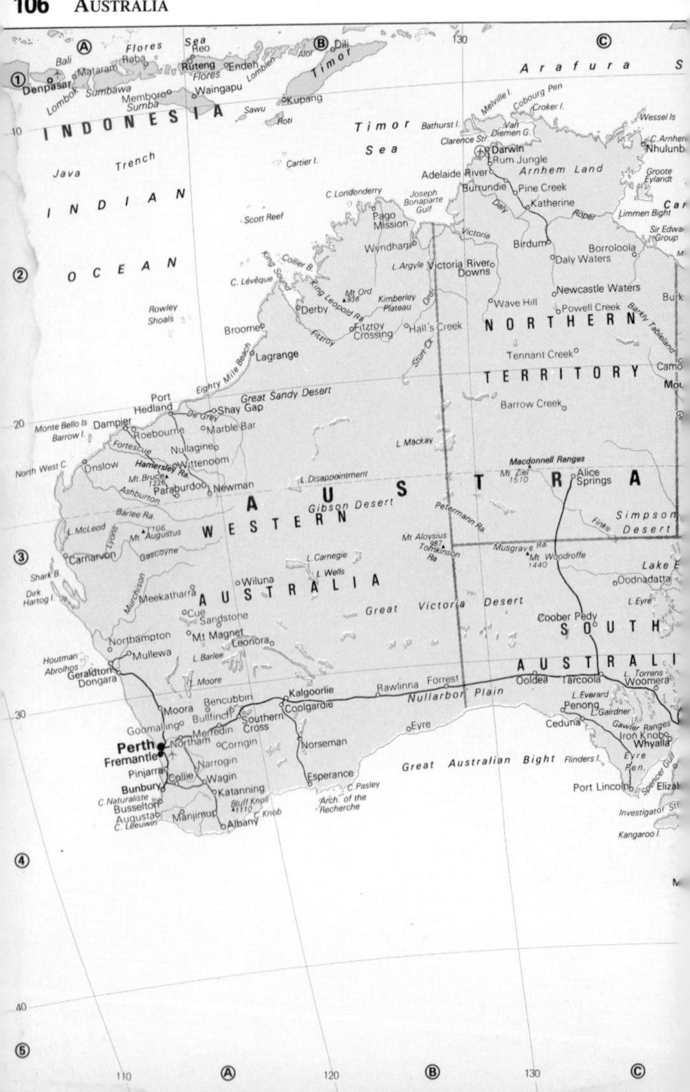
INDONESIA
Flores Sea
Reo
Bali
Raba
Ruteng
Endeh
Dili
Alor
Timor
Denpasar
Mataram
Lombok
Sumbawa
Flores
Lomblen
Memboro
Waingapu
Sumba
Kupang
Sawu
Roti
Arafura Sea
Timor Sea
Java Trench
INDIAN OCEAN
Cartier I.
Bathurst I.
Melville I.
Cobourg Pen
Croker I.
Van Diemen G.
Clarence Str.
Darwin
Rum Jungle
Adelaide River
Arnhem Land
Wessel Is
C. Arnhem
Nhulunbuy
Groote Eylandt
Burrundie
Pine Creek
Katherine
Daly
Roper
Limmen Bight
C. Londonderry
Joseph Bonaparte Gulf
Scott Reef
Pago Mission
Wyndham
Victoria
Birdum
Borroloola
Daly Waters
Sir Edward Pellew Group
King Sound
Collier B.
L. Argyle
Victoria River Downs
C. Lévêque
King Leopold Ra.
Mt Ord 936
Kimberley Plateau
Ord
Newcastle Waters
Wave Hill
Powell Creek
Barkly Tableland
Rowley Shoals
Derby
Broome
Fitzroy
Fitzroy Crossing
Hall's Creek
NORTHERN TERRITORY
Lagrange
Eighty Mile Beach
Sturt Cr.
Tennant Creek
Port Hedland
Great Sandy Desert
De Grey
Shay Gap
Barrow Creek
Monte Bello Is
Barrow I.
Dampier
Roebourne
Marble Bar
Fortescue
Nullagine
L. Mackay
North West C.
Onslow
Hamersley Ra.
Wittenoom
Mt. Bruce 1226
Paraburdoo
Newman
L. Disappointment
Macdonnell Ranges
Mt. Ziel 1510
Alice Springs
Ashburton
AUSTRALIA
Gibson Desert
Petermann Ra.
Barlee Ra.
WESTERN AUSTRALIA
Finke
Simpson Desert
L. McLeod
Mt. Augustus 1106
Lyons
Mt Aloysius 987
Tomkinson Ra
Musgrave Ra.
Mt Woodroffe 1440
Carnarvon
Gascoyne
L. Carnegie
L. Wells
Lake Eyre
Shark B.
Wiluna
Oodnadatta
Dirk Hartog I.
Murchison
Meekatharra
Great Victoria Desert
L. Eyre
Cue
Sandstone
Coober Pedy
SOUTH AUSTRALIA
Northampton
Mt Magnet
Leonora
Houtman Abrolhos
Mullewa
L. Barlee
Geraldton
Dongara
L. Moore
Ooldea
Tarcoola
L. Torrens
Woomera
Rawlinna
Forrest
Kalgoorlie
Nullarbor Plain
L. Everard
Moora
Bencubbin
Coolgardie
Penong
L. Gairdner
Goomalling
Bullfinch
Southern Cross
Eyre
Ceduna
Gawler Ranges
Merredin
Iron Knob
Perth
Northam
Corrigin
Norseman
Whyalla
Fremantle
Narrogin
Great Australian Bight
Flinders I.
Eyre Pen.
Pinjarra
Collie
Wagin
Esperance
Spencer Gulf
Bunbury
Katanning
C. Pasley
Port Lincoln
C. Naturaliste
Busselton
Bluff Knoll 1110
Arch. of the Recherche
Augusta
Manjimup
C. Knob
Investigator St
C. Leeuwin
Albany
Kangaroo I.
110
120
130
10
20
30
40

200   400   600   800 km

200   400 mils

Gulf of Papua
Daru
Saibai I.
Popondetta **PAPUA**
Port Moresby
Kokoda
D'Entrecasteaux
Woodlark
Torres Strait
C. York
Wales
Somerset
NEW GUINEA
Owen Stanley Range
Kupiano
Alotau
Samarai
Misima Louisiade
Arch.
Tagula
Rossel

New Georgia   Santa Isabel   **SOLOMON ISLANDS**
Malaita   Stewart Is.
Florida Is.
Guadalcanal   Honiara   Maramasike
San Cristobal
Rennell

Cape
C. Grenville
York
Iron Range
Coen
Peninsula
Mitchell River
Laura
Cooktown

Coral Sea Island Territories
Willis Group

C   o   r   a   l

Mt Bartle Frere 1612
Cairns
Innisfail
Ravenshoe
Forsayth
Palm Is.
Ingham
Townsville
Charters Towers
Hughenden
Ayr
Proserpine
Collinsville
Bowen

S   e   a

Coringa Is.

Marion Reef
Iles Chesterfield (Fr.)

Recifs d'Entrecasteaux
Iles Belep
Muéo   Uvéa
Nouvelle Calédonie
Bourail
Noumea
Ile des Pins

Richmond
Winton
Normanton
Gregory Range
Mackay
Sarina
Northumberland Is.
Swain Reefs
Bellona Reefs

QUEENSLAND
Clermont
Longreach
Emerald
Barcaldine   Mount Morgan
Blackall
Rockhampton
Gladstone
Cato
Tropic of Capricorn

Windorah
Theodore
Taroom
Bundaberg
Fraser I. or Gt Sandy I.
Maryborough
Gympie

P   A   C   I   F   I   C

Quilpie
Charleville
Roma
Milparinka
Paroo
Cunnamulla
St George
Toowoomba
Dalby
Mitchell
Warwick
Brisbane
Ipswich

O   C   E   A   N

Bourke
Walgett
Moree
Goondiwindi
Stanthorpe
Glen Innes
Casino
Lismore
Grafton

Wilcannia
Broken Hill
Cobar
Narrabri
Armidale
Tamworth
Port Macquarie

Norfolk I. (Aust.)

Menindee
Ivanhoe
Nyngan
Dubbo
Mt Barrington 1585
Taree
Lord Howe I. (Aust.)

NEW SOUTH WALES
Cessnock
Maitland
Newcastle
Orange
Bathurst   Lithgow

Griffith
Sydney
Wollongong

Hay
Wagga Wagga
Canberra
Goulburn

Deniliquin
Albury
Kosciuszko 2230
Bombala
C. Howe

Murray
Shepparton
Bendigo
Australian Alps

VICTORIA
Ballarat
Melbourne
Morwell
Sale
Bairnsdale

Geelong
Colac
Wonthaggi
Wilson's Prom.

King I.   **Bass Strait**
Furneaux Group
Flinders I.
C. Barren

T   A   S   M   A   N

C. Grim
Smithton
Burnie
Devonport
Queenstown
Launceston
St Mary's

S   E   A

Mt Ossa 1617
TASMANIA
Geeveston
Hobart

South West C.   South East C.

NEW ZEALAND
C. Farewell
Westport   Nelson
South Island
Greymouth

150   160

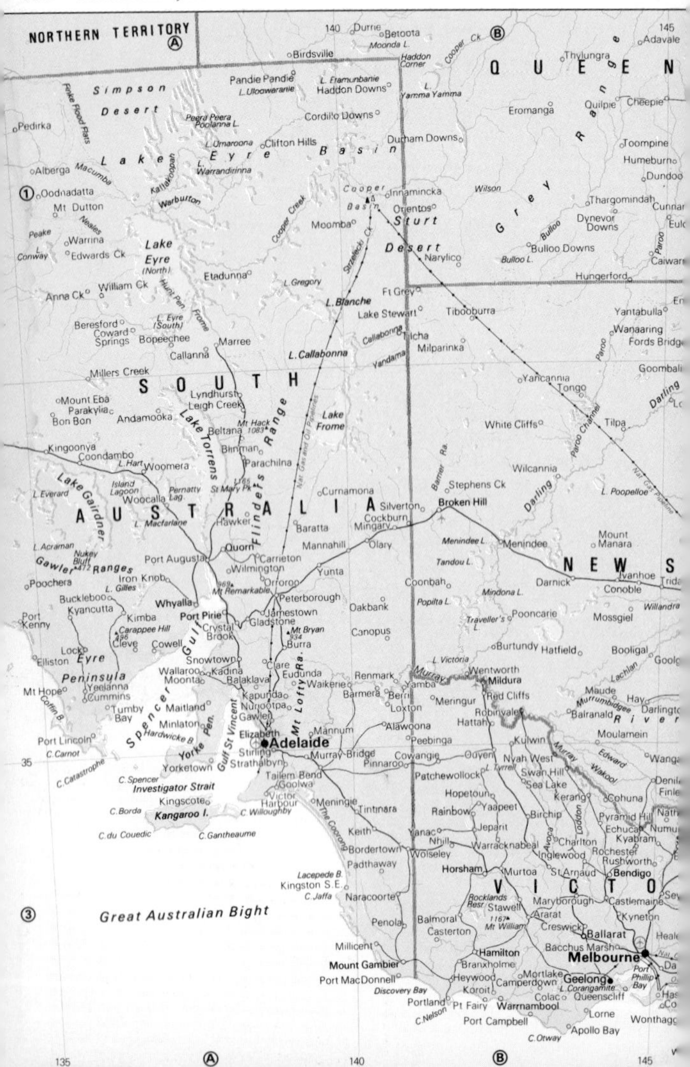

NORTHERN TERRITORY
A
B
140
145
135
35
1
3
Durrie
Betoota
Moonda L.
Birdsville
Haddon Corner
Cooper Ck
Adavale
Thylungra
QUEENSLAND
Simpson Desert
Pandie Pandie
L. Ulloowaranie
L. Framunbanie
Haddon Downs
L. Yamma Yamma
Eromanga
Quilpie
Cheepie
Pedirka
Peera Peera Poolanna L.
Cordillo Downs
Durham Downs
Toompine
L. Umaroona
Clifton Hills
Lake Eyre Basin
Humeburn
Alberga
Macumba
L. Warrandirinna
Dundoo
Kallakoopah
Oodnadatta
Warburton
Cooper Basin
Innamincka
Wilson
Grey Range
Thargomindah
Cunnamulla
Mt Dutton
Neales
Cooper Creek
Orientos
Sturt Desert
Dynevor Downs
Peake
Warrina
Moomba
Strzelecki Ck
Bulloo
Paroo
L. Conway
Edwards Ck
Lake Eyre (North)
Narylico
Bulloo Downs
Bulloo L.
Caiwarro
Etadunna
Hungerford
William Ck
L. Gregory
Anna Ck
Hunt Pen.
Ft Grey
L. Blanche
Lake Stewart
Tibooburra
Yantabulla
Beresford
L. Eyre (South)
Frome
Wanaaring
Coward Springs
Bopeechee
Callabonna
Tilcha
Fords Bridge
Marree
Milparinka
Callanna
L. Callabonna
Yandama
Millers Creek
SOUTH AUSTRALIA
Goombalie
Yancannia
Tongo
Darling
Lyndhurst
Mount Eba
Leigh Creek
Parakylia
Lake Frome
Bon Bon
Andamooka
Lake Torrens
Mt Hack 1083
White Cliffs
Tilpa
Beltana
Flinders Range
Paroo Channel
Kingoonya
Blinman
Nat. Gas and Oil Pipelines
Coondambo
Barrier Ra.
L. Hart
Parachilna
Woomera
Wilcannia
Lake Gairdner
Island Lagoon
Pernatty Lag.
St Mary Pk 1165
Curnamona
Stephens Ck
L. Everard
Woocalla
Silverton
Broken Hill
L. Poopelloe
Nat. Gas Pipeline
L. Macfarlane
Hawker
Cockburn
Baratta
Mingary
Mannahill
Olary
Menindee L.
Menindee
Mount Manara
L. Acraman
Quorn
Nukey Bluff 472
Gawler Ranges
Port Augusta
Carrieton
Tandou L.
NEW S
Wilmington
Yunta
Ivanhoe
Iron Knob
Orroroo
Coonbah
Darnick
Poochera
L. Gilles
969 Mt Remarkable
Mindona L.
Conoble
Buckleboo
Peterborough
Whyalla
Popilta L.
Oakbank
Willandra
Kyancutta
Port Pirie
Jamestown
Gladstone
Pooncarie
Port Kenny
Kimba
Traveller's L.
Mossgiel
Crystal Brook
Mt Bryan 934
Carappee Hill 496
Canopus
Cleve
Cowell
Burra
Burtundy
Hatfield
Booligal
Lock
Gulf
Eyre Peninsula
Snowtown
Clare
L. Victoria
Elliston
Wallaroo
Kadina
Murray
Wentworth
Lachlan
Moonta
Balaklava
Eudunda
Renmark
Mildura
Yeelanna
Waikerie
Yamba
Mt Hope
Cummins
Kapunda
Barmera
Berri
Red Cliffs
Maude
Hay
Coffin B.
Spencer
Maitland
Mt Lofty Ra.
Murrumbidgee
Tumby Bay
Nuriootpa
Loxton
Meringur
Robinvale
Balranald
Darlington Point
Gawler
River
Minlaton
Yorke Pen.
Gulf St Vincent
Hattah
Hardwicke B.
Alawoona
Port Lincoln
Elizabeth
Mannum
Moulamein
Adelaide
Peebinga
Kulwin
C. Carnot
Stirling
Murray Bridge
Cowangie
Ouyen
Nyah West
Edward
Wanganella
Yorketown
Strathalbyn
Pinnaroo
L. Tyrrell
Swan Hill
Wakool
C. Catastrophe
Tailem Bend
Patchewollock
Sea Lake
Deniliquin
C. Spencer
Goolwa
Finley
Investigator Strait
Victor Harbour
Hopetoun
Kerang
Cohuna
Kingscote
Meningie
Tintinara
Yaapeet
Loddon
C. Borda
Kangaroo I.
C. Willoughby
Rainbow
Birchip
Pyramid Hill
Nathalia
The Coorong
Echuca
Numurkah
C. du Couedic
C. Gantheaume
Jeparit
Avoca
Keith
Yanac
Kyabram
Nhill
Warracknabeal
Charlton
Bordertown
Rochester
Wolseley
Inglewood
Padthaway
Rushworth
Horsham
Murtoa
St Arnaud
Bendigo
Lacepede B.
Kingston S.E.
VICTORIA
C. Jaffa
Naracoorte
Rocklands Resr
Maryborough
Castlemaine
Seymour
Stawell
Great Australian Bight
Ararat
Kyneton
Penola
Balmoral
1167 Mt William
Creswick
Casterton
Ballarat
Healesville
Millicent
Hamilton
Bacchus Marsh
Mount Gambier
Branxholme
Melbourne
Heywood
Mortlake
Geelong
Port Phillip Bay
Port MacDonnell
Koroit
Camperdown
L. Corangamite
Discovery Bay
Colac
Queenscliff
Portland
Pt Fairy
Warrnambool
C. Nelson
Lorne
Port Campbell
Wonthaggi
Apollo Bay
C. Otway

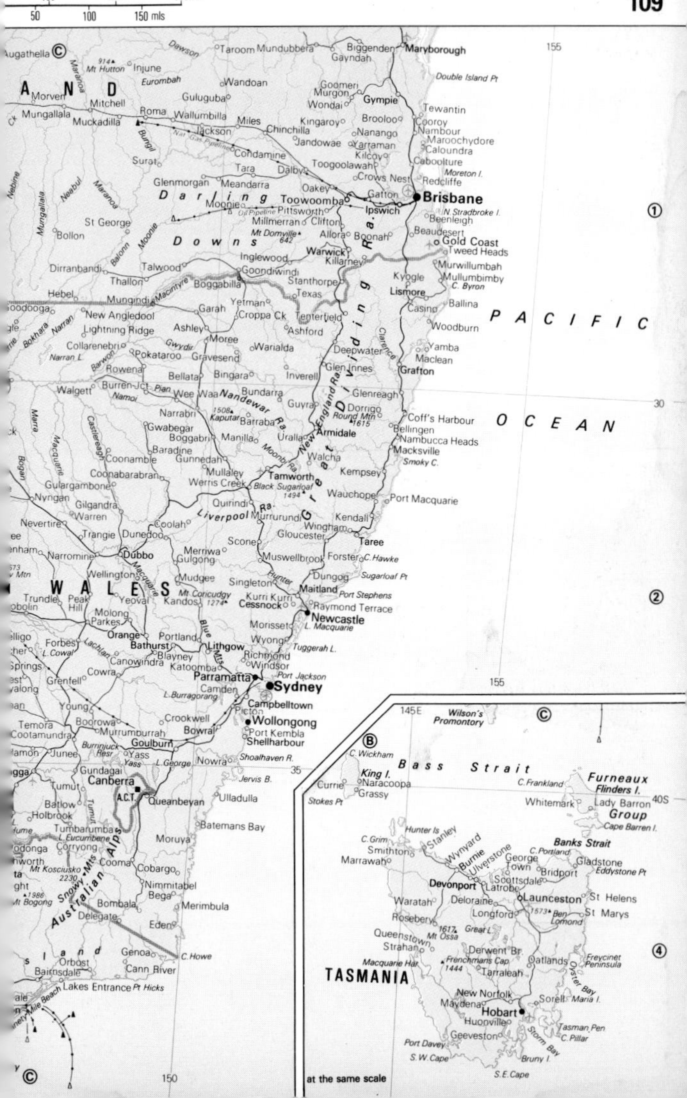

Scale bars: 100, 200, 300 km / 50, 100, 150 mls

QUEENSLAND / NEW SOUTH WALES / TASMANIA region map

Augathella · Mt Hutton 914 · Injune · Taroom · Mundubbera · Biggenden · Gayndah · **Maryborough** · Double Island Pt

Morven · Mitchell · Euromdah · Wandoan · Goomeri · Murgon · Wondai · Tewantin · Coroy · Nambour · Maroochydore · Caloundra · Kilcoy · Woodford · Redcliffe · Moreton I.

AND · Mungallala · Muckadilla · Roma · Wallumbilla · Miles · Chinchilla · Jandowae · Kingaroy · Nanango · Yarraman · Crows Nest · Toogoolawah · Caboolture

Neabul · Surat · Condamine · Dalby · Oakey · **Brisbane** · Ipswich · N. Stradbroke I.

St George · Glenmorgan · Meandarra · Moonie · Pittsworth · **Toowoomba** · Gatton · Beenleigh

Bollon · Dirranbandi · Talwood · Baton · Millmerran · Clifton · Allora · Boonah · **Gold Coast** · Tweed Heads

Hebel · Thallon · Mungindi · Inglewood · Goondiwindi · Warwick · Killarney · Murwillumbah · Mullumbimby · C. Byron

Boggabilla · Texas · Stanthorpe · Kyogle · Lismore · Ballina

New Angledool · Ashley · Garah · Yetman · Croppa Ck · Tenterfield · Casino · Woodburn

Lightning Ridge · Collarenebri · Gwydir · Moree · Ashford · Deepwater · Glen Innes · Yamba · Grafton

Walgett · Rowena · Burren Jct · Wee Waa · Narrabri · Pian · Bellata · Bingara · Inverell · Dorrigo · Round Mtn 1615 · Coff's Harbour

Nandewar Ra · Guyra · Bellingen · Nambucca Heads · Macksville · Smoky C.

Pilliga · Boggabri · Barraba · Manilla · Armidale · Walcha · Kempsey · Port Macquarie

Coonamble · Gwabegar · Baradine · Gunnedah · Mullaley · Tamworth · Black Sugarloaf 1494 · Wauchope

WALES · Gulargambone · Coonabarabran · Werris Creek · Quirindi · Kendall

Nyngan · Gilgandra · Warren · Coolah · Murrurundi · Gloucester · Taree · C. Hawke

Nevertire · Trangie · Dunedoo · Merriwa · Scone · Forster · Tuncurry

Narromine · **Dubbo** · Wellington · Gulgong · Muswellbrook · Dungog · Sugarloaf Pt

Trundle · Mudgee · Singleton · Maitland · Port Stephens

Parkes · Molong · Kandos · Kurri Kurri · Cessnock · **Newcastle** · Raymond Terrace

Forbes · Orange · Portland · Lithgow · Morisset · Wyong · Tuggerah L.

Grenfell · Cowra · Bathurst · Blayney · Canowindra · Richmond · Windsor · **Parramatta** · **Sydney** · Port Jackson

Young · Boorowa · Crookwell · Camden · Campbelltown · Picton · **Wollongong** · Shellharbour

Temora · Cootamundra · Harden · **Canberra** · ACT · Goulburn · Bowral · Kiama · Shoalhaven H.

Wagga Wagga · Junee · Gundagai · Yass · Queanbeyan · Nowra · Jervis B.

Holbrook · Batlow · Tumut · Cooma · Ulladulla

Tumbarumba · Mt Kosciusko 2230 · Nimmitabel · Bega · Batemans Bay

Corryong · Snowy Mtns · Bombala · Merimbula · Moruya

Mt Bogong 1986 · Delegate · Eden · C. Howe

Orbost · Genoa · Cann River · Bairnsdale · Lakes Entrance · Pt Hicks

TASMANIA (at the same scale)

Wilson's Promontory · C. Wickham · King I. · Naracoopa · Grassy · Currie · Stokes Pt

Bass Strait · C. Frankland · **Furneaux** · **Flinders I.** · Lady Barron · Cape Barren I.

Hunter I. · Stanley · Smithton · Wynyard · Burnie · Ulverstone · Bridport · Banks Strait · Eddystone Pt

Marrawah · Waratah · Devonport · Latrobe · Scottsdale · Launceston · St Helens

Queenstown · Mt Ossa 1617 · Deloraine · Longford · Great L. · Ben Lomond 1573 · St Marys

Rosebery · Strahan · Macquarie Hbr · Mt Field 1444 · New Norfolk · Oatlands · Freycinet Peninsula

Frenchmans Cap · Derwent Br · Tarraleah · Sorell · Maria I.

Maydena · **Hobart** · Huonville · Geeveston · Tasman Pen · C. Pillar

Port Davey · S.W. Cape · Bruny I. · S.E. Cape

P A C I F I C   O C E A N

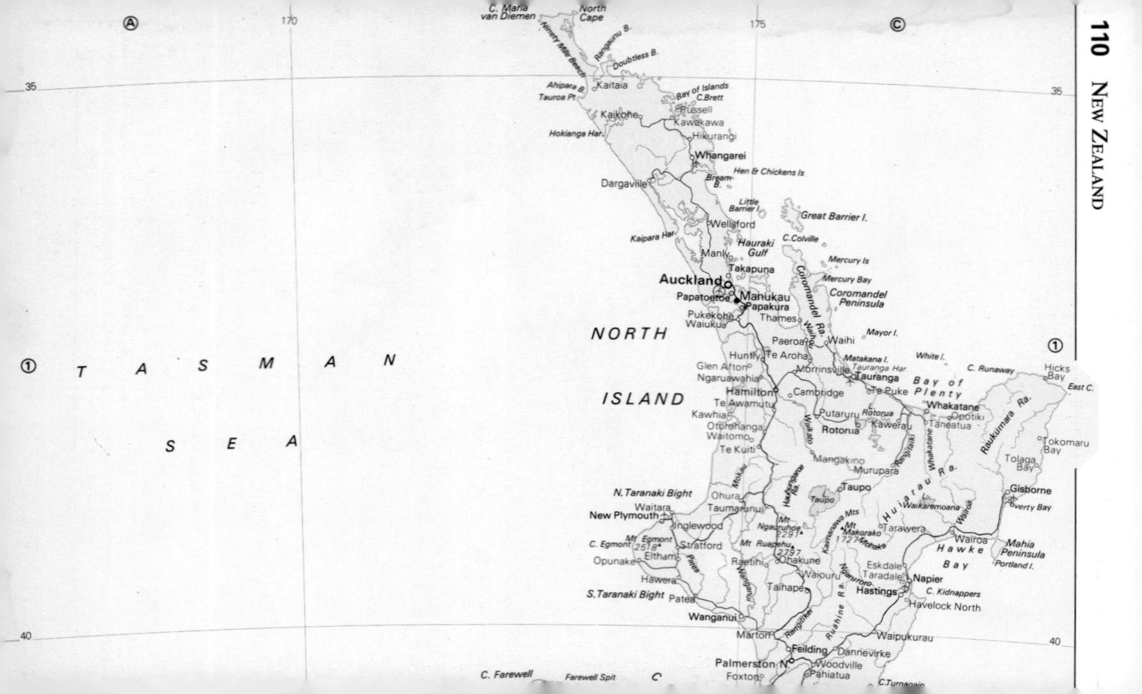
TASMAN SEA
NORTH ISLAND
North Cape
C. Maria van Diemen
Ninety Mile Beach
Rangaunu B.
Doubtless B.
Ahipara B.
Tauroa Pt
Kaitaia
Kaikohe
Hokianga Har.
Bay of Islands
C.Brett
Russell
Kawakawa
Hikurangi
Whangarei
Hen & Chickens Is
Bream B.
Dargaville
Little Barrier I.
Great Barrier I.
Wellsford
Kaipara Har.
Hauraki Gulf
C.Colville
Manly
Mercury Is
Takapuna
Mercury Bay
Auckland
Coromandel Ra.
Coromandel Peninsula
Papatoetoe
Manukau
Papakura
Pukekohe
Waiuku
Thames
Mayor I.
Paeroa
Waihi
Huntly
Te Aroha
Matakana I.
White I.
Glen Afton
Ngaruawahia
Morrinsville
Tauranga Har.
Tauranga
C. Runaway
Hicks Bay
East C.
Hamilton
Cambridge
Te Puke
Bay of Plenty
Te Awamutu
Kawhia
Putaruru
L. Rotorua
Whakatane
Opotiki
Otorohanga
Kawerau
Taneatua
Raukumara Ra.
Waitomo
Rotorua
Tokomaru Bay
Te Kuiti
Waikato
Tolaga Bay
Mangakino
Murupara
Mokau
N.Taranaki Bight
Taupo
L. Taupo
Huiarau Ra.
Gisborne
Poverty Bay
Ohura
Waitara
Taumarunui
L. Waikaremoana
Wairoa
New Plymouth
Inglewood
Mt Ngauruhoe 2291
Kaimanawa Mts
Mt Makorako 1727
Tarawera
Mt Egmont 2518
C. Egmont
Stratford
Mt Ruapehu 2797
Mahia Peninsula
Hawke Bay
Portland I.
Eltham
Opunake
Raetihi
Ohakune
Eskdale
Napier
Taradale
Waiouru
Hawera
Taihape
Hastings
C. Kidnappers
S.Taranaki Bight
Patea
Havelock North
Wanganui
Ruahine Ra.
Rangitikei
Marton
Waipukurau
Feilding
Dannevirke
Palmerston N.
Woodville
Foxton
Pahiatua
C. Farewell
Farewell Spit
C.Turnagain

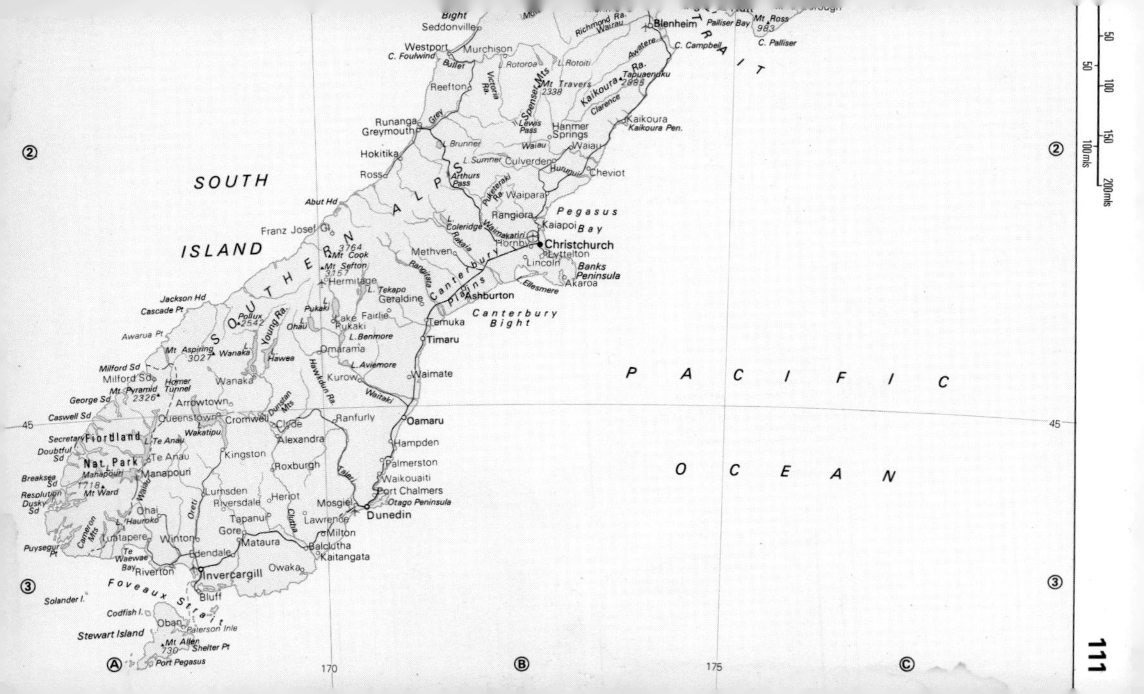

50 100 150 200mls
50 100mls

45

②

③

©

P A C I F I C

O C E A N

®

175

170

45

45

SOUTH

ISLAND

S O U T H E R N

A L P S

T R A I T

Mt. Ross 933
Pallister Bay
C. Palliser
C. Campbell

Blenheim
Kaikoura
Kaikoura Pen.
Cheviot
Pegasus Bay

Seddonville
Westport
C. Foulwind
Murchison
Ballra
Reefton

Murchison

Hanmer
Springs
Hanmer
Rotoroa L.
Rotoiti
Amuri Pass
Mt 2338

Waiau
Waiau
Rangiora
Waipara

Christchurch
Lincoln
Lyttelton
Banks
Peninsula
Akaroa

Victoria Ra.

Greymouth
Runanga
Hokitika
Ross

Brunner L.
Arthurs Pass
Bealey
Sumner L.
Culverden
Coleridge L.
Darfield
Rolleston
Rakaia
Leeston
Ellesmere

Methven
Rakaia
Ashburton

Canterbury
Bight

Abut Hd

Franz Josef
Gn.
Mt Cook 3754
Mt Sefton
2348

Teasman Gl.
Hermitage
Fairlie
L. Benmore
Kurow

Tekapo L.
Tekapo
Geraldine
Pukaki L.
Pukaki
Temuka
Timaru

Waimate
Oamaru

Jackson Hd
Mt Aspiring 3027

Haast Pa.
Haast
Wanaka L.
Hawea
Wanaka
Cromwell
Clyde
Alexandra
Roxburgh

Hamden
Palmerston
Waikouaiti
Port Chalmers
Dunedin
Mosgiel
Waihola

Cascade Pt
Awarua Pt

Hollyford
Milford Sd
Milford
George Sd
Caswell Sd

Te Anau
L.
Mt Earnslaw 2728
Queenstown
Arrowtown
Kingston

Lumsden
Riversdale
Gore
Mataura

Tapanui
Heriot
Clutha R.
Lawrence
Balclutha
Kaitangata
Owaka

Doubtful Sd
Secretary I.
Resolution I.
Breaksea Sd
Dusky Sd

Nat. Park
Fiordland
Manapouri
Manapouri L.
Mt Ward
Te Ao
Te Anau
Mavora

Winton
Otautau

Invercargill
Bluff

Mt Tutoko 2726

Dagg Sd

Puysegur Pt

Oban
Stewart Island
Port Pegasus

Foveaux Strait

Codfish I.
Solander I.
Shelter Pt
Jackson Pt

②

③

②

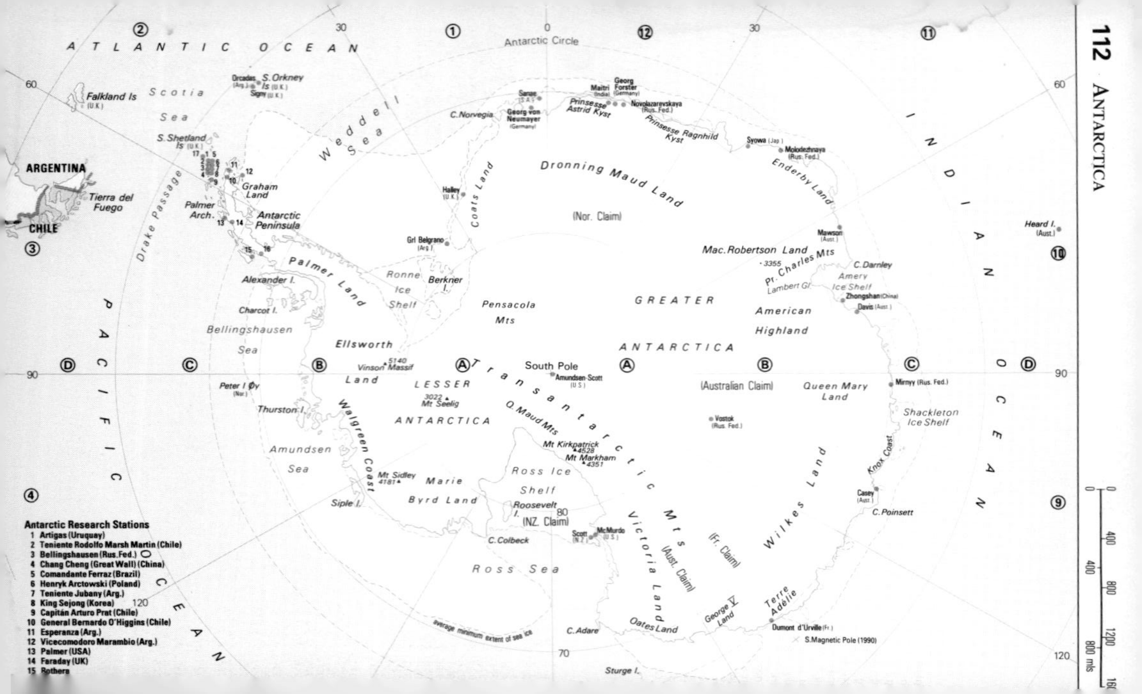
ATLANTIC OCEAN
INDIAN OCEAN
PACIFIC OCEAN
Antarctic Circle
Falkland Is (U.K.)
S. Orkney Is (U.K.)
Orcadas (Arg.)
Signy (U.K.)
Scotia Sea
S. Shetland Is (U.K.)
ARGENTINA
Tierra del Fuego
CHILE
Drake Passage
Weddell Sea
Graham Land
Palmer Arch.
Antarctic Peninsula
Palmer Land
Alexander I.
Charcot I.
Bellingshausen Sea
Peter I Øy (Nor.)
Thurston I.
Amundsen Sea
Ellsworth Land
Vinson Massif 5140
Walgreen Coast
Siple I.
Mt Sidley 4181
Marie Byrd Land
Ronne Ice Shelf
Berkner I.
Grl Belgrano (Arg.)
Halley (U.K.)
Coats Land
C. Norvegia
Sanae (S.A.)
Georg von Neumayer (Germany)
Maitri (India)
Georg Forster (Germany)
Novolazarevskaya (Rus. Fed.)
Prinsesse Astrid Kyst
Prinsesse Ragnhild Kyst
Syowa (Jap.)
Molodezhnaya (Rus. Fed.)
Enderby Land
Dronning Maud Land
(Nor. Claim)
Mawson (Aust.)
Mac. Robertson Land
Pr. Charles Mts
3355
Lambert Gl.
C. Darnley
Amery Ice Shelf
Zhongshan (China)
Davis (Aust.)
Heard I. (Aust.)
Pensacola Mts
GREATER ANTARCTICA
American Highland
South Pole
Amundsen-Scott (U.S.)
LESSER ANTARCTICA
3022 Mt Seelig
Transantarctic Mts
Q. Maud Mts
Mt Kirkpatrick 4528
Mt Markham 4351
Ross Ice Shelf
Roosevelt I.
(NZ. Claim)
Scott (N.Z.)
McMurdo (U.S.)
C. Colbeck
Ross Sea
average minimum extent of sea ice
C. Adare
Sturge I.
Oates Land
Victoria Land
(Aust. Claim)
(Fr. Claim)
George V Land
Terre Adélie
Dumont d'Urville (Fr.)
S. Magnetic Pole (1990)
(Australian Claim)
Vostok (Rus. Fed.)
Queen Mary Land
Mirnyy (Rus. Fed.)
Shackleton Ice Shelf
Knox Coast
Casey (Aust.)
C. Poinsett
Wilkes Land
0 400 800 1200 1600 kms
0 400 800 mls
Antarctic Research Stations
1 Artigas (Uruguay)
2 Teniente Rodolfo Marsh Martin (Chile)
3 Bellingshausen (Rus. Fed.)
4 Chang Cheng (Great Wall) (China)
5 Comandante Ferraz (Brazil)
6 Henryk Arctowski (Poland)
7 Teniente Jubany (Arg.)
8 King Sejong (Korea)
9 Capitán Arturo Prat (Chile)
10 General Bernardo O'Higgins (Chile)
11 Esperanza (Arg.)
12 Vicecomodoro Marambio (Arg.)
13 Palmer (USA)
14 Faraday (UK)
15 Rothera

Index

In the index, the first number refers to the page, and the following letter and number to the section of the map in which the index entry can be found. For example, 48C2 **Paris** means that Paris can be found on page 48 where column C and row 2 meet.

Abbreviations used in the index

'ghan	Afghanistan	Hung	Hungary	Pol	Poland	Arch	Archipelago
b	Albania	Ind	Indonesia	Port	Portugal	B	Bay
g	Algeria	Irish Rep	Ireland	Rom	Romania	C	Cape
nt	Antarctica	Leb	Lebanon	Russian Fed	Russian	Chan	Channel
'g	Argentina	Lib	Liberia		Federation	Gl	Glacier
ıst	Australia	Liech	Liechtenstein	S Arabia	Saudi Arabia	I(s)	Island(s)
ıng	Bangladesh	Lux	Luxembourg	Scot	Scotland	Lg	Lagoon
lg	Belgium	Madag	Madagascar	Sen	Senegal	L	Lake
l	Bolivia	Malay	Malaysia	S Africa	South Africa	Mt(s)	Mountain(s)
lg	Bulgaria	Maur	Mauritania	Switz	Switzerland	O	Ocean
rk	Burkina	Mor	Morocco	Tanz	Tanzania	P	Pass
mb	Cambodia	Mozam	Mozambique	Thai	Thailand	Pen	Peninsula
n	Canada	Neth	Netherlands	Turk	Turkey	Plat	Plateau
R	Central African Republic	NZ	New Zealand	USA	United States	Pt	Point
n	Denmark	Nic	Nicaragua		of America	Res	Reservoir
m Rep	Dominican Republic	N Ire	Northern Ireland	Urug	Uruguay	R	River
Sal	El Salvador	Nig	Nigeria	Ven	Venezuela	S	Sea
g	England	Nor	Norway	Viet	Vietnam	Sd	Sound
Guinea	Equatorial Guinea	Pak	Pakistan	Yugos	Yugoslavia	Str	Strait
ı	Ethiopia	PNG	Papua New Guinea	Zim	Zimbabwe	V	Valley
ı	Finland	Par	Paraguay				
rm	Germany	Phil	Philippines				

A

57B2 **Aachen** Germany
46C1 **Aalst** Belg
38K6 **Äänekoski** Fin
47C1 **Aarau** Switz
47B1 **Aare** *R* Switz
72A3 **Aba** China
97C4 **Aba** Nig
99D2 **Aba** Zaïre
91A3 **Abādān** Iran
90B3 **Abādeh** Iran
96B1 **Abadla** Alg
35B1 **Abaeté** Brazil
35B1 **Abaeté** *R* Brazil
31B2 **Abaetetuba** Brazil
72D1 **Abagnar Qi** China
97C4 **Abakaliki** Nig
63B2 **Abakan** Russian Fed
97C3 **Abala** Niger
96C2 **Abalessa** Alg
32C6 **Abancay** Peru
90B3 **Abarqū** Iran
74E2 **Abashiri** Japan
74E2 **Abashiri-wan** *B* Japan
71F4 **Abau** PNG
99D2 **Abaya** *L* Eth
99D1 **Abbai** *R* Eth
99E1 **Abbe** *L* Eth
48C1 **Abbeville** France
19B4 **Abbeville** Louisiana, USA
17B1 **Abbeville** S Carolina, USA
45B2 **Abbeyfeale** Irish Rep
47C2 **Abbiategrasso** Italy
20B1 **Abbotsford** Can
84C2 **Abbottabad** Pak
61H3 **Abdulino** Russian Fed
98C1 **Abéché** Chad
39F7 **Åbenrå** Den
97C4 **Abeokuta** Nig
99D2 **Abera** Eth
43B3 **Aberaeron** Wales
15C3 **Aberdeen** Maryland, USA
100B4 **Aberdeen** S Africa
44C3 **Aberdeen** Scot
8D2 **Aberdeen** S Dakota, USA
8A2 **Aberdeen** Washington, USA
4J3 **Aberdeen L** Can
44C3 **Aberfeldy** Scot
43C4 **Abergavenny** Wales
43B3 **Aberystwyth** Wales
81C4 **Abhā** S Arabia
90A2 **Abhar** Iran
97B4 **Abidjan** Ivory Coast
18A2 **Abilene** Kansas, USA
9D3 **Abilene** Texas, USA
43D4 **Abingdon** Eng
7B4 **Abitibi** *R* Can
7C5 **Abitibi,L** Can
61F5 **Abkhazskaya Respublika**, Georgia
84C2 **Abohar** India
97C4 **Abomey** Benin
98B2 **Abong Mbang** Cam
79A4 **Aborlan** Phil
98B1 **Abou Deïa** Chad
91A4 **Abqaiq** S Arabia
50A2 **Abrantes** Port
95C2 **Abri** Sudan
106A3 **Abrolhos** *Is* Aust
8B2 **Absaroka Range** *Mts* USA
91B5 **Abū al Abyad** *I* UAE
91A4 **Abū 'Ali** *I* S Arabia
91B5 **Abū Dhabi** UAE
95C3 **Abu Hamed** Sudan
97C4 **Abuja** Nig
33D5 **Abunã** Brazil
32D6 **Abunã** *R* Bol
93D3 **Abú Sukhayr** Iraq
111B2 **Abut Head** *C* NZ
95C3 **Abu 'Urug** *Well* Sudan
99D1 **Abuye Meda** *Mt* Eth
99C1 **Abu Zabad** Sudan
99D2 **Abwong** Sudan
56B1 **Åby** Den
94B3 **Aby 'Aweigîla** *Well* Egypt
99C2 **Abyei** Sudan
24B2 **Acambaro** Mexico
24B2 **Acaponeta** Mexico
24B3 **Acapulco** Mexico
31D2 **Acaraú** Brazil
32D2 **Acarigua** Ven
24C3 **Acatlán** Mexico
23B2 **Acatzingo** Mexico
97B4 **Accra** Ghana
85D4 **Achalpur** India
29B4 **Achao** Chile
47D1 **Achensee** *L* Austria
46E2 **Achern** Germany
41A3 **Achill** *I* Irish Rep
63B2 **Achinsk** Russian Fed
53C3 **Acireale** Italy
26C2 **Acklins** *I* Caribbean S
32C6 **Acobamba** Peru
29B2 **Aconcagua** *Mt* Chile
31D3 **Acopiara** Brazil
88B4 **Açores** *Is* Atlantic O
A Coruña = La Coruña
47C2 **Acqui** Italy
108A2 **Acraman,L** Aust
Acre = 'Akko
32C5 **Acre** State, Brazil
22C3 **Acton** USA
23B1 **Actopan** Mexico
19A3 **Ada** USA
50B1 **Adaja** *R* Spain
91C5 **Adam** Oman
35A2 **Adamantina** Brazil
98B2 **Adamaoua** Region, Nig/Cam
47D1 **Adamello** *Mt* Italy
16C1 **Adams** USA
87B3 **Adam's Bridge** India/Sri Lanka
13D2 **Adams L** Can
8A2 **Adams,Mt** USA
87C3 **Adam's Peak** *Mt* Sri Lanka
81C4 **'Adan** Yemen
92C2 **Adana** Turk
60D5 **Adapazari** Turk
112B7 **Adare,C** Ant
108B1 **Adavale** Aust
47C2 **Adda** *R* Italy
91A4 **Ad Dahna'** Region, S Arabia
96A2 **Ad Dakhla** Mor
81C4 **Ad Dālī'** Yemen
91B4 **Ad Damman** S Arabia
91A4 **Ad Dibdibah** Region, S Arabia
91A5 **Ad Dilam** S Arabia
91A5 **Ad Dir'iyah** S Arabia
93D3 **Ad Dīwanīyah** Iraq
93D3 **Ad Duwayd** S Arabia
106C4 **Adelaide** Aust
4J3 **Adelaide Pen** Can
22D3 **Adelanto** USA
Aden = 'Adan
81C4 **Aden,G of** Yemen/Somalia
97C3 **Aderbissinat** Niger
94C2 **Adhra** Syria
71E4 **Adi** *I* Indon
52B1 **Adige** *R* Italy
99D1 **Adigrat** Eth
85D5 **Adilābād** India
20B2 **Adin** USA
15D2 **Adirondack Mts** USA
99D2 **Ādīs Ābeba** Eth
95C3 **Adi Ugai** Eritrea
93C2 **Adıyaman** Turk
54C1 **Adjud** Rom
4E4 **Admiralty I** USA
6B2 **Admiralty Inlet** *B* Can
87B1 **Ādoni** India
48B3 **Adour** *R* France
96A2 **Adrar** Region, Maur
96C2 **Adrar** *Mts* Alg
96A2 **Adrar Soutouf** Region, Mor
98C1 **Adré** Chad
95A2 **Adri** Libya
47E2 **Adria** Italy

14B2 **Adrian** Michigan, USA
52B2 **Adriatic S** S Europe
99D1 **Ādwa** Eth
97B4 **Adzopé** Ivory Coast
55B3 **Aegean** *S* Greece
80E2 **Afghanistan** Republic, Asia
99E2 **Afgooye** Somalia
97C4 **Afikpo** Nig
38G6 **Åfjord** Nor
96C1 **Aflou** Alg
99E2 **Afmadu** Somalia
97A3 **Afollé** Region, Maur
94B2 **Afula** Israel
92B2 **Afyon** Turk
95A3 **Agadem** Niger
97C3 **Agadez** Niger
96B1 **Agadir** Mor
85D4 **Agar** India
86C2 **Agartala** India
20B1 **Agassiz** Can
97B4 **Agboville** Ivory Coast
93E1 **Agdam** Azerbaijan
75B1 **Agematsu** Japan
48C3 **Agen** France
90A3 **Agha Jārī** Iran
96A2 **Aghwinit** *Well* Mor
47D2 **Agno** *R* Italy
47E1 **Agordo** Italy
48C3 **Agout** *R* France
85D3 **Āgra** India
93D2 **Ağri** Turk
53C2 **Agri** *R* Italy
53B3 **Agrigento** Italy
55B3 **Agrínion** Greece
34A3 **Agrio** *R* Chile
53B2 **Agropoli** Italy
61H2 **Agryz** Russian Fed
6E3 **Agto** Greenland
27D3 **Aguadilla** Puerto Rico
24B1 **Agua Prieta** Mexico
24B2 **Aguascalientes** Mexico
23A1 **Aguascalientes** State, Mexico
35C1 **Aguas Formosas** Brazil
50A1 **Agueda** Port
96C3 **Aguelhok** Mali
50B2 **Aguilas** Spain
23A2 **Aguililla** Mexico
100B4 **Agulhas,C** S Africa
79C4 **Agusan** *R* Phil
Ahaggar = Hoggar
93E2 **Ahar** Iran
110B1 **Ahipara B** NZ
85C4 **Ahmadābād** India
87A1 **Ahmadnagar** India
99E2 **Ahmar** *Mts* Eth
46D1 **Ahr** *R* Germany
46D1 **Ahrgebirge** Region, Germany
23A1 **Ahuacatlán** Mexico
23A1 **Ahualulco** Mexico
39G7 **Åhus** Sweden
90B2 **Ahuvān** Iran
90A3 **Ahvāz** Iran
26A4 **Aiajuela** Costa Rica
47B1 **Aigle** Switz
47B2 **Aiguille d'Arves** *Mt* France
47B2 **Aiguille de la Grand Sassière** *Mt* France
75B1 **Aikawa** Japan
17B1 **Aiken** USA
73A5 **Ailao Shan** *Upland* China
35C1 **Aimorés** Brazil
96B1 **Aïn Beni Mathar** Mor
95B2 **Ain Dalla** *Well* Egypt
51C2 **Aïn el Hadjel** Alg
95A3 **Aïn Galakka** Chad
96B1 **Aïn Sefra** Alg
92B4 **'Ain Sukhna** Egypt
75A2 **Aioi** Japan
96B2 **Aioun Abd el Malek** *Well* Maur
97B3 **Aïoun El Atrouss** Maur
30C2 **Aiquile** Bol
97C3 **Aïr** *Desert Region* Niger
13E2 **Airdrie** Can
46B1 **Aire** France
42D3 **Aire** *R* Eng
46C2 **Aire** *R* France
6C3 **Airforce I** Can
47C1 **Airolo** Switz
4E3 **Aishihik** Can
12G2 **Aishihik L** Can
46B2 **Aisne** Department, France
49C2 **Aisne** *R* France
71F4 **Aitape** PNG
58D1 **Aiviekste** *R* Latvia
72B2 **Aixa Zuogi** China
49D3 **Aix-en-Provence** France
47A2 **Aix-les-Bains** France
86B2 **Aiyar Res** India
55B3 **Aíyion** Greece
55B3 **Aíyna** *I* Greece
86C2 **Āīzawl** India
100A3 **Aizeb** *R* Namibia
74E3 **Aizu-Wakamatsu** Japan
52A2 **Ajaccio** Corse
23B2 **Ajalpan** Mexico
95B1 **Ajdābiyā** Libya
74E2 **Ajigasawa** Japan
94B2 **Ajlūn** Jordan
91C4 **Ajman** UAE
85C3 **Ajmer** India
9B3 **Ajo** USA
23A2 **Ajuchitan** Mexico
55C3 **Ak** *R* Turk
75B1 **Akaishi-sanchi** *Mts* Japan
87B1 **Akalkot** India
111B2 **Akaroa** NZ
75A2 **Akashi** Japan
61J3 **Akbulak** Russian Fed
93C2 **Akçakale** Turk
96A2 **Akchar** *Watercourse* Maur
55C3 **Akdağ** *Mt* Turk
98C2 **Aketi** Zaïre
93D1 **Akhalkalaki** Georgia
93D1 **Akhalsikhe** Georgia
55B3 **Akharnái** Greece
12D3 **Akhiok** USA
92A2 **Akhisar** Turk
58D1 **Akhiste** Latvia
95C2 **Akhmîm** Egypt
61G4 **Akhtubinsk** Russian Fed
60D4 **Akhtyrka** Ukraine
75A2 **Aki** Japan
7B4 **Akimiski I** Can
74E3 **Akita** Japan
96A3 **Akjoujt** Maur
94B2 **'Akko** Israel
4E3 **Aklavik** USA
97B3 **Aklé Aouana** *Desert Region* Maur
99D2 **Akobo** Sudan
99D2 **Akobo** *R* Sudan
84B1 **Akoha** Afghan
85D4 **Akola** India
85D4 **Akot** India
6D3 **Akpatok I** Can
55B3 **Ákra Kafirévs** *C* Greece
55B3 **Ákra Maléa** *C* Greece
38A2 **Akranes** Iceland
55C3 **Ákra Sídheros** *C* Greece
55B3 **Ákra Spátha** *C* Greece
55B3 **Ákra Taínaron** *C* Greece
10B2 **Akron** USA
94A1 **Akrotiri B** Cyprus
84D1 **Aksai Chin** *Mts* China
92B2 **Aksaray** Turk
61H3 **Aksay** Kazakhstan
84D1 **Aksayquin Hu** *L* China
92B2 **Akşehir** Turk
92B2 **Akseki** Turk
63D2 **Aksenovo Zilovskoye** Russian Fed
68D1 **Aksha** Russian Fed
82C1 **Aksu** China
61H5 **Aktau** Kazakhstan
65J5 **Aktogay** Kazakhstan
61J4 **Aktumsyk** Kazakhstan
65G4 **Aktyubinsk** Kazakhstan
38B1 **Akureyri** Iceland
Akyab = Sittwe
65K5 **Akzhal** Kazakhstan
11B3 **Alabama** State, USA
11B3 **Alabama** *R* USA
17A1 **Alabaster** USA
92C2 **Ala Dağlari** *Mts* Turk
61F5 **Alagir** Russian Fed
47B2 **Alagna** Italy
31D3 **Alagoas** State, Brazil
31D4 **Alagoinhas** Brazil
51B1 **Alagón** Spain
93E4 **Al Ahmadi** Kuwait
25D3 **Alajuela** Costa Rica
12B2 **Alakanuk** USA
38L5 **Alakurtti** Russian Fed
93E3 **Al Amārah** Iraq
21A2 **Alameda** USA
23B1 **Alamo** Mexico
9C3 **Alamogordo** USA
9C3 **Alamosa** USA
39H6 **Åland** *I* Fin
92B2 **Alanya** Turk
17B1 **Alapaha** *R* USA
65H4 **Alapayevsk** Russian Fed
92A2 **Alaşehir** Turk
68C3 **Ala Shan** *Mts* China
4C3 **Alaska** State, USA
4D4 **Alaska,G of** USA
12C3 **Alaska Pen** USA
4C3 **Alaska Range** *Mts* USA
52A2 **Alassio** Italy
12D1 **Alatna** *R* USA
61G3 **Alatyr** Russian Fed
108B2 **Alawoona** Aust
91C5 **Al'Ayn** UAE
82B2 **Alayskiy Khrebet** *Mts* Tajikistan
49D3 **Alba** Italy
92C2 **Al Bāb** Syria
51B2 **Albacete** Spain
50A1 **Alba de Tormes** Spain
93D2 **Al Badi** Iraq
54B1 **Alba Iulia** Rom
54A2 **Albania** Republic, Europe
106A4 **Albany** Aust
17B1 **Albany** Georgia, USA
15D2 **Albany** New York, USA
8A2 **Albany** Oregon, USA
7B4 **Albany** *R* Can
34B2 **Albardón** Arg
91C5 **Al Batinah** Region, Oman
71F5 **Albatross B** Aust
95B1 **Al Bayḍā** Libya
11C3 **Albemarle Sd** USA
50B1 **Alberche** *R* Spain
108A1 **Alberga** Aust
46B1 **Albert** France
5G4 **Alberta** Province, Can
99D2 **Albert,L** Uganda/Zaïre
10A2 **Albert Lea** USA
99D2 **Albert Nile** *R* Uganda
49D2 **Albertville** France
48C3 **Albi** France
18B1 **Albia** USA
33G2 **Albina** Suriname
14B2 **Albion** Michigan, USA
15C2 **Albion** New York, USA
92C4 **Al Bi'r** S Arabia
91A5 **Al Biyadh** Region, S Arabia
50B2 **Alborán** *I* Spain
39G7 **Ålborg** Den
93D3 **Al Bū Kamāl** Syria
47C1 **Albula** *R* Switz
9C3 **Albuquerque** USA
91C5 **Al Buraymi** Oman
95A1 **Al Burayqah** Libya
95B1 **Al Burdī** Libya
107D4 **Albury** Aust
93E3 **Al Buşayyah** Iraq
50B1 **Alcalá de Henares** Spain
53B3 **Alcamo** Italy
51B1 **Alcaniz** Spain
31C2 **Alcântara** Brazil
50B2 **Alcaraz** Spain
50B2 **Alcázar de San Juan** Spain
51B2 **Alcira** Spain
35D1 **Alcobaça** Brazil
50B1 **Alcolea de Pinar** Spain
51B2 **Alcoy** Spain
51C2 **Alcudia** Spain
89J8 **Aldabra** *Is* Indian O
63E2 **Aldan** Russian Fed
63E2 **Aldanskoye Nagor'y** *Upland* Russian Fed
43E3 **Aldeburgh** Eng
48B2 **Alderney** *I* UK
43D4 **Aldershot** Eng
97A3 **Aleg** Maur
30E4 **Alegrete** Brazil
34C2 **Alejandro Roca** Arg
30H6 **Alejandro Selkirk** *I* Chile
63G2 **Aleksandrovsk Sakhalinskiy** Russian Fed
65J4 **Alekseyevka** Kazakhstan
60E3 **Aleksin** Russian Fed
58B1 **Ålem** Sweden
35C2 **Além Paraíba** Brazil
49C2 **Alençon** France
21C4 **Alenuihaha Chan** Hawaiian Is
Aleppo = Ḥalab
6D1 **Alert** Can
49C3 **Alès** France
52A2 **Alessandria** Italy
64B3 **Ålesund** Nor
12C3 **Aleutian Range** *Mts* USA
4E4 **Alexander Arch** USA
100A3 **Alexander Bay** S Africa
17A1 **Alexander City** USA
112C3 **Alexander I** Ant
111A3 **Alexandra** NZ
29G8 **Alexandra,C** South Georgia
6C2 **Alexandra Fjord** Ca
95B1 **Alexandria** Egypt
11A3 **Alexandria** Louisiana, USA
10A2 **Alexandria** Minnesota, USA
10C3 **Alexandria** Virginia, USA
55C2 **Alexandroúpolis** Greece
13C2 **Alexis Creek** Can
94B2 **Aley** Leb
65K4 **Aleysk** Russian Fed
93D3 **Al Fallūjah** Iraq
51B1 **Alfaro** Spain
54C2 **Alfatar** Bulg
93E3 **Al Fāw** Iraq
35B2 **Alfensas** Brazil
55B3 **Alfiós** *R* Greece
47D2 **Alfonsine** Italy
35C2 **Alfonzo Cláudio** Brazil
35C2 **Alfredo Chaves** Br
61J4 **Alga** Kazakhstan
34B3 **Algarrobo del Águil** Arg
50A2 **Algeciras** Spain
96C1 **Alger** Alg
96B2 **Algeria** Republic, Africa
53A2 **Alghero** Sardegna
Algiers = Alger
15C1 **Algonquin Park** Ca
91C5 **Al Hadd** Oman
93D3 **Al Hadithah** Iraq
92C3 **Al Hadithah** S Arab
93D2 **Al Haḍr** Iraq

91C5 **Al Hajar al Gharbī** *Mts* Oman
91C5 **Al Hajar ash Sharqī** *Mts* Oman
93C3 **Al Hamad** *Desert Region* Jordan/ S Arabia
93E4 **Al Haniyah** *Desert Region* Iraq
91A5 **Al Harīq** S Arabia
93C3 **Al Harrah** *Desert Region* S Arabia
95A2 **Al Harūj al Aswad** *Upland* Libya
91A4 **Al Hasa** Region, S Arabia
93D2 **Al Hasakah** Syria
93C4 **Al Hawjā'** S Arabia
93E3 **Al Hayy** Iraq
94C2 **Al Hījānah** Syria
93D3 **Al Hillah** Iraq
91A5 **Al Hillah** S Arabia
96B1 **Al Hoceima** Mor
91A4 **Al Hufūf** S Arabia
91B5 **Al Humrah** Region, UAE
91C5 **Al Huwatsah** Oman
90A2 **Aliābad** Iran
91C4 **Aliabad** Iran
55B2 **Aliákmon** *R* Greece
93E3 **Alī al Gharbī** Iraq
87A1 **Alībāg** India
51B2 **Alicante** Spain
9D4 **Alice** USA
06C3 **Alice Springs** Aust
53B3 **Alicudi** *I* Italy
84D3 **Aligarh** India
90A3 **Aligūdarz** Iran
84B2 **Ali-Khel** Afghan
55C3 **Alimniá** *I* Greece
86B1 **Alīpur Duār** India
14B2 **Aliquippa** USA
22B2 **Alisal** USA
93C3 **Al' Isawiyah** S Arabia
00B4 **Aliwal North** S Africa
95B2 **Al Jaghbūb** Libya
93D3 **Al Jālamīd** S Arabia
95B2 **Al Jawf** Libya
93C4 **Al Jawf** S Arabia
93D2 **Al Jazīrah** *Desert Region* Syria/Iraq
50A2 **Aljezur** Port
91A4 **Al Jubayl** S Arabia
91C5 **Al Kāmil** Oman
93D2 **Al Khābūr** *R* Syria
91C5 **Al Khābūrah** Oman
93D3 **Al Khālis** Iraq
91C4 **Al Khasab** Oman
91B4 **Al Khawr** Qatar
95A1 **Al Khums** Libya
91B5 **Al Kidan** Region, S Arabia
94C2 **Al Kiswah** Syria
56A2 **Alkmaar** Neth
95B2 **Al Kufrah Oasis** Libya
93E3 **Al Kūt** Iraq
92C2 **Al Lādhiqīyah** Syria
86A1 **Allahābād** India
94C2 **Al Lajāh** *Mt* Syria
2D1 **Allakaket** USA
76B2 **Allanmyo** Burma
95C2 **'Allaqi** *Watercourse* Egypt
17B1 **Allatoona L** USA
15C2 **Allegheny** *R* USA
10C3 **Allegheny Mts** USA
17B1 **Allendale** USA
11A3 **Allen,Mt** NZ
15C2 **Allentown** USA
87B3 **Alleppey** India
49C2 **Aller** *R* France
57D1 **Allgäu** *Mts* Germany
8C2 **Alliance** USA
91C3 **Al Līth** S Arabia
91B5 **Al Liwā** Region, UAE
99D1 **Allora** Aust
14B2 **Alma** Michigan, USA
82B1 **Alma Ata** Kazakhstan
50A2 **Almada** Port
Al Madinah = Medina
71F2 **Almagan** *I* Pacific O
91B4 **Al Manāmah** Bahrain
93D3 **Al Ma'nīyah** Iraq
21A1 **Almanor,L** USA
51B2 **Almansa** Spain
13B1 **Alma Peak** *Mt* Can
91B5 **Al Māriyyah** UAE
95B1 **Al Marj** Libya
Almaty = Alma Ata
93D2 **Al Mawşil** Iraq
50B1 **Almazán** Spain
35C1 **Almenara** Brazil
50B2 **Almeria** Spain
61H3 **Al'met'yevsk** Russian Fed
56C1 **Älmhult** Sweden
93E3 **Al Miqdādīyah** Iraq
112C3 **Almirante Brown** *Base* Ant
34A1 **Almirante Latorre** Chile
55B3 **Almirós** Greece
91A4 **Al Mish'āb** S Arabia
50A2 **Almodôvar** Port
84D3 **Almora** India
91A4 **Al Mubarraz** S Arabia
92C4 **Al Mudawwara** Jordan
91C5 **Al Mudaybi** Oman
91B4 **Al Muharraq** Bahrain
81C4 **Al Mukallā** Yemen
81C4 **Al Mukhā** Yemen
93D3 **Al Musayyib** Iraq
44B3 **Alness** Scot
93E3 **Al Nu'mānīyah** Iraq
42D2 **Alnwick** Eng
71D4 **Alor** *I* Indon
77C4 **Alor Setar** Malay
Alost = Aalst
107E2 **Alotau** PNG
106B3 **Aloysius,Mt** Aust
34C3 **Alpachiri** Arg
14B1 **Alpena** USA
47B2 **Alpes du Valais** *Mts* Switz
52B1 **Alpi Dolomitiche** *Mts* Italy
47B2 **Alpi Graie** *Mts* Italy
9C3 **Alpine** Texas, USA
47C1 **Alpi Orobie** *Mts* Italy
47B2 **Alpi Pennine** *Mts* Italy
47C1 **Alpi Retiche** *Mts* Switz
47D1 **Alpi Venoste** *Mts* Italy
52A1 **Alps** *Mts* Europe
95A1 **Al Qaddāhiyah** Libya
94C1 **Al Qadmūs** Syria
93D3 **Al Qā'im** Iraq
93C4 **Al Qalībah** S Arabia
93D2 **Al Qāmishlī** Syria
95A1 **Al Qaryah Ash Sharqiyah** Libya
92C3 **Al Qaryatayn** Syria
91A4 **Al Qātif** S Arabia
95A2 **Al Qatrūn** Libya
91A4 **Al Qayşāmah** S Arabia
94C2 **Al Quatayfah** Syria
50A2 **Alqueva** *R* Port
92C3 **Al Qunaytirah** Syria
81C4 **Al Qunfidhah** S Arabia
93E3 **Al Qurnah** Iraq
94C1 **Al Quşayr** Syria
92C3 **Al Qutayfah** Syria
56B1 **Als** *I* Den
49D2 **Alsace** Region, France
57B2 **Alsfeld** Germany
42C2 **Alston** Eng
38J5 **Alta** Nor
29D2 **Alta Gracia** Arg
27D5 **Altagracia de Orituco** Ven
68A2 **Altai** *Mts* Mongolia
17B1 **Altamaha** *R* USA
33G4 **Altamira** Brazil
23B1 **Altamira** Mexico
53C2 **Altamura** Italy
68C1 **Altanbulag** Mongolia
71F4 **Altape** PNG
24B2 **Altata** Mexico
63A3 **Altay** China
63B3 **Altay** Mongolia
63A2 **Altay** *Mts* Russian Fed
47C1 **Altdorf** Switz
46D1 **Altenkirchen** Germany
34B3 **Altiplanicie del Payún** *Plat* Arg
47B1 **Altkirch** France
101C2 **Alto Molócue** Mozam
10A3 **Alton** USA
15C2 **Altoona** USA
34B2 **Alto Pencoso** *Mts* Arg
35A1 **Alto Sucuriú** Brazil
23B2 **Altotonga** Mexico
23A2 **Altoyac de Alvarez** Mexico
82C2 **Altun Shan** *Mts* China
20B2 **Alturas** USA
9D3 **Altus** USA
91B5 **Al'Ubaylah** S Arabia
93C4 **Al Urayq** *Desert Region* S Arabia
91B5 **Al'Uruq al Mu'taridah** Region, S Arabia
9D2 **Alva** USA
23B2 **Alvarado** Mexico
19A3 **Alvarado** USA
39G6 **Älvdalen** Sweden
19A4 **Alvin** USA
38J5 **Alvsbyn** Sweden
80B3 **Al Wajh** S Arabia
85D3 **Alwar** India
93D3 **Al Widyān** *Desert Region* Iraq/S Arabia
72A2 **Alxa Yougi** China
93E2 **Alyat** Azerbaijan
39J8 **Alytus** Lithuania
46E2 **Alzey** Germany
23B2 **Amacuzac** *R* Mexico
99D2 **Amadi** Sudan
93D2 **Amādīyah** Iraq
6C3 **Amadjuak L** Can
74B4 **Amakusa-shotō** *I* Japan
39G7 **Åmål** Sweden
63D2 **Amalat** *R* Russian Fed
55B3 **Amaliás** Greece
85D4 **Amalner** India
69E4 **Amami** *I* Japan
69E4 **Amami gunto** *Arch* Japan
100C4 **Amanzimtoti** S Africa
33G3 **Amapá** Brazil
33G3 **Amapá** State, Brazil
9C3 **Amarillo** USA
60E5 **Amasya** Turk
23A1 **Amatitan** Mexico
Amazonas = Solimões
32D4 **Amazonas** State, Brazil
28C3 **Amazonas** *R* Brazil
84D2 **Ambāla** India
87C3 **Ambalangoda** Sri Lanka
101D3 **Ambalavao** Madag
98B2 **Ambam** Cam
101D2 **Ambanja** Madag
1C7 **Ambarchik** Russian Fed
32B4 **Ambato** Ecuador
101D2 **Ambato-Boeny** Madag
101D2 **Ambatolampy** Madag
101D2 **Ambatondrazaka** Madag
57C3 **Amberg** Germany
25D3 **Ambergris Cay** *I* Belize
86A2 **Ambikāpur** India
101D2 **Ambilobe** Madag
101D3 **Amboasary** Madag
101D2 **Ambodifototra** Madag
101D3 **Ambohimahasoa** Madag
71D4 **Ambon** Indon
101D3 **Ambositra** Madag
101D3 **Ambovombe** Madag
98B3 **Ambriz** Angola
98C1 **Am Dam** Chad
64H3 **Amderma** Russian Fed
24B2 **Ameca** Mexico
23B2 **Amecacameca** Mexico
34C2 **Ameghino** Arg
56B2 **Ameland** *I* Neth
16C2 **Amenia** USA
112B10 **American Highland** *Upland* Ant
105H4 **American Samoa** *Is* Pacific O
17B1 **Americus** USA
101G1 **Amersfoort** S Africa
112C10 **Amery Ice Shelf** Ant
55B3 **Amfilokhía** Greece
55B3 **Amfissa** Greece
63F1 **Amga** Russian Fed
63F1 **Amgal** *R* Russian Fed
69F2 **Amgu** Russian Fed
69F1 **Amgun'** *R* Russian Fed
99D1 **Amhara** *Region* Eth
7D5 **Amherst** Can
16C1 **Amherst** Massachusetts, USA
Amherst = Kyaikkami
87B2 **Amhūr** India
48C2 **Amiens** France
75B1 **Amino** Japan
94B1 **Amioune** Leb
89K8 **Amirante Is** Indian O
86B1 **Amlekhgan** Nepal
92C3 **Amman** Jordan
38K6 **Ämmänsaario** Fin
56B2 **Ammersfoort** Neth
90B2 **Amol** Iran
55C3 **Amorgós** *I* Greece
7C5 **Amos** Can
Amoy = Xiamen
101D3 **Ampanihy** Madag
35B2 **Amparo** Brazil
51C1 **Amposta** Spain
85D4 **Amrāvati** India
85C4 **Amreli** India
84C2 **Amritsar** India
56A2 **Amsterdam** Neth
101H1 **Amsterdam** S Africa
15D2 **Amsterdam** USA
98C1 **Am Timan** Chad
88L3 **Amu Darya** *R* Uzbekistan
6A2 **Amund Ringes I** Can
4F2 **Amundsen G** Can
112B4 **Amundsen S** Ant
80E **Amundsen-Scott** *Base* Ant
78D3 **Amuntai** Indon
63E2 **Amur** *R* Russian Fed
33E2 **Anaco** Ven
8B2 **Anaconda** USA
20B1 **Anacortes** USA
55C3 **Anáfi** *I* Greece
93D3 **'Anah** Iraq
21B3 **Anaheim** USA
87B2 **Anaimalai Hills** India
83C4 **Anakapalle** India
12E1 **Anaktuvuk P** USA
101D2 **Analalaya** Madag
92B2 **Anamur** Turk
75A2 **Anan** Japan
87B2 **Anantapur** India
84D2 **Anantnag** India
31B5 **Anápolis** Brazil
90C3 **Anār** Iran
90B3 **Anārak** Iran
71F2 **Anatahan** *I* Pacific O
30D4 **Añatuya** Arg
74B3 **Anbyŏn** N Korea
22C4 **Ancapa Is** USA
4D3 **Anchorage** USA
30C2 **Ancohuma** *Mt* Bol
32B6 **Ancón** Peru
52B2 **Ancona** Italy
16C1 **Ancram** USA
29B4 **Ancud** Chile
34A3 **Andacollo** Arg
108A1 **Andado** Aust
32C6 **Andahuaylas** Peru
38F6 **Andalsnes** Nor
50A2 **Andalucia** Region, Spain
17A1 **Andalusia** USA

83D4 **Andaman Is** Burma
83D4 **Andaman S** Burma
108A2 **Andamooka** Aust
38H5 **Andenes** Nor
47C1 **Andermatt** Switz
57B2 **Andernach** Germany
14A2 **Anderson** Indiana, USA
18B2 **Anderson** Missouri, USA
17B1 **Anderson** S Carolina, USA
4F3 **Anderson** *R* Can
87B1 **Andhra Pradesh** State, India
55B3 **Andikíthira** *I* Greece
65J5 **Andizhan** Uzbekistan
65H6 **Andkhui** Afghan
74B3 **Andong** S Korea
51C1 **Andorra** Principality, SW Europe
51C1 **Andorra-La-Vella** Andorra
43D4 **Andover** Eng
35A2 **Andradina** Brazil
12B2 **Andreafsky** USA
92B2 **Andreas,C** Cyprus
53C2 **Andria** Italy
11C4 **Andros** *I* The Bahamas
55B3 **Ándros** *I* Greece
87A2 **Androth** *I* India
50B2 **Andújar** Spain
100A2 **Andulo** Angola
97C4 **Anécho** Togo
97C3 **Anéfis** Mali
34B3 **Añelo** Arg
63C2 **Angarsk** Russian Fed
38H6 **Ånge** Sweden
24A2 **Angel de la Guarda** *I* Mexico
79B2 **Angeles** Phil
39G7 **Angelholm** Sweden
109C1 **Angellala Creek** *R* Aust
22B1 **Angels Camp** USA
71E4 **Angemuk** *Mt* Indon
48B2 **Angers** France
76C3 **Angkor** *Hist Site* Camb
41C3 **Anglesey** *I* Wales
19A4 **Angleton** USA
6G3 **Angmagssalik** Greenland
101D2 **Angoche** Mozam
29B3 **Angol** Chile
14B2 **Angola** Indiana, USA
100A2 **Angola** Republic, Africa
103H6 **Angola Basin** Atlantic O
12H3 **Angoon** USA
48C2 **Angoulême** France
96A1 **Angra do Heroismo** Açores
35C2 **Angra dos Reis** Brazil
34C3 **Anguil** Arg
27E3 **Anguilla** *I* Caribbean S
26B2 **Anguilla Cays** *Is* Caribbean S
86B2 **Angul** India
99C3 **Angumu** Zaïre
56C1 **Anholt** *I* Den
73C4 **Anhua** China
72D3 **Anhui** Province, China
12C2 **Aniak** USA
35B1 **Anicuns** Brazil
46B2 **Anizy-le-Château** France
4C3 **Anjak** USA
48B2 **Anjou** Region, France
101D2 **Anjouan** *I* Comoros
101D2 **Anjozorobe** Madag
74B3 **Anju** N Korea
72B3 **Ankang** China
92B2 **Ankara** Turk
101D2 **Ankaratra** *Mt* Madag
101D3 **Ankazoabo** Madag
101D2 **Ankazobe** Madag
56C2 **Anklam** Germany
76D3 **An Loc** Viet
73B4 **Anlong** China
73C3 **Anlu** China
18C2 **Anna** USA
96C1 **'Annaba** Alg
92C3 **An Nabk** S Arabia
92C3 **An Nabk** Syria
108A1 **Anna Creek** Aust
80C3 **An Nafūd** *Desert* S Arabia
93D3 **An Najaf** Iraq
42C2 **Annan** Scot
15C3 **Annapolis** USA
86A1 **Annapurna** *Mt* Nepal
14B2 **Ann Arbor** USA
94C1 **An Nāsirah** Syria
93E3 **An Nāsirīyah** Iraq
47B2 **Annecy** France
47B1 **Annemasse** France
76D3 **An Nhon** Viet
73A5 **Anning** China
17A1 **Anniston** USA
89E8 **Annobon** *I* Eq Guinea
49C2 **Annonay** France
27J1 **Annotto Bay** Jamaica
73D3 **Anqing** China
72B2 **Ansai** China
57C3 **Ansbach** Germany
26C3 **Anse d'Hainault** Haiti
72E1 **Anshan** China
73B4 **Anshun** China
97C3 **Ansongo** Mali
14B3 **Ansted** USA
92C2 **Antakya** Turk
101E2 **Antalaha** Madag
92B2 **Antalya** Turk
92B2 **Antalya Körfezi** *B* Turk
101D2 **Antananarivo** Madag
112C1 **Antarctic Circle** Ant
112C3 **Antarctic Pen** Ant
50B2 **Antequera** Spain
96B2 **Anti-Atlas** *Mts* Mor
7D5 **Anticosti, Î. d'** Can
27E3 **Antigua** *I* Caribbean S
Anti Lebanon = Jebel esh Sharqi
21A2 **Antioch** USA
19A3 **Antlers** USA
30B3 **Antofagasta** Chile
45C1 **Antrim** County, N Ire
45C1 **Antrim** N Ire
45C1 **Antrim Hills** N Ire
101D2 **Antseranana** Madag
101D2 **Antsirabe** Madag
101D2 **Antsohiny** Madag
76D3 **An Tuc** Viet
46C1 **Antwerpen** Belg
45C2 **An Uaimh** Irish Rep
84C3 **Anupgarh** India
87C3 **Anuradhapura** Sri Lanka
Anvers = Antwerpen
4B3 **Anvik** USA
63B3 **Anxi** China
72C2 **Anyang** China
72A3 **A'nyêmaqên Shan** *Upland* China
47C2 **Anza** *R* Italy
13E1 **Anzac** Can
65K4 **Anzhero-Sudzhensk** Russian Fed
53B2 **Anzio** Italy
74E2 **Aomori** Japan
52A1 **Aosta** Italy
97B3 **Aoukar** *Desert Region* Maur
96C2 **Aoulef** Alg
95A2 **Aozou** Chad
30E3 **Apa** *R* Brazil/Par
11B4 **Apalachee B** USA
17B2 **Apalachicola** USA
17A2 **Apalachicola B** USA
23B2 **Apan** Mexico
64E3 **Apatity** Russian Fed
32C3 **Apaporis** *R* Colombia
35A2 **Aparecida do Taboado** Brazil
79B2 **Aparri** Phil
54A1 **Apatin** Croatia
64E3 **Apatity** Russian Fed
24B3 **Apatzingan** Mexico
56B2 **Apeldoorn** Neth
35B2 **Apiai** Brazil
33F2 **Apoera** Surinam
108B3 **Apollo Bay** Aust
79C4 **Apo,Mt** *Mt* Phil
17B2 **Apopka,L** USA
30F2 **Aporé** *R* Brazil
10A2 **Apostle Is** USA
10A2 **Apostle L** USA
23A1 **Apozol** Mexico
11B3 **Appalachian Mts** USA
52B2 **Appennino Abruzzese** *Mts* Italy
52A2 **Appennino Ligure** *Mts* Italy
53C2 **Appennino Lucano** *Mts* Italy
53B2 **Appennino Napoletano** *Mts* Italy
52B2 **Appennino Tosco-Emilliano** *Mts* Italy
52B2 **Appennino Umbro-Marchigiano** *Mts* Italy
47C1 **Appenzell** Switz
42C2 **Appleby** Eng
14A2 **Appleton** Wisconsin, USA
30F3 **Apucarana** Brazil
23B1 **Apulco** Mexico
32D2 **Apure** *R* Ven
32C6 **Apurimac** *R* Peru
92C4 **'Aqaba** Jordan
92B4 **'Aqaba,G of** Egypt/S Arabia
90B3 **'Aqdā** Iran
30E3 **Aquidauana** Brazil
23A2 **Aquila** Mexico
86A1 **Ara** India
17A1 **Arab** USA
81D4 **Arabian** *S* Asia/Arabian Pen
31D4 **Aracajú** Brazil
30E3 **Aracanguy, Mts de** Par
31D2 **Aracati** Brazil
30F3 **Araçatuba** Brazil
50A2 **Aracena** Spain
31C5 **Araçuai** Brazil
94B3 **Arad** Israel
60B4 **Arad** Rom
98C1 **Arada** Chad
91B5 **'Arādah** UAE
106C1 **Arafura S** Indon/Aust
30F2 **Aragarças** Brazil
51B1 **Aragón** Region, Spain
50B1 **Aragon** *R* Spain
33G6 **Araguaia** *R* Brazil
31B3 **Araguaína** Brazil
31B5 **Araguari** Brazil
35B1 **Araguari** *R* Brazil
75B1 **Arai** Japan
96C2 **Arak** Alg
90A3 **Arāk** Iran
76A2 **Arakan Yoma** *Mts* Burma
87B2 **Arakkonam** India
65G5 **Aral Sea** Kazakhstan/Uzbekistan
80E1 **Aral'sk** Kazakhstan
Aral'skoye More = Aral S
40B2 **Aran** *I* Irish Rep
50B1 **Aranda de Duero** Spain
23A1 **Arandas** Mexico
50B1 **Aranjuez** Spain
75A2 **Arao** Japan
97B3 **Araouane** Mali
29E2 **Arapey** *R* Urug
31D4 **Arapiraca** Brazil
35A2 **Araporgas** Brazil
30G4 **Ararangua** Brazil
31B6 **Araraquara** Brazil
35B2 **Araras** Brazil
107D4 **Ararat** Aust
93D2 **Ararat** Armenia
93E2 **Aras** *R* Azerbaijan
75C1 **Arato** Japan
32D2 **Arauca** *R* Ven
34A3 **Arauco** Chile
32C2 **Arauea** Colombia
85C4 **Arāvalli Range** *Mts* India
31B5 **Araxá** Brazil
99D2 **Arba Minch** Eth
53A3 **Arbatax** Sardegna
93D2 **Arbīl** Iraq
47A1 **Arbois** France
39H6 **Arbrå** Sweden
44C3 **Arbroath** Scot
47A1 **Arc** France
47B2 **Arc** *R* France
48B3 **Arcachon** France
17B2 **Arcadia** USA
20B2 **Arcata** USA
23A2 **Arcelia** Mexico
26B2 **Archipiélago de Camaguey** *Arch* Cuba
29B6 **Archipiélago de la Reina Adelaida** *Arc[h]* Chile
29B4 **Archipiélago de las Chones** *Arch* Chile
32B2 **Archipiélago de las Perlas** *Arch* Panam[a]
35B2 **Arcos** Brazil
50A2 **Arcos de la Fronter[a]** Spain
6B2 **Arctic Bay** Can
1C1 **Arctic Circle**
4E3 **Arctic Red** Can
4E3 **Arctic Red R** Can
4D3 **Arctic Village** USA
54C2 **Arda** *R* Bulg
65F6 **Ardabīl** Iran
93D1 **Ardahan** Turk
39F6 **Ardal** Nor
96C2 **Ardar des Iforas** *Upland* Alg/Mali
45C2 **Ardee** Irish Rep
90B3 **Ardekān** Iran
46C2 **Ardennes** Department, France
57A2 **Ardennes** Region, Belg
90B3 **Ardestan** Iran
92C3 **Ardh es Suwwan** *Desert Region* Jordan
50A2 **Ardila** *R* Port
109C2 **Ardlethan** Aust
9D3 **Ardmore** USA
44A3 **Ardnamurchan** *Pt* Scot
46A1 **Ardres** France
44B3 **Ardrishaig** Scot
42B2 **Ardrossan** Scot
27D3 **Arecibo** Puerto Ric[o]
31D2 **Areia Branca** Brazil
21A2 **Arena,Pt** USA
39F7 **Arendal** Nor
30B2 **Arequipa** Peru
52B2 **Arezzo** Italy
52B2 **Argenta** Italy
49C2 **Argentan** France
46B2 **Argenteuil** France
28C7 **Argentina** Republi[c] S America
103F7 **Argentine Basin** Atlantic O
48C2 **Argenton-sur-Creu[se]** France
54C2 **Argeş** *R* Rom
84B2 **Arghardab** *R* Afgh[an]
55B3 **Argolikós Kólpos** [G] Greece
46C2 **Argonne** Region, France
55B3 **Árgos** Greece
55B3 **Argostólion** Greec[e]
22B3 **Arguello,Pt** USA
106B2 **Argyle,L** Aust
56C1 **Århus** Den
100A3 **Ariamsvlei** Namibi[a]
50B1 **Arian zón** *R* Spain
34C2 **Arias** Arg
97B3 **Aribinda** Burkina
30B2 **Arica** Chile
84C2 **Arifwala** Pak
Arihā = Jericho
27L1 **Arima** Trinidad
35B1 **Arinos** Brazil

33F6 **Arinos** *R* Brazil
23A2 **Ario de Rosales** Mexico
27L1 **Aripo,Mt** Trinidad
33E5 **Aripuana** Brazil
33E5 **Aripuaná** *R* Brazil
44B3 **Arisaig** Scot
87B2 **Ariskere** India
13B2 **Aristazabal I** Can
34B3 **Arizona** Arg
9B3 **Arizona** State, USA
39G7 **Årjäng** Sweden
61F3 **Arkadak** Russian Fed
19B3 **Arkadelphia** USA
65H4 **Arkaly** Kazakhstan
11A3 **Arkansas** State, USA
11A3 **Arkansas** *R* USA
18A2 **Arkansas City** USA
64F3 **Arkhangel'sk** Russian Fed
41B3 **Arklow** Irish Rep
47D1 **Arlberg P** Austria
49C3 **Arles** France
19A3 **Arlington** Texas, USA
15C3 **Arlington** Virginia, USA
20B1 **Arlington** Washington, USA
97C3 **Arlit** Niger
57B3 **Arlon** Belg
Armageddon = Megiddo
45C1 **Armagh** County, N Ire
45C1 **Armagh** N Ire
61F5 **Armavir** Russian Fed
23A2 **Armena** Mexico
32B3 **Armenia** Colombia
65F5 **Armenia** Republic, Europe
07E4 **Armidale** Aust
13D2 **Armstrong** Can
7C3 **Arnaud** *R* Can
92B2 **Arnauti** *C* Cyprus
56B2 **Arnhem** Neth
06C2 **Arnhem,C** Aust
06C2 **Arnhem Land** Aust
22B1 **Arnold** USA
15C1 **Arnprior** Can
46E1 **Arnsberg** Germany
00A3 **Aroab** Namibia
47C2 **Arona** Italy
12B2 **Aropuk L** USA
52A1 **Arosa** Switz
97A3 **Arquipélago dos Bijagós** *Arch* Guinea-Bissau
93D3 **Ar Ramādī** Iraq
42B2 **Arran** *I* Scot
93C2 **Ar Raqqah** Syria
95A2 **Ar Rāqūbah** Libya
49C1 **Arras** France
96A2 **Arrecife** Canary Is
34C2 **Arrecifes** Arg
23A1 **Arriaga** Mexico
93E3 **Ar Rifā't** Iraq
93E3 **Ar Rihāb** *Desert Region* Iraq
91A5 **Ar Riyāḍ** S Arabia
44B3 **Arrochar** Scot
1A2 **Arrowtown** NZ
23B1 **Arroyo Seco** Mexico
91B4 **Ar Ru'ays** Qatar
91C5 **Ar Rustaq** Oman
93D3 **Ar Rutbah** Iraq
47D2 **Arsiero** Italy
49D2 **Arsizio** Italy
1G2 **Arsk** Russian Fed
55B3 **Árta** Greece
3A2 **Arteaga** Mexico
63B2 **Artemovsk** Russian Fed
3D2 **Artemovskiy** Russian Fed
9C3 **Artesia** USA
1B2 **Arthurs P** NZ
2C2 **Artigas** *Base* Ant
29E2 **Artigas** Urug
4H3 **Artillery L** Can
8C1 **Artois** Region, France
2C2 **Arturo Prat** *Base* Ant
3D1 **Artvin** Turk
99D2 **Aru** Zaïre
33G6 **Aruanã** Brazil
27C4 **Aruba** *I* Caribbean S
86B1 **Arun** *R* Nepal
86C1 **Arunāchal Pradesh** Union Territory, India
87B3 **Aruppukkottai** India
99D3 **Arusha** Tanz
98C2 **Aruwimi** *R* Zaïre
68C2 **Arvayheer** Mongolia
47B2 **Arve** *R* France
7C5 **Arvida** Can
38H5 **Arvidsjaur** Sweden
39G7 **Arvika** Sweden
21B2 **Arvin** USA
94B1 **Arwad** *I* Syria
61F2 **Arzamas** Russian Fed
84C2 **Asadabad** Afghan
75A2 **Asahi** *R* Japan
74E2 **Asahi dake** *Mt* Japan
74E2 **Asahikawa** Japan
86B2 **Asansol** India
95A2 **Asawanwah** *Well* Libya
61K2 **Asbest** Russian Fed
15D2 **Asbury Park** USA
103H5 **Ascension** *I* Atlantic O
57B3 **Aschaffenburg** Germany
56C2 **Aschersleben** Germany
52B2 **Ascoli Piceno** Italy
47C1 **Ascona** Switz
99E1 **Aseb** Eritrea
96C2 **Asedjirad** *Upland* Alg
99D2 **Āsela** Eth
38H6 **Åsele** Sweden
54B2 **Asenovgrad** Bulg
46C2 **Asfeld** France
61J2 **Asha** Russian Fed
17B1 **Ashburn** USA
111B2 **Ashburton** NZ
106A3 **Ashburton** *R* Aust
92B3 **Ashdod** Israel
19B3 **Ashdown** USA
11B3 **Asheville** USA
109D1 **Ashford** Aust
43E4 **Ashford** Eng
Ashgabat = Ashkhabad
74D3 **Ashikaga** Japan
75A2 **Ashizuri-misaki** *Pt* Japan
65G6 **Ashkhabad** Turkmenistan
10B3 **Ashland** Kentucky, USA
18A1 **Ashland** Nebraska, USA
14B2 **Ashland** Ohio, USA
8A2 **Ashland** Oregon, USA
109C1 **Ashley** Aust
16B2 **Ashokan Res** USA
94B3 **Ashqelon** Israel
93D3 **Ash Shabakh** Iraq
91C4 **Ash Sha'm** UAE
93D2 **Ash Sharqāt** Iraq
93E3 **Ash Shatrah** Iraq
81C4 **Ash Shihr** Yemen
91A4 **Ash Shumlul** S Arabia
14B2 **Ashtabula** USA
7D4 **Ashuanipi L** Can
92C3 **'Aşī** *R* Syria
47D2 **Asiago** Italy
53A2 **Asinara** *I* Medit S
65K4 **Asino** Russian Fed
93D2 **Aşkale** Turk
39G7 **Askersund** Sweden
84C1 **Asmar** Afghan
95C3 **Asmera** Eritrea
75A2 **Aso** Japan
99D1 **Asosa** Eth
111A2 **Aspiring,Mt** NZ
93C2 **As Sabkhah** Syria
91A5 **As Salamiyah** S Arabia
92C2 **As Salamīyah** Syria
93D3 **As Salmān** Iraq
86C1 **Assam** State, India
93E3 **As Samāwah** Iraq
91B5 **As Şanām** Region, S Arabia
94C2 **As Sanamayn** Syria
56B2 **Assen** Neth
56B1 **Assens** Den
95A1 **As Sidrah** Libya
5H5 **Assiniboia** Can
5G4 **Assiniboine,Mt** Can
30F3 **Assis** Brazil
93C3 **As Sukhnah** Syria
93E2 **As Sulaymānīyah** Iraq
91A5 **As Summan** Region, S Arabia
99E3 **Assumption** *I* Seychelles
92C3 **As Suwaydā'** Syria
93D3 **As Suwayrah** Iraq
93E2 **Astara** Azerbaijan
52A2 **Asti** Italy
55C3 **Astipálaia** *I* Greece
50A1 **Astorga** Spain
8A2 **Astoria** USA
61G4 **Astrakhan'** Russian Fed
50A1 **Asturias** Region, Spain
30E4 **Asunción** Par
99D2 **Aswa** *R* Uganda
80B3 **Aswân** Egypt
95C2 **Aswân High Dam** Egypt
95C2 **Asyût** Egypt
92C3 **As Zilaf** Syria
97C4 **Atakpamé** Togo
71D4 **Atambua** Indon
6E3 **Atangmik** Greenland
96A2 **Atar** Maur
65J5 **Atasu** Kazakhstan
95C3 **Atatisk Baraji** *Res* Turkmenistan
95C3 **Atbara** Sudan
65H4 **Atbasar** Kazakhstan
11A4 **Atchafalaya B** USA
10A3 **Atchison** USA
16B3 **Atco** USA
23A1 **Atenguillo** Mexico
52B2 **Atessa** Italy
46B1 **Ath** Belg
13E2 **Athabasca** Can
5G4 **Athabasca** *R* Can
5H4 **Athabasca L** Can
45B2 **Athenry** Irish Rep
Athens = Athínai
11B3 **Athens** Georgia, USA
14B3 **Athens** Ohio, USA
19A3 **Athens** Texas, USA
55B3 **Athínai** Greece
41B3 **Athlone** Irish Rep
16C1 **Athol** USA
55B2 **Áthos** *Mt* Greece
45C2 **Athy** Irish Rep
98B1 **Ati** Chad
7A5 **Atikoken** Can
61F3 **Atkarsk** Russian Fed
18B2 **Atkins** USA
23B2 **Atlacomulco** Mexico
11B3 **Atlanta** Georgia, USA
14B2 **Atlanta** Michigan, USA
18A1 **Atlantic** USA
10C3 **Atlantic City** USA
16B2 **Atlantic Highlands** USA
103H8 **Atlantic Indian Basin** Atlantic O
103H7 **Atlantic Indian Ridge** Atlantic O
96C1 **Atlas Saharien** *Mts* Alg
4E4 **Atlin** Can
4E4 **Atlin L** Can
94B2 **'Atlit** Israel
23B2 **Atlixco** Mexico
11B3 **Atmore** USA
101D3 **Atofinandrahana** Madag
12D3 **Atognak I** USA
19A3 **Atoka** USA
23A1 **Atotonilco** Mexico
23B2 **Atoyac** *R* Mexico
32B2 **Atrato** *R* Colombia
91B5 **Attaf** Region, UAE
81C3 **At Tā'if** S Arabia
94C2 **At Tall** Syria
17A1 **Attalla** USA
7B4 **Attauapiskat** Can
7B4 **Attauapiskat** *R* Can
93D3 **At Taysīyah** *Desert Region* S Arabia
14A2 **Attica** Indiana, USA
46C2 **Attigny** France
15D2 **Attleboro** Massachusetts, USA
76D3 **Attopeu** Laos
92C4 **At Tubayq** *Upland* S Arabia
34B3 **Atuel** *R* Arg
39H7 **Atvidaberg** Sweden
22B2 **Atwater** USA
49D3 **Aubagne** France
46C2 **Aube** Department, France
49C3 **Aubenas** France
17A1 **Auburn** Alabama, USA
21A2 **Auburn** California, USA
14A2 **Auburn** Indiana, USA
18A1 **Auburn** Nebraska, USA
15C2 **Auburn** New York, USA
20B1 **Auburn** Washington, USA
48C3 **Auch** France
110B1 **Auckland** NZ
105G6 **Auckland Is** NZ
48C3 **Aude** *R* France
7B4 **Auden** Can
47B1 **Audincourt** France
109C1 **Augathella** Aust
57C3 **Augsburg** Germany
106A4 **Augusta** Aust
11B3 **Augusta** Georgia, USA
18A2 **Augusta** Kansas, USA
10D2 **Augusta** Maine, USA
12D3 **Augustine I** USA
58C2 **Augustów** Pol
106A3 **Augustus,Mt** Aust
46A2 **Aumale** France
85D3 **Auraiya** India
85D5 **Aurangābād** India
96C1 **Aurès** *Mts* Alg
48C3 **Aurillac** France
8C3 **Aurora** Colorado, USA
10B2 **Aurora** Illinois, USA
14B3 **Aurora** Indiana, USA
18B2 **Aurora** Mississippi, USA
100A3 **Aus** Namibia
14B2 **Au Sable** USA
10A2 **Austin** Minnesota, USA
21B2 **Austin** Nevada, USA
9D3 **Austin** Texas, USA
106C3 **Australia** Fed. State/ Monarchy
107D4 **Australian Alps** *Mts* Aust
37E4 **Austria** Federal Republic, Europe
46A1 **Authie** *R* France
24B3 **Autlán** Mexico
49C2 **Autun** France
49C2 **Auvergne** Region, France
49C2 **Auxerre** France
46B1 **Auxi-le-Château** France
49C2 **Avallon** France
22C4 **Avalon** USA
7E5 **Avalon Pen** Can
35B2 **Avaré** Brazil
90D3 **Avaz** Iran
94B3 **Avedat** *Hist Site* Israel
33F4 **Aveiro** Brazil
50A1 **Aveiro** Port
29E2 **Avellaneda** Arg
53B2 **Avellino** Italy
46B1 **Avesnes-sur-Helpe** France

39H6 **Avesta** Sweden
52B2 **Avezzano** Italy
44C3 **Aviemore** Scot
111B2 **Aviemore,L** NZ
47B2 **Avigliana** Italy
49C3 **Avignon** France
50B1 **Avila** Spain
50A1 **Aviles** Spain
47D1 **Avisio** *R* Italy
108B3 **Avoca** *R* Aust
43C4 **Avon** County, Eng
43D4 **Avon** *R* Dorset, Eng
43D3 **Avon** *R* Warwick, Eng
43C4 **Avonmouth** Wales
17B2 **Avon Park** USA
46B2 **Avre** *R* France
54A2 **Avtovac** Bosnia-Herzegovina
94C2 **A'waj** *R* Syria
74D4 **Awaji-shima** *B* Japan
99E2 **Awarē** Eth
111A2 **Awarua Pt** NZ
99E2 **Awash** Eth
99E2 **Awash** *R* Eth
75B1 **Awa-shima** *I* Japan
111B2 **Awatere** *R* NZ
95A2 **Awbārī** Libya
98C2 **Aweil** Sudan
95B2 **Awjilah** Libya
96A2 **Awserd** *Well* Mor
6A2 **Axel Heiburg I** Can
43C4 **Axminster** Eng
75B1 **Ayabe** Japan
29E3 **Ayacucho** Arg
32C6 **Ayacucho** Peru
65K5 **Ayaguz** Kazakhstan
82C2 **Ayakkum Hu** *L* China
50A2 **Ayamonte** Spain
63F2 **Ayan** Russian Fed
32C6 **Ayauiri** Peru
92A2 **Aydin** Turk
55C3 **Áyios Evstrátios** *I* Greece
43D4 **Aylesbury** Eng
13D2 **Aylmer,Mt** Can
94C2 **'Ayn al Fijah** Syria
93D2 **Ayn Zālah** Iraq
95B2 **Ayn Zuwayyah** *Well* Libya
99D2 **Ayod** Sudan
107D2 **Ayr** Aust
42B2 **Ayr** Scot
42B2 **Ayr** *R* Scot
42B2 **Ayre,Pt of** Eng
54C2 **Aytos** Bulg
76C3 **Aytthaya** Thai
23A1 **Ayutla** Mexico
55C3 **Ayvacik** Turk
55C3 **Ayvalik** Turk
86A1 **Azamgarh** India
97B3 **Azaouad** *Desert Region* Mali
97D3 **Azare** Nig
92C2 **A'Zāz** Syria
Azbine = Aïr
65F5 **Azerbaijan** Republic, Russian Fed
32B4 **Azogues** Ecuador
Azores = Açores
98C1 **Azoum** *R* Chad
60E4 **Azov, Sea of** Russian Fed/Ukraine
Azovskoye More = Azov, Sea of
96B1 **Azrou** Mor
34D3 **Azucena** Arg
32A2 **Azuero,Pen de** Panama
29E3 **Azúl** Arg
94C2 **Az-Zabdānī** Syria
91C5 **Az Zāhirah** *Mts* Oman
95A2 **Az Zahra** Iraq
96A2 **Azzeffal** *R* Maur
93E3 **Az Zubayr** Iraq

B

94B2 **Ba'abda** Leb
92C3 **Ba'albek** Leb
94B3 **Ba'al Hazor** *Mt* Israel
99E2 **Baardheere** Somalia
54C2 **Babadag** Rom
92A1 **Babaeski** Turk
32B4 **Babahoyo** Ecuador
81C4 **Bāb al Mandab** *Str* Djibouti/Yemen
71D4 **Babar** *I* Indon
99D3 **Babati** Tanz
60E2 **Babayevo** Russian Fed
14B2 **Baberton** USA
13B1 **Babine** *R* Can
5F4 **Babine L** Can
90B2 **Bābol** Iran
79B2 **Babuyan Chan** Phil
79B2 **Babuyan Is** Phil
31C2 **Bacabal** Brazil
71D4 **Bacan** *I* Indon
60C4 **Bačau** Rom
76D1 **Bac Can** Viet
108B3 **Bacchus Marsh** Aust
82B2 **Bachu** China
4J3 **Back** *R* Can
12J2 **Backbone Ranges** *Mts* Can
76D1 **Bac Ninh** Viet
79B3 **Bacolod** Phil
79B3 **Baco,Mt** Phil
87B2 **Badagara** India
72A1 **Badain Jaran Shamo** *Desert* China
50A2 **Badajoz** Spain
51C1 **Badalona** Spain
93D3 **Badanah** S Arabia
46D2 **Bad Bergzabern** Germany
46D1 **Bad Ems** Germany
47C1 **Baden** Switz
57B3 **Baden-Baden** Germany
57B3 **Baden-Württemberg** State, Germany
57C3 **Badgastein** Austria
22C2 **Badger** USA
57B2 **Bad-Godesberg** Germany
57B2 **Bad Hersfeld** Germany
46D1 **Bad Honnef** Germany
85B4 **Badin** Pak
52B1 **Bad Ischl** Austria
93C3 **Badiyat ash Sham** *Desert Region* Jordan/Iraq
57B3 **Bad-Kreuznach** Germany
46D1 **Bad Nevenahr-Ahrweiler** Germany
47C1 **Bad Ragaz** Switz
57C3 **Bad Tolz** Germany
87C3 **Badulla** Sri Lanka
50B2 **Baena** Spain
97A3 **Bafatá** Guinea-Bissau
4H2 **Baffin** *Region* Can
6C2 **Baffin B** Greenland/Can
6C2 **Baffin I** Can
98B2 **Bafia** Cam
97A3 **Bafing** *R* Mali
97A3 **Bafoulabé** Mali
98B2 **Bafoussam** Cam
90C3 **Bāfq** Iran
60E5 **Bafra Burun** *Pt* Turk
91C4 **Bāft** Iran
98C2 **Bafwasende** Zaïre
86A1 **Bagaha** India
87B1 **Bāgalkot** India
99D3 **Bagamoyo** Tanz
29F2 **Bagé** Brazil
93D3 **Baghdād** Iraq
86B2 **Bagherhat** Bang
91C3 **Baghīn** Iran
84B1 **Baghlan** Afghan
49C3 **Bagnols-sur-Cèze** France
97B3 **Bagoé** *R* Mali
Bagu = Pegu
79B2 **Baguio** Phil
86B1 **Bāhādurābād** India
11C4 **Bahamas,The** *Is* Caribbean S
86B2 **Baharampur** India
92A4 **Baharîya Oasis** Egypt
84C3 **Bahawalpur** Pak
84C3 **Bahawalpur** Province, Pak
85C3 **Bahawathagar** Pak
Bahia = Salvador
31C4 **Bahia** State, Brazil
29D3 **Bahía Blanca** Arg
29D3 **Bahía Blanca** *B* Arg
34A3 **Bahia Concepción** *B* Chile
35C2 **Bahia da Ilha Grande** *B* Brazil
24B2 **Bahia de Banderas** *B* Mexico
24C2 **Bahia de Campeche** *B* Mexico
25D3 **Bahia de la Ascension** *B* Mexico
24B3 **Bahia de Petacalco** *B* Mexico
96A2 **Bahia de Rio de Oro** *B* Mor
35C2 **Bahia de Sepetiba** *B* Brazil
29C6 **Bahía Grande** *B* Arg
9B4 **Bahia Kino** Mexico
24A2 **Bahia Magdalena** *B* Mexico
24A2 **Bahia Sebastia Vizcaino** *B* Mexico
99D1 **Bahar Dar** Eth
86A1 **Bahraich** India
80D3 **Bahrain** Sheikdom, Arabian Pen
93D3 **Bahr al Milh** *L* Iraq
98C2 **Bahr Aouk** *R* Chad/CAR
Bahrat Lut = Dead S
98C2 **Bahr el Arab** *Watercourse* Sudan
99D2 **Bahr el Ghazal** *R* Sudan
98B1 **Bahr el Ghazal** *Watercourse* Chad
101H1 **Baia de Maputo** *B* Mozam
31B2 **Baia de Marajó** *B* Brazil
101D2 **Baiá de Pemba** *B* Mozam
31C2 **Baia de São Marcos** *B* Brazil
50A2 **Baia de Setúbal** *B* Port
31D4 **Baia de Todos os Santos** *B* Brazil
100A2 **Baia dos Tigres** Angola
60B4 **Baia Mare** Rom
98B2 **Baïbokoum** Chad
69E2 **Baicheng** China
101E2 **Baie Antongila** *B* Madag
7D5 **Baie-Comeau** Can
101D2 **Baie de Bombetoka** *B* Madag
101D2 **Baie de Mahajamba** *B* Madag
101D3 **Baie de St Augustin** *B* Madag
94B2 **Baie de St Georges** *B* Leb
10D2 **Baie des Chaleurs** *B* Can
7C4 **Baie-du-Poste** Can
72B3 **Baihe** China
72C3 **Bai He** *R* China
93D3 **Ba'ījī** Iraq
86A2 **Baikunthpur** India
Baile Atha Cliath = Dublin
54B2 **Băilesti** Rom
46B1 **Bailleul** France
72A3 **Baima** China
17B1 **Bainbridge** USA
12B2 **Baird Inlet** USA
4B3 **Baird Mts** USA
72D1 **Bairin Youqi** China
72D1 **Bairin Zuoqi** China
107D4 **Bairnsdale** Aust
79B4 **Bais** Phil
54A1 **Baja** Hung
9B3 **Baja California** State, Mexico
24A1 **Baja California** *Pen* Mexico
61J2 **Bakal** Russian Fed
98C2 **Bakala** CAR
97A3 **Bakel** Sen
8C2 **Baker** Montana, US
8B2 **Baker** Oregon, USA
6A3 **Baker Foreland** *Pt* Can
4J3 **Baker L** Can
4J3 **Baker Lake** Can
8A2 **Baker,Mt** USA
9B3 **Bakersfield** USA
90C2 **Bakharden** Turkmenistan
90C2 **Bakhardok** Turkmenistan
60D3 **Bakhmach** Ukraine
38C1 **Bakkaflói** *B* Icelanc
99D2 **Bako** Eth
98C2 **Bakouma** CAR
65F5 **Baku** Azerbaijan
Baky = Baku
92B2 **Balâ** Turk
79A4 **Balabac** *I* Phil
70C3 **Balabac** *Str* Malay
78C2 **Balaikarangan** Indo
108A2 **Balaklava** Aust
61G3 **Balakovo** Russian Fed
86A2 **Balāngīr** India
61F3 **Balashov** Russian Fed
86B2 **Balasore** India
80A3 **Balât** Egypt
52C1 **Balaton** *L* Hung
45C2 **Balbriggan** Irish Re
29E3 **Balcarce** Arg
54C2 **Balchik** Bulg
111B3 **Balclutha** NZ
18B2 **Bald Knob** USA
17B1 **Baldwin** USA
9C3 **Baldy Peak** *Mt* US
Balearic Is = Islas Baleares
78C2 **Baleh** *R* Malay
79B2 **Baler** Phil
61H2 **Balezino** Russian F
106A1 **Bali** *I* Indon
92A2 **Balıkesir** Turk
93C2 **Balīkh** *R* Syria
78D3 **Balikpapan** Indon
79B2 **Balintang Chan** Ph
78C4 **Bali S** Indon
35A1 **Baliza** Brazil
84B1 **Balkh** Afghan
65J5 **Balkhash** Kazakhst
44B3 **Ballachulish** Scot
45B2 **Ballaghaderreen** Irish Rep
42B2 **Ballantrae** Scot
4G2 **Ballantyne Str** Can
87B2 **Ballapur** India
107D4 **Ballarat** Aust
44C3 **Ballater** Scot
112C7 **Balleny Is** Ant
86A1 **Ballia** India
109D1 **Ballina** Aust
41B3 **Ballina** Irish Rep
45B2 **Ballinasloe** Irish R
45B2 **Ballinrobe** Irish Re
55A2 **Ballsh** Alb
45B1 **Ballycastle** Irish R
45C1 **Ballycastle** N Ire
45C1 **Ballymena** N Ire
45C1 **Ballymoney** N Ire
45B1 **Ballyshannon** Irish Rep
45B2 **Ballyvaghan** Irish Rep
108B3 **Balmoral** Aust
34C2 **Balnearia** Arg
84B3 **Balochistān** Regio. Pak
100A2 **Balombo** Angola
109C1 **Balonn** *R* Aust
85C3 **Balotra** India
86A1 **Balrāmpur** India
107D4 **Balranald** Aust
31B3 **Balsas** Brazil
23B2 **Balsas** Mexico
24B3 **Balsas** *R* Mexico
60C4 **Balta** Ukraine
39H7 **Baltic S** N Europe

92B3 **Baltîm** Egypt
45B3 **Baltimore** Irish Rep
10C3 **Baltimore** USA
86B1 **Bālurghāt** India
61H4 **Balykshi** Kazakhstan
91C4 **Bam** Iran
98B1 **Bama** Nig
97B3 **Bamako** Mali
98C2 **Bambari** CAR
17B1 **Bamberg** USA
57C3 **Bamberg** Germany
98C2 **Bambili** Zaïre
35B2 **Bambui** Brazil
98B2 **Bamenda** Cam
13C3 **Bamfield** Can
98B2 **Bamingui** *R* CAR
98B2 **Bamingui Bangoran** *National Park* CAR
84B2 **Bamiyan** Afghan
91D4 **Bampur** Iran
91D4 **Bampur** *R* Iran
98C2 **Banalia** Zaïre
97B3 **Banamba** Mali
76C3 **Ban Aranyaprathet** Thai
76C2 **Ban Ban** Laos
77C4 **Ban Betong** Thai
45C1 **Banbridge** N Ire
43D3 **Banbury** Eng
44C3 **Banchory** Scot
25D3 **Banco Chinchorro** *Is* Mexico
15C1 **Bancroft** Can
86A1 **Bānda** India
70A3 **Banda Aceh** Indon
97B4 **Bandama** *R* Ivory Coast
91C4 **Bandar Abbās** Iran
90A2 **Bandar Anzalī** Iran
99F2 **Bandarbeyla** Somalia
91B4 **Bandar-e Daylam** Iran
91B4 **Bandar-e Lengheh** Iran
91B4 **Bandar-e Māqām** Iran
91B4 **Bandar-e Rig** Iran
90B2 **Bandar-e Torkoman** Iran
91A3 **Bandar Khomeynī** Iran
78C2 **Bandar Seri Begawan** Brunei
71D4 **Banda S** Indon
91C4 **Band Bonī** Iran
35C2 **Bandeira** *Mt* Brazil
97B3 **Bandiagara** Mali
60C5 **Bandirma** Turk
45B3 **Bandon** Irish Rep
98B3 **Bandundu** Zaïre
78B4 **Bandung** Indon
25E2 **Banes** Cuba
13D2 **Banff** Can
44C3 **Banff** Scot
5G4 **Banff** *R* Can
13D2 **Banff Nat Pk** Can
87B2 **Bangalore** India
98C2 **Bangassou** CAR
70C3 **Banggi** *I* Malay
95B1 **Banghāzī** Libya
76D2 **Bang Hieng** *R* Laos
78B3 **Bangka** *I* Indon
78A3 **Bangko** Indon
76C3 **Bangkok** Thai
82C3 **Bangladesh** Republic, Asia
84D2 **Bangong Co** *L* China
10D2 **Bangor** Maine, USA
45D1 **Bangor** N Ire
16B2 **Bangor** Pennsylvania, USA
42B3 **Bangor** Wales
78D3 **Bangsalsembera** Indon
76B3 **Bang Saphan Yai** Thai
79B2 **Bangued** Phil
98B2 **Bangui** CAR
00C2 **Bangweulu** *L* Zambia
77C4 **Ban Hat Yai** Thai
76C2 **Ban Hin Heup** Laos
76C1 **Ban Houei Sai** Laos
76B3 **Ban Hua Hin** Thai
97B3 **Bani** *R* Mali
97C3 **Bani Bangou** Niger
95A1 **Banī Walīd** Libya
92C2 **Bāniyās** Syria
94B2 **Baniyas** Syria
52C2 **Banja Luka** Bosnia-Herzegovina
78C3 **Banjarmasin** Indon
97A3 **Banjul** The Gambia
77B4 **Ban Kantang** Thai
76D2 **Ban Khemmarat** Laos
77B4 **Ban Khok Kloi** Thai
71F5 **Banks I** Aust
5E4 **Banks I** British Columbia, Can
4F2 **Banks I** Northwest Territories, Can
20C1 **Banks L** USA
111B2 **Banks Pen** NZ
109C4 **Banks Str** Aust
86B2 **Bankura** India
76B2 **Ban Mae Sariang** Thai
76B2 **Ban Mae Sot** Thai
76D3 **Ban Me Thuot** Viet
45C1 **Bann** *R* N Ire
77B4 **Ban Na San** Thai
84C2 **Bannu** Pak
34A3 **Baños Maule** Chile
76C2 **Ban Pak Neun** Laos
77C4 **Ban Pak Phanang** Thai
76D3 **Ban Ru Kroy** Camb
76B3 **Ban Sai Yok** Thai
76C3 **Ban Sattahip** Thai
59B3 **Banská Bystrica** Slovakia
85C4 **Bānswāra** India
77B4 **Ban Tha Kham** Thai
76D2 **Ban Thateng** Laos
76C2 **Ban Tha Tum** Thai
41B3 **Bantry** Irish Rep
41A3 **Bantry** *B* Irish Rep
76D3 **Ban Ya Soup** Viet
78C4 **Banyuwangi** Indon
72C3 **Baofeng** China
76C1 **Bao Ha** Viet
72B3 **Baoji** China
76D3 **Bao Loc** Viet
68B4 **Baoshan** China
72C1 **Baotou** China
87C1 **Bāpatla** India
46B1 **Bapaume** France
93D3 **Ba'Qūbah** Iraq
32J7 **Baquerizo Morena** Ecuador
54A2 **Bar** Montenegro, Yugos
99D1 **Bara** Sudan
99E2 **Baraawe** Somalia
78D3 **Barabai** Indon
86A1 **Bāra Banki** India
65J4 **Barabinsk** Russian Fed
65J4 **Barabinskaya Step** *Steppe* Kazakhstan/Russian Fed
50B1 **Baracaldo** Spain
26C2 **Baracoa** Cuba
94C2 **Baradá** *R* Syria
109C2 **Baradine** Aust
87A1 **Bārāmati** India
84C2 **Baramula** Pak
85D3 **Bārān** India
79B3 **Barangas** Phil
4E4 **Baranof I** USA
60C3 **Baranovichi** Belorussia
108A2 **Baratta** Aust
86B1 **Barauni** India
31C6 **Barbacena** Brazil
27F4 **Barbados** *I* Caribbean S
51C1 **Barbastro** Spain
101H1 **Barberton** S Africa
48B2 **Barbezieux** France
32C2 **Barbòsa** Colombia
27E3 **Barbuda** *I* Caribbean S
107D3 **Barcaldine** Aust
Barce = Al Marj
53C3 **Barcellona** Italy
51C1 **Barcelona** Spain
33E1 **Barcelona** Ven
107D3 **Barcoo** *R* Aust
34B3 **Barda del Medio** Arg
95A2 **Bardai** Chad
29C3 **Bardas Blancas** Arg
86B2 **Barddhamān** India
59C3 **Bardejov** Slovakia
47C2 **Bardi** Italy
47B2 **Bardonecchia** Italy
43B3 **Bardsey** *I* Wales
84D3 **Bareilly** India
64D2 **Barentsøya** *I* Barents S
64E2 **Barents S** Russian Fed
95C3 **Barentu** Eritrea
86A2 **Bargarh** India
47B2 **Barge** Italy
63D2 **Barguzin** Russian Fed
63D2 **Barguzin** *R* Russian Fed
86B2 **Barhi** India
53C2 **Bari** Italy
51D2 **Barika** Alg
32C2 **Barinas** Ven
86B2 **Baripāda** India
85C4 **Bari Sādri** India
86C2 **Barisal** Bang
78C3 **Barito** *R* Indon
95A2 **Barjuj** *Watercourse* Libya
73A3 **Barkam** China
18C2 **Barkley,L** USA
13B3 **Barkley Sd** Can
100B4 **Barkly East** S Africa
106C2 **Barkly Tableland** *Mts* Aust
46C2 **Bar-le-Duc** France
106A3 **Barlee,L** Aust
106A3 **Barlee Range** *Mts* Aust
53C2 **Barletta** Italy
85C3 **Barmer** India
108B2 **Barmera** Aust
43B3 **Barmouth** Wales
42D2 **Barnard Castle** Eng
65K4 **Barnaul** Russian Fed
16B3 **Barnegat** USA
16B3 **Barnegat B** USA
6C2 **Barnes Icecap** Can
17B1 **Barnesville** Georgia, USA
14B3 **Barnesville** Ohio, USA
42D3 **Barnsley** Eng
43B4 **Barnstaple** Eng
97C4 **Baro** Nig
86C1 **Barpeta** India
32D1 **Barquisimeto** Ven
31C4 **Barra** Brazil
44A3 **Barra** *I* Scot
109D2 **Barraba** Aust
23A2 **Barra de Navidad** Mexico
35C2 **Barra de Piraí** Brazil
35A1 **Barragem de São Simão** *Res* Brazil
35A1 **Barra do Garças** Brazil
35B1 **Barragem Agua Vermelha** *Res* Brazil
50A2 **Barragem do Castelo do Bode** *Res* Port
50A2 **Barragem do Maranhão** *Res* Port
35A2 **Barragem Três Irmãos** *Res* Brazil
44A3 **Barra Head** *Pt* Scot
31C6 **Barra Mansa** Brazil
32B6 **Barranca** Peru
32C2 **Barrancabermeja** Colombia
33E2 **Barrancas** Ven
30E4 **Barranqueras** Arg
32C1 **Barranquilla** Colombia
44A3 **Barra,Sound of** *Chan* Scot
16C1 **Barre** USA
34B2 **Barreal** Arg
31C4 **Barreiras** Brazil
50A2 **Barreiro** Port
31D3 **Barreiros** Brazil
107D5 **Barren,C** Aust
12D3 **Barren Is** USA
31B6 **Barretos** Brazil
13E2 **Barrhead** Can
14C2 **Barrie** Can
13C2 **Barrière** Can
108B2 **Barrier Range** *Mts* Aust
107E4 **Barrington,Mt** Aust
27N2 **Barrouaillie** St Vincent and the Grenadines
4C2 **Barrow** USA
45C2 **Barrow** *R* Irish Rep
106C3 **Barrow Creek** Aust
106A3 **Barrow I** Aust
42C2 **Barrow-in-Furness** Eng
4C2 **Barrow,Pt** USA
6A2 **Barrow Str** Can
15C1 **Barry's Bay** Can
87B1 **Barsi** India
9B3 **Barstow** USA
49C2 **Bar-sur-Aube** France
33F2 **Bartica** Guyana
92B1 **Bartın** Turk
107D2 **Bartle Frere,Mt** Aust
9D3 **Bartlesville** USA
101C3 **Bartolomeu Dias** Mozam
58C2 **Bartoszyce** Pol
78C4 **Barung** *I* Indon
85D4 **Barwāh** India
85C4 **Barwāni** India
109C1 **Barwon** *R* Aust
61G3 **Barysh** Russian Fed
98B2 **Basankusu** Zaïre
34D2 **Basavilbas** Arg
79B1 **Basco** Phil
52A1 **Basel** Switz
53C2 **Basento** *R* Italy
13E2 **Bashaw** Can
79B1 **Bashi Chan** Phil
61H3 **Bashkortostan** Russian Fed
79B4 **Basilan** *I* Phil
43E4 **Basildon** Eng
43D4 **Basingstoke** Eng
8B2 **Basin Region** USA
93E3 **Basra** Iraq
46D2 **Bas-Rhin** Department, France
76D3 **Bassac** *R* Camb
13E2 **Bassano** Can
52B1 **Bassano** Italy
47D2 **Bassano del Grappa** Italy
97C4 **Bassari** Togo
101C3 **Bassas da India** *I* Mozam Chan
76A2 **Bassein** Burma
27E3 **Basse Terre** Guadeloupe
97C4 **Bassila** Benin
22C2 **Bass Lake** USA
107D4 **Bass Str** Aust
39G7 **Båstad** Sweden
91B4 **Bastak** Iran
86A1 **Basti** India
52A2 **Bastia** Corse
57B3 **Bastogne** Belg
19B3 **Bastrop** Louisiana, USA
19A3 **Bastrop** Texas, USA
98A2 **Bata** Eq Guinea
78C3 **Batakan** Indon
84D2 **Batala** India
68B3 **Batang** China
98B2 **Batangafo** CAR
79B1 **Batan Is** Phil
35B2 **Batatais** Brazil
15C2 **Batavia** USA
109D3 **Batemans Bay** Aust
17B1 **Batesburg** USA
18B2 **Batesville** Arkansas, USA
19C3 **Batesville** Mississippi, USA
43C4 **Bath** Eng
15C2 **Bath** New York, USA
98B1 **Batha** *R* Chad
107D4 **Bathurst** Aust
7D5 **Bathurst** Can

4F2 Bathurst,C Can
106C2 Bathurst I Aust
4H2 Bathurst I Can
4H3 Bathurst Inlet B Can
97B3 Batié Burkina
90B3 Bātlāq-e-Gavkhūnī Salt Flat Iran
109C3 Batlow Aust
93D2 Batman Turk
96C1 Batna Alg
11A3 Baton Rouge USA
94B1 Batroun Leb
76C3 Battambang Camb
87C3 Batticaloa Sri Lanka
13F2 Battle R Can
10B2 Battle Creek USA
7E4 Battle Harbour Can
20C2 Battle Mountain USA
78D2 Batukelau Indon
65F5 Batumi Georgia
77C5 Batu Pahat Malay
78A3 Baturaja Indon
94B2 Bat Yam Israel
71D4 Baubau Indon
97C3 Bauchi Nig
47B2 Bauges Mts France
7E4 Bauld,C Can
47B1 Baumes-les-Dames France
63D2 Baunt Russian Fed
31B6 Bauru Brazil
35A1 Baus Brazil
57C2 Bautzen Germany
78C4 Baween I Indon
95B2 Bawîti Egypt
97B3 Bawku Ghana
76B2 Bawlake Burma
108A2 Bawlen Aust
17B1 Baxley USA
25E2 Bayamo Cuba
78D4 Bayan Indon
68C2 Bayandzürh Mongolia
68B3 Bayan Har Shan Mts China
72A1 Bayan Mod China
72B1 Bayan Obo China
47A2 Bayard P France
12J3 Bayard,Mt Can
63D3 Bayasgalant Mongolia
79B3 Baybay Phil
93D1 Bayburt Turk
10B2 Bay City Michigan, USA
19A4 Bay City Texas, USA
92B2 Bay Dağlari Turk
64H3 Baydaratskaya Guba B Russian Fed
99E2 Baydhabo Somalia
48B2 Bayeux France
47D1 Bayerische Alpen Mts Germany
57C3 Bayern State, Germany
92C3 Bāyir Jordan
63C2 Baykalskiy Khrebet Mts Russian Fed
63B1 Baykit Russian Fed
63B3 Baylik Shan Mts China/Mongolia
61J3 Baymak Russian Fed
79B2 Bayombang Phil
48B3 Bayonne France
57C3 Bayreuth Germany
19C3 Bay St Louis USA
15D2 Bay Shore USA
15C1 Bays,L of Can
68A2 Baytik Shan Mts China
Bayt Lahm = Bethlehem
19B4 Baytown USA
50B2 Baza Spain
59D3 Bazaliya Ukraine
48B3 Bazas France
73B3 Bazhong China
91D4 Bazmān Iran
94C1 Bcharre Leb
16B3 Beach Haven USA
43E4 Beachy Head Eng
16C2 Beacon USA
101D2 Bealanana Madag
18B1 Beardstown USA
Bear I = Bjørnøya
22B1 Bear Valley USA
8D2 Beatrice USA
44C2 Beatrice Oilfield N Sea
13C1 Beatton R Can
5F4 Beatton River Can
29E6 Beauchene Is Falkland Is
109D1 Beaudesert Aust
1B5 Beaufort S Can
100B4 Beaufort West S Africa
15D1 Beauharnois Can
44B3 Beauly Scot
21B3 Beaumont California, USA
11A3 Beaumont Texas, USA
49C2 Beaune France
48C2 Beauvais France
13F1 Beauval Can
12E1 Beaver Alaska, USA
13F2 Beaver R Saskatchewan, Can
4D3 Beaver Creek Can
12E1 Beaver Creek USA
18C2 Beaver Dam Kentucky, USA
13E2 Beaverhill L Can
14A1 Beaver I USA
18B2 Beaver L USA
13D1 Beaverlodge Can
85C3 Beawar India
34B2 Beazley Arg
35B2 Bebedouro Brazil
43E3 Beccles Eng
54B1 Bečej Serbia, Yugos
96B1 Béchar Alg
12C3 Becharof L USA
11B3 Beckley USA
43D3 Bedford County, Eng
43D3 Bedford Eng
14A3 Bedford Indiana, USA
27M2 Bedford Pt Grenada
4D2 Beechey Pt USA
109C3 Beechworth Aust
109D1 Beenleigh Aust
92B3 Beersheba Israel
Beèr Sheva = Beersheba
94B3 Beér Sheva R Israel
9D4 Beeville USA
98C2 Befale Zaïre
101D2 Befandriana Madag
109C3 Bega Aust
91B3 Behbehān Iran
12H3 Behm Canal Sd USA
90B2 Behshahr Iran
84B2 Behsud Afghan
69E2 Bei'an China
73B5 Beihai China
72D2 Beijing China
76E1 Beiliu China
73B4 Beipan Jiang R China
72E1 Beipiao China
Beira = Sofala
92C3 Beirut Leb
68B2 Bei Shan Mts China
94B2 Beit ed Dīne Leb
94B3 Beit Jala Israel
50A2 Beja Port
96C1 Beja Tunisia
96C1 Bejaïa Alg
50A1 Béjar Spain
90C3 Bejestān Iran
59C3 Békéscsaba Hung
101D3 Bekily Madag
86A1 Bela India
85B3 Bela Pak
78C2 Belaga Malay
16A3 Bel Air USA
87B1 Belamoalli India
71D3 Belang Indon
70A3 Belangpidie Indon
Belarus = Belorussia
Belau = Palau Is.
101C3 Bela Vista Mozam
70A3 Belawan Indon
61J2 Belaya R Ukraine
6A2 Belcher Chan Can
7C4 Belcher Is Can
84B1 Belchiragh Afghan
61H3 Belebey Russian Fed
99E2 Beled Weyne Somalia
31B2 Belém Brazil
32B3 Belén Colombia
34D2 Belén Urug
9C3 Belen USA
45D1 Belfast N Ire
101H1 Belfast S Africa
45D1 Belfast Lough Estuary N Ire
99D1 Bēlfodiyo Eth
42D2 Belford Eng
49D2 Belfort France
87A1 Belgaum India
56A2 Belgium Kingdom, N W Europe
60E3 Belgorod Russian Fed
60D4 Belgorod Dnestrovskiy Ukraine
Belgrade = Beograd
95A2 Bel Hedan Libya
78B3 Belinyu Indon
78B3 Belitung I Indon
25D3 Belize Belize
25D3 Belize Republic, Cent America
48C2 Bellac France
5F4 Bella Coola Can
47C2 Bellagio Italy
19A4 Bellaire USA
47C1 Bellano Italy
87B1 Bellary India
109C1 Bellata Aust
47B2 Belledonne Mts France
8C2 Belle Fourche USA
49D2 Bellegarde France
17B2 Belle Glade USA
7E4 Belle I Can
48B2 Belle-Ile I France
7E4 Belle Isle,Str of Can
7C5 Belleville Can
18A2 Belleville Kansas, USA
20B1 Bellevue Washington, USA
109D2 Bellingen Aust
8A2 Bellingham USA
112C2 Bellingshausen Base Ant
112C3 Bellingshausen S Ant
52A1 Bellinzona Switz
32B2 Bello Colombia
107E3 Bellona Reefs Nouvelle Calédonie
22B1 Bellota USA
15D2 Bellows Falls USA
6B3 Bell Pen Can
52B1 Belluno Italy
29D2 Bell Ville Arg
31D5 Belmonte Brazil
25D3 Belmopan Belize
45B1 Belmullet Irish Rep
69E1 Belogorsk Russian Fed
101D3 Beloha Madag
31C5 Belo Horizonte Brazil
10B2 Beloit Wisconsin, USA
64E3 Belomorsk Russian Fed
61J3 Beloretsk Russian Fed
60C3 Belorussia Republic, Europe
101D2 Belo-Tsiribihina Madag
64E3 Beloye More S Russian Fed
60E1 Beloye Ozero L Russian Fed
60E1 Belozersk Russian Fed
14B3 Belpre USA
108A2 Beltana Aust
19A3 Belton USA
59D3 Bel'tsy Moldova
16B2 Belvidere New Jersey, USA
98B3 Bembe Angola
97C3 Bembéréke Benin
10A2 Bemidji USA
39G6 Bena Nor
98C3 Bena Dibele Zaïre
108C3 Benalla Aust
44B3 Ben Attow Mt Scot
50A1 Benavente Spain
44A3 Benbecula I Scot
106A4 Bencubbin Aust
8A2 Bend USA
44B3 Ben Dearg Mt Scot
60C4 Bendery Moldova
107D4 Bendigo Aust
57C3 Benešov Czech Republic
53B2 Benevento Italy
83C4 Bengal,B of Asia
96D1 Ben Gardane Tunisi
72D3 Bengbu China
78A2 Bengkalis Indon
78A3 Bengkulu Indon
100A2 Benguela Angola
92B3 Benha Egypt
44B2 Ben Hope Mt Scot
99C2 Beni Zaïre
32D6 Béni R Bol
96B1 Beni Abbes Alg
51C1 Benicarló Spain
7A5 Benidji USA
51B2 Benidorm Spain
51C2 Beni Mansour Alg
95C2 Beni Mazar Egypt
96B1 Beni Mellal Mor
97C4 Benin Republic, Africa
97C4 Benin City Nig
95C2 Beni Suef Egypt
44B2 Ben Kilbreck Mt Sc
44B3 Ben Lawers Mt UK
109C4 Ben Lomond Mt Aust
44C3 Ben Macdui Mt Sc
44B2 Ben More Assynt M Scot
111B2 Benmore,L NZ
44B3 Ben Nevis Mt Scot
15D2 Bennington USA
94B2 Bennt Jbail Leb
98B2 Bénoué R Cam
9B3 Benson Arizona, US
99C2 Bentiu Sudan
19B3 Benton Arkansas, USA
18C2 Benton Kentucky, USA
14A2 Benton Harbor US
97C4 Benue R Nig
45B1 Benwee Hd C Irish Rep
44B3 Ben Wyvis Mt Sco
72E1 Benxi China
54B2 Beograd Serbia, Yugos
86A2 Beohāri India
74C4 Beppu Japan
55A2 Berat Alb
95C3 Berber Sudan
99E1 Berbera Somalia
98B2 Berbérati CAR
46A1 Berck France
60C4 Berdichev Ukraine
60E4 Berdyansk Ukraine
97B4 Berekum Ghana
22B2 Berenda USA
5J4 Berens R Can
5J4 Berens River Can
108A1 Beresford Aust
59C3 Berettyoújfalu Hun
58D2 Bereza Belorussia
59C3 Berezhany Ukraine
65G4 Berezniki Russian Fed
60D4 Berezovka Ukraine
64H3 Berezovo Russian Fed
92A2 Bergama Turk
52A1 Bergamo Italy
39F6 Bergen Nor
46C1 Bergen op Zoom Neth
48C3 Bergerac France
46D1 Bergisch-Gladbach Germany
12F2 Bering Gl USA

1C6 **Bering Str** USA/ Russian Fed
91C4 **Berīzak** Iran
50B2 **Berja** Spain
8A3 **Berkeley** USA
112B2 **Berkner I** Ant
54B2 **Berkovitsa** Bulg
43D4 **Berkshire** County, Eng
16C1 **Berkshire Hills** USA
13D2 **Berland** *R* Can
56C2 **Berlin** Germany
56C2 **Berlin** State, Germany
15D2 **Berlin** New Hampshire, USA
30D3 **Bermejo** Bol
30D4 **Bermejo** *R* Arg
3M5 **Bermuda** *I* Atlantic O
52A1 **Bern** Switz
16B2 **Bernardsville** USA
34C3 **Bernasconi** Arg
56C2 **Bernburg** Germany
47B1 **Berner Oberland** *Mts* Switz
6B2 **Bernier B** Can
57C3 **Berounka** *R* Czech Republic
108B2 **Berri** Aust
96C1 **Berriane** Alg
48C2 **Berry** Region, France
22A1 **Berryessa,L** USA
11C4 **Berry Is** The Bahamas
98B2 **Bertoua** Cam
45B2 **Bertraghboy B** Irish Rep
15C2 **Berwick** USA
42C2 **Berwick-upon-Tweed** Eng
43C3 **Berwyn** *Mts* Wales
01D2 **Besalampy** Madag
49D2 **Besançon** France
59C3 **Beskidy Zachodnie** *Mts* Pol
93C2 **Besni** Turk
94B3 **Besor** *R* Israel
11B3 **Bessemer** USA
01D2 **Betafo** Madag
50A1 **Betanzos** Spain
94B3 **Bet Guvrin** Israel
01G1 **Bethal** S Africa
00A3 **Bethanie** Namibia
18B1 **Bethany** Missouri, USA
18A2 **Bethany** Oklahoma, USA
4B3 **Bethel** Alaska, USA
16C2 **Bethel** Connecticut, USA
14B2 **Bethel Park** USA
15C3 **Bethesda** USA
94B3 **Bethlehem** Israel
01G1 **Bethlehem** S Africa
15C2 **Bethlehem** USA
48C1 **Bethune** France
01D3 **Betioky** Madag
08B1 **Betoota** Aust
98B2 **Betou** Congo
82A1 **Betpak Dala** *Steppe* Kazakhstan
01D3 **Betroka** Madag
7D5 **Betsiamites** Can
86A1 **Bettiah** India
12D1 **Bettles** USA
47C2 **Béttola** Italy
85D4 **Bētul** India
85D3 **Betwa** *R* India
46D1 **Betzdorf** Germany
12C3 **Beverley,L** USA
16D1 **Beverly** USA
21B3 **Beverly Hills** USA
97B4 **Beyla** Guinea
87B2 **Beypore** India
Beyrouth = Beirut
92B2 **Beyşehir** Turk
92B2 **Beyşehir Gölü** *L* Turk
94B2 **Beyt Shean** Israel
47C1 **Bezau** Austria
60E2 **Bezhetsk** Russian Fed
49C3 **Béziers** France
90C2 **Bezmein** Turkmenistan
63C2 **Beznosova** Russian Fed
86B1 **Bhadgaon** Nepal
87C1 **Bhadrāchalam** India
86B2 **Bhadrakh** India
87B2 **Bhadra Res** India
87B2 **Bhadrāvati** India
84B3 **Bhag** Pak
86B1 **Bhāgalpur** India
84C2 **Bhakkar** Pak
82D3 **Bhamo** Burma
85D4 **Bhandāra** India
85D3 **Bharatpur** India
85C4 **Bharūch** India
86B2 **Bhātiāpāra Ghat** Bang
84C2 **Bhatinda** India
87A2 **Bhatkal** India
86B2 **Bhātpāra** India
85C4 **Bhāvnagar** India
84C2 **Bhera** Pak
86A1 **Bheri** *R* Nepal
86A2 **Bhilai** India
85C3 **Bhīlwāra** India
87C1 **Bhīmavaram** India
85D3 **Bhind** India
84D3 **Bhiwāni** India
87B1 **Bhongir** India
85D4 **Bhopāl** India
86B2 **Bhubaneshwar** India
85B4 **Bhuj** India
85D4 **Bhusāwal** India
82C3 **Bhutan** Kingdom, Asia
71E4 **Biak** *I* Indon
58C2 **Biala Podlaska** Pol
58B2 **Bialograd** Pol
58C2 **Bialystok** Pol
38A1 **Biargtangar** *C* Iceland
90C2 **Bīarjmand** Iran
48B3 **Biarritz** France
47C1 **Biasca** Switz
92B4 **Biba** Egypt
74E2 **Bibai** Japan
100A2 **Bibala** Angola
57B3 **Biberach** Germany
97B4 **Bibiani** Ghana
54C1 **Bicaz** Rom
97C4 **Bida** Nig
87B1 **Bīdar** India
91C5 **Bidbid** Oman
43B4 **Bideford** Eng
43B4 **Bideford B** Eng
96C2 **Bidon 5** Alg
58C2 **Biebrza** Pol
52A1 **Biel** Switz
59B2 **Bielawa** Pol
56B2 **Bielefeld** Germany
47B1 **Bieler See** *L* Switz
52A1 **Biella** Italy
58C2 **Bielsk Podlaski** Pol
76D3 **Bien Hoa** Viet
53B2 **Biferno** *R* Italy
92A1 **Biga** Turk
55C3 **Bigadiç** Turk
19C3 **Big Black** *R* USA
18A1 **Big Blue** *R* USA
17B2 **Big Cypress Swamp** USA
4D3 **Big Delta** USA
49D2 **Bigent** Germany
13F2 **Biggar** Can
5H4 **Biggar Kindersley** Can
109D1 **Biggenden** Aust
12G3 **Bigger,Mt** Can
8C2 **Bighorn** *R* USA
76C3 **Bight of Bangkok** *B* Thai
97C4 **Bight of Benin** *B* W Africa
97C4 **Bight of Biafra** *B* Cam
6C3 **Big I** Can
47C1 **Bignasco** Switz
97A3 **Bignona** Sen
21B2 **Big Pine** USA
17B2 **Big Pine Key** USA
22C3 **Big Pine Mt** USA
14A2 **Big Rapids** USA
5H4 **Big River** Can
9C3 **Big Spring** USA
7A4 **Big Trout L** Can
7B4 **Big Trout Lake** Can
52C2 **Bihać** Bosnia-Herzegovina
86B1 **Bihār** India
86B2 **Bihar** State, India
99D3 **Biharamulo** Tanz
60B4 **Bihor** *Mt* Rom
87B1 **Bijāpur** India
87C1 **Bijāpur** India
90A2 **Bījār** Iran
86A1 **Bijauri** Nepal
54A2 **Bijeljina** Bosnia-Herzegovina
73B4 **Bijie** China
84D3 **Bijnor** India
84C3 **Bijnot** Pak
84C3 **Bikāner** India
94B2 **Bikfaya** Leb
69F2 **Bikin** Russian Fed
98B3 **Bikoro** Zaïre
85C3 **Bilara** India
84D2 **Bilaspur** India
86A2 **Bilāspur** India
76B3 **Bilauktaung Range** *Mts* Thai
50B1 **Bilbao** Spain
Bilbo = Bilbao
59B3 **Bílé** *R* Czech Republic
54A2 **Bileća** Bosnia-Herzegovina
92B1 **Bilecik** Turk
98C2 **Bili** *R* Zaïre
79B3 **Biliran** *I* Phil
8C2 **Billings** USA
95A3 **Bilma** Niger
11B3 **Biloxi** USA
98C1 **Biltine** Chad
85D4 **Bina-Etawa** India
79B3 **Binalbagan** Phil
101C2 **Bindura** Zim
100B2 **Binga** Zim
101C2 **Binga** *Mt* Zim
109D1 **Bingara** Aust
57B3 **Bingen** Germany
10C2 **Binghamton** USA
78D1 **Bingkor** Malay
93D2 **Bingöl** Turk
72D3 **Binhai** China
78A2 **Bintan** *I* Indon
78A3 **Bintuhan** Indon
78C2 **Bintulu** Malay
29B3 **Bió Bió** *R* Chile
102J4 **Bioko** *I* Atlantic O
87B1 **Bīr** India
95B2 **Bîr Abu Husein** *Well* Egypt
95B2 **Bi'r al Harash** *Well* Libya
98C1 **Birao** CAR
86B1 **Biratnagar** Nepal
12E1 **Birch Creek** USA
108B3 **Birchip** Aust
5G4 **Birch Mts** Can
7A4 **Bird** Can
106C3 **Birdsville** Aust
106C2 **Birdum** Aust
86A1 **Birganj** Nepal
94A3 **Bîr Gifgâfa** *Well* Egypt
94A3 **Bîr Hasana** *Well* Egypt
35A2 **Birigui** Brazil
90C3 **Birjand** Iran
92B4 **Birkat Qarun** *L* Egypt
46D2 **Birkenfeld** Germany
42C3 **Birkenhead** Eng
60C4 **Bîrlad** Rom
94A3 **Bir Lahfân** *Well* Egypt
43C3 **Birmingham** Eng
11B3 **Birmingham** USA
95B2 **Bîr Misâha** *Well* Egypt
96A2 **Bir Moghrein** Maur
97C3 **Birnin Kebbi** Nig
97C3 **Birni N'Konni** Nig
69F2 **Birobidzhan** Russian Fed
45C2 **Birr** Irish Rep
51C2 **Bir Rabalou** Alg
109C1 **Birrie** *R* Aust
44C2 **Birsay** Scot
61J2 **Birsk** Russian Fed
95B2 **Bîr Tarfâwi** *Well* Egypt
63B2 **Biryusa** Russian Fed
39J7 **Biržai** Lithuania
96B2 **Bir Zreigat** *Well* Maur
48A2 **Biscay,B of** France/ Spain
17B2 **Biscayne B** USA
46D2 **Bischwiller** France
73B4 **Bishan** China
82B1 **Bishkek** Kirghizia
8B3 **Bishop** USA
42D2 **Bishop Auckland** Eng
43E4 **Bishop's Stortford** Eng
86A2 **Bishrāmpur** India
96C1 **Biskra** Alg
79C4 **Bislig** Phil
8C2 **Bismarck** USA
90A3 **Bīsotūn** Iran
97A3 **Bissau** Guinea-Bissau
10A1 **Bissett** Can
5G4 **Bistcho L** Can
54C1 **Bistrita** *R* Rom
98B2 **Bitam** Gabon
57B3 **Bitburg** Germany
46D2 **Bitche** France
93D2 **Bitlis** Turk
55B2 **Bitola** Macedonia
56C2 **Bitterfeld** Germany
100A4 **Bitterfontein** S Africa
92B3 **Bitter Lakes** Egypt
8B2 **Bitteroot Range** *Mts* USA
74D3 **Biwa-ko** *L* Japan
99E1 **Biyo Kaboba** Eth
65K4 **Biysk** Russian Fed
96C1 **Bizerte** Tunisia
51C2 **Bj bou Arréridj** Alg
52C1 **Bjelovar** Croatia
96B2 **Bj Flye Ste Marie** Alg
64C2 **Bjørnøya** *I* Barents S
12F1 **Black** *R* USA
18B2 **Black** *R* USA
107D3 **Blackall** Aust
42C3 **Blackburn** Eng
4D3 **Blackburn,Mt** USA
13E2 **Black Diamond** Can
5H5 **Black Hills** USA
44B3 **Black Isle** *Pen* Scot
27R3 **Blackman's** Barbados
43C4 **Black Mts** Wales
43C3 **Blackpool** Eng
27H1 **Black River** Jamaica
8B2 **Black Rock Desert** USA
65E5 **Black S** Asia/Europe
45A1 **Blacksod B** Irish Rep
109D2 **Black Sugarloaf** *Mt* Aust
97B3 **Black Volta** *R* Ghana
41B3 **Blackwater** *R* Irish Rep
18A2 **Blackwell** USA
54B2 **Blagoevgrad** Bulg
63E2 **Blagoveshchensk** Russian Fed
20B1 **Blaine** USA
44C3 **Blair Atholl** Scot
44C3 **Blairgowrie** Scot
17B1 **Blakely** USA
108A1 **Blanche,L** Aust
34A2 **Blanco** *R* Arg
34B1 **Blanco** *R* Arg
8A2 **Blanco,C** USA
7E4 **Blanc Sablon** Can
43C4 **Blandford Forum** Eng
46A2 **Blangy-sur-Bresle** France
46B1 **Blankenberge** Belg
101C2 **Blantyre** Malawi
48B2 **Blaye** France
109C2 **Blayney** Aust
111B2 **Blenheim** NZ
96C1 **Blida** Alg
14B1 **Blind River** Can
108A2 **Blinman** Aust
78C4 **Blitar** Indon
15D2 **Block I** USA
16D2 **Block Island Sd** USA

101G1 **Bloemfontein** S Africa
101G1 **Bloemhof** S Africa
101G1 **Bloemhof Dam** *Res* S Africa
33F3 **Blommesteinmeer** *L* Surinam
38A1 **Blonduós** Iceland
45B1 **Bloody Foreland** *C* Irish Rep
14A3 **Bloomfield** Indiana, USA
18B1 **Bloomfield** Iowa, USA
10B2 **Bloomington** Illinois, USA
14A3 **Bloomington** Indiana, USA
16A2 **Bloomsburg** USA
78C4 **Blora** Indon
6H3 **Blosseville Kyst** *Mts* Greenland
57B3 **Bludenz** Austria
11B3 **Bluefield** USA
32A1 **Bluefields** Nic
26B3 **Blue Mountain Peak** *Mt* Jamaica
16A2 **Blue Mt** USA
109D2 **Blue Mts** Aust
27J1 **Blue Mts** Jamaica
8A2 **Blue Mts** USA
Blue Nile = Bahr el Azraq
99D1 **Blue Nile** *R* Sudan
4G3 **Bluenose L** Can
11B3 **Blue Ridge Mts** USA
13D2 **Blue River** Can
45B1 **Blue Stack** *Mt* Irish Rep
111A3 **Bluff** NZ
106A4 **Bluff Knoll** *Mt* Aust
30G4 **Blumenau** Brazil
49D2 **Blundez** Austria
20B2 **Bly** USA
12E3 **Blying Sd** USA
42D2 **Blyth** Eng
9B3 **Blythe** USA
11B3 **Blytheville** USA
97A4 **Bo** Sierra Leone
79B3 **Boac** Phil
72D2 **Boading** China
14B2 **Boardman** USA
63C3 **Boatou** China
33E3 **Boa Vista** Brazil
97A4 **Boa Vista** *I* Cape Verde
76E1 **Bobai** China
47C2 **Bóbbio** Italy
97B3 **Bobo Dioulasso** Burkina
60C3 **Bobruysk** Belorussia
17B2 **Boca Chica Key** *I* USA
32D5 **Bôca do Acre** Brazil
35C1 **Bocaiúva** Brazil
98B2 **Bocaranga** CAR
17B2 **Boca Raton** USA
59C3 **Bochnia** Pol
56B2 **Bocholt** Germany
46D1 **Bochum** Germany
100A2 **Bocoio** Angola
98B2 **Boda** CAR
63D2 **Bodaybo** Russian Fed
21A2 **Bodega Head** *Pt* USA
95A3 **Bodélé** *Region* Chad
38J5 **Boden** Sweden
47C1 **Bodensee** *L* Switz/ Germany
87B1 **Bodhan** India
87B2 **Bodināyakkanūr** India
43B4 **Bodmin** Eng
43B4 **Bodmin Moor** *Upland* Eng
38G5 **Bodø** Nor
55C3 **Bodrum** Turk
98C3 **Boende** Zaïre
97A3 **Boffa** Guinea
76B2 **Bogale** Burma
19C3 **Bogalusa** USA
109C2 **Bogan** *R* Aust
97B3 **Bogandé** Burkina
6H3 **Bogarnes** Iceland
92C2 **Boğazlıyan** Turk
61K2 **Bogdanovich** Russian Fed
68A2 **Bogda Shan** *Mt* China
100A3 **Bogenfels** Namibia
109D1 **Boggabilla** Aust
109C2 **Boggabri** Aust
45B2 **Boggeragh Mts** Irish Rep
79B3 **Bogo** Phil
109C3 **Bogong,Mt** Aust
78B4 **Bogor** Indon
61H2 **Bogorodskoye** Russian Fed
32C3 **Bogotá** Colombia
63A2 **Bogotol** Russian Fed
86B2 **Bogra** Bang
72D2 **Bo Hai** *B* China
46B2 **Bohain-en-Vermandois** France
72D2 **Bohai Wan** *B* China
57C3 **Böhmer-Wald** *Upland* Germany
79B4 **Bohol** *I* Phil
79B4 **Bohol S** Phil
35A1 **Bois** *R* Brazil
14B1 **Bois Blanc I** USA
8B2 **Boise** USA
96A2 **Bojador,C** Mor
79B2 **Bojeador,C** Phil
90C2 **Bojnūrd** Iran
97A3 **Boké** Guinea
109C1 **Bokhara** *R* Aust
39F7 **Boknafjord** *Inlet* Nor
98B3 **Boko** Congo
76C3 **Bokor** Camb
98C3 **Bokungu** Zaïre
98B1 **Bol** Chad
23A1 **Bolaānos** Mexico
97A3 **Bolama** Guinea-Bissau
23A1 **Bolanos** *R* Mexico
48C2 **Bolbec** France
97B4 **Bole** Ghana
59B2 **Boleslawiec** Pol
97B3 **Bolgatanga** Ghana
60C4 **Bolgrad** Ukraine
34C3 **Bolivar** Arg
18B2 **Bolivar** Missouri, USA
18C2 **Bolivar** Tennessee, USA
30C2 **Bolivia** Republic, S America
38H6 **Bollnas** Sweden
109C1 **Bollon** Aust
32C2 **Bollvar** *Mt* Ven
52B2 **Bologna** Italy
60D2 **Bologoye** Russian Fed
69F2 **Bolon'** Russian Fed
61G3 **Bol'shoy Irgiz** *R* Russian Fed
74C2 **Bol'shoy Kamen** Russian Fed
Bol'shoy Kavkaz =Caucasus
61G4 **Bol'shoy Uzen** *R* Kazakhstan
9C4 **Bolson de Mapimi** *Desert* Mexico
43C3 **Bolton** Eng
92B1 **Bolu** Turk
38A1 **Bolungarvik** Iceland
92B2 **Bolvadin** Turk
52B1 **Bolzano** Italy
98B3 **Boma** Zaïre
107D4 **Bombala** Aust
87A1 **Bombay** India
99D2 **Bombo** Uganda
35B1 **Bom Despacho** Brazil
86C1 **Bomdila** India
97A4 **Bomi Hills** Lib
31C4 **Bom Jesus da Lapa** Brazil
63E2 **Bomnak** Russian Fed
99C2 **Bomokandi** *R* Zaïre
98C2 **Bomu** *R* CAR/Zaïre
27D4 **Bonaire** *I* Caribbean S
12F2 **Bona,Mt** USA
25D3 **Bonanza** Nic
7E5 **Bonavista** Can
108A2 **Bon Bon** Aust
98C2 **Bondo** Zaïre
97B4 **Bondoukou** Ivory Coast
Bône = 'Annaba
33E3 **Bonfim** Guyana
98C2 **Bongandanga** Zaïre
98B1 **Bongor** Chad
19A3 **Bonham** USA
53A2 **Bonifacio** Corse
52A2 **Bonifacio,Str of** *Chan* Medit S
Bonin Is = Ogasawara Gunto
17B2 **Bonita Springs** USA
57B2 **Bonn** Germany
20C1 **Bonners Ferry** USA
12H1 **Bonnet Plume** *R* Can
13E2 **Bonnyville** Can
97A4 **Bonthe** Sierra Leone
99E1 **Booaaso** Somalia
108B2 **Booligal** Aust
109D1 **Boonah** Aust
15C2 **Boonville** USA
109C2 **Boorowa** Aust
6A2 **Boothia,G of** Can
6A2 **Boothia Pen** Can
98B3 **Booué** Gabon
108A1 **Bopeechee** Aust
99D2 **Bor** Sudan
92B2 **Bor** Turk
54B2 **Bor** Serbia, Yugos
8B2 **Borah Peak** *Mt* USA
39G7 **Borås** Sweden
91B4 **Borāzjān** Iran
108A3 **Borda,C** Aust
48B3 **Bordeaux** France
4G2 **Borden I** Can
6B2 **Borden Pen** Can
16B2 **Bordentown** USA
42C2 **Borders** Region, Scot
108B3 **Bordertown** Aust
96C2 **Bordi Omar Dris** Alg
8D1 **Borens River** Can
38A2 **Borgarnes** Iceland
9C3 **Borger** USA
39H7 **Borgholm** Sweden
47C2 **Borgosia** Italy
47D1 **Borgo Valsugana** Italy
59C3 **Borislav** Ukraine
61F3 **Borisoglebsk** Russian Fed
60C3 **Borisov** Belorussia
60E3 **Borisovka** Russian Fed
95A3 **Borkou** *Region* Chad
39H6 **Borlänge** Sweden
47C2 **Bormida** Italy
47D1 **Bormio** Italy
67F5 **Borneo** *I* Malay/ Indon
39H7 **Bornholm** *I* Den
55C3 **Bornova** Turk
98C2 **Boro** *R* Sudan
97B3 **Boromo** Burkina
60D2 **Borovichi** Russian Fed
106C2 **Borroloola** Aust
54B1 **Borsa** Rom
90A3 **Borūjed** Iran
90B3 **Borūjen** Iran
58B2 **Bory Tucholskie** Region, Pol
63D2 **Borzya** Russian Fed
73B5 **Bose** China
101G1 **Boshof** S Africa
54A2 **Bosna** *R* Bosnia-Herzegovina
37E4 **Bosnia-Herzegovina** Republic, Europe
75C1 **Bōsō-hantō** *B* Japan
Bosporus = Karadeniz Boğazi
51C2 **Bosquet** Alg
98B2 **Bossangoa** CAR
98B2 **Bossèmbélé** CAR
19B3 **Bossier City** USA
65K5 **Bosten Hu** *L* China
43D3 **Boston** Eng
10C2 **Boston** USA
11A3 **Boston Mts** USA
85C4 **Botād** India
54B2 **Botevgrad** Bulg
101G1 **Bothaville** S Africa
64C3 **Bothnia,G of** Sweden/Fin
100B3 **Botletli** *R* Botswana
60C4 **Botosani** Rom
100B3 **Botswana** Republic, Africa
53C3 **Botte Donato** *Mt* Italy
46D1 **Bottrop** Germany
35B2 **Botucatu** Brazil
7E5 **Botwood** Can
89D7 **Bouaké** Ivory Coast
98B2 **Bouar** CAR
96B1 **Bouârfa** Mor
98B2 **Bouca** CAR
51C2 **Boufarik** Alg
Bougie = Bejaïa
97B3 **Bougouni** Mali
46C2 **Bouillon** France
96B2 **Bou Izakarn** Mor
46D2 **Boulay-Moselle** France
8C2 **Boulder** Colorado, USA
9B3 **Boulder City** USA
22A2 **Boulder Creek** USA
48C1 **Boulogne** France
98B2 **Boumba** *R* CAR
97B4 **Bouna** Ivory Coast
8B3 **Boundary Peak** *Mt* USA
97B4 **Boundiali** Ivory Coa
107F3 **Bourail** Nouvelle Calédonie
97B3 **Bourem** Mali
49D2 **Bourg** France
49D2 **Bourg de Péage** France
48C2 **Bourges** France
48C3 **Bourg-Madame** France
49C2 **Bourgogne** Region, France
47B2 **Bourg-St-Maurice** France
108C2 **Bourke** Aust
43D4 **Bournemouth** Eng
96C1 **Bou Saâda** Alg
98B1 **Bousso** Chad
97A3 **Boutilmit** Maur
103J7 **Bouvet I** Atlantic O
34D2 **Bovril** Arg
13E2 **Bow** *R* Can
107D2 **Bowen** Aust
19A3 **Bowie** Texas, USA
13E2 **Bow Island** Can
11B3 **Bowling Green** Kentucky, USA
18B2 **Bowling Green** Missouri, USA
14B2 **Bowling Green** Ohi USA
15C3 **Bowling Green** Virginia, USA
15C2 **Bowmanville** Can
109D2 **Bowral** Aust
13C2 **Bowron** *R* Can
72D3 **Bo Xian** China
72D2 **Boxing** China
92B1 **Boyabat** Turk
98B2 **Boyali** CAR
5J4 **Boyd** Can
16B2 **Boyertown** USA
13E2 **Boyle** Can
41B3 **Boyle** Irish Rep
45C2 **Boyne** *R* Irish Rep
17B2 **Boynoton Beach** USA
98C2 **Boyoma Falls** Zaïre
55C3 **Bozca Ada** *I* Turk
55C3 **Boz Dağlari** *Mts* Turk
8B2 **Bozeman** USA
Bozen = Bolzano
98B2 **Bozene** Zaïre
98B2 **Bozoum** CAR
47B2 **Bra** Italy
52C2 **Brač** *I* Croatia
15C1 **Bracebridge** Can
95A2 **Brach** Libya
38H6 **Bräcke** Sweden
17B2 **Bradenton** USA

42D3 **Bradford** Eng
44E1 **Brae** Scot
44C3 **Braemar** Scot
50A1 **Braga** Port
34C3 **Bragado** Arg
50A1 **Bragana** Port
31B2 **Bragança** Brazil
35B2 **Bragança Paulista** Brazil
86C2 **Brahman-Baria** Bang
86B2 **Brāhmani** *R* India
86C1 **Brahmaputra** *R* India
7E5 **Braie Verte** Can
60C4 **Brăila** Rom
10A2 **Brainerd** USA
97A3 **Brakna** Region, Maur
5F4 **Bralorne** Can
14C2 **Brampton** Can
33E3 **Branco** *R* Brazil
100A3 **Brandberg** *Mt* Namibia
56C2 **Brandenburg** Germany
56C2 **Brandenburg** State, Germany
101G1 **Brandfort** S Africa
8D2 **Brandon** Can
100B4 **Brandvlei** S Africa
57C2 **Brandys nad Lebem** Czech Republic
58B2 **Braniewo** Pol
10B2 **Brantford** Can
108B3 **Branxholme** Aust
7D5 **Bras D'Or L** Can
35C1 **Brasíla de Minas** Brazil
32D6 **Brasiléia** Brazil
31B5 **Brasilia** Brazil
54C1 **Brasov** Rom
78D1 **Brassay Range** *Mts* Malay
59B3 **Bratislava** Slovakia
63C2 **Bratsk** Russian Fed
15D2 **Brattleboro** USA
56C2 **Braunschweig** Germany
97A4 **Brava** *I* Cape Verde
9B3 **Brawley** USA
45C2 **Bray** Irish Rep
6C3 **Bray I** Can
13D2 **Brazeau** *R* Can
13D2 **Brazeau,Mt** Can
28D4 **Brazil** Republic, S America
103G5 **Brazil Basin** Atlantic O
9D3 **Brazos** *R* USA
98B3 **Brazzaville** Congo
57C3 **Brdy** *Upland* Czech Republic
111A3 **Breaksea Sd** NZ
110B1 **Bream B** NZ
78B4 **Brebes** Indon
44C3 **Brechin** Scot
46C1 **Brecht** Belg
59B3 **Břeclav** Czech Republic
43C4 **Brecon** Wales
43C4 **Brecon Beacons** *Mts* Wales
43B3 **Brecon Beacons Nat Pk** Wales
56A2 **Breda** Neth
100B4 **Bredasdorp** S Africa
38H6 **Bredbyn** Sweden
61J3 **Bredy** Russian Fed
15C2 **Breezewood** USA
47C1 **Bregenz** Austria
47C1 **Bregenzer Ache** *R* Austria
38A1 **Breiðafjörður** *B* Iceland
47C2 **Brembo** *R* Italy
17A1 **Bremen** USA
56B2 **Bremen** Germany
56B2 **Bremerhaven** Germany
20B1 **Bremerton** USA
19A3 **Brenham** USA
57C3 **Brenner** *P* Austria/ Italy
47D2 **Breno** Italy
47D2 **Brenta** *R* Italy
22B2 **Brentwood** USA
52B1 **Brescia** Italy
Breslau = Wrocław
47D1 **Bressanone** Italy
44E1 **Bressay** *I* Scot
48B2 **Bressuire** France
58C2 **Brest** Belorussia
48B2 **Brest** France
48B2 **Bretagne** Region, France
46B2 **Breteuil** France
16B2 **Breton Woods** USA
110B1 **Brett,C** NZ
109C1 **Brewarrina** Aust
16C2 **Brewster** New York, USA
20C1 **Brewster** Washington, USA
101G1 **Breyten** S Africa
52C1 **Brežice** Slovenia
98C2 **Bria** CAR
49D3 **Briancon** France
49C2 **Briare** France
21B2 **Bridgeport** California, USA
15D2 **Bridgeport** Connecticut, USA
19A3 **Bridgeport** Texas, USA
22C1 **Bridgeport Res** USA
16B3 **Bridgeton** USA
27F4 **Bridgetown** Barbados
7D5 **Bridgewater** Can
16D2 **Bridgewater** USA
43C4 **Bridgwater** Eng
43C4 **Bridgwater B** Eng
42D2 **Bridlington** Eng
109C4 **Bridport** Aust
47B1 **Brienzer See** *L* Switz
46C2 **Briey** France
52A1 **Brig** Switz
8B2 **Brigham City** USA
109C3 **Bright** Aust
43D4 **Brighton** Eng
46E1 **Brilon** Germany
55A2 **Brindisi** Italy
19B3 **Brinkley** USA
107E3 **Brisbane** Aust
15D2 **Bristol** Connecticut, USA
43C4 **Bristol** Eng
15D2 **Bristol** Pennsylvania, USA
16D2 **Bristol** Rhode Island, USA
11B3 **Bristol** Tennessee, USA
12B3 **Bristol B** USA
43B4 **Bristol Chan** Eng/ Wales
4D3 **British** *Mts* USA
5F4 **British Columbia** Province, Can
6B1 **British Empire Range** *Mts* Can
101G1 **Brits** S Africa
100B4 **Britstown** S Africa
48C2 **Brive** France
59B3 **Brno** Czech Republic
17B1 **Broad** *R* USA
7C4 **Broadback** *R* Can
44A2 **Broad Bay** *Inlet* Scot
44B3 **Broadford** Scot
5H4 **Brochet** Can
4G2 **Brock I** Can
15C2 **Brockport** USA
16D1 **Brockton** USA
15C2 **Brockville** Can
6B2 **Brodeur Pen** Can
42B2 **Brodick** Scot
58B2 **Brodnica** Pol
60C3 **Brody** Ukraine
19B3 **Broken Bow** Oklahoma, USA
19B3 **Broken Bow L** USA
107D4 **Broken Hill** Aust
47C2 **Broni** Italy
38G5 **Brønnøysund** Nor
16C2 **Bronx** Borough, New York, USA
79A4 **Brooke's Point** Phil
18B2 **Brookfield** Missouri, USA
11A3 **Brookhaven** USA
20B2 **Brookings** Oregon, USA
8D2 **Brookings** South Dakota, USA
16D1 **Brookline** USA
16C2 **Brooklyn** Borough, New York, USA
5G4 **Brooks** Can
12C3 **Brooks,L** USA
12A1 **Brooks Mt** USA
4C3 **Brooks Range** *Mts* USA
17B2 **Brooksville** USA
109D1 **Brooloo** Aust
106B2 **Broome** Aust
44C2 **Brora** Scot
20B2 **Brothers** USA
95A3 **Broulkou** Chad
13E3 **Browning** USA
9D4 **Brownsville** USA
9D3 **Brownwood** USA
46B1 **Bruay-en-Artois** France
106A3 **Bruce,Mt** Aust
14B1 **Bruce Pen** Can
59B3 **Brück an der Mur** Austria
Bruges = Brugge
46B1 **Brugge** Belg
46D1 **Brühl** Germany
78C2 **Brunei** Sultanate, S E Asia
52B1 **Brunico** Italy
111B2 **Brunner,L** NZ
11B3 **Brunswick** Georgia, USA
18B2 **Brunswick** Mississippi, USA
29B6 **Brunswick,Pen de** Chile
109C4 **Bruny I** Aust
61F1 **Brusenets** Russian Fed
26A3 **Brus Laguna** Honduras
Brüssel = Bruxelles
56A2 **Bruxelles** Belg
9D3 **Bryan** USA
108A2 **Bryan,Mt** Aust
60D3 **Bryansk** Russian Fed
19B3 **Bryant** USA
59B2 **Brzeg** Pol
93E4 **Būbīyan** *I* Kuwait/ Iraq
99D3 **Bubu** *R* Tanz
32C2 **Bucaramanga** Colombia
44D3 **Buchan** *Oilfield* N Sea
97A4 **Buchanan** Lib
44D3 **Buchan Deep** N Sea
6C2 **Buchan G** Can
40C2 **Buchan Ness** *Pen* Scot
7E5 **Buchans** Can
34C2 **Buchardo** Arg
Bucharest = Bucureşti
47C1 **Buchs** Switz
43D3 **Buckingham** Eng
12B1 **Buckland** USA
12B1 **Buckland** *R* USA
108A2 **Buckleboo** Aust
98B3 **Buco Zau** Congo
54C2 **Bucureşti** Rom
59B3 **Budapest** Hung
84D3 **Budaun** India
43B4 **Bude** Eng
19B3 **Bude** USA
61F5 **Budennovsk** Russian Fed
54A2 **Budva** Montenegro, Yugos
98A2 **Buéa** Cam
22B3 **Buellton** USA
34B2 **Buena Esperanza** Arg
32B3 **Buenaventura** Colombia
23A2 **Buenavista** Mexico
29E2 **Buenos Aires** Arg
29D3 **Buenos Aires** State, Arg
18B2 **Buffalo** Mississipi, USA
10C2 **Buffalo** New York, USA
8C2 **Buffalo** South Dakota, USA
19A3 **Buffalo** Texas, USA
8C2 **Buffalo** Wyoming, USA
101H1 **Buffalo** *R* S Africa
13E2 **Buffalo L** Alberta, Can
5G3 **Buffalo L** Northwest Territories, Can
5H4 **Buffalo Narrows** Can
17B1 **Buford** USA
54C2 **Buftea** Rom
59C2 **Bug** *R* Pol/Ukraine
32B3 **Buga** Colombia
90B2 **Bugdayli** Turkmenistan
61H3 **Bugulma** Russian Fed
61H3 **Buguruslan** Russian Fed
93C2 **Buhayrat al Asad** *Res* Syria
41C3 **Builth Wells** Wales
34A2 **Buin** Chile
99C3 **Bujumbura** Burundi
98C3 **Bukama** Zaïre
99C3 **Bukavu** Zaïre
80E2 **Bukhara** Uzbekistan
78C2 **Bukit Batubrok** *Mt* Indon
70B4 **Bukittinggi** Indon
99D3 **Bukoba** Tanz
78D3 **Buku Gandadiwata** *Mt* Indon
71E4 **Bula** Indon
79B3 **Bulan** Phil
84D3 **Bulandshahr** India
100B3 **Bulawayo** Zim
55C3 **Buldan** Turk
85D4 **Buldāna** India
68C2 **Bulgan** Mongolia
54B2 **Bulgaria** Republic, Europe
47B1 **Bulle** Switz
111B2 **Buller** *R* NZ
109C3 **Buller,Mt** Aust
106A4 **Bullfinch** Aust
108B1 **Bulloo** *R* Aust
108B1 **Bulloo Downs** Aust
108B1 **Bulloo L** Aust
18B2 **Bull Shoals Res** USA
34A3 **Bulnes** Chile
71F4 **Bulolo** PNG
101G1 **Bultfontein** S Africa
98C2 **Bumba** Zaïre
76B2 **Bumphal Dam** Thai
99D2 **Buna** Kenya
106A4 **Bunbury** Aust
45C1 **Buncrana** Irish Rep
107E3 **Bundaberg** Aust
109D2 **Bundarra** Aust
85D3 **Būndi** India
45B1 **Bundoran** Irish Rep
109C1 **Bungil** *R* Aust
98B3 **Bungo** Angola
75A2 **Bungo-suidō** *Str* Japan
70B3 **Bunguran** *I* Ind
99D2 **Bunia** Zaïre
18B2 **Bunker** USA
19B3 **Bunkie** USA
17B2 **Bunnell** USA
78C3 **Buntok** Indon
71D3 **Buol** Indon
94C2 **Burāq** Syria
98C1 **Buram** Sudan
99E2 **Burao** Somalia
79B3 **Burauen** Phil
80C3 **Buraydah** S Arabia
21B3 **Burbank** USA
109C2 **Burcher** Aust
92B2 **Burdur** Turk
63F3 **Bureinskiy Khrebet** *Mts* Russian Fed
56C2 **Burg** Germany
54C2 **Burgas** Bulg
17C1 **Burgaw** USA
47B1 **Burgdorf** Switz
100B4 **Burgersdorp** S Africa
50B1 **Burgos** Spain
58B1 **Burgsvik** Sweden

55C3 **Burhaniye** Turk
85D4 **Burhānpur** India
79B3 **Burias** *I* Phil
76C2 **Buriram** Thai
35B1 **Buritis** Brazil
13B2 **Burke Chan** Can
106C2 **Burketown** Aust
97B3 **Burkina** Republic, Africa
15C1 **Burks Falls** Can
8B2 **Burley** USA
10A2 **Burlington** Iowa, USA
16B2 **Burlington** New Jersey, USA
10C2 **Burlington** Vermont, USA
20B1 **Burlington** Washington, USA
83D3 **Burma** Republic, Asia
20B2 **Burney** USA
16A2 **Burnham** USA
107D5 **Burnie** Aust
42C3 **Burnley** Eng
20C2 **Burns** USA
5F4 **Burns Lake** Can
82C1 **Burqin** China
108A2 **Burra** Aust
109D2 **Burragorang,L** Aust
44C2 **Burray** *I* Scot
109C2 **Burren Junction** Aust
109C2 **Burrinjuck Res** Aust
60C5 **Bursa** Turk
80B3 **Bur Safâga** Egypt
Bûr Sa'îd = Port Said
14B2 **Burton** USA
43D3 **Burton upon Trent** Eng
38J6 **Burtrask** Sweden
108B2 **Burtundy** Aust
71D4 **Buru** Indon
99C3 **Burundi** Republic, Africa
78A2 **Burung** Indon
63D2 **Buryatskaya Respublika,** Russian Fed
99D1 **Burye** Eth
61H4 **Burynshik** Kazakhstan
43E3 **Bury St Edmunds** Eng
91B4 **Būshehr** Iran
98B3 **Busira** *R* Zaïre
58C2 **Buskozdroj** Pol
94C2 **Busrā ash Shām** Syria
106A4 **Busselton** Aust
49D2 **Busto** Italy
52A1 **Busto Arsizio** Italy
79A3 **Busuanga** *I* Phil
98C2 **Buta** Zaïre
34B3 **Buta Ranquil** Arg
99C3 **Butare** Rwanda
42B2 **Bute** *I* Scot
69E2 **Butha Qi** China
14C2 **Butler** USA
8B2 **Butte** USA
77C4 **Butterworth** Malay
40B2 **Butt of Lewis** *C* Scot
6D3 **Button Is** Can
79C4 **Butuan** Phil
71D4 **Butung** *I* Indon
61F3 **Buturlinovka** Russian Fed
86A1 **Butwal** Nepal
99E2 **Buulo Barde** Somalia
99E2 **Buur Hakaba** Somalia
61F2 **Buy** Russian Fed
72B1 **Buyant Ovvo** Mongolia
61G5 **Buynaksk** Russian Fed
63D3 **Buyr Nuur** *L* Mongolia
93D2 **Büyük Ağri** *Mt* Turk
92A2 **Büyük Menderes** *R* Turk
54C1 **Buzău** Rom
54C1 **Buzau** *R* Rom
61H3 **Buzuluk** Russian Fed
16D2 **Buzzards B** USA
54C2 **Byala** Bulg
54B2 **Byala Slatina** Bulg
4H2 **Byam Martin** *Chan* Can
4H2 **Byam Martin I** Can
Byblos = Jubail
94B1 **Byblos** Hist Site, Leb
58B2 **Bydgoszcz** Pol
39F7 **Bygland** Nor
6C2 **Bylot I** Can
109C2 **Byrock** Aust
22B2 **Byron** USA
109D1 **Byron,C** Aust
59B2 **Bytom** Pol

C

30E4 **Caacupé** Par
100A2 **Caála** Angola
13B2 **Caamano Sd** Can
30E4 **Caazapá** Par
79B2 **Cabanatuan** Phil
31E3 **Cabedelo** Brazil
50A2 **Cabeza del Buey** Spain
34C3 **Cabildo** Arg
34A2 **Cabildo** Chile
32C1 **Cabimas** Ven
98B3 **Cabinda** Angola
98B3 **Cabinda** Province, Angola
27C3 **Cabo Beata** Dom Rep
51C2 **Cabo Binibeca** *C* Spain
53A3 **Cabo Carbonara** *C* Sardegna
34A3 **Cabo Carranza** *C* Chile
50A2 **Cabo Carvoeiro** *C* Port
9B3 **Cabo Colnett** *C* Mexico
32B2 **Cabo Corrientes** *C* Colombia
24B2 **Cabo Corrientes** *C* Mexico
26B3 **Cabo Cruz** *C* Cuba
50B1 **Cabo de Ajo** *C* Spain
51C1 **Cabo de Caballeria** *C* Spain
51C1 **Cabo de Creus** *C* Spain
50B2 **Cabo de Gata** *C* Spain
29C7 **Cabo de Hornos** *C* Chile
51C2 **Cabo de la Nao** *C* Spain
50A1 **Cabo de Peñas** *C* Spain
50A2 **Cabo de Roca** *C* Port
51C2 **Cabo de Salinas** *C* Spain
35C2 **Cabo de São Tomé** *C* Brazil
50A2 **Cabo de São Vicente** *C* Port
50A2 **Cabo de Sines** *C* Port
51C1 **Cabo de Tortosa** *C* Spain
29C4 **Cabo Dos Bahias** *C* Arg
50A2 **Cabo Espichel** *C* Port
9B4 **Cabo Falso** *C* Mexico
51B2 **Cabo Ferrat** *C* Alg
50A1 **Cabo Finisterre** *C* Spain
51C1 **Cabo Formentor** *C* Spain
35C2 **Cabo Frio** Brazil
35C2 **Cabo Frio** *C* Brazil
26A4 **Cabo Gracias à Dios** Honduras
31B2 **Cabo Maguarinho** *C* Brazil
50A2 **Cabo Negro** *C* Mor
109D1 **Caboolture** Aust
33G3 **Cabo Orange** *C* Brazil
21B3 **Cabo Punta Banda** *C* Mexico
101C2 **Cabora Bassa Dam** Mozam
24A1 **Caborca** Mexico
24C2 **Cabo Rojo** *C* Mexico
23B1 **Cabos** Mexico
29C6 **Cabo San Diego** *C* Arg
32A4 **Cabo San Lorenzo** *C* Ecuador
53A3 **Cabo Teulada** *C* Sardegna
50A2 **Cabo Trafalgar** *C* Spain
50B2 **Cabo Tres Forcas** *C* Mor
29C5 **Cabo Tres Puntas** *C* Arg
7D5 **Cabot Str** Can
50B2 **Cabra** Spain
50A1 **Cabreira** *Mt* Port
51C2 **Cabrera** *I* Spain
34A3 **Cabrero** Chile
51B2 **Cabriel** *R* Spain
23B2 **Cacahuamilpa** Mexico
54B2 **Čačak** Serbia, Yugos
23B2 **C A Carillo** Mexico
30E2 **Cáceres** Brazil
50A2 **Caceres** Spain
18B2 **Cache** *R* USA
13C2 **Cache Creek** Can
30C4 **Cachi** Arg
33G5 **Cachimbo** Brazil
31D4 **Cachoeira** Brazil
35A1 **Cachoeira Alta** Brazil
31D3 **Cachoeira de Paulo Alfonso** *Waterfall* Brazil
29F2 **Cachoeira do Sul** Brazil
31C6 **Cachoeiro de Itapemirim** Brazil
22C3 **Cachuma,L** USA
100A2 **Cacolo** Angola
100A2 **Caconda** Angola
35A1 **Caçu** Brazil
100A2 **Caculuvar** *R* Angola
59B3 **Čadca** Slovakia
43C3 **Cader Idris** *Mts* Wales
10B2 **Cadillac** USA
79B3 **Cadiz** Phil
50A2 **Cadiz** Spain
48B2 **Caen** France
42B3 **Caernarfon** Wales
43B3 **Caernarfon B** Wales
94B2 **Caesarea** *Hist Site* Israel
31C4 **Caetité** Brazil
30C4 **Cafayate** Arg
92B2 **Caga Tepe** Turk
79B2 **Cagayan** *R* Phil
79B4 **Cagayan de Oro** Phil
79B4 **Cagayan Is** Phil
53A3 **Cagliari** Sardegna
27D3 **Caguas** Puerto Rico
45B3 **Caha Mts** Irish Rep
45A3 **Cahersiveen** Irish Rep
45C2 **Cahir** Irish Rep
45C2 **Cahone Pt** Irish Rep
48C3 **Cahors** France
101C2 **Caia** Mozam
100B2 **Caianda** Angola
35A1 **Caiapó** *R* Brazil
35A1 **Caiapônia** Brazil
31D3 **Caicó** Brazil
26C2 **Caicos Is** Caribbean S
11C4 **Caicos Pass** The Bahamas
12C2 **Cairn Mt** USA
44C3 **Cairngorms** *Mts* Scot
107D2 **Cairns** Aust
92B3 **Cairo** Egypt
11B3 **Cairo** USA
108B1 **Caiwarro** Aust
32B5 **Cajabamba** Peru
32B5 **Cajamarca** Peru
27D5 **Calabozo** Ven
54B2 **Calafat** Rom
29B6 **Calafate** Arg
79B3 **Calagua Is** Phil
51B1 **Calahorra** Spain
48C1 **Calais** France
30C3 **Calama** Chile
32C3 **Calamar** Colombia
79A3 **Calamian Group** *Is* Phil
98B3 **Calandula** Angola
70A3 **Calang** Indon
95B2 **Calanscio Sand Sea** Libya
79B3 **Calapan** Phil
54C2 **Calarasi** Rom
51B1 **Calatayud** Spain
22B2 **Calaveras Res** USA
79B3 **Calbayog** Phil
19B4 **Calcasieu L** USA
86B2 **Calcutta** India
50A2 **Caldas da Rainha** Port
31B5 **Caldas Novas** Brazil
30B4 **Caldera** Chile
8B2 **Caldwell** USA
29C5 **Caleta Olivia** Arg
9B3 **Calexico** USA
5G4 **Calgary** Can
17B1 **Calhoun** USA
17B1 **Calhoun Falls** USA
32B3 **Cali** Colombia
87B2 **Calicut** India
8B3 **Caliente** Nevada, USA
8A3 **California** State, USA
22C3 **California Aqueduct** USA
87B2 **Calimera,Pt** India
34B2 **Calingasta** Arg
22A1 **Calistoga** USA
108B1 **Callabonna** *R* Aust
108A1 **Callabonna,L** Aust
15C1 **Callander** Can
44B3 **Callander** Scot
108A1 **Callanna** Aust
32B6 **Callao** Peru
13E1 **Calling L** Can
23B1 **Calnali** Mexico
17B2 **Caloosahatchee** *R* USA
109D1 **Caloundra** Aust
23B2 **Calpulalpan** Mexico
53B3 **Caltanissetta** Italy
98B3 **Caluango** Angola
100A2 **Calulo** Angola
100A2 **Caluquembe** Angola
99F1 **Caluula** Somalia
13B2 **Calvert I** Can
52A2 **Calvi** Corse
23A1 **Calvillo** Mexico
100A4 **Calvinia** S Africa
25E2 **Camagüey** Cuba
25E2 **Camagüey,Arch de** Cuba
30B2 **Camaná** Peru
30C3 **Camargo** Bol
22C3 **Camarillo** USA
29C4 **Camarones** Arg
20B1 **Camas** USA
98B3 **Camaxilo** Angola
98B3 **Cambatela** Angola
76C3 **Cambodia** Republic, S E Asia
43B4 **Camborne** Eng
49C1 **Cambrai** France
43C3 **Cambrian Mts** Wales
14B2 **Cambridge** Can
43D3 **Cambridge** County, Eng
43E3 **Cambridge** Eng
27H1 **Cambridge** Jamaica
15C3 **Cambridge** Maryland, USA
15D2 **Cambridge** Massachussets, USA
110C1 **Cambridge** NZ
14B2 **Cambridge** Ohio, USA
4H3 **Cambridge Bay** Can
60E5 **Cam Burun** *Pt* Turk
11A3 **Camden** Arkansas, USA
109D2 **Camden** Aust
15D3 **Camden** New Jersey, USA
17B1 **Camden** South Carolina, USA
18B2 **Cameron** Missouri, USA

19A3 **Cameron** Texas, USA
4H2 **Cameron I** Can
111A3 **Cameron Mts** NZ
98A2 **Cameroon** Federal Republic, Africa
98A2 **Cameroun** *Mt* Cam
31B2 **Cametá** Brazil
79B4 **Camiguin** *I* Phil
79B2 **Camiling** Phil
17B1 **Camilla** USA
22B1 **Camino** USA
30D3 **Camiri** Bol
31C2 **Camocim** Brazil
98C3 **Camissombo** Angola
106C2 **Camooweal** Aust
34D2 **Campana** Arg
29A5 **Campana** *I* Chile
13B2 **Campania I** Can
111B2 **Campbell,C** NZ
13B2 **Campbell I** Can
105G6 **Campbell I** NZ
4E3 **Campbell,Mt** Can
84C2 **Campbellpore** Pak
5F5 **Campbell River** Can
7D5 **Campbellton** Can
109D2 **Campbelltown** Aust
42B2 **Campbeltown** Scot
25C3 **Campeche** Mexico
108B3 **Camperdown** Aust
31D3 **Campina Grande** Brazil
31B6 **Campinas** Brazil
35B1 **Campina Verde** Brazil
98A2 **Campo** Cam
53B2 **Campobasso** Italy
35B2 **Campo Belo** Brazil
35B1 **Campo Florido** Brazil
30D4 **Campo Gallo** Arg
30F3 **Campo Grande** Brazil
31C2 **Campo Maior** Brazil
30F3 **Campo Mourão** Brazil
35C2 **Campos** Brazil
35B1 **Campos Altos** Brazil
47D1 **Campo Tures** Italy
76D3 **Cam Ranh** Viet
5G4 **Camrose** Can
100A2 **Camucuio** Angola
27K1 **Canaan** Tobago
16C1 **Canaan** USA
100A2 **Canacupa** Angola
2F3 **Canada** Dominion, N America
29D2 **Cañada de Gomez** Arg
9C3 **Canadian** *R* USA
60C5 **Canakkale** Turk
34B3 **Canalejas** Arg
13D2 **Canal Flats** Can
24A1 **Cananea** Mexico
102G3 **Canary Basin** Atlantic O
Canary Is = Islas Canarias
23A2 **Canas** Mexico
24B2 **Canatlán** Mexico
11B4 **Canaveral,C** USA
31D5 **Canavieiras** Brazil
107D4 **Canberra** Aust
20B2 **Canby** California, USA
55C3 **Çandarli Körfezi** *B* Turk
16C2 **Candlewood,L** USA
29E2 **Canelones** Urug
18A2 **Caney** USA
100A2 **Cangamba** Angola
100B2 **Cangombe** Angola
72D2 **Cangzhou** China
7D4 **Caniapiscau** *R* Can
53B3 **Canicatti** Italy
31D2 **Canindé** Brazil
92B1 **Çankırı** Turk
13D2 **Canmore** Can
44A3 **Canna** *I* Scot
87B2 **Cannanore** India
49D3 **Cannes** France
109C3 **Cann River** Aust
30F4 **Canõas** Brazil
13F1 **Canoe L** Can
9C3 **Canon City** USA
108B2 **Canopus** Aust
5H4 **Canora** Can
109C2 **Canowindra** Aust
45C2 **Cansore Pt** Irish Rep
43E4 **Canterbury** Eng
111B2 **Canterbury Bight** *B* NZ
111B2 **Canterbury Plains** NZ
77D4 **Can Tho** Viet
Canton = Guangzhou
19C3 **Canton** Mississippi, USA
18B1 **Canton** Missouri, USA
10B2 **Canton** Ohio, USA
12E2 **Cantwell** USA
20C2 **Canyon City** USA
12J2 **Canyon Range** *Mts* Can
20B2 **Canyonville** USA
98C3 **Canzar** Angola
76D1 **Cao Bang** Viet
31B2 **Capanema** Brazil
35B2 **Capão Bonito** Brazil
48B3 **Capbreton** France
24B2 **Cap Corrientes** *C* Mexico
52A2 **Cap Corse** *C* Corse
48B2 **Cap de la Hague** *C* France
15D1 **Cap-de-la-Madeleine** Can
6C3 **Cap de Nouvelle-France** *C* Can
51C2 **Capdepera** Spain
23A2 **Cap de Tancitiario** *C* Mexico
109C4 **Cape Barren I** Aust
103J6 **Cape Basin** Atlantic O
7E5 **Cape Breton I** Can
97B4 **Cape Coast** Ghana
15D2 **Cape Cod B** USA
6C3 **Cape Dorset** Can
17C1 **Cape Fear** *R* USA
18C2 **Cape Girardeau** USA
6B3 **Cape Henrietta Maria** Can
Cape Horn = Cabo de Hornos
104E3 **Cape Johnston Depth** Pacific O
35C1 **Capelinha** Brazil
4B3 **Cape Lisburne** USA
100A2 **Capelongo** Angola
15D3 **Cape May** USA
5F5 **Cape Mendocino** USA
98B3 **Capenda Camulemba** Angola
4F2 **Cape Perry** Can
7A4 **Cape Tatnam** Can
100A4 **Cape Town** S Africa
102G4 **Cape Verde** *Is* Atlantic O
102G4 **Cape Verde Basin** Atlantic O
12F3 **Cape Yakataga** USA
107D2 **Cape York Pen** Aust
46A1 **Cap Gris Nez** *C* France
26C3 **Cap-Haitien** Haiti
31B2 **Capim** *R* Brazil
112C2 **Capitán Arturo Prat** *Base* Ant
27P2 **Cap Moule à Chique** *C* St Lucia
53C3 **Capo Isola de Correnti** *C* Italy
53C3 **Capo Rizzuto** *C* Italy
55A3 **Capo Santa Maria di Leuca** *C* Italy
53B3 **Capo San Vito** Italy
53C3 **Capo Spartivento** *C* Italy
27P2 **Cap Pt** St Lucia
53B2 **Capri** *I* Italy
100B2 **Caprivi Strip** Region, Namibia
52A2 **Cap Rosso** *C* Corse
102H4 **Cap Vert** *C* Sen
32C4 **Caquetá** *R* Colombia
54B2 **Caracal** Rom
33E3 **Caracaraí** Brazil
32D1 **Caracas** Ven
35B2 **Caraguatatuba** Brazil
29B3 **Carahue** Chile
35C1 **Caraí** Brazil
35C2 **Carandaí** Brazil
31C6 **Carangola** Brazil
54B1 **Caransebeş** Rom
108A2 **Carappee Hill** *Mt* Aust
26A3 **Caratasca** Honduras
35C1 **Caratinga** Brazil
51B2 **Caravaca** Spain
35D1 **Caravelas** Brazil
18C2 **Carbondale** Illinois, USA
53A3 **Carbonia** Sardegna
7E5 **Carborear** Can
5G4 **Carcaion** Can
99E1 **Carcar Mts** Somalia
48C3 **Carcassonne** France
4E3 **Carcross** Can
23B2 **Cardel** Mexico
25D2 **Cardenas** Cuba
23B1 **Cárdenas** Mexico
43C4 **Cardiff** Wales
43B3 **Cardigan** Wales
43B3 **Cardigan B** Wales
13E2 **Cardston** Can
54B1 **Carei** Rom
33F4 **Careiro** Brazil
34A2 **Carén** Chile
14B2 **Carey** USA
48B2 **Carhaix-Plouguer** France
29D3 **Carhué** Arg
31C6 **Cariacica** Brazil
5J4 **Caribou** Can
5G4 **Caribou Mts** Alberta, Can
5F4 **Caribou Mts** British Columbia, Can
79B3 **Carigara** Phil
46C2 **Carignan** France
33E1 **Caripito** Ven
15C1 **Carleton Place** Can
101G1 **Carletonville** S Africa
18C2 **Carlinville** USA
42C2 **Carlisle** Eng
15C2 **Carlisle** USA
34C3 **Carlos** Arg
35C1 **Carlos Chagas** Brazil
45C2 **Carlow** County, Irish Rep
45C2 **Carlow** Irish Rep
21B3 **Carlsbad** California, USA
9C3 **Carlsbad** New Mexico, USA
5H5 **Carlyle** Can
12G2 **Carmacks** Can
47B2 **Carmagnola** Italy
43B4 **Carmarthen** Wales
43B4 **Carmarthen B** Wales
22B2 **Carmel** California, USA
16C2 **Carmel** New York, USA
94B2 **Carmel,Mt** Israel
34D2 **Carmelo** Urug
22B2 **Carmel Valley** USA
9B4 **Carmen** *I* Mexico
29D4 **Carmen de Patagones** Arg
18C2 **Carmi** USA
21A2 **Carmichael** USA
35B1 **Carmo do Paranaiba** Brazil
50A2 **Carmona** Spain
106A3 **Carnarvon** Aust
100B4 **Carnarvon** S Africa
35D1 **Carncacá** Brazil
45C1 **Carndonagh** Irish Rep
106B3 **Carnegi,L** Aust
98B2 **Carnot** CAR
108A2 **Carnot,C** Aust
17B2 **Carol City** USA
31B3 **Carolina** Brazil
101H1 **Carolina** S Africa
17C1 **Carolina Beach** USA
104F3 **Caroline Is** Pacific O
60B4 **Carpathians** *Mts* E Europe
59D3 **Carpatii Orientali** *Mts* Rom
106C2 **Carpentaria,G of** Aust
83C5 **Carpenter Ridge** Indian O
49D3 **Carpentras** France
52B2 **Carpi** Italy
22C3 **Carpinteria** USA
17B2 **Carrabelle** USA
52B2 **Carrara** Italy
41B3 **Carrauntoohill** *Mt* Irish Rep
45C2 **Carrickmacross** Irish Rep
45B2 **Carrick on Shannon** Irish Rep
45C2 **Carrick-on-Suir** Irish Rep
108A2 **Carrieton** Aust
8D2 **Carrington** USA
50B1 **Carrión** *R* Spain
10A2 **Carroll** USA
17A1 **Carrollton** Georgia, USA
14A3 **Carrollton** Kentucky, USA
18B2 **Carrollton** Missouri, USA
18C2 **Carruthersville** USA
60E5 **Carsamba** Turk
92B2 **Carsamba** *R* Turk
8B3 **Carson City** USA
14B2 **Carsonville** USA
26B4 **Cartagena** Colombia
51B2 **Cartagena** Spain
32B3 **Cartago** Colombia
25D4 **Cartago** Costa Rica
111C2 **Carterton** NZ
18B2 **Carthage** Missouri, USA
15C2 **Carthage** New York, USA
19B3 **Carthage** Texas, USA
106B2 **Cartier I** Timor S
7E4 **Cartwright** Can
31D3 **Caruaru** Brazil
33E1 **Carúpano** Ven
46B1 **Carvin** France
34A2 **Casablanca** Chile
96B1 **Casablanca** Mor
35B2 **Casa Branca** Brazil
9B3 **Casa Grande** USA
52A1 **Casale Monferrato** Italy
47D2 **Casalmaggiore** Italy
34C3 **Casares** Arg
13C3 **Cascade Mts** Can/USA
111A2 **Cascade Pt** NZ
8A2 **Cascade Range** *Mts* USA
30F3 **Cascavel** Brazil
53B2 **Caserta** Italy
112C9 **Casey** *Base* Ant
45C2 **Cashel** Irish Rep
34C2 **Casilda** Arg
107E3 **Casino** Aust
32B5 **Casma** Peru
51B1 **Caspe** Spain
8C2 **Casper** USA
61G4 **Caspian Depression** *Region* Kazakhstan
65G6 **Caspian S** Asia/Europe
14C3 **Cass** USA
100B2 **Cassamba** Angola
46B1 **Cassel** France
12J3 **Cassiar** Can
4E3 **Cassiar Mts** Can
35A1 **Cassilândia** Brazil
53B2 **Cassino** Italy
22C3 **Castaic** USA
34B2 **Castaño** *R* Arg
47D2 **Castelfranco** Italy
49D3 **Castellane** France
34D3 **Castelli** Arg
51B2 **Castellon de la Plana** Spain
31C3 **Castelo** Brazil
50A2 **Castelo Branco** Port
48C3 **Castelsarrasin** France
53B3 **Castelvetrano** Italy
108B3 **Casterton** Aust

50B2 **Castilla La Nueva** Region, Spain
50B1 **Castilla La Vieja** Region, Spain
41B3 **Castlebar** Irish Rep
44A3 **Castlebay** Scot
42C2 **Castle Douglas** Scot
20C1 **Castlegar** Can
45B2 **Castleisland** Irish Rep
108B3 **Castlemain** Aust
45B2 **Castlerea** Irish Rep
109C2 **Castlereagh** Aust
48C3 **Castres-sur-l'Agout** France
27E4 **Castries** St Lucia
29B4 **Castro** Arg
30F3 **Castro** Brazil
31D4 **Castro Alves** Brazil
53C3 **Castrovillari** Italy
22B2 **Castroville** USA
111A2 **Caswell Sd** NZ
25E2 **Cat** *I* The Bahamas
79B3 **Catabalogan** Phil
32A5 **Catacaos** Peru
35C2 **Cataguases** Brazil
19B3 **Catahoula L** USA
35B1 **Catalão** Brazil
51C1 **Cataluña** Region, Spain
30C4 **Catamarca** Arg
30C4 **Catamarca** State, Arg
101C2 **Catandica** Mozam
79B3 **Catanduanes** *I* Phil
31B6 **Catanduva** Brazil
53C3 **Catania** Italy
53C3 **Catanzaro** Italy
79B3 **Catarman** Phil
108A2 **Catastrophe,C** Aust
26C5 **Catatumbo** *R* Ven
16A2 **Catawissa** USA
23B2 **Catemaco** Mexico
49D3 **Cater** Corse
52A2 **Cateraggio** Corse
98B3 **Catete** Angola
97A3 **Catio** Guinea-Bissau
7A4 **Cat Lake** Can
13D3 **Catlegar** Can
107E3 **Cato** *I* Aust
25D2 **Catoche,C** Mexico
16A3 **Catoctin Mt** USA
15C3 **Catonsville** USA
34C3 **Catrilo** Arg
15D2 **Catskill** USA
15D2 **Catskill Mts** USA
32C2 **Cauca** *R* Colombia
31D2 **Caucaia** Brazil
32B2 **Caucasia** Colombia
65F5 **Caucasus** *Mts* Georgia
46B1 **Caudry** France
98B3 **Caungula** Angola
29B3 **Cauquenes** Chile
87B2 **Cauvery** *R* India
49D3 **Cavaillon** France
47D1 **Cavalese** Italy
97B4 **Cavally** *R* Lib
45C2 **Cavan** County, Irish Rep
45C2 **Cavan** Irish Rep
79B3 **Cavite** Phil
31C2 **Caxias** Brazil
32C4 **Caxias** Brazil
30F4 **Caxias do Sul** Brazil
98B3 **Caxito** Angola
17B1 **Cayce** USA
93D1 **Çayeli** Turk
33G3 **Cayenne** French Guiana
46A1 **Cayeux-sur-Mer** France
25E3 **Cayman Brac** *I* Caribbean S
26A3 **Cayman Is** Caribbean S
26A3 **Cayman Trench** Caribbean S
99E2 **Caynabo** Somalia
25E2 **Cayo Romana** *I* Cuba
25D3 **Cayos Miskitos** *Is* Nic
26A2 **Cay Sal** *I* Caribbean S
100B2 **Cazombo** Angola
Ceará = Fortaleza
31C3 **Ceara** State, Brazil
79B3 **Cebu** Phil
79B3 **Cebu** *I* Phil
16B3 **Cecilton** USA
52B2 **Cecina** Italy
8B3 **Cedar City** USA
19A3 **Cedar Creek Res** USA
5J4 **Cedar L** Can
10A2 **Cedar Rapids** USA
17A1 **Cedartown** USA
24A2 **Cedros** *I* Mexico
106C4 **Ceduna** Aust
99E2 **Ceelbuur** Somalia
99E1 **Ceerigaabo** Somalia
53B3 **Cefalù** Italy
59B3 **Cegléd** Hung
100A2 **Cela** Angola
24B2 **Celaya** Mexico
Celebes = Sulawesi
70C3 **Celebes S** S E Asia
14B2 **Celina** USA
52C1 **Celje** Slovenia
56C2 **Celle** Germany
71E4 **Cendrawasih** *Pen* Indon
47C2 **Ceno** *R* Italy
19B3 **Center** USA
16C2 **Center Moriches** USA
17A1 **Center Point** USA
47D2 **Cento** Italy
44B3 **Central** Region, Scot
98B2 **Central African Republic** Africa
16D2 **Central Falls** USA
18C2 **Centralia** Illinois, USA
8A2 **Centralia** Washington, USA
20B2 **Central Point** USA
71F4 **Central Range** *Mts* PNG
16A3 **Centreville** Maryland, USA
78C4 **Cepu** Indon
Ceram = Seram
71D4 **Ceram Sea** Indon
34C3 **Cereales** Arg
31B5 **Ceres** Brazil
100A4 **Ceres** S Africa
22B2 **Ceres** USA
48C2 **Cergy-Pontoise** France
53C2 **Cerignola** Italy
60C5 **Cernavodă** Rom
9C4 **Cerralvo** *I* Mexico
23A1 **Cerritos** Mexico
34B2 **Cerro Aconcagua** *Mt* Arg
23B1 **Cerro Azul** Mexico
34A3 **Cerro Campanario** *Mt* Chile
34C2 **Cerro Champaqui** *Mt* Arg
23A2 **Cerro Cuachaia** *Mt* Mexico
23B1 **Cerro de Astillero** Mexico
34B2 **Cerro de Olivares** *Mt* Arg
32B6 **Cerro de Pasco** Peru
27D3 **Cerro de Punta** *Mt* Puerto Rico
23A2 **Cerro El Cantado** *Mt* Mexico
34B3 **Cerro El Nevado** *Mt* Arg
23A2 **Cerro Grande** *Mts* Mexico
34A2 **Cerro Juncal** *Mt* Arg/Chile
23A1 **Cerro la Ardilla** *Mts* Mexico
34B1 **Cerro las Tortolas** *Mt* Chile
23A2 **Cerro Laurel** *Mt* Mexico
34A2 **Cerro Mercedario** *Mt* Arg
34A3 **Cerro Mora** *Mt* Chile
27C4 **Cerron** *Mt* Ven
34B3 **Cerro Payún** *Mt* Arg
23B2 **Cerro Penón del Rosario** *Mt* Mexico
34B2 **Cerro Sosneado** *Mt* Arg
23A2 **Cerro Teotepec** *Mt* Mexico
34B2 **Cerro Tupungato** *Mt* Arg
23B2 **Cerro Yucuyacau** *Mt* Mexico
47C2 **Cervo** *R* Italy
52B2 **Cesena** Italy
60B2 **Çēsis** Latvia
57C3 **České Budejovice** Czech Republic
59B3 **Českomoravská Vysocina** *Mts* Czech Republic
55C3 **Çeşme** Turk
107E4 **Cessnock** Aust
52C2 **Cetina** *R* Croatia
96B1 **Ceuta** N W Africa
92C2 **Ceyham** Turk
92C2 **Ceyhan** *R* Turk
93C2 **Ceylanpınar** Turk
Ceylon = Sri Lanka
63B2 **Chaa-Khol** Russian Fed
48C2 **Chaâteaudun** France
47B1 **Chablais** Region, France
34C2 **Chacabuco** Arg
32B5 **Chachapoyas** Peru
34B3 **Chacharramendi** Arg
84C3 **Chachran** Pak
30D4 **Chaco** State, Arg
98B1 **Chad** Republic, Africa
98B1 **Chad** *L* C Africa
34B3 **Chadileuvu** *R* Arg
8C2 **Chadron** USA
18C2 **Chaffee** USA
85A3 **Chagai** Pak
63F2 **Chagda** Russian Fed
84B2 **Chaghcharan** Afghan
104B4 **Chagos Arch** Indian O
27L1 **Chaguanas** Trinidad
91D4 **Chāh Bahār** Iran
76C2 **Chai Badan** Thai
76C3 **Chaine des Cardamomes** *Mts* Camb
98C4 **Chaine des Mitumba** *Mts* Zaïre
76C2 **Chaiyaphum** Thai
34D2 **Chajari** Arg
84C2 **Chakwal** Pak
30B2 **Chala** Peru
100C2 **Chalabesa** Zambia
84A2 **Chalap Dalam** *Mts* Afghan
73C4 **Chaling** China
85C4 **Chālisgaon** India
12F1 **Chalkyitsik** USA
46C2 **Challerange** France
46C2 **Châlons sur Marne** France
49C2 **Chalon sur Saône** France
57C3 **Cham** Germany
84B2 **Chaman** Pak
84D2 **Chamba** India
85D3 **Chambal** *R* India
15C3 **Chambersburg** USA
49D2 **Chambéry** France
46B2 **Chambly** France
85A3 **Chambor Kalat** Pak
90B3 **Chamgordan** Iran
34B2 **Chamical** Arg
47B2 **Chamonix** France
86A2 **Champa** India
49C2 **Champagne** Region, France
101G1 **Champagne Castle** *Mt* Lesotho
47A1 **Champagnole** France
10B2 **Champaign** USA
76D3 **Champassak** Laos
10C2 **Champlain,L** USA
87B2 **Chāmrājnagar** India
30B4 **Chañaral** Chile
34A3 **Chanco** Chile
4D3 **Chandalar** USA
4D3 **Chandalar** *R* USA
84D2 **Chandīgarh** India
86C2 **Chandpur** Bang
85D5 **Chandrapur** India
91D4 **Chānf** Iran
101C2 **Changara** Mozam
74B2 **Changbai** China
69E2 **Changchun** China
73C4 **Changde** China
68E4 **Chang-hua** Taiwan
76D2 **Changjiang** China
73D3 **Chang Jiang** *R* China
74B2 **Changjin** N Korea
73C4 **Changsha** China
72E3 **Changshu** China
74A2 **Changtu** China
72B2 **Changwu** China
74B3 **Changyŏn** N Korea
72C2 **Changzhi** China
73E3 **Changzhou** China
48B2 **Channel Is** Europe
9B3 **Channel Is** USA
7E5 **Channel Port-aux-Basques** Can
76C3 **Chanthaburi** Thai
46B2 **Chantilly** France
18A2 **Chanute** USA
73D5 **Chaoàn** China
73D5 **Chao'an** China
73D3 **Chao Hu** *L* China
76C3 **Chao Phraya** *R* Thai
72E1 **Chaoyang** China
31C4 **Chapada Diamantina** *Mts* Brazil
31C2 **Chapadinha** Brazil
23A1 **Chapala** Mexico
23A1 **Chapala,Lac de** *L* Mexico
61H3 **Chapayevo** Kazakhstan
30F4 **Chapecó** Brazil
27H1 **Chapeltown** Jamaic
7B5 **Chapleau** Can
61E3 **Chaplygin** Russian Fed
112C3 **Charcot I** Ant
80E2 **Chardzhou** Turkmenistan
48C2 **Charente** *R* France
98B1 **Chari** *R* Chad
98B1 **Chari Baguirmi** Region, Chad
84B1 **Charikar** Afghan
18B1 **Chariton** *R* USA
33F2 **Charity** Guyana
85D3 **Charkhāri** India
46C1 **Charleroi** Belg
18C2 **Charleston** Illinois, USA
18C2 **Charleston** Missouri USA
11C3 **Charleston** S Carolina, USA
10B3 **Charleston** W Virginia, USA
98C3 **Charlesville** Zaïre
107D3 **Charleville** Aust
49C2 **Charleville-Mézières** France
14A1 **Charlevoix** USA
14B2 **Charlotte** Michigan, USA
11B3 **Charlotte** N Carolin USA
17B2 **Charlotte Harbor** *B* USA
10C3 **Charlottesville** USA
7D5 **Charlottetown** Can
27K1 **Charlotteville** Tobago
108B3 **Charlton** Aust
10C1 **Charlton I** Can
84C2 **Charsadda** Pak
107D3 **Charters Towers** Aust
48C2 **Chartres** France
29E3 **Chascomús** Arg
13D2 **Chase** Can
48B2 **Châteaubriant** France
48C2 **Châteaudun** France
48B2 **Châteaulin** France
48C2 **Châteauroux** Franc

46D2 **Château-Salins** France
49C2 **Château-Thierry** France
46C1 **Châtelet** Belg
48C2 **Châtellerault** France
43E4 **Chatham** Eng
7D5 **Chatham** New Brunswick, Can
16C1 **Chatham** New York, USA
14B2 **Chatham** Ontario, Can
13A2 **Chatham Sd** Can
12H3 **Chatham Str** USA
49C2 **Châtillon** France
47B2 **Châtillon** Italy
16B3 **Chatsworth** USA
17B1 **Chattahoochee** USA
17A1 **Chattahoochee** *R* USA
11B3 **Chattanooga** USA
76A1 **Chauk** Burma
49D2 **Chaumont** France
46B2 **Chauny** France
77D3 **Chau Phu** Viet
50A1 **Chaves** Port
61H2 **Chaykovskiy** Russian Fed
50B2 **Chazaouet** Alg
34C2 **Chazón** Arg
32C2 **Chcontá** Colombia
57C2 **Cheb** Czech Republic
65F4 **Cheboksary** Russian Fed
10B2 **Cheboygan** USA
74B3 **Chech'on** S Korea
85C3 **Chechro** Pak
18A2 **Checotah** USA
76A2 **Cheduba** *I* Burma
108B1 **Cheepie** Aust
96B2 **Chegga** Maur
100C2 **Chegutu** Zim
20B1 **Chehalis** USA
74B4 **Cheju** S Korea
74B4 **Cheju do** *I* S Korea
74B4 **Cheju-haehyŏp** *Str* S Korea
63F2 **Chekunda** Russian Fed
20B1 **Chelan,L** USA
90B2 **Cheleken** Turkmenistan
34B3 **Chelforo** Arg
80D1 **Chelkar** Kazakhstan
59C2 **Chelm** Pol
58B2 **Chelmno** Pol
43E4 **Chelmsford** Eng
43C4 **Cheltenham** Eng
65H4 **Chelyabinsk** Russian Fed
101C2 **Chemba** Mozam
57C2 **Chemnitz** Germany
84D2 **Chenab** *R* India/Pak
96B2 **Chenachane** Alg
20C1 **Cheney** USA
18A2 **Cheney Res** USA
72D1 **Chengda** China
73A3 **Chengdu** China
72E2 **Chengshan Jiao** *Pt* China
73C4 **Chenxi** China
73C4 **Chen Xian** China
73D3 **Cheo Xian** China
32B5 **Chepén** Peru
34B2 **Chepes** Arg
48C2 **Cher** *R* France
23A2 **Cheran** Mexico
17C1 **Cheraw** USA
48B2 **Cherbourg** France
96C1 **Cherchell** Alg
63C2 **Cheremkhovo** Russian Fed
60E2 **Cherepovets** Russian Fed
60D4 **Cherkassy** Ukraine
61F5 **Cherkessk** Russian Fed
60D3 **Chernigov** Ukraine
60D2 **Chernobyl** Ukraine
60C4 **Chernovtsy** Ukraine
61J2 **Chernushka** Russian Fed
60B3 **Chernyakhovsk** Russian Fed
61G4 **Chernyye Zemli** Region, Russian Fed
18A2 **Cherokees,L o'the** USA
34A3 **Cherquenco** Chile
86C1 **Cherrapunji** India
60C3 **Cherven'** Belorussia
59C2 **Chervonograd** Ukraine
10C3 **Chesapeake** *B* USA
42C3 **Cheshire** County, Eng
16C1 **Cheshire** USA
64F3 **Chëshskaya Guba** *B* Russian Fed
21A1 **Chester** California, USA
42C3 **Chester** Eng
18C2 **Chester** Illinois, USA
16C1 **Chester** Massachusets, USA
15C3 **Chester** Pennsylvania, USA
17B1 **Chester** S Carolina, USA
16A3 **Chester** *R* USA
42D3 **Chesterfield** Eng
6A3 **Chesterfield Inlet** Can
16A3 **Chestertown** USA
25D3 **Chetumal** Mexico
13C1 **Chetwynd** Can
12A2 **Chevak** USA
111B2 **Cheviot** NZ
40C2 **Cheviots** *Hills* Eng/Scot
13D3 **Chewelah** USA
8C2 **Cheyenne** USA
86A1 **Chhapra** India
86C1 **Chhātak** Bang
85D4 **Chhatarpur** India
85D4 **Chhindwāra** India
86B1 **Chhuka** Bhutan
73E5 **Chia'i** Taiwan
100A2 **Chiange** Angola
76C2 **Chiang Kham** Thai
76B2 **Chiang Mai** Thai
47C1 **Chiavenna** Italy
74E3 **Chiba** Japan
86B2 **Chībāsa** India
100A2 **Chibia** Angola
7C4 **Chibougamou** Can
75A1 **Chiburi-jima** *I* Japan
101C3 **Chibuto** Mozam
10B2 **Chicago** USA
14A2 **Chicago Heights** USA
12G3 **Chichagof I** USA
43D4 **Chichester** Eng
75B1 **Chichibu** Japan
69G4 **Chichi-jima** *I* Japan
11B3 **Chickamauga L** USA
19C3 **Chickasawhay** *R* USA
9D3 **Chickasha** USA
12F2 **Chicken** USA
32A5 **Chiclayo** Peru
8A3 **Chico** USA
29C4 **Chico** *R* Arg
101C2 **Chicoa** Mozam
15D2 **Chicopee** USA
7C5 **Chicoutimi** Can
101C3 **Chicualacuala** Mozam
87B2 **Chidambaram** India
6D3 **Chidley,C** Can
17B2 **Chiefland** USA
99C3 **Chiengi** Zambia
47B2 **Chieri** Italy
46C2 **Chiers** *R* France
47C1 **Chiesa** Italy
47D2 **Chiese** *R* Italy
52B2 **Chieti** Italy
72D1 **Chifeng** China
12C3 **Chiginigak,Mt** USA
4C3 **Chigmit Mts** USA
23B2 **Chignahuapán** Mexico
12C3 **Chignik** USA
24B2 **Chihuahua** Mexico
87B2 **Chik Ballāpur** India
87B2 **Chikmagalūr** India
12C2 **Chikuminuk L** USA
101C2 **Chikwawa** Malawi
76A1 **Chi-kyaw** Burma
87C1 **Chilakalūrupet** India
23B2 **Chilapa** Mexico
87B3 **Chilaw** Sri Lanka
28B6 **Chile** Republic
34B2 **Chilecito** Mendoza, Arg
100B2 **Chililabombwe** Zambia
86B2 **Chilka** *L* India
13C2 **Chilko** *R* Can
5F4 **Chilko L** Can
13C2 **Chilkotin** *R* Can
34A3 **Chillán** Chile
34D3 **Chillar** Arg
18B2 **Chillicothe** Missouri, USA
14B3 **Chillicothe** Ohio, USA
13C3 **Chilliwack** Can
86B1 **Chilmari** India
101C2 **Chilongozi** Zambia
20B2 **Chiloquin** USA
24C3 **Chilpancingo** Mexico
43D4 **Chiltern Hills** *Upland* Eng
14A2 **Chilton** USA
101C2 **Chilumba** Malawi
69E4 **Chi-lung** Taiwan
101C2 **Chilwa** *L* Malawi
100C2 **Chimanimani** Zim
46C1 **Chimay** Belg
65G5 **Chimbay** Uzbekistan
32B4 **Chimborazo** *Mt* Ecuador
32B5 **Chimbote** Peru
65H5 **Chimkent** Kazakhstan
101C2 **Chimoio** Mozam
67E3 **China** Republic, Asia
China National Republic = Taiwan
25D3 **Chinandega** Nic
32B6 **Chincha Alta** Peru
109D1 **Chinchilla** Aust
101C2 **Chinde** Mozam
86C2 **Chindwin** *R* Burma
100B2 **Chingola** Zambia
100A2 **Chinguar** Angola
96A2 **Chinguetti** Maur
74B3 **Chinhae** S Korea
100C2 **Chinhoyi** Zim
12D3 **Chiniak,C** USA
84C2 **Chiniot** Pak
74B3 **Chinju** S Korea
98C2 **Chinko** *R* CAR
75B1 **Chino** Japan
101C2 **Chinsali** Zambia
52B1 **Chioggia** Italy
101C2 **Chipata** Zambia
101C3 **Chipinge** Zim
87A1 **Chiplūn** India
43C4 **Chippenham** Eng
10A2 **Chippewa Falls** USA
32A4 **Chira** *R* Peru
87C1 **Chīrāla** India
101C3 **Chiredzi** Zim
95A2 **Chirfa** Niger
32A2 **Chiriqui** *Mt* Panama
54C2 **Chirpan** Bulg
32A2 **Chirripo Grande** *Mt* Costa Rica
100B2 **Chirundu** Zim
100B2 **Chisamba** Zambia
7C4 **Chisasibi** Can
73B4 **Chishui He** *R* China
Chişinău = Kishinev
47B2 **Chisone** *R* Italy
61H2 **Chistopol** Russian Fed
68D1 **Chita** Russian Fed
100A2 **Chitado** Angola
100A2 **Chitembo** Angola
12F2 **Chitina** USA
12F2 **Chitina** *R* USA
87B2 **Chitradurga** India
84C1 **Chitral** Pak
32A2 **Chitré** Panama
86C2 **Chittagong** Bang
85C4 **Chittaurgarh** India
87B2 **Chittoor** India
100B2 **Chiume** Angola
47D1 **Chiusa** Italy
47B2 **Chivasso** Italy
100C2 **Chivhu** Zim
29D2 **Chivilcoy** Arg
100C2 **Chivu** Zim
75A1 **Chizu** Japan
29C3 **Choele Choel** Arg
34C3 **Choique** Arg
24B2 **Choix** Mexico
58B2 **Chojnice** Pol
99D1 **Choke** *Mts* Eth
48B2 **Cholet** France
23B2 **Cholula** Mexico
100B2 **Choma** Zambia
86B1 **Chomo Yummo** *Mt* China/India
57C2 **Chomutov** Czech Republic
63C1 **Chona** *R* Russian Fed
74B3 **Ch'ŏnan** S Korea
76C3 **Chon Buri** Thai
32A4 **Chone** Ecuador
74B2 **Ch'ŏngjin** N Korea
74B3 **Chongju** N Korea
74B3 **Ch'ŏngju** S Korea
100A2 **Chongoroi** Angola
73B4 **Chongqing** China
74B3 **Chŏngŭp** S Korea
74B3 **Chŏnju** S Korea
86B1 **Chooyu** *Mt* China/Nepal
59D3 **Chortkov** Ukraine
74B3 **Ch'ŏrwŏn** N Korea
59B2 **Chorzow** Pol
74E3 **Choshi** Japan
34A3 **Chos-Malal** Arg
58B2 **Choszczno** Pol
86A2 **Chotanāgpur** Region, India
96C1 **Chott Melrhir** Alg
22B2 **Chowchilla** USA
63D3 **Choybalsan** Mongolia
6A3 **Chrantrey Inlet** *B* Can
111B2 **Christchurch** NZ
101G1 **Christiana** S Africa
6D2 **Christian,C** Can
12H3 **Christian Sd** USA
6E3 **Christianshab** Greenland
104D4 **Christmas I** Indian O
65J5 **Chu** Kazakhstan
65J5 **Chu** *R* Kazakhstan
29C4 **Chubut** State, Arg
29C4 **Chubut** *R* Arg
60D2 **Chudovo** Russian Fed
Chudskoye Ozero = Peipus, Lake
4D3 **Chugach Mts** USA
12E2 **Chugiak** USA
75A1 **Chūgoku-sanchi** *Mts* Japan
29F2 **Chuí** Brazil
29B3 **Chuillán** Chile
77C5 **Chukai** Malay
76D2 **Chu Lai** Viet
21B3 **Chula Vista** USA
12E2 **Chulitna** USA
63E2 **Chulman** Russian Fed
32A5 **Chulucanas** Peru
30C2 **Chulumani** Bol
65K4 **Chulym** Russian Fed
63A2 **Chulym** *R* Russian Fed
63B2 **Chuma** *R* Russian Fed
84D2 **Chumar** India
63F2 **Chumikan** Russian Fed
77B3 **Chumphon** Thai
74B3 **Ch'unch'ŏn** S Korea
86B2 **Chunchura** India
74B3 **Ch'ungju** S Korea
Chungking = Chongqing
99D3 **Chunya** Tanz
63C1 **Chunya** *R* Russian Fed
27L1 **Chupara Pt** Trinidad
30C3 **Chuquicamata** Chile
52A1 **Chur** Switz

86C2 **Churāchāndpur** India
7A4 **Churchill** Can
7D4 **Churchill** *R* Labrador, Can
7A4 **Churchill** *R* Manitoba, Can
7A4 **Churchill,C** Can
7D4 **Churchill Falls** Can
5H4 **Churchill L** Can
84C3 **Chūru** India
23A2 **Churumuco** Mexico
61J2 **Chusovoy** Russian Fed
61G2 **Chuvashskaya Respublika,** Russian Fed
68B4 **Chuxiong** China
76D3 **Chu Yang Sin** *Mt* Viet
78B4 **Cianjur** Indon
47D2 **Ciano d'Enza** Italy
35A2 **Cianorte** Brazil
58C2 **Ciechanów** Pol
25E2 **Ciego de Avila** Cuba
32C1 **Ciénaga** Colombia
25D2 **Cienfuegos** Cuba
59B3 **Cieszyn** Pol
51B2 **Cieza** Spain
92B2 **Cihanbeyli** Turk
23A2 **Cihuatlán** Mexico
78B4 **Cijulang** Indon
78B4 **Cilacap** Indon
54C1 **Cimpina** Rom
51C1 **Çinca** *R* Spain
52C2 **Činčer** *Mt* Bosnia-Herzegovina
10B3 **Cincinnati** USA
54B1 **Cindrelu** *Mt* Rom
55C3 **Cine** *R* Turk
46C1 **Ciney** Belg
34B3 **Cipolletti** Arg
4D3 **Circle** Alaska, USA
14B3 **Circleville** USA
78B4 **Cirebon** Indon
43D4 **Cirencester** Eng
47D2 **Citadella** Italy
24C3 **Citlaltepetl** *Mt* Mexico
100A4 **Citrusdal** S Africa
52B2 **Citta del Vaticano** Italy
52B2 **Città di Castello** Italy
24B2 **Ciudad Acuña** Mexico
23A2 **Ciudad Altamirano** Mexico
33E2 **Ciudad Bolivar** Ven
24B2 **Ciudad Camargo** Mexico
25C3 **Ciudad del Carmen** Mexico
23B1 **Ciudad del Maiz** Mexico
51C1 **Ciudadela** Spain
33E2 **Ciudad Guayana** Ven
24B3 **Ciudad Guzman** Mexico
23A2 **Ciudad Hidalgo** Mexico
24B1 **Ciudad Juárez** Mexico
9C4 **Ciudad Lerdo** Mexico
24C2 **Ciudad Madero** Mexico
23B2 **Ciudad Mendoza** Mexico
24B2 **Ciudad Obregon** Mexico
27C4 **Ciudad Ojeda** Ven
33E2 **Ciudad Piar** Ven
50B2 **Ciudad Real** Spain
50A1 **Ciudad Rodrigo** Spain
24C2 **Ciudad Valles** Mexico
24C2 **Ciudad Victoria** Mexico
52B2 **Civitavecchia** Italy
93D2 **Cizre** Turk
43E4 **Clacton-on-Sea** Eng
5G4 **Claire,L** Can
14C2 **Clairton** USA
47A1 **Clairvaux** France
17A1 **Clanton** USA
100A4 **Clanwilliam** S Africa
45C2 **Clara** Irish Rep
34D3 **Claraz** Arg
45B2 **Clare** County, Irish Rep
14B2 **Clare** USA
45A2 **Clare** *I* Irish Rep
15D2 **Claremont** USA
18A2 **Claremore** USA
45B2 **Claremorris** Irish Rep
109D1 **Clarence** *R* Aust
111B2 **Clarence** *R* NZ
106C2 **Clarence Str** Aust
12H3 **Clarence Str** USA
19B3 **Clarendon** USA
7E5 **Clarenville** Can
5G4 **Claresholm** Can
18A1 **Clarinda** USA
15C2 **Clarion** Pennsylvania, USA
24A3 **Clarión** *I* Mexico
15C2 **Clarion** *R* USA
105J3 **Clarion Fracture Zone** Pacific O
11B3 **Clark Hill Res** USA
14B2 **Clark,Pt** Can
14B3 **Clarksburg** USA
11A3 **Clarksdale** USA
12C3 **Clarks Point** USA
20C1 **Clarkston** USA
18B2 **Clarksville** Arkansas, USA
35A1 **Claro** *R* Brazil
29D3 **Claromecó** Arg
18A2 **Clay Center** USA
44D2 **Claymore** *Oilfield* N Sea
13B3 **Clayoquot Sd** Can
9C3 **Clayton** New Mexico, USA
15C2 **Clayton** New York, USA
41B3 **Clear** *C* Irish Rep
12E3 **Cleare,C** USA
13D1 **Clear Hills** *Mts* Can
21A2 **Clear L** USA
20B2 **Clear Lake Res** USA
13D2 **Clearwater** Can
11B4 **Clearwater** USA
13E1 **Clearwater** *R* Can
13C2 **Clearwater L** Can
9D3 **Cleburne** USA
42E2 **Cleeton** *Oilfield* North Sea
22B1 **Clements** USA
79A3 **Cleopatra Needle** *Mt* Phil
107D3 **Clermont** Aust
46B2 **Clermont** France
46C2 **Clermont-en-Argonne** France
49C2 **Clermont-Ferrand** France
46D1 **Clervaux** Germany
47D1 **Cles** Italy
108A2 **Cleve** Aust
42D2 **Cleveland** County, Eng
19B3 **Cleveland** Mississippi, USA
10B2 **Cleveland** Ohio, USA
11B3 **Cleveland** Tennessee, USA
19A3 **Cleveland** Texas, USA
41B3 **Clew** *B* Irish Rep
45A2 **Clifden** Irish Rep
109D1 **Clifton** Aust
16B2 **Clifton** New Jersey, USA
108A1 **Clifton Hills** Aust
13F3 **Climax** Can
18B2 **Clinton** Arkansas, USA
5F4 **Clinton** Can
16C2 **Clinton** Connecticut, USA
16D1 **Clinton** Massachusetts, USA
19B3 **Clinton** Mississippi, USA
18B2 **Clinton** Missouri, USA
16B2 **Clinton** New Jersey, USA
4H3 **Clinton-Colden L** Can
24B3 **Clipperton I** Pacific O
30C2 **Cliza** Bol
45B3 **Clonakilty** Irish Rep
107D3 **Cloncurry** Aust
45C1 **Clones** Irish Rep
45C2 **Clonmel** Irish Rep
10A2 **Cloquet** USA
12C2 **Cloudy Mt** USA
22C2 **Clovis** California, USA
9C3 **Clovis** New Mexico, USA
60B4 **Cluj** Rom
54B1 **Cluj-Napoca** Rom
47B1 **Cluses** France
47C2 **Clusone** Italy
111A3 **Clutha** *R* NZ
43C3 **Clwyd** County, Wales
6D2 **Clyde** Can
111A3 **Clyde** NZ
42B2 **Clyde** *R* Scot
23A2 **Coahuayana** Mexico
23A2 **Coalcomán** Mexico
13E2 **Coaldale** Can
21B2 **Coaldale** USA
21A2 **Coalinga** USA
33E5 **Coari** *R* Brazil
17A1 **Coastal Plain** USA
4E4 **Coast Mts** Can
8A2 **Coast Ranges** *Mts* USA
42B2 **Coatbridge** Scot
23B2 **Coatepec** Mexico
16B3 **Coatesville** USA
15D1 **Coaticook** Can
6B3 **Coats I** Can
112B1 **Coats Land** Region, Ant
25C3 **Coatzacoalcos** Mexico
7C5 **Cobalt** Can
25C3 **Cobán** Guatemala
107D4 **Cobar** Aust
109C3 **Cobargo** Aust
45B3 **Cobh** Irish Rep
32D6 **Cobija** Bol
16B1 **Cobleskill** USA
51B2 **Cobo de Palos** *C* Spain
7C5 **Cobourg** Can
106C2 **Cobourg Pen** Aust
57C2 **Coburg** Germany
32B4 **Coca** Ecuador
17B2 **Coca** USA
30C2 **Cochabamba** Bol
46D1 **Cochem** Germany
87B3 **Cochin** India
13E2 **Cochrane** Alberta, Can
7B5 **Cochrane** Ontario, Can
108B2 **Cockburn** Aust
16A3 **Cockeysville** USA
27H1 **Cockpit Country,The** Jamaica
25D3 **Coco** *R* Honduras/Nic
98A2 **Cocobeach** Gabon
27L1 **Cocos B** Trinidad
104C4 **Cocos Is** Indian O
23A1 **Cocula** Mexico
10C2 **Cod,C** USA
111A3 **Codfish I** NZ
7D4 **Cod I** Can
47E2 **Codigoro** Italy
31C2 **Codó** Brazil
47C2 **Codogno** Italy
8C2 **Cody** USA
56B2 **Coesfeld** Germany
8B2 **Coeur d'Alene** USA
9D3 **Coffeyville** USA
108A2 **Coffin B** Aust
109D2 **Coff's Harbour** Aust
23B2 **Cofre de Perote** *Mt* Mexico
48B2 **Cognac** France
15D2 **Cohoes** USA
108B3 **Cohuna** Aust
29B5 **Coihaique** Chile
87B2 **Coimbatore** India
50A1 **Coimbra** Port
32A3 **Cojimies** Ecuador
107D4 **Colac** Aust
31C5 **Colatina** Brazil
112B6 **Colbeck,C** Ant
43E4 **Colchester** Eng
16C2 **Colchester** USA
47B1 **Col de la Faucille** France
13E2 **Cold L** Can
52A1 **Col du Grand St Bernard** *P* Italy/Switz
47B2 **Col du Lautaret** *P* France
52A1 **Col du Mont Cenis** *P* France/Italy
14B2 **Coldwater** USA
12F1 **Coleen** *R* USA
14B2 **Coleman** Michigan, USA
101G1 **Colenso** S Africa
45C1 **Coleraine** N Ire
111B2 **Coleridge,L** NZ
100B4 **Colesberg** S Africa
22C1 **Coleville** USA
21A2 **Colfax** California, USA
19B3 **Colfax** Louisiana, USA
20C1 **Colfax** Washington, USA
24B3 **Colima** Mexico
23A2 **Colima** State, Mexico
34A2 **Colina** Chile
44A3 **Coll** *I* Scot
109C1 **Collarenebri** Aust
52A2 **Colle de Tende** *P* France/Italy
12E2 **College** USA
17B1 **College Park** Georgia, USA
16A3 **College Park** Washington, USA
19A3 **College Station** USA
106A4 **Collie** Aust
106B2 **Collier B** Aust
46A1 **Collines de L'Artois** *Mts* France
46B2 **Collines De Thiérache** France
14B2 **Collingwood** Can
110B2 **Collingwood** NZ
19C3 **Collins** Mississippi, USA
4H2 **Collinson Pen** Can
107D3 **Collinsville** Aust
18C2 **Collinsville** Illinois, USA
18A2 **Collinsville** Oklahoma, USA
34A3 **Collipulli** Chile
49D2 **Colmar** France
Cologne = Köln
35B2 **Colômbia** Brazil
32B3 **Colombia** Republic, S America
15C3 **Colombia** USA
87B3 **Colombo** Sri Lanka
25D2 **Colon** Cuba
32B2 **Colón** Panama
29E2 **Colonia** Urug
34D2 **Colonia del Sacramento** Urug
34B3 **Colonia 25 de Mayo** Arg
29C5 **Colonia Las Heras** Arg
44A3 **Colonsay** *I* Scot
23A1 **Colontlán** Mexico
27E5 **Coloradito** Ven
8C3 **Colorado** State, USA
9B3 **Colorado** *R* Arizona USA
29D3 **Colorado** *R* Buenos Aires, Arg
9D3 **Colorado** *R* Texas, USA
9B3 **Colorado Plat** USA
8C3 **Colorado Springs** USA
22D3 **Colton** USA
16A3 **Columbia** Maryland, USA

19C3 **Columbia** Mississippi, USA
10A3 **Columbia** Missouri, USA
15C2 **Columbia** Pennsylvania, USA
11B3 **Columbia** S Carolina, USA
11B3 **Columbia** Tennessee, USA
13D2 **Columbia** *R* Can
8A2 **Columbia** *R* USA
5G4 **Columbia,Mt** Can
20C1 **Columbia Plat** USA
11B3 **Columbus** Georgia, USA
14A3 **Columbus** Indiana, USA
11B3 **Columbus** Mississippi, USA
8D2 **Columbus** Nebraska, USA
10B2 **Columbus** Ohio, USA
19A4 **Columbus** Texas, USA
20C1 **Colville** USA
4C3 **Colville** *R* USA
110C1 **Colville,C** NZ
4F3 **Colville L** Can
42C3 **Colwyn Bay** Wales
47E2 **Comacchio** Italy
22B1 **Comanche Res** USA
112C2 **Comandante Ferraz** *Base* Ant
25D3 **Comayagua** Honduras
34A2 **Combarbalá** Chile
45C2 **Comeragh** *Mts* Irish Rep
86C2 **Comilla** Bang
25C3 **Comitán** Mexico
46C2 **Commercy** France
6B3 **Committees B** Can
52A1 **Como** Italy
29C5 **Comodoro Rivadavia** Arg
23A1 **Comonfort** Mexico
87B3 **Comorin,C** India
101D2 **Comoros** *Is* Indian O
49C2 **Compiègne** France
23A1 **Compostela** Mexico
34B2 **Comte Salas** Arg
86C1 **Cona** China
97A4 **Conakry** Guinea
34B2 **Concarán** Arg
48B2 **Concarneau** France
35D1 **Conceiçao da Barra** Brazil
31B3 **Conceição do Araguaia** Brazil
35C1 **Conceiçao do Mato Dentro** Brazil
29B3 **Concepción** Chile
30E3 **Concepción** Par
29E2 **Concepción** *R* Arg
24B2 **Concepcion del Oro** Mexico
34D2 **Concepcion del Uruguay** Arg
9A3 **Conception,Pt** USA
35B2 **Conchas** Brazil
9C4 **Conchos** *R* Mexico
21A2 **Concord** California, USA
10C2 **Concord** New Hampshire, USA
29E2 **Concordia** Arg
8D3 **Concordia** USA
20B1 **Concrete** USA
109D1 **Condamine** Aust
107D4 **Condobolin** Aust
20B1 **Condon** USA
46C1 **Condroz** *Mts* Belg
17A1 **Conecuh** *R* USA
47E2 **Conegliano** Italy
89F8 **Congo** Republic, Africa
89F8 **Congo** *R* Congo
Congo,R = Zaïre
14B1 **Coniston** Can
45B2 **Connaught** Region, Irish Rep
14B2 **Conneaut** USA
10C2 **Connecticut** State, USA
15D2 **Connecticut** *R* USA
15C2 **Connellsville** USA
45B2 **Connemara,Mts of** Irish Rep
14A3 **Connersville** USA
108B2 **Conoble** Aust
19A3 **Conroe** USA
35C2 **Conselheiro Lafaiete** Brazil
77D4 **Con Son** *Is* Viet
Constance,L = Bodensee
60C5 **Constanta** Rom
96C1 **Constantine** Alg
12C3 **Constantine,C** USA
29B3 **Constitución** Chile
13F3 **Consul** Can
47E2 **Contarina** Italy
31C4 **Contas** *R* Brazil
23B2 **Contreras** Mexico
4H3 **Contuoyto L** Can
11A3 **Conway** Arkansas, USA
15D2 **Conway** New Hampshire, USA
17C1 **Conway** South Carolina, USA
108A1 **Conway,L** Aust
42C3 **Conwy** Wales
106C3 **Coober Pedy** Aust
110B2 **Cook** *Str* NZ
13B2 **Cook,C** Can
4C3 **Cook Inlet** *B* USA
105H4 **Cook Is** Pacific O
111B2 **Cook,Mt** NZ
107D2 **Cooktown** Aust
109C2 **Coolabah** Aust
108C1 **Cooladdi** Aust
109C2 **Coolah** Aust
109C2 **Coolamon** Aust
106B4 **Coolgardie** Aust
109C3 **Cooma** Aust
109C2 **Coonabarabran** Aust
109C2 **Coonambie** Aust
108B2 **Coonbah** Aust
108A2 **Coondambo** Aust
108C1 **Coongoola** Aust
87B2 **Coonoor** India
108B1 **Cooper Basin** Aust
106C3 **Cooper Creek** Aust
108B1 **Cooper Creek** *R* Aust
108A3 **Coorong,The** Aust
109D1 **Cooroy** Aust
20B2 **Coos B** USA
20B2 **Coos Bay** USA
107D4 **Cootamundra** Aust
45C1 **Cootehill** Irish Rep
23B2 **Copala** Mexico
23B2 **Copalillo** Mexico
Copenhagen = København
30B4 **Copiapó** Chile
47D2 **Copparo** Italy
12F2 **Copper** *R* USA
4D3 **Copper Centre** USA
14B1 **Copper Cliff** Can
Coppermine = Qurlurtuuk
4G3 **Coppermine** *R* Can
Coquilhatville = Mbandaka
30B4 **Coquimbo** Chile
54B2 **Corabia** Rom
17B2 **Coral Gables** USA
6B3 **Coral Harbour** Can
107D2 **Coral S** Aust/PNG
104F4 **Coral Sea Basin** Pacific O
107E2 **Coral Sea Island Territories** Aust
108B3 **Corangamite,L** Aust
33F3 **Corantijn** *R* Surinam/Guyana
46B2 **Corbeil-Essonnes** France
50A1 **Corcubion** Spain
11B3 **Cordele** USA
50A1 **Cordillera Cantabrica** *Mts* Spain
26C3 **Cordillera Central** *Mts* Dom Rep
79B2 **Cordillera Central** *Mts* Phil
34B2 **Cordillera de Ansita** *Mts* Arg
32B5 **Cordillera de los Andes** *Mts* Peru
30C4 **Cordillera del Toro** *Mt* Arg
32C2 **Cordillera de Mérida** Ven
34A3 **Cordillera de Viento** *Mts* Arg
25D3 **Cordillera Isabelia** *Mts* Nic
32B3 **Cordillera Occidental** *Mts* Colombia
32B3 **Cordillera Oriental** *Mts* Colombia
108B1 **Cordillo Downs** Aust
29D2 **Córdoba** Arg
24C3 **Córdoba** Mexico
50B2 **Córdoba** Spain
29D2 **Córdoba** State, Arg
4D3 **Cordova** USA
Corfu = Kérkira
109D2 **Coricudgy,Mt** Aust
53C3 **Corigliano Calabro** Italy
11B3 **Corinth** Mississippi, USA
31C5 **Corinto** Brazil
45B2 **Cork** County, Irish Rep
41B3 **Cork** Irish Rep
92A1 **Çorlu** Turk
31C5 **Cornel Fabriciano** Brazil
35A2 **Cornelio Procópio** Brazil
7E5 **Corner Brook** Can
109C3 **Corner Inlet** *B* Aust
15C2 **Corning** USA
7C5 **Cornwall** Can
43B4 **Cornwall** County, Eng
43B4 **Cornwall,C** Eng
4H2 **Cornwall I** Can
6A2 **Cornwallis I** Can
32D1 **Coro** Ven
31C2 **Coroatá** Brazil
30C2 **Coroico** Bol
35B1 **Coromandel** Brazil
87C2 **Coromandel Coast** India
110C1 **Coromandel Pen** NZ
110C1 **Coromandel Range** *Mts* NZ
22D4 **Corona** California, USA
13E2 **Coronation** Can
4G3 **Coronation G** Can
34C2 **Coronda** Arg
29B3 **Coronel** Chile
34D3 **Coronel Brandsen** Arg
34C3 **Coronel Dorrego** Arg
35C1 **Coronel Fabriciano** Brazil
30E4 **Coronel Oviedo** Par
29D3 **Coronel Pringles** Arg
34C3 **Coronel Suárez** Arg
34D3 **Coronel Vidal** Arg
30B2 **Coropuna** *Mt* Peru
109C3 **Corowa** Aust
49D3 **Corps** France
9D4 **Corpus Christi** USA
9D4 **Corpus Christi,L** USA
79B3 **Corregidor** *I* Phil
35A1 **Corrente** *R* Mato Grosso, Brazil
30E4 **Corrientes** Arg
30E4 **Corrientes** State, Arg
19B3 **Corrigan** USA
106A4 **Corrigin** Aust
107E2 **Corringe Is** Aust
109C3 **Corryong** Aust
52A2 **Corse** *I* Medit S
42B2 **Corsewall** *Pt* Scot
Corsica = Corse
9D3 **Corsicana** USA
52A2 **Corte** Corse
9C3 **Cortez** USA
52B1 **Cortina d'Ampezzo** Italy
15C2 **Cortland** USA
23A2 **Coruca de Catalan** Mexico
93D1 **Çoruh** *R* Turk
60E5 **Çorum** Turk
30E2 **Corumbá** Brazil
35B1 **Corumba** *R* Brazil
35B1 **Corumbaiba** Brazil
20B2 **Corvallis** USA
96A1 **Corvo** *I* Açores
43C3 **Corwen** Wales
23B2 **Coscomatopec** Mexico
53C3 **Cosenza** Italy
101D1 **Cosmoledo** *Is* Seychelles
34C2 **Cosquín** Arg
51B2 **Costa Blanca** Region, Spain
51C1 **Costa Brava** Region, Spain
50B2 **Costa de la Luz** Region, Spain
50B2 **Costa del Sol** Region, Spain
22D4 **Costa Mesa** USA
25D3 **Costa Rica** Republic, Cent America
79B4 **Cotabato** Phil
30C3 **Cotagaita** Bol
49D3 **Côte d'Azur** Region, France
46C2 **Côtes de Meuse** *Mts* France
97C4 **Cotonou** Benin
32B4 **Cotopaxi** *Mt* Ecuador
43C4 **Cotswold Hills** *Upland* Eng
20B2 **Cottage Grove** USA
56C2 **Cottbus** Germany
108A3 **Couedic,C du** Aust
20C1 **Couer d'Alene L** USA
46B2 **Coulommiers** France
15C1 **Coulonge** *R* Can
22B2 **Coulterville** USA
4B3 **Council** USA
8D2 **Council Bluffs** USA
58C1 **Courland Lagoon** *Lg* Lithuania/Russian Fed
47B2 **Courmayeur** Italy
13B3 **Courtenay** Can
Courtrai = Kortrijk
48B2 **Coutances** France
43D3 **Coventry** Eng
50A1 **Covilhã** Spain
17B1 **Covington** Georgia, USA
19B3 **Covington** Louisiana, USA
109C2 **Cowal,L** Aust
108B3 **Cowangie** Aust
15D1 **Cowansville** Can
108A1 **Coward Springs** Aust
108A2 **Cowell** Aust
108C3 **Cowes** Aust
20B1 **Cowichan L** Can
20B1 **Cowiltz** *R* USA
109C2 **Cowra** Aust
30F2 **Coxim** Brazil
16C1 **Coxsackie** USA
86C2 **Cox's Bazar** Bang
22B2 **Coyote** USA
23A2 **Coyuca de Benitez** Mexico
59B2 **Cracow** Pol
100B4 **Cradock** S Africa
8C2 **Craig** USA
57C3 **Crailsheim** Germany
54B2 **Craiova** Rom
15D2 **Cranberry L** USA
5G5 **Cranbrook** Can
20C2 **Crane** Oregon, USA
16D2 **Cranston** USA
20B2 **Crater L** USA
20B2 **Crater Lake Nat Pk** USA
31C3 **Crateus** Brazil
31D3 **Crato** Brazil
14A2 **Crawfordsville** USA
17B1 **Crawfordville** USA
43D4 **Crawley** Eng
5H4 **Cree L** Can
46B2 **Creil** France

47C2 **Crema** Italy
52B1 **Cremona** Italy
46B2 **Crépy-en-Valois** France
52B2 **Cres** *I* Yugos
20B2 **Crescent City** USA
34C2 **Crespo** Arg
13D3 **Creston** Can
18B1 **Creston** USA
17A1 **Crestview** USA
108B3 **Creswick** Aust
47A1 **Crêt de la Neige** *Mt* France
Crete = Kríti
18A1 **Crete** USA
55B3 **Crete,S of** Greece
48C2 **Creuse** *R* France
43C3 **Crewe** Eng
44B3 **Crianlarich** Scot
30G4 **Criciuma** Brazil
44C3 **Crieff** Scot
12G3 **Crillon,Mt** USA
35B1 **Cristalina** Brazil
52C1 **Croatia** Republic, Europe
78D1 **Crocker Range** *Mts* Malay
19A3 **Crockett** USA
106C2 **Croker I** Aust
44C3 **Cromarty** Scot
43E3 **Cromer** Eng
111A3 **Cromwell** NZ
11C4 **Crooked** *I* The Bahamas
13C2 **Crooked** *R* Can
8D2 **Crookston** USA
109C2 **Crookwell** Aust
109D1 **Croppa Creek** Aust
11A3 **Crossett** USA
12G3 **Cross Sd** USA
53C3 **Crotone** Italy
19B3 **Crowley** USA
27K1 **Crown Pt** Tobago
109D1 **Crows Nest** Aust
107D2 **Croydon** Aust
43D4 **Croydon** Eng
104B5 **Crozet Basin** Indian O
4F2 **Crozier Chan** Can
30F4 **Cruz Alta** Brazil
25E3 **Cruz,C** Cuba
29D2 **Cruz del Eje** Arg
35C2 **Cruzeiro** Brazil
32C5 **Cruzeiro do Sul** Brazil
13C1 **Crysdale,Mt** Can
108A2 **Crystal Brook** Aust
18B2 **Crystal City** Missouri, USA
14A1 **Crystal Falls** USA
101C2 **Cuamba** Mozam
100B2 **Cuando** *R* Angola
100A2 **Cuangar** Angola
Cuango,R = Kwango,R
34C2 **Cuarto** *R* Arg
24B2 **Cuauhtémoc** Mexico
23B2 **Cuautla** Mexico
25D2 **Cuba** Republic, Caribbean S
100A2 **Cubango** *R* Angola
100A2 **Cuchi** Angola
100A2 **Cuchi** *R* Angola
34C3 **Cuchillo Có** Arg
32D3 **Cucui** Brazil
32C2 **Cúcuta** Colombia
87B2 **Cuddalore** India
87B2 **Cuddapah** India
106A3 **Cue** Aust
32B4 **Cuenca** Ecuador
51B1 **Cuenca** Spain
24C3 **Cuernavaca** Mexico
19A4 **Cuero** USA
30E2 **Cuiabá** Brazil
30E2 **Cuiabá** *R* Brazil
23B2 **Cuicatlan** Mexico
35C1 **Cuieté** *R* Brazil
44A3 **Cuillin Hills** *Mts* Scot
98B3 **Cuilo** *R* Angola
100A2 **Cuito** *R* Angola
100A2 **Cuito Cunavale** Angola
23A2 **Cuitzeo** Mexico
77D3 **Cu Lao Hon** *I* Viet
109C3 **Culcairn** Aust
109C1 **Culgoa** *R* Aust
24B2 **Culiacán** Mexico
79A3 **Culion** *I* Phil
17A1 **Cullman** USA
47A2 **Culoz** France
15C3 **Culpeper** USA
32J7 **Culpepper** *I* Ecuador
17B2 **Culter Ridge** USA
111B2 **Culverden** NZ
33E1 **Cumaná** Ven
10C3 **Cumberland** Maryland, USA
11B3 **Cumberland** *R* USA
6D3 **Cumberland Pen** Can
6D3 **Cumbernauld Sd** Can
42C2 **Cumbria** Eng
21A2 **Cummings** USA
108A2 **Cummins** Aust
42B2 **Cumnock** Scot
34A3 **Cunco** Chile
100A2 **Cunene** *R* Angola/ Namibia
52A2 **Cuneo** Italy
107D3 **Cunnamulla** Aust
44C3 **Çupar** Scot
54B2 **Čuprija** Serbia, Yugos
27D4 **Curaçao** *I* Caribbean S
34A3 **Curacautin** Chile
34B3 **Curaco** *R* Arg
34A3 **Curanilahue** Chile
34A3 **Curepto** Chile
29B2 **Curicó** Chile
30G4 **Curitiba** Brazil
108A2 **Curnamona** Aust
100A2 **Curoca** *R* Angola
31C5 **Curvelo** Brazil
18A2 **Cushing** USA
13D2 **Cutbank** *R* Can
17B1 **Cuthbert** USA
34B3 **Cutral-Có** Arg
86B2 **Cuttack** India
100A2 **Cuvelai** Angola
56B2 **Cuxhaven** Germany
14B2 **Cuyahoga Falls** USA
79B3 **Cuyo Is** Phil
32C6 **Cuzco** Peru
99C3 **Cyangugu** Zaïre
Cyclades = Kikládhes
13F3 **Cypress Hills** *Mts* Can
92B3 **Cyprus** Republic, Medit S
6D3 **Cyrus Field B** Can
59B3 **Czech Republic** Republic, Europe
59B2 **Częstochowa** Pol

D

76C1 **Da** *R* Viet
69E2 **Da'an** China
94C3 **Dab'a** Jordan
27C4 **Dabajuro** Ven
99E2 **Dabaro** Somalia
73B3 **Daba Shan** *Mts* China
99D1 **Dabat** Eth
85C4 **Dabhoi** India
73C3 **Dabie Shan** *Mts* China
97A3 **Dabola** Guinea
97B4 **Dabou** Ivory Coast
59B2 **Dabrowa Gorn** Pol
57C3 **Dachau** Germany
52B1 **Dachstein** *Mt* Austria
73A3 **Dada He** *R* China
17B2 **Dade City** USA
84B3 **Dadhar** Pak
85B3 **Dadu** Pak
68C3 **Dadu He** *R* China
79B3 **Daet** Phil
73B4 **Dafang** China
76B2 **Daga** *R* Burma
99E2 **Dagabur** Eth
97A3 **Dagana** Sen
65F5 **Dagestanskaya Respublic,** Russian Fed
79B2 **Dagupan** Phil
92B4 **Dahab** Egypt
63E3 **Da Hinggan Ling** *Mts* China
17B1 **Dahlonega** USA
85C4 **Dāhod** India
86A1 **Dailekh** Nepal
34C3 **Daireaux** Arg
69F4 **Daitō** *Is* Pacific O
106C3 **Dajarra** Aust
97A3 **Dakar** Sen
95B2 **Dakhla Oasis** Egypt
97C3 **Dakoro** Niger
54B2 **Dakovica** Serbia, Yugos
54A1 **Dakovo** Croatia
100B2 **Dala** Angola
97A3 **Dalaba** Guinea
72D1 **Dalai Nur** *L* China
68C2 **Dalandzadgad** Mongolia
79B3 **Dalanganem Is** Phil
76D3 **Da Lat** Viet
72A1 **Dalay** Mongolia
107E3 **Dalby** Aust
39F7 **Dalen** Nor
42C2 **Dales,The** *Upland* Eng
17A1 **Daleville** USA
9C3 **Dalhart** USA
4E2 **Dalhousie,C** Can
72E2 **Dalian** China
9D3 **Dallas** USA
20B1 **Dalles,The** USA
5E4 **Dall I** USA
86A2 **Dalli Rajhara** India
97C3 **Dallol** *R* Niger
97C3 **Dallol Bosso** *R* Niger
52C2 **Dalmatia** *Region* Bosnia-Herzegovina
69F2 **Dal'nerechensk** Russian Fed
97B4 **Daloa** Ivory Coast
73B4 **Dalou Shan** *Mts* China
86A2 **Dāltenganj** India
17B1 **Dalton** Georgia, USA
16C1 **Dalton** Massachusetts, USA
106C2 **Daly** *R* Aust
21A2 **Daly City** USA
106C2 **Daly Waters** Aust
79B4 **Damaguete** Phil
85C4 **Damān** India
92B3 **Damanhûr** Egypt
71D4 **Damar** *I* Indon
98B2 **Damara** CAR
92C3 **Damascus** Syria
16A3 **Damascus** USA
97D3 **Damaturu** Nig
90B2 **Damavand** Iran
98B3 **Damba** Angola
87C3 **Dambulla** Sri Lanka
90B2 **Damghan** Iran
85D4 **Damoh** India
99E2 **Damot** Eth
94B2 **Damour** Leb
106A3 **Dampier** Aust
94B3 **Danā** Jordan
22C2 **Dana,Mt** USA
97B4 **Danané** Lib
76D2 **Da Nang** Viet
79B3 **Danao** Phil
70A3 **Danau Tobu** *L* Indon
71D4 **Danau Tuwuti** *L* Indon
73A3 **Danbu** China
15D2 **Danbury** USA
86A1 **Dandeldhura** Nepal
87A1 **Dandeli** India
108C3 **Dandenong** Aust
74A2 **Dandong** China
100A4 **Danger Pt** S Africa
99D1 **Dangila** Eth
6D1 **Danguard Jenson Land** *Region* Can
7E4 **Daniels Harbour** Can
6G3 **Dannebrogs Øy** *I* Greenland
110C2 **Dannevirke** NZ
87C1 **Dantewāra** India
Danube = Donau
10B2 **Danville** Illinois, USA
11B3 **Danville** Kentucky, USA
16A2 **Danville** Pennsylvania, USA
11C3 **Danville** Virginia, USA
Danzig = Gdańsk
73C4 **Dao Xian** China
73B4 **Daozhen** China
79B4 **Dapiak,Mt** Phil
79B4 **Dapitan** Phil
68B3 **Da Qaidam** China
69E2 **Daqing** China
94C2 **Dar'a** Syria
91B4 **Dārāb** Iran
95A1 **Daraj** Libya
90B3 **Dārān** Iran
92C3 **Dar'ā Salkhad** Syria
86B1 **Darbhanga** India
22C1 **Dardanelle** USA
18B2 **Dardanelle,L** USA
Dar-el-Beida = Casablanca
99D3 **Dar es Salaam** Tanz
110B1 **Dargaville** NZ
17B1 **Darien** USA
Darjeeling = Dārjiling
86B1 **Dārjiling** India
107D4 **Darling** *R* Aust
109C1 **Darling Downs** Aust
6C1 **Darling Pen** Can
108B2 **Darlington** Aust
42D2 **Darlington** Eng
17C1 **Darlington** USA
57B3 **Darmstadt** Germany
95B1 **Darnah** Libya
108B2 **Darnick** Aust
4F3 **Darnley B** Can
112C10 **Darnley,C** Ant
51B1 **Daroca** Spain
98C2 **Dar Rounga** Region, CAR
43C4 **Dart** *R* Eng
41C3 **Dartmoor** *Moorland* Eng
43C4 **Dartmoor Nat Pk** Eng
7D5 **Dartmouth** Can
43C4 **Dartmouth** Eng
107D1 **Daru** PNG
52C1 **Daruvar** Croatia
106C2 **Darwin** Aust
91B4 **Daryacheh-ye Bakhtegan** *L* Iran
91B4 **Daryacheh-ye Mahārlū** *L* Iran
90B3 **Daryācheh-ye Namak** *Salt Flat* Iran
90D3 **Daryacheh-ye-Sistan** *Salt L* Iran/Afghan
91B4 **Daryacheh-ye Tashk** *L* Iran
80C2 **Daryācheh-ye Orūmīyeh** *L* Iran
91C4 **Dārzīn** Iran
91B4 **Das** *I* UAE
73C3 **Dashennonglia** *Mt* China
90C2 **Dasht** Iran
90B3 **Dasht-e-Kavir** *Salt Desert* Iran
90C3 **Dasht-e Lut** *Salt Desert* Iran
90D3 **Dasht-e Naomid** *Desert Region* Iran
85D3 **Datia** India
72A2 **Datong** China
72C1 **Datong** China
72A2 **Datong He** *R* China
79B4 **Datu Piang** Phil
39K7 **Daugava** *R* Latvia
60C2 **Daugavpils** Latvia
6D1 **Dauguard Jensen Land** Greenland
84A1 **Daulatabad** Afghan
85D3 **Daulpur** India
46D1 **Daun** Germany
87A1 **Daund** India
5H4 **Dauphin** Can
16A2 **Dauphin** USA
49D2 **Dauphiné** Region, France
97C3 **Daura** Nig
85D3 **Dausa** India
87B2 **Dāvangere** India
79C4 **Davao** Phil
79C4 **Davao G** Phil
22A2 **Davenport** California, USA

10A2 **Davenport** Iowa, USA
32A2 **David** Panama
4D3 **Davidson Mts** USA
21A2 **Davis** USA
112C10 **Davis** *Base* Ant
7D4 **Davis Inlet** Can
6E3 **Davis Str** Greenland/Can
61J3 **Davlekanovo** Russian Fed
47C1 **Davos** Switz
99E2 **Dawa** *R* Eth
73A4 **Dawan** China
84B2 **Dawat Yar** Afghan
Dawei = Tavoy
91B4 **Dawḩat Salwah** *B* Qatar/S Arabia
76B2 **Dawna Range** *Mts* Burma
4E3 **Dawson** Can
17B1 **Dawson** Georgia, USA
107D3 **Dawson** *R* Aust
5F4 **Dawson Creek** Can
13D2 **Dawson,Mt** Can
12G2 **Dawson Range** *Mts* Can
73A3 **Dawu** China
73C3 **Dawu** China
48B3 **Dax** France
73B3 **Daxian** China
73B5 **Daxin** China
73A3 **Daxue Shan** *Mts* China
73C4 **Dayong** China
94C2 **Dayr'Alī** Syria
94C1 **Dayr'Atīyah** Syria
93D2 **Dayr az Zawr** Syria
10B3 **Dayton** Ohio, USA
19B4 **Dayton** Texas, USA
20C1 **Dayton** Washington, USA
11B4 **Daytona Beach** USA
73C4 **Dayu** China
78D3 **Dayu** Indon
72D2 **Da Yunhe** *R* China
20C2 **Dayville** USA
73B3 **Dazhu** China
100B4 **De Aar** S Africa
26C2 **Deadman's Cay** The Bahamas
92C3 **Dead S** Israel/Jordan
46A1 **Deal** Eng
101G1 **Dealesville** S Africa
13B2 **Dean** *R* Can
13B2 **Dean Chan** Can
34C2 **Deán Funes** Arg
14B2 **Dearborn** USA
4F3 **Dease Arm** *B* Can
4E4 **Dease Lake** Can
9B3 **Death V** USA
48C2 **Deauville** France
97B4 **Debakala** Ivory Coast
12B2 **Debauch Mt** USA
27L1 **Débé** Trinidad
59C2 **Debica** Pol
58C2 **Deblin** Pol
97B3 **Débo,L** Mali
59C3 **Debrecen** Hung
99D2 **Debre Birhan** Eth
99D1 **Debre Markos** Eth
99D1 **Debre Tabor** Eth
11B3 **Decatur** Alabama, USA
17B1 **Decatur** Georgia, USA
10B3 **Decatur** Illinois, USA
14B2 **Decatur** Indiana, USA
48C3 **Decazeville** France
73A4 **Dechang** China
97B3 **Dédougou** Burkina
101C2 **Dedza** Malawi
42B2 **Dee** *R* Dumfries and Galloway, Scot
42C3 **Dee** *R* Eng/Wales
44C3 **Dee** *R* Grampian, Scot
15C1 **Deep River** Can
16C2 **Deep River** USA
109D1 **Deepwater** Aust
7E5 **Deer Lake** Can
8B2 **Deer Lodge** USA
34D3 **Defferrari** Arg
17A1 **De Funiak Springs** USA
68B3 **Dêgê** China
99E1 **Degeh Bur** Eth
106A3 **De Grey** *R* Aust
91B3 **Deh Bīd** Iran
84B1 **Dehi** Afghan
96D1 **Dehibat** Tunisia
87B3 **Dehiwala-Mt Lavinia** Sri Lanka
90A3 **Dehlorān** Iran
84D2 **Dehra Dūn** India
86A2 **Dehri** India
98C2 **Deim Zubeir** Sudan
94B2 **Deir Abu Sa'id** Jordan
94C1 **Deir el Ahmar** Leb
60B4 **Dej** Rom
19B3 **De Kalb** Texas, USA
63G2 **De Kastri** Russian Fed
98C3 **Dekese** Zaïre
98B2 **Dekoa** CAR
106B1 **Dekusi** Indon
9B3 **Delano** USA
10C3 **Delaware** State, USA
14B2 **Delaware** USA
15C2 **Delaware** *R* USA
10C3 **Delaware B** USA
109C3 **Delegate** Aust
47B1 **Delemont** Switz
101D2 **Delgado** *C* Mozam
84D3 **Delhi** India
15D2 **Delhi** New York, USA
92B1 **Delice** Turk
24B2 **Delicias** Mexico
90B3 **Delījān** Iran
47B1 **Delle** France
22D4 **Del Mar** USA
39F8 **Delmenhorst** Germany
4B3 **De Long** *Mts* USA
109C4 **Deloraine** Aust
5H5 **Deloraine** Can
17B2 **Delray Beach** USA
9C4 **Del Rio** USA
8B3 **Delta** USA
12E2 **Delta** *R* USA
12E2 **Delta Junction** USA
99D2 **Dembī Dolo** Eth
46C1 **Demer** *R* Belg
9C3 **Deming** USA
54C2 **Demirköy** Turk
49C1 **Denain** France
82A2 **Denau** Uzbekistan
42C3 **Denbigh** Wales
12B2 **Denbigh,C** USA
78B3 **Dendang** Indon
46C1 **Dendermond** Belg
99D2 **Dendi** *Mt* Eth
46B1 **Dèndre** *R* Belg
72B1 **Dengkou** China
72C3 **Deng Xian** China
Den Haag = 's-Gravenhage
27H1 **Denham,Mt** Jamaica
56A2 **Den Helder** Neth
51C2 **Denia** Spain
107D4 **Deniliquin** Aust
20C2 **Denio** USA
9D3 **Denison** Texas, USA
12D3 **Denison,Mt** USA
92A2 **Denizli** Turk
39F7 **Denmark** Kingdom, Europe
1C1 **Denmark Str** Greenland/Iceland
27P2 **Dennery** St Lucia
78D4 **Denpasar** Indon
16B3 **Denton** Maryland, USA
9D3 **Denton** Texas, USA
107E1 **D'Entrecasteaux Is** PNG
47B1 **Dents du Midi** *Mt* Switz
8C3 **Denver** USA
98B2 **Déo** *R* Cam
86B2 **Deoghar** India
85C5 **Deolāli** India
84D1 **Deosai Plain** India
95B3 **Dépression du Mourdi** Chad
19B3 **De Queen** USA
84C3 **Dera** Pak
84B3 **Dera Bugti** Pak
84C2 **Dera Ismail Khan** Pak
106B2 **Derby** Aust
16C2 **Derby** Connecticut, USA
43D3 **Derby** County, Eng
43D3 **Derby** Eng
18A2 **Derby** Kansas, USA
60E3 **Dergachi** Ukraine
19B3 **De Ridder** USA
Derna = Darnah
95C3 **Derudeb** Sudan
109C4 **Derwent Bridge** Aust
34B2 **Desaguadero** Arg
34B2 **Desaguadero** *R* Arg
30C2 **Désaguadero** *R* Bol
21B3 **Descanso** Mexico
20B2 **Deschutes** *R* USA
99D1 **Desē** Eth
29C5 **Deseado** Arg
29C5 **Deseado** *R* Arg
47D2 **Desenzano** Italy
96A1 **Deserta Grande** *I* Medeira
30C4 **Desierto de Atacama** *Desert* Chile
18B2 **Desloge** USA
10A2 **Des Moines** Iowa, USA
60D3 **Desna** *R* Russian Fed
29B6 **Desolación** *I* Chile
14A2 **Des Plaines** USA
56C2 **Dessau** Germany
12G2 **Destruction Bay** Can
46A1 **Desvres** France
54B1 **Deta** Rom
100B2 **Dete** Zim
10B2 **Detroit** USA
76D3 **Det Udom** Thai
54B1 **Deva** Rom
56B2 **Deventer** Neth
44C3 **Deveron** *R* Scot
85C3 **Devikot** India
22C2 **Devil Postpile Nat Mon** USA
22C1 **Devils Gate** *P* USA
Devil's Island = Isla du Diable
8D2 **Devils Lake** USA
12H3 **Devils Paw** *Mt* Can
43D4 **Devizes** Eng
85D3 **Devli** India
55B2 **Devoll** *R* Alb
43B4 **Devon** County, Eng
6A2 **Devon I** Can
107D5 **Devonport** Aust
86C1 **Dewangiri** Bhutan
85D4 **Dewās** India
101G1 **Dewetsdorp** S Africa
11B3 **Dewey Res** USA
19B3 **De Witt** USA
18C2 **Dexter** Missouri, USA
73A3 **Deyang** China
90C3 **Deyhuk** Iran
90A3 **Dezfūl** Iran
72D2 **Dezhou** China
90A2 **Dezh Shāhpūr** Iran
91B4 **Dhahran** S Arabia
86C2 **Dhākā** Bang
87B2 **Dhamavaram** India
86A2 **Dhamtari** India
86B2 **Dhanbād** India
86A1 **Dhangarhi** Nepal
86B1 **Dhankuta** Nepal
85D4 **Dhār** India
87B2 **Dharmapuri** India
84D2 **Dharmshala** India
97B3 **Dhar Oualata** *Desert Region* Maur
86A1 **Dhaulagiri** *Mt* Nepal
86B2 **Dhenkānāi** India
94B3 **Dhibah** Jordan
55C3 **Dhíkti Óri** *Mt* Greece
55C3 **Dhodhekánisos** *Is* Greece
55B3 **Dhomokós** Greece
87B1 **Dhone** India
85C4 **Dhoraji** India
85C4 **Dhrāngadhra** India
86B1 **Dhuburi** India
85C4 **Dhule** India
22B2 **Diablo,Mt** USA
21A2 **Diablo Range** *Mts* USA
34C2 **Diamante** Arg
34B2 **Diamante** *R* Arg
31C5 **Diamantina** Brazil
107D3 **Diamantina** *R* Aust
86B2 **Diamond Harbours** India
22B1 **Diamond Springs** USA
91C4 **Dibā** UAE
98C3 **Dibaya** Zaïre
86C1 **Dibrugarh** India
8C2 **Dickinson** USA
15C2 **Dickson City** USA
93D2 **Dicle** *R* Turk
13E2 **Didsbury** Can
85C3 **Dīdwāna** India
97B3 **Diebougou** Burkina
46D2 **Diekirch** Lux
97B3 **Diéma** Mali
76C1 **Dien Bien Phu** Viet
56B2 **Diepholz** Germany
48C2 **Dieppe** France
46C1 **Diest** Belg
46D2 **Dieuze** France
7D5 **Digby** Can
49D3 **Digne-les-Bains** France
49C2 **Digoin** France
79C4 **Digos** Phil
71E4 **Digul** *R* Indon
86C1 **Dihang** *R* India
Dijlah = Tigris
49C2 **Dijon** France
98B2 **Dik** Chad
99E1 **Dikhil** Djibouti
46B1 **Diksmuide** Belg
1B10 **Dikson** Russian Fed
82A2 **Dilaram** Afghan
106B1 **Dili** Indon
76D3 **Di Linh** Viet
46E1 **Dillenburg** Germany
99C1 **Dilling** Sudan
12C3 **Dillingham** USA
8B2 **Dillon** USA
16A2 **Dillsburg** USA
100B2 **Dilolo** Zaïre
Dimashq = Damascus
98C3 **Dimbelenge** Zaïre
97B4 **Dimbokro** Ivory Coast
54C2 **Dimitrovgrad** Bulg
61G3 **Dimitrovgrad** Russian Fed
94B3 **Dimona** Israel
86C1 **Dimpāpur** India
79C3 **Dinagat** *I* Phil
86B1 **Dinajpur** India
48B2 **Dinan** France
46C1 **Dinant** Belg
92B2 **Dinar** Turk
99D1 **Dinder** *R* Sudan
87B2 **Dindigul** India
72B2 **Dingbian** China
86B1 **Dinggyê** China
41A3 **Dingle** Irish Rep
41A3 **Dingle** *B* Irish Rep
97A3 **Dinguiraye** Guinea
44B3 **Dingwall** Scot
72A2 **Dingxi** China
72D2 **Ding Xian** China
76D1 **Dinh Lap** Viet
22C2 **Dinuba** USA
97A3 **Diouloulou** Sen
86C1 **Diphu** India
99E2 **Dirē Dawa** Eth
106A3 **Dirk Hartog** *I* Aust
95A3 **Dirkou** Niger
109C1 **Dirranbandi** Aust
99E2 **Dirri** Somalia
29G8 **Disappointment,C** South Georgia
20B1 **Disappointment,C** USA
106B3 **Disappointment,L** Aust
108B3 **Discovery B** Aust

103J7 **Discovery Tablemount** Atlantic O
47C1 **Disentis Muster** Switz
6E3 **Disko** Greenland
6E3 **Disko Bugt** *B* Greenland
6E3 **Diskorjord** Greenland
58D1 **Disna** *R* Belorussia
35B1 **Distrito Federal** Federal District, Brazil
85C4 **Diu** India
79C4 **Diuat Mts** Phil
31C6 **Divinópolis** Brazil
61F4 **Divnoye** Russian Fed
93C2 **Divriği** Turk
22B1 **Dixon** California, USA
5E4 **Dixon Entrance** *Sd* Can/USA
13D1 **Dixonville** Can
93E3 **Diyālā** *R* Iraq
65F6 **Diyarbakir** Turk
90A3 **Diz** *R* Iran
98B2 **Dja** *R* Cam
96C1 **Djadi** *R* Alg
95A2 **Djado,Plat du** Niger
98B3 **Djambala** Congo
96C2 **Djanet** Alg
50A2 **Djebel Bouhalla** *Mt* Mor
96C1 **Djelfa** Alg
98C2 **Djéma** CAR
97B3 **Djenné** Mali
97B3 **Djibo** Burkina
99E1 **Djibouti** Djibouti
99E1 **Djibouti** Republic, E Africa
98C2 **Djolu** Zaïre
97C4 **Djougou** Benin
99D2 **Djugu** Zaïre
38C2 **Djúpivogur** Iceland
51C2 **Djurdjura** *Mts* Alg
60E2 **Dmitrov** Russian Fed
Dnepr = Dnieper
60D4 **Dneprodzerzhinsk** Ukraine
60E4 **Dnepropetrovsk** Ukraine
60C3 **Dneprovskaya Nizmennost'** Region, Belorussia
Dnestr = Dniester
60D4 **Dnieper** *R* Ukraine
60B4 **Dniester** *R* Ukraine
60D2 **Dno** Russian Fed
98B2 **Doba** Chad
58C1 **Dobele** Latvia
34C3 **Doblas** Arg
71E4 **Dobo** Indon
54A2 **Doboj** Bosnia-Herzegovina
54B2 **Dobreta-Turnu-Severin** Rom
54C2 **Dobrich** Bulg
60D3 **Dobrush** Belorussia
31C5 **Doce** *R* Brazil
30D3 **Doctor R P Peña** Arg
87B2 **Dod** India
87B2 **Doda Betta** *Mt* India
Dodecanese = Sporádhes
9C3 **Dodge City** USA
99D3 **Dodoma** Tanz
75A1 **Dōgo** *I* Japan
97C3 **Dogondoutchi** Niger
93D2 **Doğubayazit** Turk
91B4 **Doha** Qatar
7C5 **Dolbeau** Can
49D2 **Dôle** France
43C3 **Dolgellau** Wales
47D1 **Dolomitche** *Mts* Italy
99E2 **Dolo Odo** Eth
29E3 **Dolores** Arg
34D2 **Dolores** Urug
23A1 **Dolores Hidalgo** Mexico
4G3 **Dolphin and Union Str** Can
29E6 **Dolphin,C** Falkland Is
71E4 **Dom** *Mt* Indon
65G4 **Dombarovskiy** Russian Fed
38F6 **Dombas** Nor
46D2 **Dombasle-sur-Meurthe** France
54A1 **Dombóvár** Hung
48B2 **Domfront** France
27E3 **Dominica** *I* Caribbean S
27C3 **Dominican Republic** Caribbean S
6C3 **Dominion,C** Can
7E4 **Domino** Can
68D1 **Domna** Russian Fed
52A1 **Domodossola** Italy
78D4 **Dompu** Indon
29B3 **Domuyo** *Mt* Arg
109D1 **Domville,Mt** Aust
44C3 **Don** *R* Scot
61F4 **Don** *R* Russian Fed
45C1 **Donaghadee** N Ire
57C3 **Donau** *R* Germany
57C3 **Donauwörth** Germany
50A2 **Don Benito** Spain
42D3 **Doncaster** Eng
98B3 **Dondo** Angola
101C2 **Dondo** Mozam
87C3 **Dondra Head** *C* Sri Lanka
45B1 **Donegal** County, Irish Rep
40B3 **Donegal** Irish Rep
40B3 **Donegal** *B* Irish Rep
45B1 **Donegal** *Mts* Irish Rep
60E4 **Donetsk** Ukraine
73C4 **Dong'an** China
106A3 **Dongara** Aust
73A4 **Dongchuan** China
76D2 **Dongfang** China
74B2 **Dongfeng** China
70C4 **Donggala** Indon
68B3 **Donggi Cona** *L* China
74A3 **Donggou** China
73C5 **Donghai Dao** *I* China
72A1 **Dong He** *R* China
76D2 **Dong Hoi** Viet
73C5 **Dong Jiang** *R* China
95C3 **Dongola** Sudan
73D5 **Dongshan** China
68D4 **Dongsha Qundao** *I* China
72C2 **Dongsheng** China
72E3 **Dongtai** China
73C4 **Dongting Hu** *L* China
73B5 **Dongxing** China
73D3 **Dongzhi** China
18B2 **Doniphan** USA
52C2 **Donji Vakuf** Bosnia-Herzegovina
38G5 **Dönna** *I* Nor
21A2 **Donner** *P* USA
46D2 **Donnersberg** *Mt* Germany
101G1 **Donnybrook** S Africa
Donostia = San Sebastian
22B2 **Don Pedro Res** USA
12D1 **Doonerak,Mt** USA
79B4 **Dopolong** Phil
73A3 **Do Qu** *R* China
47B2 **Dora Baltea** *R* Italy
49D2 **Dorbirn** Austria
43C4 **Dorchester** Eng
6C3 **Dorchester,C** Can
48C2 **Dordogne** *R* France
56A2 **Dordrecht** Neth
13F2 **Dore** *L* Can
13F2 **Dore Lake** Can
97B3 **Dori** Burkina
46B2 **Dormans** France
57B3 **Dornbirn** Austria
44B3 **Dornoch** Scot
44B3 **Dornoch Firth** *Estuary* Scot
38H6 **Dorotea** Sweden
109D2 **Dorrigo** Aust
20B2 **Dorris** USA
43C4 **Dorset** County, Eng
46D1 **Dorsten** Germany
56B2 **Dortmund** Germany
98C2 **Doruma** Zaïre
63D2 **Dosatuy** Russian Fed
84B1 **Doshi** Afghan
22B2 **Dos Palos** USA
97C3 **Dosso** Niger
65G5 **Dossor** Kazakhstan
11B3 **Dothan** USA
49C1 **Douai** France
98A2 **Douala** Cam
109D1 **Double Island Pt** Aust
49D2 **Doubs** *R* France
111A3 **Doubtful Sd** NZ
97B3 **Douentza** Mali
9C3 **Douglas** Arizona, USA
42B2 **Douglas** Eng
17B1 **Douglas** Georgia, USA
8C2 **Douglas** Wyoming, USA
12A1 **Douglas,C** USA
13B2 **Douglas Chan** Can
12D3 **Douglas,Mt** USA
46B1 **Doullens** France
45C1 **Doun** County, N Ire
30F3 **Dourados** Brazil
50A1 **Douro** *R* Port
15C3 **Dover** Delaware, USA
43E4 **Dover** Eng
15D2 **Dover** New Hampshire, USA
16B2 **Dover** New Jersey, USA
14B2 **Dover** Ohio, USA
43D3 **Dover** *R* Eng
41D3 **Dover,Str of** UK/France
16B3 **Downington** USA
42B2 **Downpatrick** N Ire
13C2 **Downton,Mt** Can
16B2 **Doylestown** USA
75A1 **Dōzen** *I* Japan
96A2 **Dr'aa** *R* Mor
35A2 **Dracena** Brazil
16D1 **Dracut** USA
49D3 **Draguignan** France
101C3 **Drakensberg** *Mts* S Africa
101G1 **Drakensberg** *Mt* S Africa
103E7 **Drake Pass** Pacific/Atlantic O
55B2 **Dráma** Greece
39G7 **Drammen** Nor
38A1 **Drangajökull** Iceland
52C1 **Drava** *R* Slovenia
13D2 **Drayton Valley** Can
49C2 **Dreaux** France
57C2 **Dresden** Germany
48C2 **Dreux** France
20C2 **Drewsey** USA
54B2 **Drin** *R* Alb
54A2 **Drina** *R* Bosnia-Herzegovina/Serbia
58D1 **Drissa** *R* Belorussia
45C2 **Drogheda** Irish Rep
59C3 **Drogobych** Ukraine
112B12 **Dronning Maud Land** Region, Ant
30D3 **Dr P.P. Pená** Par
5G4 **Drumheller** Can
14B1 **Drummond I** USA
15D1 **Drummondville** Can
58C2 **Druskininksi** Lithuania
12G3 **Dry B** USA
7A5 **Dryden** Can
27H1 **Dry Harbour Mts** Jamaica
76B3 **Duang** *I* Burma
91C4 **Dubai** UAE
5H3 **Dubawnt** *R* Can
4H3 **Dubawnt L** Can
107D4 **Dubbo** Aust
45C2 **Dublin** County, Irish Rep
45C2 **Dublin** Irish Rep
17B1 **Dublin** USA
60E2 **Dubna** Russian Fed
60C3 **Dubno** Ukraine
15C2 **Du Bois** USA
13B2 **Dubose,Mt** Can
58D2 **Dubrovica** Ukraine
54A2 **Dubrovnik** Croatia
10A2 **Dubuque** USA
46D2 **Dudelange** Lux
1C10 **Dudinka** Russian Fec
43C3 **Dudley** Eng
97B4 **Duekoué** Ivory Coast
50B1 **Duero** *R* Spain
44C3 **Dufftown** Scot
52B2 **Dugi Otok** *I* Croatia
56B2 **Duisburg** Germany
93E3 **Dūkan** Iraq
99D2 **Duk Faiwil** Sudan
91B4 **Dukhān** Qatar
73A4 **Dukou** China
68B3 **Dulan** China
34C2 **Dulce** *R* Arg
78C2 **Dulit Range** *Mts* Malay
86C2 **Dullabchara** India
10A2 **Duluth** USA
94C2 **Dūmā** Syria
78A2 **Dumai** Indon
79A3 **Dumaran** *I* Phil
9C3 **Dumas** USA
94C2 **Dumayr** Syria
42B2 **Dumbarton** Scot
42C2 **Dumfries** Scot
42B2 **Dumfries and Galloway** Region, Scot
86B2 **Dumka** India
15C1 **Dumoine,L** Can
112C8 **Dumont d'Urville** *Base* Ant
95C1 **Dumyat** Egypt
54C2 **Dunărea** *R* Rom
45C2 **Dunary Head** *Pt* Irish Rep
54B2 **Dunav** *R* Bulg
59D3 **Dunayevtsy** Ukraine
13C3 **Duncan** Can
16A2 **Duncannon** USA
44C2 **Duncansby Head** *Pt* Scot
45C1 **Dundalk** Irish Rep
16A3 **Dundalk** USA
45C2 **Dundalk B** Irish Rep
6D2 **Dundas** Greenland
4G2 **Dundas Pen** Can
71E5 **Dundas Str** Aust
101H1 **Dundee** S Africa
44C3 **Dundee** Scot
108B1 **Dundoo** Aust
42B2 **Dundrum** *B* N Ire
111B3 **Dunedin** NZ
17B2 **Dunedin** USA
109C2 **Dunedoo** Aust
44C3 **Dunfermline** Scot
85C4 **Dungarpur** India
45C2 **Dungarvan** Irish Rep
43E4 **Dungeness** Eng
109D2 **Dungog** Aust
99C2 **Dungu** Zaïre
95C2 **Dungunab** Sudan
68B2 **Dunhuang** China
46B1 **Dunkerque** France
10C2 **Dunkirk** USA
99D1 **Dunkur** Eth
97B4 **Dunkwa** Ghana
41B3 **Dun Laoghaire** Irish Rep
45B3 **Dunmanway** Irish Rep
26B1 **Dunmore Town** The Bahamas
44C2 **Dunnet Head** *Pt* Sc
42C2 **Duns** Scot
20B2 **Dunsmuir** USA
111A2 **Dunstan Mts** NZ
46C2 **Dun-sur-Meuse** France
72D1 **Duolun** China
18C2 **Du Quoin** USA
94B3 **Dura** Israel
49D3 **Durance** *R* France
24B2 **Durango** Mexico
50B1 **Durango** Spain
9C3 **Durango** USA
29E2 **Durano** Urug
9D3 **Durant** USA
94C1 **Duraykīsh** Syria
101H1 **Durban** S Africa
46D1 **Duren** Germany
86A2 **Durg** India
86B2 **Durgapur** India
42D2 **Durham** County, Er

42D2 **Durham** Eng
11C3 **Durham** N Carolina, USA
16D1 **Durham** New Hampshire, USA
108B1 **Durham Downs** Aust
54A2 **Durmitor** *Mt* Montenegro, Yugos
44B2 **Durness** Scot
55A2 **Durrës** Alb
108B1 **Durrie** Aust
45A3 **Dursey** *I* Irish Rep
55C3 **Dursunbey** Turk
110B2 **D'Urville I** NZ
90D2 **Dushak** Turkmenistan
73B4 **Dushan** China
82A2 **Dushanbe** Tajikistan
111A3 **Dusky Sd** NZ
56B2 **Düsseldorf** Germany
73B4 **Duyun** China
92B1 **Düzce** Turk
60C2 **Dvina** *R* Latvia
85B4 **Dwärka** India
6D3 **Dyer,C** Can
11B3 **Dyersburg** USA
43B3 **Dyfed** County, Wales
61F5 **Dykh Tau** *Mt* Russian Fed
108B1 **Dynevor Downs** Aust
68B2 **Dzag** Mongolia
63C3 **Dzamin Uüd** Mongolia
101D2 **Dzaoudzi** Mayotte
68C2 **Dzarnïn Uüd** Mongolia
68B2 **Dzavhan Gol** *R* Mongolia
80E1 **Dzehezkazgan** Kazakhstan
61F2 **Dzerzhinsk** Russian Fed
63E2 **Dzhalinda** Russian Fed
65J5 **Dzhambul** Kazakhstan
60D4 **Dzhankoy** Ukraine
Dzharkent = Panfilov
65H4 **Dzhezkazgan** Kazakhstan
84B1 **Dzhilikul'** Tajikistan
65J5 **Dzhungarskiy Alatau** *Mts* Kazakhstan
59B2 **Dzierzoniow** Pol
63B3 **Dzüyl** Mongolia
82C1 **Dzungaria** Basin, China

E

7B4 **Eabamet L** Can
12F2 **Eagle** Alaska, USA
20B2 **Eagle L** California, USA
19A3 **Eagle Mountain L** USA
9C4 **Eagle Pass** USA
4E3 **Eagle Plain** Can
12E2 **Eagle River** USA
21B2 **Earlimart** USA
17B1 **Easley** USA
15C2 **East Aurora** USA
43E4 **Eastbourne** Eng
14A2 **East Chicago** USA
69E3 **East China Sea** China/Japan
83B4 **Eastern Ghats** *Mts* India
29E6 **East Falkland** *I* Falkland Is
12E1 **East Fork** *R* USA
21B2 **Eastgate** USA
16C1 **Easthampton** USA
16C2 **East Hampton** USA
14A2 **East Lake** USA
14B2 **East Liverpool** USA
00B4 **East London** S Africa
7C4 **Eastmain** Can
7C4 **Eastmain** *R* Can
17B1 **Eastman** USA
15C3 **Easton** Maryland, USA
15C2 **Easton** Pennsylvania, USA
16B2 **East Orange** USA
105L4 **East Pacific Ridge** Pacific O
17B1 **East Point** USA
42D3 **East Retford** Eng
11A3 **East St Louis** USA
1B7 **East Siberian S** Russian Fed
43E4 **East Sussex** County, Eng
17B1 **Eatonton** USA
10A2 **Eau Claire** USA
71F3 **Eauripik** *I* Pacific O
23B1 **Ebano** Mexico
98B2 **Ebebiyin** Eq Guinea
56C2 **Eberswalde** Germany
73A4 **Ebian** China
65K5 **Ebinur** *L* China
53C2 **Eboli** Italy
98B2 **Ebolowa** Cam
51B1 **Ebro** *R* Spain
92A1 **Eceabat** Turk
96C1 **Ech Cheliff** Alg
72D2 **Eching** China
20C1 **Echo** USA
4G3 **Echo Bay** Can
46D2 **Echternach** Lux
108B3 **Echuca** Aust
50A2 **Ecija** Spain
6B2 **Eclipse Sd** Can
32B4 **Ecuador** Republic, S America
99E1 **Ed** Eritrea
44C2 **Eday** *I* Scot
98C1 **Ed Da'ein** Sudan
95C3 **Ed Damer** Sudan
95C3 **Ed Debba** Sudan
44B2 **Eddrachillis** *B* Scot
99D1 **Ed Dueim** Sudan
109C4 **Eddystone Pt** Aust
98A2 **Edea** Cam
109C3 **Eden** Aust
42C2 **Eden** *R* Eng
101G1 **Edenburg** S Africa
111A3 **Edendale** NZ
46E2 **Edenkoben** Germany
46E1 **Eder** *R* Germany
6D3 **Edgell I** Can
64D2 **Edgeøya** *I* Barents S
16A3 **Edgewood** USA
94B3 **Edh Dhahiriya** Israel
55B2 **Edhessa** Greece
44C3 **Edinburgh** Scot
60C5 **Edirne** Turk
17B1 **Edisto** *R* USA
13D2 **Edith Cavell,Mt** Can
20B1 **Edmonds** USA
5G4 **Edmonton** Can
7D5 **Edmundston** Can
19A4 **Edna** USA
12H3 **Edna Bay** USA
52B1 **Edolo** Italy
94B3 **Edom** Region, Jordan
92A2 **Edremit** Turk
55C3 **Edremit Körfezi** *B* Turk
68B2 **Edrengiyn Nuruu** *Mts* Mongolia
5G4 **Edson** Can
34C3 **Eduardo Castex** Arg
12J2 **Eduni,Mt** Can
108B3 **Edward** *R* Aust
99C3 **Edward,L** Uganda/Zaïre
108A1 **Edwards Creek** Aust
9C3 **Edwards Plat** USA
18C2 **Edwardsville** USA
12H3 **Edziza,Mt** Can
12B2 **Eek** USA
46B1 **Eeklo** Belg
10B3 **Effingham** USA
6E3 **Egedesminde** Greenland
12C3 **Egegik** USA
59C3 **Eger** Hung
39F7 **Egersund** Nor
16B3 **Egg Harbor City** USA
4G2 **Eglinton I** Can
110B1 **Egmont,C** NZ
110B1 **Egmont,Mt** NZ
92B2 **Eğridir Gölü** *L* Turk
95B2 **Egypt** Republic, Africa
50B1 **Eibar** Spain
49C2 **Eibeuf** France
46D1 **Eifel** Region, Germany
44A3 **Eigg** *I* Scot
83B5 **Eight Degree Chan** Indian O
106B2 **Eighty Mile Beach** Aust
108C3 **Eildon,L** Aust
56B2 **Eindhoven** Neth
47C1 **Einsiedeln** Switz
94B3 **Ein Yahav** Israel
57C2 **Eisenach** Germany
57C3 **Eisenerz** Austria
46D1 **Eitorf** Germany
72A1 **Ejin qi** China
23B2 **Ejutla** Mexico
110C2 **Eketahuna** NZ
65J4 **Ekibastuz** Kazakhstan
63F2 **Ekimchan** Russian Fed
92B3 **Ek Mahalla el Kubra** Egypt
39H7 **Eksjo** Sweden
10B1 **Ekwen** *R* Can
92A3 **El'Alamein** Egypt
92B3 **El'Arîsh** Egypt
92B4 **Elat** Israel
95B3 **El'Atrun Oasis** Sudan
93C2 **Elazig** Turk
92C3 **El Azraq** Jordan
52B2 **Elba** *I* Italy
95C2 **El Balyana** Egypt
32C2 **El Banco** Colombia
55B2 **Elbasan** Alb
27D5 **El Baúl** Ven
57C2 **Elbe** *R* Germany
94C1 **El Bega'a** *R* Leb
14A2 **Elberta** USA
8C3 **Elbert,Mt** USA
17B1 **Elberton** USA
92C2 **Elbistan** Turk
58D2 **Elblag** Pol
29B4 **El Bolson** Arg
61F5 **Elbrus** *Mt* Russian Fed
Elburz Mts = Reshteh-ye Alborz
21B3 **El Cajon** USA
19A4 **El Campo** USA
51B2 **Elche** Spain
51B2 **Elda** Spain
32B3 **El Diviso** Colombia
96B2 **El Djouf** *Desert Region* Maur
18B2 **Eldon** USA
11A3 **El Dorado** Arkansas, USA
35B2 **Eldorado** Brazil
9D3 **El Dorado** Kansas, USA
24B2 **El Dorado** Mexico
33E2 **El Dorado** Ven
99D2 **Eldoret** Kenya
22C1 **Eleanor,L** USA
96B2 **El Eglab** Region, Alg
50B1 **El Escorial** Spain
93D2 **Eleşkirt** Turk
11C4 **Eleuthera** *I* The Bahamas
92B4 **El Faiyûm** Egypt
96B2 **El Farsia** *Well* Mor
98C1 **El Fasher** Sudan
92B4 **El Fashn** Egypt
50A1 **El Ferrol del Caudillo** Spain
99C1 **El Fula** Sudan
96C1 **El Gassi** Alg
99D1 **El Geteina** Sudan
99D1 **El Gezîra** Region, Sudan
94B3 **El Ghor** *V* Israel/Jordan
10B2 **Elgin** Illinois, USA
44C3 **Elgin** Scot
92B3 **El Gîza** Egypt
96C1 **El Golea** Alg
99D2 **Elgon,Mt** Uganda/Kenya
99E2 **El Goran** Eth
23A2 **El Grullo** Mexico
96B2 **El Guettara** *Well* Mali
96B2 **El Haricha** *Desert Region* Mali
92A4 **El Harra** Egypt
51C2 **El Harrach** Alg
99D1 **El Hawata** Sudan
23B1 **El Higo** Mexico
34A3 **El Huecu** Arg
92B4 **El'Igma** *Desert Region* Egypt
12B2 **Elim** USA
4H2 **Elira,C** Can
Elisabethville = Lubumbashi
39K6 **Elisenvaara** Fin
El Iskandarîya = Alexandria
61F4 **Elista** Russian Fed
106C4 **Elizabeth** Aust
15D2 **Elizabeth** USA
11C3 **Elizabeth City** USA
17C1 **Elizabethtown** N Carolina, USA
16A2 **Elizabethtown** Pennsylvania, USA
96B1 **El Jadida** Mor
92C3 **El Jafr** Jordan
99D1 **El Jebelein** Sudan
96D1 **El Jem** Tunisia
58C2 **Elk** Pol
16B3 **Elk** *R* Maryland, USA
14B3 **Elk** *R* W Virginia, USA
95C3 **El Kamlin** Sudan
22B1 **Elk Grove** USA
El Khalil = Hebron
80B3 **El Khârga** Egypt
80B3 **El-Khârga Oasis** Egypt
14A2 **Elkhart** USA
96B2 **El Khenachich** *Desert Region* Mali
54C2 **Elkhovo** Bulg
14C3 **Elkins** USA
8B2 **Elko** USA
16B3 **Elkton** USA
92B3 **El Kuntilla** Egypt
99C1 **El Lagowa** Sudan
4H2 **Ellef Ringnes I** Can
8A2 **Ellensburg** USA
16B2 **Ellenville** USA
6B2 **Ellesmere I** Can
111B2 **Ellesmere,L** NZ
16A3 **Ellicott City** USA
100B4 **Elliot** S Africa
7B5 **Elliot Lake** Can
94B3 **El Lisan** *Pen* Jordan
112B3 **Ellsworth Land** *Region* Ant
95B1 **El Maghra** *L* Egypt
92B3 **El Mansûra** Egypt
16B3 **Elmer** USA
96B3 **El Merelé** *Desert Region* Maur
34B2 **El Milagro** Arg
94B1 **El Mîna** Leb
92B4 **El Minya** Egypt
22B1 **Elmira** California, USA
10C2 **Elmira** New York, USA
96B2 **El Mreitl** *Well* Maur
56B2 **Elmshorn** Germany
98C1 **El Muglad** Sudan
96B2 **El Mzereb** *Well* Mali
79A3 **El Nido** Phil
99D1 **El Obeid** Sudan
23A2 **El Oro** Mexico
96C1 **El Oued** Alg
9C3 **El Paso** USA
21A2 **El Porta** USA
22C2 **El Portal** USA
50A2 **El Puerto del Sta Maria** Spain
El Qâhira = Cairo
El Quds = Jerusalem
94B3 **El Quseima** Egypt
9D3 **El Reno** USA
4E3 **Elsa** Can
25D3 **El Salvador** Republic, Cent America
22D4 **Elsinore L** USA
34B3 **El Sosneade** Arg

57C2 **Elsterwerde** Germany
El Suweis = Suez
50A1 **El Teleno** *Mt* Spain
110B1 **Eltham** NZ
33E2 **El Tigre** Ven
92B4 **El Tîh** *Desert Region* Egypt
34C2 **El Tio** Arg
20C1 **Eltopia** USA
92B4 **El Tûr** Egypt
87C1 **Elūru** India
50A2 **Elvas** Port
32C5 **Elvira** Brazil
34A2 **El Volcán** Chile
14A2 **Elwood** USA
43E3 **Ely** Eng
10A2 **Ely** Minnesota, USA
8B3 **Ely** Nevada, USA
14B2 **Elyria** USA
90B2 **Emāmrūd** Iran
84B1 **Emām Sāheb** Afghan
58B1 **Eman** *R* Sweden
61J4 **Emba** Kazakhstan
61J4 **Emba** *R* Kazakhstan
29C3 **Embalse Cerros Colorados** *L* Arg
51B2 **Embalse de Alarcón** *Res* Spain
50A2 **Embalse de Alcántarà** *Res* Spain
50A1 **Embalse de Almendra** *Res* Spain
50A2 **Embalse de Garcia de Sola** *Res* Spain
33E2 **Embalse de Guri** *L* Ven
51B1 **Embalse de Mequinenza** *Res* Spain
50A1 **Embalse de Ricobayo** *Res* Spain
29E2 **Embalse de Rio Negro** *Res* Urug
29C3 **Embalse El Chocón** *L* Arg
29C4 **Embalse Florentine Ameghino** *L* Arg
50A1 **Embalse Gabriel y Galan** *Res* Spain
30D3 **Embarcación** Arg
5G4 **Embarras Portage** Can
47B2 **Embrun** France
99D3 **Embu** Kenya
56B2 **Emden** Germany
73A4 **Emei** China
107D3 **Emerald** Aust
7D4 **Emeri** Can
5J5 **Emerson** Can
21B1 **Emigrant P** USA
95A3 **Emi Koussi** *Mt* Chad
34B3 **Emilo Mitre** Arg
92B2 **Emirdağ** Turk
16B2 **Emmaus** USA
56B2 **Emmen** Neth
20C2 **Emmett** USA
16A3 **Emmitsburg** USA
12B2 **Emmonak** USA
9C4 **Emory Peak** *Mt* USA
24A2 **Empalme** Mexico
101H1 **Empangeni** S Africa
30E4 **Empedrado** Arg
105G1 **Emperor Seamount Chain** Pacific O
18A2 **Emporia** Kansas, USA
56B2 **Ems** *R* Germany
44B2 **Enard** *B* Scot
23A1 **Encarnacion** Mexico
30E4 **Encarnación** Par
97B4 **Enchi** Ghana
22D4 **Encinitas** USA
35C1 **Encruzilhada** Brazil
106B1 **Endeh** Indon
13D2 **Enderby** Can
112C11 **Enderby Land** Region, Ant
15C2 **Endicott** USA
12D1 **Endicott Mts** USA
47D1 **Engadin** *Mts* Switz
79B2 **Engaño,C** Phil
94B3 **En Gedi** Israel
47C1 **Engelberg** Switz
78A4 **Enggano** *I* Indon
41C3 **England** Country, UK
7E4 **Englee** Can
41C3 **English Channel** Eng/France
97B3 **Enji** *Well* Maur
39H7 **Enkoping** Sweden
53B3 **Enna** Italy
99C1 **En Nahud** Sudan
95B3 **Ennedi** *Region* Chad
109C1 **Enngonia** Aust
41B3 **Ennis** Irish Rep
19A3 **Ennis** Texas, USA
45C2 **Enniscorthy** Irish Rep
45C1 **Enniskillen** N Ire
45B2 **Ennistimon** Irish Rep
94B2 **Enn Nâqoûra** Leb
57C3 **Enns** *R* Austria
39F8 **Enschede** Neth
24A1 **Ensenada** Mexico
73B3 **Enshi** China
99D2 **Entebbe** Uganda
17A1 **Enterprise** Alabama, USA
20C1 **Enterprise** Oregon, USA
97C4 **Enugu** Nig
75B1 **Enzan** Japan
49C2 **Epernay** France
16A2 **Ephrata** Pennsylvania, USA
20C1 **Ephrata** Washington, USA
49D2 **Épinal** France
46A2 **Epte** *R* France
100A3 **Epukiro** Namibia
34C3 **Epu pel** Arg
90B3 **Eqlid** Iran
89D7 **Equator**
98A2 **Equatorial Guinea** Republic, Africa
47C2 **Erba** Italy
46D2 **Erbeskopf** *Mt* Germany
34A3 **Ercilla** Chile
93D2 **Erciş** Turk
92C2 **Erciyas Daglari** *Mt* Turk
74B2 **Erdaobaihe** China
72C1 **Erdene** Mongolia
68C2 **Erdenet** Mongolia
95B3 **Erdi** *Region* Chad
30F4 **Erechim** Brazil
92B1 **Ereğli** Turk
92B2 **Ereğli** Turk
68D2 **Erenhot** China
50B1 **Eresma** *R* Spain
46D1 **Erft** *R* Germany
57C2 **Erfurt** Germany
93C2 **Ergani** Turk
96B2 **Erg Chech** *Desert Region* Alg
95A3 **Erg du Djourab** *Desert* Chad
97D3 **Erg Du Ténéré** *Desert Region* Niger
92A1 **Ergene** *R* Turk
96B2 **Erg Iguidi** *Region* Alg
58D1 **Ergli** Latvia
98B1 **Erguig** *R* Chad
68D1 **Ergun'** *R* China/Russian Fed
63E2 **Ergun Zuoqi** China
95C3 **Eriba** Sudan
10C2 **Erie** USA
10B2 **Erie,L** Can/USA
42B2 **Erin Port** Eng
44A3 **Eriskay** *I* Scot
99D1 **Eritrea** Republic,Africa
46D1 **Erkelenz** Germany
57C3 **Erlangen** Germany
19B3 **Erling,L** USA
101G1 **Ermelo** S Africa
87B3 **Ernākulam** India
87B2 **Erode** India
108B1 **Eromanga** Aust
96B1 **Er Rachidia** Mor
99D1 **Er Rahad** Sudan
101C2 **Errego** Mozam
40B2 **Errigal** *Mt* Irish Rep
41A3 **Erris Head** *Pt* Irish Rep
99D1 **Er Roseires** Sudan
94B2 **Er Rummān** Jordan
57C2 **Erzgebirge** *Upland* Germany
93C2 **Erzincan** Turk
65F6 **Erzurum** Turk
48C3 **Esara** *R* Spain
56B1 **Esbjerg** Den
9C4 **Escalón** Mexico
10B2 **Escanaba** USA
25C3 **Escárcega** Mexico
46C2 **Esch** Lux
21B3 **Escondido** USA
24B2 **Escuinapa** Mexico
25C3 **Escuintla** Guatemala
98B2 **Eséka** Cam
51C1 **Esera** *R* Spain
90B3 **Eşfahān** Iran
101H1 **Eshowe** S Africa
110C1 **Eskdale** NZ
38C1 **Eskifjörður** Iceland
39H7 **Eskilstuna** Sweden
4E3 **Eskimo L** Can
7A3 **Eskimo Point** Can
92B2 **Eskisehir** Turk
50A1 **Esla** *R* Spain
29A5 **Esmeralda** *I* Chile
32B3 **Esmeraldas** Ecuador
26B2 **Esmerelda** Cuba
49C3 **Espalion** France
14B1 **Espanola** Can
32J7 **Española** *I* Ecuador
106B4 **Esperance** Aust
34C2 **Esperanza** Arg
112C2 **Esperanza** *Base* Ant
35C1 **Espírito Santo** State, Brazil
101C3 **Espungabera** Mozam
29B4 **Esquel** Arg
20B1 **Esquimalt** Can
34D2 **Esquina** Arg
94C2 **Es Samra** Jordan
96B1 **Essaourira** Mor
96A2 **Es Semara** Mor
56B2 **Essen** Germany
33F3 **Essequibo** *R* Guyana
43E4 **Essex** County, Eng
14B2 **Essexville** USA
57B3 **Esslingen** Germany
46B2 **Essonne** France
31D4 **Estância** Brazil
101G1 **Estcourt** S Africa
47D2 **Este** Italy
46B2 **Esternay** France
30D3 **Esteros** Par
5H5 **Estevan** Can
17B1 **Estill** USA
60B2 **Estonia** Republic, Europe
29B6 **Estrecho de Magallanes** *Str* Chile
50A2 **Estremoz** Port
59B3 **Esztergom** Hung
108A1 **Etadunna** Aust
46C2 **Etam** France
48C2 **Etampes** France
108A1 **Etamunbanie,L** Aust
46A1 **Etaples** France
85D3 **Etāwah** India
99D2 **Ethiopia** Republic, Africa
23B2 **Etla** Mexico
53B3 **Etna** *Mt* Italy
12H3 **Etolin I** USA
12A2 **Etolin Str** USA
6C2 **Eton** Can
100A2 **Etosha Nat Pk** Namibia
100A2 **Etosha Pan** *Salt L* Namibia
17B1 **Etowah** *R* USA
46D2 **Ettelbruck** Lux
109C2 **Euabalong** Aust
14B2 **Euclid** USA
109C3 **Eucumbene,L** Aust
108A2 **Eudunda** Aust
19A2 **Eufala L** USA
17A1 **Eufaula** USA
8A2 **Eugene** USA
108C1 **Eulo** Aust
19B3 **Eunice** Louisiana, USA
46D1 **Eupen** Germany
93D3 **Euphrates** *R* Iraq
19C3 **Eupora** USA
48C2 **Eure** *R* France
20B2 **Eureka** California, USA
6B1 **Eureka** Can
8B3 **Eureka** Nevada, USA
6B2 **Eureka** *Sd* Can
108C3 **Euroa** Aust
109C1 **Eurombah** *R* Aust
101D3 **Europa** *I* Mozam Chan
57B2 **Euskirchen** Germany
13B2 **Eutsuk L** Can
13D2 **Evansburg** Can
6B1 **Evans,C** Can
7C4 **Evans,L** Can
6B3 **Evans Str** Can
14A2 **Evanston** Illinois, USA
8B2 **Evanston** Wyoming, USA
11B3 **Evansville** Indiana, USA
101G1 **Evaton** S Africa
106C4 **Everard,L** Aust
82C3 **Everest,Mt** China/Nepal
8A2 **Everett** Washington, USA
16C1 **Everett,Mt** USA
11B4 **Everglades,The** *Swamp* USA
43D3 **Evesham** Eng
98B2 **Evinayong** Eq Guine
39F7 **Evje** Nor
47B1 **Evolène** Switz
50A2 **Évora** Port
48C2 **Évreux** France
55B3 **Évvoia** *I* Greece
98B3 **Ewo** Congo
22C1 **Excelisor Mt** USA
18B2 **Excelsior Springs** USA
21B2 **Exeter** California, USA
43C4 **Exeter** Eng
15D2 **Exeter** New Hampshire, USA
43C4 **Exmoor Nat Pk** Eng
43C4 **Exmouth** Eng
50A2 **Extremadura** Regio Spain
25E2 **Exuma Sd** The Bahamas
99D3 **Eyasi** *L* Tanz
42C2 **Eyemouth** Scot
99E2 **Eyl** Somalia
106B4 **Eyre** Aust
106C3 **Eyre Creek** *R* Aust
106C3 **Eyre,L** Aust
106C4 **Eyre Pen** Aust
79B3 **Eyte** *I* Phil
23A1 **Ezatlan** Mexico
55C3 **Ezine** Turk

F

4G3 **Faber L** Can
39G7 **Fåborg** Den
52B2 **Fabriano** Italy
95A3 **Fachi** Niger
95B3 **Fada** Chad
97C3 **Fada N'Gourma** Burkina
52B2 **Faenza** Italy
6E3 **Faeringehavn** Greenland
98B2 **Fafa** *R* CAR
99E2 **Fafan** *R* Eth
54B1 **Făgăraş** Rom
46C1 **Fagnes** Region, Be
97B3 **Faguibine,L** *L* Mal
91C5 **Fahud** Oman
96A1 **Faiol** *I* Açores
4D3 **Fairbanks** USA
14B3 **Fairborn** USA
8D2 **Fairbury** USA
16A3 **Fairfax** USA
21A2 **Fairfield** California USA
16C2 **Fairfield** Connectic USA
14B3 **Fairfield** Ohio, USA
45C1 **Fair Head** *Pt* N Ire
40C2 **Fair Isle** *I* Scot
111B2 **Fairlie** NZ

14B3 **Fairmont** W Virginia, USA
13D1 **Fairview** Can
4E4 **Fairweather,Mt** USA
71F3 **Fais** *I* Pacific O
84C2 **Faisalabad** Pak
8C2 **Faith** USA
44E1 **Faither,The** *Pen* Scot
86A1 **Faizābād** India
43E3 **Fakenham** Eng
39G7 **Faköping** Sweden
86C2 **Falam** Burma
24C2 **Falcon Res** Mexico/USA
97A3 **Falémé** *R* Mali/Sen
39G7 **Falkenberg** Sweden
42C2 **Falkirk** Scot
29D6 **Falkland Is** Dependency, S Atlantic
29E6 **Falkland Sd** Falkland Is
22D4 **Fallbrook** USA
8B3 **Fallon** USA
15D2 **Fall River** USA
18A1 **Falls City** USA
43B4 **Falmouth** Eng
27H1 **Falmouth** Jamaica
16D2 **Falmouth** Massachusetts, USA
100A4 **False B** S Africa
24A2 **Falso,C** Mexico
56C2 **Falster** *I* Den
54C1 **Fălticeni** Rom
39H6 **Falun** Sweden
92B2 **Famagusta** Cyprus
46C1 **Famenne** Region, Belg
76B2 **Fang** Thai
99D2 **Fangak** Sudan
73E5 **Fang liao** Taiwan
52B2 **Fano** Italy
112C3 **Faraday** *Base* Ant
99C2 **Faradje** Zaïre
101D3 **Farafangana** Madag
95B2 **Farafra Oasis** Egypt
80E2 **Farah** Afghan
71F2 **Farallon de Medinilla** *I* Pacific O
97A3 **Faranah** Guinea
71F3 **Faraulep** *I* Pacific O
43D4 **Fareham** Eng
Farewell,C = Kap Farvel
107G5 **Farewell,C** NZ
110B2 **Farewell Spit** *Pt* NZ
8D2 **Fargo** USA
94B2 **Fari'a** *R* Israel
10A2 **Faribault** USA
86B2 **Faridpur** Bang
90C2 **Farīmān** Iran
18B2 **Farmington** Missouri, USA
9C3 **Farmington** New Mexico, USA
22B2 **Farmington Res** USA
42D2 **Farne Deep** N Sea
13D2 **Farnham,Mt** Can
12H2 **Faro** Can
50A2 **Faro** Port
39H7 **Fåro** *I* Sweden
89K9 **Farquhar** *Is* Indian O
44B3 **Farrar** *R* Scot
14B2 **Farrell** USA
55B3 **Fársala** Greece
91B4 **Fasā** Iran
45B3 **Fastnet Rock** Irish Rep
60C3 **Fastov** Ukraine
86A1 **Fatehpur** India
13D1 **Father** Can
30F2 **Fatima du Sul** Brazil
101G1 **Fauresmith** S Africa
47B2 **Faverges** France
7B4 **Fawn** *R* Can
38H6 **Fax** *R* Sweden
38A2 **Faxaflói** *B* Iceland
95A3 **Faya** Chad
11A3 **Fayetteville** Arkansas, USA
11C3 **Fayetteville** N Carolina, USA
93E4 **Faylakah** *I* Kuwait
84C2 **Fāzilka** India
96A2 **Fdérik** Maur
11C3 **Fear,C** USA
21A2 **Feather Middle Fork** *R* USA
48C2 **Fécamp** France
34D2 **Federación** Arg
34D2 **Federal** Arg
71F3 **Federated States of Micronesia** *Is* Pacific O
56C2 **Fehmarn** *I* Germany
32C5 **Feijó** Brazil
73C5 **Feilai Xai Bei Jiang** *R* China
110C2 **Feilding** NZ
100C2 **Feira** Zambia
31D4 **Feira de Santan** Brazil
92C2 **Feke** Turk
57B3 **Feldkirch** Austria
34D2 **Feliciano** *R* Arg
41D3 **Felixstowe** Eng
47D1 **Feltre** Italy
38G6 **Femund** *L* Nor
74A2 **Fengcheng** China
73B4 **Fengdu** China
72D1 **Fenging** China
73B3 **Fengjie** China
72B3 **Feng Xian** China
72C1 **Fengzhen** China
72C2 **Fen He** *R* China
101D2 **Fenoarivo Atsinanana** Madag
60E5 **Feodosiya** Ukraine
90C3 **Ferdow** Iran
46B2 **Fère-Champenoise** France
82B2 **Fergana** Uzbekistan
45C1 **Fermanagh** County, N Ire
45B2 **Fermoy** Irish Rep
47D1 **Fern** *Mt* Austria
32J7 **Fernandina** *I* Ecuador
17B1 **Fernandina Beach** USA
103G5 **Fernando de Noronha** *I* Atlantic O
35A2 **Fernandópolis** Brazil
20B1 **Ferndale** USA
21B2 **Fernley** USA
52B2 **Ferrara** Italy
32B5 **Ferreñafe** Peru
19B3 **Ferriday** USA
96B1 **Fès** Mor
18B2 **Festus** USA
54C2 **Fetești** Rom
92A2 **Fethiye** Turk
61H5 **Fetisovo** Kazakhstan
44E1 **Fetlar** *I* Scot
84C1 **Feyzabad** Afghan
101D3 **Fianarantsoa** Madag
99D2 **Fichē** Eth
101G1 **Ficksburg** S Africa
47D2 **Fidenza** Italy
55A2 **Fier** Alb
47D1 **Fiera Di Primeiro** Italy
44C3 **Fife** Region, Scot
44C3 **Fife Ness** *Pen* Scot
48C3 **Figeac** France
50A1 **Figueira da Foz** Port
51C1 **Figueras** Spain
Figueres = Figueras
96B1 **Figuig** Mor
105G4 **Fiji** *Is* Pacific O
30D3 **Filadelfia** Par
54B2 **Filiași** Rom
55B3 **Filiatrá** Greece
53B3 **Filicudi** *I* Italy
21B3 **Fillmore** California, USA
44B3 **Findhorn** *R* Scot
10B2 **Findlay** USA
13D2 **Findlay,Mt** Can
15C2 **Finger Lakes** USA
101C2 **Fingoè** Mozam
92B2 **Finike** Turk
106C3 **Finke** *R* Aust
108A1 **Finke Flood Flats** Aust
64D3 **Finland** Republic, N Europe
39J7 **Finland,G of** N Europe
5F4 **Finlay** *R* Can
5F4 **Finlay Forks** Can
108C3 **Finley** Aust
38H5 **Finnsnes** Nor
71F4 **Finschhafen** PNG
47C1 **Finsteraarhorn** *Mt* Switz
56C2 **Finsterwalde** Germany
45C1 **Fintona** N Ire
111A3 **Fiordland Nat Pk** NZ
94B2 **Fiq** Syria
93C2 **Firat** *R* Turk
22B2 **Firebaugh** USA
52B2 **Firenze** Italy
34C2 **Firmat** Arg
85D3 **Firozābād** India
84C2 **Firozpur** India
39H7 **Firspång** Sweden
42B2 **Firth of Clyde** *Estuary* Scot
44C3 **Firth of Forth** *Estuary* Scot
44A3 **Firth of Lorn** *Estuary* Scot
40C2 **Firth of Tay** *Estuary* Scot
91B4 **Firūzābād** Iran
100A3 **Fish** *R* Namibia
22C2 **Fish Camp** USA
16C2 **Fishers I** USA
6B3 **Fisher Str** Can
43B4 **Fishguard** Wales
6E3 **Fiskenaesset** Greenland
46B2 **Fismes** France
15D2 **Fitchburg** USA
44E2 **Fitful Head** *Pt* Scot
17B1 **Fitzgerald** USA
106B2 **Fitzroy** *R* Aust
106B2 **Fitzroy Crossing** Aust
14B1 **Fitzwilliam I** Can
Fiume = Rijeka
99C3 **Fizi** Zaïre
9B3 **Flagstaff** USA
42D2 **Flamborough Head** *C* Eng
8C2 **Flaming Gorge Res** USA
44A2 **Flannan Isles** *Is* Scot
12J2 **Flat** *R* Can
13E3 **Flathead** *R* USA
8B2 **Flathead L** USA
18B2 **Flat River** USA
8A2 **Flattery,C** USA
42C3 **Fleetwood** Eng
39F7 **Flekkefjord** Nor
69G4 **Fleming Deep** Pacific O
16B2 **Flemington** USA
56B2 **Flensburg** Germany
47B1 **Fleurier** Switz
106C4 **Flinders** *I* Aust
107D4 **Flinders** *I* Aust
107D2 **Flinders** *R* Aust
106C4 **Flinders Range** *Mts* Aust
5H4 **Flin Flon** Can
10B2 **Flint** USA
42C3 **Flint** Wales
11B3 **Flint** *R* USA
46B1 **Flixecourt** France
17A1 **Florala** USA
Florence = Firenze
11B3 **Florence** Alabama, USA
18A2 **Florence** Kansas, USA
20B2 **Florence** Oregon, USA
11C3 **Florence** S Carolina, USA
32B3 **Florencia** Colombia
46C2 **Florenville** Belg
25D3 **Flores** Guatemala
96A1 **Flores** *I* Açores
106B1 **Flores** *I* Indon
34D3 **Flores** *R* Arg
70C4 **Flores S** Indon
31C3 **Floriano** Brazil
30G4 **Florianópolis** Brazil
25D2 **Florida** State, USA
29E2 **Florida** Urug
17B2 **Florida B** USA
17B2 **Florida City** USA
107E1 **Florida Is** Solomon Is
11B4 **Florida Keys** *Is* USA
11B4 **Florida,Strs of** USA
55B2 **Flórina** Greece
38F6 **Florø** Nor
47D1 **Fluchthorn** *Mt* Austria
54C1 **Focsani** Rom
53C2 **Foggia** Italy
97A4 **Fogo** *I* Cape Verde
48C3 **Foix** France
6C3 **Foley I** Can
52B2 **Foligno** Italy
43E4 **Folkestone** Eng
17B1 **Folkston** USA
52B2 **Follonica** Italy
22B1 **Folsom** USA
22B1 **Folsom L** *L* USA
5H4 **Fond-du-Lac** Can
10B2 **Fond du Lac** USA
48C2 **Fontainebleau** France
18B2 **Fontenac** USA
48B2 **Fontenay-le-Comte** France
52C1 **Fonyód** Hung
Foochow = Fuzhou
12D2 **Foraker,Mt** USA
46D2 **Forbach** France
109C2 **Forbes** Aust
97C4 **Forcados** Nig
38F6 **Forde** Nor
108C1 **Fords Bridge** Aust
19B3 **Fordyce** USA
97A4 **Forécariah** Guinea
6G3 **Forel,Mt** Greenland
14B2 **Forest** Can
17B1 **Forest Park** USA
22A1 **Forestville** USA
44C3 **Forfar** Scot
46A2 **Forges-les-Eaux** France
20B1 **Forks** USA
52B2 **Forlì** Italy
51C2 **Formentera** *I* Spain
53B2 **Formia** Italy
96A1 **Formigas** *I* Açores
Formosa = Taiwan
30E4 **Formosa** Arg
31B5 **Formosa** Brazil
30D3 **Formosa** State, Arg
73D5 **Formosa Str** Taiwan/China
47D2 **Fornovo di Taro** Italy
38D3 **Føroyar** *Is* N Atlantic O
44C3 **Forres** Scot
106B4 **Forrest** Aust
11A3 **Forrest City** USA
107D2 **Forsayth** Aust
39J6 **Forssa** Fin
109D2 **Forster** Aust
18B2 **Forsyth** Missouri, USA
84C3 **Fort Abbas** Pak
7B4 **Fort Albany** Can
31D2 **Fortaleza** Brazil
44B3 **Fort Augustus** Scot
100B4 **Fort Beaufort** S Africa
21A2 **Fort Bragg** USA
8C2 **Fort Collins** USA
15C1 **Fort Coulogne** Can
27E4 **Fort de France** Martinique
17A1 **Fort Deposit** USA
10A2 **Fort Dodge** USA
106A3 **Fortescue** *R* Aust
7A5 **Fort Frances** Can
4F3 **Fort Franklin** Can
4F3 **Fort Good Hope** Can
108B1 **Fort Grey** Aust
44B3 **Forth** *R* Scot
7B4 **Fort Hope** Can
34B3 **Fortin Uno** Arg
4F3 **Fort Laird** Can
96C1 **Fort Lallemand** Alg
Fort Lamy = Ndjamena
11B4 **Fort Lauderdale** USA
4F3 **Fort Liard** Can

5G4 **Fort Mackay** Can
5G5 **Fort Macleod** Can
5G4 **Fort McMurray** Can
4E3 **Fort McPherson** Can
18B2 **Fort Madison** USA
8C2 **Fort Morgan** USA
11B4 **Fort Myers** USA
5F4 **Fort Nelson** Can
4F3 **Fort Norman** Can
17A1 **Fort Payne** USA
8C2 **Fort Peck Res** USA
11B4 **Fort Pierce** USA
4G3 **Fort Providence** Can
5G3 **Fort Resolution** Can
98B3 **Fort Rousset** Congo
5F4 **Fort St James** Can
13C1 **Fort St John** Can
13E2 **Fort Saskatchewan** Can
18B2 **Fort Scott** USA
4E3 **Fort Selkirk** Can
7B4 **Fort Severn** Can
61H5 **Fort Shevchenko** Kazakhstan
4F3 **Fort Simpson** Can
5G3 **Fort Smith** Can
4G3 **Fort Smith** Region, Can
11A3 **Fort Smith** USA
9C3 **Fort Stockton** USA
20B2 **Fortuna** California, USA
5G4 **Fort Vermillion** Can
17A1 **Fort Walton Beach** USA
10B2 **Fort Wayne** USA
44B3 **Fort William** Scot
9D3 **Fort Worth** USA
12F2 **Fortymile** *R* USA
12E1 **Fort Yukon** USA
73C5 **Foshan** China
47B2 **Fossano** Italy
12G3 **Foster,Mt** USA
98B3 **Fougamou** Gabon
48B2 **Fougères** France
44D1 **Foula** *I* Scot
43E4 **Foulness I** Eng
111B2 **Foulwind,C** NZ
98B2 **Foumban** Cam
49C1 **Fourmies** France
55C3 **Foúrnoi** *I* Greece
97A3 **Fouta Djallon** *Mts* Guinea
111B3 **Foveaux** *Str* NZ
43B4 **Fowey** Eng
13D2 **Fox Creek** Can
6B3 **Foxe Basin** *G* Can
6B3 **Foxe Chan** Can
6C3 **Foxe Pen** Can
110C2 **Foxton** NZ
13F2 **Fox Valley** Can
45B2 **Foynes** Irish Rep
100A2 **Foz do Cuene** Angola
30F4 **Foz do Iquaçu** Brazil
16A2 **Frackville** USA
34B2 **Fraga** Arg
16D1 **Framingham** USA
31B6 **Franca** Brazil
49C2 **France** Republic, Europe
10A2 **Frances** Can
12J2 **Frances** *R* Can
49D2 **Franche Comté** Region, France
100B3 **Francistown** Botswana
13B2 **Francois L** Can
14A2 **Frankfort** Indiana, USA
11B3 **Frankfort** Kentucky, USA
101G1 **Frankfort** S Africa
57B2 **Frankfurt** Germany
46E1 **Frankfurt am Main** Germany
56C2 **Frankfurt-an-der-Oder** Germany
57C3 **Fränkischer Alb** *Upland* Germany
14A3 **Franklin** Indiana, USA
19B4 **Franklin** Louisiana, USA
16D1 **Franklin** Massachusetts, USA
16B2 **Franklin** New Jersey, USA
14C2 **Franklin** Pennsylvania, USA
4F2 **Franklin B** Can
20C1 **Franklin D Roosevelt** *L* USA
4F3 **Franklin Mts** Can
4J2 **Franklin Str** Can
111B2 **Franz Josef Glacier** NZ
Franz-Joseph-Land = Zemlya Frantsa Iosifa
5F5 **Fraser** *R* Can
44C3 **Fraserburgh** Scot
107E3 **Fraser I** Aust
13B2 **Fraser L** Can
47B1 **Frasne** France
47C1 **Frauenfield** Switz
34D2 **Fray Bentos** Urug
40C2 **Frazerburgh** Scot
16B3 **Frederica** USA
56B1 **Fredericia** Den
15C3 **Frederick** Maryland, USA
15C3 **Fredericksburg** Virginia, USA
12H3 **Frederick Sd** USA
18B2 **Fredericktown** USA
7D5 **Fredericton** Can
6E3 **Frederikshab** Greenland
39G7 **Frederikshavn** Den
15C2 **Fredonia** USA
39G7 **Fredrikstad** Nor
16B2 **Freehold** USA
26B1 **Freeport** The Bahamas
19A4 **Freeport** Texas, USA
97A4 **Freetown** Sierra Leone
57B3 **Freiburg** Germany
57C3 **Freistadt** Austria
106A4 **Fremantle** Aust
22B2 **Fremont** California, USA
18A1 **Fremont** Nebraska, USA
14B2 **Fremont** Ohio, USA
33G3 **French Guiana** Dependency, S America
109C4 **Frenchmans Cap** *Mt* Aust
105J4 **French Polynesia** *Is* Pacific O
24B2 **Fresnillo** Mexico
8B3 **Fresno** USA
22C2 **Fresno** *R* USA
47A1 **Fretigney** France
46B1 **Frévent** France
109C4 **Freycinet Pen** Aust
97A3 **Fria** Guinea
22C2 **Friant** USA
22C2 **Friant Dam** USA
52A1 **Fribourg** Switz
57B3 **Friedrichshafen** Germany
6D3 **Frobisher B** Can
6D3 **Frobisher Bay** Can
5H4 **Frobisher L** Can
61F4 **Frolovo** Russian Fed
43C4 **Frome** Eng
108A1 **Frome** *R* Aust
43C4 **Frome** *R* Eng
106C4 **Frome,L** Aust
25C3 **Frontera** Mexico
15C3 **Front Royal** USA
53B2 **Frosinone** Italy
73C5 **Fuchuan** China
73E4 **Fuding** China
24B2 **Fuerte** *R* Mexico
30E3 **Fuerte Olimpo** Par
96A2 **Fuerteventura** *I* Canary Is
72C2 **Fugu** China
68A2 **Fuhai** China
91C4 **Fujairah** UAE
75B1 **Fuji** Japan
73D4 **Fujian** Province, China
69F2 **Fujin** China
75B1 **Fujinomiya** Japan
74D3 **Fuji-san** *Mt* Japan
75B1 **Fujisawa** Japan
75B1 **Fuji-Yoshida** Japan
63A3 **Fukang** China
74C3 **Fukuchiyima** Japan
74D3 **Fukui** Japan
74C4 **Fukuoka** Japan
74E3 **Fukushima** Japan
74C4 **Fukuyama** Japan
57B2 **Fulda** Germany
57B2 **Fulda** *R* Germany
73B4 **Fuling** China
27L1 **Fullarton** Trinidad
22D4 **Fullerton** USA
18C2 **Fulton** Kentucky, USA
15C2 **Fulton** New York, USA
46C1 **Fumay** France
75C1 **Funabashi** Japan
96A1 **Funchal** Medeira
35C1 **Fundão** Brazil
7D5 **Fundy,B of** Can
101C3 **Funhalouro** Mozam
72D3 **Funing** China
73B5 **Funing** China
97C3 **Funtua** Nig
73D4 **Fuqing** China
101C2 **Furancungo** Mozam
91C4 **Fürg** Iran
47C1 **Furka** *P* Switz
107D5 **Furneaux Group** *Is* Aust
56C2 **Fürstenwalde** Germany
57C3 **Fürth** Germany
74D3 **Furukawa** Japan
6B3 **Fury and Hecla St** Can
74A2 **Fushun** Liaoning, China
73A4 **Fushun** Sichuan, China
74B2 **Fusong** China
57C3 **Füssen** Germany
72E2 **Fu Xian** China
72E1 **Fuxin** China
72D3 **Fuyang** China
72E1 **Fuyuan** Liaoning, China
73A4 **Fuyuan** Yunnan, China
68A2 **Fuyun** China
73D4 **Fuzhou** China
56C1 **Fyn** *I* Den

G

99E2 **Gaalkacyo** Somalia
21B2 **Gabbs** USA
100A2 **Gabela** Angola
96D1 **Gabe's** Tunisia
22B2 **Gabilan Range** *Mts* USA
98B3 **Gabon** Republic, Africa
100B3 **Gaborone** Botswana
54C2 **Gabrovo** Bulg
91B3 **Gach Sārān** Iran
17A1 **Gadsden** Alabama, USA
10A1 **Gads L** Can
53B2 **Gaeta** Italy
71F3 **Gaferut** *I* Pacific O
96C1 **Gafsa** Tunisia
60D2 **Gagarin** Russian Fed
97B4 **Gagnoa** Ivory Coast
7D4 **Gagnon** Can
61F5 **Gagra** Georgia
86B1 **Gaibanda** India
29C4 **Gaimán** Arg
17B2 **Gainesville** Florida, USA
17B1 **Gainesville** Georgia, USA
19A3 **Gainesville** Texas, USA
42D3 **Gainsborough** Eng
108A2 **Gairdner,L** Aust
44B3 **Gairloch** Scot
16A3 **Gaithersburg** USA
87B1 **Gajendragarh** India
73D4 **Ga Jiang** *R* China
99D3 **Galana** *R* Kenya
103D5 **Galapagos Is** Pacific O
42C2 **Galashiels** Scot
54C1 **Galaţi** Rom
4C3 **Galena** Alaska, USA
18B2 **Galena** Kansas, USA
27L1 **Galeota Pt** Trinidad
27L1 **Galera Pt** Trinidad
10A2 **Galesburg** USA
15C2 **Galeton** USA
61F2 **Galich** Russian Fed
50A1 **Galicia** Region, Spain
Galilee,S of = Tiberias,L
27J1 **Galina Pt** Jamaica
99D1 **Gallabat** Sudan
47C2 **Gallarate** Italy
87C3 **Galle** Sri Lanka
51B1 **Gállego** *R* Spain
Gallipoli = Gelibolu
55A2 **Gallipoli** Italy
38J5 **Gällivare** Sweden
42B2 **Galloway** District
42B2 **Galloway,Mull of** *C* Scot
8C3 **Gallup** USA
22B1 **Galt** USA
96A2 **Galtat Zemmour** Mo
25C2 **Galveston** USA
11A4 **Galveston B** USA
34C2 **Galvez** Arg
49D3 **Galvi** Corse
45B2 **Galway** County, Irish Rep
41B3 **Galway** Irish Rep
41B3 **Galway** *B* Irish Rep
86B1 **Gamba** China
97B3 **Gambaga** Ghana
4A3 **Gambell** USA
97A3 **Gambia** *R* The Gambia/Sen
97A3 **Gambia,The** Republic, Africa
98B3 **Gamboma** Congo
100A2 **Gambos** Angola
87C3 **Gampola** Sri Lanka
99E2 **Ganale Dorya** *R* Eth
15C2 **Gananoque** Can
Gand = Gent
100A2 **Ganda** Angola
98C3 **Gandajika** Zaïre
84B3 **Gandava** Pak
7E5 **Gander** Can
85C4 **Gāndhīdhām** India
85C4 **Gāndhīnagar** India
85D4 **Gāndhi Sāgar** *L* India
51B2 **Gandia** Spain
86B2 **Ganga** *R* India
85C3 **Ganganar** India
86C2 **Gangaw** Burma
72A2 **Gangca** China
82C2 **Gangdise Shan** *Mts* China
Ganges = Ganga
86B1 **Gangtok** India
72B3 **Gangu** China
8C2 **Gannett Peak** *Mt* USA
72B2 **Ganquan** China
108A3 **Gantheaume** *C* Aus
39K8 **Gantsevichi** Belorussia
73D4 **Ganzhou** China
97C3 **Gao** Mali
72A2 **Gaolan** China
72C2 **Gaoping** China
97B3 **Gaoua** Burkina
97A3 **Gaoual** Guinea
72D3 **Gaoyou Hu** *L* China
73C5 **Gaozhou** China
49D3 **Gap** France
79B2 **Gapan** Phil
84D2 **Gar** China
109C1 **Garah** Aust
31D3 **Garanhuns** Brazil
21A1 **Garberville** USA
35B2 **Garça** Brazil
35A2 **Garcias** Brazil
47D2 **Garda** Italy
9C3 **Garden City** USA
14A1 **Garden Pen** USA
34D3 **Gardey** Arg
84B2 **Gardez** Afghan

16C2 **Gardiners I** USA
16D1 **Gardner** USA
47D2 **Gardone** Italy
47D2 **Gargano** Italy
85D4 **Garhākota** India
61K2 **Gari** Russian Fed
00A4 **Garies** S Africa
99D3 **Garissa** Kenya
19A3 **Garland** USA
57C3 **Garmisch-Partenkirchen** Germany
90B2 **Garmsar** Iran
18A2 **Garnett** USA
8B2 **Garnett Peak** *Mt* USA
48C3 **Garonne** *R* France
44B3 **Garry** *R* Scot
78B4 **Garut** Indon
86A2 **Garwa** India
14A2 **Gary** USA
82C2 **Garyarsa** China
4H3 **Gary L** Can
19A3 **Garza-Little Elm** *Res* USA
90B2 **Gasan Kuli** Turkmenistan
48B3 **Gascogne** Region, France
18B2 **Gasconade** *R* USA
06A3 **Gascoyne** *R* Aust
98B2 **Gashaka** Nig
97D3 **Gashua** Nig
10D2 **Gaspé** Can
10D2 **Gaspé,C. de** Can
94A1 **Gata,C** Cyprus
60C2 **Gatchina** Russian Fed
42D2 **Gateshead** Eng
19A3 **Gatesville** USA
15C1 **Gatineau** Can
15C1 **Gatineau** *R* Can
09D1 **Gatton** Aust
86C1 **Gauháti** India
58C1 **Gauja** *R* Latvia
86A1 **Gauri Phanta** India
22B3 **Gaviota** USA
39H6 **Gävle** Sweden
08A2 **Gawler Ranges** *Mts* Aust
72A1 **Gaxun Nur** *L* China
86A2 **Gaya** India
97C3 **Gaya** Niger
14B1 **Gaylord** USA
09D1 **Gayndah** Aust
61H1 **Gayny** Russian Fed
60C4 **Gaysin** Ukraine
92B3 **Gaza** Israel
92C2 **Gaziantep** Turk
97B4 **Gbaringa** Lib
58B2 **Gdańsk** Pol
58B2 **Gdańsk,G of** Pol
39K7 **Gdov** Russian Fed
58B2 **Gdynia** Pol
94A3 **Gebel Halâl** *Mt* Egypt
95C2 **Gebel Hamata** *Mt* Egypt
92B4 **Gebel Katherina** *Mt* Egypt
94A3 **Gebel Libni** *Mt* Egypt
94A3 **Gebel Maghâra** *Mt* Egypt
99D1 **Gedaref** Sudan
55C3 **Gediz** *R* Turk
56C2 **Gedser** Den
46C1 **Geel** Belg
08B3 **Geelong** Aust
09C4 **Geeveston** Aust
97D3 **Geidam** Nig
56D1 **Geilenkirchen** Germany
99D3 **Geita** Tanz
73A5 **Gejiu** China
53B3 **Gela** Italy
99E2 **Geladī** Eth
46D1 **Geldern** Germany
55C2 **Gelibolu** Turk
92B2 **Gelidonya Burun** Turk
6D1 **Gelsenkirchen** Germany
39F8 **Gelting** Germany
77C5 **Gemas** Malay
46C1 **Gembloux** Belg
98B2 **Gemena** Zaïre
92C2 **Gemerek** Turk
92A1 **Gemlik** Turk
52B1 **Gemona** Italy
100B3 **Gemsbok** *Nat Pk* Botswana
98C1 **Geneina** Sudan
34C3 **General Acha** Arg
34C3 **General Alvear** Buenos Aires, Arg
34B2 **General Alvear** Mendoza, Arg
34C2 **General Arenales** Arg
34D3 **General Belgrano** Arg
112B2 **General Belgrano** *Base* Ant
112C2 **General Bernardo O'Higgins** *Base* Ant
34D3 **General Conesa** Buenos Aires, Arg
30D3 **General Eugenio A Garay** Par
34D3 **General Guido** Arg
34C3 **General La Madrid** Arg
34C2 **General Levalle** Arg
30C4 **General Manuel Belgrano** *Mt* Arg
34D3 **General Paz** Buenos Aires, Arg
34C3 **General Pico** Arg
34C2 **General Pinto** Arg
34D3 **General Pirán** Arg
29C3 **General Roca** Arg
112C3 **General San Martin** *Base* Ant
79C4 **General Santos** Phil
34C3 **General Viamonte** Arg
34C3 **General Villegas** Arg
15C2 **Genesee** *R* USA
15C2 **Geneseo** USA
Geneva = Genève
18A1 **Geneva** Nebraska, USA
15C2 **Geneva** New York, USA
Geneva,L of = LacLéman
52A1 **Genève** Switz
50B2 **Genil** *R* Spain
Genoa = Genova
109C3 **Genoa** Aust
52A2 **Genova** Italy
32J7 **Genovesa** *I* Ecuador
46B1 **Gent** Belg
78B4 **Genteng** Indon
56C2 **Genthin** Germany
93E1 **Geokchay** Azerbaijan
100B4 **George** S Africa
7D4 **George** *R* Can
109C2 **George,L** Aust
17B2 **George,L** Florida, USA
15D2 **George,L** New York, USA
111A2 **George Sd** NZ
109C4 **George Town** Aust
15C3 **Georgetown** Delaware, USA
33F2 **Georgetown** Guyana
14B3 **Georgetown** Kentucky, USA
77C4 **George Town** Malay
27N2 **Georgetown** St Vincent and the Grenadines
17C1 **Georgetown** S Carolina, USA
19A3 **Georgetown** Texas, USA
97A3 **Georgetown** The Gambia
112C8 **George V Land** Region, Ant
65F5 **Georgia** Republic, Europe
112C12 **Georg Forster** *Base* Ant
17B1 **Georgia** State, USA
14B1 **Georgian B** Can
13C3 **Georgia,Str of** Can
106C3 **Georgina** *R* Aust
61F5 **Georgiyevsk** Russian Fed
57C2 **Gera** Germany
46B1 **Geraardsbergen** Belg
111B2 **Geraldine** NZ
106A3 **Geraldton** Aust
10B2 **Geraldton** Can
94B3 **Gerar** *R* Israel
4C3 **Gerdine,Mt** USA
12E2 **Gerdova Peak** *Mt* USA
77C4 **Gerik** Malay
60B4 **Gerlachovsky** *Mt* Pol
13C1 **Germanson Lodge** Can
56C2 **Germany** Republic, Europe
101G1 **Germiston** S Africa
46D1 **Gerolstein** Germany
51C1 **Gerona** Spain
46E1 **Geseke** Germany
99E2 **Gestro** *R* Eth
50B1 **Getafe** Spain
16A3 **Gettysburg** Pennsylvania, USA
93D2 **Gevaş** Turk
55B2 **Gevgeliija** Macedonia
47B1 **Gex** France
94C2 **Ghabāghib** Syria
96C1 **Ghadamis** Libya
90B2 **Ghaem Shahr** Iran
86A1 **Ghāghara** *R* India
97B4 **Ghana** Republic, Africa
100B3 **Ghanzi** Botswana
96C1 **Ghardaïa** Alg
95A1 **Gharyan** Libya
95A2 **Ghāt** Libya
84D3 **Ghāziābād** India
84C3 **Ghazi Khan** Pak
84B2 **Ghazni** Afghan
54C1 **Gheorgheni** Rom
88E4 **Ghudamis** Alg
90D3 **Ghurian** Afghan
95B2 **Gialo** Libya
99E2 **Giamame** Somalia
53C3 **Giarre** Italy
100A3 **Gibeon** Namibia
50A2 **Gibraltar** Colony, SW Europe
50A2 **Gibraltar,Str of** Spain/Africa
106B3 **Gibson Desert** Aust
20B1 **Gibsons** Can
87B1 **Giddalūr** India
99D2 **Gīdolē** Eth
57B2 **Giessen** Germany
17B2 **Gifford** USA
74D3 **Gifu** Japan
42B2 **Gigha** *I* Scot
52B2 **Giglio** *I* Italy
50A1 **Gijón** Spain
107D2 **Gilbert** *R* Aust
13C2 **Gilbert,Mt** Can
101C2 **Gilé** Mozam
94B2 **Gilead** Region, Jordan
95B2 **Gilf Kebir Plat** Egypt
109C2 **Gilgandra** Aust
84C1 **Gilgit** Pak
84C1 **Gilgit** *R* Pak
108C2 **Gilgunnia** Aust
7A4 **Gillam** Can
108A2 **Gilles** *L* Aust
13B2 **Gill I** Can
14A1 **Gills Rock** USA
14A2 **Gilman** USA
22B2 **Gilroy** USA
8D1 **Gimli** Can
101H1 **Gingindlovu** S Africa
79C4 **Gingoog** Phil
99E2 **Gīnīr** Eth
55B3 **Gióna** *Mt* Greece
109C3 **Gippsland** *Mts* Aust
14B2 **Girard** USA
32C3 **Girardot** Colombia
44C3 **Girdle Ness** *Pen* Scot
93C1 **Giresun** Turk
85C4 **Gir Hills** India
98B2 **Giri** *R* Zaïre
86B2 **Girīdīh** India
Girona = Gerona
48B2 **Gironde** *R* France
42B2 **Girvan** Scot
111C2 **Gisborne** NZ
46A2 **Gisors** France
99C3 **Gitega** Burundi
Giuba,R = Juba,R
54C2 **Giurgiu** Rom
46C1 **Givet** Belg
58C2 **Gizycko** Pol
55B2 **Gjirokastër** Alb
4J3 **Gjoatlaven** Can
39G6 **Gjøvik** Nor
7D5 **Glace Bay** Can
12G3 **Glacier Bay Nat Mon** USA
13E3 **Glacier Nat Pk** USA/Can
20B1 **Glacier Peak** *Mt* USA
6B2 **Glacier Str** Can
107E3 **Gladstone** Queensland, Aust
108A2 **Gladstone** S Aust, Aust
109C4 **Gladstone** Tasmania, Aust
14A1 **Gladstone** USA
38A1 **Glama** *Mt* Iceland
39G6 **Glåma** *R* Nor
46D2 **Glan** *R* Germany
47C1 **Glarner** *Mts* Switz
47C1 **Glarus** Switz
18A2 **Glasco** USA
8C2 **Glasgow** Montana, USA
42B2 **Glasgow** Scot
16B3 **Glassboro** USA
43C4 **Glastonbury** Eng
61H2 **Glazov** Russian Fed
59B3 **Gleisdorf** Austria
110C1 **Glen Afton** NZ
16A3 **Glen Burnie** USA
101H1 **Glencoe** S Africa
9B3 **Glendale** Arizona, USA
22C3 **Glendale** California, USA
12E2 **Glenhallen** USA
109D1 **Glen Innes** Aust
109C1 **Glenmorgan** Aust
109D2 **Glenreagh** Aust
16A3 **Glen Rock** USA
19A3 **Glen Rose** USA
44C3 **Glenrothes** UK
15D2 **Glens Falls** USA
45B1 **Glenties** Irish Rep
19B3 **Glenwood** Arkansas, USA
8C3 **Glenwood Springs** USA
39F6 **Glittertind** *Mt* Nor
59B2 **Gliwice** Pol
9B3 **Globe** USA
58B2 **Głogów** Pol
38G5 **Glomfjord** Nor
109D2 **Gloucester** Aust
43C4 **Gloucester** Eng
16D1 **Gloucester** USA
58D1 **Glubokoye** Belorussia
60D3 **Glukhov** Russian Fed
59B3 **Gmünd** Austria
57C3 **Gmunden** Austria
58B2 **Gniezno** Pol
100A3 **Goabeg** Namibia
87A1 **Goa, Daman and Diu** Union Territory, India
86C1 **Goālpāra** India
99D2 **Goba** Eth
100A3 **Gobabis** Namibia
34C2 **Gobernador Crespo** Arg
34B3 **Gobernador Duval** Arg
72B1 **Gobi** *Desert* China/Mongolia
75B2 **Gobo** Japan
87B1 **Godag** India
87C1 **Godāvari** *R* India
14B2 **Goderich** Can
6E3 **Godhavn** Greenland
85C4 **Godhra** India
34B2 **Godoy Cruz** Arg

7A4 **Gods L** Can
6E3 **Godthab** Greenland
Godwin Austen = K2
35B1 **Goiandira** Brazil
35B1 **Goianésia** Brazil
35B1 **Goiânia** Brazil
35A1 **Goiás** Brazil
31B4 **Goiás** State, Brazil
35A2 **Goio-Erê** Brazil
99D2 **Gojab** *R* Eth
55C2 **Gökçeada** *I* Turk
55C3 **Gökova Körfezi** *B* Turk
92C2 **Göksun** Turk
63C3 **Gol** *R* Mongolia
86C1 **Golāghāt** India
93C2 **Gölbaşi** Turk
20C2 **Golconda** USA
20B2 **Gold Beach** USA
109D1 **Gold Coast** Aust
13D2 **Golden** Can
110B2 **Golden B** NZ
20B1 **Goldendale** USA
22A2 **Golden Gate** *Chan* USA
19B4 **Golden Meadow** USA
21B2 **Goldfield** USA
13B3 **Gold River** Can
56C2 **Goleniów** Pol
22C3 **Goleta** USA
52A2 **Golfe d'Ajaccio** *G* Corse
96D1 **Golfe de Gabes** *G* Tunisia
Golfe de Gascogne = Biscay,Bay of
52A2 **Golfe de St Florent** *G* Corse
48B2 **Golfe de St-Malo** *B* France
49C3 **Golfe du Lion** *G* France
29B4 **Golfo Corcovado** *G* Chile
50B2 **Golfo de Almeira** *G* Spain
29B4 **Golfo de Ancud** *G* Chile
25D2 **Golfo de Batabano** *G* Cuba
50A2 **Golfo de Cadiz** *G* Spain
53A3 **Golfo de Cagliari** *G* Sardegna
24A1 **Golfo de California** *G* Mexico
25D4 **Golfo de Chiriqui** *G* Panama
25D3 **Golfo de Fonseca** Honduras
26B2 **Golfo de Guacanayabo** *G* Cuba
32A4 **Golfo de Guayaquil** *G* Ecuador
26B5 **Golfo del Darien** *G* Colombia/Panama
32A2 **Golfo de los Mosquitos** *G* Panama
25D3 **Golfo del Papagaya** *G* Nic
51B2 **Golfo de Mazarrón** *G* Spain
25D4 **Golfo de Nicoya** *G* Costa Rica
53A3 **Golfo de Oristano** *G* Sardegna
25E4 **Golfo de Panamá** *G* Panama
25D3 **Golfo de Papagayo** *G* Costa Rica
27E4 **Golfo de Paria** *G* Ven
29B5 **Golfo de Penas** *G* Chile
49D3 **Golfo de St Florent** Corse
51C1 **Golfo de San Jorge** *G* Spain
24C3 **Golfo de Tehuantepec** *G* Mexico
32B3 **Golfo de Torugas** *G* Colombia
32B2 **Golfo de Uraba** *G* Colombia
51C2 **Golfo de Valencia** *G* Spain
27C4 **Golfo de Venezuela** *G* Ven
52A2 **Golfo di Genova** *G* Italy
53C3 **Golfo di Policastro** *G* Italy
53C3 **Golfo di Squillace** *G* Italy
53C2 **Golfo di Taranto** *G* Italy
52B1 **Golfo di Venezia** *G* Italy
25D4 **Golfo Dulce** *G* Costa Rica
29C5 **Golfo San Jorge** *G* Arg
29D4 **Golfo San Matías** *G* Arg
68B3 **Golmud** China
99E2 **Golocha** Eth
12B2 **Golovin B** USA
74F2 **Golovnino** Russian Fed
99C3 **Goma** Zaïre
97D3 **Gombe** Nig
60D3 **Gomel** Belorussia
96A2 **Gomera** *I* Canary Is
24B2 **Gómez Palacio** Mexico
63E2 **Gonam** *R* Russian Fed
90C2 **Gonbad-e Kāvūs** Iran
86A1 **Gonda** India
85C4 **Gondal** India
99D1 **Gonder** Eth
92A1 **Gönen** Turk
55C3 **Gonen** *R* Turk
73A4 **Gongga Shan** *Mt* China
72A2 **Gonghe** China
97D3 **Gongola** *R* Nig
22B2 **Gonzales** California, USA
19A4 **Gonzales** Texas, USA
34C3 **Gonzalez Chaves** Arg
13C2 **Good Hope Mt** Can
8C2 **Goodland** USA
12B3 **Goodnews Bay** USA
109C1 **Goodooga** *R* Aust
42D3 **Goole** Eng
108C2 **Goolgowi** Aust
108A3 **Goolwa** Aust
106A4 **Goomalling** Aust
108C2 **Goombalie** Aust
109D1 **Goomer** Aust
109D1 **Goomeri** Aust
109D1 **Goondiwindi** Aust
7E4 **Goose Bay** Can
17C1 **Goose Creek** USA
20B2 **Goose L** USA
87B1 **Gooty** India
63C2 **Gora Munku Sardyk** *Mt* Mongolia/ Russian Fed
64H3 **Gora Narodnaya** *Mt* Russian Fed
64G3 **Gora Tel'pos-iz** Russian Fed
54A2 **Goražde** Bosnia-Herzegovina
4D3 **Gordon** USA
13E1 **Gordon L** Can
15C3 **Gordonsville** USA
98B2 **Goré** Chad
99D2 **Gorē** Eth
111A3 **Gore** NZ
63F2 **Gore Topko** *Mt* Russian Fed
45C2 **Gorey** Irish Rep
90B2 **Gorgān** Iran
93E2 **Goris** Armenia
52B1 **Gorizia** Italy
Gor'kiy = Nizniy Novgorod
61F2 **Gor'kovskoye Vodokhranilishche** *Res* Russian Fed
57C2 **Gorlitz** Germany
60E4 **Gorlovka** Ukraine
22C3 **Gorman** USA
54C2 **Gorna Orjahovica** Bulg
68A1 **Gorno-Altaysk** Russian Fed
69G2 **Gornozavodsk** Russian Fed
61F2 **Gorodets** Russian Fed
59C3 **Gorodok** Ukraine
59D3 **Gorodok** Ukraine
71F4 **Goroka** PNG
86A1 **Gorokhpur** India
101C2 **Gorongosa** Mozam
71D3 **Gorontalo** Indon
61K2 **Goro Yurma** *Mt* Russian Fed
45B2 **Gort** Irish Rep
63C2 **Goryachinsk** Russian Fed
59D3 **Goryn'** *R* Ukraine
59C2 **Góry Świetokrzyskie** *Upland* Pol
64G3 **Gory Tel'pos-iz'** *Mt* Russian Fed
39H8 **Gorzów Wielkopolski** Pol
74E2 **Goshogawara** Japan
52C2 **Gospić** Croatia
54B2 **Gostivar** Macedonia
58B2 **Gostynin** Pol
39G7 **Göteborg** Sweden
98B2 **Gotel** *Mts* Nig
39H7 **Gotland** *I* Sweden
74B4 **Gotō-retto** *I* Japan
39H7 **Gotska Sandön** *I* Sweden
74C3 **Gōtsu** Japan
98B1 **Goudoumaria** Niger
103H7 **Gough I** Atlantic O
109C2 **Goulburn** Aust
97B3 **Goumbou** Mali
97B3 **Goundam** Mali
98B1 **Gouré** Niger
97B3 **Gourma Rharous** Mali
46A2 **Gournay-en-Bray** France
95A3 **Gouro** Chad
71E5 **Gove Pen** Aust
60B4 **Goverla** *Mt* Ukraine
35C1 **Governador Valadares** Brazil
86A2 **Govind Ballabh Paht Sāgar** *L* India
15C2 **Gowanda** USA
84B3 **Gowārān** Afghan
30E4 **Goya** Arg
98C1 **Goz-Beïda** Chad
53B3 **Gozo** *I* Medit S
95C3 **Goz Regeb** Sudan
100B4 **Graaff-Reinet** S Africa
15C1 **Gracefield** Can
109D1 **Grafton** Aust
8D2 **Grafton** N Dakota, USA
14B3 **Grafton** W Virginia, USA
5E4 **Graham** *I* Can
13C1 **Graham** *R* Can
13E1 **Graham L** Can
100B4 **Grahamstown** S Africa
31B3 **Grajaú** Brazil
58C2 **Grajewo** Pol
55B2 **Grámmos** *Mt* Greece/Alb
44C3 **Grampian** Region, Scot
44B3 **Grampian** *Mts* Scot
32C3 **Granada** Colombia
25D3 **Granada** Nic
50B2 **Granada** Spain
15D1 **Granby** Can
96A2 **Gran Canaria** *I* Canary Is
30D4 **Gran Chaco** *Region* Arg
14A2 **Grand** *R* Michigan, USA
18B1 **Grand** *R* Missouri, USA
27Q2 **Grand B** Dominica
11C4 **Grand Bahama** *I* The Bahamas
7E5 **Grand Bank** Can
102F2 **Grand Banks** Atlantic O
97B4 **Grand Bassam** Ivory Coast
9B3 **Grand Canyon** USA
26A3 **Grand Cayman** *I* Caribbean S
13E2 **Grand Centre** Can
20C1 **Grand Coulee** USA
34B3 **Grande** *R* Arg
31C4 **Grande** *R* Bahia, Brazil
35B1 **Grande** *R* Minas Gerais/São Paulo, Brazil
13D2 **Grande Cache** Can
47A2 **Grande Chartreuse** Region, France
101D2 **Grande Comore** *I* Comoros
13D1 **Grande Prairie** Can
19A3 **Grande Prairie** USA
95A3 **Grand Erg de Bilma** *Desert* Niger
96B2 **Grand erg Occident** *Mts* Alg
96C2 **Grand erg Oriental** *Mts* Alg
7C4 **Grande Rivière de la Baleine** *R* Can
20C1 **Grande Ronde** *R* USA
7D5 **Grand Falls** New Brunswick, Can
7E5 **Grand Falls** Newfoundland, Can
20C1 **Grand Forks** Can
8D2 **Grand Forks** USA
16B1 **Grand Gorge** USA
14A2 **Grand Haven** USA
19C3 **Grand Isle** USA
19B4 **Grand L** USA
15D1 **Grand Mère** Can
50A2 **Grândola** Port
5J4 **Grand Rapids** Can
14A2 **Grand Rapids** Michigan, USA
10A2 **Grand Rapids** Minnesota, USA
47B2 **Grand St Bernard** Italy/Switz
8B2 **Grand Teton** *Mt* USA
8B2 **Grand Teton Nat Pk** USA
46A2 **Grandvilliers** France
25D1 **Grangeburg** USA
51C1 **Granollérs** Spain
52A1 **Gran Paradiso** *Mt* Italy
47D1 **Gran Pilastro** *Mt* Austria/Italy
43D3 **Grantham** Eng
21B2 **Grant,Mt** USA
44C3 **Grantown-on-Spey** Scot
9C3 **Grants** USA
20B2 **Grants Pass** USA
48B2 **Granville** France
5H4 **Granville L** Can
35C1 **Grão Mogol** Brazil
49D3 **Grasse** France
21A2 **Grass Valley** USA
5H5 **Gravelbourg** Can
46B1 **Gravelines** France
100C3 **Gravelotte** S Africa
15C2 **Gravenhurst** Can
109D1 **Gravesend** Aust
12H3 **Gravina I** USA
12B2 **Grayling** USA
20B1 **Grays Harbor** *B* USA
14B3 **Grayson** USA
18C2 **Grayville** USA
59B3 **Graz** Austria
27H1 **Great** *R* Jamaica
11C4 **Great Abaco** *I* The Bahamas

106B4 **Great Australian Bight** *G* Aust
16B3 **Great B** New Jersey, USA
25E2 **Great Bahama Bank** The Bahamas
110C1 **Great Barrier I** NZ
107D2 **Great Barrier Reef** *Is* Aust
16C1 **Great Barrington** USA
4F3 **Great Bear L** Can
9D2 **Great Bend** USA
107D3 **Great Dividing Range** *Mts* Aust
42D2 **Great Driffield** Eng
16B3 **Great Egg Harbor** *B* USA
12B10 **Greater Antarctic** Region, Ant
26B2 **Greater Antilles** *Is* Caribbean S
43D4 **Greater London** Metropolitan County, Eng
43C3 **Greater Manchester** County, Eng
25E2 **Great Exuma** *I* The Bahamas
8B2 **Great Falls** USA
44B3 **Great Glen** *V* Scot
86B1 **Great Himalayan Range** *Mts* Asia
11C4 **Great Inagua** *I* The Bahamas
100B4 **Great Karroo** *Mts* S Africa
109C4 **Great L** Aust
100A3 **Great Namaland** Region, Namibia
42C3 **Great Ormes Head** *C* Wales
11C4 **Great Ragged** *I* The Bahamas
99D3 **Great Ruaha** *R* Tanz
15D2 **Great Sacandaga L** USA
8B2 **Great Salt L** USA
95B2 **Great Sand Sea** Libya/Egypt
106B3 **Great Sandy Desert** Aust
8A2 **Great Sandy Desert** USA
Great Sandy I = Fraser I
4G3 **Great Slave L** Can
16C2 **Great South B** USA
106B3 **Great Victoria Desert** Aust
112C2 **Great Wall** *Base* Ant
72B2 **Great Wall** China
43E3 **Great Yarmouth** Eng
94B1 **Greco,C** Cyprus
55B3 **Greece** Republic, Europe
15C2 **Greece** USA
8C2 **Greeley** USA
6B1 **Greely Fjord** Can
14A1 **Green B** USA
14A2 **Green Bay** USA
14A3 **Greencastle** Indiana, USA
16C1 **Greenfield** Massachusetts, USA
14A2 **Greenfield** Wisconsin, USA
13F2 **Green Lake** Can
6F2 **Greenland** Dependency, N Atlantic O
102H1 **Greenland Basin** Greenland S
1B1 **Greenland S** Greenland
42B2 **Greenock** Scot
16C2 **Greenport** USA
16B3 **Greensboro** Maryland, USA
11C3 **Greensboro** N Carolina, USA
15C2 **Greensburg** Pennsylvania, USA
44B3 **Greenstone** *Pt* Scot
18C2 **Greenup** USA
17A1 **Greenville** Alabama, USA
97B4 **Greenville** Lib
19B3 **Greenville** Mississippi, USA
16D1 **Greenville** N Hampshire, USA
14B2 **Greenville** Ohio, USA
17B1 **Greenville** S Carolina, USA
19A3 **Greenville** Texas, USA
43E4 **Greenwich** Eng
16C2 **Greenwich** USA
16B3 **Greenwood** Delaware, USA
19B3 **Greenwood** Mississippi, USA
17B1 **Greenwood** S Carolina, USA
18B2 **Greers Ferry L** USA
108A1 **Gregory,L** Aust
107D2 **Gregory Range** *Mts* Aust
56C2 **Greifswald** Germany
64F3 **Gremikha** Russian Fed
56C1 **Grenå** Den
19C3 **Grenada** USA
27E4 **Grenada** *I* Caribbean S
109C2 **Grenfell** Aust
49D2 **Grenoble** France
27M2 **Grenville** Grenada
107D2 **Grenville,C** Aust
20B1 **Gresham** USA
78C4 **Gresik** Jawa, Indon
78A3 **Gresik** Sumatera, Indon
19B4 **Gretna** USA
111B2 **Grey** *R* NZ
12G2 **Grey Hunter Pk** *Mt* Can
7E4 **Grey Is** Can
16C1 **Greylock,Mt** USA
111B2 **Greymouth** NZ
107D3 **Grey Range** *Mts* Aust
45C2 **Greystones** Irish Rep
101H1 **Greytown** S Africa
101F1 **Griekwastad** S Africa
17B1 **Griffin** USA
108C2 **Griffith** Aust
107D5 **Grim,C** Aust
15C2 **Grimsby** Can
42D3 **Grimsby** Eng
38B1 **Grimsey** *I* Iceland
13D1 **Grimshaw** Can
39F7 **Grimstad** Nor
47C1 **Grindelwald** Switz
6A2 **Grinnell Pen** Can
6B2 **Grise Fjord** Can
61H1 **Griva** Russian Fed
39J7 **Grobina** Latvia
58C2 **Grodno** Belorussia
86A1 **Gromati** *R* India
56B2 **Groningen** Neth
106C2 **Groote Eylandt** *I* Aust
100A2 **Grootfontein** Namibia
100B3 **Grootvloer** *Salt L* S Africa
27P2 **Gros Islet** St Lucia
46E1 **Grosser Feldberg** *Mt* Germany
52B2 **Grosseto** Italy
46E2 **Gross-Gerau** Germany
57C3 **Grossglockner** *Mt* Austria
47E1 **Gross Venediger** *Mt* Austria
12C3 **Grosvenor,L** USA
22B2 **Groveland** USA
21A2 **Grover City** USA
15D2 **Groveton** USA
61G5 **Groznyy** Russian Fed
58B2 **Grudziądz** Pol
100A3 **Grünau** Namibia
44E2 **Grutness** Scot
61F3 **Gryazi** Russian Fed
61E2 **Gryazovets** Russian Fed
29G8 **Grytviken** South Georgia
45A2 **Gt Blasket** *I* Irish Rep
35C2 **Guaçuí** Brazil
23A1 **Guadalajara** Mexico
50B1 **Guadalajara** Spain
107E1 **Guadalcanal** *I* Solomon Is
50B2 **Guadalimar** *R* Spain
51B1 **Guadalope** *R* Spain
50B2 **Guadalqivir** *R* Spain
24B2 **Guadalupe** Mexico
3G6 **Guadalupe** *I* Mexico
27E3 **Guadeloupe** *I* Caribbean S
50B2 **Guadian** *R* Spain
50A2 **Guadiana** *R* Port
50B2 **Guadix** Spain
32D6 **Guajará Mirim** Brazil
32C1 **Guajira,Pen de** Colombia
32B4 **Gualaceo** Ecuador
34D2 **Gualeguay** Arg
34D2 **Gualeguaychú** Arg
71F2 **Guam** *I* Pacific O
34C3 **Guamini** Arg
77C5 **Gua Musang** Malay
23A1 **Guanajuato** Mexico
23A1 **Guanajuato** State, Mexico
32D2 **Guanare** Ven
25D2 **Guane** Cuba
73C5 **Guangdong** Province, China
73A3 **Guanghan** China
72C3 **Guanghua** China
73A4 **Guangmao Shan** *Mt* China
73B5 **Guangnan** China
72B3 **Guangyuan** China
73D4 **Guangze** China
67F3 **Guangzhou** China
35C1 **Guanhães** Brazil
32D3 **Guania** *R* Colombia
27E5 **Guanipa** *R* Ven
26B2 **Guantánamo** Cuba
72D1 **Guanting Shuiku** *Res* China
73B5 **Guanxi** Province, China
73A3 **Guan Xian** China
32B2 **Guapa** Colombia
33E6 **Guaporé** *R* Brazil/Bol
30C2 **Guaquí** Bol
32B4 **Guaranda** Ecuador
30F4 **Guarapuava** Brazil
35B2 **Guaratinguetá** Brazil
50A1 **Guarda** Port
35B1 **Guarda Mor** Brazil
9C4 **Guasave** Mexico
47D2 **Guastalla** Italy
25C3 **Guatemala** Guatemala
25C3 **Guatemala** Republic, Cent America
34C3 **Guatraché** Arg
32C3 **Guavrare** *R* Colombia
35B2 **Guaxupé** Brazil
27L1 **Guayaguayare** Trinidad
32A4 **Guayaquil** Ecuador
24A2 **Guaymas** Mexico
34D2 **Guayquiraro** *R* Arg
100B2 **Guba** Zaïre
99E2 **Guban** *Region* Somalia
79B3 **Gubat** Phil
56C2 **Gubin** Pol
87B2 **Güdür** India
14B2 **Guelpho** Can
26A2 **Guenabacoa** Cuba
98C1 **Guéréda** Chad
48C2 **Guéret** France
40B2 **Guernsey** *I* UK
23A2 **Guerrero** State, Mexico
99D2 **Gughe** *Mt* Eth
63E2 **Gugigu** China
71F2 **Guguan** *I* Pacific O
109C2 **Guiargambone** Aust
73C4 **Guidong** China
97B4 **Guiglo** Ivory Coast
73C5 **Gui Jiang** *R* China
43D4 **Guildford** Eng
73C4 **Guilin** China
47B2 **Guillestre** France
72A2 **Guinan** China
97A3 **Guinea** Republic, Africa
102H4 **Guinea Basin** Atlantic O
97A3 **Guinea-Bissau** Republic, Africa
97C4 **Guinea,G of** W Africa
26A2 **Güines** Cuba
97B3 **Guir** *Well* Mali
84C2 **Guiranwala** Pak
33E1 **Güiria** Ven
46B2 **Guise** France
79C3 **Guiuan** Phil
73B5 **Gui Xian** China
73B4 **Guiyang** China
73B4 **Guizhou** Province, China
85C4 **Gujarāt** State, India
84C2 **Gujrat** Pak
87B1 **Gulbarga** India
58D1 **Gulbene** Latvia
87B1 **Guledagudda** India
80D3 **Gulf,The** S W Asia
109C2 **Gulgong** Aust
73B4 **Gulin** China
12E2 **Gulkana** USA
12E2 **Gulkana** *R* USA
13E2 **Gull L** Can
13F2 **Gull Lake** Can
55C3 **Güllük Körfezi** *B* Turk
99D2 **Gulu** Uganda
109C1 **Guluguba** Aust
97C3 **Gumel** Nig
46D1 **Gummersbach** Germany
86A2 **Gumpla** India
93C1 **Gümüşhane** Turk
85D4 **Guna** India
99D1 **Guna** *Mt* Eth
109C3 **Gundagai** Aust
98B3 **Gungu** Zaïre
6H3 **Gunnbjørn Fjeld** *Mt* Greenland
109D2 **Gunnedah** Aust
87B1 **Guntakal** India
17A1 **Guntersville** USA
17A1 **Guntersville L** USA
87C1 **Guntūr** India
77C5 **Gunung Batu Putch** *Mt* Malay
78D3 **Gunung Besar** *Mt* Indon
78D2 **Gunung Bulu** *Mt* Indon
78A3 **Gunung Gedang** *Mt* Indon
78C2 **Gunung Lawit** *Mt* Malay
78C4 **Gunung Lawu** *Mt* Indon
78D2 **Gunung Menyapa** *Mt* Indon
78D2 **Gunung Niapa** *Mt* Indon
78A3 **Gunung Patah** *Mt* Indon
78C4 **Gunung Raung** *Mt* Indon
78A3 **Gunung Resag** *Mt* Indon
78D3 **Gunung Sarempaka** *Mt* Indon
78C4 **Gunung Sumbing** *Mt* Indon
77C5 **Gunung Tahan** *Mt* Malay
78A2 **Gunung Talakmau** *Mt* Indon
100A2 **Gunza** Angola
72D3 **Guoyang** China
84D2 **Gurdāspur** India
84D3 **Gurgaon** India
86A1 **Gurkha** Nepal
92C2 **Gürün** Turk
31B2 **Gurupi** *R* Brazil

100C2 **Guruve** Zim
72A1 **Gurvan Sayhan Uul** *Upland* Mongolia
61H4 **Gur'yev** Kazakhstan
97C3 **Gusau** Nig
58C2 **Gusev** Russian Fed
74A3 **Gushan** China
61F2 **Gus'khrustalnyy** Russian Fed
12G3 **Gustavus** USA
22B2 **Gustine** USA
11B3 **Guston** USA
56B2 **Gütersloh** Germany
18C2 **Guthrie** Kentucky, USA
18A2 **Guthrie** Oklahoma, USA
23B1 **Gutiérrez Zamora** Mexico
33F3 **Guyana** Republic, S America
102F4 **Guyana Basin** Atlantic O
72C1 **Guyang** China
48B3 **Guyenne** Region, France
9C3 **Guymon** USA
109D2 **Guyra** Aust
72B2 **Guyuan** China
109C2 **Gwabegar** Aust
85D3 **Gwalior** India
100B3 **Gwanda** Zim
98C2 **Gwane** Zaïre
82A3 **Gwardar** Pak
45B1 **Gweebarra B** Irish Rep
89G9 **Gwelo** Zim
43C4 **Gwent** County, Wales
100B2 **Gweru** Zim
109C1 **Gwydir** *R* Aust
43C3 **Gwynedd** Wales
65F5 **Gyandzha** Azerbaijan
86B1 **Gyangzê** China
68B3 **Gyaring Hu** *L* China
64J2 **Gydanskiy Poluostrov** *Pen* Russian Fed
86B1 **Gyirong** China
6F3 **Gyldenløues** Greenland
109D1 **Gympie** Aust
59B3 **Gyöngyös** Hung
59B3 **Györ** Hung

H

38K6 **Haapajärvi** Fin
60B2 **Haapsalu** Estonia
56A2 **Haarlem** Neth
46D1 **Haarstrang** Region, Germany
25D2 **Habana** Cuba
86C2 **Habiganj** Bang
74D4 **Hachijō-jima** *I* Japan
75B1 **Hachiman** Japan
74E2 **Hachinohe** Japan
75B1 **Hachioji** Japan
16B2 **Hackettstown** USA
108A2 **Hack,Mt** *Mt* Aust
42C2 **Haddington** Scot
108B1 **Haddon Corner** Aust
108B1 **Haddon Downs** Aust
97D3 **Hadejia** Nig
97C3 **Hadejia** *R* Nig
94B2 **Hadera** Israel
56B1 **Haderslev** Den
81D4 **Hadiboh** Socotra
4H2 **Hadley B** Can
73B5 **Hadong** Vietnam
81C4 **Hadramawt** Region, Yemen
56C1 **Hadsund** Den
74B3 **Haeju** N Korea
91A4 **Hafar al Bātin** S Arabia
6D2 **Haffners Bjerg** *Mt* Greenland
84C2 **Hafizabad** Pak
86C1 **Hāflong** India
38A2 **Hafnafjörður** Iceland
12B3 **Hagemeister** *I* USA
56B2 **Hagen** Germany
15C3 **Hagerstown** USA
75A2 **Hagi** Japan
73A5 **Ha Giang** Vietnam
46D2 **Hagondange** France
45B2 **Hags Hd** *C* Irish Rep
46D2 **Haguenan** France
96A2 **Hagunia** *Well* Mor
69G4 **Haha-jima** *I* Japan
68B3 **Hah Xil Hu** *L* China
74A2 **Haicheng** China
76D1 **Hai Duong** Viet
94B2 **Haifa** Israel
94B2 **Haifa,B of** Israel
72D2 **Hai He** *R* China
73C5 **Haikang** China
76E1 **Haikou** China
80C3 **Ha'il** S Arabia
86C2 **Hailākāndi** India
63D3 **Hailar** China
74B2 **Hailong** China
69E2 **Hailun** China
38J5 **Hailuoto** *I* Fin
76D2 **Hainan** *I* China
12G3 **Haines** USA
12G2 **Haines Junction** Can
59B3 **Hainfeld** Austria
73B5 **Haiphong** Vietnam
26C3 **Haiti** Republic, Caribbean S
95C3 **Haiya** Sudan
72A2 **Haiyan** China
72B2 **Haiyuan** China
72D3 **Haizhou Wan** *B* China
59C3 **Hajdúböszörmény** Hung
75B1 **Hajiki-saki** *Pt* Japan
86C2 **Haka** Burma
21C4 **Hakalau** Hawaiian Is
93D2 **Hakkâri** Turk
74E2 **Hakodate** Japan
Hakwa = Haka
75B1 **Hakui** Japan
75B1 **Haku-san** *Mt* Japan
92C2 **Ḩalab** Syria
93E3 **Ḩalabja** Iraq
95C2 **Halaib** Sudan
94C1 **Halba** Leb
68B2 **Halban** Mongolia
56C2 **Halberstadt** Germany
79B3 **Halcon,Mt** Phil
39G7 **Halden** Nor
86B2 **Haldia** India
84D3 **Haldwāni** India
13C1 **Halfway** *R* Can
7D5 **Halifax** Can
42D3 **Halifax** Eng
6D1 **Hall Basin** *Sd* Can
6B3 **Hall Beach** Can
46C1 **Halle** Belg
56C2 **Halle** Germany
112B1 **Halley** *Base* Ant
39F6 **Hallingdal** *R* Nor
6D3 **Hall Pen** Can
106B2 **Hall's Creek** Aust
71D3 **Halmahera** *I* Indon
39G7 **Halmstad** Sweden
56B2 **Haltern** Germany
38J5 **Halti** *Mt* Nor
42C2 **Haltwhistle** Eng
91B4 **Halul** *I* Qatar
94B3 **Haluza** *Hist Site* Israel
75A2 **Hamada** Japan
96C2 **Hamada de Tinrhert** *Desert Region* Alg
96B2 **Hamada du Dra** *Upland* Alg
90A3 **Hamadān** Iran
96B2 **Hamada Tounassine** Region, Alg
92C2 **Ḩamāh** Syria
75B2 **Hamamatsu** Japan
39G6 **Hamar** Nor
87C3 **Hambantota** Sri Lanka
19B3 **Hamburg** Arkansas, USA
18A1 **Hamburg** Iowa, USA
16B2 **Hamburg** Pennsylvania, USA
56B2 **Hamburg** Germany
16C2 **Hamden** USA
39J6 **Hämeeninna** Fin
106A3 **Hamersley Range** *Mts* Aust
74B2 **Hamgyong Sanmaek** *Mts* N Korea
74B2 **Hamhŭng** N Korea
68B2 **Hami** China
94B1 **Hamīdīyah** Syria
108B3 **Hamilton** Aust
14C2 **Hamilton** Can
110C1 **Hamilton** NZ
14B3 **Hamilton** Ohio, USA
42B2 **Hamilton** Scot
22B2 **Hamilton,Mt** USA
38K6 **Hamina** Fin
86A1 **Hamirpur** India
56B2 **Hamm** Germany
95A2 **Hammādāh al Hamra** *Upland* Libya
38H6 **Hammerdal** Sweden
38J4 **Hammerfest** Nor
14A2 **Hammond** Illinois, USA
19B3 **Hammond** Louisiana, USA
16B3 **Hammonton** USA
111B3 **Hampden** NZ
43D4 **Hampshire** County, Eng
19B3 **Hampton** Arkansas, USA
91C4 **Hāmūn-e Jaz Mūrīan** *L* Iran
84B3 **Hamun-i-Lora** *Salt L* Pak
21C4 **Hana** Hawaiian Is
21C4 **Hanalei** Hawaiian Is
74E3 **Hanamaki** Japan
72C2 **Hancheng** China
73C3 **Hanchuan** China
15C3 **Hancock** Maryland, USA
10B2 **Hancock** Michigan, USA
75B2 **Handa** Japan
72C2 **Handan** China
99D3 **Handeni** Tanz
72B2 **Hanggin Qi** China
39J7 **Hangö** Fin
73E3 **Hangzhou** China
73E3 **Hangzhou Wan** *B* China
111B2 **Hanmer Springs** NZ
13E2 **Hanna** Can
18B2 **Hannibal** USA
56B2 **Hannover** Germany
39G7 **Hanöbukten** *B* Sweden
76D1 **Hanoi** Viet
16A3 **Hanover** USA
29B6 **Hanover** *I* Chile
72B3 **Han Shui** China
73C3 **Han Shui** *R* China
85D3 **Hānsi** India
68C2 **Hantay** Mongolia
72B3 **Hanzhong** China
86B2 **Hāora** India
38J5 **Haparanda** Sweden
86C1 **Hāpoli** India
92C4 **Haql** S Arabia
91A5 **Haradh** S Arabia
99E2 **Hara Fanna** Eth
75C1 **Haramachi** Japan
101C2 **Harare** Zim
98C1 **Harazé** Chad
14B2 **Harbor Beach** USA
85D4 **Harda** India
39F6 **Hardangerfjord** *Inlet* Nor
46D2 **Hardt** Region, Germany
108A2 **Hardwicke B** Aust
18B2 **Hardy** USA
99E2 **Harēr** Eth
99E2 **Hargeysa** Somalia
94B3 **Har Hakippa** *Mt* Israel
68B3 **Harhu** *L* China
78A3 **Hari** *R* Indon
75A2 **Harima-nada** *B* Japan
56B2 **Harlingen** Neth
9D4 **Harlingen** USA
43E4 **Harlow** Eng
94B2 **Har Meron** *Mt* Israel
20C2 **Harney Basin** USA
20C2 **Harney L** USA
38H6 **Härnösand** Sweden
63B3 **Har Nuur** *L* Mongol
97B4 **Harper** Lib
12F2 **Harper,Mt** USA
15C3 **Harpers Ferry** USA
94B3 **Har Ramon** *Mt* Israel
7C4 **Harricanaw** *R* Can
16B3 **Harrington** USA
7E4 **Harrington Harbour** Can
44A3 **Harris** *District* Scot
18C2 **Harrisburg** Illinois, USA
16A2 **Harrisburg** Pennsylvania, USA
101G1 **Harrismith** S Africa
18B2 **Harrison** USA
15C3 **Harrisonburg** USA
7E4 **Harrison,C** Can
13C3 **Harrison L** Can
18B2 **Harrisonville** USA
44A3 **Harris,Sound of** *Ch* Scot
14B2 **Harrisville** USA
42D3 **Harrogate** Eng
94B3 **Har Saggi** *Mt* Israel
38H5 **Harstad** Nor
12G2 **Hart** *R* Can
39F6 **Hårteigen** *Mt* Nor
16C2 **Hartford** Connectic USA
14A2 **Hartford** Michigan, USA
38G6 **Hartkjølen** *Mt* Nor
108A2 **Hart,L** Aust
43B4 **Hartland Pt** Eng
42D2 **Hartlepool** Eng
19A3 **Hartshorne** USA
17B1 **Hartwell Res** USA
101F1 **Hartz** *R* S Africa
68B2 **Har Us Nuur** *L* Mongolia
43E4 **Harwich** Eng
84D3 **Haryāna** State, Indi
94B3 **Hāsā** Jordan
94B2 **Hāsbaiya** Leb
43D4 **Haselmere** Eng
75B2 **Hashimoto** Japan
90A2 **Hashtpar** Iran
90A2 **Hashtrūd** Iran
87B2 **Hassan** India
56B2 **Hasselt** Belg
96C2 **Hassi Inifel** Alg
96B2 **Hassi Mdakane** *We* Alg
96C1 **Hassi Messaoud** Al
108C3 **Hastings** Aust
43E4 **Hastings** Eng
8D2 **Hastings** Nebraska, USA
110C1 **Hastings** NZ
108B2 **Hatfield** Aust
12B1 **Hatham Inlet** USA
85D3 **Hāthras** India
76D2 **Ha Tinh** Viet
108B2 **Hattah** Aust
11C3 **Hatteras,C** USA
19C3 **Hattiesburg** USA
59B3 **Hatvan** Hung
76D3 **Hau Bon** Viet
99E2 **Haud** Region, Eth
39F7 **Haugesund** Nor
110C1 **Hauhungaroa Rang** *Mts* NZ
13F1 **Haultain** *R* Can
110B1 **Hauraki G** NZ
111A3 **Hauroko,L** NZ
47C1 **Hausstock** *Mt* Swi
96B1 **Haut Atlas** *Mts* Mo
98C2 **Haute Kotto** Regio CAR
46C1 **Hautes Fagnes** *Mts* Belg
46B1 **Hautmont** Belg
96B1 **Hauts Plateaux** *Mts* Alg
90D3 **Hauzdar** Iran
18B1 **Havana** USA
Havana = Habana
87B3 **Havankulam** Sri Lanka

110C1 **Havelock North** NZ
43B4 **Haverfordwest** Wales
16D1 **Haverhill** USA
87B2 **Hāveri** India
16C2 **Haverstraw** USA
59B3 **Havlíčkův Brod** Czech Republic
8C2 **Havre** USA
16A3 **Havre de Grace** USA
7D4 **Havre-St-Pierre** Can
54C2 **Havsa** Turk
21C4 **Hawaii** *I* Hawaiian Is
21C4 **Hawaii Volcanoes Nat Pk** Hawaiian Is
11A2 **Hawea,L** NZ
10B1 **Hawera** NZ
42C2 **Hawick** Scot
11A2 **Hawkdun Range** *Mts* NZ
10C1 **Hawke B** NZ
09D2 **Hawke,C** Aust
08A2 **Hawker** Aust
76B1 **Hawng Luk** Burma
93D3 **Hawr al Habbaniyah** *L* Iraq
93E3 **Hawr al Hammár** *L* Iraq
21B2 **Hawthorne** USA
08B2 **Hay** Aust
5G3 **Hay** *R* Can
46D2 **Hayange** France
4B3 **Haycock** USA
7A4 **Hayes** *R* Can
6D2 **Hayes Halvø** *Region* Greenland
12E2 **Hayes,Mt** USA
5G3 **Hay River** Can
18A2 **Haysville** USA
22A2 **Hayward** California, USA
86B2 **Hazāribāg** India
46B1 **Hazebrouck** France
19B3 **Hazelhurst** USA
4G2 **Hazel Str** Can
5F4 **Hazelton** Can
13B1 **Hazelton Mts** Can
6C1 **Hazen L** Can
94B3 **Hazeva** Israel
16B2 **Hazleton** USA
22A1 **Healdsburg** USA
08C3 **Healesville** Aust
12E2 **Healy** USA
04B6 **Heard I** Indian O
19A3 **Hearne** USA
10B2 **Hearst** Can
72D2 **Hebei** Province, China
09C1 **Hebel** Aust
72C2 **Hebi** China
72C2 **Hebian** China
7D4 **Hebron** Can
94B3 **Hebron** Israel
18A1 **Hebron** Nebraska, USA
5E4 **Hecate** *Str* Can
12H3 **Heceta I** USA
73B5 **Hechi** China
4G2 **Hecla and Griper B** Can
11C2 **Hector,Mt** NZ
38G6 **Hede** Sweden
39H6 **Hedemora** Sweden
20C1 **He Devil Mt** USA
56B2 **Heerenveen** Neth
46C1 **Heerlen** Neth
Hefa = Haifa
3D3 **Hefei** China
73B4 **Hefeng** China
69F2 **Hegang** China
75B1 **Hegura-jima** *I* Japan
94B3 **Heidan** *R* Jordan
6B2 **Heide** Germany
1G1 **Heidelberg** Transvaal, S Africa
7B3 **Heidelberg** Germany
73E2 **Heihe** China
1G1 **Heilbron** S Africa
7B3 **Heilbronn** Germany
56C2 **Heiligenstadt** Germany
8K6 **Heinola** Fin
3B4 **Hejiang** China
6J3 **Hekla** *Mt* Iceland
76C1 **Hekou** Viet
73A5 **Hekou Yaozou Zizhixian** China
72B2 **Helan** China
72B2 **Helan Shan** *Mt* China
19B3 **Helena** Arkansas, USA
8B2 **Helena** Montana, USA
22D3 **Helendale** USA
71E3 **Helen Reef** *I* Pacific O
44B3 **Helensburgh** Scot
91B4 **Helleh** *R* Iran
51B2 **Hellin** Spain
20C1 **Hells Canyon** *R* USA
46D1 **Hellweg** Region, Germany
22B2 **Helm** USA
80E2 **Helmand** *R* Afghan
100A3 **Helmeringhausen** Namibia
46C1 **Helmond** Neth
44C2 **Helmsdale** Scot
74B2 **Helong** China
39G7 **Helsingborg** Sweden
Helsingfors = Helsinki
56C1 **Helsingør** Den
38J6 **Helsinki** Fin
43B4 **Helston** Eng
92B4 **Helwân** Egypt
19A3 **Hempstead** USA
39H7 **Hemse** Sweden
72A3 **Henan** China
72C3 **Henan** Province, China
110B1 **Hen and Chicken Is** NZ
14A3 **Henderson** Kentucky, USA
9B3 **Henderson** Nevada, USA
19B3 **Henderson** Texas, USA
73E5 **Heng-ch'un** Taiwan
68B4 **Hengduan Shan** *Mts* China
56B2 **Hengelo** Neth
72B2 **Hengshan** China
72D2 **Hengshui** China
76D1 **Heng Xian** China
73C4 **Hengyang** China
77A4 **Henhoaha** Nicobar Is
43D4 **Henley-on-Thames** Eng
16B3 **Henlopen,C** USA
7B4 **Henrietta Maria,C** Can
18A2 **Henryetta** USA
112C2 **Henryk Arctowski** *Base* Ant
6D3 **Henry Kater Pen** Can
68C2 **Hentiyn Nuruu** *Mts* Mongolia
76B2 **Henzada** Burma
73B5 **Hepu** China
80E2 **Herat** Afghan
5H4 **Herbert** Can
110C2 **Herbertville** NZ
46E1 **Herborn** Germany
26A4 **Heredia** Costa Rica
43C3 **Hereford** Eng
43C3 **Hereford & Worcester** County, Eng
46C1 **Herentals** Belg
47B1 **Héricourt** France
18A2 **Herington** USA
111A3 **Heriot** NZ
47C1 **Herisau** Switz
15D2 **Herkimer** USA
44E1 **Herma Ness** *Pen* Scot
109C2 **Hermidale** Aust
111B2 **Hermitage** NZ
Hermon,Mt = Jebel ash Shaykh
24A2 **Hermosillo** Mexico
16A2 **Herndon** Pennsylvania, USA
22C2 **Herndon** California, USA
46D1 **Herne** Germany
56B1 **Herning** Den
90A2 **Herowābad** Iran
50A2 **Herrera del Duque** Spain
16A2 **Hershey** USA
43D4 **Hertford** County, Eng
94B2 **Herzliyya** Israel
46C1 **Hesbaye** Region, Belg
46B1 **Hesdin** France
72B2 **Heshui** China
22D3 **Hesperia** USA
12H2 **Hess** *R* Can
57B2 **Hessen** State, Germany
22C2 **Hetch Hetchy Res** USA
42C2 **Hexham** Eng
73C5 **He Xian** China
73C5 **Heyuan** China
108B3 **Heywood** Aust
72D2 **Heze** China
17B2 **Hialeah** USA
10A2 **Hibbing** USA
110C1 **Hicks Bay** NZ
109C3 **Hicks,Pt** Aust
23B1 **Hidalgo** State, Mexico
24B2 **Hidalgo del Parral** Mexico
35B1 **Hidrolândia** Brazil
96A2 **Hierro** *I* Canary Is
75C1 **Higashine** Japan
74B4 **Higashi-suidō** *Str* Japan
20B2 **High Desert** USA
19B4 **High Island** USA
44B3 **Highland** Region, Scot
22D3 **Highland** USA
22C1 **Highland Peak** *Mt* USA
16B2 **Highlands Falls** USA
11B3 **High Point** USA
13D1 **High Prairie** Can
5G4 **High River** Can
17B2 **High Springs** USA
16B2 **Hightstown** USA
43D4 **High Wycombe** Eng
39J7 **Hiiumaa** *I* Estonia
80B3 **Hijaž** Region, S Arabia
75B2 **Hikigawa** Japan
75B1 **Hikone** Japan
110B1 **Hikurangi** NZ
9C4 **Hildago** Mexico
9C4 **Hildago del Parral** Mexico
56B2 **Hildesheim** Germany
27R3 **Hillaby,Mt** Barbados
56C1 **Hillerød** Den
14B3 **Hillsboro** Ohio, USA
20B1 **Hillsboro** Oregon, USA
19A3 **Hillsboro** Texas, USA
108C2 **Hillston** Aust
44E1 **Hillswick** Scot
21C4 **Hilo** Hawaiian Is
93C2 **Hilvan** Turk
56B2 **Hilversum** Neth
84D2 **Himachal Pradesh** State, India
82B3 **Himalaya** *Mts* Asia
85C4 **Himatnagar** India
74C4 **Himeji** Japan
74D3 **Himi** Japan
92C3 **Himş** Syria
12E2 **Hinchinbrook Entrance** USA
12E2 **Hinchinbrook I** USA
85D3 **Hindaun** India
84B1 **Hindu Kush** *Mts* Afghan
87B2 **Hindupur** India
13D1 **Hines Creek** Can
85D4 **Hinganghāt** India
69E2 **Hinggan Ling** *Upland* China
85B3 **Hingol** *R* Pak
85D5 **Hingoli** India
38H5 **Hinnøya** *I* Nor
16C1 **Hinsdale** USA
13D2 **Hinton** Can
34B2 **Hipolito Irigoyen** Arg
86A2 **Hirakud Res** India
92B2 **Hirfanli Baraji** *Res* Turk
87B2 **Hirihar** India
74E2 **Hirosaki** Japan
74C4 **Hiroshima** Japan
46C2 **Hirson** France
54C2 **Hîrşova** Rom
56B1 **Hirtshals** Den
84D3 **Hisār** India
26C3 **Hispaniola** *I* Caribbean S
94C1 **Hisyah** Syria
93D3 **Hīt** Iraq
74E3 **Hitachi** Japan
75C1 **Hitachi-Ota** Japan
43D4 **Hitchin** Eng
38F6 **Hitra** *I* Nor
75A2 **Hiuchi-nada** *B* Japan
75A2 **Hiwasa** Japan
56B1 **Hjørring** Den
76B1 **Hka** *R* Burma
97C4 **Ho** Ghana
76D1 **Hoa Binh** Viet
76D3 **Hoa Da** Viet
109C4 **Hobart** Aust
9C3 **Hobbs** USA
56B1 **Hobro** Den
13C2 **Hobson L** Can
99E2 **Hobyo** Somalia
76D3 **Ho Chi Minh** Viet
57C3 **Hochkonig** *Mt* Austria
54B1 **Hódmezó'hely** Hung
59B3 **Hodonin** Czech Republic
74B2 **Hoeryong** N Korea
57C2 **Hof** Germany
38B2 **Hofsjökull** *Mts* Iceland
74C4 **Hōfu** Japan
96C2 **Hoggar** *Upland* Alg
46D1 **Hohe Acht** *Mt* Germany
72C1 **Hohhot** China
6J3 **Höhn** Iceland
68B3 **Hoh Sai Hu** *L* China
82C2 **Hoh Xil Shan** *Mts* China
99D2 **Hoima** Uganda
86C1 **Hojāi** India
75A2 **Hojo** Japan
110B1 **Hokianga Harbour** *B* NZ
111B2 **Hokitika** NZ
74E2 **Hokkaidō** Japan
90C2 **Hokmābād** Iran
109C3 **Holbrook** Aust
9B3 **Holbrook** USA
19A2 **Holdenville** USA
87B2 **Hole Narsipur** India
27R3 **Holetown** Barbados
26B2 **Holguín** Cuba
111B2 **Holitika** NZ
12C2 **Holitna** *R* USA
59B3 **Hollabrunn** Austria
14A2 **Holland** USA
22B2 **Hollister** USA
19C3 **Holly Springs** USA
22C3 **Hollywood** California, USA
17B2 **Hollywood** Florida, USA
4G2 **Holman Island** Can
38J6 **Holmsund** Sweden
94B2 **Holon** Israel
56B1 **Holstebro** Den
6E3 **Holsteinborg** Greenland
14B2 **Holt** USA
18A2 **Holton** USA
12C2 **Holy Cross** USA
42B3 **Holyhead** Wales
42D2 **Holy I** Eng
43B3 **Holy I** Wales
16C1 **Holyoke** Massachusetts, USA
86C2 **Homalin** Burma
6D3 **Home B** Can
12D3 **Homer** Alaska, USA
19B3 **Homer** Louisiana, USA
111A2 **Homer Tunnel** NZ
17B1 **Homerville** USA

17B2 **Homestead** USA
17A1 **Homewood** USA
87B1 **Homnābād** India
101C3 **Homoine** Mozam
25D3 **Hondo** *R* Mexico
25D3 **Honduras** Republic, Cent America
25D3 **Honduras,G of** Honduras
39G6 **Hønefoss** Nor
15C2 **Honesdale** USA
21A1 **Honey L** USA
76C1 **Hong** *R* Viet
76D1 **Hon Gai** Viet
73A4 **Hongguo** China
73C4 **Hong Hu** *L* China
72B2 **Honghui** China
73C4 **Hongjiang** China
73C5 **Hong Kong** Colony, S E Asia
68D2 **Hongor** Mongolia
73B5 **Hongshui He** *R* China
72A3 **Hongyuan** China
72D3 **Hongze Hu** *L* China
107E1 **Honiara** Solomon Is
77C4 **Hon Khoai** *I* Camb
76D3 **Hon Lan** *I* Viet
38K4 **Honnigsvåg** Nor
21C4 **Honolulu** Hawaiian Is
77C4 **Hon Panjang** *I* Viet
74D3 **Honshu** *I* Japan
20B1 **Hood,Mt** USA
20B1 **Hood River** USA
45C2 **Hook Head** *C* Irish Rep
12G3 **Hoonah** USA
12A2 **Hooper Bay** USA
101G1 **Hoopstad** S Africa
56A2 **Hoorn** Neth
9B3 **Hoover Dam** USA
12E2 **Hope** Alaska, USA
19B3 **Hope** Arkansas, USA
13C3 **Hope** Can
7D4 **Hopedale** Can
64D2 **Hopen** *I* Barents S
6D3 **Hopes Advance,C** Can
108B3 **Hopetoun** Aust
100B3 **Hopetown** S Africa
18C2 **Hopkinsville** USA
20B1 **Hoquiam** USA
93D1 **Horasan** Turk
99F1 **Hordiyo** Somalia
47C1 **Horgen** Switz
105H5 **Horizon Depth** Pacific O
91C4 **Hormuz,Str of** Oman/Iran
59B3 **Horn** Austria
6H3 **Horn** *C* Iceland
38H5 **Hornavan** *L* Sweden
19B3 **Hornbeck** USA
20B2 **Hornbrook** USA
111B2 **Hornby** NZ
7B5 **Hornepayne** Can
4F3 **Horn Mts** Can
42D3 **Hornsea** Eng
72B1 **Horn Uul** *Mt* Mongolia
30E3 **Horqueta** Par
15C2 **Horseheads** USA
56C1 **Horsens** Den
20B1 **Horseshoe Bay** Can
108B3 **Horsham** Aust
43D4 **Horsham** Eng
39G7 **Horten** Nor
4F3 **Horton** *R* Can
78C2 **Hose Mts** Malay
85D4 **Hoshangābād** India
84D2 **Hoshiārpur** India
87B1 **Hospet** India
29C7 **Hoste** *I* Chile
82B2 **Hotan** China
19B3 **Hot Springs** Arkansas, USA
8C2 **Hot Springs** S. Dakota, USA
4G3 **Hottah** Can
46A2 **Houdan** France
72C2 **Houma** China
19B4 **Houma** USA
16C2 **Housatonic** *R* USA
13B2 **Houston** Can
19C3 **Houston** Mississippi, USA
19A4 **Houston** Texas, USA
106A3 **Houtman** *Is* Aust
68B2 **Hovd** Mongolia
68C1 **Hövsgol Nuur** *L* Mongolia
14A2 **Howard City** USA
12C1 **Howard P** USA
109C3 **Howe,C** Aust
101H1 **Howick** S Africa
44C2 **Hoy** *I* Scot
39F6 **Høyanger** Nor
59B2 **Hradeç-Královė** Czech Republic
59B3 **Hranice** Czech Republic
59B3 **Hron** *R* Slovakia
73E5 **Hsin-chu** Taiwan
73E5 **Hsüeh Shan** *Mt* Taiwan
72B2 **Huachi** China
32B6 **Huacho** Peru
72C1 **Huade** China
72D3 **Huaibei** China
72D3 **Huaibin** China
72D3 **Huai He** *R* China
73C4 **Huaihua** China
73C5 **Huaiji** China
72D3 **Huainan** China
69E4 **Hua-lien** Taiwan
32B5 **Huallaga** *R* Peru
32B5 **Huallanca** Peru
32B5 **Huamachuco** Peru
100A2 **Huambo** Angola
30C2 **Huanay** Bol
32B5 **Huancabamba** Peru
32B6 **Huancavelica** Peru
32B6 **Huancayo** Peru
73D3 **Huangchuan** China
Huang Hai = Yellow S
72D2 **Huang He** *R* China
72B2 **Huangling** China
76D2 **Huangliu** China
73C3 **Huangpi** China
73D4 **Huangshan** China
73D3 **Huangshi** China
34C3 **Huanguelén** Arg
73E4 **Huangyan** China
74B2 **Huanren** China
32B5 **Huānuco** Peru
30C2 **Huanuni** Bol
72B2 **Huan Xian** China
32B5 **Huaráz** Peru
32B6 **Huarmey** Peru
32B5 **Huascarán** *Mt* Peru
30B4 **Huasco** Chile
23B2 **Huatusco** Mexico
23B1 **Huauchinango** Mexico
23B2 **Huautla** Mexico
72C2 **Hua Xian** China
24B2 **Huayapan** *R* Mexico
73C3 **Hubei** Province, China
87B1 **Hubli** India
34C3 **Hucal** Arg
74B2 **Huch'ang** N Korea
42D3 **Huddersfield** Eng
39H6 **Hudiksvall** Sweden
17B2 **Hudson** Florida, USA
14B2 **Hudson** Michigan, USA
16C1 **Hudson** New York, USA
16C1 **Hudson** *R* USA
7B4 **Hudson B** Can
5H4 **Hudson Bay** Can
13C1 **Hudson's Hope** Can
6C3 **Hudson Str** Can
76D2 **Hue** Viet
23B1 **Huejutla** Mexico
50A2 **Huelva** Spain
23A2 **Hueramo** Mexico
51B2 **Húercal Overa** Spain
51B1 **Huesca** Spain
23B2 **Huexotla** *Hist Site* Mexico
107D3 **Hughenden** Aust
12D1 **Hughes** USA
86B2 **Hugli** *R* India
19A3 **Hugo** USA
73D4 **Hui'an** China
110C1 **Huiarau Range** *Mts* NZ
74B2 **Huich'ŏn** N Korea
74B2 **Huifa He** *R* China
32B3 **Huila** *Mt* Colombia
73D5 **Huilai** China
73A4 **Huili** China
74B2 **Huinan** China
34C2 **Huinca Renancó** Arg
25C3 **Huixtla** Mexico
73A4 **Huize** China
73C5 **Huizhou** China
23B2 **Hujuápan de Léon** Mexico
69F2 **Hulin** China
15C1 **Hull** Can
42D3 **Hull** Eng
58B1 **Hultsfred** Sweden
63D3 **Hulun Nur** *L* China
69E1 **Huma** China
33E5 **Humaita** Brazil
100B4 **Humansdorp** S Africa
42D3 **Humber** *R* Eng
42D3 **Humberside** County, Eng
5H4 **Humboldt** Can
20C2 **Humboldt** *R* USA
20B2 **Humboldt B** USA
6D2 **Humboldt Gletscher** *Gl* Greenland
21B2 **Humboldt L** USA
108C1 **Humeburn** Aust
109C3 **Hume,L** Aust
100A2 **Humpata** Angola
22C2 **Humphreys** USA
38A1 **Húnaflóri** *B* Iceland
73C4 **Hunan** Province, China
74C2 **Hunchun** China
13C2 **Hundred Mile House** Can
54B1 **Hunedoara** Rom
59B3 **Hungary** Republic, Europe
108B1 **Hungerford** Aust
74B3 **Hŭngnam** N Korea
74B2 **Hunjiang** China
46D2 **Hunsrück** Mts, Germany
109D2 **Hunter** *R* Aust
13B2 **Hunter I** Can
109C4 **Hunter Is** Aust
12D2 **Hunter,Mt** USA
14A3 **Huntingburg** USA
43D3 **Huntingdon** Eng
14A2 **Huntingdon** Indiana, USA
14B3 **Huntington** W Virginia, USA
22C4 **Huntington Beach** USA
22C2 **Huntington L** USA
110C1 **Huntly** NZ
44C3 **Huntly** Scot
12J2 **Hunt,Mt** Can
108A1 **Hunt Pen** Aust
17A1 **Huntsville** Alabama, USA
15C1 **Huntsville** Can
19A3 **Huntsville** Texas, USA
76D2 **Huong Khe** Viet
71F4 **Huon Peninsula** *Pen* PNG
109C4 **Huonville** Anst
14B1 **Hurd,C** Can
80B3 **Hurghada** Egypt
8D2 **Huron** S. Dakota, USA
14B1 **Huron,L** Can/USA
34A2 **Hurtado** Chile
111B2 **Hurunui** *R* NZ
38B1 **Husavik** Iceland
54C1 **Huşi** Rom
39G7 **Huskvarna** Sweden
12C1 **Huslia** USA
94B2 **Husn** Jordan
56B2 **Husum** Germany
109C1 **Hutton,Mt** Aust
72D2 **Hutuo He** *R* China
46C1 **Huy** Belg
72A2 **Huzhu** China
52C2 **Hvar** *I* Croatia
100B2 **Hwange** Zim
100B2 **Hwange Nat Pk** Zim
15D2 **Hyannis** USA
68B2 **Hyaryas Nuur** *L* Mongolia
5E4 **Hydaburg** Can
16C2 **Hyde Park** USA
87B1 **Hyderābād** India
85B3 **Hyderabad** Pak
49D3 **Hyères** France
12J2 **Hyland** *R* Can
8B2 **Hyndman Peak** *Mt* USA
38K6 **Hyrynsalmi** Fin
13D1 **Hythe** Can
74C4 **Hyūga** Japan
39J6 **Hyvikää** Fin

I

31C4 **Iaçu** Brazil
54C2 **Ialomiţa** *R* Rom
54C1 **Iaşi** Rom
97C4 **Ibadan** Nig
32B3 **Ibagué** Colombia
54B2 **Ibar** *R* Montenegro Serbia, Yugos
32B3 **Ibarra** Ecuador
35B1 **Ibiá** Brazil
30E4 **Ibicui** *R* Brazil
34D2 **Ibicuy** Arg
51C2 **Ibiza** Spain
51C2 **Ibiza** *I* Spain
101D2 **Ibo** Mozam
31C4 **Ibotirama** Brazil
91C5 **'Ibrī** Oman
32B6 **Ica** Peru
32D4 **Icá** *R* Brazil
32D3 **Icana** Brazil
38A1 **Iceland** Republic, N Atlantic O
13C2 **Ice Mt** Can
87A1 **Ichalkaranji** India
74E3 **Ichihara** Japan
75B1 **Ichinomiya** Japan
74E3 **Ichinoseki** Japan
12F3 **Icy B** USA
4B2 **Icy C** USA
19B3 **Idabell** USA
8B2 **Idaho Falls** USA
20B2 **Idanha** USA
46D2 **Idar Oberstein** Germany
95A2 **Idehan Marzūg** *Desert* Libya
95A2 **Idehan Ubari** *Dese* Libya
96C2 **Idelés** Alg
68B2 **Iderlym Gol** *R* Mongolia
95C2 **Idfu** Egypt
55B3 **Ídhi Óros** *Mt* Gree
55B3 **Ídhra** *I* Greece
98B3 **Idiofa** Zaïre
12C2 **Iditarod** *R* USA
92C2 **Idlib** Syria
39K7 **Idritsa** Russian Fe
100B4 **Idutywa** S Africa
55C3 **Ierápetra** Greece
46B1 **Ieper** Belg
63D2 **Iet Oktyobr'ya** Russian Fed
99D3 **Ifakara** Tanz
71F3 **Ifalik** *I* Pacific O
101D3 **Ifanadiana** Madag
97C4 **Ife** Nig
97C3 **Iférouane** Niger
78C2 **Igan** Malay
35B2 **Igaranava** Brazil
93E2 **Igdir** Iran
39H6 **Iggesund** Sweden
34B2 **Iglesia** Arg
53A3 **Iglesias** Sardegna
6B3 **Igloolik** Can
10A2 **Ignace** Can
55B3 **Igoumenítsa** Gree
61H2 **Igra** Russian Fed
23B2 **Iguala** Mexico
35B2 **Iguape** Brazil
35B2 **Iguatama** Brazil
31D3 **Iguatu** Brazil
98A3 **Iguéla** Gabon
101D3 **Ihosy** Madag
74D3 **Iida** Japan
75B1 **Iide-san** *Mt* Japan
38K6 **Iisalmi** Fin

75A2 **Iizuka** Japan
97C4 **Ijebu Ode** Nig
56B2 **Ijsselmeer** *S* Neth
55C3 **Ikaría** *I* Greece
74E2 **Ikeda** Japan
98C3 **Ikela** Zaïre
54B2 **Ikhtiman** Bulg
12D3 **Ikolik,C** USA
01D2 **Ikopa** *R* Madag
79B2 **Ilagan** Phil
90A3 **Ilām** Iran
47C1 **Ilanz** Switz
13F1 **Île à la Crosse** Can
13F1 **Île à la Crosse,L** Can
39G8 **Ilebo** Zaïre
96D1 **Île de Jerba** *I* Tunisia
48B2 **Ile de Noirmoutier** *I* France
48B2 **Ile de Ré** *I* France
07F3 **Île des Pins** *I* Nouvelle Calédonie
48A2 **Ile d'Ouessant** *I* France
48B2 **Ile d'Yeu** *I* France
61J3 **Ilek** *R* Russian Fed
07F2 **Îles Bélèp** Nouvelle Calédonie
07E2 **Îles Chesterfield** Nouvelle Calédonie
9D3 **Iles d'Hyères** *Is* France
3B4 **Ilfracombe** Eng
92B1 **Ilgaz Dağları** *Mts* Turk
01C3 **Ilha Bazaruto** *I* Mozam
3G3 **Ilha De Maracá** *I* Brazil
3G4 **Ilha de Marajó** *I* Brazil
35B2 **Ilha de São Sebastião** *I* Brazil
3G6 **Ilha do Bananal** *Region* Brazil
35C2 **Ilha Grande** *I* Brazil
35B2 **Ilha Santo Amaro** *I* Brazil
6A1 **Ilhas Selvegens** *I* Atlantic O
5A2 **Ilha Solteira Dam** Brazil
1D4 **Ilhéus** Brazil
2C3 **Iliamna L** USA
2D2 **Iliamna V** USA
9B4 **Iligan** Phil
3C2 **Ilim** *R* Russian Fed
3C2 **Ilim** Russian Fed
3G3 **Il'inskiy** Russian Fed
5B3 **Iliodhrómia** *I* Greece
9B4 **Illana B** Phil
4A2 **Illapel** Chile
4A2 **Illapel** *R* Chile
7C3 **Illéla** Niger
7D1 **Iller** *R* Germany
4C4 **Illiamna L** USA
0A2 **Illinois** State, USA
8B2 **Illinois** *R* USA
6C2 **Illizi** Alg
0B2 **Ilo** Peru
9B3 **Iloilo** Phil
8L6 **Ilomantsi** Fin
7C4 **Ilorin** Nig
5A2 **Imabari** Japan
5B1 **Imalchi** Japan
0C1 **Imatra** Fin
0G4 **Imbituba** Brazil
9E2 **Imi** Eth
0C2 **Imlay** USA
7D1 **Immenstadt** Germany
2B2 **Imola** Italy
1B3 **Imperatriz** Brazil
2A2 **Imperia** Italy
3B2 **Impfondo** Congo
6C2 **Imphāl** India
7D1 **Imst** Austria
2B1 **Imuruk L** USA
5B1 **Ina** Japan
6C2 **In Afahleleh** *Well* Alg
5B2 **Inamba-jima** *I* Japan
6C2 **In Amenas** Alg
3K5 **Inari** Fin
3K5 **Inarijärvi** *L* Fin
75C1 **Inawashiro-ko** *L* Japan
96C2 **In Belbel** Alg
60E5 **Ince Burun** *Pt* Turk
92B2 **Incekum Burun** *Pt* Turk
74B3 **Inch'ŏn** S Korea
96B2 **In Dagouber** *Well* Mali
35B1 **Indaia** *R* Brazil
38H6 **Indals** *R* Sweden
21B2 **Independence** California, USA
18A2 **Independence** Kansas, USA
18B2 **Independence** Missouri, USA
78A3 **Inderagiri** *R* Indon
61H4 **Inderborskly** Kazakhstan
83B3 **India** Federal Republic, Asia
14A2 **Indiana** State, USA
15C2 **Indiana** USA
104C6 **Indian-Antarctic Ridge** Indian O
14A3 **Indianapolis** USA
Indian Desert = Thar Desert
7E4 **Indian Harbour** Can
104B4 **Indian O**
18B1 **Indianola** Iowa, USA
19B3 **Indianola** Mississippi, USA
35B1 **Indianópolis** Brazil
76D2 **Indo China** Region, S E Asia
70C4 **Indonesia** Republic, S E Asia
85D4 **Indore** India
78B4 **Indramayu** Indon
48C2 **Indre** *R* France
85B3 **Indus** *R* Pak
60D5 **Inebdu** Turk
96C2 **In Ebeggi** *Well* Alg
96C2 **In Ecker** Alg
92A1 **Inegöl** Turk
96D2 **In Ezzane** Alg
97C3 **Ingal** Niger
14B2 **Ingersoll** Can
107D2 **Ingham** Aust
6D2 **Inglefield Land** *Region* Can
110B1 **Inglewood** NZ
109D1 **Inglewood** Queensland, Aust
22C4 **Inglewood** USA
108B3 **Inglewood** Victoria, Aust
38B2 **Ingólfshöfði** *I* Iceland
57C3 **Ingolstadt** Germany
86B2 **Ingrāj Bāzār** India
96C3 **In-Guezzam** *Well* Alg
101C3 **Inhambane** Mozam
101C3 **Inharrime** Mozam
35B1 **Inhumas** Brazil
32D3 **Inirida** *R* Colombia
45A2 **Inishbofin** *I* Irish Rep
45A1 **Inishkea** *I* Irish Rep
45B2 **Inishmaan** *I* Irish Rep
45B2 **Inishmore** *I* Irish Rep
45B1 **Inishmurray** *I* Irish Rep
45C1 **Inishowen** District, Irish Rep
45A2 **Inishshark** *I* Irish Rep
45A2 **Inishturk** *I* Irish Rep
109C1 **Injune** Aust
12H3 **Inklin** Can
12H3 **Inklin** *R* Can
12C1 **Inland L** USA
47D1 **Inn** *R* Austria
108B1 **Innamincka** Aust
68C2 **Inner Mongolia** Autonomous Region, China
107D2 **Innisfail** Aust
12C2 **Innoko** *R* USA
57C3 **Innsbruck** Austria
98B3 **Inongo** Zaïre
58B2 **Inowrocław** Pol
96C2 **In Salah** Alg
47B1 **Interlaken** Switz
24C3 **Intexpec** Mexico
47C2 **Intra** Italy
78D3 **Intu** Indon
75C1 **Inubo-saki** *C* Japan
7C4 **Inukjuak** Can
4E3 **Inuvik** Can
4F3 **Inuvik** *Region* Can
44B3 **Inveraray** Scot
111A3 **Invercargill** NZ
109D1 **Inverell** Aust
13D2 **Invermere** Can
44B3 **Inverness** Scot
44C3 **Inverurie** Scot
108A3 **Investigator Str** Aust
68A1 **Inya** Russian Fed
21B2 **Inyokern** USA
98B3 **Inzia** *R* Zaïre
55B3 **Ioánnina** Greece
18A2 **Iola** USA
44A3 **Iona** *I* Scot
100A2 **Iôna Nat Pk** Angola
20C1 **Ione** USA
Ionian Is = Ioníoi Nísoi
55A3 **Ionian S** Italy/Greece
55B3 **Ioníoi Nísoi** *Is* Greece
55C3 **Íos** *I* Greece
10A2 **Iowa** *R* USA
10A2 **Iowa City** USA
35B1 **Ipameri** Brazil
35C1 **Ipanema** Brazil
61F4 **Ipatovo** Russian Fed
32B3 **Ipiales** Colombia
77C5 **Ipoh** Malay
30F2 **Iporá** Brazil
55C2 **Ipsala** Turk
109D1 **Ipswich** Aust
43E3 **Ipswich** Eng
16D1 **Ipswich** USA
30B3 **Iquique** Chile
32C4 **Iquitos** Peru
55C3 **Iráklion** Greece
80D2 **Iran** Republic, S W Asia
91D4 **Irānshahr** Iran
23A1 **Irapuato** Mexico
93D3 **Iraq** Republic, S W Asia
95A2 **Irā Wan** *Watercourse* Libya
94B2 **Irbid** Jordan
61K2 **Irbit** Russian Fed
36C3 **Ireland** Republic, NW Europe
33F3 **Ireng** *R* Guyana
74B3 **Iri** S Korea
71E4 **Irian Jaya** Province, Indon
95B3 **Iriba** Chad
79B3 **Iriga** Phil
99D3 **Iringa** Tanz
69E4 **Iriomote** *I* Japan
33G5 **Iriri** *R* Brazil
42B3 **Irish S** Eng/Irish Rep
12D1 **Irkillik** *R* USA
63C2 **Irkutsk** Russian Fed
65J4 **Irlysh** *R* Kazakhstan
108A2 **Iron Knob** Aust
14A1 **Iron Mountain** USA
107D2 **Iron Range** Aust
14A1 **Iron River** USA
14B3 **Irontown** USA
10A2 **Ironwood** USA
10B2 **Iroquois Falls** Can
75B2 **Iro-zaki** *C* Japan
76A2 **Irrawaddy,Mouths of the** Burma
65H4 **Irtysh** *R* Russian Fed
51B1 **Irun** Spain
42B2 **Irvine** Scot
19A3 **Irving** USA
79B4 **Isabela** Phil
32J7 **Isabela** *I* Ecuador
4H2 **Isachsen** Can
4H2 **Isachsen,C** Can
6H3 **Ísafjörður** Iceland
74C4 **Isahaya** Japan
98C2 **Isangi** Zaïre
47D1 **Isar** *R* Germany
47D1 **Isarco** *R* Italy
44E1 **Isbister** Scot
47D1 **Ischgl** Austria
53B2 **Ischia** *I* Italy
75B2 **Ise** Japan
47D2 **Iseo** Italy
46D1 **Iserlohn** Germany
53B2 **Isernia** Italy
75B2 **Ise-wan** *B* Japan
69E4 **Ishigaki** *I* Japan
74E2 **Ishikari** *R* Japan
74E2 **Ishikari-wan** *B* Japan
65H4 **Ishim** Russian Fed
65H4 **Ishim** *R* Kazakhstan
74E3 **Ishinomaki** Japan
75C1 **Ishioka** Japan
84C1 **Ishkashim** Afghan
14A1 **Ishpeming** USA
65J4 **Isil'kul** Russian Fed
99D2 **Isiolo** Kenya
98C2 **Isiro** Zaïre
92C2 **Iskenderun** Turk
92C2 **Iskenferun Körfezi** *B* Turk
92B1 **İskilip** Turk
65K4 **Iskitim** Russian Fed
54B2 **Iskur** *R* Bulg
12H3 **Iskut** *R* Can/USA
23B2 **Isla** Mexico
34C3 **Isla Bermejo** *I* Arg
27E4 **Isla Blanquilla** Ven
32A2 **Isla Coiba** *I* Panama
9B4 **Isla de Cedros** *I* Mexico
29B4 **Isla de Chiloé** *I* Chile
25D2 **Isla de Cozumel** *I* Mexico
26C3 **Isla de la Gonâve** Cuba
26A2 **Isla de la Juventud** *I* Cuba
34D2 **Isla de las Lechiguanas** *I* Arg
3K8 **Isla del Coco** *I* Costa Rica
25D3 **Isla del Maiz** *I* Caribbean S
23B1 **Isla de Lobos** *I* Mexico
29D6 **Isla de los Estados** *I* Arg
28E2 **Isla de Marajó** *I* Brazil
105L5 **Isla de Pascua** *I* Pacific O
26A4 **Isla de Providencia** *I* Caribbean S
26A4 **Isla de San Andres** *I* Caribbean S
30G4 **Isla de Santa Catarina** *I* Brazil
33G2 **Isla du Diable** *I* French Guiana
31E2 **Isla Fernando de Noronha** *I* Brazil
29C6 **Isla Grande de Tierra del Fuego** *I* Arg/Chile
27D4 **Isla la Tortuga** *I* Ven
84C2 **Islamabad** Pak
24A2 **Isla Magdalena** *I* Mexico
27E4 **Isla Margarita** Ven
34A3 **Isla Mocha** Chile
17B2 **Islamorada** USA
10A1 **Island L** Can
108A2 **Island Lg** Aust
110B1 **Islands,B of** NZ
32A4 **Isla Puná** *I* Ecuador
103D6 **Isla San Ambrosia** *I* Pacific O
103D6 **Isla San Felix** *I* Pacific O
24A2 **Isla Santa Margarita** *I* Mexico
34A3 **Isla Santa Maria** *I* Chile
51C2 **Islas Baleares** *Is* Spain
96A2 **Islas Canarias** *Is* Atlantic O
51C2 **Islas Columbretes** *Is* Spain
25D3 **Islas de la Bahia** *Is* Honduras
26A4 **Islas del Maíz** *Is* Caribbean S
33E1 **Islas de Margarita** *Is* Ven

29C7 **Islas Diego Ramírez** *Is* Chile
32J7 **Islas Galapagos** *Is* Pacific O
30H6 **Islas Juan Fernández** Chile
32D1 **Islas los Roques** *Is* Ven
Islas Malvinas = Falkland Is
105L3 **Islas Revilla Gigedo** *Is* Pacific O
29C7 **Islas Wollaston** *Is* Chile
97A3 **Isla Tidra** *I* Maur
29B5 **Isla Wellington** *I* Chile
48C2 **Isle** *R* France
104B5 **Isle Amsterdam** *I* Indian O
43D4 **Isle of Wight** *I* Eng
10B2 **Isle Royale** *I* USA
104B5 **Isle St Paul** *I* Indian O
104A6 **Îsles Crozet** *I* Indian O
105J4 **Îsles de la Société** Pacific O
105K5 **Îsles Gambier** *Is* Pacific O
101D2 **Isles Glorieuses** *Is* Madag
104B6 **Îsles Kerguelen** *Is* Indian O
105K4 **Îsles Marquises** *Is* Pacific O
105J4 **Îsles Tuamotu** *Is* Pacific O
105J5 **Îsles Tubai** *Is* Pacific O
22B1 **Isleton** USA
92B3 **Ismâ'ilîya** Egypt
101D3 **Isoanala** Madag
101C2 **Isoka** Zambia
53B3 **Isola Egadi** *I* Italy
52B2 **Isola Ponziane** *I* Italy
53B3 **Isole Lipari** *Is* Italy
52C2 **Isoles Tremiti** *Is* Italy
75B1 **Isosaki** Japan
92B2 **Isparta** Turk
94B2 **Israel** Republic, S W Asia
51C2 **Isser** *R* Alg
48C2 **Issoire** France
49C2 **Issoudun** France
92A1 **Istanbul** Turk
55B3 **Istiáia** Greece
25C3 **Istmo de Tehuantepec** *Isthmus* Mexico
17B2 **Istokpoga,L** USA
52B1 **Istra** *Pen* Croatia
35B1 **Itaberai** Brazil
35C1 **Itabira** Brazil
35C2 **Itabirito** Brazil
31D4 **Itabuna** Brazil
33F4 **Itacoatiara** Brazil
32B2 **Itagui** Colombia
33F4 **Itaituba** Brazil
30G4 **Itajaí** Brazil
35B2 **Itajuba** Brazil
52B2 **Italy** Repubic, Europe
35D1 **Itamaraju** Brazil
35C1 **Itamarandiba** Brazil
35C1 **Itambacuri** Brazil
35C1 **Itambé** *Mt* Brazil
86C1 **Itānagar** India
35B2 **Itanhaém** Brazil
35C1 **Itanhém** Brazil
35C1 **Itanhém** *R* Brazil
35C1 **Itaobím** Brazil
35B2 **Itapecerica** Brazil
35C2 **Itaperuna** Brazil
31C5 **Itapetinga** Brazil
35B2 **Itapetininga** Brazil
35B2 **Itapeva** Brazil
31D2 **Itapipoca** Brazil
35B1 **Itapuranga** Brazil
30E4 **Itaqui** Brazil
35C1 **Itarantim** Brazil
35B2 **Itararé** Brazil
35B2 **Itararé** *R* Brazil
35C2 **Itaúna** Brazil
33E6 **Iténez** *R* Brazil/Bol
15C2 **Ithaca** USA
98C2 **Itimbiri** *R* Zaïre
35C1 **Itinga** Brazil
6E3 **Itivdleg** Greenland
75B2 **Ito** Japan
74D3 **Itoigawa** Japan
33E6 **Itonomas** *R* Bol
35B2 **Itu** Brazil
35B1 **Itumbiara** Brazil
35A1 **Iturama** Brazil
30C3 **Iturbe** Arg
35B1 **Iturutaba** Brazil
56B2 **Itzehoe** Germany
58D2 **Ivacevichi** Belorussia
35A2 **Ivai** *R* Brazil
38K5 **Ivalo** Fin
54A2 **Ivangrad** Montenegro, Yugos
108B2 **Ivanhoe** Aust
59C3 **Ivano-Frankovsk** Ukraine
61F2 **Ivanovo** Russian Fed
65H3 **Ivdel'** Russian Fed
98B2 **Ivindo** *R* Gabon
101D3 **Ivohibe** Madag
101D2 **Ivongo Soanierana** Madag
97B4 **Ivory Coast** Republic, Africa
52A1 **Ivrea** Italy
6C3 **Ivujivik** Can
74E3 **Iwaki** Japan
74C4 **Iwakuni** Japan
74E2 **Iwanai** Japan
97C4 **Iwo** Nig
69G4 **Iwo Jima** *I* Japan
23B1 **Ixmiquilpa** Mexico
23A2 **Ixtapa** Mexico
23A1 **Ixtlán** Mexico
75A2 **Iyo** Japan
75A2 **Iyo-nada** *B* Japan
65G4 **Izhevsk** Russian Fed
64G3 **Izhma** Russian Fed
91C5 **Izkī** Oman
60C4 **Izmail** Ukraine
92A2 **İzmir** Turk
55C3 **İzmir Körfezi** *B* Turk
92A1 **İzmit** Turk
92A1 **İznik** Turk
55C2 **Iznik Golü** *L* Turk
94C2 **Izra'** Syria
23B2 **Izúcar de Matamoros** Mexico
75B2 **Izumi-sano** Japan
75A1 **Izumo** Japan
74D4 **Izu-shotō** *Is* Japan

J

95B1 **Jabal al Akhdar** *Mts* Libya
94C2 **Jabal al 'Arab** Syria
95A2 **Jabal as Sawdā** *Mts* Libya
91B5 **Jabal az Zannah** UAE
94C1 **Jabal Halīmah** *Mt* Leb/Syria
83B3 **Jabalpur** India
59B2 **Jablonec nad Nisou** Czech Republic
31D3 **Jaboatão** Brazil
35B2 **Jaboticabal** Brazil
51B1 **Jaca** Spain
23B1 **Jacala** Mexico
33F5 **Jacareacanga** Brazil
35B2 **Jacarei** Brazil
30F3 **Jacarezinho** Brazil
29C2 **Jáchal** Arg
35C1 **Jacinto** Brazil
13F2 **Jackfish L** Can
109C1 **Jackson** Aust
22B1 **Jackson** California, USA
14B2 **Jackson** Michigan, USA
19B3 **Jackson** Mississippi, USA
18C2 **Jackson** Missouri, USA
14B3 **Jackson** Ohio, USA
11B3 **Jackson** Tennessee, USA
111B2 **Jackson,C** NZ
111A2 **Jackson Head** *Pt* NZ
19B3 **Jacksonville** Arkansas, USA
17B1 **Jacksonville** Florida, USA
18B2 **Jacksonville** Illinois, USA
17C1 **Jacksonville** N Carolina, USA
19A3 **Jacksonville** Texas, USA
17B1 **Jacksonville Beach** USA
26C3 **Jacmel** Haiti
84B3 **Jacobabad** Pak
31C4 **Jacobina** Brazil
23A2 **Jacona** Mexico
Jadotville = Likasi
32B5 **Jaén** Peru
50B2 **Jaén** Spain
Jaffa = Tel Aviv Yafo
108A3 **Jaffa,C** Aust
87B3 **Jaffna** Sri Lanka
86B2 **Jagannathganj Ghat** Bang
87C1 **Jagdalpur** India
91C4 **Jagin** *R* Iran
87B1 **Jagtial** India
29F2 **Jaguarão** *R* Brazil
35B2 **Jaguariaíva** Brazil
91B4 **Jahrom** Iran
85D5 **Jāina** India
72A2 **Jainca** China
85D3 **Jaipur** India
85C3 **Jaisalmer** India
90C2 **Jajarm** Iran
52C2 **Jajce** Bosnia-Herzegovina
78B4 **Jakarta** Indon
6E3 **Jakobshavn** Greenland
38J6 **Jakobstad** Fin
23B2 **Jalaca** Mexico
84B2 **Jalai-Kut** Afghan
84D2 **Jalandhar** India
23B2 **Jalapa** Mexico
35A2 **Jales** Brazil
86B1 **Jaleswar** Nepal
85D4 **Jalgaon** India
97D4 **Jalingo** Nig
51B1 **Jalón** *R* Spain
85C3 **Jālor** India
23A1 **Jalostotitlan** Mexico
86B1 **Jalpāiguri** India
23B1 **Jalpan** Mexico
95B2 **Jālū Oasis** Libya
32A4 **Jama** Ecuador
26B3 **Jamaica** *I* Caribbean S
26B3 **Jamaica Chan** Caribbean S
86B2 **Jamalpur** Bang
78A3 **Jambi** Indon
85C4 **Jambussar** India
7B4 **James B** Can
5J5 **Jameston** USA
108A2 **Jamestown** Aust
8D2 **Jamestown** N. Dakota, USA
15C2 **Jamestown** New York, USA
16D2 **Jamestown** Rhode Island, USA
23B2 **Jamiltepec** Mexico
87B1 **Jamkhandi** India
84C2 **Jammu** India
84D2 **Jammu and Kashmir** State, India
85B4 **Jamnagar** India
84C3 **Jampur** Pak
38K6 **Jämsä** Fin
86B2 **Jamshedpur** India
86B1 **Janakpur** Nepal
35C1 **Janaúba** Brazil
90B3 **Jandaq** Iran
109D1 **Jandowae** Aust
1B1 **Jan Mayen** *I* Norwegian S
35C1 **Januária** Brazil
85D4 **Jaora** India
51 **Japan** Empire, E Asia
74C3 **Japan,S of** S E Asia
104F2 **Japan Trench** Pacific O
32D4 **Japurá** *R* Brazil
93C2 **Jarābulus** Syria
35B1 **Jaraguá** Brazil
50B1 **Jarama** *R* Spain
94B2 **Jarash** Jordan
30E3 **Jardim** Brazil
51B2 **Jardin** *R* Spain
26B2 **Jardines de la Rein[a]** *Is* Cuba
Jargalant = Hovd
33G3 **Jari** *R* Brazil
86C1 **Jaria Jhānjail** Bang
46C2 **Jarny** France
58B2 **Jarocin** Pol
59C2 **Jaroslaw** Pol
38G6 **Järpen** Sweden
72B2 **Jartai** China
85C4 **Jasdan** India
97C4 **Jasikan** Ghana
91C4 **Jāsk** Iran
59C3 **Jaslo** Pol
29D6 **Jason Is** Falkland I[s]
18B2 **Jasper** Arkansas, USA
13D2 **Jasper** Can
17B1 **Jasper** Florida, US[A]
14A3 **Jasper** Indiana, US[A]
19B3 **Jasper** Texas, USA
13D2 **Jasper Nat Pk** Can
58B2 **Jastrowie** Pol
35A1 **Jatai** Brazil
51B2 **Játiva** Spain
35B2 **Jau** Brazil
32B6 **Jauja** Peru
86A1 **Jaunpur** India
Java = Jawa
87B2 **Javadi Hills** India
Javari = Yavari
70B4 **Java S** Indon
106A2 **Java Trench** Indon
78B4 **Jawa** *I* Indon
71F4 **Jayapura** Indon
94C2 **Jayrūd** Syria
96B2 **Jbel Ouarkziz** *Mts* Mor
96B1 **Jbel Sarhro** *Mt* M[or]
19B4 **Jeanerette** USA
97C4 **Jebba** Nig
93D2 **Jebel 'Abd al 'Azīz** *Mt* Syria
95B3 **Jebel Abyad** Suda[n]
91C5 **Jebel Akhdar** *Mt* Oman
92C4 **Jebel al Lawz** *Mt* S Arabia
94B2 **Jebel ash Shaykh** Syria
95C2 **Jebel Asoteriba** *M[t]* Sudan
94B3 **Jebel Ed Dabab** *M[t]* Jordan
94B3 **Jebel el Ata'ita** *M[t]* Jordan
92C3 **Jebel esh Sharqi** Leb/Syria
94C3 **Jebel Ithrīyat** *Mt* Jordan
91C5 **Jebel Ja'lan** *Mt* Oman
94B2 **Jebel Liban** *Mts*
94C2 **Jebel Ma'lūlā** *Mt* Syria
98C1 **Jebel Marra** *Mt* Sudan
94C3 **Jebel Mudeisisat** Jordan
95C2 **Jebel Oda** *Mt* Su[dan]
94B3 **Jebel Qasr ed Dei[r]** *Mt* Jordan
94B2 **Jebel Um ed Dara[j]** *Mt* Jordan
95B2 **Jebel Uweinat** *M[t]* Sudan
42C2 **Jedburgh** Scot
Jedda = Jiddah
59C2 **Jedrzejów** Pol
19B3 **Jefferson** Texas, USA
11A3 **Jefferson City** US[A]
8B3 **Jefferson,Mt** US[A]
14A3 **Jeffersonville** US[A]
60C2 **Jekabpils** Latvia
59B2 **Jelena Gora** Pol
60B2 **Jelgava** Latvia

78C4 **Jember** Indon
57C2 **Jena** Germany
78B2 **Jenaja** *I* Indon
47D1 **Jenbach** Austria
94B2 **Jenin** Israel
19B3 **Jennings** USA
59B2 **Jeseniky** *Upland* Czech Republic
6F3 **Jensen Nunatakker** *Mt* Greenland
6B3 **Jens Munk** *I* Can
08B3 **Jeparit** Aust
31D4 **Jequié** Brazil
35C1 **Jequital** *R* Brazil
35C1 **Jequitinhonha** Brazil
31C5 **Jequitinhonha** *R* Brazil
50A2 **Jerez de la Frontera** Spain
50A2 **Jerez de los Caballeros** Spain
94B3 **Jericho** Israel
08C3 **Jerilderie** Aust
48B2 **Jersey** *I* UK
10C2 **Jersey City** USA
15C2 **Jersey Shore** USA
18B2 **Jerseyville** USA
92C3 **Jerusalem** Israel
09D3 **Jervis B** Aust
13C2 **Jervis Inlet** *Sd* Can
52B1 **Jesenice** Slovenia
86B2 **Jessore** Bang
11B3 **Jesup** USA
34C2 **Jesus Maria** Arg
6D2 **Jewett City** USA
54A2 **Jezerce** *Mt* Alb
58C2 **Jezioro Mamry** *L* Pol
58C2 **Jezioro Śniardwy** *L* Pol
94B2 **Jezzine** Leb
85C4 **Jhābua** India
85D4 **Jhālāwār** India
84C2 **Jhang Maghiana** Pak
85D3 **Jhānsi** India
86A2 **Jhārsuguda** India
84C2 **Jhelum** Pak
84C2 **Jhelum** *R* Pak
11C3 **J H Kerr L** USA
4D3 **Jhunjhunūn** India
69F2 **Jiamusi** China
73C4 **Ji'an** Jiangxi, China
74B2 **Ji'an** Jilin, China
3D4 **Jiande** China
3B4 **Jiang'an** China
3D4 **Jiangbiancun** China
3A5 **Jiangcheng** China
3B3 **Jiang Jiang** *R* China
3C5 **Jiangmen** China
2D3 **Jiangsu** Province, China
3C4 **Jiangxi** Province, China
3A3 **Jiangyou** China
2D1 **Jianping** China
3A5 **Jianshui** China
3D4 **Jian Xi** *R* China
3D4 **Jianyang** China
2E2 **Jiaonan** China
2E2 **Jiao Xian** China
2E2 **Jiaozhou Wan** *B* China
2C2 **Jiaozuo** China
3E3 **Jiaxiang** China
8B3 **Jiayuguan** China
1B3 **Jiddah** S Arabia
2D3 **Jieshou** China
2C2 **Jiexiu** China
2A3 **Jigzhi** China
9B3 **Jihlava** Czech Republic
9E2 **Jilib** Somalia
9E2 **Jilin** China
1B1 **Jiloca** *R* Spain
9D2 **Jima** Eth
9C4 **Jiménez** Coahuila, Mexico
2D2 **Jinan** China
4D3 **Jind** India
2B2 **Jingbian** China
3D4 **Jingdezhen** China
3C1 **Jinghong** China
3C3 **Jingmen** China
2B2 **Jingning** China
3B4 **Jing Xiang** China
73D4 **Jinhua** China
72C1 **Jining** Nei Monggol, China
72D2 **Jining** Shandong, China
99D2 **Jinja** Uganda
76C1 **Jinping** China
73A4 **Jinsha Jiang** *R* China
73C4 **Jinshi** China
72E1 **Jinxi** China
72E2 **Jin Xian** China
72E1 **Jinzhou** China
33E5 **Jiparaná** *R* Brazil
32A4 **Jipijapa** Ecuador
23A2 **Jiquilpan** Mexico
91C4 **Jīroft** Iran
99E2 **Jirriban** Somalia
73B4 **Jishou** China
92C2 **Jisr ash Shughūr** Syria
54B2 **Jiu** *R* Rom
73D4 **Jiujiang** China
73A4 **Jiulong** China
73D4 **Jiulong Jiang** *R* China
69F2 **Jixi** China
94B3 **Jiza** Jordan
81C4 **Jīzan** S Arabia
97A3 **Joal** Sen
35C1 **João Monlevade** Brazil
31E3 **João Pessoa** Brazil
35B1 **João Pirheiro** Brazil
34B2 **Jocoli** Arg
85C3 **Jodhpur** India
38K6 **Joensuu** Fin
46C2 **Joeuf** France
13D2 **Joffre,Mt** Can
86B1 **Jogbani** India
87A2 **Jog Falls** India
101G1 **Johannesburg** S Africa
21B2 **Johannesburg** USA
6C2 **Johan Pen** Can
12D1 **John** *R* USA
20C2 **John Day** USA
20B1 **John Day** *R* USA
44C2 **John O'Groats** Scot
18A2 **John Redmond Res** USA
11B3 **Johnson City** Tennessee, USA
17B1 **Johnston** USA
27N2 **Johnston Pt** St Vincent and the Grenadines
15C2 **Johnstown** Pennsylvania, USA
77C5 **Johor Bharu** Malay
49C2 **Joigny** France
30G4 **Joinville** Brazil
61H3 **Jok** *R* Russian Fed
38H5 **Jokkmokk** Sweden
93E2 **Jolfa** Iran
10B2 **Joliet** USA
7C5 **Joliette** Can
79B4 **Jolo** Phil
79B4 **Jolo** *I* Phil
82D2 **Joma** *Mt* China
58C1 **Jonava** Lithuania
72A3 **Jonê** China
11A3 **Jonesboro** Arkansas, USA
19B3 **Jonesboro** Louisiana, USA
6B2 **Jones Sd** Can
58C1 **Joniśkis** Lithuania
39G7 **Jönköping** Sweden
11A3 **Joplin** USA
92C3 **Jordan** Kingdom, S W Asia
94B2 **Jordan** *R* Israel
20C2 **Jordan Valley** USA
86C1 **Jorhāt** India
38J5 **Jörn** Sweden
78C3 **Jorong** Indon
39F7 **Jørpeland** Nor
79B3 **Jose Pañganiban** Phil
106B2 **Joseph Bonaparte G** Aust
64B3 **Jotunheimen** *Mt* Nor
94B2 **Jouai'ya** Leb
94B2 **Jounié** Leb
86C1 **Jowal** India
99E2 **Jowhar** Somalia
12H2 **Joy,Mt** Can
5F5 **Juan de Fuca,Str of** Can/USA
101D2 **Juan de Nova** *I* Mozam Chan
34D3 **Juárez** Arg
31C3 **Juàzeiro** Brazil
31D3 **Juazeiro do Norte** Brazil
99D2 **Juba** Sudan
99E2 **Juba** *R* Somalia
94B1 **Jubail** Leb
93D3 **Jubbah** S Arabia
96A2 **Juby,C** Mor
51B2 **Jucar** *R* Spain
23B2 **Juchatengo** Mexico
23A1 **Juchipila** *R* Mexico
23A1 **Juchitlan** Mexico
57C3 **Judenburg** Austria
30B2 **Juilaca** Peru
73C4 **Juiling Shan** *Hills* China
31C6 **Juiz de Fora** Brazil
30C3 **Jujuy** State, Arg
30C2 **Juli** Peru
33F3 **Julianatop** *Mt* Surinam
6F3 **Julianehab** Greenland
46D1 **Jülich** Germany
86A1 **Jumla** Nepal
94B3 **Jum Suwwāna** *Mt* Jordan
85C4 **Jūnāgadh** India
72D2 **Junan** China
9D3 **Junction City** USA
31B6 **Jundiaí** Brazil
4E4 **Juneau** USA
107D4 **Junee** Aust
22C2 **June Lake** USA
52A1 **Jungfrau** *Mt* Switz
16A2 **Juniata** *R* USA
29D2 **Junín** Arg
73A4 **Junlian** China
31B6 **Juquiá** Brazil
99C2 **Jur** *R* Sudan
42B2 **Jura** *I* Scot
49D2 **Jura** *Mts* France
44B3 **Jura,Sound of** *Chan* Scot
94B3 **Jurf ed Darāwīsh** Jordan
65K4 **Jurga** Russian Fed
60B2 **Jūrmala** Latvia
32D4 **Juruá** *R* Brazil
33F6 **Juruena** *R* Brazil
94C1 **Jūsīyah** Syria
34B2 **Justo Daract** Arg
32D4 **Jutai** *R* Brazil
25D3 **Juticalpa** Honduras
Jutland = Jylland
90C3 **Jūymand** Iran
56B1 **Jylland** *Pen* Den
38K6 **Jyväskyla** Fin

K

82B2 **K2** *Mt* China/India
90C2 **Kaakhka** Turkmenistan
101H1 **Kaapmuiden** S Africa
71D4 **Kabaena** *I* Indon
97A4 **Kabala** Sierra Leone
99D3 **Kabale** Rwanda
98C3 **Kabalo** Zaïre
98C3 **Kabambare** Zaïre
99D2 **Kabarole** Uganda
98C3 **Kabinda** Zaïre
90A3 **Kabir Kuh** *Mts* Iran
100B2 **Kabompo** Zambia
100B2 **Kabompo** *R* Zambia
98C3 **Kabongo** Zaïre
84B2 **Kabul** Afghan
85B4 **Kachchh,G of** India
61J2 **Kachkanar** Russian Fed
63C2 **Kachug** Russian Fed
76B3 **Kadan** Burma
78D3 **Kadapongan** *I* Indon
85C4 **Kadi** India
108A2 **Kadina** Aust
92B2 **Kadinhanı** Turk
87B2 **Kadiri** India
60E4 **Kadiyevka** Ukraine
100B2 **Kadoma** Zim
99C1 **Kadugli** Sudan
97C3 **Kaduna** Nig
97C3 **Kaduna** *R* Nig
87B2 **Kadūr** India
97A3 **Kaédi** Maur
21C4 **Kaena Pt** Hawaiian Is
74B3 **Kaesŏng** N Korea
97C4 **Kafanchan** Nig
97A3 **Kaffrine** Sen
94C1 **Kafrūn Bashūr** Syria
100B2 **Kafue** Zambia
100B2 **Kafue** *R* Zambia
100B2 **Kafue Nat Pk** Zambia
74D3 **Kaga** Japan
65H6 **Kagan** Kazakhstan
93D1 **Kağizman** Turk
74C4 **Kagoshima** Japan
90C2 **Kāhak** Iran
99D3 **Kahama** Tanz
84B3 **Kahan** Pak
78C3 **Kahayan** *R* Indon
98B3 **Kahemba** Zaïre
46E1 **Kahler Asten** *Mt* Germany
91C4 **Kahnūj** Iran
18B1 **Kahoka** USA
21C4 **Kahoolawe** *I* Hawaiian Is
92C2 **Kahramanmaraş** Turk
21C4 **Kahuku Pt** Hawaiian Is
111B2 **Kaiapoi** NZ
33F2 **Kaieteur Fall** Guyana
72C3 **Kaifeng** China
110B1 **Kaikohe** NZ
111B2 **Kaikoura** NZ
111B2 **Kaikoura Pen** NZ
111B2 **Kaikoura Range** *Mts* NZ
73B4 **Kaili** China
21C4 **Kailua** Hawaiian Is
71E4 **Kaimana** Indon
75B2 **Kainan** Japan
97C3 **Kainji Res** Nig
110B1 **Kaipara Harbour** *B* NZ
73C5 **Kaiping** China
96D1 **Kairouan** Tunisia
22C2 **Kaiser Peak** *Mt* USA
57B3 **Kaiserslautern** Germany
74B2 **Kaishantun** China
58D2 **Kaisiadorys** Lithuania
110B1 **Kaitaia** NZ
111A3 **Kaitangata** NZ
84D3 **Kaithal** India
21C4 **Kaiwi Chan** Hawaiian Is
73B3 **Kai Xian** China
73A5 **Kaiyuan** Liaoning, China
74A2 **Kaiyuan** Yunnan, China
12C2 **Kaiyuh Mts** USA
38K6 **Kajaani** Fin
84B2 **Kajaki** Afghan
99D3 **Kajiado** Kenya
84B2 **Kajrān** Afghan
99D1 **Kaka** Sudan
99D2 **Kakamega** Kenya
75A2 **Kake** Japan
12H3 **Kake** USA
12D3 **Kakhonak** USA
65E5 **Kakhovskoye Vodokhranilishche** *Res* Ukraine
91B4 **Kākī** Iran
87C1 **Kākināda** India
75A2 **Kakogawa** Japan
4D2 **Kaktovik** USA
75C1 **Kakuda** Japan
Kalaallit Nunaat = Greenland
55B3 **Kalabáka** Greece
78D1 **Kalabakan** Malay
100B2 **Kalabo** Zambia
61F3 **Kalach** Russian Fed
61F4 **Kalach-na-Donu** Russian Fed
86C2 **Kaladan** *R* Burma
21C4 **Ka Lae** *C* Hawaiian Is

100B3 **Kalahari Desert** Botswana
38J6 **Kalajoki** Fin
63D2 **Kalakan** Russian Fed
70A3 **Kalakepen** Indon
84C1 **Kalam** Pak
55B3 **Kalámai** Greece
10B2 **Kalamazoo** USA
84B3 **Kalat** Pak
92B1 **Kalecik** Turk
78D3 **Kalembau** *I* Indon
99C3 **Kalémié** Zaïre
38L5 **Kalevala** Russian Fed
86C2 **Kalewa** Burma
12D2 **Kalgin I** USA
106B4 **Kalgoorlie** Aust
78B4 **Kalianda** Indon
79B3 **Kalibo** Phil
98C3 **Kalima** Zaïre
78C3 **Kalimantan** Province, Indon
55C3 **Kálimnos** *I* Greece
86B1 **Kälimpang** India
60B3 **Kaliningrad** Russian Fed
60C3 **Kalinkovichi** Belorussia
8B2 **Kalispell** USA
58B2 **Kalisz** Pol
99D3 **Kaliua** Tanz
38J5 **Kalix** *R* Sweden
100A3 **Kalkfeld** Namibia
100A3 **Kalkrand** Namibia
108A1 **Kallakoopah** *R* Aust
38K6 **Kallávesi** *L* Fin
55C3 **Kallonis Kólpos** *B* Greece
39H7 **Kalmar** Sweden
61G4 **Kalmytskaya Respublika,** Russian Fed
100B2 **Kalomo** Zambia
18B1 **Kalona** USA
13B2 **Kalone Peak** *Mt* Can
87A2 **Kalpeni** *I* India
85D3 **Kālpi** India
53A3 **Kalsat Khasba** Tunisia
12B2 **Kalskag** USA
12C2 **Kaltag** USA
60E3 **Kaluga** Russian Fed
39G7 **Kalundborg** Den
59C3 **Kalush** Ukraine
87B2 **Kalyandurg** India
60E2 **Kalyazin** Russian Fed
61H1 **Kama** *R* Russian Fed
74E3 **Kamaishi** Japan
84C2 **Kamalia** Pak
110C1 **Kamanawa Mts** NZ
100A2 **Kamanjab** Namibia
84D2 **Kamat** *Mt* India
87B3 **Kamban** India
61H2 **Kambarka** Russian Fed
97A4 **Kambia** Sierra Leone
59D3 **Kamenets Podolskiy** Ukraine
61F3 **Kamenka** Russian Fed
65K4 **Kamen-na-Obi** Russian Fed
61K2 **Kamensk-Ural'skiy** Russian Fed
5H3 **Kamilukuak L** Can
98C3 **Kamina** Zaïre
7A3 **Kaminak L** Can
75C1 **Kaminoyama** Japan
5F4 **Kamloops** Can
93E1 **Kamo** Armenia
75C1 **Kamogawa** Japan
99D2 **Kampala** Uganda
77C5 **Kampar** Malay
78A2 **Kampar** *R* Indon
56B2 **Kampen** Neth
76B2 **Kamphaeng Phet** Thai
77C3 **Kampot** Camb
91D4 **Kamsaptar** Iran
61J2 **Kamskoye Vodokhranilishche** *Res* Russian Fed
85D4 **Kāmthi** India
61G3 **Kamyshin** Russian Fed
61K2 **Kamyshlov** Russian Fed
7C4 **Kanaaupscow** *R* Can
98C3 **Kananga** Zaïre
61G2 **Kanash** Russian Fed
75B1 **Kanayama** Japan
74D3 **Kanazawa** Japan
4C3 **Kanbisha** USA
87B2 **Kānchipuram** India
84B2 **Kandahar** Afghan
64E3 **Kandalaksha** Russian Fed
38L5 **Kandalakshskaya Guba** *B* Russian Fed
97C3 **Kandi** Benin
109C2 **Kandos** Aust
87C3 **Kandy** Sri Lanka
15C2 **Kane** USA
6C1 **Kane Basin** *B* Can
98B1 **Kanem** *Desert Region* Chad
97B3 **Kangaba** Mali
92C2 **Kangal** Turk
6E3 **Kangâmiut** Greenland
91B4 **Kangān** Iran
77C4 **Kangar** Malay
106C4 **Kangaroo I** Aust
6E3 **Kangâtsiaq** Greenland
90A3 **Kangavar** Iran
72C1 **Kangbao** China
82C3 **Kangchenjunga** *Mt* Nepal
73A4 **Kangding** China
6G3 **Kangerdlugssuaq** *B* Greenland
6G3 **Kangerdlugssvatsaiq** *B* Greenland
99D2 **Kangetet** Kenya
74B2 **Kanggye** N Korea
7D4 **Kangiqsualujjuaq** Can
6C3 **Kangiqsujuaq** Can
7C3 **Kangirsuk** Can
74B3 **Kangnüng** S Korea
98B2 **Kango** Gabon
68B4 **Kangto** *Mt* China
72B3 **Kang Xian** China
77D4 **Kanh Hung** Viet
98C3 **Kaniama** Zaïre
87B1 **Kani Giri** India
39J6 **Kankaanpää** Fin
14A2 **Kankakee** USA
14A2 **Kankakee** *R* USA
97B3 **Kankan** Guinea
86A2 **Kānker** India
87B3 **Kanniyākuman** India
97C3 **Kano** Nig
74C4 **Kanoya** Japan
86A1 **Kānpur** India
9D3 **Kansas** State, USA
18A2 **Kansas** *R* USA
10A3 **Kansas City** USA
73D5 **Kanshi** China
63B2 **Kansk** Russian Fed
97C3 **Kantchari** Burkina
86B2 **Kanthi** India
12D2 **Kantishna** USA
12D2 **Kantishna** *R* USA
100B3 **Kanye** Botswana
68D4 **Kao-hsiung** Taiwan
100A2 **Kaoka Veld** *Plain* Namibia
97A3 **Kaolack** Sen
100B2 **Kaoma** Zambia
21C4 **Kapaau** Hawaiian Is
98C3 **Kapanga** Zaïre
6F3 **Kap Cort Adelaer** *C* Greenland
6H3 **Kap Dalton** *C* Greenland
39H7 **Kapellskär** Sweden
6F3 **Kap Farvel** *C* Greenland
6G3 **Kap Gustav Holm** *C* Greenland
100B2 **Kapiri** Zambia
78C2 **Kapit** Malay
19B3 **Kaplan** USA
57C3 **Kaplice** Czech Republic
77B4 **Kapoe** Thai
99C3 **Kapona** Zaïre
52C1 **Kaposvár** Hung
6C2 **Kap Parry** *C* Can
6H3 **Kap Ravn** *C* Greenland
78B3 **Kapuas** *R* Indon
108A2 **Kapunda** Aust
84D2 **Kapurthala** India
7B5 **Kapuskasing** Can
109D2 **Kaputar** *Mt* Aust
93E2 **Kapydzhik** *Mt* Armenia
6D2 **Kap York** *C* Greenland
92B1 **Karabük** Turk
55C2 **Karacabey** Turk
85B4 **Karachi** Pak
87A1 **Karād** India
60E5 **Kara Daglari** *Mt* Turk
54C5 **Karadeniz Boğazi** *Sd* Turk
68D1 **Karaftit** Russian Fed
65J5 **Karaganda** Kazakhstan
65J5 **Karagayly** Kazakhstan
87B2 **Kāraikāl** India
90B2 **Karaj** Iran
92C3 **Karak** Jordan
65G5 **Kara Kalpakskaya Respublika,** Uzbekistan
84D1 **Karakax He** *R* China
71D3 **Karakelong** *I* Indon
84D1 **Karakoram** *Mts* India
84D1 **Karakoram** *P* India/China
97A3 **Karakoro** *R* Maur/Sen
65G6 **Karakumy** *Desert* Russian Fed
94B3 **Karama** Jordan
92B2 **Karaman** Turk
65K5 **Karamay** China
111B2 **Karamea** NZ
111B2 **Karamea Bight** *B* NZ
85D4 **Kāranja** India
92B2 **Karapınar** Turk
64H2 **Kara S** Russian Fed
100A3 **Karasburg** Namibia
38K5 **Karasjok** Nor
65J4 **Karasuk** Russian Fed
92C2 **Karataş** Turk
65H5 **Kara Tau** *Mts* Kazakhstan
76B3 **Karathuri** Burma
74B4 **Karatsu** Japan
91B4 **Karāz** Iran
93D3 **Karbalā'** Iraq
59C3 **Karcag** Hung
55B3 **Kardhítsa** Greece
64E3 **Karel'skaya Respublika,** Russian Fed
38J5 **Karesvando** Sweden
96B2 **Karet** *Desert Region* Maur
65K4 **Kargasok** Russian Fed
97D3 **Kari** Nig
100B2 **Kariba** Zim
100B2 **Kariba** *L* Zim/Zambia
100B2 **Kariba Dam** Zim/Zambia
95C3 **Karima** Sudan
78B3 **Karimata** *I* Indon
86C2 **Karimganj** Bang
87B1 **Karīmnagar** India
99E1 **Karin** Somalia
39J6 **Karis** Fin
99C3 **Karishimbe** *Mt* Zaïre
55B3 **Káristos** Greece
87A2 **Kārkal** India
71F4 **Karkar** *I* PNG
90A3 **Karkheh** *R* Iran
60D4 **Karkinitskiy Zaliv** *B* Ukraine
63B3 **Karlik Shan** *Mt* China
58B2 **Karlino** Pol
52C2 **Karlobag** Croatia
52C1 **Karlovac** Croatia
54B2 **Karlovo** Bulg
57C2 **Karlovy Vary** Czech Republic
39G7 **Karlshamn** Sweden
39G7 **Karlskoga** Sweden
39H7 **Karlskrona** Sweden
57B3 **Karlsruhe** Germany
39G7 **Karlstad** Sweden
12D3 **Karluk** USA
86C2 **Karnafuli Res** Bang
84D3 **Karnal** India
87A1 **Karnataka** State, India
54C2 **Karnobat** Bulg
100B2 **Karoi** Zim
99D3 **Karonga** Malawi
95C3 **Karora** Sudan
78D3 **Karossa** Indon
55C3 **Kárpathos** *I* Greece
6E2 **Karrats Fjord** Greenland
93D1 **Kars** Turk
65H4 **Karsakpay** Kazakhstan
58D1 **Kärsava** Latvia
80E2 **Karshi** Uzbekistan
38J6 **Karstula** Fin
94B1 **Kartaba** Leb
54C2 **Kartal** Turk
61K3 **Kartaly** Russian Fe
90A3 **Kārūn** *R* Iran
86A1 **Karwa** India
87A2 **Kārwār** India
68D1 **Karymskoye** Russian Fed
98B3 **Kasai** *R* Zaïre
100B2 **Kasaji** Zaïre
101C2 **Kasama** Zambia
99D3 **Kasanga** Tanz
87A2 **Kāsaragod** India
5H3 **Kasba L** Can
100B2 **Kasempa** Zambia
100B2 **Kasenga** Zaïre
99D2 **Kasese** Uganda
90B3 **Kāshān** Iran
12C2 **Kashegelok** USA
82B2 **Kashi** China
84D3 **Kāshipur** India
74D3 **Kashiwazaki** Japa
90C2 **Kashmar** Iran
66D3 **Kashmir** State, Ind
61F3 **Kasimov** Russian F
18C2 **Kaskaskia** *R* USA
38J6 **Kaskinen** Fin
61K2 **Kasli** Russian Fed
5G5 **Kaslo** Can
98C3 **Kasonga** Zaïre
98B3 **Kasongo-Lunda** Zε
55C3 **Kásos** *I* Greece
Kaspiyskiy = **Lagar**
95C3 **Kassala** Sudan
56B2 **Kassel** Germany
96C1 **Kasserine** Tunisia
100A2 **Kassinga** Angola
92B1 **Kastamonou** Turk
55B3 **Kastélli** Greece
92A2 **Kastellorizon** *I* Greece
55B2 **Kastoría** Greece
55C3 **Kástron** Greece
74D3 **Kasugai** Japan
75A1 **Kasumi** Japan
101C2 **Kasungu** Malawi
84C2 **Kasur** Pak
100B2 **Kataba** Zambia
98C3 **Katako-kombe** Za
4D3 **Katalla** USA
63G2 **Katangli** Russian
106A4 **Katanning** Aust
55B2 **Katerini** Greece
5E4 **Kates Needle** *Mt* Can/USA
82D3 **Katha** Burma
106C2 **Katherine** Aust
85C4 **Kāthiāwār** *Pen* In
86B1 **Kathmandu** Nepa
84D2 **Kathua** India
86B1 **Katihār** India
100B2 **Katima Mulilo** Namibia
4C4 **Katmai,Mt** USA
12D3 **Katmai Nat Mon** USA
86A2 **Katni** India
109D2 **Katoomba** Aust
59B2 **Katowice** Pol
39H7 **Katrineholm** Swe

97C3 **Katsina** Nig
97C4 **Katsina Ala** Nig
75C1 **Katsuta** Japan
75C1 **Katsuura** Japan
75B1 **Katsuy** Japan
65H6 **Kattakurgan** Uzbekistan
39G7 **Kattegat** *Str* Den/Sweden
21C4 **Kauai** *I* Hawaiian Is
21C4 **Kauai Chan** Hawaiian Is
21C4 **Kaulakahi Chan** Hawaiian Is
21C4 **Kaunakaki** Hawaiian Is
60B3 **Kaunas** Lithuania
97C3 **Kaura Namoda** Nig
38J5 **Kautokeino** Nor
55B2 **Kavadarci** Macedonia
55A2 **Kavajë** Alb
87B2 **Kavali** India
55B2 **Kaválla** Greece
85B4 **Kāvda** India
75B1 **Kawagoe** Japan
75B1 **Kawaguchi** Japan
10B1 **Kawakawa** NZ
99C3 **Kawambwa** Zambia
86A2 **Kawardha** India
15C2 **Kawartha Lakes** Can
74D3 **Kawasaki** Japan
10C1 **Kawerau** NZ
10B1 **Kawhia** NZ
97B3 **Kaya** Burkina
12F3 **Kayak I** USA
78D2 **Kayan** *R* Indon
87B3 **Kāyankulam** India
97A3 **Kayes** Mali
92C2 **Kayseri** Turk
1B8 **Kazach'ye** Russian Fed
93E1 **Kazakh** Azerbaijan
65G5 **Kazakhstan** Republic, Asia
61G2 **Kazan'** Russian Fed
54C2 **Kazanlŭk** Bulg
69G4 **Kazan Retto** *Is* Japan
91B4 **Kāzerūn** Iran
61H1 **Kazhim** Russian Fed
93E1 **Kazi Magomed** Azerbaijan
59C3 **Kazincbarcika** Hung
55B3 **Kéa** *I* Greece
21C4 **Kealaikahiki Chan** Hawaiian Is
8D2 **Kearney** USA
93C2 **Keban Baraji** *Res* Turk
97A3 **Kébémer** Sen
96C1 **Kebili** Tunisia
94C1 **Kebīr** *R* Leb/Syria
38H5 **Kebrekaise** *Mt* Sweden
59B3 **Kecskemét** Hung
58C1 **Kedainiai** Lithuania
97A3 **Kédougou** Sen
12J2 **Keele** *R* Can
2H2 **Keele Pk** *Mt* Can
21B2 **Keeler** USA
5D2 **Keene** New Hampshire, USA
0A3 **Keetmanshoop** Namibia
8C1 **Keewanee** USA
6A3 **Keewatin** *Region* Can
5B3 **Kefallinía** *I* Greece
4B2 **Kefar Sava** Israel
7C4 **Keffi** Nig
8A2 **Keflavik** Iceland
5G4 **Keg River** Can
6B1 **Kehsi Mansam** Burma
8B3 **Keith** Aust
4C3 **Keith** Scot
4F3 **Keith Arm** *B* Can
6D3 **Kekertuk** Can
5D3 **Kekri** India
7C5 **Kelang** Malay
7C4 **Kelantan** *R* Malay
4B1 **Kelif** Turkmenistan
2C1 **Kelkit** *R* Turk
8B3 **Kellé** Congo
4F2 **Kellet,C** Can
20C1 **Kellogg** USA
64D3 **Kelloselka** Fin
45C2 **Kells** Irish Rep
42B2 **Kells Range** *Hills* Scot
58C1 **Kelme** Lithuania
5G5 **Kelowna** Can
5F4 **Kelsey Bay** Can
42C2 **Kelso** Scot
20B1 **Kelso** USA
64E3 **Kem'** Russian Fed
38L6 **Kem'** *R* Russian Fed
97B3 **Ke Macina** Mali
13B2 **Kemano** Can
65K4 **Kemerovo** Russian Fed
38J5 **Kemi** Fin
38K5 **Kemi** *R* Fin
38K5 **Kemijärvi** Fin
46C1 **Kempen** Region, Belg
26B2 **Kemps Bay** The Bahamas
109D2 **Kempsey** Aust
57C3 **Kempten** Germany
12D2 **Kenai** USA
12D3 **Kenai Mts** USA
12D2 **Kenai Pen** USA
99D2 **Kenamuke Swamp** Sudan
42C2 **Kendal** Eng
109D2 **Kendall** Aust
71D4 **Kendari** Indon
78C3 **Kendawangan** Indon
86B2 **Kendrāpāra** India
20C1 **Kendrick** USA
97A4 **Kenema** Sierra Leone
98B3 **Kenge** Zaïre
76B1 **Kengtung** Burma
100B3 **Kenhardt** S Africa
97A3 **Kéniéba** Mali
96B1 **Kenitra** Mor
45B3 **Kenmare** Irish Rep
45B3 **Kenmare** *R* Irish Rep
19B4 **Kenner** USA
18C2 **Kennett** USA
16B3 **Kennett Square** USA
20C1 **Kennewick** USA
5F4 **Kenny Dam** Can
7A5 **Kenora** Can
10B2 **Kenosha** USA
43E4 **Kent** County, Eng
20B1 **Kent** Washington, USA
14A2 **Kentland** USA
14B2 **Kenton** USA
4H3 **Kent Pen** Can
11B3 **Kentucky** State, USA
11B3 **Kentucky L** USA
19B3 **Kentwood** Louisiana, USA
14A2 **Kentwood** Michigan, USA
99D2 **Kenya** Republic, Africa
Kenya,Mt = Kirinyaga
18B1 **Keokuk** USA
86A2 **Keonchi** India
86B2 **Keonjhargarh** India
71E4 **Kepaluan Tanimbar** *Arch* Indon
6H3 **Keplavik** Iceland
59B2 **Kepno** Pol
78B2 **Kepulauan Anambas** *Arch* Indon
71E4 **Kepulauan Aru** *Arch* Indon
78B2 **Kepulauan Badas** *Is* Indon
71E4 **Kepulauan Banda** *Arch* Indon
71D4 **Kepulauan Banggai** *I* Indon
78B2 **Kepulauan Bunguran Seletan** *Arch* Indon
71E4 **Kepulauan Kai** *Arch* Indon
71D4 **Kepulauan Leti** *I* Indon
78A3 **Kepulauan Lingga** *Is* Indon
70A4 **Kepulauan Mentawi** *Arch* Indon
78A2 **Kepulauan Riau** *Arch* Indon
78D4 **Kepulauan Sabalana** *Arch* Indon
71D3 **Kepulauan Sangihe** *Arch* Indon
71D4 **Kepulauan Sula** *I* Indon
71D3 **Kepulauan Talaud** *Arch* Indon
78B2 **Kepulauan Tambelan** *Is* Indon
71E4 **Kepulauan Tanimbar** *I* Indon
71D4 **Kepulauan Togian** *I* Indon
71D4 **Kepulauan Tukambesi** *Is* Indon
87B2 **Kerala** State, India
108B3 **Kerang** Aust
39K6 **Kerava** Fin
60E4 **Kerch'** Ukraine
71F4 **Kerema** PNG
20C1 **Keremeps** Can
95C3 **Keren** Eritrea
104B6 **Kerguelen Ridge** Indian O
99D3 **Kericho** Kenya
70B4 **Kerinci** *Mt* Indon
99D2 **Kerio** *R* Kenya
80E2 **Kerki** Turkmenistan
55A3 **Kérkira** Greece
55A3 **Kérkira** *I* Greece
91C3 **Kerman** Iran
22B2 **Kerman** USA
90A3 **Kermānshāh** Iran
21B2 **Kern** *R* USA
13F2 **Kerrobert** Can
45B2 **Kerry** County, Irish Rep
17B1 **Kershaw** USA
78B3 **Kertamulia** Indon
63D3 **Kerulen** *R* Mongolia
96B2 **Kerzaz** Alg
55C2 **Keşan** Turk
74E3 **Kesennuma** Japan
38L5 **Kesten 'ga** Russian Fed
42C2 **Keswick** Eng
65K4 **Ket** *R* Russian Fed
97C4 **Kéta** Ghana
78C3 **Ketapang** Indon
5E4 **Ketchikan** USA
97C3 **Ketia** Niger
85B4 **Keti Bandar** Pak
58C2 **Kętrzyn** Pol
43D3 **Kettering** Eng
14B3 **Kettering** USA
20C1 **Kettle** *R* Can
20C1 **Kettle River Range** *Mts* USA
7C3 **Kettlestone B** Can
90C3 **Kevir-i Namak** *Salt Flat* Iran
14A2 **Kewaunee** USA
14B1 **Key Harbour** Can
17B2 **Key Largo** USA
11B4 **Key West** USA
63C2 **Kezhma** Russian Fed
54A1 **K'félegháza** Hung
12B2 **Kgun L** USA
94C2 **Khabab** Syria
62H3 **Khabarovsk** Russian Fed
85B3 **Khairpur** Pak
85B3 **Khairpur** Region, Pak
100B3 **Khakhea** Botswana
55C3 **Khálki** *I* Greece
55B2 **Khalkidhíki** *Pen* Greece
55B3 **Khalkís** Greece
61G2 **Khalturin** Russian Fed
85C4 **Khambhāt,G of** India
85D4 **Khāmgaon** India
76C2 **Kham Keut** Laos
87C1 **Khammam** India
90A2 **Khamseh** *Mts* Iran
76C2 **Khan** *R* Laos
84B1 **Khanabad** Afghan
93E3 **Khānaqīn** Iraq
85D4 **Khandwa** India
84C2 **Khanewal** Pak
94C3 **Khan ez Zabib** Jordan
77D4 **Khanh Hung** Viet
55B3 **Khaniá** Greece
84C3 **Khanpur** Pak
65H3 **Khanty-Mansiysk** Russian Fed
94B3 **Khan Yunis** Egypt
84D1 **Khapalu** India
68C2 **Khapcheranga** Russian Fed
61G4 **Kharabali** Russian Fed
86B2 **Kharagpur** India
91C4 **Khāran** Iran
84B3 **Kharan** Pak
90B3 **Kharānaq** Iran
91B4 **Khārg** *Is* Iran
95C2 **Khârga Oasis** Egypt
85D4 **Khargon** India
60E4 **Khar'kov** Ukraine
54C2 **Kharmanli** Bulg
61F2 **Kharovsk** Russian Fed
95C3 **Khartoum** Sudan
95C3 **Khartoum North** Sudan
74C2 **Khasan** Russian Fed
95C3 **Khashm el Girba** Sudan
86C1 **Khasi-Jaīntīa Hills** India
54C2 **Khaskovo** Bulg
1B9 **Khatanga** Russian Fed
76B3 **Khawsa** Burma
76C2 **Khe Bo** Viet
85C4 **Khed Brahma** India
51C2 **Khemis** Alg
96B1 **Khenifra** Mor
51D2 **Kherrata** Alg
60D4 **Kherson** Ukraine
63D2 **Khilok** Russian Fed
55C3 **Khíos** Greece
55C3 **Khíos** *I* Greece
60C4 **Khmel'nitskiy** Ukraine
59C3 **Khodorov** Ukraine
84B1 **Kholm** Afghan
76D3 **Khong** Laos
91B4 **Khonj** Iran
69F2 **Khor** Russian Fed
91A3 **Khoramshahr** Iran
91B5 **Khōr Duwayhin** *B* UAE
84C1 **Khorog** Tajikistan
90A3 **Khorramābad** Iran
90C3 **Khosf** Iran
84B2 **Khost** Pak
60C4 **Khotin** Ukraine
12C2 **Khotol** *Mt* USA
60C3 **Khoyniki** Belorussia
63F2 **Khrebet Dzhugdzhur** *Mts* Russian Fed
90C2 **Khrebet Kopet Dag** *Mts* Turkmenistan
64H3 **Khrebet Pay-khoy** *Mts* Russian Fed
82C1 **Khrebet Tarbagatay** *Mts* Kazakhstan
63E2 **Khrebet Tukuringra** *Mts* Russian Fed
82A1 **Khudzhand** Tajikistan
86B2 **Khulna** Bang
84D1 **Khunjerab** *P* China/India
90B3 **Khunsar** Iran
91A4 **Khurays** S Arabia
86B2 **Khurda** India
84D3 **Khurja** India
84C2 **Khushab** Pak
94B2 **Khushnīyah** Syria
59C3 **Khust** Ukraine
99C1 **Khuwei** Sudan
85B3 **Khuzdar** Pak
90D3 **Khvāf** Iran
61G3 **Khvalynsk** Russian Fed
90C3 **Khvor** Iran
91B4 **Khvormūj** Iran
93D2 **Khvoy** Iran
84C1 **Khwaja Muhammad** *Mts* Afghan
84C2 **Khyber P** Afghan/Pak

99C3 **Kiambi** Zaïre
19A3 **Kiamichi** *R* USA
12B1 **Kiana** USA
98B3 **Kibangou** Congo
99D3 **Kibaya** Tanz
98C3 **Kibombo** Zaïre
99D3 **Kibondo** Tanz
99D3 **Kibungu** Rwanda
55B2 **Kičevo** Macedonia
5G4 **Kicking Horse P** Can
97C3 **Kidal** Mali
43C3 **Kidderminster** Eng
97A3 **Kidira** Sen
110C1 **Kidnappers,C** NZ
56C2 **Kiel** Germany
59C2 **Kielce** Pol
56C2 **Kieler Bucht** *B* Germany
Kiev = Kiyev
80E2 **Kifab** Uzbekistan
97A3 **Kiffa** Maur
89H8 **Kigali** Rwanda
12A2 **Kigluaik Mts** USA
99C3 **Kigoma** Tanz
75B2 **Kii-sanchi** *Mts* Japan
74C4 **Kii-suido** *B* Japan
54B1 **Kikinda** Serbia, Yugos
55B3 **Kikládhes** *Is* Greece
71F4 **Kikori** PNG
98B3 **Kikwit** Zaïre
21C4 **Kilauea Crater** *Mt* Hawaiian Is
4C3 **Kilbuck Mts** USA
74B2 **Kilchu** N Korea
109D1 **Kilcoy** Aust
45C2 **Kildare** County, Irish Rep
45C2 **Kildare** Irish Rep
19B3 **Kilgore** USA
99D3 **Kilifi** Kenya
99D3 **Kilimanjaro** *Mt* Tanz
99D3 **Kilindoni** Tanz
92C2 **Kilis** Turk
45B2 **Kilkee** Irish Rep
45C2 **Kilkenny** County, Irish Rep
45C2 **Kilkenny** Irish Rep
45B2 **Kilkieran B** Irish Rep
55B2 **Kilkís** Greece
45B1 **Killala B** Irish Rep
45B2 **Killaloe** Irish Rep
109D1 **Killarney** Aust
41B3 **Killarney** Irish Rep
19A3 **Killeen** USA
12D1 **Killik** *R* USA
44B3 **Killin** Scot
55B3 **Killíni** *Mt* Greece
45B1 **Killybegs** Irish Rep
42B2 **Kilmarnock** Scot
61H2 **Kil'mez** Russian Fed
99D3 **Kilosa** Tanz
41B3 **Kilrush** Irish Rep
99C3 **Kilwa** Zaïre
99D3 **Kilwa Kisiwani** Tanz
99D3 **Kilwa Kivinje** Tanz
108A2 **Kimba** Aust
12F2 **Kimball,Mt** USA
13D3 **Kimberley** Can
101F1 **Kimberley** S Africa
106B2 **Kimberley Plat** Aust
74B2 **Kimch'aek** N Korea
74B3 **Kimch'ŏn** S Korea
55B3 **Kími** Greece
60E2 **Kimry** Russian Fed
70C3 **Kinabalu** *Mt* Malay
78D1 **Kinabatangan** *R* Malay
14B2 **Kincardine** Can
13B1 **Kincolith** Can
19B3 **Kinder** USA
13F2 **Kindersley** Can
97A3 **Kindia** Guinea
98C3 **Kindu** Zaïre
61H3 **Kinel'** Russian Fed
61F2 **Kineshma** Russian Fed
109D1 **Kingaroy** Aust
21A2 **King City** USA
5F4 **Kingcome Inlet** Can
7C4 **King George Is** Can
107D4 **King I** Aust
13B2 **King I** Can
106B2 **King Leopold Range** *Mts* Aust
9B3 **Kingman** USA
98C3 **Kingombe** Zaïre
108A2 **Kingoonya** Aust
22C2 **Kingsburg** USA
21B2 **Kings Canyon Nat Pk** USA
108A3 **Kingscote** Aust
106B2 **King Sd** Aust
112C2 **King Sejong** *Base* Ant
14A1 **Kingsford** USA
17B1 **Kingsland** USA
43E3 **King's Lynn** Eng
16C2 **Kings Park** USA
8B2 **Kings Peak** *Mt* USA
107C4 **Kingston** Aust
7C5 **Kingston** Can
25E3 **Kingston** Jamaica
15D2 **Kingston** New York, USA
111A3 **Kingston** NZ
27E4 **Kingstown** St Vincent and the Grenadines
9D4 **Kingsville** USA
44B3 **Kingussie** Scot
4J3 **King William I** Can
100B4 **King William's Town** S Africa
98B3 **Kinkala** Congo
39G7 **Kinna** Sweden
44D3 **Kinnairds Head** *Pt* Scot
75B1 **Kinomoto** Japan
44C3 **Kinross** Scot
45B3 **Kinsale** Irish Rep
98B3 **Kinshasa** Zaïre
78D3 **Kintap** Indon
42B2 **Kintyre** *Pen* Scot
13D1 **Kinuso** Can
99D2 **Kinyeti** *Mt* Sudan
55B3 **Kiparissía** Greece
55B3 **Kiparissiakós Kólpos** *G* Greece
15C1 **Kipawa,L** Can
99D3 **Kipili** Tanz
12B3 **Kipnuk** USA
45C2 **Kippure** *Mt* Irish Rep
100B2 **Kipushi** Zaïre
63C2 **Kirensk** Russian Fed
65J5 **Kirghizia** Republic, Asia
82B1 **Kirgizskiy Khrebet** *Mts* Kirghizia
98B3 **Kiri** Zaïre
105G4 **Kiribati** *Is* Pacific O
92B2 **Kırıkkale** Turk
99D3 **Kirinyaga** *Mt* Kenya
60D2 **Kirishi** Russian Fed
85B3 **Kirithar Range** *Mts* Pak
55C3 **Kirkağaç** Turk
90A2 **Kirk Bulāg Dāgh** *Mt* Iran
42C2 **Kirkby** Eng
44C3 **Kirkcaldy** Scot
42B2 **Kirkcudbright** Scot
38K5 **Kirkenes** Nor
7B5 **Kirkland Lake** Can
112A **Kirkpatrick,Mt** Ant
10A2 **Kirksville** USA
93D2 **Kirkūk** Iraq
44C2 **Kirkwall** Scot
18B2 **Kirkwood** USA
60D3 **Kirov** Russian Fed
61G2 **Kirov** Russian Fed
93D1 **Kirovakan** Armenia
61J2 **Kirovgrad** Russian Fed
60D4 **Kirovograd** Ukraine
61H2 **Kirs** Russian Fed
92B2 **Kırşehir** Turk
56C2 **Kiruna** Sweden
75B1 **Kiryū** Japan
98C2 **Kisangani** Zaïre
75B1 **Kisarazu** Japan
86B1 **Kishanganj** India
85C3 **Kishangarh** India
60C4 **Kishinev** Moldova
75B2 **Kishiwada** Japan
99D3 **Kisii** Kenya
99D3 **Kisiju** Tanz
59B3 **Kiskunhalas** Hung
65F5 **Kislovodsk** Russian Fed
99E3 **Kismaayo** Somalia
75B1 **Kiso-sammyaku** *Mts* Japan
97A4 **Kissidougou** Guinea
17B2 **Kissimmee,L** USA
99D3 **Kisumu** Kenya
59C3 **Kisvárda** Hung
97B3 **Kita** Mali
65H6 **Kitab** Uzbekistan
75C1 **Kitakata** Japan
74C4 **Kita-Kyūshū** Japan
99D2 **Kitale** Kenya
69G4 **Kitalo** *I* Japan
74E2 **Kitami** Japan
7B5 **Kitchener** Can
99D2 **Kitgum** Uganda
55B3 **Kíthira** *I* Greece
55B3 **Kíthnos** *I* Greece
94A1 **Kiti,C** Cyprus
4H3 **Kitikmeot** *Region* Can
5F4 **Kitimat** Can
38K5 **Kitnen** *R* Fin
75A2 **Kitsuki** Japan
15C2 **Kittanning** USA
38J5 **Kittilä** Fin
99D3 **Kitunda** Tanz
13B1 **Kitwanga** Can
100B2 **Kitwe** Zambia
57C3 **Kitzbühel** Austria
47E1 **Kitzbühler Alpen** *Mts* Austria
57C3 **Kitzingen** Germany
98C3 **Kiumbi** Zaïre
12B1 **Kivalina** USA
59D2 **Kivercy** Ukraine
99C3 **Kivu,L** Zaïre/Rwanda
4B3 **Kiwalik** USA
60D3 **Kiyev** Ukraine
61J2 **Kizel** Russian Fed
92C2 **Kizil** *R* Turk
80D2 **Kizyl-Arvat** Turkmenistan
90B2 **Kizyl-Atrek** Turkmenistan
57C2 **Kladno** Czech Republic
57C3 **Klagenfurt** Austria
60B2 **Klaipēda** Lithuania
8A2 **Klamath** USA
20B2 **Klamath** *R* USA
8A2 **Klamath Falls** USA
20B2 **Klamath Mts** USA
57C3 **Klatovy** Czech Republic
12H3 **Klawak** USA
94B1 **Kleiat** Leb
101G1 **Klerksdorp** S Africa
60E2 **Klin** Russian Fed
58B1 **Klintehamn** Sweden
60D3 **Klintsy** Russian Fed
52C2 **Ključ** Bosnia-Herzegovina
59B2 **Klodzko** Pol
12G2 **Klondike** *R* Can/USA
4D3 **Klondike Plat** Can/USA
59B3 **Klosterneuburg** Austria
12G2 **Kluane** *R* Can
12G2 **Kluane L** Can
12G2 **Kluane Nat Pk** Can
59B2 **Kluczbork** Pol
12G3 **Klukwan** USA
12E2 **Klutina L** USA
12E2 **Knight I** USA
43C3 **Knighton** Wales
52C2 **Knin** Croatia
106A4 **Knob,C** Aust
46B1 **Knokke-Heist** Belg
112C9 **Knox Coast** Ant
11B3 **Knoxville** Tennessee, USA
6H3 **Knud Ramsussens Land** *Region* Greenland
78B3 **Koba** Indon
6F3 **Kobbermirebugt** Greenland
74D4 **Kobe** Japan
56C1 **København** Den
57B2 **Koblenz** Germany
60B3 **Kobrin** Russian Fed
71E4 **Kobroör** *I* Indon
12C1 **Kobuk** *R* USA
54B2 **Kočani** Macedonia
76C3 **Ko Chang** *I* Thai
86B1 **Koch Bihār** India
47D1 **Kochel** Germany
6C3 **Koch I** Can
Kochi = Cochin
74C4 **Kōchi** Japan
12D3 **Kodiak** USA
12D3 **Kodiak I** USA
87B2 **Kodiyakkari** India
99D2 **Kodok** Sudan
100A3 **Koes** Namibia
101G1 **Koffiefontein** S Africa
97B4 **Koforidua** Ghana
74D3 **Kōfu** Japan
75B1 **Koga** Japan
39G7 **Køge** Den
84C2 **Kohat** Pak
84B2 **Koh-i-Baba** *Mts* Afghan
84B1 **Koh-i-Hisar** *Mts* Afghan
84B2 **Koh-i-Khurd** *Mt* Afghan
86C1 **Kohīma** India
84B1 **Koh-i-Mazar** *Mt* Afghan
84B3 **Kohlu** Pak
60C2 **Kohtla Järve** Eston
75B1 **Koide** Japan
12F2 **Koidern** Can
77A4 **Koihoa** *Is* Nicobar
74B4 **Kōje-do** *I* S Korea
65H4 **Kokchetav** Kazakhstan
39J6 **Kokemaki** *L* Fin
38J6 **Kokkola** Fin
107D1 **Kokoda** PNG
14A2 **Kokomo** USA
71E4 **Kokonau** Indon
65K5 **Kokpekty** Kazakhstan
7D4 **Koksoak** *R* Can
100B4 **Kokstad** S Africa
76C3 **Ko Kut** *I* Thai
38L5 **Kola** Russian Fed
71D4 **Kolaka** Indon
77B4 **Ko Lanta** *I* Thai
Kollam = Quilon
87B2 **Kolār** India
87B2 **Kolār Gold Fields** India
97A3 **Kolda** Sen
39F7 **Kolding** Den
87A1 **Kolhāpur** India
12C3 **Koliganek** USA
59B2 **Kolín** Czech Repub
57B2 **Köln** Germany
58B2 **Kolo** Pol
58B2 **Kolobrzeg** Pol
97B3 **Kolokani** Mali
60E2 **Kolomna** Russian Fed
60C4 **Kolomyya** Ukraine
65K4 **Kolpashevo** Russian Fed
55C3 **Kólpos Merabéllou** Greece
55B2 **Kólpos Singitikós** Greece
55B2 **Kólpos Strimonikó** *G* Greece
55B2 **Kólpos Toronaíos** Greece
38L5 **Kol'skiy Poluostro** *Pen* Russian Fed
38G6 **Kolvereid** Nor
100B2 **Kolwezi** Zaïre
1C7 **Kolyma** *R* Russian Fed
54B2 **Kom** *Mt* Bulg/Ser Yugos
99D2 **Koma** Eth
97D3 **Komaduga Gana** Nig
59B3 **Komárno** Slovakia
101H1 **Komati** *R* S Africa
74D3 **Komatsu** Japan

75A2 **Komatsushima** Japan
64G3 **Komi Respublika,** Russian Fed
70C4 **Komodo** *I* Indon
71E4 **Komoran** *I* Indon
75B1 **Komoro** Japan
55C2 **Komotiní** Greece
76D3 **Kompong Cham** Camb
76C3 **Kompong Chhnang** *Mts* Camb
77C3 **Kompong Som** Camb
76C3 **Kompong Thom** Camb
76D3 **Kompong Trabek** Camb
63F2 **Komsomol'sk na Amure** Russian Fed
65H4 **Konda** *R* Russian Fed
99D3 **Kondoa** Tanz
87B1 **Kondukūr** India
6G3 **Kong Christian IX Land** *Region* Greenland
6F3 **Kong Frederik VI Kyst** *Mts* Greenland
64C2 **Kong Karls Land** *Is* Barents S
78D2 **Kongkemul** *Mt* Indon
98C3 **Kongolo** Zaïre
39F7 **Kongsberg** Den
39G6 **Kongsvinger** Nor
Königsberg = Kaliningrad
58B2 **Konin** Pol
54A2 **Konjic** Bosnia-Herzegovina
61F1 **Konosha** Russian Fed
75B1 **Konosu** Japan
60D3 **Konotop** Ukraine
59C2 **Końskie** Pol
49D2 **Konstanz** Germany
97C3 **Kontagora** Nig
76D3 **Kontum** Viet
92B2 **Konya** Turk
13D3 **Kootenay** *R* Can
35C5 **Kopargaon** India
6J3 **Kópasker** Iceland
38A2 **Kópavogur** Iceland
52B1 **Koper** Slovenia
90D2 **Kopet Dag** *Mts* Iran/Turkmenistan
61K2 **Kopeysk** Russian Fed
77C4 **Ko Phangan** *I* Thai
77B4 **Ko Phuket** *I* Thai
39H7 **Köping** Sweden
87B1 **Koppal** India
52C1 **Koprivnica** Croatia
85B4 **Korangi** Pak
87C1 **Koraput** India
86A2 **Korba** India
57B2 **Korbach** Germany
4B3 **Korbuk** *R* USA
55B2 **Korçë** Alb
52C2 **Korčula** *I* Croatia
72E2 **Korea B** China/Korea
74B4 **Korea Str** S Korea/Japan
59D2 **Korec** Ukraine
92B1 **Körğlu Tepesi** *Mt* Turk
97B4 **Korhogo** Ivory Coast
85B4 **Kori Creek** India
55B3 **Korinthiakós Kólpos** *G* Greece
55B3 **Kórinthos** Greece
74E3 **Kōriyama** Japan
61K3 **Korkino** Russian Fed
92B2 **Korkuteli** Turk
82C1 **Korla** China
52C2 **Kornat** *I* Croatia
90D5 **Köroğlu Tepesi** *Mt* Turk
99D3 **Korogwe** Tanz
33B3 **Koroit** Aust
71E3 **Koror** Palau Is, Pacific O
59C3 **Körös** *R* Hung
60C3 **Korosten** Ukraine
95A3 **Koro Toro** Chad
12B3 **Korovin** *I* USA
69G2 **Korsakov** Russian Fed
39G7 **Korsør** Den
46B1 **Kortrijk** Belg
55C3 **Kós** *I* Greece
77C4 **Ko Samui** *I* Thai
58B2 **Koscierzyna** Pol
107D4 **Kosciusko** *Mt* Aust
12H3 **Kosciusko I** USA
74B4 **Koshikijima-retto** *I* Japan
59C3 **Košice** Slovakia
74B3 **Kosong** N Korea
54B2 **Kosovo** Aut Republic, Serbia, Yugos
97B4 **Kossou** *L* Ivory Coast
101G1 **Koster** S Africa
99D1 **Kosti** Sudan
59D2 **Kostopol'** Ukraine
61F2 **Kostroma** Russian Fed
56C2 **Kostrzyn** Pol
39H8 **Koszalin** Pol
85D3 **Kota** India
78A4 **Kotaagung** Indon
78C3 **Kotabaharu** Indon
78D3 **Kotabaru** Indon
77C4 **Kota Bharu** Malay
78A3 **Kotabum** Indon
84C2 **Kot Addu** Pak
78D1 **Kota Kinabulu** Malay
87C1 **Kotapad** India
61G2 **Kotel'nich** Russian Fed
61F4 **Kotel'nikovo** Russian Fed
39K6 **Kotka** Fin
64F3 **Kotlas** Russian Fed
12B2 **Kotlik** USA
54A2 **Kotor** Montenegro, Yugos
60C4 **Kotovsk** Ukraine
85B3 **Kotri** Pak
87C1 **Kottagūdem** India
87B3 **Kottayam** India
98C2 **Kotto** *R* CAR
87B2 **Kottūru** India
12B1 **Kotzebue** USA
4B3 **Kotzebue Sd** USA
97C3 **Kouande** Benin
98C2 **Kouango** CAR
97B3 **Koudougou** Burkina
98B3 **Koulamoutou** Gabon
97B3 **Koulikoro** Mali
97B3 **Koupéla** Burkina
33G2 **Kourou** French Guiana
97B3 **Kouroussa** Guinea
98B1 **Kousséri** Cam
39K6 **Kouvola** Fin
38L5 **Kovdor** Russian Fed
60B3 **Kovel'** Ukraine
Kovno = Kaunas
61F2 **Kovrov** Russian Fed
61F3 **Kovylkino** Russian Fed
60E1 **Kovzha** *R* Russian Fed
77C4 **Ko Way** *I* Thai
73C5 **Kowloon** Hong Kong
84B2 **Kowt-e-Ashrow** Afghan
92A2 **Köyceğğiz** Turk
38L5 **Koydor** Russian Fed
87A1 **Koyna Res** India
12B2 **Koyuk** USA
12B1 **Koyuk** *R* USA
12C2 **Koyukuk** USA
12C1 **Koyukuk** *R* USA
92C2 **Kozan** Turk
55B2 **Kozańi** Greece
Kozhikode = Calicut
61G2 **Koz'modemyansk** Russian Fed
75B2 **Kōzu-shima** *I* Japan
39F7 **Kragerø** Nor
54B2 **Kragujevac** Serbia, Yugos
77B3 **Kra,Isthmus of** Burma/Malay
Krakatau = Rakata
94C1 **Krak des Chevaliers** *Hist Site* Syria
Kraków = Cracow
54B2 **Kraljevo** Serbia, Yugos
60E4 **Kramatorsk** Ukraine
38H6 **Kramfors** Sweden
52B1 **Kranj** Slovenia
61G1 **Krasavino** Russian Fed
64G2 **Krasino** Russian Fed
59C2 **Kraśnik** Pol
61G3 **Krasnoarmeysk** Russian Fed
60E5 **Krasnodar** Russian Fed
61J2 **Krasnokamsk** Russian Fed
61K2 **Krasnotur'insk** Russian Fed
61J2 **Krasnoufimsk** Russian Fed
61J3 **Krasnousol'-skiy** Russian Fed
65G3 **Krasnovishersk** Russian Fed
65G5 **Krasnovodsk** Turkmenistan
63B2 **Krasnoyarsk** Russian Fed
59C2 **Krasnystaw** Pol
61G3 **Krasnyy Kut** Russian Fed
60E4 **Krasnyy Luch** Ukraine
61G4 **Krasnyy Yar** Russian Fed
76D3 **Kratie** Camb
6E2 **Kraulshavn** Greenland
56B2 **Krefeld** Germany
60D4 **Kremenchug** Ukraine
60D4 **Kremenchugskoye Vodokhranilische** *Res* Ukraine
59D2 **Kremenets** Ukraine
98A2 **Kribi** Cam
60D3 **Krichev** Belorussia
47E1 **Krimml** Austria
87B1 **Krishna** *R* India
87B2 **Krishnagiri** India
86B2 **Krishnangar** India
39F7 **Kristiansand** Nor
39G7 **Kristianstad** Sweden
64B3 **Kristiansund** Nor
39G7 **Kristinehamn** Sweden
38J6 **Kristiinankaupunki** Fin
55B3 **Kríti** *I* Greece
60D4 **Krivoy Rog** Ukraine
52B1 **Krk** *I* Croatia
6G3 **Kronpris Frederik Bjerge** *Mts* Greenland
39K7 **Kronshtadt** Russian Fed
101G1 **Kroonstad** S Africa
65F5 **Kropotkin** Russian Fed
101G1 **Krugersdorp** S Africa
78A4 **Krui** Indon
55A2 **Kruje** Alb
58D2 **Krupki** Belorussia
12B1 **Krusenstern,C** USA
54B2 **Kruševac** Serbia, Yugos
39K7 **Krustpils** Latvia
12G3 **Kruzof I** USA
65E5 **Krym** *Pen* Ukraine
60E5 **Krymsk** Russian Fed
58B2 **Krzyz** Pol
96C1 **Ksar El Boukhari** Alg
96B1 **Ksar el Kebir** Mor
70A3 **Kuala** Indon
77C5 **Kuala Dungun** Malay
77C4 **Kuala Kerai** Malay
77C5 **Kuala Kubu Baharu** Malay
77C5 **Kuala Lipis** Malay
77C5 **Kuala Lumpur** Malay
77C4 **Kuala Trengganu** Malay
78D1 **Kuamut** Malay
74A2 **Kuandian** China
77C5 **Kuantan** Malay
93E1 **Kuba** Azerbaijan
71F4 **Kubar** PNG
78C2 **Kuching** Malay
70C3 **Kudat** Malay
78C4 **Kudus** Indon
61H2 **Kudymkar** Russian Fed
57C3 **Kufstein** Austria
90C3 **Kuh Duren** *Upland* Iran
91C4 **Kūh e Bazmān** *Mt* Iran
90B3 **Kūh-e Dinar** *Mt* Iran
90C2 **Kūh-e-Hazār Masjed** *Mts* Iran
91C4 **Kūh-e Jebāl Barez** *Mts* Iran
90B3 **Kūh-e Karkas** *Mts* Iran
91C4 **Kuh-e Laleh Zar** *Mt* Iran
90A2 **Kūh-e Sahand** *Mt* Iran
91D4 **Kuh e Taftān** *Mt* Iran
90A2 **Kūhhaye Sabalan** *Mts* Iran
90A3 **Kūhhā-ye Zāgros** *Mts* Iran
38K6 **Kuhmo** Fin
90B3 **Kūhpāyeh** Iran
90C3 **Kūhpāyeh** *Mt* Iran
91C4 **Kūh ye Bashākerd** *Mts* Iran
90A2 **Kūh ye Sabalan** *Mt* Iran
100A3 **Kuibis** Namibia
4B4 **Kuigillingok** USA
100A2 **Kuito** Angola
12H3 **Kuiu I** USA
74E2 **Kuji** Japan
75A2 **Kuju-san** *Mt* Japan
12C3 **Kukaklek L** USA
54B2 **Kukës** Alb
77C5 **Kukup** Malay
91C4 **Kūl** *R* Iran
55C3 **Kula** Turk
61J4 **Kulakshi** Kazakhstan
99D2 **Kulal,Mt** Kenya
55B2 **Kulata** Bulg
60B2 **Kuldīga** Latvia
61H4 **Kul'sary** Kazakhstan
84D2 **Kulu** India
92B2 **Kulu** Turk
65J4 **Kulunda** Russian Fed
108B2 **Kulwin** Aust
61G5 **Kuma** *R* Russian Fed
75B1 **Kumagaya** Japan
78C3 **Kumai** Indon
74C4 **Kumamoto** Japan
75B2 **Kumano** Japan
54B2 **Kumanovo** Macedonia
63E2 **Kumara** China
97B4 **Kumasi** Ghana
65F5 **Kumayri** Armenia
98A2 **Kumba** Cam
87B2 **Kumbakonam** India
61J3 **Kumertau** Russian Fed
74B3 **Kŭmhwa** S Korea
39H7 **Kumla** Sweden
87A2 **Kumta** India
82C1 **Kümüx** China
84C2 **Kunar** *R* Afghan
39K7 **Kunda** Estonia
87A2 **Kundāpura** India
85C4 **Kundla** India
84B1 **Kunduz** Afghan
89F9 **Kunene** *R* Angola
39G7 **Kungsbacka** Sweden
61J2 **Kungur** Russian Fed
76B1 **Kunhing** Burma
82B2 **Kunlun Shan** *Mts* China
73A4 **Kunming** China
74B3 **Kunsan** S Korea
38K6 **Kuopio** Fin
52C1 **Kupa** *R* Croatia/Bosnia-Herzegovina
106B2 **Kupang** Indon
107D2 **Kupiano** PNG
12H3 **Kupreanof I** USA

60E4 **Kupyansk** Ukraine
82C1 **Kuqa** China
75B1 **Kurabe** Japan
74C4 **Kurashiki** Japan
75A1 **Kurayoshi** Japan
54C2 **Kürdzhali** Bulg
74C4 **Kure** Japan
60B2 **Kuressaare** Estonia
63A1 **Kureyka** *R* Russian Fed
65H4 **Kurgan** Russian Fed
88K6 **Kuria Muria Is** Oman
38J6 **Kurikka** Fin
Kuril Is = Kuril'skoye Osrova
69H2 **Kuril'skiye Ostrova** Russian Fed
87B1 **Kurnool** India
75C1 **Kuroiso** Japan
111B2 **Kurow** NZ
109D2 **Kurri Kurri** Aust
60E3 **Kursk** Russian Fed
Kurskiy Zaliv = Courland Lagoon
68A2 **Kuruktag** *R* China
100B3 **Kuruman** S Africa
74C4 **Kurume** Japan
87C3 **Kurunegala** Sri Lanka
65K5 **Kurunktag** *R* China
61J2 **Kusa** Russian Fed
55C3 **Kuşadasi Körfezi** *B* Turk
55C2 **Kus Golü** *L* Turk
74D4 **Kushimoto** Japan
74E2 **Kushiro** Japan
86B2 **Kushtia** Bang
61H3 **Kushum** *R* Kazakhstan
80E2 **Kushra** Afgan
65G4 **Kushva** Russian Fed
12B2 **Kuskokwim** *R* USA
12B3 **Kuskokwim B** USA
12C2 **Kuskokwim Mts** USA
86A1 **Kusma** Nepal
74E2 **Kussharo-ko** *L* Japan
65H4 **Kustanay** Kazakhstan
92A2 **Kütahya** Turk
78D3 **Kutai** *R* Indon
59B3 **Kutná Hora** Czech Republic
58B2 **Kutno** Pol
98B3 **Kutu** Zaïre
86C2 **Kutubdia I** Bang
98C1 **Kutum** Sudan
7D4 **Kuujjuaq** Can
7C4 **Kuujjuarapik** Can
38K5 **Kuusamo** Fin
61J3 **Kuvandyk** Russian Fed
93E4 **Kuwait** Kuwait
80C3 **Kuwait** Sheikdom, S W Asia
75B1 **Kuwana** Japan
Kuybyshev = Samara
65J4 **Kuybyshev** Russian Fed
61G3 **Kuybyshevskoye Vodokhranilishche** *Res* Russian Fed
63C2 **Kuytun** Russian Fed
60E5 **Kuzey Anadolu Daglari** *Mts* Turk
61G3 **Kuznetsk** Russian Fed
38J4 **Kvaenangen** *Sd* Nor
12C3 **Kvichak** USA
12C3 **Kvichak** *R* USA
12C3 **Kvichak B** USA
38G5 **Kvigtind** *Mt* Nor
38H5 **Kvikkjokk** Sweden
99D3 **Kwale** Kenya
74B3 **Kwangju** S Korea
98B3 **Kwango** *R* Zaïre
100B2 **Kwekwe** Zim
12B2 **Kwethluk** USA
12B2 **Kwethluk** *R* USA
58B2 **Kwidzyn** Pol
71E4 **Kwoka** *Mt* Indon
108C3 **Kyabram** Aust
76B2 **Kyaikkami** Burma
76B2 **Kyaikto** Burma
68C1 **Kyakhta** Russian Fed
108A2 **Kyancutta** Aust
76B1 **Kyaukme** Burma
76B1 **Kyauk-padaung** Burma
76A2 **Kyaukpyu** Burma
40B2 **Kyle of Lochalsh** Scot
46D1 **Kyll** *R* Germany
108B3 **Kyneton** Aust
99D2 **Kyoga** *L* Uganda
109D1 **Kyogle** Aust
74B3 **Kyŏngju** S Korea
74D3 **Kyoto** Japan
Kyrgyzstan = Kirghizia
65H4 **Kyshtym** Russian Fed
74C4 **Kyūshū** *I* Japan
104E3 **Kyushu-Palau Ridge** Pacific O
54B2 **Kyustendil** Bulg
68B1 **Kyzyl** Russian Fed
65H5 **Kyzylkum** *Desert* Uzbekistan
65H5 **Kzyl Orda** Kazakhstan

L

99E2 **Laascaanood** Somalia
46E1 **Laasphe** Germany
99E1 **Laasqoray** Somalia
33E1 **La Asunción** Ven
96A2 **Laâyoune** Mor
23A1 **La Barca** Mexico
97A3 **Labé** Guinea
59B2 **Labe** *R* Czech Republic
15D1 **Labelle** Can
17B2 **La Belle** USA
12G2 **Laberge,L** Can
78D1 **Labi** Brunei
13E2 **la Biche,L** Can
61F5 **Labinsk** Russian Fed
94C1 **Laboué** Leb
34C2 **Laboulaye** Arg
7D4 **Labrador** *Region* Can
7D4 **Labrador City** Can
7E4 **Labrador S** Greenland/Can
33E5 **Lábrea** Brazil
78D1 **Labuan** *I* Malay
78B4 **Labuhan** Indon
76A2 **Labutta** Burma
65H3 **Labytnangi** Russian Fed
7C4 **Lac á L'eau Claire** Can
46B2 **La Capelle** France
34C2 **La Carlota** Arg
79B3 **La Carlota** Phil
12J1 **Lac Belot** *L* Can
7C4 **Lac Bienville** *L* Can
83B4 **Laccadive Is** India
47B2 **Lac d'Annecy** *L* France
4G3 **Lac de Gras** *L* Can
47B1 **Lac de Joux** *L* Switz
47B1 **Lac de Neuchâtel** *L* Switz
23A2 **Lac de Patzcuaro** *L* Mexico
23A2 **Lac de Sayula** *L* Mexico
4F3 **Lac des Bois** *L* Can
47A2 **Lac du Bourget** *L* France
25D3 **La Ceiba** Honduras
108A3 **Lacepede B** Aust
48C2 **La Châtre** France
47B1 **La-Chaux-de-Fonds** Switz
94B3 **Lachish** *Hist Site* Israel
107D4 **Lachlan** *R* Aust
32B2 **La Chorrera** Panama
15D1 **Lachute** Can
7D4 **Lac Joseph** *L* Can
15C2 **Lackawanna** USA
5G4 **Lac la Biche** Can
4G3 **Lac la Martre** *L* Can
5H4 **Lac la Ronge** *L* Can
52A1 **Lac Léman** *L* Switz/France
10C1 **Lac Manouane** *L* Can
15D1 **Lac Megantic** Can
7C4 **Lac Mistassini** *L* Can
13E2 **Lacombe** Can
15D2 **Laconia** USA
50A1 **La Coruña** Spain
10A2 **La Crosse** USA
9C3 **La Cruces** USA
7A4 **Lac Seul** *L* Can
18B2 **La Cygne** USA
84D2 **Ladākh Range** India
85C3 **Lādnūn** India
73B5 **Ladong** China
60D1 **Ladozhskoye Ozero** *L* Ukraine
6B2 **Lady Ann Str** Can
109C4 **Lady Barron** Aust
101G1 **Ladybrand** S Africa
13C3 **Ladysmith** Can
101G1 **Ladysmith** S Africa
71F4 **Lae** PNG
76C3 **Laem Ngop** Thai
56C1 **Laesø** *I* Den
10B2 **Lafayette** Indiana, USA
11A3 **Lafayette** Louisiana, USA
46B2 **La Fère** France
46B2 **La-Ferté-sous-Jouarre** France
97C4 **Lafia** Nig
97C4 **Lafiagi** Nig
48B2 **La Flèche** France
96C1 **La Galite** *I* Tunisia
61G4 **Lagan'** Russian Fed
56C1 **Lagan** *R* Sweden
31D4 **Lagarto** Brazil
96C1 **Laghouat** Alg
35C2 **Lagoa de Araruama** Brazil
29F2 **Lagoa dos Patos** *Lg* Brazil
35C2 **Lagoa Feia** Brazil
32B4 **Lago Agrio** Ecuador
35C1 **Lagoa Juparanã** *L* Brazil
29D2 **Lagoa mar Chiguita** *L* Arg
29F2 **Lagoa Mirim** *L* Brazil/Urug
29B6 **Lago Argentino** *L* Arg
29B5 **Lago Buenos Aries** *L* Arg
29B5 **Lago Cochrane** *L* Arg/Chile
29C5 **Lago Colhué Huapi** *L* Arg
24B2 **Lago de Chapala** *L* Mexico
32A2 **Lago de Chiriqui** *L* Panama
23A2 **Lago de Cuitzeo** *L* Mexico
29B3 **Lago de la Laja** *L* Chile
53A2 **Lago del Coghinas** *L* Sardegna
32C2 **Lago de Maracaibo** *L* Ven
25D3 **Lago de Nicaragua** *L* Nic
32A1 **Lago de Perlas** *L* Nic
52B2 **Lago di Bolsena** *L* Italy
52B2 **Lago di Bracciano** *L* Italy
52A1 **Lago di Como** *L* Italy
47D2 **Lago d'Idro** *L* Italy
52B1 **Lago di Garda** *L* Italy
47C2 **Lago di Lecco** *L* Italy
47C2 **Lago di Lugano** *L* Italy
47D2 **Lago d'Iseo** *L* Italy
47C2 **Lago d'Orta** *L* Italy
29B5 **Lago General Carrera** *L* Chile
52A1 **Lago Maggiore** *L* Italy
29C5 **Lago Musters** *L* Arg
48B3 **Lagon** France
29B4 **Lago Nahuel Haupi** Arg
29B5 **Lago O'Higgins** *L* Chile
53A2 **Lago Omodeo** *L* Sardegna
30C2 **Lago Poopó** *L* Bol
29B4 **Lago Ranco** *L* Chile
32D6 **Lago Rogaguado** *L* Bol
97C4 **Lagos** Nig
50A2 **Lagos** Port
29B5 **Lago San Martin** *L* Arg/Chile
24B2 **Lagos de Moreno** Mexico
30C2 **Lago Titicaca** Bol/Peru
29B5 **Lago Viedma** *L* Ar
8B2 **La Grande** USA
106B2 **Lagrange** Aust
11B3 **La Grange** Georgia USA
14A3 **La Grange** Kentuck USA
19A4 **La Grange** Texas, USA
33E2 **La Gran Sabana** *M* Ven
47B2 **La Grave** France
48B3 **Lagronño** Spain
34A3 **Laguna Aluminé** *L* Arg
21B3 **Laguna Beach** US
34C3 **Laguna Colorada Grande** *L* Arg
79B3 **Laguna de Bay** *Lg* Phil
25D3 **Laguna de Caratas** *Lg* Honduras
25D4 **Laguna de Chiriqui** Panama
25D3 **Laguna de Managu** *L* Nic
25D3 **Laguna de Nicarag** *L* Nic
26A4 **Laguna de Perlas** Nic
23B1 **Laguna de Pueblo Viejo** *L* Mexico
24C2 **Laguna de Tamiah** *Lg* Mexico
25C3 **Laguna de Términ** *Lg* Mexico
23A1 **Laguna de Yuriria** Mexico
23B1 **Laguna le Altamir** Mexico
24C2 **Laguna Madre** *Lg* Mexico
34C2 **Laguna Mar Chiqu** *L* Arg
29B4 **Laguna Nahuel Hu** *L* Arg
34C2 **Laguna Paiva** Arg
29B4 **Laguna Ranco** Ch
9C4 **Laguna Seca** Mex
23B1 **Laguna Tortugas** Mexico
70C3 **Lahad Datu** Malay
78A3 **Lahat** Indon
38J6 **Lahia** Fin
90B2 **Lāhījān** Iran
46D1 **Lahn** *R* Germany
46D1 **Lahnstein** Germa
84C2 **Lahore** Pak
39K6 **Lahti** Fin
23A2 **La Huerta** Mexico
98B2 **Lai** Chad
73B5 **Laibin** China
76C1 **Lai Chau** Viet
100B4 **Laingsburg** S Afri
44B2 **Lairg** Scot
78A3 **Lais** Indon
79C4 **Lais** Phil
72E2 **Laiyang** China
72D2 **Laizhou Wan** *B* China
34A3 **Laja** *R* Chile
30F4 **Lajes** Brazil
22D4 **La Jolla** USA
9C3 **La Junta** USA
109C2 **Lake Cargelligo**
11A3 **Lake Charles** US

17B1 **Lake City** Florida, USA
17C1 **Lake City** S Carolina, USA
42C2 **Lake District** Region, Eng
22D4 **Lake Elsinore** USA
106C3 **Lake Eyre Basin** Aust
15C2 **Lakefield** Can
6D3 **Lake Harbour** Can
22C3 **Lake Hughes** USA
16B2 **Lakehurst** USA
19A4 **Lake Jackson** USA
13E2 **Lake la Biche** Can
17B2 **Lakeland** USA
7A5 **Lake of the Woods** Can
20B1 **Lake Oswego** USA
21A2 **Lakeport** USA
19B3 **Lake Providence** USA
111B2 **Lake Pukaki** NZ
109C3 **Lakes Entrance** Aust
22C2 **Lakeshore** USA
108B1 **Lake Stewart** Aust
15C1 **Lake Traverse** Can
8A2 **Lakeview** USA
20B1 **Lakeview Mt** Can
19B3 **Lake Village** USA
17B2 **Lake Wales** USA
22C4 **Lakewood** California, USA
16B2 **Lakewood** New Jersey, USA
14B2 **Lakewood** Ohio, USA
17B2 **Lake Worth** USA
86A1 **Lakhīmpur** India
85B4 **Lakhpat** India
84C2 **Lakki** Pak
55B3 **Lakonikós Kólpos** *G* Greece
97B4 **Lakota** Ivory Coast
38K4 **Laksefjord** *Inlet* Nor
38K4 **Lakselv** Nor
34C2 **La Laguna** Arg
32A4 **La Libertad** Ecuador
34A2 **La Ligua** Chile
50A2 **La Linea** Spain
85D4 **Lalitpur** India
5H4 **La Loche** Can
13F1 **la Loche,L** Can
46C1 **La Louvière** Belg
26A4 **La Luz** Nic
7C5 **La Malbaie** Can
23B2 **La Malinche** *Mt* Mexico
50B2 **La Mancha** Region, Spain
9C3 **Lamar** Colorado, USA
18B2 **Lamar** Missouri, USA
19A4 **La Marque** USA
98B3 **Lambaréné** Gabon
32A5 **Lambayeque** Peru
2B10 **Lambert Gl** Ant
16B2 **Lambertville** USA
4F2 **Lamblon,C** Can
47C2 **Lambro** *R* Italy
76C2 **Lam Chi** *R* Thai
50A1 **Lamego** Port
47B2 **La Meije** *Mt* France
32B6 **La Merced** Peru
21B3 **La Mesa** USA
55B3 **Lamía** Greece
42C2 **Lammermuir Hills** Scot
39G7 **Lammhult** Sweden
79B3 **Lamon B** Phil
18B1 **Lamoni** USA
71F3 **Lamotrek** *I* Pacific O
43B3 **Lampeter** Wales
99E3 **Lamu** Kenya
47D1 **Lana** Italy
21C4 **Lanai** *I* Hawaiian Is
21C4 **Lanai City** Hawaiian Is
42C2 **Lanark** Scot
76B3 **Lanbi** *I* Burma
76C1 **Lancang** *R* China
42C3 **Lancashire** County, Eng
21B3 **Lancaster** California, USA
42C2 **Lancaster** Eng
18B1 **Lancaster** Mississippi, USA
15D2 **Lancaster** New Hampshire, USA
14B3 **Lancaster** Ohio, USA
10C3 **Lancaster** Pennsylvania, USA
17B1 **Lancaster** S Carolina, USA
6B2 **Lancaster Sd** Can
78B3 **Landak** *R* Indon
46E2 **Landan** Germany
57C3 **Landeck** Austria
8C2 **Lander** USA
34C2 **Landeta** Arg
57C3 **Landsberg** Germany
4F2 **Lands End** *C* Can
43B4 **Land's End** *Pt* Eng
57C3 **Landshut** Germany
39G7 **Làndskrona** Sweden
17A1 **Lanett** USA
56B2 **Langenhagen** Germany
47B1 **Langenthal** Switz
42C2 **Langholm** Scot
38A2 **Langjökull** *Mts* Iceland
77B4 **Langkawi** *I* Malay
13C3 **Langley** Can
108C1 **Langlo** *R* Aust
47B1 **Langnau** Switz
49D2 **Langres** France
70A3 **langsa** Indon
68C2 **Lang Shan** *Mts* China
76D1 **Lang Son** Viet
48C3 **Languedoc** Region, France
29B3 **Lanin** *Mt* Arg
79B4 **Lanoa,L** *L* Phil
16B2 **Lansdale** USA
7B4 **Lansdowne House** Can
16B2 **Lansford** USA
10B2 **Lansing** USA
47B2 **Lanslebourg** France
96A2 **Lanzarote** *I* Canary Is
72A2 **Lanzhou** China
47B2 **Lanzo Torinese** Italy
79B2 **Laoag** Phil
76C1 **Lao Cai** Viet
72D1 **Laoha He** *R* China
45C2 **Laois** County, Irish Rep
46B2 **Laon** France
32B6 **La Oroya** Peru
76C2 **Laos** Republic, S E Asia
49C2 **Lapalisse** France
32B2 **La Palma** Panama
96A2 **La Palma** *I* Canary Is
34B3 **La Pampa** State, Arg
33E2 **La Paragua** Ven
29E2 **La Paz** Arg
34B2 **La Paz** Arg
30C2 **La Paz** Bol
24A2 **La Paz** Mexico
69G2 **La Perouse Str** Japan/Russian Fed
23A1 **La Piedad** Mexico
20B2 **La Pine** USA
19B3 **Laplace** USA
23A2 **la Placita** Mexico
29E2 **La Plata** Arg
13F1 **La Plonge,L** Can
14A2 **La Porte** USA
39K6 **Lappeenranta** Fin
38H5 **Lappland** *Region* Sweden/Fin
34C3 **Laprida** Arg
1B8 **Laptev S** Russian Fed
38J6 **Lapua** Fin
79B3 **Lapu-Lapu** Phil
9B4 **La Purisma** Mexico
95B2 **Laqiya Arba'in** *Well* Sudan
30C3 **La Quiaca** Arg
52B2 **L'Aquila** Italy
91B4 **Lār** Iran
96B1 **Larache** Mor
8C2 **Laramie** USA
8C2 **Laramie Range** *Mts* USA
50B2 **Larca** Spain
9D4 **Laredo** USA
91B4 **Larestan** Region, Iran
Largeau = Faya
47B2 **L'Argentière** France
17B2 **Largo** USA
42B2 **Largs** Scot
90A2 **Lārī** Iran
30C4 **La Rioja** Arg
30C4 **La Rioja** State, Arg
55B3 **Lárisa** Greece
85B3 **Larkana** Pak
92B3 **Larnaca** Cyprus
94A1 **Larnaca B** Cyprus
45D1 **Larne** N Ire
50A1 **La Robla** Spain
46C1 **La Roche-en-Ardenne** Belg
48B2 **La Rochelle** France
47B1 **La Roche-sur-Foron** France
48B2 **La Roche-sur-Yon** France
51B2 **La Roda** Spain
27D3 **La Romana** Dom Rep
5H4 **La Ronge** Can
5H4 **La Ronge,L** Can
39F7 **Larvik** Nor
65J3 **Laryak** Russian Fed
50B2 **La Sagra** *Mt* Spain
15D1 **La Salle** Can
18C1 **La Salle** USA
7C5 **La Sarre** Can
34C1 **Las Avispas** Arg
34A2 **Las Cabras** Chile
5G4 **Lascombe** Can
9C3 **Las Cruces** USA
26C3 **La Selle** *Mt* Haiti
72B2 **Lasengmia** China
30B4 **La Serena** Chile
29E3 **Las Flores** Arg
76B1 **Lashio** Burma
53C3 **La Sila** *Mts* Italy
90B2 **Lāsjerd** Iran
34A3 **Las Lajas** Chile
50A2 **Las Marismas** *Marshland* Spain
96A2 **Las Palmas de Gran Canaria** Canary Is
52A2 **La Spezia** Italy
29C4 **Las Plumas** Arg
34C2 **Las Rosas** Arg
20B2 **Lassen Peak** *Mt* USA
20B2 **Lassen Volcanic Nat Pk** USA
23B2 **las Tinai** Mexico
98B3 **Lastoursville** Gabon
52C2 **Lastovo** *I* Croatia
24B2 **Las Tres Marias** *Is* Mexico
34C2 **Las Varillas** Arg
9C3 **Las Vegas** USA
Latakia = Al Lādhiqīyah
53B2 **Latina** Italy
34B2 **La Toma** Arg
32D1 **La Tortuga** *I* Ven
79B2 **La Trinidad** Phil
109C4 **Latrobe** Aust
94B3 **Latrun** Israel
7C5 **La Tuque** Can
87B1 **Lātūr** India
60B2 **Latvia** Republic, Europe
107D5 **Launceston** Aust
43B4 **Launceston** Eng
29B4 **La Unión** Chile
25D3 **La Union** El Salvador
23A2 **La Union** Mexico
32B5 **La Unión** Peru
107D2 **Laura** Aust
15C3 **Laurel** Delaware, USA
16A3 **Laurel** Maryland, USA
11B3 **Laurel** Mississippi, USA
17B1 **Laurens** USA
17C1 **Laurinburg** USA
52A1 **Lausanne** Switz
78D3 **Laut** *I* Indon
29B5 **Lautaro** *Mt* Chile
46D2 **Lauterecken** Germany
15D1 **Laval** Can
48B2 **Laval** France
22B2 **Laveaga Peak** *Mt* USA
47C2 **Laveno** Italy
31B6 **Lavras** Brazil
4A3 **Lavrentiya** Russian Fed
101H1 **Lavumisa** Swaziland
78D1 **Lawas** Malay
76B1 **Lawksawk** Burma
18A2 **Lawrence** Kansas, USA
15D2 **Lawrence** Massachusetts, USA
111A3 **Lawrence** NZ
14A3 **Lawrenceville** Illinois, USA
9D3 **Lawton** USA
91A5 **Layla** S Arabia
99D2 **Laylo** Sudan
23A2 **Lázaro Cárdenas** Mexico
99E1 **Laz Daua** Somalia
79B4 **Lazi** Phil
8C2 **Lead** USA
13F2 **Leader** Can
18A2 **Leavenworth** USA
58B2 **Leba** Pol
18B2 **Lebanon** Missouri, USA
20B2 **Lebanon** Oregon, USA
15C2 **Lebanon** Pennsylvania, USA
92C3 **Lebanon** Republic, S W Asia
101C3 **Lebombo** *Mts* Mozam/S Africa/ Swaziland
58B2 **Lebork** Pol
47A2 **Le Bourg-d'Oisans** France
47B1 **Le Brassus** Switz
29B3 **Lebu** Chile
47B1 **Le Buet** *Mt* France
46B1 **Le Cateau** France
55A2 **Lecce** Italy
52A1 **Lecco** Italy
47D1 **Lech** *R* Austria
47D1 **Lechtaler Alpen** *Mts* Austria
49C2 **Le Creusot** France
43C3 **Ledbury** Eng
13E2 **Leduc** Can
16C1 **Lee** USA
45B3 **Lee** *R* Irish Rep
41C3 **Leeds** Eng
43C3 **Leek** Eng
56B2 **Leer** Germany
17B2 **Leesburg** Florida, USA
16A3 **Leesburg** Virginia, USA
19B3 **Leesville** USA
109C2 **Leeton** Aust
56B2 **Leeuwarden** Neth
106A4 **Leeuwin,C** Aust
22C2 **Lee Vining** USA
27E3 **Leeward Is** Caribbean S
94A1 **Lefkara** Cyprus
79B3 **Legazpi** Phil
47D2 **Legnago** Italy
59B2 **Legnica** Pol
33F2 **Leguan Inlet** Guyana
32C4 **Leguizamo** Colombia
84D2 **Leh** India
48C2 **Le Havre** France
16B2 **Lehigh** *R* USA
16B2 **Lehighton** USA
84C2 **Leiah** Pak
59B3 **Leibnitz** Austria
43D3 **Leicester** County, Eng
43D3 **Leicester** Eng
107C2 **Leichhardt** *R* Aust
56A2 **Leiden** Neth
46B1 **Leie** *R* Belg
106C4 **Leigh Creek** Aust
43D4 **Leighton Buzzard** Eng

56B2 **Leine** *R* Germany
45C2 **Leinster** Region, Irish Rep
57C2 **Leipzig** Germany
50A2 **Leiria** Port
39F7 **Leirvik** Nor
45B1 **Leitrim** County, Irish Rep
73C4 **Leiyang** China
73B5 **Leizhou Bandao** *Pen* China
73C5 **Leizhou Wan** *B* China
56A2 **Lek** *R* Neth
96C1 **Le Kef** Tunisia
19B3 **Leland** USA
54A2 **Lelija** *Mt* Bosnia-Herzegovina
47B1 **Le Locle** France
48C2 **Le Mans** France
6D3 **Lemicux Is** Can
8C2 **Lemmon** USA
21B2 **Lemoore** USA
49C2 **Lempdes** France
86C2 **Lemro** *R* Burma
52C2 **Le Murge** Region, Italy
63C2 **Lena** *R* Russian Fed
38L6 **Lendery** Russian Fed
73C4 **Lengshujiang** China
Leningrad = Sankt-Peterburg
112B7 **Leningradskaya** *Base* Ant
61H3 **Leninogorsk** Tatarskaya Respublika, Russian Fed
68A1 **Leninogorsk** Kazakhstan
65K4 **Leninsk-Kuznetskiy** Russian Fed
69F2 **Leninskoye** Russian Fed
65F6 **Lenkoran'** Azerbaijan
46E1 **Lenne** *R* Germany
16C1 **Lenox** USA
46B1 **Lens** France
63D1 **Lensk** Russian Fed
53B3 **Lentini** Italy
76B3 **Lenya** *R* Burma
52B1 **Leoben** Austria
43C3 **Leominster** Eng
16D1 **Leominster** USA
24B2 **Leon** Mexico
25D3 **León** Nic
50A1 **Leon** Region, Spain
50A1 **León** Spain
100A3 **Leonardville** Namibia
106B3 **Leonora** Aust
35C2 **Leopoldina** Brazil
Léopoldville = Kinshasa
60C3 **Lepel** Belorussia
73D4 **Leping** China
49C2 **Le Puy-en-Velay** France
98B2 **Léré** Chad
101G1 **Leribe** Lesotho
47C2 **Lerici** Italy
51C1 **Lérida** Spain
23A1 **Lerma** *R* Mexico
47D1 **Lermoos** Austria
55C3 **Léros** *I* Greece
44E1 **Lerwick** Scot
46A2 **Les Andelys** France
26C3 **Les Cayes** Haiti
47B2 **Les Ecrins** *Mt* France
73A4 **Leshan** China
54B2 **Leskovac** Serbia, Yugos
48B3 **Les Landes** Region, France
101G1 **Leslie** S Africa
61H2 **Lesnoy** Russian Fed
63B2 **Lesosibirsk** Russian Fed
101G1 **Lesotho** Kingdom, S Africa
69F2 **Lesozavodsk** Russian Fed
48B2 **Les Sables-d'Olonne** France
112A **Lesser Antarctica** Region, Ant
27D4 **Lesser Antilles** *Is* Caribbean S
65F5 **Lesser Caucasus** *Mts* Azerbaijan/Georgia
13E1 **Lesser Slave L** Can
55C3 **Lésvos** *I* Greece
58B2 **Leszno** Pol
86C2 **Letha Range** *Mts* Burma
5G5 **Lethbridge** Can
33F3 **Lethem** Guyana
59D3 **Letichev** Ukraine
63D2 **Let Oktyobr'ya** Russian Fed
78B2 **Letong** Indon
46A1 **Le Touquet-Paris-Plage** France
76B2 **Letpadan** Burma
48C1 **Le Tréport** France
47B1 **Leuk** Switz
57A2 **Leuven** Belg
55B3 **Levádhia** Greece
38G6 **Levanger** Nor
47B2 **Levanna** *Mt* Italy
71D5 **Lévèque,C** Aust
46D1 **Leverkusen** Germany
59B3 **Levice** Slovakia
47D1 **Levico** Italy
110C2 **Levin** NZ
7C5 **Lévis** Can
15D2 **Levittown** USA
55B3 **Lévka ·ri** *Mt* Greece
55B3 **Levkás** Greece
55B3 **Levkás** *I* Greece
106B2 **Lévêque,C** Aust
54C2 **Levski** Bulg
43E4 **Lewes** Eng
40B2 **Lewis** *I* Scot
16A2 **Lewisburg** USA
111B2 **Lewis P** NZ
8B2 **Lewis Range** *Mts* USA
8B2 **Lewiston** Idaho, USA
10C2 **Lewiston** Maine, USA
8C2 **Lewistown** Montana, USA
15C2 **Lewistown** Pennsylvania, USA
19B3 **Lewisville** USA
11B3 **Lexington** Kentucky, USA
18B2 **Lexington** Missouri, USA
15C3 **Lexington Park** USA
79C3 **Leyte G** Phil
54A2 **Lezhe** Alb
82D3 **Lhasa** China
86B1 **Lhazê** China
70A3 **Lhokseumawe** Indon
86C1 **Lhozhag** China
68B4 **Lhunze** China
Liancourt Rocks = Tok-do
79C4 **Lianga** Phil
72B3 **Liangdang** China
73C5 **Lianjiang** China
73C5 **Lianping** China
73C5 **Lian Xian** China
72D3 **Lianyungang** China
72E1 **Liaoding Bandao** *Pen* China
72E1 **Liaodong Wan** *B* China
72E1 **Liao He** *R* China
72E1 **Liaoning** Province, China
72E1 **Liaoyang** China
72E1 **Liaoyuan** China
74B2 **Liaoyuang** China
4F3 **Liard** *R* Can
4F4 **Liard River** Can
46C2 **Liart** France
98B2 **Libenge** Zaïre
9C3 **Liberal** USA
57C2 **Liberec** Czech Republic
97A4 **Liberia** Republic, Africa
18B2 **Liberty** Missouri, USA
15D2 **Liberty** New York, USA
19B3 **Liberty** Texas, USA
48B3 **Libourne** France
23B2 **Libres** Mexico
98A2 **Libreville** Gabon
95A2 **Libya** Republic, Africa
95B2 **Libyan Desert** Libya
95B1 **Libyan Plat** Egypt
53B3 **Licata** Italy
43D3 **Lichfield** Eng
101C2 **Lichinga** Mozam
101G1 **Lichtenburg** S Africa
14B3 **Licking** *R* USA
22B2 **Lick Observatory** USA
60C3 **Lida** Belorussia
39G7 **Lidköping** Sweden
53B2 **Lido di Ostia** Italy
52A1 **Liechtenstein** Principality, Europe
57B2 **Liège** Belg
58C1 **Lielupe** *R* Latvia
98C2 **Lienart** Zaïre
57C3 **Lienz** Austria
60B2 **Liepāja** Latvia
46C1 **Lier** Belg
47B1 **Liestal** Switz
15C1 **Liévre** *R* Can
57C3 **Liezen** Austria
45C2 **Liffey** *R* Irish Rep
45C1 **Lifford** Irish Rep
107F3 **Lifu** *I* Nouvelle Calédonie
109C1 **Lightning Ridge** Aust
46C2 **Ligny-en-Barrois** France
101C2 **Ligonha** *R* Mozam
47C2 **Liguria** Region, Italy
52A2 **Ligurian** *S* Italy
21C4 **Lihue** Hawaiian Is
100B2 **Likasi** Zaïre
49C1 **Lille** France
39G6 **Lillehammer** Nor
46B1 **Lillers** France
39G7 **Lillestøm** Nor
13C2 **Lillooet** Can
13C2 **Lillooet** *R* Can
101C2 **Lilongwe** Malawi
79B4 **Liloy** Phil
54A2 **Lim** *R* Montenegro/Serbia, Yugos
32B6 **Lima** Peru
50A1 **Lima** Spain
10B2 **Lima** USA
92B3 **Limassol** Cyprus
45C1 **Limavady** N Ire
34B3 **Limay** *R* Arg
34B3 **Limay Mahuida** Arg
98A2 **Limbe** Cam
101C2 **Limbe** Malawi
57B2 **Limburg** W Gem
31B6 **Limeira** Brazil
45B2 **Limerick** County, Irish Rep
41B3 **Limerick** Irish Rep
56B1 **Limfjorden** *L* Den
106C2 **Limmen Bight** *B* Aust
55C3 **Límnos** *I* Greece
31D3 **Limoeiro** Brazil
48C2 **Limoges** France
25D4 **Limón** Costa Rica
8C3 **Limon** USA
48C2 **Limousin** Region, France
79A3 **Linapacan Str** Phil
29B3 **Linares** Chile
9D4 **Linares** Mexico
50B2 **Linares** Spain
68B4 **Lincang** China
29D2 **Lincoln** Arg
18A1 **Lincoln** California, USA
42D3 **Lincoln** County, Eng
42D3 **Lincoln** Eng
18C1 **Lincoln** Illinois, USA
8D2 **Lincoln** Nebraska, USA
15D2 **Lincoln** New Hampshire, USA
111B2 **Lincoln** NZ
80A **Lincoln** *S* Greenland
20B2 **Lincoln City** USA
14B2 **Lincoln Park** USA
52A2 **L'Incudina** *Mt* Corse
57B3 **Lindau** Germany
33F2 **Linden** Guyana
39F7 **Lindesnes** *C* Nor
99D3 **Lindi** Tanz
98C2 **Lindi** *R* Zaïre
101G1 **Lindley** S Africa
55C3 **Lindos** Greece
15C2 **Lindsay** Can
105J3 **Line Is** Pacific O
72C2 **Linfen** China
76D2 **Lingao** China
79B2 **Lingayen** Phil
56B2 **Lingen** Germany
73C4 **Lingling** China
73B5 **Lingshan** China
72C2 **Lingshi** China
97A3 **Linguère** Sen
73E4 **Linhai** Rhejiang, China
31D5 **Linhares** Brazil
72B1 **Linhe** China
74B2 **Linjiang** China
39H7 **Linköping** Sweden
72D2 **Linqing** China
35B2 **Lins** Brazil
72A2 **Lintao** China
47C1 **Linthal** Switz
68D2 **Linxi** China
72A2 **Linxia** China
57C3 **Linz** Austria
79B3 **Lipa** Phil
53B3 **Lipari** *I* Italy
61E3 **Lipetsk** Russian Fec
54B1 **Lipova** Rom
56B2 **Lippe** *R* Germany
46E1 **Lippstadt** Germany
99D2 **Lira** Uganda
98B3 **Liranga** Congo
98C2 **Lisala** Zaïre
50A2 **Lisboa** Port
Lisbon = Lisboa
45C1 **Lisburn** N Ire
45B2 **Liscannor B** Irish R
73D4 **Lishui** China
73C4 **Li Shui** *R* China
60E4 **Lisichansk** Ukraine
48C2 **Lisieux** France
60E3 **Liski** Russian Fed
46B2 **L'Isle-Adam** France
47B1 **L'Isle-sur-le-Doubs** France
107E3 **Lismore** Aust
45B2 **Listowel** Irish Rep
73B5 **Litang** China
94B2 **Lītanī** *R* Leb
33G3 **Litani** *R* Surinam
18C2 **Litchfield** USA
107E4 **Lithgow** Aust
60B2 **Lithuania** Republic, Europe
16A2 **Lititz** USA
69F2 **Litovko** Russian Fe
19A3 **Little** *R* USA
11C4 **Little Abaco** *I* The Bahamas
110C1 **Little Barrier I** NZ
13E2 **Little Bow** *R* Can
25D3 **Little Cayman** *I* Caribbean S
16B3 **Little Egg Harbor** *B* USA
26C2 **Little Inagua** *I* Caribbean S
77A4 **Little Nicobar** *I* Nicobar Is
11A3 **Little Rock** USA
22D3 **Littlerock** USA
13D2 **Little Smoky** Can
13D2 **Little Smoky** *R* Ca
16A3 **Littlestown** USA
15D2 **Littleton** New Hampshire, USA
74B2 **Liuhe** China
73B5 **Liuzhou** China
55B3 **Livanátais** Greece
58D1 **Līvāni** Latvia
12E1 **Livengood** USA
17B1 **Live Oak** USA
21A2 **Livermore** USA
7D5 **Liverpool** Can
42C3 **Liverpool** Eng

4E2 **Liverpool B** Can
42C3 **Liverpool B** Eng
6C2 **Liverpool,C** Can
109D2 **Liverpool Range** *Mts* Aust
8B2 **Livingston** Montana, USA
19B3 **Livingston** Texas, USA
44C4 **Livingston** UK
Livingstone = Maramba
19A3 **Livingston,L** USA
52C2 **Livno** Bosnia-Herzegovina
60E3 **Livny** Russian Fed
14B2 **Livonia** USA
52B2 **Livorno** Italy
99D3 **Liwale** Tanz
52B1 **Ljubljana** Slovenia
38G6 **Ljungan** *R* Sweden
39G7 **Ljungby** Sweden
39H6 **Ljusdal** Sweden
38H6 **Ljusnan** *R* Sweden
43C4 **Llandeilo** Wales
43C4 **Llandovery** Wales
43C3 **Llandrindod Wells** Wales
42C3 **Llandudno** Wales
43B4 **Llanelli** Wales
43C3 **Llangollen** Wales
9C3 **Llano Estacado** *Plat* USA
32C2 **Llanos** Region, Colombia/Ven
30D2 **Llanos de Chiquitos** Region, Bol
Lleida = Lérida
50A2 **Llerena** Spain
43B3 **Lleyn** *Pen* Wales
89E7 **Llorin** Nig
5H4 **Lloydminster** Can
30C3 **Llullaillaco** *Mt* Arg/Chile
30C3 **Loa** *R* Chile
49C2 **Loan** France
98B3 **Loange** *R* Zaïre
00B3 **Lobatse** Botswana
98B2 **Lobaye** *R* CAR
34D3 **Loberia** Arg
00A2 **Lobito** Angola
34D3 **Lobos** Arg
47B2 **Locano** Italy
47C1 **Locarno** Switz
44B3 **Loch Awe** *L* Scot
44A3 **Lochboisdale** Scot
44A3 **Loch Bracadale** *Inlet* Scot
44B3 **Loch Broom** *Estuary* Scot
42B2 **Loch Doon** *L* Scot
44B3 **Loch Earn** *L* Scot
44B2 **Loch Eriboll** *Inlet* Scot
44B3 **Loch Ericht** *L* Scot
48C2 **Loches** France
44B3 **Loch Etive** *Inlet* Scot
44B3 **Loch Ewe** *Inlet* Scot
44B3 **Loch Fyne** *Inlet* Scot
44B3 **Loch Hourn** *Inlet* Scot
44B2 **Lochinver** Scot
44B3 **Loch Katrine** *L* Scot
44C3 **Loch Leven** *L* Scot
44B3 **Loch Linnhe** *Inlet* Scot
44B3 **Loch Lochy** *L* Scot
44B3 **Loch Lomond** *L* Scot
44B3 **Loch Long** *Inlet* Scot
44A3 **Lochmaddy** Scot
44B3 **Loch Maree** *L* Scot
44B3 **Loch Morar** *L* Scot
44C3 **Lochnagar** *Mt* Scot
44B3 **Loch Ness** *L* Scot
44B3 **Loch Rannoch** *L* Scot
44A2 **Loch Roag** *Inlet* Scot
44B3 **Loch Sheil** *L* Scot
44B2 **Loch Shin** *L* Scot
44A3 **Loch Snizort** *Inlet* Scot
44B3 **Loch Sunart** *Inlet* Scot
44B3 **Loch Tay** *L* Scot
44B3 **Loch Torridon** *Inlet* Scot
108A2 **Lock** Aust
42C2 **Lockerbie** Scot
15C2 **Lock Haven** USA
15C2 **Lockport** USA
76D3 **Loc Ninh** Viet
53C3 **Locri** Italy
94B3 **Lod** Israel
108B3 **Loddon** *R* Aust
60D1 **Lodeynoye Pole** Russian Fed
84C3 **Lodhran** Pak
52A1 **Lodi** Italy
21A2 **Lodi** USA
98C3 **Lodja** Zaïre
47B1 **Lods** France
99D2 **Lodwar** Kenya
58B2 **Łódź** Pol
38G5 **Lofoten** *Is* Nor
8B2 **Logan** Utah, USA
4D3 **Logan,Mt** Can
14A2 **Logansport** Indiana, USA
19B3 **Logansport** Louisiana, USA
50B1 **Logroño** Spain
86A2 **Lohārdaga** India
39J6 **Lohja** Fin
76B2 **Loikaw** Burma
39J6 **Loimaa** Fin
48C2 **Loir** *R* France
49C2 **Loire** *R* France
32B4 **Loja** Ecuador
50B2 **Loja** Spain
38K5 **Lokan Tekojärvi** *Res* Fin
46B1 **Lokeren** Belg
99D2 **Lokitaung** Kenya
58D1 **Loknya** Russian Fed
98C3 **Lokolo** *R* Zaïre
98C3 **Lokoro** *R* Zaïre
6D3 **Loks Land** *I* Can
56C2 **Lolland** *I* Den
54B2 **Lom** Bulg
98C3 **Lomami** *R* Zaïre
97A4 **Loma Mts** Sierra Leone/Guinea
47C2 **Lombardia** Region, Italy
71D4 **Lomblen** *I* Indon
78D4 **Lombok** *I* Indon
97C4 **Lomé** Togo
98C3 **Lomela** Zaïre
98C3 **Lomela** *R* Zaïre
60C2 **Lomonosov** Russian Fed
47B1 **Lomont** Region, France
21A3 **Lompoc** USA
58C2 **Łomza** Pol
87A1 **Lonāvale** India
29B3 **Loncoche** Chile
7B5 **London** Can
43D4 **London** Eng
45C1 **Londonderry** County, N Ire
45C1 **Londonderry** N Ire
29B7 **Londonderry** *I* Chile
106B2 **Londonderry,C** Aust
30C4 **Londres** Arg
30F3 **Londrina** Brazil
21B2 **Lone Pine** USA
11C4 **Long** *I* The Bahamas
71F4 **Long** *I* PNG
78C2 **Long Akah** Malay
47E1 **Longarone** Italy
34A3 **Longavi** *Mt* Chile
27H2 **Long B** Jamaica
17C1 **Long B** USA
9B3 **Long Beach** California, USA
15D2 **Long Beach** New York, USA
15D2 **Long Branch** USA
73D5 **Longchuan** China
20C2 **Long Creek** USA
109C4 **Longford** Aust
45C2 **Longford** County, Irish Rep
45C2 **Longford** Irish Rep
44D3 **Long Forties** *Region* N Sea
72D1 **Longhua** China
7C4 **Long I** Can
10C2 **Long I** USA
16C2 **Long Island Sd** USA
7B4 **Longlac** Can
73B5 **Longlin** China
8C2 **Longmont** USA
78D2 **Longnawan** Indon
29B3 **Longquimay** Chile
107D3 **Longreach** Aust
72A2 **Longshou Shan** *Upland* China
42C2 **Longtown** Eng
15D1 **Longueuil** Can
34A3 **Longuimay** Chile
46C2 **Longuyon** France
11A3 **Longview** Texas, USA
8A2 **Longview** Washington, USA
46C2 **Longwy** France
72A3 **Longxi** China
77D3 **Long Xuyen** Viet
73D4 **Longyan** China
73B5 **Longzhou** China
47D2 **Lonigo** Italy
49D2 **Lons-le-Saunier** France
11C3 **Lookout,C** USA
99D3 **Loolmalasin** *Mt* Tanz
13D1 **Loon** *R* Can
45B2 **Loop Hd** *C* Irish Rep
76C3 **Lop Buri** Thai
98A3 **Lopez** *C* Gabon
68B2 **Lop Nur** *L* China
50A2 **Lora del Rio** Spain
10B2 **Lorain** USA
84B2 **Loralai** Pak
90B3 **Lordegān** Iran
107E4 **Lord Howe** *I* Aust
105G5 **Lord Howe Rise** Pacific O
6A3 **Lord Mayor B** Can
9C3 **Lordsburg** USA
35B2 **Lorena** Brazil
47E2 **Loreo** Italy
23A1 **Loreto** Mexico
48B2 **Lorient** France
108B3 **Lorne** Aust
57B3 **Lörrach** Germany
49D2 **Lorraine** *Region* France
9C3 **Los Alamos** USA
34A2 **Los Andes** Chile
29B3 **Los Angeles** Chile
9B3 **Los Angeles** USA
21A2 **Los Banos** USA
34B2 **Los Cerrillos** Arg
21A2 **Los Gatos** USA
52B2 **Lošinj** *I* Croatia
29B3 **Los Lagos** Chile
24B2 **Los Mochis** Mexico
22B3 **Los Olivos** USA
34A3 **Los Sauces** Chile
44C3 **Lossiemouth** Scot
27E4 **Los Testigos** *Is* Ven
29B2 **Los Vilos** Chile
48C3 **Lot** *R* France
34A3 **Lota** Chile
42C2 **Lothian** Region, Scot
99D2 **Lotikipi Plain** Sudan/Kenya
98C3 **Loto** Zaïre
47B1 **Lötschberg Tunnel** Switz
38K5 **Lotta** *R* Fin/Russian Fed
48B2 **Loudéac** France
97A3 **Louga** Sen
41B3 **Lough Allen** *L* Irish Rep
45C2 **Lough Boderg** *L* Irish Rep
43D3 **Loughborough** Eng
45C2 **Lough Bowna** *L* Irish Rep
45C1 **Lough Carlingford** *L* N Ire
41B3 **Lough Conn** *L* Irish Rep
41B3 **Lough Corrib** *L* Irish Rep
41B3 **Lough Derg** *L* Irish Rep
45C2 **Lough Derravaragh** *L* Irish Rep
4H2 **Loughead I** Can
45C2 **Lough Ennell** *L* Irish Rep
41B3 **Lough Erne** *L* N Ire
40B2 **Lough Foyle** *Estuary* N Ire/Irish Rep
40B3 **Lough Neagh** *L* N Ire
45C1 **Lough Oughter** *L* Irish Rep
45B2 **Loughrea** Irish Rep
45C2 **Lough Ree** *L* Irish Rep
45C2 **Lough Sheelin** *L* Irish Rep
42B2 **Lough Strangford** *L* Irish Rep
45C1 **Lough Swilly** *Estuary* Irish Rep
14B3 **Louisa** USA
70C3 **Louisa Reef** *I* S E Asia
12E2 **Louise,L** USA
107E2 **Louisiade Arch** Solomon Is
11A3 **Louisiana** State, USA
17B1 **Louisville** Georgia, USA
11B3 **Louisville** Kentucky, USA
38L5 **Loukhi** Russian Fed
48B3 **Lourdes** France
108C2 **Louth** Aust
45C2 **Louth** County, Irish Rep
42D3 **Louth** Eng
Louvain = Leuven
48C2 **Louviers** France
60D2 **Lovat** *R* Russian Fed
54B2 **Lovech** Bulg
21B1 **Lovelock** USA
52B1 **Lóvere** Italy
9C3 **Lovington** USA
38L5 **Lovozero** Russian Fed
6B3 **Low,C** Can
10C2 **Lowell** Massachusetts, USA
20B2 **Lowell** Oregon, USA
16D1 **Lowell** USA
111B2 **Lower Hutt** NZ
43E3 **Lowestoft** Eng
58B2 **Łowicz** Pol
108B2 **Loxton** Aust
5F4 **Loyd George,Mt** Can
54A2 **Loznica** Serbia, Yugos
23A2 **Loz Reyes** Mexico
65H3 **Lozva** *R* Russian Fed
100B2 **Luacano** Angola
98C3 **Luachimo** Angola
98C3 **Lualaba** *R* Zaïre
100B2 **Luampa** Zambia
100B2 **Luân** Angola
73D3 **Lu'an** China
98B3 **Luanda** Angola
100A2 **Luando** *R* Angola
100B2 **Luanginga** *R* Angola
76C1 **Luang Namtha** Laos
76C2 **Luang Prabang** Laos
98B3 **Luangue** *R* Angola
100C2 **Luangwa** *R* Zambia
72D1 **Luan He** *R* China
72D1 **Luanping** China
100B2 **Luanshya** Zambia
100B2 **Luapula** *R* Zaïre
50A1 **Luarca** Spain
98B3 **Lubalo** Angola
58D2 **L'uban** Belorussia
79B3 **Lubang Is** Phil
100A2 **Lubango** Angola
9C3 **Lubbock** USA
56C2 **Lübeck** Germany
98C3 **Lubefu** Zaïre
98C3 **Lubefu** *R* Zaïre
99C3 **Lubero** Zaïre
98C3 **Lubilash** *R* Zaïre
59C2 **Lublin** Pol
60D3 **Lubny** Ukraine
78C2 **Lubok Antu** Malay
98C3 **Lubudi** Zaïre
98C3 **Lubudi** *R* Zaïre

78A3 **Lubuklinggau** Indon
100B2 **Lubumbashi** Zaïre
98C3 **Lubutu** Zaïre
79B3 **Lucban** Phil
52B2 **Lucca** Italy
42B2 **Luce** *B* Scot
19C3 **Lucedale** USA
79B3 **Lucena** Phil
59B3 **Lucenec** Slovakia
Lucerne = Luzern
73C5 **Luchuan** China
56C2 **Luckenwalde** Germany
101F1 **Luckhoff** S Africa
86A1 **Lucknow** India
100B2 **Lucusse** Angola
46D1 **Lüdenscheid** Germany
100A3 **Lüderitz** Namibia
84D2 **Ludhiana** India
14A2 **Ludington** USA
43C3 **Ludlow** Eng
54C2 **Ludogorie** *Upland* Bulg
17B1 **Ludowici** USA
54B1 **Luduş** Rom
39H6 **Ludvika** Sweden
57B3 **Ludwigsburg** Germany
57B3 **Ludwigshafen** Germany
56C2 **Ludwigslust** Germany
98C3 **Luebo** Zaïre
98C3 **Luema** *R* Zaïre
98C3 **Luembe** *R* Angola
100A2 **Luena** Angola
100B2 **Luene** *R* Angola
72B3 **Lüeyang** China
73D5 **Lufeng** China
11A3 **Lufkin** USA
60C2 **Luga** Russian Fed
60C2 **Luga** *R* Russian Fed
52A1 **Lugano** Switz
60E4 **Lugansk** Ukraine
101C2 **Lugela** Mozam
101C2 **Lugenda** *R* Mozam
50A1 **Lugo** Spain
54B1 **Lugoj** Rom
72A3 **Luhuo** China
98B3 **Lui** *R* Angola
100B2 **Luiana** Angola
100B2 **Luiana** *R* Angola
Luichow Peninsula = Leizhou Bandao
47C2 **Luino** Italy
98B2 **Luionga** *R* Zaïre
72B2 **Luipan Shan** *Upland* China
100B2 **Luishia** Zaïre
68B4 **Luixi** China
98C3 **Luiza** Zaïre
34B2 **Luján** Arg
34D2 **Luján** Arg
73D3 **Lujiang** China
98B3 **Lukenie** *R* Zaïre
64E4 **Luki** Russian Fed
98B3 **Lukolela** Zaïre
58C2 **Łuków** Pol
98C3 **Lukuga** *R* Zaïre
100B2 **Lukulu** Zambia
38J5 **Lule** *R* Sweden
38J5 **Luleå** Sweden
54C2 **Lüleburgaz** Turk
72C2 **Lüliang Shan** *Mts* China
19A4 **Luling** USA
98C2 **Lulonga** *R* Zaïre
Luluabourg = Kananga
100B2 **Lumbala Kaquengue** Angola
11C3 **Lumberton** USA
78D1 **Lumbis** Indon
86C1 **Lumding** India
100B2 **Lumeje** Angola
111A3 **Lumsden** NZ
39G7 **Lund** Sweden
101C2 **Lundazi** Zambia
43B4 **Lundy** *I* Eng
56C2 **Lüneburg** Germany
46D2 **Lunéville** France
100B2 **Lunga** *R* Zambia
86C2 **Lunglei** India
100A2 **Lungue Bungo** *R* Angola
58D2 **Luninec** Belorussia
98B3 **Luobomo** Congo
73B5 **Luocheng** China
73C5 **Luoding** China
72C3 **Luohe** China
72C3 **Luo He** *R* Henan, China
72B2 **Luo He** *R* Shaanxi, China
73C4 **Luoxiao Shan** *Hills* China
72C3 **Luoyang** China
98B3 **Luozi** Zaïre
100B2 **Lupane** Zim
101C2 **Lupilichi** Mozam
Lu Qu = Tao He
30E4 **Luque** Par
45C1 **Lurgan** N Ire
101C2 **Lurio** *R* Mozam
90A3 **Luristan** Region, Iran
100B2 **Lusaka** Zambia
98C3 **Lusambo** Zaïre
55A2 **Lushnjë** Alb
99D3 **Lushoto** Tanz
68B4 **Lushui** China
72E2 **Lüshun** China
43D4 **Luton** Eng
60C3 **Lutsk** Ukraine
99E2 **Luuq** Somalia
99C3 **Luvua** *R* Zaïre
99D3 **Luwegu** *R* Tanz
100C2 **Luwingu** Zambia
71D4 **Luwuk** Indon
46D2 **Luxembourg** Grand Duchy, N W Europe
49D2 **Luxembourg** Lux
73A5 **Luxi** China
95C2 **Luxor** Egypt
61G1 **Luza** Russian Fed
61G1 **Luza** *R* Russian Fed
52A1 **Luzern** Switz
73B5 **Luzhai** China
73B4 **Luzhi** China
73B4 **Luzhou** China
35B1 **Luziânia** Brazil
79B2 **Luzon** *I* Phil
79B1 **Luzon Str** Phil
59C3 **L'vov** Ukraine
44C2 **Lybster** Scot
38H6 **Lycksele** Sweden
100B3 **Lydenburg** S Africa
8B3 **Lyell,Mt** USA
16A2 **Lykens** USA
43C4 **Lyme B** Eng
43C4 **Lyme Regis** Eng
11C3 **Lynchburg** USA
108A2 **Lyndhurst** Aust
15D2 **Lynn** USA
12G3 **Lynn Canal** *Sd* USA
17A1 **Lynn Haven** USA
5H4 **Lynn Lake** Can
5H3 **Lynx L** Can
49C2 **Lyon** France
12G3 **Lyon Canal** *Sd* USA
17B1 **Lyons** Georgia, USA
106A3 **Lyons** *R* Aust
47B2 **Lys** *R* Italy
61J2 **Lys'va** Russian Fed
111B2 **Lyttelton** NZ
13C2 **Lytton** Can
22A1 **Lytton** USA
58D2 **Lyubeshov** Ukraine
60E2 **Lyublino** Russian Fed

M

76C1 **Ma** *R* Viet
94B2 **Ma'agan** Jordan
94B2 **Ma'alot Tarshīha** Israel
92C3 **Ma'an** Jordan
73D3 **Ma'anshan** China
92C2 **Ma'arrat an Nu'mān** Syria
46C1 **Maas** *R* Neth
46C1 **Maaseik** Belg
79B3 **Maasin** Phil
57B2 **Maastricht** Neth
101C3 **Mabalane** Mozam
33F2 **Mabaruma** Guyana
42E3 **Mablethorpe** Eng
101C3 **Mabote** Mozam
58C2 **Mabrita** Belorussia
58D2 **M'adel** Belorussia
35C2 **Macaé** Brazil
9D3 **McAlester** USA
9D4 **McAllen** USA
101C2 **Macaloge** Mozam
33G3 **Macapá** Brazil
35C1 **Macarani** Brazil
32B4 **Macas** Ecuador
31D3 **Macaú** Brazil
73C5 **Macau** Dependency, China
98C2 **M'Bari** *R* CAR
13C2 **McBride** Can
12F2 **McCarthy** USA
13A2 **McCauley I** Can
42C3 **Macclesfield** Eng
6B1 **McClintock B** Can
4H2 **McClintock Chan** Can
16A2 **McClure** USA
22B2 **McClure,L** USA
4G2 **McClure Str** Can
19B3 **McComb** USA
8C2 **McCook** USA
6C2 **Macculloch,C** Can
13C1 **McCusker,Mt** Can
4F4 **McDame** Can
20C2 **McDermitt** USA
13E2 **Macdonald** *R* Can
106C3 **Macdonnell Ranges** *Mts* Aust
50A1 **Macedo de Cavaleiros** Port
55B2 **Macedonia** Republic, Europe
31D3 **Maceió** Brazil
97B4 **Macenta** Guinea
52B2 **Macerata** Italy
108A2 **Macfarlane,L** Aust
19B3 **McGehee** USA
45B3 **MacGillycuddys Reeks** *Mts* Irish Rep
4C3 **McGrath** USA
35B2 **Machado** Brazil
101C3 **Machaíla** Mozam
99D3 **Machakos** Kenya
32B4 **Machala** Ecuador
101C3 **Machaze** Mozam
87B1 **Mācherla** India
94B2 **Machgharab** Leb
87C1 **Machilīpatnam** India
32C1 **Machiques** Ven
32C6 **Machu-Picchu** *Hist Site* Peru
101C3 **Macia** Mozam
109C1 **MacIntyre** *R* Aust
107D3 **Mackay** Aust
106B3 **Mackay,L** Aust
14C2 **McKeesport** USA
13C1 **Mackenzie** Can
4F3 **Mackenzie** *R* Can
4E3 **Mackenzie B** Can
4G2 **Mackenzie King I** Can
4E3 **Mackenzie Mts** Can
14B1 **Mackinac,Str of** USA
14B1 **Mackinaw City** USA
12D2 **McKinley,Mt** USA
19A3 **McKinney** USA
6C2 **Mackinson Inlet** *B* Can
109D2 **Macksville** Aust
20B2 **Mclaoughlin,Mt** USA
109D1 **Maclean** Aust
100B4 **Maclear** S Africa
5G4 **McLennan** Can
13D2 **McLeod** *R* Can
4G3 **McLeod B** Can
106A3 **McLeod,L** Aust
13C1 **McLeod Lake** Can
4E3 **Macmillan** *R* Can
12H2 **Macmillan P** Can
20B1 **McMinnville** Oregon, USA
112B7 **McMurdo** *Base* Ant
13D2 **McNaughton L** Can
18B1 **Macomb** USA
53A2 **Macomer** Sardegna
101C2 **Macomia** Mozam
49C2 **Mâcon** France
11B3 **Macon** Georgia, USA
18B2 **Macon** Missouri, USA
100B2 **Macondo** Angola
18A2 **McPherson** USA
104F6 **Macquarie** *Is* Aust
109C2 **Macquarie** *R* Aust
109C4 **Macquarie Harbour** Aust
109D2 **Macquarie,L** Aust
17B1 **McRae** USA
112B11 **Mac. Robertson Lan[d]** Region, Ant
45B3 **Macroom** Irish Rep
96C1 **M'Sila** Alg
4G3 **McTavish Arm** *B* Can
108A1 **Macumba** *R* Aust
47C2 **Macunaga** Italy
4F3 **McVicar Arm** *B* Can
59B3 **M'yaróvár** Hung
94B3 **Mādabā** Jordan
95A3 **Madadi** *Well* Chad
89J10 **Madagascar** *I* Indian O
95A2 **Madama** Niger
71F4 **Madang** PNG
97C3 **Madaoua** Niger
86C2 **Madaripur** Bang
90B2 **Madau** Turkmenista[n]
15C1 **Madawaska** *R* Can
96A1 **Madeira** *I* Atlantic [O]
33E5 **Madeira** *R* Brazil
7D5 **Madeleine, Îsle de l[a]** Can
24B2 **Madera** Mexico
21A2 **Madera** USA
87A1 **Madgaon** India
86B1 **Madhubani** India
86A2 **Madhya Pradesh** State, India
87B2 **Madikeri** India
98B3 **Madimba** Zaïre
98B3 **Madingo Kayes** Congo
98B3 **Madingou** Congo
10B3 **Madison** Indiana, USA
10B2 **Madison** Wisconsi[n] USA
18C2 **Madisonville** Kentucky, USA
19A3 **Madisonville** Texas USA
78C4 **Madiun** Indon
99D2 **Mado Gashi** Kenya
47D1 **Madonna Di Campiglio** Italy
87C2 **Madras** India
20B2 **Madras** USA
29A6 **Madre de Dios** *I* Chile
32D6 **Madre de Dios** *R* B[ol]
50B1 **Madrid** Spain
50B2 **Madridejos** Spain
78C4 **Madura** *I* Indon
87B3 **Madurai** India
75B1 **Maebashi** Japan
76B3 **Mae Khlong** *R* Tha[i]
77B4 **Mae Nam Lunang** Thai
76C2 **Mae Nam Mun** *R* Thai
76B2 **Mae Nam Ping** *R* Thai
101D2 **Maevatanana** Mad
101G1 **Mafeteng** Lesotho
109C3 **Maffra** Aust
99D3 **Mafia** *I* Tanz
101G1 **Mafikeng** S Africa
30G4 **Mafra** Brazil
92C3 **Mafraq** Jordan
32C2 **Magangué** Colomb[ia]
34D3 **Magdalena** Arg
24A1 **Magdalena** Mexic[o]
26C4 **Magdalena** *R* Colombia
78D1 **Magdalena,Mt** Ma[l]
56C2 **Magdeburg** Germ[any]
31C6 **Magé** Brazil
78C4 **Magelang** Indon
47C1 **Maggia** *R* Switz
92B4 **Maghâgha** Egypt
45C1 **Magherafelt** N Ire
55A2 **Maglie** Italy
61J3 **Magnitogorsk** Russian Fed
19B3 **Magnolia** USA
101C2 **Magoé** Mozam

15D1 **Magog** Can
23B1 **Magosal** Mexico
13E2 **Magrath** Can
7A3 **Maguse River** Can
76B1 **Magwe** Burma
90A2 **Mahābād** Iran
86B1 **Mahabharat Range** *Mts* Nepal
87A1 **Mahād** India
85D4 **Mahadeo Hills** India
101D2 **Mahajanga** Madag
100B3 **Mahalapye** Botswana
86A2 **Mahānadi** *R* India
101D2 **Mahanoro** Madag
16A2 **Mahanoy City** USA
87A1 **Maharashtra** State, India
86A2 **Māhāsamund** India
76C2 **Maha Sarakham** Thai
101D2 **Mahavavy** *R* Madag
87B1 **Mahbūbnagar** India
96D1 **Mahdia** Tunisia
87B2 **Mahe** India
85D4 **Mahekar** India
101D2 **Mahéli** *I* Comoros
86A2 **Mahendragarh** India
99D3 **Mahenge** Tanz
85C4 **Mahesāna** India
110C1 **Mahia Pen** NZ
85D3 **Mahoba** India
51C2 **Mahón** Spain
12J1 **Mahony L** Can
96D1 **Mahrés** Tunisia
85C4 **Mahuva** India
32C1 **Maicao** Colombia
47B1 **Maîche** France
43E4 **Maidstone** Eng
98B1 **Maiduguri** Nig
86A2 **Maihar** India
86C2 **Maijdi** Bang
76B3 **Mail Kyun** *I* Burma
84A1 **Maimana** Afghan
14B1 **Main Chan** Can
98B3 **Mai-Ndombe** *L* Zaïre
10D2 **Maine** State, USA
48B2 **Maine** *Region* France
44C2 **Mainland** *I* Scot
85D3 **Mainpuri** India
46A2 **Maintenon** France
101D2 **Maintirano** Madag
57B2 **Mainz** Germany
97A4 **Maio** *I* Cape Verde
29C2 **Maipó** *Mt* Arg/Chile
34D3 **Maipú** Arg
32D1 **Maiquetía** Ven
47B2 **Maira** *R* Italy
86C1 **Mairābāri** India
86C2 **Maiskhal I** Bang
107E4 **Maitland** New South Wales, Aust
108A2 **Maitland** S Australia, Aust
12C12 **Maitri** *Base* Ant
74D3 **Maizuru** Japan
70C4 **Majene** Indon
30B2 **Majes** *R* Peru
99D2 **Maji** Eth
72D2 **Majia He** *R* China
Majunga = Mahajanga
70C4 **Makale** Indon
86B1 **Makalu** *Mt* China/Nepal
98B2 **Makanza** Zaïre
52C2 **Makarska** Croatia
61F2 **Makaryev** Russian Fed
Makassar = Ujung Pandang
78D3 **Makassar Str** Indon
61H4 **Makat** Kazakhstan
97A4 **Makeni** Sierra Leone
60E4 **Makeyevka** Ukraine
100B3 **Makgadikgadi** *Salt Pan* Botswana
61G5 **Makhachkala** Russian Fed
99D3 **Makindu** Kenya
88H5 **Makkah** S Arabia
7E4 **Makkovik** Can
59C3 **Makó** Hung
98B2 **Makokou** Gabon
110C1 **Makorako,Mt** NZ
98B2 **Makoua** Congo
85C3 **Makrāna** India
85A3 **Makran Coast Range** *Mts* Pak
96C1 **Makthar** Tunisia
93D2 **Mākū** Iran
98C3 **Makumbi** Zaïre
74C4 **Makurazaki** Japan
97C4 **Makurdi** Nig
79B4 **Malabang** Phil
87A2 **Malabar Coast** India
89E7 **Malabo** Bioko
77C5 **Malacca,Str of** S E Asia
32C2 **Málaga** Colombia
50B2 **Malaga** Spain
101D3 **Malaimbandy** Madag
107F1 **Malaita** *I* Solomon Is
99D2 **Malakal** Sudan
84C2 **Malakand** Pak
78C4 **Malang** Indon
98B3 **Malange** Angola
97C3 **Malanville** Benin
39H7 **Mälaren** *L* Sweden
34B3 **Malargüe** Arg
12F3 **Malaspina Gl** USA
93C2 **Malatya** Turk
101C2 **Malawi** Republic, Africa
Malawi,L = Nyasa,L
79C4 **Malaybalay** Phil
90A3 **Malāyer** Iran
70B3 **Malaysia** Federation, S E Asia
93D2 **Malazgirt** Turk
58B2 **Malbork** Pol
56C2 **Malchin** Germany
18C2 **Malden** USA
83B5 **Maldives Is** Indian O
104B4 **Maldives Ridge** Indian O
29F2 **Maldonado** Urug
47D1 **Male** Italy
85C4 **Malegaon** India
59B3 **Malé Karpaty** *Upland* Slovakia
101C2 **Malema** Mozam
84B2 **Mālestān** Afghan
38H5 **Malgomaj** *L* Sweden
95B3 **Malha** *Well* Sudan
20C2 **Malheur L** USA
97B3 **Mali** Republic, Africa
78D1 **Malinau** Indon
99E3 **Malindi** Kenya
Malines = Mechelen
40B2 **Malin Head** *Pt* Irish Rep
86A2 **Malkala Range** *Mts* India
85D4 **Malkāpur** India
55C2 **Malkara** Turk
54C2 **Malko Tūrnovo** Bulg
44B3 **Mallaig** Scot
95C2 **Mallawi** Egypt
47D1 **Málles Venosta** Italy
51C2 **Mallorca** *I* Spain
45B2 **Mallow** Irish Rep
38G6 **Malm** Nor
38J5 **Malmberget** Sweden
46D1 **Malmédy** Germany
43C4 **Malmesbury** Eng
100A4 **Malmesbury** S Africa
39G7 **Malmö** Sweden
61G2 **Malmyzh** Russian Fed
79B3 **Malolos** Phil
15D2 **Malone** USA
101G1 **Maloti Mts** Lesotho
38F6 **Måloy** Nor
28A2 **Malpelo** *I* Colombia
34A2 **Malpo** *R* Chile
85D3 **Mālpura** India
8C2 **Malta** Montana, USA
53B3 **Malta** *Chan* Malta/Italy
53B3 **Malta** *I* Medit S
100A3 **Maltahöhe** Namibia
42D2 **Malton** Eng
39G6 **Malung** Sweden
87A1 **Mālvan** India
19B3 **Malvern** USA
85D4 **Malwa Plat** India
61G4 **Malyy Uzen'** *R* Kazakhstan
63D2 **Mama** Russian Fed
61H2 **Mamadysh** Russian Fed
99C2 **Mambasa** Zaïre
71E4 **Mamberamo** *R* Indon
98B2 **Mambéré** *R* CAR
98A2 **Mamfé** Cam
33D6 **Mamoré** *R* Bol
97A3 **Mamou** Guinea
101D2 **Mampikony** Madag
97B4 **Mampong** Ghana
94B3 **Mamshit** *Hist Site* Israel
100B3 **Mamuno** Botswana
97B4 **Man** Ivory Coast
21C4 **Mana** Hawaiian Is
101D3 **Manabo** Madag
33E4 **Manacapuru** Brazil
51C2 **Manacor** Spain
71D3 **Manado** Indon
25D3 **Managua** Nic
101D3 **Manakara** Madag
101D2 **Mananara** Madag
101D3 **Mananjary** Madag
111A3 **Manapouri** NZ
111A3 **Manapouri,L** NZ
86C1 **Manas** Bhutan
82C1 **Manas** China
65K5 **Manas Hu** *L* China
86A1 **Manaslu** *Mt* Nepal
16B2 **Manasquan** USA
33F4 **Manaus** Brazil
92B2 **Manavgat** Turk
93C2 **Manbij** Syria
42B2 **Man,Calf of** *I* Eng
87B1 **Mancheral** India
15D2 **Manchester** Connecticut, USA
42C3 **Manchester** Eng
10C2 **Manchester** New Hampshire, USA
16A2 **Manchester** Pennsylvania, USA
69E2 **Manchuria** Hist Region, China
91B4 **Mand** *R* Iran
101C2 **Manda** Tanz
35A2 **Mandaguari** Brazil
39F7 **Mandal** Nor
76B1 **Mandalay** Burma
68C2 **Mandalgovĭ** Mongolia
8C2 **Mandan** USA
14A2 **Mandelona** USA
99E2 **Mandera** Eth
26B3 **Mandeville** Jamaica
101C2 **Mandimba** Mozam
86A2 **Mandla** India
101D2 **Mandritsara** Madag
85D4 **Mandsaur** India
53C2 **Manduria** Italy
85B4 **Māndvi** India
87B2 **Mandya** India
58D2 **Manevichi** Ukraine
42D3 **Manfield** Eng
53C2 **Manfredonia** Italy
98B1 **Manga** *Desert Region* Niger
110C1 **Mangakino** NZ
54C2 **Mangalia** Rom
98B1 **Mangalmé** Chad
87A2 **Mangalore** India
78B3 **Manggar** Indon
68B3 **Mangnia** China
101C2 **Mangoche** Malawi
101D3 **Mangoky** *R* Madag
71D4 **Mangole** *I* Indon
85B4 **Māngral** India
63E2 **Mangui** China
8D3 **Manhattan** USA
31C6 **Manhuacu** Brazil
101D2 **Mania** *R* Madag
101C2 **Manica** Mozam
7D5 **Manicouagan** *R* Can
91A4 **Manifah** S Arabia
79B3 **Manila** Phil
109D2 **Manilla** Aust
97B3 **Maninian** Ivory Coast
86C2 **Manipur** State, India
86C2 **Manipur** *R* Burma
92A2 **Manisa** Turk
41C3 **Man,Isle of** Irish S
14A2 **Manistee** USA
14A2 **Manistee** *R* USA
14A1 **Manistique** USA
5H4 **Manitoba** Province, Can
5J4 **Manitoba,L** Can
13F2 **Manito L** Can
14A1 **Manitou Is** USA
7B5 **Manitoulin** *I* Can
14A2 **Manitowoc** USA
15C1 **Maniwaki** Can
32B2 **Manizales** Colombia
101D3 **Manja** Madag
106A4 **Manjimup** Aust
87B1 **Mānjra** *R* India
10A2 **Mankato** USA
97B4 **Mankono** Ivory Coast
12D2 **Manley Hot Springs** USA
110B1 **Manly** NZ
85C4 **Manmād** India
78A3 **Manna** Indon
108A2 **Mannahill** Aust
87B3 **Mannar** Sri Lanka
87B3 **Mannār,G of** India
87B2 **Mannārgudi** India
57B3 **Mannheim** Germany
13D1 **Manning** Can
17B1 **Manning** USA
108A2 **Mannum** Aust
97A4 **Mano** Sierra Leone
71E4 **Manokwari** Indon
98C3 **Manono** Zaïre
76B3 **Manoron** Burma
75B1 **Mano-wan** *B* Japan
74B2 **Manp'o** N Korea
84D3 **Mānsa** India
100B2 **Mansa** Zambia
6B3 **Mansel I** Can
19B2 **Mansfield** Arkansas, USA
108C3 **Mansfield** Aust
19B3 **Mansfield** Louisiana, USA
16D1 **Mansfield** Massachusetts, USA
10B2 **Mansfield** Ohio, USA
15C2 **Mansfield** Pennsylvania, USA
71E2 **Mansyu Deep** Pacific O
32A4 **Manta** Ecuador
79A4 **Mantalingajan,Mt** Phil
32B6 **Mantaro** *R* Peru
22B2 **Manteca** USA
48C2 **Mantes** France
52B1 **Mantova** Italy
38J6 **Mäntta** Fin
61F2 **Manturovo** Russian Fed
35A2 **Manuel Ribas** Brazil
79B4 **Manukan** Phil
110B1 **Manukau** NZ
71F4 **Manus** *I* Pacific O
50B2 **Manzanares** Spain
25E2 **Manzanillo** Cuba
24B3 **Manzanillo** Mexico
63D3 **Manzhouli** China
94C3 **Manzil** Jordan
101C3 **Manzini** Swaziland
98B1 **Mao** Chad
72A2 **Maomao Shan** *Mt* China
73C5 **Maoming** China
101C3 **Mapai** Mozam
71E3 **Mapia** *Is* Pacific O
79A4 **Mapin** *I* Phil
5H5 **Maple Creek** Can
101H1 **Maputo** Mozam
101H1 **Maputo** *R* Mozam
Ma Qu = Huange He
72A3 **Maqu** China
86B1 **Maquan He** *R* China
98B3 **Maquela do Zombo** Angola
29C4 **Maquinchao** Arg
31B3 **Marabá** Brazil
32C1 **Maracaibo** Ven
32D1 **Maracay** Ven
95A2 **Marādah** Libya
97C3 **Maradi** Niger
90A2 **Marāgheh** Iran

99D2 **Maralal** Kenya
107F1 **Maramasike** *I* Solomon Is
100B2 **Maramba** Zambia
90A2 **Marand** Iran
31B2 **Maranhõa** State, Brazil
109C1 **Maranoa** *R* Aust
32B4 **Marañón** *R* Peru
7B5 **Marathon** Can
17B2 **Marathon** Florida, USA
78D2 **Maratua** *I* Indon
23A2 **Maravatio** Mexico
79B4 **Marawi** Phil
34B2 **Marayes** Arg
50B2 **Marbella** Spain
106A3 **Marble Bar** Aust
100B3 **Marblehall** S Africa
16D1 **Marblehead** USA
57B2 **Marburg** Germany
57B2 **Marche** Belg
50A2 **Marchean** Spain
46C1 **Marche-en-Famenne** Belg
32J7 **Marchena** *I* Ecuador
17B2 **Marco** USA
34C2 **Marcos Juárez** Arg
12E2 **Marcus Baker,Mt** USA
15D2 **Marcy,Mt** USA
84C2 **Mardan** Pak
29E3 **Mar del Plata** Arg
93D2 **Mardin** Turk
99D1 **Mareb** *R* Eritrea/Eth
16B1 **Margaretville** USA
43E4 **Margate** Eng
54B1 **Marghita** Rom
109C4 **Maria I** Aust
104F3 **Mariana** *Is* Pacific O
13E1 **Mariana Lake** Can
104F3 **Marianas Trench** Pacific O
86C1 **Mariāni** India
19B3 **Marianna** Arkansas, USA
17A1 **Marianna** Florida, USA
7G4 **Maria Van Diemen,C** NZ
59B3 **Mariazell** Austria
52C1 **Maribor** Slovenia
99C2 **Maridi** Sudan
112B5 **Marie Byrd Land** Region, Ant
27E3 **Marie Galante** *I* Caribbean S
39H6 **Mariehamn** Fin
46C1 **Mariembourg** Belg
33G2 **Marienburg** Surinam
100A3 **Mariental** Namibia
39G7 **Mariestad** Sweden
17B1 **Marietta** Georgia, USA
14B3 **Marietta** Ohio, USA
19A3 **Marietta** Oklahoma, USA
27Q2 **Marigot** Dominica
60B3 **Marijampole** Lithuania
31B6 **Marilia** Brazil
98B3 **Marimba** Angola
79B3 **Marinduque** *I* Phil
10B2 **Marinette** USA
30F3 **Maringá** Brazil
98C2 **Maringa** *R* Zaïre
18B2 **Marion** Arkansas, USA
18C2 **Marion** Illinois, USA
10B2 **Marion** Indiana, USA
10B2 **Marion** Ohio, USA
17C1 **Marion** S Carolina, USA
11B3 **Marion,L** USA
107E2 **Marion Reef** Aust
21B2 **Mariposa** USA
22B2 **Mariposa** *R* USA
22B2 **Mariposa Res** USA
60C5 **Marista** *R* Bulg
60E4 **Mariupol'** Ukraine
61G2 **Mariyskaya Respublika,** Russian Fed
94B2 **Marjayoun** Leb
58D2 **Marjina Gorki** Belorussia
94B3 **Marka** Jordan
99E2 **Marka** Somalia
56C1 **Markaryd** Sweden
43C3 **Market Drayton** Eng
43D3 **Market Harborough** Eng
112A **Markham,Mt** Ant
22C1 **Markleeville** USA
16D1 **Marlboro** Massachusetts, USA
107D3 **Marlborough** Aust
46B2 **Marle** France
19A3 **Marlin** USA
48C3 **Marmande** France
55C2 **Marmara Adi** *I* Turk
92A1 **Marmara,S of** Turk
55C3 **Marmaris** Turk
14B3 **Marmet** USA
52B1 **Marmolada** *Mt* Italy
12D3 **Marmot B** USA
47A1 **Marnay** France
46B2 **Marne** Department, France
46B2 **Marne** *R* France
98B2 **Maro** Chad
101D2 **Maroantsetra** Madag
101C2 **Marondera** Zim
33G3 **Maroni** *R* French Guiana
109D1 **Maroochydore** Aust
98B1 **Maroua** Cam
101D2 **Marovoay** Madag
11B4 **Marquesas Keys** *Is* USA
10B2 **Marquette** USA
46A1 **Marquise** France
109C2 **Marra** *R* Aust
101H1 **Marracuene** Mozam
96B1 **Marrakech** Mor
106C3 **Marree** Aust
19B4 **Marrero** USA
101C2 **Marromeu** Mozam
101C2 **Marrupa** Mozam
95C2 **Marsa Alam** Egypt
99D2 **Marsabit** Kenya
53B3 **Marsala** Italy
49D3 **Marseille** France
12B2 **Marshall** Alaska, USA
14A3 **Marshall** Illinois, USA
14B2 **Marshall** Michigan, USA
18B2 **Marshall** Missouri, USA
11A3 **Marshall** Texas, USA
105G3 **Marshall Is** Pacific O
18B2 **Marshfield** Missouri, USA
26B1 **Marsh Harbour** The Bahamas
19B4 **Marsh I** USA
12H2 **Marsh L** Can
76B2 **Martaban,G of** Burma
78A3 **Martapura** Indon
78C3 **Martapura** Indon
15D2 **Martha's Vineyard** *I* USA
49D2 **Martigny** Switz
59B3 **Martin** Slovakia
111C2 **Martinborough** NZ
34B3 **Martín de Loyola** Arg
23B1 **Martínez de la Torre** Mexico
27E4 **Martinique** *I* Caribbean S
17A1 **Martin,L** USA
15C3 **Martinsburg** USA
14B2 **Martins Ferry** USA
103G6 **Martin Vaz** *I* Atlantic O
49D3 **Martiques** France
110C2 **Marton** NZ
50B2 **Martos** Spain
78D1 **Marudi** Malay
84B2 **Maruf** Afghan
75A2 **Marugame** Japan
85C3 **Mārwār** India
65H6 **Mary** Turkmenistan
107E3 **Maryborough** Queensland, Aust
108B3 **Maryborough** Victoria, Aust
5F4 **Mary Henry,Mt** Can
10C3 **Maryland** State, USA
42C2 **Maryport** Eng
21A2 **Marysville** California, USA
18A2 **Marysville** Kansas, USA
20B1 **Marysville** Washington, USA
10A2 **Maryville** Iowa, USA
18B1 **Maryville** Missouri, USA
95A2 **Marzuq** Libya
Masada = Mezada
94B2 **Mas'adah** Syria
99D3 **Masai Steppe** *Upland* Tanz
99D3 **Masaka** Uganda
93E2 **Masally** Azerbaijan
74B3 **Masan** S Korea
101C2 **Masasi** Tanz
25D3 **Masaya** Nic
79B3 **Masbate** Phil
79B3 **Masbate** *I* Phil
96C1 **Mascara** Alg
23A1 **Mascota** Mexico
35D1 **Mascote** Brazil
101G1 **Maseru** Lesotho
66C3 **Mashad** Iran
84B2 **Mashaki** Afghan
90C2 **Mashhad** Iran
98B3 **Masi-Manimba** Zaïre
99D2 **Masindi** Uganda
99C3 **Masisi** Zaïre
90A3 **Masjed Soleyman** Iran
101E2 **Masoala** *C* Madag
10A2 **Mason City** USA
91C5 **Masqat** Oman
52B2 **Massa** Italy
10C2 **Massachusetts** State, USA
15D2 **Massachusetts B** USA
98B1 **Massakori** Chad
101C3 **Massangena** Mozam
Massawa = Mits'iwa
15D2 **Massena** USA
98B1 **Massénya** Chad
14B1 **Massey** Can
49C2 **Massif Central** *Mts* France
98B2 **Massif de l'Adamaoua** *Mts* Cam
26C3 **Massif de la Hotte** *Mts* Haiti
101D3 **Massif de l'Isalo** *Upland* Madag
98C2 **Massif des Bongo** *Upland* CAR
49D2 **Massif du Pelvoux** *Mts* France
101D2 **Massif du Tsaratanana** *Mt* Madag
14B2 **Massillon** USA
97B3 **Massina** Region, Mali
101C3 **Massinga** Mozam
101C3 **Massingir** Mozam
61H4 **Masteksay** Kazakhstan
111C2 **Masterton** NZ
74C4 **Masuda** Japan
98B3 **Masuku** Gabon
100C3 **Masvingo** Zim
92C2 **Maşyāf** Syria
98B3 **Matadi** Zaïre
25D3 **Matagalpa** Nic
7C4 **Matagami** Can
9D4 **Matagorda B** USA
110C1 **Matakana I** NZ
100A2 **Matala** Angola
87C3 **Matale** Sri Lanka
97A3 **Matam** Sen
97C3 **Matameye** Niger
24C2 **Matamoros** Mexico
95B2 **Ma'tan as Sarra** *Well* Libya
7D5 **Matane** Can
25D2 **Matanzas** Cuba
34A2 **Mataquito** *R* Chile
87C3 **Matara** Sri Lanka
106A1 **Mataram** Indon
30B2 **Matarani** Peru
51C1 **Mataró** Spain
111A3 **Mataura** NZ
24B2 **Matehuala** Mexico
27L1 **Matelot** Trinidad
53C2 **Matera** Italy
59C3 **Mátészalka** Hung
85D3 **Mathura** India
79C4 **Mati** Phil
78D3 **Matisiri** *I* Indon
43D3 **Matlock** Eng
33F6 **Mato Grosso** Brazil
33F6 **Mato Grosso** State, Brazil
30E2 **Mato Grosso do Sul** State, Brazil
101H1 **Matola** Mozam
91C5 **Matrah** Oman
92A3 **Matrûh** Egypt
74C3 **Matsue** Japan
74E2 **Matsumae** Japan
74D3 **Matsumoto** Japan
74D4 **Matsusaka** Japan
74C4 **Matsuyama** Japan
7B5 **Mattagami** *R* Can
15C1 **Mattawa** Can
52A1 **Matterhorn** *Mt* Italy/Switz
26C2 **Matthew Town** The Bahamas
16C2 **Mattituck** USA
18C2 **Mattoon** USA
84B2 **Matun** Afghan
27L1 **Matura B** Trinidad
33E2 **Maturin** Ven
86A1 **Mau** India
101C2 **Maúa** Mozam
49C1 **Maubeuge** France
108B2 **Maude** Aust
103J8 **Maud Seamount** Atlantic O
21C4 **Maui** *I* Hawaiian Is
34A3 **Maule** *R* Chile
14B2 **Maumee** USA
14B2 **Maumee** *R* USA
100B2 **Maun** Botswana
21C4 **Mauna Kea** *Mt* Hawaiian Is
21C4 **Mauna Loa** *Mt* Hawaiian Is
4F3 **Maunoir** *L* Can
4F3 **Maunoir,L** Can
48C2 **Mauriac** France
96A2 **Mauritania** Republic Africa
100E3 **Mauritius** *I* Indian O
100B2 **Mavinga** Angola
86C2 **Mawlaik** Burma
Mawlamyine = Moulmein
112C10 **Mawson** *Base* Ant
78B3 **Maya** *I* Indon
63F2 **Maya** *R* Russian Fe
93D2 **Mayādīn** Syria
11C4 **Mayaguana** *I* The Bahamas
27D3 **Mayagüez** Puerto Rico
97C3 **Mayahi** Niger
98B3 **Mayama** Congo
90C2 **Mayamey** Iran
42B2 **Maybole** Scot
10C3 **May,C** USA
109C4 **Maydena** Aust
46D1 **Mayen** Germany
48B2 **Mayenne** France
13D2 **Mayerthorpe** Can
18C2 **Mayfield** USA
61E5 **Maykop** Russian Fe
65H6 **Maymaneh** Afghan
76B1 **Maymyo** Burma
4E3 **Mayo** Can
45B2 **Mayo** County, Irish Rep
16A3 **Mayo** USA
45B1 **Mayo,Mts of** Irish Rep
79B3 **Mayon** *Mt* Phil
51C2 **Mayor** *Mt* Spain
34C3 **Mayor Buratovich** Arg
110C1 **Mayor I** NZ
30D2 **Mayor P Lagerenza** Par

101D2 **Mayotte** *I* Indian O
27H2 **May Pen** Jamaica
16B3 **May Point,C** USA
47D1 **Mayrhofen** Austria
16B3 **Mays Landing** USA
14B3 **Maysville** USA
98B3 **Mayumba** Gabon
100B2 **Mazabuka** Zambia
84D1 **Mazar** China
94B3 **Mazār** Jordan
53B3 **Mazara del Vallo** Italy
84B1 **Mazar-i-Sharif** Afghan
24B2 **Mazatlán** Mexico
60B2 **Mazeikiai** Lithuania
94B3 **Mazra** Jordan
101C3 **Mbabane** Swaziland
98B2 **Mbaïki** CAR
99D3 **Mbala** Zambia
100B3 **Mbalabala** Zim
99D2 **Mbale** Uganda
98B2 **Mbalmayo** Cam
98B2 **Mbam** *R* Cam
101C2 **Mbamba Bay** Tanz
98B2 **Mbandaka** Zaïre
98B3 **Mbanza Congo** Angola
98B3 **Mbanza-Ngungu** Zaïre
99D3 **Mbarara** Uganda
98B2 **Mbènza** Congo
98B2 **Mbére** *R* Cam
99D3 **Mbeya** Tanz
98B3 **Mbinda** Congo
97A3 **Mbout** Maur
98C3 **Mbuji-Mayi** Zaïre
99D3 **Mbulu** Tanz
96B2 **Mcherrah** Region, Alg
101C2 **Mchinji** Malawi
76D3 **Mdrak** Viet
9B3 **Mead,L** USA
5H4 **Meadow Lake** Can
14B2 **Meadville** USA
7E4 **Mealy Mts** Can
109C1 **Meandarra** Aust
5G4 **Meander River** Can
45C2 **Meath** County, Irish Rep
49C2 **Meaux** France
16C1 **Mechanicville** USA
56A2 **Mechelen** Belg
96B1 **Mecheria** Alg
56C2 **Mecklenburg-Vorpommern** *State* Germany
56C2 **Mecklenburger Bucht** *B* Germany
101C2 **Meconta** Mozam
101C2 **Mecuburi** Mozam
101D2 **Mecufi** Mozam
101C2 **Mecula** Mozam
70A3 **Medan** Indon
34C3 **Medanos** Arg
34D2 **Médanos** Arg
13E2 **Medecine Hat** Can
32B2 **Medellin** Colombia
96D1 **Medenine** Tunisia
8A2 **Medford** USA
54C2 **Medgidia** Rom
34B2 **Media Agua** Arg
54B1 **Mediaş** Rom
20C1 **Medical Lake** USA
5G5 **Medicine Hat** Can
35C1 **Medina** Brazil
80B3 **Medina** S Arabia
50B1 **Medinaceli** Spain
50B1 **Medina del Campo** Spain
50A1 **Medina de Rio Seco** Spain
86B2 **Medinīpur** India
88E4 **Mediterranean S** Europe
13F2 **Medley** Can
61J3 **Mednogorsk** Russian Fed
86D1 **Mêdog** China
98B2 **Medouneu** Gabon
61F3 **Medvedista** *R* Russian Fed
64E3 **Medvezh'yegorsk** Russian Fed
106A3 **Meekatharra** Aust
84D3 **Meerut** India
99D2 **Mēga** Eth
55B3 **Megalópolis** Greece
55B3 **Mégara** Greece
86C1 **Meghālaya** State, India
86C2 **Meghna** *R* Bang
94B2 **Megiddo** *Hist Site* Israel
91B4 **Mehran** *R* Iran
90B3 **Mehriz** Iran
35B1 **Meia Ponte** *R* Brazil
98B2 **Meiganga** Cam
76B1 **Meiktila** Burma
47C1 **Meiringen** Switz
73A4 **Meishan** China
57C2 **Meissen** Germany
73D5 **Mei Xian** China
73D5 **Meizhou** China
30B3 **Mejillones** Chile
98B2 **Mekambo** Gabon
99D1 **Mek'elē** Eth
96B1 **Meknès** Mor
76D3 **Mekong** *R* Camb
97C3 **Mekrou** *R* Benin
77C5 **Melaka** Malay
104F4 **Melanesia** *Region* Pacific O
78C3 **Melawi** *R* Indon
107D4 **Melbourne** Aust
11B4 **Melbourne** USA
9C4 **Melchor Muźguiz** Mexico
61J3 **Meleuz** Russian Fed
98B1 **Melfi** Chad
5H4 **Melfort** Can
96B1 **Melilla** N W Africa
29B4 **Melimoyu** *Mt* Chile
34C2 **Melincué** Arg
34A2 **Melipilla** Chile
60E4 **Melitopol'** Ukraine
6D2 **Meliville Bugt** *B* Greenland
99D2 **Melka Guba** Eth
101H1 **Melmoth** S Africa
34C2 **Melo** Arg
29F2 **Melo** Urug
22B2 **Melones Res** USA
12D1 **Melozitna** *R* USA
47C1 **Mels** Switz
43D3 **Melton Mowbry** Eng
49C2 **Melun** France
5H4 **Melville** Can
27Q2 **Melville,C** Dominica
4F3 **Melville Hills** *Mts* Can
106C2 **Melville I** Aust
4G2 **Melville I** Can
7E4 **Melville,L** Can
6B3 **Melville Pen** Can
45B1 **Melvin,L** Irish Rep
101D2 **Memba** Mozam
106A1 **Memboro** Indon
57C3 **Memmingen** Germany
78B2 **Mempawan** Indon
11B3 **Memphis** Tennessee, USA
19B3 **Mena** USA
43B3 **Menai Str** Wales
97C3 **Ménaka** Mali
14A2 **Menasha** USA
78C3 **Mendawai** *R* Indon
49C3 **Mende** France
99D2 **Mendebo** *Mts* Eth
43C4 **Mendip Hills** *Upland* Eng
20B2 **Mendocino,C** USA
105J2 **Mendocino Seascarp** Pacific O
22B2 **Mendota** California, USA
29C2 **Mendoza** Arg
29C3 **Mendoza** State, Arg
55C3 **Menemen** Turk
46B1 **Menen** Belg
72D3 **Mengcheng** China
78B3 **Menggala** Indon
76B1 **Menghai** China
73A5 **Mengla** China
76B1 **Menglian** China
73A5 **Mengzi** China
107D4 **Menindee** Aust
108B2 **Menindee L** Aust
108A3 **Meningie** Aust
14A1 **Menominee** USA
14A2 **Menomonee Falls** USA
100A2 **Menongue** Angola
51C1 **Menorca** *I* Spain
12F2 **Mentasta Mts** USA
78B3 **Mentok** Indon
14B2 **Mentor** USA
46B2 **Ménu** France
72A2 **Menyuan** China
61H2 **Menzelinsk** Russian Fed
56B2 **Meppen** Germany
78D2 **Merah** Indon
18B2 **Meramec** *R* USA
52B1 **Merano** Italy
71F4 **Merauke** Indon
8A3 **Merced** USA
22B2 **Merced** *R* USA
29B2 **Mercedario** *Mt* Chile
29C2 **Mercedes** Arg
29E2 **Mercedes** Buenos Aires, Arg
30E4 **Mercedes** Corrientes, Arg
29E2 **Mercedes** Urug
110C1 **Mercury B** NZ
110C1 **Mercury Is** NZ
4F2 **Mercy B** Can
6D3 **Mercy,C** Can
99E2 **Meregh** Somalia
76B3 **Mergui** Burma
76B3 **Mergui Arch** Burma
25D2 **Mérida** Mexico
50A2 **Mérida** Spain
32C2 **Mérida** Ven
11B3 **Meridian** USA
109C3 **Merimbula** Aust
108B2 **Meringur** Aust
95C3 **Merowe** Sudan
106A4 **Merredin** Aust
42B2 **Merrick** *Mt* Scot
14A2 **Merrillville** USA
13C2 **Merritt** Can
17B2 **Merritt Island** USA
109D2 **Merriwa** Aust
99E1 **Mersa Fatma** Eritrea
51B2 **Mers el Kebir** Alg
42C3 **Mersey** *R* Eng
42C3 **Merseyside** Metropolitan County, Eng
92B2 **Mersin** Turk
77C5 **Mersing** Malay
85C3 **Merta** India
43C4 **Merthyr Tydfil** Wales
50A2 **Mertola** Port
99D3 **Meru** *Mt* Tanz
60E5 **Merzifon** Turk
46D2 **Merzig** Germany
9B3 **Mesa** USA
46E1 **Meschede** Germany
93D1 **Mescit Dağ** *Mt* Turk
12C3 **Meshik** USA
99C2 **Meshra Er Req** Sudan
47C1 **Mesocco** Switz
55B3 **Mesolóngion** Greece
19A3 **Mesquite** Texas, USA
101C2 **Messalo** *R* Mozam
53C3 **Messina** Italy
100B3 **Messina** S Africa
55B3 **Messíni** Greece
55B3 **Messiniakós Kólpos** *G* Greece
54B2 **Mesta** *R* Bulg
52B1 **Mestre** Italy
32C3 **Meta** *R* Colombia
60D2 **Meta** *R* Russian Fed
32D2 **Meta** *R* Ven
6C3 **Meta Incognito Pen** Can
19B4 **Metairie** USA
20C1 **Metaline Falls** USA
30D4 **Metán** Arg
101C2 **Metangula** Mozam
53C2 **Metaponto** Italy
44C3 **Methil** Scot
16D1 **Methuen** USA
111B2 **Methven** NZ
12H3 **Metlakatla** USA
18C2 **Metropolis** USA
87B2 **Mettūr** India
49D2 **Metz** France
70A3 **Meulaboh** Indon
46A2 **Meulan** France
46C2 **Meuse** Department, France
49D2 **Meuse** *R* France
19A3 **Mexia** USA
24A1 **Mexicali** Mexico
24B2 **Mexico** Federal Republic, Cent America
24C3 **México** Mexico
23A2 **México** State, Mexico
18B2 **Mexico** USA
24C2 **Mexico,G of** Cent America
94B3 **Mezada** *Hist Site* Israel
23B2 **Mezcala** Mexico
64F3 **Mezen'** Russian Fed
64G2 **Mezhdusharskiy, Ostrov** *I* Russian Fed
85D4 **Mhow** India
23B2 **Miahuatlán** Mexico
11B4 **Miami** Florida, USA
18B2 **Miami** Oklahoma, USA
11B4 **Miami Beach** USA
90A2 **Miandowāb** Iran
101D2 **Miandrivazo** Madag
90A2 **Mīāneh** Iran
84C2 **Mianwali** Pak
73A3 **Mianyang** China
73C3 **Mianyang** China
73A3 **Mianzhu** China
72E2 **Miaodao Qundao** *Arch* China
73B4 **Miao Ling** *Upland* China
61K3 **Miass** Russian Fed
59C3 **Michalovce** Slovakia
27D3 **Miches** Dom Rep
10B2 **Michigan** State, USA
14A2 **Michigan City** USA
10B2 **Michigan,L** USA
7B5 **Michipicoten I** Can
23A2 **Michoacan** State, Mexico
54C2 **Michurin** Bulg
61F3 **Michurinsk** Russian Fed
104F3 **Micronesia** *Region* Pacific O
78B2 **Midai** *I* Indon
102F4 **Mid Atlantic Ridge** Atlantic O
46B1 **Middelburg** Neth
20B2 **Middle Alkali L** USA
16D2 **Middleboro** USA
100B4 **Middleburg** Cape Province, S Africa
16A2 **Middleburg** Pennsylvania, USA
101G1 **Middleburg** Transvaal, S Africa
16B1 **Middleburgh** USA
15D2 **Middlebury** USA
11B3 **Middlesboro** USA
42D2 **Middlesbrough** Eng
16C2 **Middletown** Connecticut, USA
16B3 **Middletown** Delaware, USA
15D2 **Middletown** New York, USA
14B3 **Middletown** Ohio, USA
16A2 **Middletown** Pennsylvania, USA
96B1 **Midelt** Mor
43C4 **Mid Glamorgan** County, Wales
104B4 **Mid Indian Basin** Indian O
104B4 **Mid Indian Ridge** Indian O
7C5 **Midland** Can
14B2 **Midland** Michigan, USA
9C3 **Midland** Texas, USA
101D3 **Midongy Atsimo** Madag

105G2 **Mid Pacific Mts** Pacific O
20C2 **Midvale** USA
105H2 **Midway Is** Pacific O
18A2 **Midwest City** USA
93D2 **Midyat** Turk
54B2 **Midžor** *Mt* Serbia, Yugos
59B2 **Mielec** Pol
54C1 **Miercurea-Ciuc** Rom
50A1 **Mieres** Spain
16A2 **Mifflintown** USA
75A2 **Mihara** Japan
72D1 **Mijun Shuiku** *Res* China
54B2 **Mikhaylovgrad** Bulg
61F3 **Mikhaylovka** Russian Fed
65J4 **Mikhaylovskiy** Russian Fed
38K6 **Mikkeli** Fin
55C3 **Míkonos** *I* Greece
59B3 **Mikulov** Czech Republic
99D3 **Mikumi** Tanz
74D3 **Mikuni-sammyaku** *Mts* Japan
75B2 **Mikura-jima** *I* Japan
32B4 **Milagro** Ecuador
Milan = Milano
51C2 **Milana** Alg
101C2 **Milange** Mozam
52A1 **Milano** Italy
92A2 **Milas** Turk
107D4 **Mildura** Aust
73A5 **Mile** China
93D3 **Mileh Tharthār** *L* Iraq
107E3 **Miles** Aust
8C2 **Miles City** USA
16C2 **Milford** Connecticut, USA
15C3 **Milford** Delaware, USA
15D2 **Milford** Massachusetts, USA
18A1 **Milford** Nebraska, USA
16B2 **Milford** Pennsylvania, USA
43B4 **Milford Haven** Wales
43B4 **Milford Haven** *Sd* Wales
18A2 **Milford L** USA
111A2 **Milford Sd** NZ
13E2 **Milk River** Can
49C3 **Millau** France
16C2 **Millbrook** USA
17B1 **Milledgeville** USA
12F2 **Miller,Mt** USA
61F4 **Millerovo** Russian Fed
16A2 **Millersburg** USA
108A1 **Millers Creek** Aust
16C1 **Millers Falls** USA
16C2 **Millerton** USA
22C2 **Millerton L** USA
108B3 **Millicent** Aust
109D1 **Millmerran** Aust
45B2 **Milltown Malbay** Irish Rep
22A2 **Mill Valley** USA
15D3 **Millville** USA
6H2 **Milne Land** *I* Greenland
21C4 **Milolii** Hawaiian Is
55B3 **Milos** *I* Greece
107D3 **Milparinka** Aust
16A2 **Milroy** USA
111A3 **Milton** NZ
16A2 **Milton** Pennsylvania, USA
10B2 **Milwaukee** USA
51C2 **Mina** *R* Alg
93E4 **Mīnā' al Ahmadī** Kuwait
91C4 **Mīnāb** Iran
74C4 **Minamata** Japan
78A2 **Minas** Indon
29E2 **Minas** Urug
31B5 **Minas Gerais** State, Brazil
35C1 **Minas Novas** Brazil
25C3 **Minatitlan** Mexico
76A1 **Minbu** Burma
76A1 **Minbya** Burma
34A2 **Mincha** Chile
44A3 **Minch,Little** *Sd* Scot
44A2 **Minch,North** *Sd* Scot
40B2 **Minch,The** *Sd* Scot
12D2 **Minchumina,L** USA
47D2 **Mincio** *R* Italy
79B4 **Mindanao** *I* Phil
19B3 **Minden** Louisiana, USA
56B2 **Minden** Germany
108B2 **Mindona L** Aust
79B3 **Mindoro** *I* Phil
79B3 **Mindoro Str** Phil
45C3 **Mine Hd** *C* Irish Rep
43C4 **Minehead** Eng
30F2 **Mineiros** Brazil
19A3 **Mineola** USA
23B1 **Mineral de Monte** Mexico
16A2 **Minersville** USA
108B2 **Mingary** Aust
72A2 **Minhe** China
87A3 **Minicoy** *I* India
73D4 **Min Jiang** *R* Fujian, China
73A4 **Min Jiang** *R* Sichuan, China
22C2 **Minkler** USA
108A2 **Minlaton** Aust
72A2 **Minle** China
97C4 **Minna** Nig
10A2 **Minneapolis** USA
5J4 **Minnedosa** Can
10A2 **Minnesota** State, USA
50A1 **Miño** *R* Spain
8C2 **Minot** USA
72A2 **Minqin** China
72A3 **Min Shan** *Upland* China
60C3 **Minsk** Belorussia
58C2 **Mińsk Mazowiecki** Pol
12E2 **Minto** USA
4G2 **Minto Inlet** *B* Can
7C4 **Minto,L** Can
63B2 **Minusinsk** Russian Fed
72A3 **Min Xian** China
7E5 **Miquelon** Can
22D3 **Mirage L** USA
87A1 **Miraj** India
29E3 **Miramar** Arg
84B2 **Miram Shah** Pak
50B1 **Miranda de Ebro** Spain
47D2 **Mirandola** Italy
84B2 **Mir Bachchen Kūt** Afghan
78D1 **Miri** Malay
96A3 **Mirik,C** Maur
63A1 **Mirnoye** Russian Fed
63D1 **Mirnyy** Russian Fed
112C9 **Mirnyy** *Base* Ant
84C2 **Mirpur** Pak
85B3 **Mirpur Khas** Pak
55B3 **Mirtoan S** Greece
74B3 **Miryang** S Korea
86A1 **Mirzāpur** India
23B2 **Misantla** Mexico
84C1 **Misgar** Pak
14A2 **Mishawaka** USA
12B1 **Misheguk Mt** USA
75A2 **Mi-shima** *I* Japan
107E2 **Misima** *I* Solomon Is
30F4 **Misiones** State, Arg
59C3 **Miskolc** Hung
94C2 **Mismīyah** Syria
71E4 **Misoöl** *I* Indon
95A1 **Misrātah** Libya
7B5 **Missinaibi** *R* Can
20B1 **Mission City** Can
15C2 **Mississauga** Can
11A3 **Mississippi** State, USA
11A3 **Mississippi** *R* USA
19C3 **Mississippi Delta** USA
8B2 **Missoula** USA
96B1 **Missour** Mor
11A3 **Missouri** State, USA
10A2 **Missouri** *R* USA
10C1 **Mistassini,L** Can
30B2 **Misti** *Mt* Peru
109C1 **Mitchell** Aust
8D2 **Mitchell** USA
107D2 **Mitchell** *R* Aust
11B3 **Mitchell,Mt** USA
45B2 **Mitchelstown** Irish Rep
84C3 **Mithankot** Pak
55C3 **Mitilíni** Greece
23B2 **Mitla** Mexico
54B2 **Mitrovica** Serbia, Yugos
95C3 **Mits'iwa** Eritrea
32C3 **Mitu** Colombia
99C3 **Mitumbar** *Mts* Zaïre
98C3 **Mitwaba** Zaïre
98B2 **Mitzic** Gabon
75B1 **Miura** Japan
72C3 **Mi Xian** China
69F3 **Miyake** *I* Japan
75B2 **Miyake-jima** *I* Japan
69E4 **Miyako** *I* Japan
74C4 **Miyakonojō** Japan
74C4 **Miyazaki** Japan
75B1 **Miyazu** Japan
74C4 **Miyoshi** Japan
72D1 **Miyun** China
99D2 **Mīzan Teferi** Eth
95A1 **Mizdah** Libya
45B3 **Mizen Hd** *C* Irish Rep
54C1 **Mizil** Rom
86C2 **Mizo Hills** India
86C2 **Mizoram** Union Territory, India
94B3 **Mizpe Ramon** Israel
112B11 **Mizuho** *Base* Ant
74E3 **Mizusawa** Japan
39H7 **Mjolby** Sweden
100B2 **Mkushi** Zambia
101H1 **Mkuzi** S Africa
57C2 **Mladá Boleslav** Czech Republic
58C2 **Mława** Pol
52C2 **Mljet** *I* Croatia
100B3 **Mmabatho** S Africa
84D2 **Mnadi** India
97A4 **Moa** *R* Sierra Leone
94B3 **Moab** Region, Jordan
9C3 **Moab** USA
98B3 **Moanda** Congo
98B3 **Moanda** Gabon
99C3 **Moba** Zaïre
75C1 **Mobara** Japan
98C2 **Mobaye** CAR
98C2 **Mobayi** Zaïre
10A3 **Moberly** USA
11B3 **Mobile** USA
11B3 **Mobile B** USA
8C2 **Mobridge** USA
101D2 **Moçambique** Mozam
76C1 **Moc Chau** Viet
100B3 **Mochudi** Botswana
101D2 **Mocimboa da Praia** Mozam
32B3 **Mocoa** Colombia
35B2 **Mococa** Brazil
34D2 **Mocoreta** *R* Arg
23B1 **Moctezuma** *R* Mexico
101C2 **Mocuba** Mozam
47B2 **Modane** France
101G1 **Modder** *R* S Africa
52B2 **Modena** Italy
46D2 **Moder** *R* France
8A3 **Modesto** USA
22B2 **Modesto Res** USA
53B3 **Modica** Italy
59B3 **Mödling** Austria
107D4 **Moe** Aust
47C1 **Moesa** *R* Switz
42C2 **Moffat** Scot
84D2 **Moga** India
35B2 **Mogi das Cruzes** Brazil
60C3 **Mogilev** Belorussia
60C4 **Mogilev Podolskiy** Ukraine
35B2 **Mogi-Mirim** Brazil
101D2 **Mogincual** Mozam
47E2 **Mogliano** Italy
34B2 **Mogna** Arg
68D1 **Mogocha** Russian Fed
65K4 **Mogochin** Russian Fed
50A2 **Moguer** Spain
110C1 **Mohaka** *R* NZ
86C2 **Mohanganj** Bang
15D2 **Mohawk** *R* USA
99D3 **Mohoro** Tanz
65J5 **Mointy** Kazakhstan
38G5 **Mo i Rana** Nor
48C3 **Moissac** France
21B2 **Mojave** USA
22D3 **Mojave** *R* USA
9B3 **Mojave Desert** USA
78C4 **Mojokerto** Indon
86B1 **Mokama** India
110B1 **Mokau** *R* NZ
22B1 **Mokelumne Aqueduct** USA
22B1 **Mokelumne Hill** USA
22B1 **Mokelumne North Fork** *R* USA
101G1 **Mokhotlong** Lesotho
96D1 **Moknine** Tunisia
86C1 **Mokokchūng** India
98B1 **Mokolo** Cam
74B4 **Mokp'o** S Korea
61F3 **Moksha** *R* Russian Fed
23B1 **Molango** Mexico
55B3 **Moláoi** Greece
38F6 **Molde** Nor
60C4 **Moldova** Republic, Europe
54B1 **Moldoveanu** *Mt* Rom
100B3 **Molepolole** Botswana
53C2 **Molfetta** Italy
34A3 **Molina** Chile
30B2 **Mollendo** Peru
60C3 **Molodechno** Belorussia
112C11 **Molodezhnaya** *Base* Ant
21C4 **Molokai** *I* Hawaiian Is
61G2 **Moloma** *R* Russian Fed
109C2 **Molong** Aust
100B3 **Molopo** *R* Botswana
98B2 **Molounddu** Cam
8D1 **Molson L** Can
71D4 **Molucca** *S* Indon
71D4 **Moluccas** *Is* Indon
101C2 **Moma** Mozam
31C3 **Mombaca** Brazil
99D3 **Mombasa** Kenya
98C2 **Mompono** Zaïre
56C2 **Mon** *I* Den
44A3 **Monach** *Is* Scot
49D3 **Monaco** Principality, Europe
44B3 **Monadhliath** *Mts* Scot
45C1 **Monaghan** County, Irish Rep
45C1 **Monaghan** Irish Rep
27D3 **Mona Pass** Caribbean S
13B2 **Monarch Mt** Can
5G4 **Monashee Mts** Can
41B3 **Monastereven** Irish Rep
47B2 **Moncalieri** Italy
31B2 **Monção** Brazil
38L5 **Monchegorsk** Russian Fed
56B2 **Mönchen-gladbach** Germany
24B2 **Monclova** Mexico
7D5 **Moncton** Can
9C4 **Monctova** Mexico
50A1 **Mondego** *R* Port
52A2 **Mondovi** Italy
27H1 **Moneague** Jamaica
14C2 **Monessen** USA
18B2 **Monett** USA
52B1 **Monfalcone** Italy

50A1 **Monforte de Lemos** Spain
98C2 **Monga** Zaïre
98C2 **Mongala** *R* Zaïre
99D2 **Mongalla** Sudan
76D1 **Mong Cai** Viet
98B1 **Mongo** Chad
68B2 **Mongolia** Republic, Asia
100B2 **Mongu** Zambia
21B2 **Monitor Range** *Mts* USA
98C3 **Monkoto** Zaïre
43C4 **Monmouth** Eng
18B1 **Monmouth** USA
13C2 **Monmouth,Mt** Can
97C4 **Mono** *R* Togo
21B2 **Mono L** USA
53C2 **Monopoli** Italy
51B1 **Monreal del Campo** Spain
19B3 **Monroe** Louisiana, USA
14B2 **Monroe** Michigan, USA
20B1 **Monroe** Washington, USA
18B2 **Monroe City** USA
97A4 **Monrovia** Lib
20D3 **Monrovia** USA
56A2 **Mons** Belg
47D2 **Monselice** Italy
16C1 **Monson** USA
58B1 **Mönsterås** Sweden
101D2 **Montagne d'Ambre** *Mt* Madag
96C1 **Montagnes des Ouled Naïl** *Mts* Alg
12E3 **Montague I** USA
49C3 **Mont Aigoual** *Mt* France
48B2 **Montaigu** France
53C3 **Montallo** *Mt* Italy
8B2 **Montana** State, USA
50A1 **Montañas de León** *Mts* Spain
49C2 **Montargis** France
48C3 **Montauban** France
15D2 **Montauk** USA
15D2 **Montauk Pt** USA
49D2 **Montbéliard** France
52A1 **Mont Blanc** *Mt* France/Italy
49C2 **Montceau les Mines** France
51C1 **Montceny** *Mt* Spain
49D3 **Mont Cinto** *Mt* Corse
46C2 **Montcornet** France
48B3 **Mont-de-Marsan** France
48C2 **Montdidier** France
30D2 **Monteagudo** Bol
33G4 **Monte Alegre** Brazil
52B2 **Monte Amiata** *Mt* Italy
47D2 **Monte Baldo** *Mt* Italy
15C1 **Montebello** Can
106A3 **Monte Bello Is** Aust
47E2 **Montebelluna** Italy
49D3 **Monte Carlo** Monaco
35B1 **Monte Carmelo** Brazil
34D2 **Monte Caseros** Arg
52B2 **Monte Cimone** *Mt* Italy
52A2 **Monte Cinto** *Mt* Corse
34B2 **Monte Coman** Arg
52B2 **Monte Corno** *Mt* Italy
27C3 **Montecristi** Dom Rep
52B2 **Montecristo** *I* Italy
23A1 **Monte Escobedo** Mexico
53C2 **Monte Gargano** *Mt* Italy
26B3 **Montego Bay** Jamaica
47D2 **Monte Grappa** *Mt* Italy
47C2 **Monte Lesima** *Mt* Italy
49C3 **Montélimar** France
53B2 **Monte Miletto** *Mt* Italy
50A2 **Montemo-o-Novo** Port
24C2 **Montemorelos** Mexico
26B5 **Montená** Colombia
54A2 **Montenegro** Republic, Yugos
35D1 **Monte Pascoal** *Mt* Brazil
34A2 **Monte Patria** Chile
53C3 **Monte Pollino** *Mt* Italy
101C2 **Montepuez** Mozam
8A3 **Monterey** California, USA
15C3 **Monterey** Virginia, USA
8A3 **Monterey B** USA
32B2 **Montería** Colombia
30D2 **Montero** Bol
47B2 **Monte Rosa** *Mt* Italy/Switz
24B2 **Monterrey** Mexico
31C5 **Montes Claros** Brazil
50B2 **Montes de Toledo** *Mts* Spain
29E2 **Montevideo** Urug
52A2 **Monte Viso** *Mt* Italy
27P2 **Mont Gimie** *Mt* St Lucia
11B3 **Montgomery** Alabama, USA
96C2 **Mont Gréboun** Niger
46C2 **Montherme** France
47B1 **Monthey** Switz
19B3 **Monticello** Arkansas, USA
16B2 **Monticello** New York, USA
9C3 **Monticello** Utah, USA
53A2 **Monti del Gennargentu** *Mt* Sardegna
47D2 **Monti Lessini** *Mts* Italy
53B3 **Monti Nebrodi** *Mts* Italy
7C5 **Mont-Laurier** Can
48C2 **Montluçon** France
7C5 **Montmagny** Can
46C2 **Montmédy** France
49C3 **Mont Mézenc** *Mt* France
46B2 **Montmirail** France
50B2 **Montoro** Spain
49D3 **Mont Pelat** *Mt* France
14B2 **Montpelier** Ohio, USA
10C2 **Montpelier** Vermont, USA
49C3 **Montpellier** France
7C5 **Montréal** Can
48C1 **Montreuil** France
52A1 **Montreux** Switz
47B1 **Mont Risoux** *Mt* France
8C3 **Montrose** Colorado, USA
40C2 **Montrose** Scot
48B2 **Mont-St-Michel** France
96B1 **Monts des Ksour** *Mts* Alg
51C3 **Monts des Ouled Neil** *Mts* Alg
51C2 **Monts du Hodna** *Mts* Alg
27E3 **Montserrat** *I* Caribbean S
10C1 **Monts Otish** *Mts* Can
12B1 **Monument Mt** USA
9B3 **Monument V** USA
98C2 **Monveda** Zaïre
76B1 **Monywa** Burma
52A1 **Monza** Italy
100B2 **Monze** Zambia
101H1 **Mooi** *R* S Africa
101G1 **Mooi River** S Africa
108B1 **Moomba** Aust
109D2 **Moonbi Range** *Mts* Aust
108B1 **Moonda L** Aust
109D1 **Moonie** Aust
109C1 **Moonie** *R* Aust
108A2 **Moonta** Aust
106A4 **Moora** Aust
106A3 **Moore,L** Aust
42C2 **Moorfoot Hills** Scot
8D2 **Moorhead** USA
22C3 **Moorpark** USA
7B4 **Moose** *R* Can
5H4 **Moose Jaw** Can
5H4 **Moosomin** Can
7B4 **Moosonee** Can
16D2 **Moosup** USA
101C2 **Mopeia** Mozam
97B3 **Mopti** Mali
30B2 **Moquegua** Peru
39G6 **Mora** Sweden
31D3 **Morada** Brazil
84D3 **Morādābād** India
35B1 **Morada Nova de Minas** *L* Brazil
101D2 **Morafenobe** Madag
101D2 **Moramanga** Madag
27J2 **Morant Bay** Jamaica
27J2 **Morant Pt** Jamaica
87B3 **Moratuwa** Sri Lanka
59B3 **Morava** *R* Austria/Slovakia
54B2 **Morava** *R* Serbia, Yugos
90C2 **Moraveh Tappeh** Iran
40C2 **Moray Firth** *Estuary* Scot
47C1 **Morbegno** Italy
85C4 **Morbi** India
93D2 **Mor Dağ** *Mt* Turk
5J5 **Morden** Can
61F3 **Mordovskaya Respublika,** Russian Fed
42C2 **Morecambe** Eng
42C2 **Morecambe B** Eng
107D3 **Moree** Aust
14B3 **Morehead** USA
47C1 **Mörel** Switz
24B3 **Morelia** Mexico
23B2 **Morelos** State, Mexico
85D3 **Morena** India
5E4 **Moresby I** Can
109D1 **Moreton I** Aust
46B2 **Moreuil** France
47B1 **Morez** France
19B4 **Morgan City** USA
22B2 **Morgan Hill** USA
14C3 **Morgantown** USA
101G1 **Morgenzon** S Africa
47B1 **Morges** Switz
46D2 **Morhange** France
74E2 **Mori** Japan
27K1 **Moriatio** Tobago
13B2 **Morice L** Can
13E2 **Morinville** Can
74E3 **Morioka** Japan
109D2 **Morisset** Aust
63D1 **Morkoka** *R* Russian Fed
48B2 **Morlaix** France
27Q2 **Morne Diablotin** *Mt* Dominica
106C2 **Mornington** *I* Aust
85B3 **Moro** Pak
96B2 **Morocco** Kingdom, Africa
79B4 **Moro G** Phil
99D3 **Morogoro** Tanz
23A1 **Moroleon** Mexico
101D3 **Morombe** Madag
26B2 **Morón** Cuba
101D3 **Morondava** Madag
50A2 **Moron de la Frontera** Spain
101D2 **Moroni** Comoros
71D3 **Morotai** *I* Indon
99D2 **Moroto** Uganda
61F4 **Morozovsk** Russian Fed
42D2 **Morpeth** Eng
19B2 **Morrilton** USA
35B1 **Morrinhos** Brazil
110C1 **Morrinsville** NZ
16B2 **Morristown** New Jersey, USA
15C2 **Morristown** New York, USA
16B2 **Morrisville** Pennsylvania, USA
21A2 **Morro Bay** USA
23A2 **Morro de Papanoa** Mexico
23A2 **Morro de Petatlán** Mexico
101C2 **Morrumbala** Mozam
101C3 **Morrumbene** Mozam
61F3 **Morshansk** Russian Fed
47C2 **Mortara** Italy
34C2 **Morteros** Arg
33G6 **Mortes** *R* Mato Grosso, Brazil
35C2 **Mortes** *R* Minas Gerais, Brazil
108B3 **Mortlake** Aust
27L1 **Moruga** Trinidad
109D3 **Moruya** Aust
109C1 **Morven** Aust
44B3 **Morvern** *Pen* Scot
109C3 **Morwell** Aust
76B3 **Moscos Is** Burma
Moscow = Moskva
20C1 **Moscow** Idaho, USA
56B2 **Mosel** *R* Germany
46D2 **Moselle** Department, France
46D2 **Moselle** *R* France
20C1 **Moses Lake** USA
111B3 **Mosgiel** NZ
99D3 **Moshi** Tanz
38G5 **Mosjøen** Nor
63G2 **Moskal'vo** Russian Fed
64E4 **Moskva** Russian Fed
35C1 **Mosquito** *R* Brazil
39G7 **Moss** Nor
98B3 **Mossaka** Congo
100B4 **Mossel Bay** S Africa
98B3 **Mossendjo** Congo
108B2 **Mossgiel** Aust
31D3 **Mossoró** Brazil
57C2 **Most** Czech Republic
96C1 **Mostaganem** Alg
54A2 **Mostar** Bosnia-Herzegovina
58C2 **Mosty** Belorussia
Mosul = Al Mawşil
39H7 **Motala** Sweden
42C2 **Motherwell** Scot
86A1 **Motihāri** India
51B2 **Motilla del Palancar** Spain
50B2 **Motril** Spain
111B2 **Motueka** NZ
111B2 **Motueka** *R* NZ
47B1 **Moudon** Switz
98B3 **Mouila** Gabon
108B2 **Moulamein** Aust
4G2 **Mould Bay** Can
49C2 **Moulins** France
76B2 **Moulmein** Burma
96B1 **Moulouya** *R* Mor
17B1 **Moultrie** USA
17C1 **Moultrie,L** USA
18C2 **Mound City** Illinois, USA
18A1 **Mound City** Missouri, USA
98B2 **Moundou** Chad
14B3 **Moundsville** USA
12J1 **Mountain** *R* Can
17A1 **Mountain Brook** USA
18B2 **Mountain Grove** USA
18B2 **Mountain Home** Arkansas, USA
22A2 **Mountain View** USA
12B2 **Mountain Village** USA
16A3 **Mount Airy** Maryland, USA
16A2 **Mount Carmel** USA
108A1 **Mount Dutton** Aust
108A2 **Mount Eba** Aust
108B3 **Mount Gambier** Aust
16B3 **Mount Holly** USA

16A2 **Mount Holly Springs** USA
108A2 **Mount Hope** Aust
106C3 **Mount Isa** Aust
108A2 **Mount Lofty Range'** *Mts* Aust
12D2 **Mount McKinley Nat Pk** USA
106A3 **Mount Magnet** Aust
108B2 **Mount Manara** Aust
107E3 **Mount Morgan** Aust
19B3 **Mount Pleasant** Texas, USA
20B1 **Mount Rainier Nat Pk** USA
43B4 **Mounts B** Eng
20B2 **Mount Shasta** USA
11B3 **Mount Vernon** Illinois, USA
19A3 **Mount Vernon** Kentucky, USA
20B1 **Mount Vernon** Washington, USA
45C1 **Mourne Mts** N Ire
98B1 **Moussoro** Chad
86B2 **Mouths of the Ganga** India/Bang
85B4 **Mouths of the Indus** Pak
77D4 **Mouths of the Mekong** Viet
97C4 **Mouths of the Niger** Nig
47B1 **Moutier** Switz
47B2 **Moûtiers** France
96C2 **Mouydir** *Mts* Alg
98B3 **Mouyondzi** Congo
46C2 **Mouzon** France
59B3 **M'óvár** Hung
23A1 **Moyahua** Mexico
99D2 **Moyale** Kenya
97A4 **Moyamba** Sierra Leone
96B1 **Moyen Atlas** *Mts* Mor
100B4 **Moyeni** Lesotho
99D2 **Moyo** Uganda
32B5 **Moyobamba** Peru
84D1 **Moyu** China
101C3 **Mozambique** Republic, Africa
101C3 **Mozambique Chan** Mozam/Madag
61H2 **Mozhga** Russian Fed
60C3 **Mozyr'** Belorussia
99D3 **Mpanda** Tanz
101C2 **Mpika** Zambia
99D3 **Mporokosa** Zambia
100B2 **Mposhi** Zambia
99D3 **Mpulungu** Zambia
99D3 **Mpwapwa** Tanz
60E3 **Mtsensk** Russian Fed
101H1 **Mtubatuba** S Africa
101D2 **Mtwara** Tanz
76C2 **Muang Chainat** Thai
76C2 **Muang Chiang Rai** Thai
76C2 **Muang Kalasin** Thai
76C2 **Muang Khon Kaen** Thai
76B2 **Muang Lampang** Thai
76B2 **Muang Lamphun** Thai
76C2 **Muang Loei** Thai
76C2 **Muang Lom Sak** Thai
76C2 **Muang Nakhon Phanom** Thai
76B2 **Muang Nakhon Sawan** Thai
76C2 **Muang Nan** Thai
76C2 **Muang Phayao** Thai
76C2 **Muang Phetchabun** Thai
76C2 **Muang Phichit** Thai
76C2 **Muang Phitsanulok** Thai
76C2 **Muang Phrae** Thai
76C2 **Muang Roi Et** Thai
76C2 **Muang Sakon Nakhon** Thai
76C3 **Muang Samut Prakan** Thai
76C2 **Muang Uthai Thani** Thai
76C2 **Muang Yasothon** Thai
77C5 **Muar** Malay
78C2 **Muara** Brunei
70B4 **Muara** Indon
78A3 **Muaralakitan** Indon
78A3 **Muaratebo** Indon
78C3 **Muaratewah** Indon
78A3 **Muarenim** Indon
76A2 **Muaungmaya** Burma
99D2 **Mubende** Uganda
100C2 **Muchinga** *Mts* Zambia
44A3 **Muck** *I* Scot
109C1 **Muckadilla** Aust
100B2 **Muconda** Angola
35D1 **Mucuri** Brazil
35C1 **Mucuri** *R* Brazil
100B2 **Mucusso** Angola
69E2 **Mudanjiang** China
109C2 **Mudgee** Aust
76B2 **Mudon** Burma
101C2 **Mueda** Mozam
107F3 **Mueo** Nouvelle Calédonie
100B2 **Mufulira** Zambia
73C4 **Mufu Shan** *Hills* China
Mugadishu = Muqdisho
93C4 **Mughayra** S Arabia
92A2 **Muğla** Turk
65G5 **Mugodzhary** *Mts* Kazakhstan
73A3 **Muguaping** China
93D3 **Muhaywir** Iraq
57C3 **Mühldorf** Germany
57C2 **Muhlhausen** Germany
38K6 **Muhos** Fin
77C4 **Mui Bai Bung** *C* Camb
45C2 **Muine Bheag** Irish Rep
100B2 **Mujimbeji** Zambia
59C3 **Mukachevo** Ukraine
78C2 **Mukah** Malay
69G4 **Muko-jima** *I* Japan
86A1 **Muktinath** Nepal
84B2 **Mukur** Afghan
18B2 **Mulberry** USA
12C2 **Mulchatna** *R* USA
34A3 **Mulchén** Chile
56C2 **Mulde** *R* Germany
71F5 **Mulgrave I** Aust
50B2 **Mulhacén** *Mt* Spain
46D1 **Mülheim** Germany
49D2 **Mulhouse** France
73A4 **Muli** China
44B3 **Mull** *I* Scot
87C3 **Mullaitvu** Sri Lanka
109C2 **Mullaley** Aust
106A3 **Mullewa** Aust
16B3 **Mullica** *R* USA
45C2 **Mullingar** Irish Rep
42B2 **Mull of Kintyre** *Pt* Scot
45C1 **Mull of Oa** *C* Scot
109D1 **Mullumbimby** Aust
100B2 **Mulobezi** Zambia
84C2 **Multan** Pak
Mumbai = Bombay
100B2 **Mumbwa** Zambia
61G4 **Mumra** Russian Fed
71D4 **Muna** *I* Indon
57C3 **München** Germany
14A2 **Muncie** USA
15C2 **Muncy** USA
56B2 **Münden** Germany
109D1 **Mundubbera** Aust
109C1 **Mungallala** Aust
109C1 **Mungallala** *R* Aust
99C2 **Mungbere** Zaïre
86A2 **Mungeli** India
86B1 **Munger** India
109C1 **Mungindi** Aust
Munich = München
14A1 **Munising** USA
29B6 **Muñoz Gomero,Pen** Chile
45B2 **Munster** Region, Irish Rep
47C1 **Münster** Switz
56B2 **Münster** Germany
54B1 **Muntii Apuseni** *Mts* Rom
54B1 **Muntii Călimanilor** *Mts* Rom
54B1 **Muntii Carpaţii Meridionali** *Mts* Rom
54B1 **Muntii Rodnei** *Mts* Rom
54B1 **Muntii Zarandului** *Mts* Rom
100B2 **Munyati** *R* Zim
93C2 **Munzur Silsilesi** *Mts* Turk
64D3 **Muomio** Fin
76C1 **Muong Khoua** Laos
76D3 **Muong Man** Viet
76D2 **Muong Nong** Laos
76C1 **Muong Ou Neua** Laos
76C1 **Muong Sai** Laos
76C2 **Muong Sen** Viet
76C1 **Muong Sing** Laos
76C1 **Muong Son** Laos
38J5 **Muonio** Fin
38J5 **Muonio** *R* Sweden/Fin
99E2 **Muqdisho** Somalia
52B1 **Mur** *R* Austria
74D3 **Murakami** Japan
29B5 **Murallón** *Mt* Arg/Chile
61G2 **Murashi** Russian Fed
93D2 **Murat** *R* Turk
53A3 **Muravera** Sardegna
75C1 **Murayama** Japan
90B3 **Murcheh Khvort** Iran
111B2 **Murchison** NZ
106A3 **Murchison** *R* Aust
51B2 **Murcia** Region, Spain
51B2 **Murcia** Spain
54B1 **Mureş** *R* Rom
46E2 **Murg** *R* Germany
65H6 **Murgab** *R* Turkmenistan
84B2 **Murgha Kibzai** Pak
109D1 **Murgon** Aust
86B2 **Muri** India
35C2 **Muriaé** Brazil
98C3 **Muriege** Angola
64E3 **Murmansk** Russian Fed
61F2 **Murom** Russian Fed
74E2 **Muroran** Japan
50A1 **Muros** Spain
74C4 **Muroto** Japan
75A2 **Muroto-zaki** *C* Japan
20C2 **Murphy** Idaho, USA
22B1 **Murphys** USA
18C2 **Murray** Kentucky, USA
108B2 **Murray** *R* Aust
13C2 **Murray** *R* Can
108A3 **Murray Bridge** Aust
71F4 **Murray,L** PNG
17B1 **Murray,L** USA
105J2 **Murray Seacarp** Pacific O
108B2 **Murrumbidgee** *R* Aust
109C2 **Murrumburrah** Aust
109D2 **Murrurundi** Aust
47B1 **Murten** Switz
108B3 **Murtoa** Aust
110C1 **Murupara** NZ
86A2 **Murwāra** India
109D1 **Murwillimbah** Aust
93D2 **Muş** Turk
54B2 **Musala** *Mt* Bulg
74B2 **Musan** N Korea
91C4 **Musandam** *Pen* Oman
Muscat = Masqat
91C5 **Muscat** Region, Oman
106C3 **Musgrave Range** *Mts* Aust
98B3 **Mushie** Zaïre
14A2 **Muskegon** USA
14A2 **Muskegon** *R* USA
18A2 **Muskogee** USA
15C2 **Muskoka,L** Can
95C3 **Musmar** Sudan
99D3 **Musoma** Tanz
8C2 **Musselshell** *R* USA
100A2 **Mussende** Angola
48C2 **Mussidan** France
55C2 **Mustafa-Kemalpasa** Turk
86A1 **Mustang** Nepal
109D2 **Muswelibrook** Aust
95B2 **Mut** Egypt
101C2 **Mutarara** Mozam
101C2 **Mutare** Zim
101C2 **Mutoko** Zim
101D2 **Mutsamudu** Comoros
100B2 **Mutshatsha** Zaïre
74E2 **Mutsu** Japan
74E2 **Mutsu-wan** *B* Japan
45B2 **Mutton** *I* Irish Rep
72B2 **Mu Us Shamo** *Desert* China
98B3 **Muxima** Angola
63D2 **Muya** Russian Fed
38L6 **Muyezerskiy** Russian Fed
99D3 **Muyinga** Burundi
98C3 **Muyumba** Zaïre
82A1 **Muyun Kum** *Desert* Kazakhstan
84C2 **Muzaffarābad** Pak
84C2 **Muzaffargarh** Pak
84D3 **Muzaffarnagar** India
86B1 **Muzaffarpur** India
64H3 **Muzhi** Russian Fed
82C2 **Muztag** *Mt* China
82B2 **Muztagata** *Mt* China
100C2 **Mvuma** Zim
99D3 **Mwanza** Tanz
98C3 **Mwanza** Zaïre
98C3 **Mweka** Zaïre
98C3 **Mwene Ditu** Zaïre
100C3 **Mwenezi** Zim
99C3 **Mwenga** Zaïre
99C3 **Mweru** *L* Zambia
100B2 **Mwinilunga** Zambia
83D4 **Myanaung** Burma
Myanma = Burma
86D2 **Myingyan** Burma
76B1 **Myingyao** Burma
76B3 **Myinmoletkat** *Mt* Burma
82D3 **Myitkyina** Burma
76B3 **Myitta** Burma
86C2 **Mymensingh** Bang
69F3 **Myojin** *I* Japan
39F6 **Myrdal** Nor
38B2 **Myrdalsjökur** *Ice Cap* Iceland
17C1 **Myrtle Beach** USA
20B2 **Myrtle Creek** USA
39G7 **Mysen** Nor
56C2 **Myśiloborz** Pol
64F3 **Mys Kanin Nos** *C* Russian Fed
59B3 **Myślenice** Pol
69H1 **Mys Lopatka** *C* Russian Fed
87B2 **Mysore** India
60D5 **Mys Sarych** *C* Ukraine
16D2 **Mystic** USA
61H5 **Mys Tyub-Karagan** *P* Kazakhstan
63G2 **Mys Yelizavety** *C* Russian Fed
64H2 **Mys Zhelaniya** *C* Russian Fed
77D3 **My Tho** Viet
20B2 **Mytle Point** USA
101C2 **Mzimba** Malawi
101C2 **Mzuzú** Malawi

N

21C4 **Naalehu** Hawaiian Is
39J6 **Naantali** Fin
45C2 **Naas** Irish Rep
75B2 **Nabari** Japan
61H2 **Naberezhnye Chelny** Russian Fed
12F2 **Nabesna** *R* USA
96D1 **Nabeul** Tunisia
94B2 **Nablus** Israel
101D2 **Nacala** Mozam
20B1 **Naches** USA
101C2 **Nachingwea** Tanz

19B3 **Nacogdoches** USA
76A3 **Nacondam** *I* Indian O
24B1 **Nacozari** Mexico
85C4 **Nadiād** India
50B2 **Nador** Mor
90B3 **Nadūshan** Iran
59C3 **Nadvornaya** Ukraine
56C1 **Naestved** Den
95B2 **Nāfūrah** Libya
75A2 **Nagahama** Japan
82D3 **Naga Hills** Burma
75B1 **Nagai** Japan
86C1 **Nāgāland** State, India
74D3 **Nagano** Japan
74D3 **Nagaoka** Japan
86C1 **Nagaon** India
87B2 **Nāgappattinam** India
85C4 **Nagar Parkar** Pak
74B4 **Nagasaki** Japan
75B2 **Nagashima** Japan
75A2 **Nagato** Japan
85C3 **Nāgaur** India
87B3 **Nāgercoil** India
85B3 **Nagha Kalat** Pak
84D3 **Nagīna** India
74D3 **Nagoya** Japan
85D4 **Nāgpur** India
82D2 **Nagqu** China
59B3 **Nagykanizsa** Hung
59B3 **Nagykörös** Hung
69E4 **Naha** Japan
8A2 **Nahaimo** Can
84D2 **Nāhan** India
4F3 **Nahanni Butte** Can
94B2 **Nahariya** Israel
90A3 **Nahāvand** Iran
46D2 **Nahe** *R* Germany
72D2 **Nahpu** China
72E1 **Naimen Qi** China
7D4 **Nain** Can
90B3 **Nā'īn** Iran
84D3 **Naini Tai** India
44C3 **Nairn** Scot
99D3 **Nairobi** Kenya
90B3 **Najafābād** Iran
74C2 **Najin** N Korea
75A2 **Nakama** Japan
74E3 **Nakaminato** Japan
75A2 **Nakamura** Japan
75B1 **Nakano** Japan
75A1 **Nakano-shima** *I* Japan
74C4 **Nakatsu** Japan
75B1 **Nakatsu-gawa** Japan
95C3 **Nak' fa** Eritrea
93E2 **Nakhichevan** Azerbaijan
92B4 **Nakhl** Egypt
74C2 **Nakhodka** Russian Fed
76C3 **Nakhon Pathom** Thai
76C3 **Nakhon Ratchasima** Thai
77C4 **Nakhon Si Thammarat** Thai
12H3 **Nakina** Can
7B4 **Nakina** Ontario, Can
12C3 **Naknek** USA
12C3 **Naknek L** USA
4C4 **Nakrek** USA
39G8 **Nakskov** Den
99D3 **Nakuru** Kenya
13D2 **Nakusp** Can
61F5 **Nal'chik** Russian Fed
87B1 **Nalgonda** India
87B1 **Nallamala Range** *Mts* India
95A1 **Nālūt** Libya
01H1 **Namaacha** Mozam
65G6 **Namak** *L* Iran
90C3 **Namakzar-e Shadad** *Salt Flat* Iran
65J5 **Namangan** Uzbekistan
01C2 **Namapa** Mozam
00A4 **Namaqualand** Region, S Africa
09D1 **Nambour** Aust
09D2 **Nambucca Heads** Aust
77D4 **Nam Can** Viet
82D2 **Nam Co** *L* China
76D1 **Nam Dinh** Viet
101C2 **Nametil** Mozam
74B4 **Namhae-do** *I* S Korea
100A2 **Namib Desert** Namibia
100A2 **Namibe** Angola
100A3 **Namibia** Republic, Africa
82D3 **Namjagbarwa Feng** *Mt* China
71D4 **Namlea** Indon
109C2 **Namoi** *R* Aust
13D1 **Nampa** Can
20C2 **Nampa** USA
97B3 **Nampala** Mali
76C2 **Nam Phong** Thai
74B3 **Namp'o** N Korea
101C2 **Nampula** Mozam
38G6 **Namsos** Nor
76B1 **Namton** Burma
86D2 **Namtu** Burma
13B2 **Namu** Can
101C2 **Namuno** Mozam
46C1 **Namur** Belg
100A2 **Namutoni** Namibia
74B3 **Namwŏn** S Korea
13C3 **Nanaimo** Can
74B2 **Nanam** N Korea
109D1 **Nanango** Aust
74D3 **Nanao** Japan
75B1 **Nanatsu-jima** *I* Japan
73B3 **Nanbu** China
73D4 **Nanchang** China
73B3 **Nanchong** China
49D2 **Nancy** France
87B1 **Nānded** India
109D2 **Nandewar Range** *Mts* Aust
85C4 **Nandurbar** India
87B1 **Nandyāl** India
98B2 **Nanga Eboko** Cam
84C1 **Nanga Parbat** *Mt* Pak
78C3 **Nangapinoh** Indon
78C3 **Nangatayap** Indon
74B2 **Nangnim Sanmaek** *Mts* N Korea
86C1 **Nang Xian** China
67F3 **Nangzhou** China
87B2 **Nanjangūd** India
72D3 **Nanjing** China
Nanking = Nanjing
75A2 **Nankoku** Japan
73C4 **Nan Ling** Region, China
76D1 **Nanliu** *R* China
73B5 **Nanning** China
6F3 **Nanortalik** Greenland
73A5 **Nanpan Jiang** *R* China
86A1 **Nānpāra** India
73D4 **Nanping** China
6A1 **Nansen Sd** Can
99D3 **Nansio** Tanz
48B2 **Nantes** France
13E2 **Nanton** Can
72E3 **Nantong** China
10C2 **Nantucket** *I* USA
35C1 **Nanuque** Brazil
72C3 **Nanyang** China
72D2 **Nanyang Hu** *L* China
99D2 **Nanyuki** Kenya
74D3 **Naoetsu** Japan
85B4 **Naokot** Pak
22A1 **Napa** USA
12B2 **Napaiskak** USA
15C2 **Napanee** Can
65K4 **Napas** Russian Fed
6E3 **Napassoq** Greenland
76D2 **Nape** Laos
110C1 **Napier** NZ
Naples = Napoli
17B2 **Naples** Florida, USA
19B3 **Naples** Texas, USA
73B5 **Napo** China
32C4 **Napo** *R* Peru/ Ecuador
53B2 **Napoli** Italy
90A2 **Naqadeh** Iran
92C4 **Naqb Ishtar** Jordan
75B2 **Nara** Japan
97B3 **Nara** Mali
107D4 **Naracoorte** Aust
23B1 **Naranjos** Mexico
87C1 **Narasarāopet** India
77C4 **Narathiwat** Thai
86C2 **Narayanganj** Bang
87B1 **Nārāyenpet** India
49C3 **Narbonne** France
84D2 **Narendranagar** India
6C2 **Nares Str** Can
58C2 **Narew** *R* Pol
75C1 **Narita** Japan
85C4 **Narmada** *R* India
84D3 **Nārnaul** India
60E2 **Naro Fominsk** Russian Fed
99D3 **Narok** Kenya
84C2 **Narowal** Pak
107D4 **Narrabri** Aust
109C1 **Narran** *L* Aust
109C1 **Narran** *R* Aust
109C2 **Narrandera** Aust
106A4 **Narrogin** Aust
109C2 **Narromine** Aust
85D4 **Narsimhapur** India
87C1 **Narsīpatnam** India
6F3 **Narssalik** Greenland
6F3 **Narssaq** Greenland
6F3 **Narssarssuaq** Greenland
75C1 **Narugo** Japan
75A2 **Naruto** Japan
60C2 **Narva** Russian Fed
38H5 **Narvik** Nor
84D3 **Narwāna** India
64G3 **Nar'yan Mar** Russian Fed
108B1 **Narylico** Aust
65J5 **Naryn** Kirghizia
97C4 **Nasarawa** Nig
103D5 **Nasca Ridge** Pacific O
16D1 **Nashua** USA
19B3 **Nashville** Arkansas, USA
11B3 **Nashville** Tennessee, USA
54A1 **Našice** Croatia
85D4 **Nāsik** India
99D2 **Nasir** Sudan
13B1 **Nass** *R* Can
26B1 **Nassau** The Bahamas
16C1 **Nassau** USA
95C2 **Nasser,L** Egypt
39G7 **Nässjö** Sweden
7C4 **Nastapoka Is** Can
100B3 **Nata** Botswana
31D3 **Natal** Brazil
70A3 **Natal** Indon
90B3 **Natanz** Iran
7D4 **Natashquan** Can
7D4 **Natashquan** *R* Can
19B3 **Natchez** USA
19B3 **Natchitoches** USA
108C3 **Nathalia** Aust
6H2 **Nathorsts Land** *Region* Greenland
13C1 **Nation** *R* Can
21B3 **National City** USA
75C1 **Natori** Japan
99D3 **Natron** *L* Tanz
106A4 **Naturaliste,C** Aust
47D1 **Nauders** Austria
56C2 **Nauen** Germany
16C2 **Naugatuck** USA
57C2 **Naumburg** Germany
94B3 **Naur** Jordan
105G4 **Nauru** *I* Pacific O
63C2 **Naushki** Russian Fed
23B1 **Nautla** Mexico
9C3 **Navajo Res** USA
50A2 **Navalmoral de la Mata** Spain
29C7 **Navarino** *I* Chile
51B1 **Navarra** Province, Spain
34D3 **Navarro** Arg
19A3 **Navasota** USA
19A3 **Navasota** *R* USA
50A1 **Navia** *R* Spain
34A2 **Navidad** Chile
85C4 **Navlakhi** India
60D3 **Navlya** Russian Fed
24B2 **Navojoa** Mexico
55B3 **Návpaktos** Greece
55B3 **Návplion** Greece
85C4 **Navsāri** India
94C2 **Nawá** Syria
86B2 **Nawāda** India
84B2 **Nawah** Afghan
85B3 **Nawrabshah** Pak
73B4 **Naxi** China
55C3 **Náxos** *I* Greece
23A1 **Nayar** Mexico
90C3 **Nay Band** Iran
91B4 **Nāy Band** Iran
74E2 **Nayoro** Japan
94B2 **Nazareth** Israel
48B2 **Nazay** France
32C6 **Nazca** Peru
92A2 **Nazilli** Turk
63B2 **Nazimovo** Russian Fed
13C2 **Nazko** *R* Can
99D2 **Nazret** Eth
91C5 **Nazwa** Oman
65J4 **Nazyvayevsk** Russian Fed
98B3 **Ndalatando** Angola
98C2 **Ndélé** CAR
98B3 **Ndendé** Gabon
98B1 **Ndjamena** Chad
98B3 **Ndjolé** Gabon
100B2 **Ndola** Zambia
109C1 **Neabul** Aust
108A1 **Neales** *R* Aust
55B3 **Neápolis** Greece
43C4 **Neath** Wales
109C1 **Nebine** *R* Aust
65G6 **Nebit Dag** Turkmenistan
8C2 **Nebraska** State, USA
18A1 **Nebraska City** USA
13C2 **Nechako** *R* Can
19A3 **Neches** *R* USA
34D3 **Necochea** Arg
86C1 **Nêdong** China
9B3 **Needles** USA
14A2 **Neenah** USA
5J4 **Neepawa** Can
46C1 **Neerpelt** Belg
63C2 **Neftelensk** Russian Fed
99D2 **Negelē** Eth
94B3 **Negev** *Desert* Israel
60B4 **Negolu** *Mt* Rom
87B3 **Negombo** Sri Lanka
76A2 **Negrais,C** Burma
32A4 **Negritos** Peru
33E4 **Negro** *R* Amazonas, Brazil
29C4 **Negro** *R* Arg
34D2 **Negro** *R* Urug
79B4 **Negros** *I* Phil
54C2 **Negru Voda** Rom
90D3 **Nehbāndan** Iran
73B4 **Neijiang** China
72B1 **Nei Monggol** Autononous Region, China
32B3 **Neiva** Colombia
99D2 **Nejo** Eth
99D2 **Nek'emtē** Eth
60D2 **Nelidovo** Russian Fed
87B2 **Nellore** India
69F2 **Nel'ma** Russian Fed
13D3 **Nelson** Can
111B2 **Nelson** NZ
7A4 **Nelson** *R* Can
108B3 **Nelson,C** Aust
12B2 **Nelson I** USA
97B3 **Néma** Maur
72A1 **Nemagt Uul** *Mt* Mongolia
58C1 **Neman** *R* Lithuania
54C1 **Nemira** *Mt* Rom
74F2 **Nemuro** Japan
63E3 **Nen** *R* China
41B3 **Nenagh** Irish Rep
12E2 **Nenana** USA
12E2 **Nenana** *R* USA
43D3 **Nene** *R* Eng
69E2 **Nenjiang** China
18A2 **Neodesha** USA

18B2 **Neosho** USA
63C2 **Nepa** Russian Fed
82C3 **Nepal** Kingdom, Asia
86A1 **Nepalganj** Nepal
45B1 **Nephin** *Mt* Irish Rep
94B3 **Neqarot** *R* Israel
34A3 **Nequén** State, Arg
68D1 **Nerchinsk** Russian Fed
52C2 **Neretva** *R* Bosnia-Herzegovina/Croatia
71F2 **Nero Deep** Pacific O
38C1 **Neskaupstaður** Iceland
46B2 **Nesle** France
7E5 **Nesleyville** Can
55B2 **Néstos** *R* Greece
94B2 **Netanya** Israel
16B2 **Netcong** USA
56B2 **Netherlands** Kingdom, Europe
3M7 **Netherlands Antilles** *Is* Caribbean S
86C2 **Netrakona** Bang
6C3 **Nettilling L** Can
56C2 **Neubrandenburg** Germany
47B1 **Neuchâtel** Switz
46C2 **Neufchâteau** Belg
48C2 **Neufchâtel** France
46A2 **Neufchâtel-en-Bray** France
56B2 **Neumünster** Germany
52C1 **Neunkirchen** Austria
46D2 **Neunkirchen** Germany
34B3 **Neuquén** Arg
29B4 **Neuquén** State, Arg
34B3 **Neuquén** *R* Arg
56C2 **Neuruppin** Germany
46D1 **Neuss** Germany
46E2 **Neustadt** Germany
56C2 **Neustadt** Germany
56C2 **Neustrelitz** Germany
46D1 **Neuwied** Germany
8B3 **Nevada** State, USA
18B2 **Nevada** USA
34A3 **Nevada de Chillán** *Mts* Arg/Chile
23A2 **Nevada de Collima** Mexico
23B2 **Nevada de Toluca** *Mt* Mexico
94B3 **Nevatim** Israel
60C2 **Nevel'** Russian Fed
49C2 **Nevers** France
109C2 **Nevertire** Aust
27E3 **Nevis** *I* Caribbean S
58D2 **Nevis** *R* Belorussia/Lithuania
92B2 **Nevşehir** Turk
61K2 **Nev'yansk** Russian Fed
101C2 **Newala** Tanz
14A3 **New Albany** Indiana, USA
19C3 **New Albany** Mississippi, USA
33F2 **New Amsterdam** Guyana
109C1 **New Angledool** Aust
15C3 **Newark** Delaware, USA
10C2 **Newark** New Jersey, USA
14B2 **Newark** Ohio, USA
43D3 **Newark-upon-Trent** Eng
15D2 **New Bedford** USA
13B2 **New Bella Bella** Can
20B1 **Newberg** USA
11C3 **New Bern** USA
17B1 **Newberry** USA
26B2 **New Bight** The Bahamas
14B3 **New Boston** USA
9D4 **New Braunfels** USA
16C2 **New Britain** USA
7D5 **New Brunswick** Province, Can
16B2 **New Brunswick** USA
16B2 **Newburgh** USA
43D4 **Newbury** Eng
16D1 **Newburyport** USA
16C2 **New Canaan** USA
109D2 **Newcastle** Aust
14A3 **New Castle** Indiana, USA
42B2 **Newcastle** N Ire
14B2 **New Castle** Pennsylvania, USA
101G1 **Newcastle** S Africa
8C2 **Newcastle** Wyoming, USA
42D2 **Newcastle upon Tyne** Eng
106C2 **Newcastle Waters** Aust
45B2 **Newcastle West** Irish Rep
84D3 **New Delhi** India
109D2 **New England Range** *Mts* Aust
12B3 **Newenham,C** USA
43D4 **New Forest,The** Eng
7D4 **Newfoundland** Province, Can
7E5 **Newfoundland** *I* Can
102F2 **Newfoundland Basin** Atlantic O
18B2 **New Franklin** USA
42B2 **New Galloway** Scot
107E1 **New Georgia** *I* Solomon Is
7D5 **New Glasgow** Can
71F4 **New Guinea** SE Asia
12D3 **Newhalen** USA
22C3 **Newhall** USA
10C2 **New Hampshire** State, USA
101H1 **New Hanover** S Africa
43E4 **Newhaven** Eng
15D2 **New Haven** USA
13B1 **New Hazelton** Can
19B3 **New Iberia** USA
10C2 **New Jersey** State, USA
7C5 **New Liskeard** Can
16C2 **New London** USA
106A3 **Newman** Aust
22B2 **Newman** USA
43E3 **Newmarket** Eng
45B2 **Newmarket** Irish Rep
15C3 **New Market** USA
9C3 **New Mexico** State, USA
16C2 **New Milford** Connecticut, USA
17B1 **Newnan** USA
109C4 **New Norfolk** Aust
11A3 **New Orleans** USA
16B2 **New Paltz** USA
14B2 **New Philadelphia** USA
110B1 **New Plymouth** NZ
18B2 **Newport** Arkansas, USA
43D4 **Newport** Eng
14B3 **Newport** Kentucky, USA
20B2 **Newport** Oregon, USA
16A2 **Newport** Pennsylvania, USA
15D2 **Newport** Rhode Island, USA
15D2 **Newport** Vermont, USA
43C4 **Newport** Wales
20C1 **Newport** Washington, USA
22D4 **Newport Beach** USA
11C3 **Newport News** USA
26B1 **New Providence** *I* Caribbean S
43B4 **Newquay** Eng
6C3 **New Quebec Crater** Can
45C2 **New Ross** Irish Rep
45C1 **Newry** N Ire
New Siberian Is = Novosibirskye Ostrova
17B2 **New Smyrna Beach** USA
107D4 **New South Wales** State, Aust
12C3 **New Stuyahok** USA
18A2 **Newton** Kansas, USA
16D1 **Newton** Massachusetts, USA
19C3 **Newton** Mississippi, USA
16B2 **Newton** New York, USA
43C4 **Newton Abbot** Eng
45C1 **Newton Stewart** N Ire
42B2 **Newton Stewart** Scot
43C3 **Newtown** Wales
42B2 **Newtownards** N Ire
16A2 **Newville** USA
5F5 **New Westminster** Can
10C2 **New York** State, USA
10C2 **New York** USA
110 **New Zealand** Dominion, SW Pacific O
105G6 **New Zealand Plat** Pacific O
61F2 **Neya** Russian Fed
91B4 **Neyrīz** Iran
90C2 **Neyshābūr** Iran
60D3 **Nezhin** Russian Fed
98B3 **Ngabé** Congo
100B3 **Ngami** *L* Botswana
110C1 **Ngaruawahia** NZ
110C1 **Ngaruroro** *R* NZ
110C1 **Ngauruhoe,Mt** NZ
98B3 **Ngo** Congo
76D2 **Ngoc Linh** *Mt* Viet
98B2 **Ngoko** *R* Cam
68B3 **Ngoring Hu** *L* China
99D3 **Ngorongoro Crater** Tanz
98B3 **N'Gounié** *R* Gabon
98B1 **Nguigmi** Niger
71E3 **Ngulu** *I* Pacific O
97D3 **Nguru** Nig
76D3 **Nha Trang** Viet
108B3 **Nhill** Aust
101H1 **Nhlangano** Swaziland
76D2 **Nhommarath** Laos
106C2 **Nhulunbuy** Aust
97B3 **Niafounké** Mali
14A1 **Niagara** USA
15C2 **Niagara Falls** Can
15C2 **Niagara Falls** USA
70C3 **Niah** Malay
97B4 **Niakaramandougou** Ivory Coast
97C3 **Niamey** Niger
99C2 **Niangara** Zaïre
98C2 **Nia Nia** Zaïre
70A3 **Nias** *I* Indon
25D3 **Nicaragua** Republic, Cent America
53C3 **Nicastro** Italy
49D3 **Nice** France
26B1 **Nicholl's Town** The Bahamas
83D5 **Nicobar Is** Indian O
92B2 **Nicosia** Cyprus
25D3 **Nicoya,Pen de** Costa Rica
58C2 **Nidzica** Pol
46D2 **Niederbronn** France
56B2 **Niedersachsen** State, Germany
99C3 **Niemba** Zaïre
56B2 **Nienburg** Germany
46D1 **Niers** *R* Germany
97B4 **Niete,Mt** Lib
33F2 **Nieuw Amsterdam** Surinam
33F2 **Nieuw Nickerie** Surinam
46B1 **Nieuwpoort** Belg
92B2 **Niğde** Turk
97C3 **Niger** Republic, Africa
97C4 **Niger** *R* Nig
97C4 **Nigeria** Federal Republic, Africa
55B2 **Nigríta** Greece
75C1 **Nihommatsu** Japan
74D3 **Niigata** Japan
74C4 **Niihama** Japan
75B2 **Nii-jima** *I* Japan
75A2 **Niimi** Japan
74D3 **Niitsu** Japan
94B3 **Nijil** Jordan
56B2 **Nijmegen** Neth
64E3 **Nikel'** Russian Fed
97C3 **Nikki** Benin
74D3 **Nikko** Japan
60D4 **Nikolayev** Ukraine
61G4 **Nikolayevsk** Russian Fed
63G2 **Nikolayevsk-na-Amure** Russian Fed
61G2 **Nikol'sk** Russian Fed
61G3 **Nikol'sk** Russian Fed
60D4 **Nikopol** Ukraine
92C1 **Niksar** Turk
91D4 **Nīkshahr** Iran
54A2 **Nikšić** Montenegro, Yugos
71D4 **Nila** *I* Indon
80B3 **Nile** *R* N E Africa
14A2 **Niles** USA
87B2 **Nilgiri Hills** India
85C4 **Nimach** India
49C3 **Nîmes** France
109C3 **Nimmitabel** Aust
99D2 **Nimule** Sudan
83B5 **Nine Degree Chan** Indian O
104C4 **Ninety-East Ridge** Indian O
109C3 **Ninety Mile Beach** Aust
73D4 **Ningde** China
73D4 **Ningdu** China
68B3 **Ningjing Shan** *Mts* China
76D1 **Ningming** China
73A4 **Ningnan** China
72B2 **Ningxia** Province, China
72B2 **Ning Xian** China
73B5 **Ninh Binh** Vietnam
107D1 **Ninigo Is** PNG
12D2 **Ninilchik** USA
8D2 **Niobrara** *R* USA
98B3 **Nioki** Zaïre
97B3 **Nioro du Sahel** Mali
48B2 **Niort** France
5H4 **Nipawin** Can
7B5 **Nipigon** Can
7B5 **Nipigon,L** Can
7B5 **Nipissing** *R* Can
14B1 **Nipissing,L** Can
87B1 **Nirmal** India
86B1 **Nirmāli** India
54B2 **Niš** Serbia, Yugos
81C4 **Nisāb** Yemen
69F4 **Nishino-shima** *I* Japan
75A1 **Nishino-shima** *I* Japan
75A2 **Nishiwaki** Japan
12G2 **Nisling** *R* Can
12H2 **Nisutlin** *R* Can
7C4 **Nitchequon** Can
31C6 **Niterói** Brazil
42C2 **Nith** *R* Scot
59B3 **Nitra** Slovakia
14B3 **Nitro** USA
78C2 **Niut** *Mt* Malay
46C1 **Nivelles** Belg
49C2 **Nivernais** Region, France
38L5 **Nivskiy** Russian Fed
87B1 **Nizāmābād** India
94B3 **Nizana** *Hist Site* Israel
61J2 **Nizhniye Sergi** Russian Fed
65F4 **Nizhniy Novgorod** Russian Fed
61F3 **Nizhniy Lomov** Russian Fed
65G4 **Nizhniy Tagil** Russian Fed
63B1 **Nizhnyaya Tunguska** *R* Russian Fed
93C2 **Nizip** Turk
100B2 **Njoko** *R* Zambia

99D3 **Njombe** Tanz
98B2 **Nkambé** Cam
101C2 **Nkhata Bay** Malawi
98B2 **Nkongsamba** Cam
97C3 **N'Konni** Niger
86C2 **Noakhali** Bang
12B1 **Noatak** USA
12C1 **Noatak** *R* USA
74C4 **Nobeoka** Japan
47D1 **Noce** *R* Italy
23A1 **Nochistlán** Mexico
23B2 **Nochixtlán** Mexico
19A3 **Nocona** USA
24A1 **Nogales** Sonora, Mexico
9B3 **Nogales** USA
23B2 **Nogales** Veracruz, Mexico
47D2 **Nogara** Italy
75A2 **Nogata** Japan
60E2 **Noginsk** Russian Fed
34D2 **Nogoyá** Arg
34D2 **Nogoyá** *R* Arg
84C3 **Nohar** India
75B2 **Nojima-zaki** *C* Japan
98B2 **Nola** CAR
61G2 **Nolinsk** Russian Fed
16D2 **Nomans Land** *I* USA
12A2 **Nome** USA
46D2 **Nomeny** France
72B1 **Nomgon** Mongolia
5H3 **Nonachol L** Can
76C2 **Nong Khai** Thai
101H1 **Nongoma** S Africa
12B1 **Noorvik** USA
13B3 **Nootka Sd** Can
98B3 **Noqui** Angola
7C5 **Noranda** Can
46B1 **Nord** Department, France
64D2 **Nordaustlandet** *I* Barents S
13D2 **Nordegg** Can
38F6 **Nordfjord** *Inlet* Nor
39F8 **Nordfriesische** *Is* Germany
56C2 **Nordhausen** Germany
56B2 **Nordhrein Westfalen** State, Germany
38J4 **Nordkapp** *C* Nor
6E3 **Nordre** Greenland
38H5 **Nord Stronfjället** *Mt* Sweden
1B9 **Nordvik** Russian Fed
45C2 **Nore** *R* Irish Rep
43E3 **Norfolk** County, Eng
8D2 **Norfolk** Nebraska, USA
11C3 **Norfolk** Virginia, USA
107F3 **Norfolk I** Aust
18B2 **Norfolk L** USA
05G5 **Norfolk Ridge** Pacific O
1C10 **Noril'sk** Russian Fed
18C1 **Normal** USA
19A2 **Norman** USA
48B2 **Normandie** Region, France
07D2 **Normanton** Aust
12J1 **Norman Wells** Can
4B3 **Norne** USA
15C2 **Norristown** USA
39H7 **Norrköping** Sweden
39H6 **Norrsundet** Sweden
39H7 **Norrtälje** Sweden
06B4 **Norseman** Aust
63F2 **Norsk** Russian Fed
02J2 **North** *S* N W Europe
42D2 **Northallerton** Eng
06A4 **Northam** Aust
02E3 **North American Basin** Atlantic O
06A3 **Northampton** Aust
43D3 **Northampton** County, Eng
43D3 **Northampton** Eng
15D2 **Northampton** USA
4G3 **North Arm** *B* Can
17B1 **North Augusta** USA
6D4 **North Aulatsvik** *I* Can
13F2 **North Battleford** Can
7C5 **North Bay** Can
20B2 **North Bend** USA
44C3 **North Berwick** Scot
7D5 **North,C** Can
7G4 **North C** NZ
11B3 **North Carolina** State, USA
20B1 **North Cascade Nat Pk** USA
14B1 **North Chan** Can
42B2 **North Chan** Ire/Scot
8C2 **North Dakota** State, USA
43E4 **North Downs** Eng
14C2 **North East** USA
102H2 **North East Atlantic Basin** Atlantic O
4B3 **Northeast C** USA
40B3 **Northern Ireland** UK
27L1 **Northern Range** *Mts* Trinidad
106C2 **Northern Territory** Aust
44C3 **North Esk** *R* Scot
16C1 **Northfield** Massachusetts, USA
12D2 **North Fork** *R* USA
110B1 **North I** NZ
74B3 **North Korea** Republic, S E Asia
North Land = Severnaya Zemlya
19B3 **North Little Rock** USA
1B4 **North Magnetic Pole** Can
17B2 **North Miami** USA
17B2 **North Miami Beach** USA
8C2 **North Platte** USA
8C2 **North Platte** *R* USA
27R3 **North Pt** Barbados
14B1 **North Pt** USA
40B2 **North Rona** *I* Scot
44C2 **North Ronaldsay** *I* Scot
13F2 **North Saskatchewan** *R* Can
40D2 **North Sea** N W Europe
4D3 **North Slope** *Region* USA
109D1 **North Stradbroke** *I* Aust
110B1 **North Taranaki Bight** *B* NZ
9C3 **North Truchas Peak** *Mt* USA
44A3 **North Uist** *I* Scot
42C2 **Northumberland** County, Eng
107E3 **Northumberland Is** Aust
7D5 **Northumberland Str** Can
20B1 **North Vancouver** Can
43E3 **North Walsham** Eng
12F2 **Northway** USA
106A3 **North West C** Aust
84C2 **North West Frontier** Province, Pak
7D4 **North West River** Can
4F3 **North West Territories** Can
42D2 **North York Moors Nat Pk** Eng
12B2 **Norton B** USA
12B2 **Norton Sd** USA
112B1 **Norvegia,C** Ant
16C2 **Norwalk** Connecticut, USA
14B2 **Norwalk** Ohio, USA
39F6 **Norway** Kingdom, Europe
5J4 **Norway House** Can
6A2 **Norwegian B** Can
102H1 **Norwegian Basin** Norewegian S
64A3 **Norwegian S** N W Europe
16C2 **Norwich** Connecticut, USA
43E3 **Norwich** Eng
16D1 **Norwood** Massachusetts, USA
14B3 **Norwood** Ohio, USA
54C2 **Nos Emine** *C* Bulg
74D2 **Noshiro** Japan
54C2 **Nos Kaliakra** *C* Bulg
44E1 **Noss** *I* Scot
91D4 **Nostrābād** Iran
101D2 **Nosy Barren** *I* Madag
101D2 **Nosy Bé** *I* Madag
101E2 **Nosy Boraha** *I* Madag
101D3 **Nosy Varika** Madag
58B2 **Notéc** *R* Pol
5G4 **Notikeuin** Can
53C3 **Noto** Italy
39F7 **Notodden** Nor
75B1 **Noto-hantō** *Pen* Japan
7E5 **Notre Dams B** Can
43D3 **Nottingham** County, Eng
43D3 **Nottingham** Eng
6C3 **Nottingham** *I* Can
6C3 **Nottingham Island** Can
96A2 **Nouadhibou** Maur
97A3 **Nouakchott** Maur
107F3 **Nouméa** Nouvelle Calédonie
97B3 **Nouna** Burkina
107F3 **Nouvelle Calédonie** *I* S W Pacific O
98B3 **Nova Caipemba** Angola
35A2 **Nova Esperança** Brazil
35C2 **Nova Friburgo** Brazil
100A2 **Nova Gaia** Angola
35B2 **Nova Granada** Brazil
35B2 **Nova Horizonte** Brazil
35C1 **Nova Lima** Brazil
Nova Lisboa = Huambo
35A2 **Nova Londrina** Brazil
101C3 **Nova Mambone** Mozam
47C2 **Novara** Italy
7D5 **Nova Scotia** Province, Can
22A1 **Novato** USA
35C1 **Nova Venécia** Brazil
60D4 **Novaya Kakhovka** Ukraine
64G2 **Novaya Zemlya** *I* Barents S
54C2 **Nova Zagora** Bulg
31C2 **Nove Russas** Brazil
54A1 **Nové Zámky** Slovakia
60D2 **Novgorod** Russian Fed
47C2 **Novi Ligure** Italy
54C2 **Novi Pazar** Bulg
54B2 **Novi Pazar** Serbia, Yugos
54A1 **Novi Sad** Serbia, Yugos
61J3 **Novoalekseyevka** Kazakhstan
61F3 **Novoanninskiy** Russian Fed
61E4 **Novocherkassk** Russian Fed
60C3 **Novograd Volynskiy** Ukraine
58D2 **Novogrudok** Russian Fed
30F4 **Novo Hamburgo** Brazil
65H5 **Novokazalinsk** Kazakhstan
65K4 **Novokuznetsk** Russian Fed
112B12 **Novolazarevskaya** *Base* Ant
52C1 **Novo Mesto** Slovenia
60E3 **Novomoskovsk** Russian Fed
60E5 **Novorossiysk** Russian Fed
65K4 **Novosibirsk** Russian Fed
1B8 **Novosibirskiye Ostrova** *I* Russian Fed
61J3 **Novotroitsk** Russian Fed
61G3 **Novo Uzensk** Russian Fed
59C2 **Novovolynsk** Ukraine
61G2 **Novo Vyatsk** Russian Fed
60D3 **Novozybkov** Russian Fed
58C2 **Novy Dwór Mazowiecki** Pol
61K2 **Novyy Lyalya** Russian Fed
61H5 **Novyy Port** Russian Fed
61H5 **Novyy Uzen** Kazakhstan
58B2 **Nowa Sól** Pol
18A2 **Nowata** USA
Nowgong = Nagaon
12D2 **Nowitna** *R* USA
109D2 **Nowra** Aust
90B2 **Now Shahr** Iran
84C2 **Nowshera** Pak
59C3 **Nowy Sącz** Pol
12H3 **Noyes I** USA
46B2 **Noyon** France
97B4 **Nsawam** Ghana
99D1 **Nuba** *Mts* Sudan
81B3 **Nubian Desert** Sudan
34A3 **Nuble** *R* Chile
9D4 **Nueces** *R* USA
5J3 **Nueltin L** Can
26A2 **Nueva Gerona** Cuba
34A3 **Nueva Imperial** Chile
9C4 **Nueva Laredo** Mexico
34D2 **Nueva Palmira** Urug
24B2 **Nueva Rosita** Mexico
26B2 **Nuevitas** Cuba
24B1 **Nuevo Casas Grandes** Mexico
24C2 **Nuevo Laredo** Mexico
99E2 **Nugaal** Region, Somalia
6E2 **Nûgâtsiaq** Greenland
6E2 **Nugssuag** *Pen* Greenland
6E2 **Nûgussaq** *I* Greenland
108A2 **Nukey Bluff** *Mt* Aust
93D3 **Nukhayb** Iraq
65G5 **Nukus** Uzbekistan
12C2 **Nulato** USA
106B4 **Nullarbor Plain** Aust
97D4 **Numan** Nig
75B1 **Numata** Japan
98C2 **Numatinna** *R* Sudan
74D3 **Numazu** Japan
71E4 **Numfoor** *I* Indon
108C3 **Numurkah** Aust
12B2 **Nunapitchuk** USA
84D2 **Nunkun** *Mt* India
53A2 **Nuoro** Sardegna
91B3 **Nurābād** Iran
47C2 **Nure** *R* Italy
108A2 **Nuriootpa** Aust
84C1 **Nuristan** *Upland* Afghan
61H3 **Nurlat** Russian Fed
38K6 **Nurmes** Fin
57C3 **Nürnberg** Germany
108C2 **Nurri,Mt** Aust
93D2 **Nusaybin** Turk
12C3 **Nushagak** *R* USA
12C3 **Nushagak B** USA
12C3 **Nushagak Pen** USA
84B3 **Nushki** Pak
7D4 **Nutak** Can
12F2 **Nutzotin Mts** USA
Nuuk = Godthåb
86A1 **Nuwakot** Nepal
87C3 **Nuwara-Eliya** Sri Lanka
6C3 **Nuyukjuak** Can

16C2 **Nyack** USA
99D2 **Nyahururu** Kenya
108B3 **Nyah West** Aust
4C3 **Nyai** USA
68B3 **Nyainqentanglha Shan** *Mts* China
99D3 **Nyakabindi** Tanz
98C1 **Nyala** Sudan
86B1 **Nyalam** China
98C2 **Nyamlell** Sudan
64F3 **Nyandoma** Russian Fed
100C2 **Nyanga** Zim
98B3 **Nyanga** *R* Gabon
101C2 **Nyasa L** Malawi/ Mozam
76B2 **Nyaunglebin** Burma
61J2 **Nyazepetrovsk** Russian Fed
39G7 **Nyborg** Den
39H7 **Nybro** Sweden
64J3 **Nyda** Russian Fed
6D1 **Nyeboes Land** *Region* Can
99D3 **Nyeri** Kenya
101C2 **Nyimba** Zambia
82D3 **Nyingchi** China
59C3 **Nyíregyháza** Hung
99D2 **Nyiru,Mt** Kenya
38J6 **Nykarleby** Fin
39F7 **Nykøbing** Den
39G8 **Nykøbing** Den
39H7 **Nyköping** Sweden
100B3 **Nylstroom** S Africa
109C2 **Nymagee** Aust
39H7 **Nynäshamn** Sweden
109C2 **Nyngan** Aust
47B1 **Nyon** Switz
98B2 **Nyong** *R* Cam
49D3 **Nyons** France
59B2 **Nysa** Pol
20C2 **Nyssa** USA
63D1 **Nyurba** Russian Fed
99D3 **Nzega** Tanz
97B4 **Nzérékore** Guinea
98B3 **N'zeto** Angola

O

6F3 **Oaggsimiut** Greenland
8C2 **Oahe Res** USA
21C4 **Oahu** *I* Hawaiian Is
108B2 **Oakbank** Aust
22B2 **Oakdale** USA
109D1 **Oakey** Aust
21A2 **Oakland** California, USA
20B2 **Oakland** Oregon, USA
14A3 **Oakland City** USA
14A2 **Oak Lawn** USA
22B2 **Oakley** California, USA
20B2 **Oakridge** USA
14C2 **Oakville** Can
111B3 **Oamaru** NZ
112B7 **Oates Land** Region, Ant
109C4 **Oatlands** Aust
23B2 **Oaxaca** Mexico
23B2 **Oaxaca** State, Mexico
65J3 **Ob'** *R* Russian Fed
75B1 **Obama** Japan
111A3 **Oban** NZ
44B3 **Oban** Scot
75C1 **Obanazawa** Japan
47D1 **Oberammergau** Germany
46D1 **Oberhausen** Germany
47D1 **Oberstdorf** Germany
71D4 **Obi** *I* Indon
33F4 **Obidos** Brazil
74E2 **Obihiro** Japan
98C2 **Obo** CAR
99E1 **Obock** Djibouti
58B2 **Oborniki** Pol
60E3 **Oboyan** Russian Fed
20B2 **O'Brien** USA
61H3 **Obshchiy Syrt** *Mts* Russian Fed
64J3 **Obskava Guba** *B* Russian Fed
97B4 **Obuasi** Ghana
17B2 **Ocala** USA
32C2 **Ocana** Colombia
50B2 **Ocaño** Spain
12G3 **Ocean C** USA
15C3 **Ocean City** Maryland, USA
16B3 **Ocean City** New Jersey, USA
5F4 **Ocean Falls** Can
22D4 **Oceanside** USA
19C3 **Ocean Springs** USA
61H2 **Ocher** Russian Fed
44C3 **Ochil Hills** Scot
17B1 **Ochlockonee** *R* USA
27H1 **Ocho Rios** Jamaica
17B1 **Ocmulgee** *R* USA
17B1 **Oconee** *R* USA
14A2 **Oconto** USA
23A1 **Ocotlán** Jalisco, Mexico
23B2 **Ocotlán** Oaxaca, Mexico
97B4 **Oda** Ghana
75A1 **Oda** Japan
38B2 **Ódáðahraun** Region, Iceland
74E2 **Odate** Japan
74D3 **Odawara** Japan
39F6 **Odda** Nor
50A2 **Odemira** Port
55C3 **Ödemiş** Turk
101G1 **Odendaalsrus** S Africa
39G7 **Odense** Den
56C2 **Oder** *R* Pol/Germany
9C3 **Odessa** Texas, USA
60D4 **Odessa** Ukraine
20C1 **Odessa** Washington, USA
97B4 **Odienné** Ivory Coast
59B2 **Odra** *R* Pol
31C3 **Oeiras** Brazil
53C2 **Ofanto** *R* Italy
94B3 **Ofaqim** Israel
45C2 **Offaly** County, Irish Rep
49D1 **Offenbach** Germany
49D2 **Offenburg** Germany
74D3 **Oga** Japan
99E2 **Ogaden** Region, Eth
74D3 **Ogaki** Japan
8C2 **Ogallala** USA
69G4 **Ogasawara Gunto** *Is* Japan
97C4 **Ogbomosho** Nig
8B2 **Ogden** Utah, USA
15C2 **Ogdensburg** USA
17B1 **Ogeechee** *R* USA
12G1 **Ogilvie** Can
4E3 **Ogilvie Mts** Can
17B1 **Oglethorpe,Mt** USA
47D2 **Oglio** *R* Italy
47B1 **Ognon** *R* France
97C4 **Ogoja** Nig
98A3 **Ogooué** *R* Gabon
58C1 **Ogre** Latvia
96B2 **Oguilet Khenachich** *Well* Mali
52C1 **Ogulin** Croatia
111A3 **Ohai** NZ
110C1 **Ohakune** NZ
96C2 **Ohanet** Alg
111A2 **Ohau,L** NZ
10B2 **Ohio** State, USA
14A3 **Ohio** *R* USA
100A2 **Ohopoho** Namibia
57C2 **Ohre** *R* Czech Republic
55B2 **Ohrid** Macedonia
55B2 **Ohridsko Jezero** *L* Macedonia/Alb
110B1 **Ohura** NZ
33G3 **Oiapoque** French Guiana
68B2 **Oijiaojing** China
14C2 **Oil City** USA
21B2 **Oildale** USA
46B2 **Oise** Department, France
49C2 **Oise** *R* France
74C4 **Oita** Japan
22C3 **Ojai** USA
24B2 **Ojinaga** Mexico
23B2 **Ojitlán** Mexico
75B1 **Ojiya** Japan
30C4 **Ojos del Salado** *Mt* Arg
23A1 **Ojueloz** Mexico
60E3 **Oka** *R* Russian Fed
100A3 **Okahandja** Namibia
20C1 **Okanagan Falls** Can
13D2 **Okanagan L** Can
20C1 **Okanogan** USA
20C1 **Okanogan** *R* USA
20B1 **Okanogan Range** *Mts* Can/USA
84C2 **Okara** Pak
100A2 **Okavango** *R* Angola/ Namibia
100B2 **Okavango Delta** *Marsh* Botswana
74D3 **Okaya** Japan
74C4 **Okayama** Japan
75B2 **Okazaki** Japan
17B2 **Okeechobee** USA
17B2 **Okeechobee,L** USA
17B1 **Okefenokee Swamp** USA
97C4 **Okene** Nig
85B4 **Okha** India
69G1 **Okha** Russian Fed
86B1 **Okhaldunga** Nepal
62J3 **Okhotsk,S of** Russian Fed
69E4 **Okinawa** *I* Japan
69E4 **Okinawa gunto** *Arch* Japan
74C3 **Oki-shoto** *Is* Japan
9D3 **Oklahoma** State, USA
18A2 **Oklahoma City** USA
18A2 **Okmulgee** USA
98B3 **Okondja** Gabon
98B3 **Okoyo** Congo
97C4 **Okpara** *R* Nig
61J4 **Oktyabr'sk** Kazakhstan
61H3 **Oktyabr'skiy** Russian Fed
74D2 **Okushiri-tō** *I* Japan
38A2 **Olafsvik** Iceland
39H7 **Öland** *I* Sweden
108B2 **Olary** Aust
18B2 **Olathe** USA
29D3 **Olavarría** Arg
53A2 **Olbia** Sardegna
12G1 **Old Crow** Can
56B2 **Oldenburg** Niedersachsen, Germany
56C2 **Oldenburg** Schleswig-Holstein, Germany
15C2 **Old Forge** USA
42C3 **Oldham** Eng
12D3 **Old Harbor** USA
41B3 **Old Head of Kinsale** *C* Scot
16C2 **Old Lyme** USA
13E2 **Olds** Can
72B1 **Öldziyt** Mongolia
15C2 **Olean** USA
63E2 **Olekma** *R* Russian Fed
63D1 **Olekminsk** Russian Fed
38L5 **Olenegorsk** Russian Fed
58D2 **Olevsk** Ukraine
69F2 **Ol'ga** Russian Fed
100A3 **Olifants** *R* Namibia
55B2 **Ólimbos** *Mt* Greece
35B2 **Olímpia** Brazil
23B2 **Olinala** Mexico
31E3 **Olinda** Brazil
34C2 **Oliva** Arg
29C2 **Olivares** *Mt* Arg
35C2 **Oliveira** Brazil
13D3 **Oliver** Can
30C3 **Ollague** Chile
30C3 **Ollagüe** *Mt* Bol
18C2 **Olney** USA
68E1 **Olochi** Russian Fed
39G7 **Olofstrom** Sweden
98B3 **Olombo** Congo
59B3 **Olomouc** Czech Republic
60D1 **Olonets** Russian Fed
79B3 **Olongapa** Phil
48B3 **Oloron Ste Marie** France
68D1 **Olovyannaya** Russian Fed
46D1 **Olpe** Germany
58C2 **Olsztyn** Pol
54B2 **Olt** *R* Rom
47B1 **Olten** Switz
20B1 **Olympia** USA
20B1 **Olympic Nat Pk** USA
Olympus = Ólimbos
20B1 **Olympus,Mt** USA
65J4 **Om'** *R* Russian Fed
75B1 **Omachi** Japan
75B2 **Omae-zaki** *C* Japan
45C1 **Omagh** N Ire
18A1 **Omaha** USA
20C1 **Omak** USA
91C5 **Oman** Sultanate, Arabian Pen
91C4 **Oman,G of** UAE
98A3 **Omboué** Gabon
99D1 **Omdurman** Sudan
23B2 **Ometepec** Mexico
99D1 **Om Häjer** Eritrea
13B1 **Omineca** *R* Can
13B1 **Omineca Mts** Can
75B1 **Omiya** Japan
12H3 **Ommaney,C** USA
4H2 **Ommanney B** Can
99D2 **Omo** *R* Eth
65J4 **Omsk** Russian Fed
74B4 **Omura** Japan
74C4 **Omuta** Japan
61H2 **Omutninsk** Russian Fed
78D3 **Onang** Indon
14B1 **Onaping L** Can
100A2 **Oncócua** Angola
100A2 **Ondangua** Namibia
59C3 **Ondava** *R* Slovakia
68D2 **Öndörhaan** Molgolia
83B5 **One and Half Degree Chan** Indian O
64E3 **Onega** Russian Fed
64E3 **Onega** *R* Russian Fed
15C2 **Oneida L** USA
8D2 **O'Neill** USA
69H2 **Onekotan** *I* Russian Fed
98C3 **Onema** Zaïre
15D2 **Oneonta** USA
54C1 **Oneşti** Rom
64E3 **Onezhskoye Ozero** Russian Fed
100A2 **Ongiva** Angola
74B3 **Ongjin** N Korea
72D1 **Ongniud Qi** China
87C1 **Ongole** India
15C2 **Onieda L** USA
101D3 **Onilahy** *R* Madag
97C4 **Onitsha** Nig
68C2 **Onjüül** Mongolia
75B1 **Ono** Japan
75B2 **Onohara-jima** *I* Japan
74C4 **Onomichi** Japan
106A3 **Onslow** Aust
17C1 **Onslow B** USA
75B1 **Ontake-san** *Mt* Japan
22D3 **Ontario** California, USA
20C2 **Ontario** Oregon, US
7A4 **Ontario** Province, Can
15C2 **Ontario,L** Can/USA
51B2 **Onteniente** Spain
106C3 **Oodnadatta** Aust
106C4 **Ooldea** Aust
18A2 **Oologah L** USA
46B1 **Oostende** Belg
46B1 **Oosterschelde** *Estuary* Neth
87B2 **Ootacamund** India
13B2 **Ootsa L** Can
69H1 **Opala** Russian Fed
98C3 **Opala** Zaïre
87C3 **Opanake** Sri Lanka
61G2 **Oparino** Russian Fe

59B3 **Opava** Czech Republic
17A1 **Opelika** USA
19B3 **Opelousas** USA
12C2 **Ophir** USA
58D1 **Opochka** Russian Fed
59B2 **Opole** Pol
Oporto = Porto
110C1 **Opotiki** NZ
17A1 **Opp** USA
38F6 **Oppdal** Nor
110B1 **Opunake** NZ
54B1 **Oradea** Rom
38B2 **Oraefajökull** *Mts* Iceland
85D3 **Orai** India
96B1 **Oran** Alg
30D3 **Orán** Arg
109C2 **Orange** Aust
22D4 **Orange** California, USA
49C3 **Orange** France
19B3 **Orange** Texas, USA
100A3 **Orange** *R* S Africa
17B1 **Orangeburg** USA
17B1 **Orange Park** USA
14B2 **Orangeville** Can
56C2 **Oranienburg** Germany
79C3 **Oras** Phil
54B1 **Orăstie** Rom
54B1 **Oravița** Rom
52B2 **Orbetello** Italy
109C3 **Orbost** Aust
46B1 **Orchies** France
47B2 **Orco** *R* Italy
106B2 **Ord** *R* Aust
106B2 **Ord,Mt** Aust
93C1 **Ordu** Turk
39H7 **Örebro** Sweden
8A2 **Oregon** State, USA
14B2 **Oregon** USA
20B1 **Oregon City** USA
39H6 **Oregrund** Sweden
60E2 **Orekhovo Zuyevo** Russian Fed
60E3 **Orel** Russian Fed
61H3 **Orenburg** Russian Fed
34D3 **Orense** Arg
50A1 **Orense** Spain
56C1 **Oresund** *Str* Den/Sweden
11A3 **Oreti** *R* NZ
55C3 **Orhaneli** *R* Turk
68C2 **Orhon Gol** *R* Mongolia
23B2 **Oriental** Mexico
108B1 **Orientos** Aust
51B2 **Orihuela** Spain
15C2 **Orillia** Can
33E2 **Orinoco** *R* Ven
86A2 **Orissa** State, India
53A3 **Oristano** Sardegna
38K6 **Orivesi** *L* Fin
33F4 **Oriximina** Brazil
23B2 **Orizaba** Mexico
35B1 **Orizona** Brazil
44C2 **Orkney** *I* Scot
35B2 **Orlândia** Brazil
17B2 **Orlando** USA
48C2 **Orléanais** *Region* France
48C2 **Orléans** France
63B2 **Orlik** Russian Fed
82A3 **Ormara** Pak
79B3 **Ormoc** Phil
17B2 **Ormond Beach** USA
46C2 **Ornain** *R* France
47B1 **Ornans** France
48B2 **Orne** *R* France
38H6 **Örnsköldsvik** Sweden
32C3 **Orocué** Colombia
94B3 **Oron** Israel
Orontes = 'Āṣī
79B4 **Oroquieta** Phil
59C3 **Orosháza** Hung
21A2 **Oroville** California, USA
20C1 **Oroville** Washington, USA
47B1 **Orsières** Switz
65G4 **Orsk** Russian Fed
38F6 **Ørsta** Nor
48B3 **Orthez** France
50A1 **Ortigueira** Spain
47D1 **Ortles** *Mts* Italy
27L1 **Ortoire** *R* Trinidad
93E2 **Orūmīyeh** Iran
30C2 **Oruro** Bol
61J2 **Osa** Russian Fed
18B2 **Osage** *R* USA
75B1 **Osaka** Japan
25D4 **Osa,Pen de** Costa Rica
18C2 **Osceola** Arkansas, USA
18B1 **Osceola** Iowa, USA
20C2 **Osgood Mts** USA
15C2 **Oshawa** Can
75B2 **Ō-shima** *I* Japan
10B2 **Oshkosh** USA
97C4 **Oshogbo** Nig
7B5 **Oshosh** USA
98B3 **Oshwe** Zaïre
54A1 **Osijek** Croatia
65K5 **Osinniki** Russian Fed
58D2 **Osipovichi** Belorussia
18B1 **Oskaloosa** USA
60A2 **Oskarshamn** Sweden
39G7 **Oslo** Nor
92C2 **Osmaniye** Turk
56B2 **Osnabrück** Germany
30F4 **Osório** Brazil
29B4 **Osorno** Chile
50B1 **Osorno** Spain
20C1 **Osoyoos** Can
13C1 **Ospika** *R* Can
107D5 **Ossa,Mt** Aust
16C2 **Ossining** USA
60D2 **Ostashkov** Russian Fed
Ostend = Oostende
38G6 **Østerdalen** *V* Nor
38G6 **Östersund** Sweden
56B2 **Ostfriesische Inseln** *Is* Germany
39H6 **Östhammär** Sweden
53B2 **Ostia** Italy
47D2 **Ostiglia** Italy
59B3 **Ostrava** Czech Republic
58B2 **Ostróda** Pol
58B2 **Ostroleka** Pol
60C2 **Ostrov** Russian Fed
64J2 **Ostrov Belyy** *I* Russian Fed
64H1 **Ostrov Greem Bell** *I* Barents S
64F3 **Ostrov Kolguyev** *I* Russian Fed
74F2 **Ostrov Kunashir** *I* Russian Fed
64F2 **Ostrov Mechdusharskiy** *I* Barents S
90B2 **Ostrov Ogurchinskiy** *I* Turkmenistan
64G1 **Ostrov Rudol'fa** *I* Barents S
64G2 **Ostrov Vaygach** *I* Russian Fed
1B7 **Ostrov Vrangelya** *I* Russian Fed
58B2 **Ostrów Wlkp.** Pol
59C2 **Ostrowiec** Pol
58C2 **Ostrów Mazowiecka** Pol
50A2 **Osuna** Spain
15C2 **Osweg** USA
15C2 **Oswego** USA
43C3 **Oswestry** Eng
59B2 **Oświęcim** Pol
75B1 **Ota** Japan
111B3 **Otago Pen** NZ
110C2 **Otaki** NZ
74E2 **Otaru** Japan
32B3 **Otavalo** Ecuador
100A2 **Otavi** Namibia
75C1 **Otawara** Japan
20C1 **Othello** USA
55B3 **Óthris** *Mt* Greece
16C1 **Otis** Massachusetts, USA
16B2 **Otisville** USA
100A3 **Otjiwarongo** Namibia
72B2 **Otog Qi** China
110C1 **Otorohanga** NZ
55A2 **Otranto** Italy
55A2 **Otranto,Str of** *Chan* Italy/Alb
14A2 **Otsego** USA
75B1 **Otsu** Japan
39F6 **Otta** Nor
39F7 **Otta** *R* Nor
15C1 **Ottawa** Can
18A2 **Ottawa** Kansas, USA
15C1 **Ottawa** *R* Can
7B4 **Ottawa Is** Can
7B4 **Otter Rapids** Can
6B1 **Otto Fjord** Can
101G1 **Ottosdal** S Africa
18B1 **Ottumwa** USA
46D2 **Ottweiler** Germany
97C4 **Oturkpo** Nig
32B5 **Otusco** Peru
108B3 **Otway,C** Aust
58C2 **Otwock** Pol
47D1 **Ötz** Austria
47D1 **Otzal** *Mts* Austria
76C1 **Ou** *R* Laos
19B3 **Ouachita** *R* USA
19B3 **Ouachita,L** USA
19B3 **Ouachita Mts** USA
96A2 **Ouadane** Maur
98C2 **Ouadda** CAR
98C1 **Ouaddai** *Desert Region* Chad
97B3 **Ouagadougou** Burkina
97B3 **Ouahigouya** Burkina
98C2 **Ouaka** CAR
97C3 **Oualam** Niger
96C2 **Ouallen** Alg
98C2 **Ouanda Djallé** CAR
96A2 **Ouarane** Region, Maur
96C1 **Ouargla** Alg
98C2 **Ouarra** *R* CAR
96B1 **Ouarzazate** Mor
51C2 **Ouassel** *R* Alg
98B2 **Oubangui** *R* Congo
46B1 **Oudenaarde** Belg
100B4 **Oudtshoorn** S Africa
51B2 **Oued Tlělat** Alg
96B1 **Oued Zem** Mor
98B2 **Ouesso** Congo
96B1 **Ouezzane** Mor
98B2 **Ouham** *R* Chad
97C4 **Ouidah** Benin
96B1 **Oujda** Mor
38J6 **Oulainen** Fin
38K5 **Oulu** Fin
38K6 **Oulu** *R* Fin
38K6 **Oulujärvi** *L* Fin
95B3 **Oum Chalouba** Chad
98B1 **Oum Hadjer** Chad
95B3 **Oum Haouach** *Watercourse* Chad
38K5 **Ounas** *R* Fin
95B3 **Ounianga Kébir** Chad
46D1 **Our** *R* Germany
46B2 **Ourcq** *R* France
Ourense = Orense
31C3 **Ouricurí** Brazil
35B2 **Ourinhos** Brazil
35C2 **Ouro Prêto** Brazil
46C1 **Ourthe** *R* Belg
42D2 **Ouse** *R* Eng
43E3 **Ouse** *R* Eng
40B2 **Outer Hebrides** *Is* Scot
22C4 **Outer Santa Barbara** *Chan* USA
100A3 **Outjo** Namibia
38K6 **Outokumpu** Fin
108B3 **Ouyen** Aust
47C2 **Ovada** Italy
34A2 **Ovalle** Chile
100A2 **Ovamboland** Region, Namibia
61H5 **Ova Tyuleni** *Is* Kazakhstan
38J5 **Övertorneå** Sweden
50A1 **Oviedo** Spain
60C3 **Ovruch** Ukraine
63E2 **Ovsyanka** Russian Fed
111A3 **Owaka** NZ
75B2 **Owase** Japan
11B3 **Owensboro** USA
21B2 **Owens L** USA
14B2 **Owen Sound** Can
107D1 **Owen Stanley Range** *Mts* PNG
97C4 **Owerri** Nig
97C4 **Owo** Nig
14B2 **Owosso** USA
20C2 **Owyhee** *R* USA
20C2 **Owyhee Mts** USA
32B6 **Oxapampa** Peru
39H7 **Oxelösund** Sweden
43D4 **Oxford** County, Eng
43D4 **Oxford** Eng
16D1 **Oxford** Massachusetts, USA
19C3 **Oxford** Mississippi, USA
45B1 **Ox Mts** Irish Rep
22C3 **Oxnard** USA
74D3 **Oyama** Japan
13E2 **Oyen** Can
98B2 **Oyem** Gabon
44B3 **Oykel** *R* Scot
39F6 **Øyre** Nor
109C4 **Oyster B** Aust
79B4 **Ozamiz** Phil
17A1 **Ozark** USA
18B2 **Ozark Plat** USA
18B2 **Ozarks,L of the** USA
59C3 **Ózd** Hung
65K5 **Ozero Alakol** *L* Kazakhstan/Russian Fed
65J5 **Ozero Balkhash** *L* Kazakhstan
63C2 **Ozero Baykal** *L* Kazakhstan
65J4 **Ozero Chany** *L* Russian Fed
69F1 **Ozero Chukchagirskoye** Russian Fed
69F1 **Ozero Evoron** Russian Fed
Ozero Chudskoye = Peipus,L
60D2 **Ozero Il'men** *L* Russian Fed
38L5 **Ozero Imandra** *L* Russian Fed
82B1 **Ozero Issyk Kul'** *L* Kirghizia
69F2 **Ozero Khanka** *L* China/Russian Fed
38L5 **Ozero Kovdozero** *L* Russian Fed
38L5 **Ozero Kuyto** *L* Russian Fed
38L5 **Ozero Pyaozero** *L* Russian Fed
65H4 **Ozero Tengiz** *L* Kazakhstan
38L5 **Ozero Topozero** *L* Russian Fed
65K5 **Ozero Zaysan** Kazakhstan
23B1 **Ozuluama** Mexico

P

100A4 **Paarl** S Africa
44A3 **Pabbay** *I* Scot
58B2 **Pabianice** Pol
86B2 **Pabna** Bang
58D2 **Pabrade** Lithuania
32B5 **Pacasmayo** Peru
23B1 **Pachuca** Mexico
105K6 **Pacific-Antarctic Ridge** Pacific O
22B2 **Pacific Grove** USA
78C4 **Pacitan** Indon
35C1 **Pacuí** *R* Brazil
70B4 **Padang** Indon
56B2 **Paderborn** Germany
5J3 **Padlei** Can
86C2 **Padma** *R* Bang
47D2 **Padova** Italy
9D4 **Padre I** USA

43B4 **Padstow** Eng
108B3 **Padthaway** Aust
Padua = Padova
14A3 **Paducah** Kentucky, USA
11B3 **Paducah** USA
38L5 **Padunskoye More** *L* Russian Fed
74A3 **Paengnyŏng-do** *I* S Korea
110C1 **Paeroa** NZ
100C3 **Pafuri** Mozam
52B2 **Pag** *I* Croatia
79B4 **Pagadian** Phil
70B4 **Pagai Selatan** *I* Indon
70B4 **Pagai Utara** *I* Indon
71F2 **Pagan** *I* Pacific O
78D3 **Pagatan** Indon
55C3 **Pagondhas** Greece
110C2 **Pahiatua** NZ
21C4 **Pahoa** Hawaiian Is
17B2 **Pahokee** USA
39K6 **Päijänna** *L* Fin
21C4 **Pailola Chan** Hawaiian Is
14B2 **Painesville** USA
9B3 **Painted Desert** USA
42B2 **Paisley** Scot
32A5 **Paita** Peru
38J5 **Pajala** Sweden
80E3 **Pakistan** Republic, Asia
76C2 **Pak Lay** Laos
86D2 **Pakokku** Burma
13E2 **Pakowki L** Can
52C1 **Pakrac** Croatia
54A1 **Paks** Hung
76C2 **Pak Sane** Laos
76D2 **Pakse** Laos
99D2 **Pakwach** Uganda
98B2 **Pala** Chad
52C2 **Palagruža** *I* Croatia
46B2 **Palaiseau** France
Palakhat = Palghat
78C3 **Palangkaraya** Indon
87B2 **Palani** India
85C4 **Palanpur** India
100B3 **Palapye** Botswana
17B2 **Palatka** USA
71E3 **Palau Is** Pacific O
76B3 **Palaw** Burma
79A4 **Palawan** *I* Phil
79A4 **Palawan Pass** Phil
87B3 **Palayankottai** India
39J7 **Paldiski** Estonia
78A3 **Palembang** Indon
50B1 **Palencia** Spain
94A1 **Paleokhorio** Cyprus
53B3 **Palermo** Italy
19A3 **Palestine** USA
86C2 **Paletwa** Burma
87B2 **Pālghāt** India
85C3 **Pāli** India
85C4 **Pālitāna** India
87B3 **Palk Str** India/ Sri Lanka
61G3 **Pallasovka** Russian Fed
38J5 **Pallastunturi** *Mt* Fin
111B2 **Palliser B** NZ
111C2 **Palliser,C** NZ
101D2 **Palma** Mozam
51C2 **Palma de Mallorca** Spain
31D3 **Palmares** Brazil
26A5 **Palmar Sur** Costa Rica
97B4 **Palmas,C** Lib
26B2 **Palma Soriano** Cuba
17B2 **Palm Bay** USA
17B2 **Palm Beach** USA
22C3 **Palmdale** USA
31D3 **Palmeira dos Indos** Brazil
12E2 **Palmer** USA
112C3 **Palmer** *Base* Ant
112C3 **Palmer Arch** Ant
112B3 **Palmer Land** *Region* Ant
111B3 **Palmerston** NZ
110C2 **Palmerston North** NZ
16B2 **Palmerton** USA
17B2 **Palmetto** USA
53C3 **Palmi** Italy
32B3 **Palmira** Colombia
107D2 **Palm Is** Aust
21B3 **Palm Springs** USA
18B2 **Palmyra** Missouri, USA
16A2 **Palmyra** Pennsylvania, USA
86B2 **Palmyras Pt** India
22A2 **Palo Alto** USA
78B2 **Paloh** Indon
99D1 **Paloích** Sudan
21B3 **Palomar Mt** USA
70D4 **Palopo** Indon
70C4 **Palu** Indon
93C2 **Palu** Turk
84D3 **Palwal** India
97C3 **Pama** Burkina
78C4 **Pamekasan** Indon
78B4 **Pameungpeuk** Indon
48C3 **Pamiers** France
82B2 **Pamir** *Mts* China
65J6 **Pamir** *R* Russian Fed
11C3 **Pamlico Sd** USA
9C3 **Pampa** USA
34B2 **Pampa de la Salinas** *Salt pan* Arg
34B3 **Pampa de la Varita** *Plain* Arg
32C2 **Pamplona** Colombia
50B1 **Pamplona** Spain
18C2 **Pana** USA
54B2 **Panagyurishte** Bulg
87A1 **Panaji** India
32B2 **Panamá** Panama
32A2 **Panama** Republic, Cent America
26B5 **Panama Canal** Panama
17A1 **Panama City** USA
21B2 **Panamint Range** *Mts* USA
21B2 **Panamint V** USA
47D2 **Panaro** *R* Italy
79B3 **Panay** *I* Phil
54B2 **Pancevo** Serbia, Yugos
79B3 **Pandan** Phil
87B1 **Pandharpur** India
108A1 **Pandie Pandie** Aust
58C1 **Panevežys** Lithuania
65K5 **Panfilov** Kazakhstan
76B1 **Pang** *R* Burma
99D3 **Pangani** Tanz
99D3 **Pangani** *R* Tanz
98C3 **Pangi** Zaïre
78B3 **Pangkalpinang** Indon
6D3 **Pangnirtung** Can
76B1 **Pangtara** Burma
79B4 **Pangutaran Group** *Is* Phil
84D3 **Panipat** India
84B2 **Panjao** Afghan
74B3 **P'anmunjŏm** N Korea
86A2 **Panna** India
35A2 **Panorama** Brazil
53B3 **Pantelleria** *I* Medit S
23B1 **Pantepec** Mexico
23B1 **Panuco** Mexico
23B1 **Pánuco** *R* Mexico
73A4 **Pan Xian** China
53C3 **Paola** Italy
18B2 **Paola** USA
14A3 **Paoli** USA
59B3 **Pápa** Hung
110B1 **Papakura** NZ
23B2 **Papaloapan** *R* Mexico
23B1 **Papantla** Mexico
44E1 **Papa Stour** *I* Scot
110B1 **Papatoetoe** NZ
44C2 **Papa Westray** *I* Scot
107D1 **Papua,G of** PNG
107D1 **Papua New Guinea** Republic, S E Asia
34A2 **Papudo** Chile
76B2 **Papun** Burma
33G4 **Para** State, Brazil
31B2 **Pará** *R* Brazil
106A3 **Paraburdoo** Aust
32B6 **Paracas,Pen de** Peru
35B1 **Paracatu** Brazil
35B1 **Paracatu** *R* Brazil
108A2 **Parachilna** Aust
84C2 **Parachinar** Pak
54B2 **Paracin** Serbia, Yugos
35C1 **Pará de Minas** Brazil
21A2 **Paradise** California, USA
18B2 **Paragould** USA
33E6 **Paraguá** *R* Bol
33E2 **Paragua** *R* Ven
30E2 **Paraguai** *R* Brazil
30E4 **Paraguari** Par
30E3 **Paraguay** Republic, S America
30E3 **Paraguay** *R* Par
31D3 **Paraiba** State, Brazil
35B2 **Paraiba** *R* Brazil
35C2 **Paraíba do Sul** *R* Brazil
97C4 **Parakou** Benin
108A2 **Parakylia** Aust
87B3 **Paramakkudi** India
33F2 **Paramaribo** Surinam
69H1 **Paramushir** *I* Russian Fed
30F3 **Paraná** State, Brazil
34C2 **Paraná** Urug
29E2 **Paraná** *R* Arg
31B4 **Paranã** *R* Brazil
35A2 **Paraná** *R* Brazil
30G4 **Paranaguá** Brazil
35A1 **Paranaiba** Brazil
35A1 **Paranaiba** *R* Brazil
35A2 **Paranapanema** *R* Brazil
35A2 **Paranavai** Brazil
79B4 **Parang** Phil
35C1 **Paraope** *R* Brazil
110B2 **Paraparaumu** NZ
87B1 **Parbhani** India
94B2 **Pardes Hanna** Israel
34D3 **Pardo** Arg
35D1 **Pardo** *R* Bahia, Brazil
35A2 **Pardo** *R* Mato Grosso do Sul, Brazil
35B1 **Pardo** *R* Minas Gerais, Brazil
35B2 **Pardo** *R* Sao Paulo, Brazil
59B2 **Pardubice** Czech Republic
69F4 **Parece Vela** *Reef* Pacific O
10C2 **Parent** Can
70C4 **Parepare** Indon
34C3 **Parera** Arg
70B4 **Pariaman** Indon
33E1 **Paria,Pen de** Ven
48C2 **Paris** France
14B3 **Paris** Kentucky, USA
19A3 **Paris** Texas, USA
14B3 **Parkersburg** USA
109C2 **Parkes** Aust
16B3 **Parkesburg** USA
14A2 **Park Forest** USA
20B1 **Parksville** Can
87B1 **Parli** India
47D2 **Parma** Italy
14B2 **Parma** USA
31C2 **Parnaiba** Brazil
31C2 **Parnaiba** *R* Brazil
55B3 **Párnon Óros** *Mts* Greece
60B2 **Pärnu** Estonia
86B1 **Paro** Bhutan
108B1 **Paroo** *R* Aust
108B2 **Paroo Channel** *R* Aust
55C3 **Páros** *I* Greece
47B2 **Parpaillon** *Mts* France
34A3 **Parral** Chile
109D2 **Parramatta** Aust
9C4 **Parras** Mexico
6B3 **Parry B** Can
4G2 **Parry Is** Can
7C5 **Parry Sd** Can
14B1 **Parry Sound** Can
57C3 **Parsberg** Germany
5F4 **Parsnip** *R* Can
18A2 **Parsons** Kansas, USA
14C3 **Parsons** West Virginia, USA
48B2 **Parthenay** France
53B3 **Partinico** Italy
74C2 **Partizansk** Russian Fed
33G4 **Paru** *R* Brazil
101G1 **Parys** S Africa
19A4 **Pasadena** Texas, USA
22C3 **Pasadena** California, USA
78D3 **Pasangkayu** Indon
76B2 **Pasawing** Burma
19C3 **Pascagoula** USA
54C1 **Paşcani** Rom
20C1 **Pasco** USA
46B1 **Pas-de-Calais** Department, France
39G8 **Pasewalk** Germany
91C4 **Pashū'īyeh** Iran
106B4 **Pasley,C** Aust
29E2 **Paso de los Toros** Urug
29B4 **Paso Limay** Arg
21A2 **Paso Robles** USA
45B3 **Passage West** Irish Rep
16B2 **Passaic** USA
57C3 **Passau** Germany
30E4 **Passo de los Libres** Arg
47D1 **Passo di Stelvio** *Mt* Italy
30F4 **Passo Fundo** Brazil
35B2 **Passos** Brazil
47B2 **Passy** France
32B4 **Pastaza** *R* Peru
34C3 **Pasteur** Arg
5H4 **Pas,The** Can
32B3 **Pasto** Colombia
12B2 **Pastol B** USA
47D2 **Pasubio** *Mt* Italy
78C4 **Pasuruan** Indon
58C1 **Pasvalys** Lithuania
85C4 **Pātan** India
86B1 **Patan** Nepal
108B3 **Patchewollock** Aus
110B1 **Patea** NZ
111B2 **Patea** *R* NZ
53B3 **Paterno** Italy
16B2 **Paterson** USA
111A3 **Paterson Inlet** *B* N
84D2 **Pathankot** India
Pathein = Bassein
84D2 **Patiāla** India
32B6 **Pativilca** Peru
55C3 **Pátmos** *I* Greece
86B1 **Patna** India
93D2 **Patnos** Turk
63D2 **Patomskoye Nagor'ye** *Upland* Russian Fed
31D3 **Patos** Brazil
35B1 **Patos de Minas** Bra
34B2 **Patquia** Arg
55B3 **Pátrai** Greece
35B1 **Patrocinio** Brazil
99E3 **Patta** *I* Kenya
78D4 **Pattallasang** Indon
77C4 **Pattani** Thai
22B2 **Patterson** Californi USA
19B4 **Patterson** Louisian USA
12H2 **Patterson,Mt** Can
22C2 **Patterson Mt** USA
13B1 **Pattullo,Mt** Can
31D3 **Patu** Brazil
86C2 **Patuakhali** Bang
25D3 **Patuca** *R* Hondura
23A2 **Patzcuaro** Mexico
48B3 **Pau** France
4F3 **Paulatuk** Can
31C3 **Paulistana** Brazil
101H1 **Paulpietersburg** S Africa
19A3 **Pauls Valley** USA
76B2 **Paungde** Burma
84D2 **Pauri** India
38H5 **Pauskie** Nor
35C1 **Pavão** Brazil
47C2 **Pavia** Italy
65J4 **Pavlodar** Kazakhst
61J2 **Pavlovka** Russian Fed

61F2 **Pavlovo** Russian Fed
61F3 **Pavlovsk** Russian Fed
78C3 **Pawan** *R* Indon
18A2 **Pawhuska** USA
16D2 **Pawtucket** USA
47B1 **Payerne** Switz
20C2 **Payette** USA
7C4 **Payne,L** Can
34D2 **Paysandu** Urug
46A2 **Pays-de-Bray** Region, France
54B2 **Pazardzhik** Bulg
13D1 **Peace** *R* Can
17B2 **Peace** *R* USA
13D1 **Peace River** Can
43D3 **Peak District Nat Pk** Eng
108A1 **Peake** *R* Aust
109C2 **Peak Hill** Aust
71E4 **Peak Mandala** *Mt* Indon
42D3 **Peak,The** *Mt* Eng
19B3 **Pearl** *R* USA
21C4 **Pearl City** Hawaiian Is
21C4 **Pearl Harbor** Hawaiian Is
4H2 **Peary Chan** Can
101C2 **Pebane** Mozam
54B2 **Peć** Serbia, Yugos
35C1 **Peçanha** Brazil
19B4 **Pecan Island** USA
38L5 **Pechenga** Russian Fed
64F3 **Pechora** *R* Russian Fed
64G3 **Pechorskoye More** *S* Russian Fed
53C3 **Pecoraro** *Mt* Italy
9C3 **Pecos** USA
9C3 **Pecos** *R* USA
59B3 **Pécs** Hung
108A1 **Pedirka** Aust
35C1 **Pedra Azul** Brazil
35B2 **Pedregulho** Brazil
26B3 **Pedro Cays** *Is* Caribbean S
30C3 **Pedro de Valdivia** Chile
30E3 **Pedro Juan Caballero** Par
34C3 **Pedro Luro** Arg
23B1 **Pedro Mentova** Mexico
87C3 **Pedro,Pt** Sri Lanka
108B2 **Peebinga** Aust
42C2 **Peebles** Scot
17C1 **Pee Dee** *R* USA
16C2 **Peekskill** USA
42B2 **Peel** Eng
12H1 **Peel** *R* Can
4J2 **Peel Sd** Can
108A1 **Peera Peera Poolanna** *L* Aust
13E1 **Peerless L** Can
71E4 **Peg Arfak** *Mt* Indon
111B2 **Pegasus B** NZ
83D4 **Pegu** Burma
78A3 **Pegunungan Barisan** *Mts* Indon
78C2 **Pegunungan Iran** *Mts* Malay/Indon
71E4 **Pegunungan Maoke** *Mts* Indon
78D3 **Pegunungan Meratus** *Mts* Indon
78C2 **Pegunungan Muller** *Mts* Indon
78C3 **Pegunungan Schwanet** *Mts* Indon
78A3 **Pegunungan Tigapuluh** *Mts* Indon
76B2 **Pegu Yoma** *Mts* Burma
34C3 **Pehuajó** Arg
Péipsi Järve = Peipus,L
39K7 **Peipus, Lake** Estonia/Russian Fed
35A2 **Peixe** *R* Sao Paulo, Brazil
72D3 **Pei Xian** China
78B4 **Pekalongan** Indon
77C5 **Pekan** Malay
78A2 **Pekanbaru** Indon
18C1 **Pekin** USA
Peking = Beijing
77C5 **Pelabohan Kelang** Malay
78D4 **Pelau Pelau Kangean** *Is* Indon
78C4 **Pelau Pelau Karimunjawa** *Arch* Indon
78D4 **Pelau Pelau Postilyon** *Is* Indon
54B1 **Peleaga** *Mt* Rom
63D2 **Peleduy** Russian Fed
14B2 **Pelee I** Can
71D4 **Peleng** *I* Indon
12G3 **Pelican** USA
69F1 **Peliny Osipenko** Russian Fed
34C3 **Pellegrini** Arg
38J5 **Pello** Fin
12H2 **Pelly** *R* Can
6A3 **Pelly Bay** Can
12G2 **Pelly Crossing** Can
12H2 **Pelly Mts** Can
30F5 **Pelotas** Brazil
30F4 **Pelotas** *R* Brazil
47B2 **Pelvoux** Region, France
78B4 **Pemalang** Indon
78A3 **Pematang** Indon
101D2 **Pemba** Mozam
99D3 **Pemba** *I* Tanz
13C2 **Pemberton** Can
13D2 **Pembina** *R* Can
15C1 **Pembroke** Can
17B1 **Pembroke** USA
43B4 **Pembroke** Wales
34A3 **Pemuco** Chile
78D2 **Penambo Range** *Mts* Malay
35A2 **Penápolis** Brazil
50A2 **Peñarroya** Spain
51B1 **Penarroya** *Mt* Spain
50A1 **Peña Trevina** *Mt* Spain
98B2 **Pende** *R* Chad
12J3 **Pendelton,Mt** Can
20C1 **Pendleton** USA
20C1 **Pend Oreille** *R* USA
31D4 **Penedo** Brazil
85D5 **Penganga** *R* India
73D5 **P'eng-hu Lieh-tao** *Is* Taiwan
72E2 **Penglai** China
73B4 **Pengshui** China
71E4 **Pengunungan Maoke** *Mts* Indon
26C4 **Península de la Guajiri** *Pen* Colombia
27E4 **Península de Paria** *Pen* Ven
77C5 **Peninsular Malaysia** Malay
10D2 **Peninsule de Gaspé** *Pen* Can
23A1 **Penjamo** Mexico
87B2 **Penner** *R* India
42C2 **Pennine Chain** *Mts* Eng
16B3 **Penns Grove** USA
10C2 **Pennsylvania** State, USA
6D3 **Penny Highlands** *Mts* Can
108B3 **Penola** Aust
106C4 **Penong** Aust
42C2 **Penrith** Eng
11B3 **Pensacola** USA
112A **Pensacola Mts** Ant
78D1 **Pensiangan** Malay
13D3 **Penticton** Can
44C2 **Pentland Firth** *Chan* Scot
42C2 **Pentland Hills** Scot
61G3 **Penza** Russian Fed
43B4 **Penzance** Eng
10B2 **Peoria** USA
78A3 **Perabumulih** Indon
77C5 **Perak** *R* Malay
78A2 **Perawang** Indon
32B3 **Pereira** Colombia
35A2 **Pereira Barreto** Brazil
61F4 **Perelazovskiy** Russian Fed
12D3 **Perenosa B** USA
34C2 **Pergamino** Arg
7C4 **Peribonca** *R* Can
48C2 **Périqueux** France
25E4 **Perlas Arch de** *Is* Panama
61J2 **Perm'** Russian Fed
Pernambuco = Recife
31D3 **Pernambuco** State, Brazil
108A2 **Pernatty Lg** Aust
54B2 **Pernik** Bulg
46B2 **Péronne** France
23B2 **Perote** Mexico
49C3 **Perpignan** France
22D4 **Perris** USA
17B1 **Perry** Florida, USA
17B1 **Perry** Georgia, USA
18A2 **Perry** Oklahoma, USA
4H3 **Perry River** Can
14B2 **Perrysburg** USA
12C3 **Perryville** Alaska, USA
18C2 **Perryville** Missouri, USA
106A4 **Perth** Aust
15C2 **Perth** Can
44C3 **Perth** Scot
16B2 **Perth Amboy** USA
32C6 **Peru** Republic, S America
18C1 **Peru** USA
103E5 **Peru-Chile Trench** Pacific O
52B2 **Perugia** Italy
52C2 **Perušic** Croatia
93D2 **Pervari** Turk
61F3 **Pervomaysk** Russian Fed
60D4 **Pervomaysk** Ukraine
61J2 **Pervoural'sk** Russian Fed
52B2 **Pesaro** Italy
22A2 **Pescadero** USA
Pescadores = P'eng-hu Lieh-tao
52B2 **Pescara** Italy
47D2 **Peschiera** Italy
84C2 **Peshawar** Pak
54B2 **Peshkopi** Alb
14A1 **Peshtigo** USA
60E2 **Pestovo** Russian Fed
94B2 **Petah Tiqwa** Israel
21A2 **Petaluma** USA
46C2 **Pétange** Lux
23A2 **Petatlán** Mexico
101C2 **Petauke** Zambia
108A2 **Peterborough** Aust
15C2 **Peterborough** Can
43D3 **Peterborough** Eng
44D3 **Peterhead** Scot
6D1 **Petermann Gletscher** *Gl* Greenland
106B3 **Petermann Range** *Mts* Aust
29B3 **Peteroa** *Mt* Arg/Chile
13F1 **Peter Pond L** Can
12H3 **Petersburg** Alaska, USA
85C4 **Petlād** India
23B2 **Petlalcingo** Mexico
25D2 **Peto** Mexico
63D2 **Petomskoye Nagor'ye** *Upland* Russian Fed
34A2 **Petorca** Chile
14B1 **Petoskey** USA
31C3 **Petrolina** Brazil
65H4 **Petropavlovsk** Kazakhstan
35C2 **Petrópolis** Brazil
61G3 **Petrovsk** Russian Fed
68C1 **Petrovsk Zabaykal'skiy** Russian Fed
64E3 **Petrozavodsk** Russian Fed
101G1 **Petrus** S Africa
101G1 **Petrusburg** S Africa
1B7 **Pevek** Russian Fed
46D2 **Pfälzer Wald** Region, Germany
57B3 **Pforzheim** Germany
84D2 **Phagwara** India
85C3 **Phalodi** India
46D2 **Phalsbourg** France
87A1 **Phaltan** India
77B4 **Phangnga** Thai
76C3 **Phanom Dang** *Mts* Camb
76D3 **Phan Rang** Viet
76D3 **Phan Thiet** Viet
17A1 **Phenix City** USA
76B3 **Phet Buri** Thai
76D3 **Phiafay** Laos
19C3 **Philadelphia** Mississippi, USA
16B2 **Philadelphia** Pennsylvania, USA
Philippeville = Skikda
46C1 **Philippeville** Belg
71D2 **Philippine S** Pacific O
71D2 **Philippines** Republic, S E Asia
104E3 **Philippine Trench** Pacific O
15C2 **Philipsburg** Pennsylvania, USA
12E1 **Philip Smith Mts** USA
79B2 **Phillipine S** Phil
6B1 **Phillips B** Can
16B2 **Phillipsburg** New Jersey, USA
6B2 **Philpots Pen** Can
76C3 **Phnom Penh** Camb
9B3 **Phoenix** Arizona, USA
16B2 **Phoenixville** USA
76C1 **Phong Saly** Laos
Phra Nakhon = Bangkok
76C2 **Phu Bia** *Mt* Laos
76D3 **Phu Cuong** Viet
77B4 **Phuket** Thai
86A2 **Phulbāni** India
76C2 **Phu Miang** *Mt* Thai
76D2 **Phu Set** *Mt* Laos
76D1 **Phu Tho** Viet
77D4 **Phu Vinh** Viet
47C2 **Piacenza** Italy
109C2 **Pian** *R* Aust
52B2 **Pianosa** *I* Italy
52C2 **Pianosa** *I* Italy
58C2 **Piaseczno** Pol
54C1 **Piatra-Neamţ** Rom
31C3 **Piaui** State, Brazil
47E2 **Piave** *R* Italy
99D2 **Pibor** *R* Sudan
99D2 **Pibor Post** Sudan
46B1 **Picardie** Region, France
19C3 **Picayune** USA
47B2 **Pic de Rochebrune** *Mt* France
34A2 **Pichilemu** Chile
34C3 **Pichi Mahuida** Arg
42D2 **Pickering** Eng
7A4 **Pickle Lake** Can
96A1 **Pico** *I* Açores
47C1 **Pico Bernina** *Mt* Switz
51C1 **Pico de Anito** *Mt* Spain
24B3 **Pico del Infiernillo** *Mt* Mexico
27C3 **Pico Duarte** *Mt* Dom Rep
31C3 **Picos** Brazil
50B1 **Picos de Europa** *Mt* Spain
109D2 **Picton** Aust
111B2 **Picton** NZ
95A2 **Pic Toussidé** *Mt* Chad
35B2 **Piedade** Brazil
22C2 **Piedra** USA
24B2 **Piedras Negras** Mexico
38K6 **Pieksämäki** Fin
38K6 **Pielinen** *L* Fin
47B2 **Piemonte** Region, Italy

8C2 **Pierre** USA
59B3 **Pieštany** Slovakia
101H1 **Pietermaritzburg** S Africa
100B3 **Pietersburg** S Africa
101H1 **Piet Retief** S Africa
60B4 **Pietrosu** *Mt* Rom
47E1 **Pieve di Cadore** Italy
13E2 **Pigeon L** Can
18B2 **Piggott** USA
34C3 **Pigüé** Arg
7A4 **Pikangikum L** Can
8C3 **Pikes Peak** USA
100A4 **Piketberg** S Africa
6F3 **Pikintaleq** Greenland
82B2 **Pik Kommunizma** *Mt* Tajikistan
98B2 **Pikounda** Congo
82C1 **Pik Pobedy** *Mt* China/Kirghizia
34D3 **Pila** Arg
58B2 **Pila** Pol
30E4 **Pilar** Par
30D3 **Pilcomayo** *R* Arg/Par
84D3 **Pīlībhīt** India
59B2 **Pilica** *R* Pol
109C4 **Pillar,C** Aust
55B3 **Pílos** Greece
12C3 **Pilot Point** USA
12B2 **Pilot Station** USA
19C3 **Pilottown** USA
33F4 **Pimenta** Brazil
77C4 **Pinang** *I* Malay
26A2 **Pinar del Rio** Cuba
34B2 **Pinas** Arg
46C1 **Pinche** Belg
13E2 **Pincher Creek** Can
31B2 **Pindaré** *R* Brazil
55B3 **Píndhos** *Mts* Greece
19B3 **Pine Bluff** USA
106C2 **Pine Creek** Aust
22C1 **Pinecrest** USA
22C2 **Pinedale** California, USA
22C2 **Pine Flat Res** USA
64F3 **Pinega** *R* Russian Fed
16A2 **Pine Grove** USA
17B2 **Pine Hills** USA
17B2 **Pine I** USA
19B3 **Pineland** USA
17B2 **Pinellas Park** USA
5G3 **Pine Point** Can
47B2 **Pinerolo** Italy
19B3 **Pines,Lo'the** USA
19B3 **Pineville** USA
72C3 **Pingdingshan** China
73B5 **Pingguo** China
72B2 **Pingliang** China
72B2 **Pingluo** China
73D4 **Pingtan Dao** *I* China
73E5 **P'ing tung** Taiwan
72A3 **Pingwu** China
73B5 **Pingxiang** Guangxi, China
73C4 **Pingxiang** Jiangxi, China
31B2 **Pinheiro** Brazil
70A3 **Pini** *I* Indon
55B3 **Piniós** *R* Greece
106A4 **Pinjarra** Aust
13C1 **Pink Mountain** Can
108B3 **Pinnaroo** Aust
Pinos,I de, I = Isla de la Juventud
21A2 **Pinos,Pt** USA
23B2 **Pinotepa Nacional** Mexico
70C4 **Pinrang** Indon
60C3 **Pinsk** Belorussia
32J7 **Pinta** *I* Ecuador
61G1 **Pinyug** Russian Fed
8B3 **Pioche** USA
52B2 **Piombino** Italy
6H3 **Piórsá** Iceland
59B2 **Piotrków Trybunalski** Pol
44E2 **Piper** *Oilfield* N Sea
21B2 **Piper Peak** *Mt* USA
10C2 **Pipmuacan Res** Can
14B2 **Piqua** USA
35B1 **Piracanjuba** Brazil
35B2 **Piracicaba** Brazil
35B2 **Piraçununga** Brazil
35B2 **Piraí do Sul** Brazil
55B3 **Piraiévs** Greece
35B2 **Pirajui** Brazil
35A1 **Piranhas** Brazil
35C1 **Pirapora** Brazil
35B1 **Pirenópolis** Brazil
35B1 **Pires do Rio** Brazil
55B3 **Pírgos** Greece
Pirineos = Pyrénees
31C2 **Piripiri** Brazil
46D2 **Pirmasens** Germany
54B2 **Pirot** Serbia, Yugos
84C2 **Pīr Panjāl Range** *Mts* Pak
71D4 **Piru** Indon
22C3 **Piru Creek** *R* USA
49E3 **Pisa** Italy
32B6 **Pisco** Peru
57C3 **Pisek** Czech Republic
84B2 **Pishin** Pak
30C4 **Pissis** *Mt* Arg
49E3 **Pistoia** Italy
50B1 **Pisuerga** *R* Spain
20B2 **Pit** *R* USA
32B3 **Pitalito** Colombia
105K5 **Pitcairn** *I* Pacific O
38H5 **Pite** *R* Sweden
38J5 **Piteå** Sweden
54B2 **Pitești** Rom
63B2 **Pit Gorodok** Russian Fed
38L6 **Pitkyaranta** Russian Fed
44C3 **Pitlochry** Scot
34A3 **Pitrutquén** Chile
13B2 **Pitt I** Can
22B1 **Pittsburg** California, USA
18B2 **Pittsburg** Kansas, USA
14C2 **Pittsburgh** USA
18B2 **Pittsfield** Illinois, USA
16C1 **Pittsfield** Massachusetts, USA
109D1 **Pittsworth** Aust
86A1 **Piuthan** Nepal
47D1 **Pizzo Redorta** *Mt* Italy
38B2 **Pjórsá** Iceland
32A5 **Pjura** Peru
7E5 **Placentia B** Can
22B1 **Placerville** USA
46B1 **Plaine des Flandres** *Plain* Belg/France
96C2 **Plaine du Tidikelt** *Desert* Region
9C3 **Plainview** Texas, USA
22B2 **Planada** USA
30F2 **Planalto de Mato Grosso** *Plat* Brazil
31D3 **Planalto do Borborema** *Plat* Brazil
32A1 **Planalto do Mato Grosso** *Mts* Brazil
19A3 **Plano** USA
17B2 **Plantation** USA
17B2 **Plant City** USA
50A1 **Plasencia** Spain
61K3 **Plast** Russian Fed
69F2 **Plastun** Russian Fed
96C2 **Plateau du Tademait** Alg
46D2 **Plateau Lorrain** *Plat* France
48C2 **Plateaux de Limousin** *Plat* France
51C2 **Plateaux du Sersou** *Plat* Alg
26C5 **Plato** Colombia
65G5 **Plato Ustyurt** *Plat* Kazakhstan
8C2 **Platte** *R* USA
15D2 **Plattsburgh** USA
18A1 **Plattsmouth** USA
57C2 **Plauen** Germany
60E3 **Plavsk** Russian Fed
23A2 **Playa Azul** Mexico
32A4 **Playas** Ecuador
23B2 **Playa Vicente** Mexico
50A1 **Plaza de Moro Almanzor** *Mt* Spain
22B2 **Pleasanton** California, USA
16B3 **Pleasantville** USA
14A3 **Pleasure Ridge Park** USA
76D3 **Pleiku** Viet
110C1 **Plenty,B of** NZ
58B2 **Pleszew** Pol
7C4 **Pletipi,L** Can
54B2 **Pleven** Bulg
54A2 **Pljevlja** Montenegro, Yugos
52C2 **Ploče** Bosnia-Herzegovina
58B2 **Płock** Pol
48B2 **Ploërmel** France
54C2 **Ploiești** Rom
60B3 **Płońsk** Pol
54B2 **Plovdiv** Bulg
20C1 **Plummer** USA
12C2 **Plummer,Mt** USA
100B3 **Plumtree** Zim
22B1 **Plymouth** California, USA
43B4 **Plymouth** Eng
14A2 **Plymouth** Indiana, USA
16D2 **Plymouth** Massachusetts, USA
15C2 **Plymouth** Pennsylvania, USA
43B4 **Plymouth Sd** Eng
43C3 **Plynlimon** *Mt* Wales
57C3 **Plzeň** Czech Republic
58B2 **Pniewy** Pol
38K6 **Pnyäselkä** *L* Fin
97B3 **Pô** Burkina
47E2 **Po** *R* Italy
97C4 **Pobé** Benin
69G2 **Pobedino** Russian Fed
8B2 **Pocatello** USA
15C3 **Pocomoke City** USA
35B2 **Pocos de Caldas** Brazil
54A2 **Podgorica** Montenegro, Yugos
47D2 **Po di Volano** *R* Italy
63B1 **Podkamennaya** *R* Russian Fed
60E2 **Podol'sk** Russian Fed
59D3 **Podol'skaya Vozvyshennost'** *Upland* Ukraine
60D1 **Podporozh'ye** Russian Fed
61F1 **Podyuga** Russian Fed
100A3 **Pofadder** S Africa
74B3 **P'ohang** S Korea
112C9 **Poinsett,C** Ant
108C2 **Point** Aust
27E3 **Pointe-à-Pitre** Guadeloupe
48B2 **Pointe de Barfleur** *Pt* France
98B3 **Pointe Noire** Congo
98A2 **Pointe Pongara** *Pt* Gabon
108B3 **Point Fairy** Aust
27L1 **Point Fortin** Trinidad
4B3 **Point Hope** USA
4G3 **Point L** Can
12B1 **Point Lay** USA
16B2 **Point Pleasant** New Jersey, USA
14B3 **Point Pleasant** W Virginia, USA
47B2 **Point St Bernard** *Mt* France
48C2 **Poitiers** France
48B2 **Poitou** Region, France
46A2 **Poix** France
85C3 **Pokaran** India
109C1 **Pokataroo** Aust
61G3 **Pokrovsk** Russian Fed
63E1 **Pokrovsk** Russian Fed
58B2 **Poland** Republic, Europe
92B2 **Polatli** Turk
78D3 **Polewali** Indon
47A1 **Poligny** France
55B2 **Políyiros** Greece
87B2 **Pollāchi** India
79B3 **Polollo Is** Phil
59D2 **Polonnye** Ukraine
58D1 **Polotsk** Russian Fed
60D4 **Poltava** Russian Fed
52C1 **Pölten** Austria
64F3 **Poluostrov Kanin** *Pen* Russian Fed
61H5 **Poluostrov Mangyshiak** *Pen* Kazakhstan
38L5 **Poluostrov Rybachiy** *Pen* Russian Fed
64H2 **Poluostrov Yamal** *Pen* Russian Fed
38L5 **Polyarnyy** Murmansk, Russian Fed
1B8 **Polyarnyy** Yakutskaya, Russian Fed
105H3 **Polynesia** *Region* Pacific O
32B5 **Pomabamba** Peru
35C2 **Pomba** *R* Brazil
22D3 **Pomona** USA
18A2 **Pomona Res** USA
17B2 **Pompano Beach** USA
16B2 **Pompton Lakes** USA
18A2 **Ponca City** USA
27D3 **Ponce** Puerto Rico
17B2 **Ponce de Leon B** USA
87B2 **Pondicherry** India
6C2 **Pond Inlet** Can
50A1 **Ponferrade** Spain
98C2 **Pongo** *R* Sudan
101H1 **Pongola** *R* S Africa
87B2 **Ponnāni** India
86C2 **Ponnyadoung Range** *Mts* Burma
13E2 **Ponoka** Can
64F3 **Ponoy** Russian Fed
48B2 **Pons** France
35D1 **Ponta da Baleia** *Pt* Brazil
96A1 **Ponta Delgada** Açores
98B3 **Ponta do Padrão** *Pt* Angola
35C2 **Ponta dos Búzios** *Pt* Brazil
30F4 **Ponta Grossa** Brazil
35B2 **Pontal** Brazil
46D2 **Pont-à-Mousson** France
30E3 **Ponta Pora** Brazil
49D2 **Pontarlier** France
19B3 **Pontchartrain,L** USA
52B2 **Pontedera** Italy
52A2 **Ponte Leccia** Corse
50A1 **Pontevedra** Spain
18C1 **Pontiac** Illinois, USA
14B2 **Pontiac** Michigan, USA
78B3 **Pontianak** Indon
48B2 **Pontivy** France
46B2 **Pontoise** France
19C3 **Pontotoc** USA
43C4 **Pontypool** Wales
43C4 **Pontypridd** Wales
43D4 **Poole** Eng
Poona = Pune
108B2 **Pooncarie** Aust
108B2 **Poopelloe,L** *L* Aust
12C2 **Poorman** USA
32B3 **Popayán** Colombia
46B1 **Poperinge** Belg
108B2 **Popilta L** Aust
18B2 **Poplar Bluff** USA
19C3 **Poplarville** USA
107D1 **Popndetta** PNG
23B2 **Popocatepetl** *Mt* Mexico
98B3 **Popokabaka** Zaïre
71F4 **Popondetta** PNG
54C2 **Popovo** Bulg
85B4 **Porbandar** India
13A2 **Porcher I** Can
12F1 **Porcupine** *R* Can/USA

52B1 **Poreč** Croatia
35A2 **Porecatu** Brazil
39J6 **Pori** Fin
111B2 **Porirua** NZ
38H5 **Porjus** Sweden
69G2 **Poronaysk** Russian Fed
47B1 **Porrentruy** Switz
38K4 **Porsangen** *Inlet* Nor
39F7 **Porsgrunn** Nor
45C1 **Portadown** N Ire
8D2 **Portage la Prairie** Can
13C3 **Port Alberni** Can
50A2 **Portalegre** Port
9C3 **Portales** USA
100B4 **Port Alfred** S Africa
13B2 **Port Alice** Can
19B3 **Port Allen** USA
20B1 **Port Angeles** USA
26B3 **Port Antonio** Jamaica
45C2 **Portarlington** Irish Rep
19B4 **Port Arthur** USA
108A2 **Port Augusta** Aust
26C3 **Port-au-Prince** Haiti
14B2 **Port Austin** USA
108B3 **Port Campbell** Aust
86B2 **Port Canning** India
7D5 **Port Cartier** Can
111B3 **Port Chalmers** NZ
17B2 **Port Charlotte** USA
16C2 **Port Chester** USA
15C2 **Port Colborne** Can
15C2 **Port Credit** Can
109C4 **Port Davey** Aust
26C3 **Port-de-Paix** Haiti
77C5 **Port Dickson** Malay
100C4 **Port Edward** S Africa
35C1 **Porteirinha** Brazil
14B2 **Port Elgin** Can
100B4 **Port Elizabeth** S Africa
27N2 **Porter Pt** St Vincent and the Grenadines
21B2 **Porterville** USA
07D4 **Port Fairy** Aust
98A3 **Port Gentil** Gabon
19B3 **Port Gibson** USA
12D3 **Port Graham** USA
20B1 **Port Hammond** Can
89E7 **Port Harcourt** Nig
13B2 **Port Hardy** Can
7D5 **Port Hawkesbury** Can
06A3 **Port Hedland** Aust
Port Heiden = Meshik
43B3 **Porthmadog** Wales
7E4 **Port Hope Simpson** Can
22C3 **Port Hueneme** USA
14B2 **Port Huron** USA
50A2 **Portimão** Port
09D2 **Port Jackson** *B* Aust
16C2 **Port Jefferson** USA
16B2 **Port Jervis** USA
09D2 **Port Kembla** Aust
14B2 **Portland** Indiana, USA
10C2 **Portland** Maine, USA
09C2 **Portland** New South Wales, Aust
20B1 **Portland** Oregon, USA
08B3 **Portland** Victoria, Aust
27H2 **Portland Bight** *B* Jamaica
43C4 **Portland Bill** *Pt* Eng
09C4 **Portland,C** Aust
13A1 **Portland Canal** Can/USA
10C1 **Portland I** NZ
27H2 **Portland Pt** Jamaica
45C2 **Port Laoise** Irish Rep
08A2 **Port Lincoln** Aust
97A4 **Port Loko** Sierra Leone
01E3 **Port Louis** Mauritius
08B3 **Port MacDonnell** Aust
13B2 **Port McNeill** Can
109D2 **Port Macquarie** Aust
12B3 **Port Moller** USA
107D1 **Port Moresby** PNG
100A3 **Port Nolloth** S Africa
16B3 **Port Norris** USA
89E7 **Port Novo** Benin
50A1 **Porto** Port
30F5 **Pôrto Alegre** Brazil
33F6 **Pôrto Artur** Brazil
30F3 **Pôrto E Cunha** Brazil
52B2 **Portoferraio** Italy
27E4 **Port of Spain** Trinidad
47D2 **Portomaggiore** Italy
97C4 **Porto Novo** Benin
20B1 **Port Orchard** USA
20B2 **Port Orford** USA
96A1 **Porto Santo** *I* Medeira
31D5 **Pôrto Seguro** Brazil
53A2 **Porto Torres** Sardegna
53A2 **Porto Vecchio** Corse
33E5 **Pôrto Velho** Brazil
111A3 **Port Pegasus** *B* NZ
108B3 **Port Phillip B** Aust
108A2 **Port Pirie** Aust
44A3 **Portree** Scot
20B1 **Port Renfrew** Can
27J2 **Port Royal** Jamaica
17B1 **Port Royal Sd** USA
45C1 **Portrush** N Ire
92B3 **Port Said** Egypt
17A2 **Port St Joe** USA
100B4 **Port St Johns** S Africa
7E4 **Port Saunders** Can
100C4 **Port Shepstone** S Africa
13A2 **Port Simpson** Can
27Q2 **Portsmouth** Dominica
43D4 **Portsmouth** Eng
14B3 **Portsmouth** Ohio, USA
11C3 **Portsmouth** Virginia, USA
109D2 **Port Stephens** *B* Aust
95C3 **Port Sudan** Sudan
19C3 **Port Sulphur** USA
38K5 **Porttipahdan Tekojärvi** *Res* Fin
50A2 **Portugal** Republic, Europe
14A2 **Port Washington** USA
77C5 **Port Weld** Malay
32D6 **Porvenir** Bol
39K6 **Porvoo** Fin
30E4 **Posadas** Arg
50A2 **Posadas** Spain
47D1 **Poschiavo** Switz
6B2 **Posheim Pen** Can
90C3 **Posht-e Badam** Iran
71D4 **Poso** Indon
58D1 **Postavy** Belorussia
14B2 **Post Clinton** USA
100B3 **Postmasburg** S Africa
52B1 **Postojna** Slovenia
74C2 **Pos'yet** Russian Fed
101G1 **Potchetstroom** S Africa
19B2 **Poteau** USA
53C2 **Potenza** Italy
100B3 **Potgietersrus** S Africa
97D3 **Potiskum** Nig
20C1 **Potlatch** USA
15C3 **Potomac** *R* USA
30C2 **Potosi** Bol
30C4 **Potrerillos** Chile
56C2 **Potsdam** Germany
16B2 **Pottstown** USA
16A2 **Pottsville** USA
16C2 **Poughkeepsie** USA
35B2 **Pouso Alegre** Brazil
110C1 **Poverty B** NZ
61F3 **Povorino** Russian Fed
7C4 **Povungnituk** Can
8C2 **Powder** *R* USA
106C2 **Powell Creek** Aust
9B3 **Powell,L** USA
13C3 **Powell River** Can
8C2 **Power** *R* USA
43C3 **Powys** County, Wales
73D4 **Poyang Hu** *L* China
92B2 **Pozantı** Turk
23B1 **Poza Rica** Mexico
58B2 **Poznań** Pol
30E3 **Pozo Colorado** Par
53B2 **Pozzuoli** Italy
97B4 **Pra** *R* Ghana
76C3 **Prachin Buri** Thai
76B3 **Prachuap Khiri Khan** Thai
59B2 **Praděd** *Mt* Czech Republic
49C3 **Pradelles** France
35D1 **Prado** Brazil
Prague = Praha
57C2 **Praha** Czech Republic
97A4 **Praia** Cape Verde
33E5 **Prainha** Brazil
18B2 **Prairie Village** USA
76C3 **Prakhon Chai** Thai
35B1 **Prata** Brazil
35B1 **Prata** *R* Brazil
Prates = Dongsha Qundao
49E3 **Prato** Italy
16B1 **Prattsville** USA
17A1 **Prattville** USA
48B1 **Prawle Pt** Eng
78D4 **Praya** Indon
47D1 **Predazzo** Italy
63B2 **Predivinsk** Russian Fed
58C2 **Pregolyu** *R* Russian Fed
76D3 **Prek Kak** Camb
56C2 **Prenzlau** Germany
76A3 **Preparis** *I* Burma
76A2 **Preparis North Chan** Burma
59B3 **Přerov** Czech Republic
23A2 **Presa del Infiernillo** Mexico
9B3 **Prescott** Arizona, USA
19B3 **Prescott** Arkansas, USA
15C2 **Prescott** Can
30D4 **Presidencia Roque Sáenz Peña** Arg
35A2 **Presidente Epitácio** Brazil
112C2 **Presidente Frei** *Base* Ant
23B2 **Presidente Migúel Aleman** *L* Mexico
35A2 **Presidente Prudente** Brazil
35A2 **Presidente Venceslau** Brazil
59C3 **Prešov** Slovakia
55B2 **Prespansko Jezero** *L* Macedonia, Yugos
10D2 **Presque Isle** USA
42C3 **Preston** Eng
8B2 **Preston** Idaho, USA
18B2 **Preston** Missouri, USA
42B2 **Prestwick** Scot
31B6 **Prêto** Brazil
35B1 **Prêto** *R* Brazil
101G1 **Pretoria** S Africa
55B3 **Préveza** Greece
76D3 **Prey Veng** Camb
8B3 **Price** USA
13B2 **Price I** Can
60D4 **Prichernomorskaya Nizmennost'** *Lowland* Ukraine
27M2 **Prickly Pt** Grenada
58C1 **Priekule** Lithuania
100B3 **Prieska** S Africa
20C1 **Priest L** USA
20C1 **Priest River** USA
55B2 **Prilep** Macedonia, Yugos
60D3 **Priluki** Ukraine
34C2 **Primero** *R* Arg
39K6 **Primorsk** Russian Fed
60E4 **Primorsko-Akhtarsk** Russian Fed
13F2 **Primrose L** Can
5H4 **Prince Albert** Can
4F2 **Prince Albert,C** Can
4G2 **Prince Albert Pen** Can
4G2 **Prince Albert Sd** Can
6C3 **Prince Charles I** Can
112B10 **Prince Charles Mts** Ant
7D5 **Prince Edward I** Can
13C2 **Prince George** Can
4H2 **Prince Gustaf Adolp S** Can
5E4 **Prince of Wales** *I* USA
71F5 **Prince of Wales I** Aust
4H2 **Prince of Wales I** Can
4G2 **Prince of Wales Str** Can
4F2 **Prince Patrick I** Can
6A2 **Prince Regent Inlet** *Str* Can
13A2 **Prince Rupert** Can
107D2 **Princess Charlotte B** Aust
13B2 **Princess Royal I** Can
27L1 **Princes Town** Trinidad
13C3 **Princeton** Can
18C2 **Princeton** Kentucky, USA
18B1 **Princeton** Missouri, USA
16B2 **Princeton** New Jersey, USA
4D3 **Prince William** USA
12E2 **Prince William Sd** USA
97C4 **Principe** *I* W Africa
20B2 **Prineville** USA
12E1 **Pringle,Mt** USA
6F3 **Prins Christian Sund** *Sd* Greenland
112B12 **Prinsesse Astrid Kyst** Region, Ant
112B12 **Prinsesse Ragnhild Kyst** Region, Ant
64B2 **Prins Karls Forland** *I* Barents S
25D3 **Prinzapolca** Nic
58D2 **Pripet** *R* Belorussia
Pripyat' = Pripet
54B2 **Priština** Serbia, Yugos
56C2 **Pritzwalk** Germany
61F3 **Privolzhskaya Vozvyshennost'** *Upland* Russian Fed
54B2 **Prizren** Serbia, Yugos
78C4 **Probolinggo** Indon
5G5 **Procatello** USA
87B2 **Proddatūr** India
25D2 **Progreso** Mexico
20B2 **Project City** USA
61F5 **Prokhladnyy** Russian Fed
65K4 **Prokop'yevsk** Russian Fed
61F4 **Proletarskaya** Russian Fed
64G2 **Proliv Karskiye Vorota** *Str* Russian Fed
83D4 **Prome** Burma
31D4 **Propriá** Brazil
20B2 **Prospect** Oregon, USA
107D3 **Prosperine** Aust
59B3 **Prostějov** Czech Republic
6E2 **Prøven** Greenland
49D3 **Provence** Region, France
16D2 **Providence** USA
15D2 **Provincetown** USA
49C2 **Provins** France
8B2 **Provo** USA

13E2 **Provost** Can
4D2 **Prudhoe Bay** USA
6D2 **Prudhoe Land** Greenland
58C2 **Pruszkow** Pol
60C4 **Prut** *R* Romania/ Moldova
60C4 **Prutul** *R* Romania
58C2 **Pruzhany** Belorussia
18A2 **Pryor** USA
59C3 **Przemys'l** Pol
55C3 **Psará** *I* Greece
60C2 **Pskov** Russian Fed
58D2 **Ptich** *R* Belorussia
55B2 **Ptolemaïs** Greece
32C5 **Pucallpa** Peru
73D4 **Pucheng** China
34A3 **Pucón** Chile
38K5 **Pudasjärvi** Fin
87B2 **Pudukkottai** India
23B2 **Puebla** Mexico
23B2 **Puebla** State, Mexico
50A1 **Puebla de Sanabria** Spain
50A1 **Puebla de Trives** Spain
9C2 **Pueblo** USA
34B3 **Puelches** Arg
34B3 **Puelén** Arg
23A2 **Puenta Ixbapa** Mexico
34B2 **Puente del Inca** Arg
32A5 **Puerta Aguja** Peru
30B2 **Puerta Coles** Peru
34B2 **Puerta de los Llanos** Arg
31D3 **Puerta do Calcanhar** *Pt* Brazil
32C1 **Puerta Gallinas** Colombia
23B2 **Puerta Maldonado** *Pt* Mexico
32A2 **Puerta Mariato** Panama
29C5 **Puerta Médanosa** *Pt* Arg
23A2 **Puerta Mongrove** Mexico
25E4 **Puerta San Blas** *Pt* Panama
23A2 **Puerta San Telmo** Mexico
29B5 **Puerto Aisén** Chile
25D4 **Puerto Armuelles** Panama
33F6 **Puerto Artur** Brazil
32B3 **Puerto Asis** Colombia
32D2 **Puerto Ayacucho** Ven
25D3 **Puerto Barrios** Guatemala
32C2 **Puerto Berrio** Colombia
32D1 **Puerto Cabello** Ven
25D3 **Puerto Cabezas** Nic
32D2 **Puerto Carreño** Colombia
25D4 **Puerto Cortes** Costa Rica
25D3 **Puerto Cortés** Honduras
96A2 **Puerto del Rosario** Canary Is
30F3 **Puerto E Cunha** Brazil
32C1 **Puerto Fijo** Ven
31B3 **Puerto Franco** Brazil
32D6 **Puerto Heath** Bol
25D2 **Puerto Juarez** Mexico
33E1 **Puerto la Cruz** Ven
50B2 **Puertollano** Spain
27C4 **Puerto Lopez** Colombia
29D4 **Puerto Madryn** Arg
32D6 **Puerto Maldonado** Peru
23B2 **Puerto Marquéz** Mexico
29B4 **Puerto Montt** Chile
30E3 **Puerto Murtinho** Brazil
29B6 **Puerto Natales** Chile
24A1 **Puerto Peñasco** Mexico
29D4 **Puerto Pirámides** Arg
27C3 **Puerto Plata** Dom Rep
79A4 **Puerto Princesa** Phil
32B3 **Puerto Rico** Colombia
27D3 **Puerto Rico** *I* Caribbean S
27D3 **Puerto Rico Trench** Caribbean S
23A2 **Puerto San Juan de Lima** Mexico
33G4 **Puerto Santanga** Brazil
30E2 **Puerto Suárez** Bol
24B2 **Puerto Vallarta** Mexico
29B4 **Puerto Varas** Chile
30D2 **Puerto Villarroel** Bol
61G3 **Pugachev** Russian Fed
84C3 **Pugal** India
51C1 **Puigcerdá** Spain
111B2 **Pukaki,L** *L* NZ
74B2 **Pukch'ŏng** N Korea
110B1 **Pukekobe** NZ
111B2 **Puketeraki Range** *Mts* NZ
52B2 **Pula** Croatia
15C2 **Pulaski** New York, USA
71E4 **Pulau Kolepom** *I* Indon
70A4 **Pulau Pulau Batu** *Is* Indon
58C2 **Pulawy** Pol
87C2 **Pulicat,L** India
84B1 **Pul-i-Khumri** Afghan
87B3 **Puliyangudi** India
20C1 **Pullman** USA
71E3 **Pulo Anna Merir** *I* Pacific O
79B2 **Pulog,Mt** Phil
38L5 **Pulozero** Russian Fed
58C2 **Pultusk** Pol
30C4 **Puna de Atacama** Arg
86B1 **Punakha** Bhutan
84C2 **Punch** Pak
87A1 **Pune** India
23A2 **Punéper** Mexico
98C3 **Punia** Zaïre
34A2 **Punitaqui** Chile
84C2 **Punjab** Province, Pak
84D2 **Punjab** State, India
30B2 **Puno** Peru
24A2 **Punta Abreojos** *Pt* Mexico
53C3 **Punta Alice** *Pt* Italy
34C3 **Punta Alta** Arg
29B6 **Punta Arenas** Chile
24A2 **Punta Baja** *Pt* Mexico
34A2 **Punta Curaumilla** *Pt* Chile
100A2 **Punta da Marca** *Pt* Angola
101C3 **Punta de Barra Falsa** *Pt* Mozam
29F2 **Punta del Este** Urug
24A2 **Punta Eugenia** *Pt* Mexico
25D3 **Punta Gorda** Belize
17B2 **Punta Gorda** USA
34A3 **Punta Lavapié** *Pt* Chile
34A2 **Punta Lengua de Vaca** *Pt* Chile
53B2 **Punta Licosa** *Pt* Italy
34A1 **Punta Poroto** *Pt* Chile
9B4 **Punta San Antonia** *Pt* Mexico
34A2 **Punta Topocalma** Chile
73C4 **Puqi** China
64J3 **Pur** *R* Russian Fed
19A2 **Purcell** USA
12C1 **Purcell Mt** USA
13D2 **Purcell Mts** Can
34A3 **Purén** Chile
86B2 **Puri** India
87B1 **Pūrna** India
86B1 **Pūrnia** India
76C3 **Pursat** Camb
23A1 **Puruandro** Mexico
33E4 **Purus** *R* Brazil
19C3 **Purvis** USA
78B4 **Purwokerto** Indon
78C4 **Purworejo** Indon
85D5 **Pusad** India
74B3 **Pusan** S Korea
60D2 **Pushkin** Russian Fed
58D1 **Pustoshka** Russian Fed
82D3 **Puta** Burma
34A2 **Putaendo** Chile
110C1 **Putaruru** NZ
73D4 **Putian** China
16D2 **Putnam** USA
87B3 **Puttalam** Sri Lanka
56C2 **Puttgarden** Germany
32B4 **Putumayo** *R* Ecuador
78C2 **Putussibau** Indon
38K6 **Puulavesl** *L* Fin
20B1 **Puyallup** USA
49C2 **Puy de Sancy** *Mt* France
111A3 **Puysegur Pt** NZ
99C3 **Pweto** Zaïre
43B3 **Pwllheli** Wales
76B2 **Pyapon** Burma
61F5 **Pyatigorsk** Russian Fed
Pyè = Prome
74B3 **P'yŏngyang** N Korea
108B3 **Pyramid Hill** Aust
21B1 **Pyramid L** USA
111A2 **Pyramid,Mt** NZ
48B3 **Pyrénées** *Mts* France
58D1 **Pytalovo** Russian Fed
76B2 **Pyu** Burma

Q

94B2 **Qabatiya** Israel
94C3 **Qā'el Hafīra** *Mud Flats* Jordan
94C3 **Qa'el Jinz** *Mud Flats* Jordan
68B3 **Qaidam Pendi** *Salt Flat* China
94C2 **Qa Khanna** *Salt Marsh* Jordan
99D1 **Qala'en Nahl** Sudan
84B2 **Qalat** Afghan
94C1 **Qal'at al Hisn** Syria
81C3 **Qal'at Bīshah** S Arabia
93E3 **Qal'at Sālih** Iraq
68B3 **Qamdo** China
99E1 **Qandala** Somalia
99E2 **Qardho** Somalia
95B2 **Qara** Egypt
90A3 **Qaṛe Shīrīn** Iran
91A4 **Qaryat al Ulyā** S Arabia
94C3 **Qasr el Kharana** Jordan
91D4 **Qasr-e-Qand** Iran
95B2 **Qasr Farafra** Egypt
94C2 **Qaṭana** Syria
91B4 **Qatar** Emirate, Arabian Pen
94C3 **Qatrāna** Jordan
95B2 **Qattāra Depression** Egypt
90C3 **Qāyen** Iran
90A2 **Qazvīn** Iran
95C2 **Qena** Egypt
90A2 **Qeydār** Iran
91B4 **Qeys** *I* Iran
94B3 **Qeziot** Israel
73B5 **Qian Jiang** *R* China
72E1 **Qian Shan** *Upland* China
72E3 **Qidong** China
73B4 **Qijiang** China
84B2 **Qila Saifullah** Pak
72A2 **Qilian** China
68B3 **Qilian Shan** China
72B3 **Qin'an** China
72E2 **Qingdao** China
72A2 **Qinghai** Province, China
68B3 **Qinghai Hu** *L* China
72D3 **Qingjiang** Jiangsu, China
73D4 **Qingjiang** Jiangxi, China
72B3 **Qing Jiang** *R* China
72C2 **Qingshuihe** China
72B2 **Qingshui He** *R* Chin
72B2 **Qingtonxia** China
72B2 **Qingyang** China
74B2 **Qingyuan** Liaoning, China
73D4 **Qingyuan** Zhejiang, China
82C2 **Qing Zang** *Upland* China
72D2 **Qinhuangdao** China
72B3 **Qin Ling** *Mts* China
73B5 **Qinzhou** China
76E2 **Qionghai** China
73A3 **Qionglai Shan** *Upland* China
76D1 **Qiongzhou Haixia** *S* China
69E2 **Qiqihar** China
94B2 **Qiryat Ata** Israel
94B3 **Qiryat Gat** Israel
94B2 **Qiryat Shemona** Israel
94B2 **Qiryat Yam** Israel
94B2 **Qishon** *R* Israel
63A3 **Qitai** China
73C4 **Qiyang** China
72B1 **Qog Qi** China
90B2 **Qolleh-ye Damavan** *Mt* Iran
90B3 **Qom** Iran
90B3 **Qomisheh** Iran
Qomolangma Feng Everest,Mt
94C1 **Qornet es Saouda** Leb
6E3 **Qôrnoq** Greenland
90A2 **Qorveh** Iran
91C4 **Qotābad** Iran
16C1 **Quabbin Res** USA
16B2 **Quakertown** USA
77C3 **Quam Phu Quoc** *I* Viet
76D2 **Quang Ngai** Viet
76D2 **Quang Tri** Viet
77D4 **Quan Long** Viet
73D5 **Quanzhou** Fujian, China
73C4 **Quanzhou** Guangxi, China
5H4 **Qu' Appelle** *R* Can
91C5 **Quarayyāt** Oman
13B2 **Quatsino Sd** Can
90C2 **Quchan** Iran
109C3 **Queanbeyan** Aust
15D1 **Québec** Can
7C4 **Quebec** Province, Can
35B1 **Quebra-Anzol** *R* Brazil
34D2 **Quebracho** Urug
30F4 **Quedas do Iguaçu** Brazil/Arg
16A3 **Queen Anne** USA
13B2 **Queen Bess,Mt** Ca
5E4 **Queen Charlotte** *Is* Can
13B2 **Queen Charlotte Sc** Can
13B2 **Queen Charlotte St** Can
4H1 **Queen Elizabeth Is** Can
112B9 **Queen Mary Land** Region, Ant
4H3 **Queen Maud G** Ca
112A **Queen Maud Mts**
16C2 **Queens** Borough, New York, USA
108B3 **Queenscliff** Aust
107D3 **Queensland** State, Aust
109C4 **Queenstown** Aust
111A3 **Queenstown** NZ
100B4 **Queenstown** S Afr
16A3 **Queenstown** USA
98B3 **Quela** Angola
101C2 **Quelimane** Mozam

34C3 **Quemuquemú** Arg
13C2 **Quensel L** Can
34D3 **Quequén** Arg
34D3 **Quequén** *R* Arg
23A1 **Querétaro** Mexico
23A1 **Queretaro** *State* Mexico
13C2 **Quesnel** Can
84B2 **Quetta** Pak
25C3 **Quezaltenango** Guatemala
79B3 **Quezon City** Phil
100A2 **Quibala** Angola
98B3 **Quibaxe** Angola
32B2 **Quibdó** Colombia
48B2 **Quiberon** France
98B3 **Quicama Nat Pk** Angola
73A4 **Quijing** China
34A2 **Quilima** Chile
34C2 **Quilino** Arg
32C6 **Quillabamba** Peru
30C2 **Quillacollo** Bol
48C3 **Quillan** France
5H4 **Quill L** Can
5H4 **Quill Lakes** Can
34A2 **Quillota** Chile
87B3 **Quilon** India
108B1 **Quilpie** Aust
34A2 **Quilpué** Chile
98B3 **Quimbele** Angola
48B2 **Quimper** France
48B2 **Quimperlé** France
21A2 **Quincy** California, USA
10A3 **Quincy** Illinois, USA
16D1 **Quincy** Massachusetts, USA
34B2 **Quines** Arg
12B3 **Quinhagak** USA
76D3 **Qui Nhon** Viet
50B2 **Quintanar de la Orden** Spain
34A2 **Quintero** Chile
34C2 **Quinto** *R* Arg
34A3 **Quirihue** Chile
100A2 **Quirima** Angola
109D2 **Quirindi** Aust
101D2 **Quissanga** Mozam
101C3 **Quissico** Mozam
32B4 **Quito** Ecuador
31D2 **Quixadá** Brazil
108A2 **Quorn** Aust
4G3 **Qurlurtuuk** Can
95C2 **Quseir** Egypt
6E3 **Qutdligssat** Greenland
Quthing = Moyeni
73B3 **Qu Xian** Sichuan, China
73D4 **Qu Xian** Zhejiang, China
76D2 **Quynh Luu** Viet
72C2 **Quzhou** China
86C1 **Qūzū** China

R

38J6 **Raahe** Fin
44A3 **Raasay** *I* Scot
44A3 **Raasay,Sound of** *Chan* Scot
99F1 **Raas Caseyr** *C* Somalia
52B2 **Rab** *I* Croatia
78D4 **Raba** Indon
59B3 **Rába** *R* Hung
96B1 **Rabat** Mor
94B3 **Rabba** Jordan
80B3 **Rabigh** S Arabia
47B2 **Racconigi** Italy
7E5 **Race,C** Can
94B2 **Rachaya** Leb
57C3 **Rachel** *Mt* Germany
76D3 **Rach Gia** Viet
14A2 **Racine** USA
59D3 **Rădăuţi** Rom
85C4 **Radhanpur** India
27L1 **Radix,Pt** Trinidad
58C2 **Radom** Pol
59B2 **Radomsko** Pol
58C1 **Radviliškis** Lithuania
4G3 **Rae** Can
86A1 **Rāe Bareli** India
6B3 **Rae Isthmus** Can
4G3 **Rae L** Can
110C1 **Raetihi** NZ
34C2 **Rafaela** Arg
94B3 **Rafah** Egypt
98C2 **Rafai** CAR
93D3 **Rafhā Al Jumaymah** S Arabia
91C3 **Rafsanjān** Iran
98C2 **Raga** Sudan
27R3 **Ragged Pt** Barbados
53B3 **Ragusa** Italy
99D1 **Rahad** *R* Sudan
84C3 **Rahimyar Khan** Pak
90B3 **Rāhjerd** Iran
34D2 **Raíces** Arg
87B1 **Rāichur** India
86A2 **Raigarh** India
108B3 **Rainbow** Aust
17A1 **Rainbow City** USA
20B1 **Rainier** USA
20B1 **Rainier,Mt** USA
10A2 **Rainy L** Can
12D2 **Rainy P** USA
10A2 **Rainy River** Can
86A2 **Raipur** India
87C1 **Rājahmundry** India
78C2 **Rajang** *R* Malay
84C3 **Rajanpur** Pak
87B3 **Rājapālaiyam** India
85C3 **Rājasthan** State, India
84D3 **Rājgarh** India
85D4 **Rājgarh** State, India
85C4 **Rājkot** India
86B2 **Rājmahāl Hills** India
86A2 **Raj Nāndgaon** India
85C4 **Rājpīpla** India
86B2 **Rajshahi** Bang
85D4 **Rajur** India
111B2 **Rakaia** *R* NZ
78B4 **Rakata** *I* Indon
82C3 **Raka Zangbo** *R* China
59C3 **Rakhov** Ukraine
100B3 **Rakops** Botswana
58D2 **Rakov** Belorussia
11C3 **Raleigh** USA
7A5 **Ralny L** Can
94B2 **Rama** Israel
94B3 **Ramallah** Israel
87B3 **Rāmanāthapuram** India
69G3 **Ramapo Deep** Pacific O
94B2 **Ramat Gan** Israel
46A2 **Rambouillet** France
86B2 **Rāmgarh** Bihar, India
85C3 **Rāmgarh** Rajosthan, India
90A3 **Rāmhormoz** Iran
94B3 **Ramla** Israel
91C5 **Ramlat Al Wahibah** Region, Oman
21B3 **Ramona** USA
84D3 **Rāmpur** India
85D4 **Rāmpura** India
90B2 **Rāmsar** Iran
42B2 **Ramsey** Eng
16B2 **Ramsey** USA
43B4 **Ramsey I** Wales
43E4 **Ramsgate** Eng
94C2 **Ramtha** Jordan
71F4 **Ramu** *R* PNG
34A2 **Rancagua** Chile
86B2 **Rānchi** India
86A2 **Rānchi Plat** India
101G1 **Randburg** S Africa
39G7 **Randers** Den
101G1 **Randfontein** S Africa
15D2 **Randolph** Vermont, USA
111B3 **Ranfurly** NZ
86C2 **Rangamati** Bang
111B2 **Rangiora** NZ
110C1 **Rangitaiki** *R* NZ
111B2 **Rangitate** *R* NZ
110C1 **Rangitikei** *R* NZ
Rangoon = Yangon
86B1 **Rangpur** India
87B2 **Rānībennur** India
8A2 **Ranier,Mt** *Mt* USA
86B2 **Rānīganj** India
109C2 **Rankins Springs** Aust
6A3 **Ranklin Inlet** Can
85B4 **Rann of Kachchh** *Flood Area* India
77B4 **Ranong** Thai
70A3 **Rantauparapat** Indon
18C1 **Rantoul** USA
49D3 **Rapallo** Italy
34A2 **Rapel** *R* Chile
6D3 **Raper,C** Can
8C2 **Rapid City** USA
14A1 **Rapid River** USA
15C3 **Rappahannock** *R* USA
47C1 **Rapperswil** Switz
16B2 **Raritan B** USA
95C2 **Ras Abu Shagara** *C* Sudan
93D2 **Ra's al 'Ayn** Syria
91C5 **Ra's al Hadd** *C* Oman
91C4 **Ras al Kaimah** UAE
91C4 **Ras-al-Kuh** *C* Iran
81D4 **Ra's al Madrakah** *C* Oman
91A4 **Ra's az Zawr** *C* S Arabia
95C2 **Rãs Bânas** *C* Egypt
94A3 **Ras Burûn** *C* Egypt
99D1 **Ras Dashan** *Mt* Eth
90A3 **Ra's-e-Barkan** *Pt* Iran
92A3 **Râs el Kenâyis** *Pt* Egypt
81D4 **Ra's Fartak** *C* Yemen
95C2 **Râs Ghârib** Egypt
99D1 **Rashad** Sudan
94B3 **Rashādīya** Jordan
92B3 **Rashîd** Egypt
90A2 **Rasht** Iran
91C5 **Ra's Jibish** *C* Oman
99E1 **Ras Khanzira** *C* Somalia
84B3 **Ras Koh** *Mt* Pak
95C2 **Râs Muhammad** *C* Egypt
96A2 **Ras Nouadhibou** *C* Maur
69H2 **Rasshua** *I* Russian Fed
61F3 **Rasskazovo** Russian Fed
91A4 **Ra's Tanāqib** *C* S Arabia
91B4 **Ra's Tannūrah** S Arabia
57B3 **Rastatt** Germany
Ras Uarc = Cabo Tres Forcas
99F1 **Ras Xaafuun** *C* Somalia
84C3 **Ratangarh** India
76B3 **Rat Buri** Thai
85D3 **Rath** India
56C2 **Rathenow** Germany
45B2 **Rathkeale** Irish Rep
45C1 **Rathlin** *I* N Ire
45B2 **Ráth Luirc** Irish Rep
85D4 **Ratlām** India
87A1 **Ratnāgiri** India
87C3 **Ratnapura** Sri Lanka
58C2 **Ratno** Ukraine
47D1 **Rattenberg** Austria
39H6 **Rättvik** Sweden
12H3 **Ratz,Mt** Can
34D3 **Rauch** Arg
110C1 **Raukumara Range** *Mts* NZ
35C2 **Raul Soares** Brazil
39J6 **Rauma** Fin
86A2 **Raurkela** India
90A3 **Ravānsar** Iran
90C3 **Rāvar** Iran
59C2 **Rava Russkaya** Ukraine
16C1 **Ravena** USA
52B2 **Ravenna** Italy
57B3 **Ravensburg** Germany
107D2 **Ravenshoe** Aust
42E2 **Ravenspurn** *Oilfield* N Sea
84C2 **Ravi** *R* Pak
84C2 **Rawalpindi** Pak
93D2 **Rawāndiz** Iraq
58B2 **Rawicz** Pol
106B4 **Rawlinna** Aust
8C2 **Rawlins** USA
29C4 **Rawson** Arg
78C3 **Raya** *Mt* Indon
87B2 **Rāyadurg** India
94C2 **Rayak** Leb
7E5 **Ray,C** Can
91C4 **Rāyen** Iran
22C2 **Raymond** California, USA
20B1 **Raymond** Washington, USA
109D2 **Raymond Terrace** Aust
12D1 **Ray Mts** USA
23B1 **Rayon** Mexico
90A2 **Razan** Iran
54C2 **Razgrad** Bulg
54C2 **Razim** *L* Rom
43D4 **Reading** Eng
16B2 **Reading** USA
4G3 **Read Island** Can
16C1 **Readsboro** USA
34B2 **Real de Padre** Arg
34C3 **Realicó** Arg
95B2 **Rebiana** *Well* Libya
95B2 **Rebiana Sand Sea** Libya
38L6 **Reboly** Russian Fed
106B4 **Recherche,Arch of the** *Is* Aust
31E3 **Recife** Brazil
107F2 **Récifs D'Entrecasteaux** Nouvelle Calédonie
46D1 **Recklinghausen** Germany
30E4 **Reconquista** Arg
19B3 **Red** *R* USA
77C4 **Redang** *I* Malay
16B2 **Red Bank** New Jersey, USA
21A1 **Red Bluff** USA
42D2 **Redcar** Eng
13E2 **Redcliff** Can
109D1 **Redcliffe** Aust
108B2 **Red Cliffs** Aust
13E2 **Red Deer** Can
13E2 **Red Deer** *R* Can
20B2 **Redding** USA
10A2 **Red L** USA
7A4 **Red Lake** Can
22D3 **Redlands** USA
16A3 **Red Lion** USA
20B2 **Redmond** USA
18A1 **Red Oak** USA
48B2 **Redon** France
22C4 **Redondo Beach** USA
12D2 **Redoubt V** USA
73B5 **Red River Delta** Vietnam
80B3 **Red Sea** Africa/ Arabian Pen
13E2 **Redwater** Can
22A2 **Redwood City** USA
14A2 **Reed City** USA
22C2 **Reedley** USA
20B2 **Reedsport** USA
111B2 **Reefton** NZ
93C2 **Refahiye** Turk
35D1 **Regência** Brazil
57C3 **Regensburg** Germany
96C2 **Reggane** Alg
53C3 **Reggio di Calabria** Italy
47D2 **Reggio Nell'Emilia** Italy
54B1 **Reghin** Rom
5H4 **Regina** Can
100A3 **Rehoboth** Namibia
15C3 **Rehoboth Beach** USA
94B3 **Rehovot** Israel
32D1 **Reicito** Ven
43D4 **Reigate** Eng
46C2 **Reims** France
5H4 **Reindeer** *R* Can
50B1 **Reinosa** Spain
16A3 **Reisterstown** USA
101G1 **Reitz** S Africa
4H3 **Reliance** Can
108A2 **Remarkable,Mt** Aust
78C4 **Rembang** Indon
91C4 **Remeshk** Iran

46D1 **Remscheid** Germany
18C2 **Rend,L** USA
56B2 **Rendsburg** Germany
15C1 **Renfrew** Can
78A3 **Rengat** Indon
34A2 **Rengo** Chile
59D3 **Reni** Ukraine
99D1 **Renk** Sudan
6H2 **Renland** *Pen* Greenland
108B2 **Renmark** Aust
107F2 **Rennell** *I* Solomon Is
48B2 **Rennes** France
21B2 **Reno** USA
47D2 **Reno** *R* Italy
15C2 **Renovo** USA
16C1 **Rensselaer** USA
20B1 **Renton** USA
70D4 **Reo** Indon
35B2 **Reprêsa de Furnas** *Dam* Brazil
30E3 **Reprêsa Ilha Grande** *Dam* Brazil
30E3 **Reprêsa Itaipu** *Dam* Brazil
35A2 **Reprêsa Porto Primavera** *Dam* Brazil
35B1 **Reprêsa Três Marias** *Dam* Brazil
20C1 **Republic** USA
41B3 **Republic of Ireland** NW Europe
6B3 **Repulse Bay** Can
15C1 **Réservoir Baskatong** *Res* Can
10C1 **Réservoir de la Grande 2** *Res* Can
10C1 **Réservoir de la Grande 3** *Res* Can
7C4 **Réservoir de la Grande 4** *Res* Can
7C5 **Réservoir Cabonga** *Res* Can
7D4 **Réservoir Caniapiscau** *Res* Can
7C5 **Réservoir Gouin** *Res* Can
10D1 **Réservoir Manicouagan** *Res* Can
90B2 **Reshteh-ye Alborz** *Mts* Iran
72A2 **Reshui** China
30E4 **Resistencia** Arg
54B1 **Resita** Rom
6A2 **Resolute** Can
111A3 **Resolution I** NZ
6D3 **Resolution Island** Can
101H1 **Ressano Garcia** Mozam
34B2 **Retamito** Arg
46C2 **Rethel** France
55B3 **Réthimnon** Greece
89K10 **Reunion** *I* Indian O
51C1 **Reus** Spain
47C1 **Reuss** *R* Switz
47D1 **Reutte** Austria
61K3 **Revda** Russian Fed
13D2 **Revelstoke** Can
24A3 **Revillagigedo** *Is* Mexico
12H3 **Revillagigedo I** USA
46C2 **Revin** France
94B3 **Revivim** Israel
86A2 **Rewa** India
84D3 **Rewari** India
8B2 **Rexburg** USA
38A2 **Reykjavik** Iceland
24C2 **Reynosa** Mexico
48B2 **Rezé** France
58D1 **Rezekne** Latvia
61K2 **Rezh** Russian Fed
47C1 **Rhätikon** *Mts* Austria/Switz
94B1 **Rhazīr** Republic, Leb
56B2 **Rhein** *R* W Europe
56B2 **Rheine** Germany
47B1 **Rheinfielden** Switz
49D2 **Rheinland Pfalz** Region, Germany
47C1 **Rheinwaldhorn** *Mt* Switz
Rhine = Rhein
16C2 **Rhinebeck** USA
10B2 **Rhinelander** USA
47C2 **Rho** Italy
15D2 **Rhode Island** State, USA
16D2 **Rhode Island Sd** USA
Rhodes = Ródhos
49C3 **Rhône** *R* France
43C3 **Rhyl** Wales
31D4 **Riachão do Jacuipe** Brazil
50A1 **Ria de Arosa** *B* Spain
50A1 **Ria de Betanzos** *B* Spain
50A1 **Ria de Corcubion** *B* Spain
50A1 **Ria de Lage** *B* Spain
50A1 **Ria de Sta Marta** *B* Spain
50A1 **Ria de Vigo** *B* Spain
84C2 **Riāsi** Pak
50A1 **Ribadeo** Spain
35A2 **Ribas do Rio Pardo** Brazil
101C2 **Ribauè** Mozam
42C3 **Ribble** *R* Eng
35B2 **Ribeira** Brazil
35B2 **Ribeirão Prêto** Brazil
32D6 **Riberalta** Bol
15C2 **Rice L** Can
10A2 **Rice Lake** USA
101H1 **Richard's Bay** S Africa
19A3 **Richardson** USA
12G1 **Richardson Mts** Can
8B3 **Richfield** USA
20C1 **Richland** USA
22A2 **Richmond** California, USA
101H1 **Richmond** Natal, S Africa
109D2 **Richmond** New South Wales, Aust
111B2 **Richmond** NZ
107D3 **Richmond** Queensland, Aust
10C3 **Richmond** Virginia, USA
111B2 **Richmond Range** *Mts* NZ
15C2 **Rideau,L** Can
17B1 **Ridgeland** USA
15C2 **Ridgway** USA
27D4 **Riecito** Ven
47D1 **Rienza** *R* Italy
57C2 **Riesa** Germany
29B6 **Riesco** *I* Chile
101F1 **Riet** *R* S Africa
52B2 **Rieti** Italy
50B2 **Rif** *Mts* Mor
58C1 **Riga** Latvia
60B2 **Riga,G of** Estonia/Latvia
91C4 **Rīgān** Iran
20C1 **Riggins** USA
7E4 **Rigolet** Can
39J6 **Riihimaki** Fin
52B1 **Rijeka** Croatia
13E2 **Rimbey** Can
39H7 **Rimbo** Sweden
52B2 **Rimini** Italy
54C1 **Rîmnicu Sărat** Rom
54B1 **Rîmnicu Vîlcea** Rom
10D2 **Rimouski** Can
23A1 **Rincón de Romos** Mexico
39F7 **Ringkøbing** Den
98A2 **Rio Benito** Eq Guinea
32D5 **Rio Branco** Brazil
24B1 **Rio Bravo del Norte** *R* Mexico/USA
32C1 **Riochacha** Colombia
35B2 **Rio Claro** Brazil
27L1 **Rio Claro** Trinidad
34C3 **Rio Colorado** Arg
34C2 **Rio Cuarto** Arg
31D4 **Rio de Jacuipe** Brazil
35C2 **Rio de Janeiro** Brazil
35C2 **Rio de Janeiro** State, Brazil
29E3 **Rio de la Plata** *Est* Arg/Urug
29C6 **Rio Gallegos** Arg
29C6 **Rio Grande** Arg
30F5 **Rio Grande** Brazil
26A4 **Rio Grande** Nic
25D3 **Rio Grande** *R* Nic
24B2 **Rio Grande** *R* Mexico/USA
23A1 **Rio Grande de Santiago** Mexico
31D3 **Rio Grande do Norte** State, Brazil
30F4 **Rio Grande do Sul** State, Brazil
103G6 **Rio Grande Rise** Atlantic O
26C4 **Riohacha** Colombia
49C2 **Riom** France
32B4 **Riombamba** Ecuador
30C2 **Rio Mulatos** Bol
29C3 **Río Negro** State, Arg
30F4 **Rio Pardo** Brazil
34C2 **Rio Tercero** Arg
33E6 **Rio Theodore Roosevelt** *R* Brazil
29B6 **Rio Turbio** Arg
35A1 **Rio Verde** Brazil
23A1 **Rio Verde** Mexico
14B3 **Ripley** Ohio, USA
14B3 **Ripley** West Virginia, USA
42D2 **Ripon** Eng
22B2 **Ripon** USA
94B3 **Rishon le Zion** Israel
16A3 **Rising Sun** USA
39F7 **Risør** Nor
6E2 **Ritenberk** Greenland
22C2 **Ritter,Mt** USA
20C1 **Ritzville** USA
34B2 **Rivadavia** Arg
34A1 **Rivadavia** Chile
34C3 **Rivadavia Gonzalez Moreno** Arg
47D2 **Riva de Garda** Italy
34C3 **Rivera** Arg
29E2 **Rivera** Urug
22B2 **Riverbank** USA
97B4 **River Cess** Lib
16C2 **Riverhead** USA
108B3 **Riverina** Aust
111A3 **Riversdale** NZ
22D4 **Riverside** USA
13B2 **Rivers Inlet** Can
111A3 **Riverton** NZ
8C2 **Riverton** USA
17B2 **Riviera Beach** USA
7C4 **Rivière aux Feuilles** *R* Can
7D4 **Rivière de la Baleine** *R* Can
7D4 **Rivière du Petit Mècatina** *R* Can
46C2 **Rivigny-sur-Ornain** France
93D1 **Rize** Turk
72D2 **Rizhao** China
Rizhskiy Zaliv = Riga,G of
39F7 **Rjukan** Nor
6B2 **Roanes Pen** Can
49C2 **Roanne** France
17A1 **Roanoke** Alabama, USA
11C3 **Roanoke** Virginia, USA
11C3 **Roanoke** *R* USA
45B3 **Roaringwater B** Irish Rep
38J6 **Robertsforz** Sweden
19B2 **Robert S Kerr Res** USA
97A4 **Robertsport** Lib
7C5 **Roberval** Can
30H6 **Robinson Crusoe** *I* Chile
108B2 **Robinvale** Aust
13D2 **Robson,Mt** Can
24A3 **Roca Partida** *I* Mexico
103G5 **Rocas** *I* Atlantic O
31E2 **Rocas** *I* Brazil
29F2 **Rocha** Urug
42C3 **Rochdale** Eng
48B2 **Rochefort** France
5G3 **Rocher River** Can
108B3 **Rochester** Aust
7C5 **Rochester** Can
43E4 **Rochester** Eng
10A2 **Rochester** Minnesota, USA
15D2 **Rochester** New Hampshire, USA
10C2 **Rochester** New York, USA
10B2 **Rockford** USA
11B3 **Rock Hill** USA
10A2 **Rock Island** USA
108B3 **Rocklands Res** Aust
17B2 **Rockledge** USA
8C2 **Rock Springs** Wyoming, USA
110B2 **Rocks Pt** NZ
109C3 **Rock,The** Aust
16C2 **Rockville** Connecticut, USA
14A3 **Rockville** Indiana, USA
16A3 **Rockville** Maryland, USA
14B1 **Rocky Island L** Can
13E2 **Rocky Mountain House** Can
8B1 **Rocky Mts** Can/USA
12B2 **Rocky Pt** USA
56C2 **Rødbyhavn** Den
34B2 **Rodeo** Arg
49C3 **Rodez** France
55C3 **Ródhos** Greece
55C3 **Ródhos** *I* Greece
52C2 **Rodi Garganico** Italy
54B2 **Rodopi Planina** *Mts* Bulg
106A3 **Roebourne** Aust
46C1 **Roermond** Neth
46B1 **Roeselare** Belg
6B3 **Roes Welcome Sd** Can
18B2 **Rogers** USA
14B1 **Rogers City** USA
20B2 **Rogue** *R* USA
85B3 **Rohn** Pak
84D3 **Rohtak** India
58C1 **Roja** Latvia
35A2 **Rolândia** Brazil
18B2 **Rolla** USA
109C1 **Roma** Aust
52B2 **Roma** Italy
47C2 **Romagnano** Italy
17C1 **Romain,C** USA
54C1 **Roman** Rom
103H5 **Romanche Gap** Atlantic O
71D4 **Romang** *I* Indon
60B4 **Romania** Republic, E Europe
17B2 **Romano,C** USA
49D2 **Romans sur Isère** France
79B3 **Romblon** Phil
Rome = Roma
17A1 **Rome** Georgia, USA
15C2 **Rome** New York, USA
49C2 **Romilly-sur-Seine** France
15C3 **Romney** USA
60D3 **Romny** Ukraine
56B1 **Rømø** *I* Den
47B1 **Romont** Switz
48C2 **Romorantin** France
50A2 **Ronda** Spain
33E6 **Rondônia** Brazil
24F6 **Rondônia** State, Brazil
30F2 **Rondonópolis** Brazil
73B4 **Rong'an** China
73B4 **Rongchang** China
72E2 **Rongcheng** China
73B4 **Rongjiang** China
73B4 **Rong Jiang** *R* China
76A1 **Rongklang Range** *Mts* Burma
39G7 **Rønne** Den
39H7 **Ronneby** Sweden
112B2 **Ronne Ice Shelf** Ant
46B1 **Ronse** Belg
46A1 **Ronthieu** Region, France
9C3 **Roof Butte** *Mt* USA

84D3 **Roorkee** India
46C1 **Roosendaal** Neth
112B6 **Roosevelt I** Ant
106C2 **Roper** *R* Aust
33E3 **Roraima** State, Brazil
33E2 **Roraime** *Mt* Ven
38G6 **Røros** Nor
47C1 **Rorschach** Switz
38G6 **Rørvik** Nor
27Q2 **Rosalie** Dominica
22C3 **Rosamond L** USA
34C2 **Rosario** Arg
31C2 **Rosário** Brazil
34D2 **Rosario del Tala** Arg
48B2 **Roscoff** France
45B2 **Roscommon** County, Irish Rep
41B3 **Roscommon** Irish Rep
45C2 **Roscrea** Irish Rep
27E3 **Roseau** Dominica
09C4 **Rosebery** Aust
20B2 **Roseburg** USA
19A4 **Rosenberg** USA
57C3 **Rosenheim** Germany
13F2 **Rosetown** Can
54B2 **Roşiori de Vede** Rom
39G7 **Roskilde** Den
60D3 **Roslavl'** Russian Fed
61E2 **Roslyatino** Russian Fed
11B2 **Ross** NZ
12H2 **Ross** *R* Can
40B3 **Rossan** *Pt* Irish Rep
53C3 **Rossano** Italy
19C3 **Ross Barnet Res** USA
15C1 **Rosseau L** *L* Can
07E2 **Rossel** *I* Solomon Is
112A **Ross Ice Shelf** Ant
20B1 **Ross L** USA
13D3 **Rossland** Can
45C2 **Rosslare** Irish Rep
11C2 **Ross,Mt** NZ
97A3 **Rosso** Maur
43C4 **Ross-on-Wye** Eng
60E4 **Rossosh** Russian Fed
4E3 **Ross River** Can
12B6 **Ross S** Ant
91B4 **Rostāq** Iran
56C2 **Rostock** Germany
Rostov = Rostov-na-Donu
61E4 **Rostov-na-Donu** Russian Fed
17B1 **Roswell** Georgia, USA
9C3 **Roswell** New Mexico, USA
71F2 **Rota** Pacific O
56B2 **Rotenburg** Niedersachsen, Germany
46E1 **Rothaar-Geb** *Region* Germany
12C3 **Rothera** *Base* Ant
42D3 **Rotherham** Eng
42B2 **Rothesay** Scot
71D5 **Roti** *I* Indon
08C2 **Roto** Aust
11B2 **Rotoiti,L** NZ
1B2 **Rotoroa,L** NZ
0C1 **Rotorua** NZ
10C1 **Rotorua,L** NZ
56A2 **Rotterdam** Neth
46B1 **Roubaix** France
48C2 **Rouen** France
42E3 **Rough** *Oilfield* N Sea
Roulers = Roeselare
01E3 **Round I** Mauritius
09D2 **Round Mt** Aust
8C2 **Roundup** USA
44C2 **Rousay** *I* Scot
48C3 **Roussillon** Region, France
10C2 **Rouyn** Can
38K5 **Rovaniemi** Fin
47D2 **Rovereto** Italy
47D2 **Rovigo** Italy
52B1 **Rovinj** Croatia
59D2 **Rovno** Ukraine
90A2 **Row'ān** Iran
09C1 **Rowena** Aust
6C3 **Rowley I** Can
96A2 **Rowley Shoals** Aust
79A3 **Roxas** Palawan, Phil
79B3 **Roxas** Panay, Phil
111A3 **Roxburgh** NZ
45C2 **Royal Canal** Irish Rep
43D3 **Royal Leamington Spa** Eng
14B2 **Royal Oak** USA
43E4 **Royal Tunbridge Wells** Eng
48B2 **Royan** France
46B2 **Roye** France
43D3 **Royston** Eng
59C3 **Rožňava** Slovakia
46B2 **Rozoy** France
61F3 **Rtishchevo** Russian Fed
99D3 **Ruaha Nat Pk** Tanz
110C1 **Ruahine Range** *Mts* NZ
110C1 **Ruapehu,Mt** NZ
65D3 **Rub al Khālī** *Desert* S Arabia
44A3 **Rubha Hunish** Scot
35A2 **Rubinéia** Brazil
65K4 **Rubtsovsk** Russian Fed
12C2 **Ruby** USA
91C4 **Rudan** Iran
90A2 **Rūdbār** Iran
69F2 **Rudnaya Pristan'** Russian Fed
54B2 **Rudoka Planina** *Mt* Macedonia
72E3 **Rudong** China
14B1 **Rudyard** USA
46A1 **Rue** France
48C2 **Ruffec** France
99D3 **Rufiji** *R* Tanz
34C2 **Rufino** Arg
97A3 **Rufisque** Sen
100B2 **Rufunsa** Zambia
43D3 **Rugby** Eng
39G8 **Rügen** *I* Germany
56B2 **Ruhr** *R* Germany
73D4 **Ruijin** China
54B2 **Rujen** *Mt* Bulg/Macedonia
99D3 **Rukwa** *L* Tanz
44A3 **Rum** *I* Scot
54A1 **Ruma** Serbia, Yugos
91A4 **Rumāh** S Arabia
98C2 **Rumbek** Sudan
26C2 **Rum Cay** *I* Caribbean S
47A2 **Rumilly** France
106C2 **Rum Jungle** Aust
101C2 **Rumphi** Malawi
111B2 **Runanga** NZ
110C1 **Runaway,C** NZ
100C3 **Rundi** *R* Zim
100A2 **Rundu** Namibia
99D3 **Rungwa** Tanz
99D3 **Rungwa** *R* Tanz
99D3 **Rungwe** *Mt* Tanz
82C2 **Ruoqiang** China
68C2 **Ruo Shui** *R* China
54C1 **Rupea** Rom
7C4 **Rupert** *R* Can
46D1 **Rur** *R* Germany
32D6 **Rurrenabaque** Bol
101C2 **Rusape** Zim
54C2 **Ruse** Bulg
18B1 **Rushville** Illinois, USA
108B3 **Rushworth** Aust
19A3 **Rusk** USA
17B2 **Ruskin** USA
110B1 **Russell** NZ
18B2 **Russellville** Arkansas, USA
18C2 **Russellville** Kentucky, USA
21A2 **Russian** *R* USA
62C3 **Russian Fed** Asia/Europe
93E1 **Rustavi** Georgia
101G1 **Rustenburg** S Africa
19B3 **Ruston** USA
99C3 **Rutana** Burundi
46E1 **Rüthen** Germany
23B2 **Rutla** Mexico
15D2 **Rutland** USA
84D2 **Rutog** China
Ruvu = Pangani
101D2 **Ruvuma** *R* Tanz/Mozam
99D2 **Ruwenzori Range** *Mts* Uganda/Zaire
101C2 **Ruya** *R* Zim
59B3 **Ružomberok** Slovakia
99C3 **Rwanda** Republic, Africa
60E3 **Ryazan'** Russian Fed
61F3 **Ryazhsk** Russian Fed
60E2 **Rybinsk** Russian Fed
60E2 **Rybinskoye Vodokhranilishche** *Res* Russian Fed
13D1 **Rycroft** Can
43D4 **Ryde** Eng
43E4 **Rye** Eng
20C2 **Rye Patch Res** USA
60D3 **Ryl'sk** Russian Fed
61G4 **Ryn Peski** *Desert* Kazakhstan
74D3 **Ryōtsu** Japan
59D3 **Ryskany** Moldova
69E4 **Ryūkyū Retto** *Arch* Japan
59C2 **Rzeszów** Pol
60D2 **Rzhev** Russian Fed

S

91B3 **Sa'ādatābād** Iran
56C2 **Saale** *R* Germany
47B1 **Saanen** Switz
46D2 **Saar** *R* Germany
46D2 **Saarbrücken** Germany
46D2 **Saarburg** Germany
39J7 **Saaremaa** *I* Estonia
46D2 **Saarland** State, Germany
46D2 **Saarlouis** Germany
34C3 **Saavedra** Arg
54A2 **Šabac** Serbia, Yugos
51C1 **Sabadell** Spain
75B1 **Sabae** Japan
78D1 **Sabah** State, Malay
26C4 **Sabanalarga** Colombia
70A3 **Sabang** Indon
87C1 **Sabari** *R* India
94B2 **Sabastiya** Israel
30C2 **Sabaya** Bol
93C3 **Sab'Bi'ār** Syria
94C2 **Sabhā** Jordan
95A2 **Sabhā** Libya
24B2 **Sabinas** Mexico
24B2 **Sabinas Hidalgo** Mexico
19A3 **Sabine** *R* USA
19B4 **Sabine L** USA
91B5 **Sabkhat Maṭṭi** *Salt Marsh* UAE
94A3 **Sabkhet El Bardawîl** *Lg* Egypt
79B3 **Sablayan** Phil
7D5 **Sable,C** Can
17B2 **Sable,C** USA
7D5 **Sable I** Can
90C2 **Sabzevār** Iran
20C1 **Sacajawea Peak** USA
10A1 **Sachigo** *R* Can
57C2 **Sachsen** State, Germany
56C2 **Sachsen-Anhalt** State, Germany
4F2 **Sachs Harbour** Can
47B1 **Säckingen** Germany
22B1 **Sacramento** USA
22B1 **Sacramento** *R* USA
21A1 **Sacramento** *V* USA
9C3 **Sacramento Mts** USA
81C4 **Sa'dah** Yemen
54B2 **Sadanski** Bulg
82D3 **Sadiya** India
50A2 **Sado** *R* Port
74D3 **Sado-shima** *I* Japan
85C3 **Sādri** India
Safad = Zefat
84A2 **Safed Koh** *Mts* Afghan
39G7 **Saffle** Sweden
92C3 **Safi** Jordan
96B1 **Safi** Mor
90D3 **Safidabeh** Iran
94C1 **Şāfītā** Syria
93E3 **Şafwān** Iraq
75A2 **Saga** Japan
76B1 **Sagaing** Burma
75B2 **Sagami-nada** *B* Japan
85D4 **Sāgar** India
16C2 **Sag Harbor** USA
14B2 **Saginaw** USA
14B2 **Saginaw B** USA
26B2 **Sagua de Tánamo** Cuba
26B2 **Sagua la Grande** Cuba
7C5 **Saguenay** *R* Can
51B2 **Sagunto** Spain
94C3 **Sahāb** Jordan
50A1 **Sahagún** Spain
96C2 **Sahara** *Desert* N Africa
84D3 **Saharanpur** India
84C2 **Sahiwal** Pak
93D3 **Şahrā al Hijārah** *Desert Region* Iraq
23A1 **Sahuayo** Mexico
107D1 **Saibai I** Aust
96C1 **Saïda** Alg
94B2 **Săida** Leb
91C4 **Sa'īdabad** Iran
51B2 **Saidia** Mor
86B1 **Saidpur** India
84C2 **Saidu** Pak
75A1 **Saigō** Japan
Saigon = Ho Chi Minh
86C2 **Saiha** India
68D2 **Saihan Tal** China
75A2 **Saijo** Japan
74C4 **Saiki** Japan
42C2 **St Abb's Head** *Pt* Scot
43D4 **St Albans** Eng
15D2 **St Albans** Vermont, USA
14B3 **St Albans** West Virginia, USA
43C4 **St Albans Head** *C* Eng
13E2 **St Albert** Can
46B1 **St Amand-les-Eaux** France
48C2 **St Amand-Mont Rond** France
17A2 **St Andrew B** USA
44C3 **St Andrews** Scot
17B1 **St Andrew Sd** USA
27H1 **St Ann's Bay** Jamaica
7E4 **St Anthony** Can
108B3 **St Arnaud** Aust
17B2 **St Augustine** USA
43B4 **St Austell** Eng
46D2 **St-Avold** France
42C2 **St Bees Head** *Pt* Eng
47B2 **St-Bonnet** France
43B4 **St Brides B** Wales
48B2 **St-Brieuc** France
15C2 **St Catharines** Can
27M2 **St Catherine,Mt** Grenada
17B1 **St Catherines I** USA
43D4 **St Catherines Pt** Eng
49C2 **St Chamond** France
18B2 **St Charles** Missouri, USA
14B2 **St Clair** USA
14B2 **St Clair,L** Can/USA
14B2 **St Clair Shores** USA
49D2 **St Claud** France
10A2 **St Cloud** USA
47B1 **Ste Croix** Switz
27E3 **St Croix** *I* Caribbean S
43B4 **St Davids Head** *Pt* Wales
46B2 **St Denis** France
101E3 **St Denis** Réunion
46C2 **St Dizier** France
12F2 **St Elias,Mt** USA
12G2 **St Elias Mts** Can
48B2 **Saintes** France
49C2 **St Étienne** France
18B2 **St Francis** *R* USA
100B4 **St Francis,C** S Africa

47C1 **St Gallen** Switz
48C3 **St-Gaudens** France
109C1 **St George** Aust
17B1 **St George** South Carolina, USA
9B3 **St George** Utah, USA
17B2 **St George I** Florida, USA
20B2 **St George,Pt** USA
15D1 **St-Georges** Can
27E4 **St George's** Grenada
45C3 **St George's Chan** Irish Rep/Wales
46A2 **St Germain-en-Laye** France
47B2 **St-Gervais** France
47C1 **St Gotthard** *P* Switz
43B4 **St Govans Head** *Pt* Wales
22A1 **St Helena** USA
103H5 **St Helena** *I* Atlantic O
100A4 **St Helena B** S Africa
17B1 **St Helena Sd** USA
109C4 **St Helens** Aust
42C3 **St Helens** Eng
20B1 **St Helens** USA
20B1 **St Helens,Mt** USA
48B2 **St Helier** Jersey
47B1 **St Hippolyte** France
46C1 **St-Hubert** Belg
7C5 **St-Hyacinthe** Can
14B1 **St Ignace** USA
43B4 **St Ives** Eng
18B2 **St James** Missouri, USA
5E4 **St James,C** Can
15D1 **St Jean** Can
48B2 **St Jean-d'Angely** France
47B2 **St-Jean-de-Maurienne** France
10C2 **St Jean,L** Can
15D1 **St-Jérôme** Can
20C1 **St Joe** *R* USA
7D5 **Saint John** Can
7E5 **St John's** Can
14B2 **St Johns** Michigan, USA
17B2 **St Johns** *R* USA
15D2 **St Johnsbury** USA
15D1 **St-Joseph** Can
19B3 **St Joseph** Louisiana, USA
14A2 **St Joseph** Michigan, USA
18B2 **St Joseph** Missouri, USA
27L1 **St Joseph** Trinidad
14B2 **St Joseph** *R* USA
14B1 **St Joseph I** Can
7A4 **St Joseph,L** Can
47B1 **St Julien** France
48C2 **St-Junien** France
46B2 **St-Just-en-Chaussée** France
4B2 **St Kilda** *I* Scot
27E3 **St Kitts-Nevis** *Is* Caribbean S
47A1 **St-Laurent** France
7D5 **St Lawrence** *R* Can
7D5 **Saint Lawrence,G of** Can
4A3 **St Lawrence I** USA
15C2 **St Lawrence Seaway** Can/USA
48B2 **St Lô** France
97A3 **St Louis** Sen
11A3 **St Louis** USA
27E4 **St Lucia** *I* Caribbean S
101H1 **St Lucia,L** S Africa
44E1 **St Magnus** *B* Scot
48B2 **St Malo** France
20C1 **St Maries** USA
27E3 **St Martin** *I* Caribbean S
108A2 **St Mary Peak** *Mt* Aust
109C4 **St Marys** Aust
15C2 **St Marys** USA
17B1 **St Marys** *R* USA
46C2 **Ste-Menehould** France
12B2 **St Michael** USA
16A3 **St Michaels** USA
47B2 **St-Michel** France
46C2 **St-Mihiel** France
47C1 **St Moritz** Switz
48B2 **St-Nazaire** France
46C1 **St-Niklaas** Belg
46B1 **St-Omer** France
13E2 **St Paul** Can
10A2 **St Paul** Minnesota, USA
97A4 **St Paul** *R* Lib
17B2 **St Petersburg** USA
7E5 **St Pierre** Can
15D1 **St Pierre,L** Can
46B1 **St-Pol-Sur-Ternoise** France
59B3 **St Pölten** Austria
46B2 **St Quentin** France
49D3 **St Raphaël** France
101D2 **St Sébastien** *C* Madag
17B1 **St Simons I** USA
17B1 **St Stephen** USA
14B2 **St Thomas** Can
49D3 **St-Tropez** France
46C1 **St Truiden** Belg
46A1 **St-Valéry-sur-Somme** France
27E4 **St Vincent and the Grenadines** *Is* Caribbean S
108A2 **St Vincent,G** Aust
46D1 **St-Vith** Germany
46D2 **St Wendel** Germany
71F2 **Saipan** *I* Pacific O
84B2 **Saiydabad** Afghan
30C2 **Sajama** *Mt* Bol
74D4 **Sakai** Japan
75A2 **Sakaidi** Japan
75A1 **Sakaiminato** Japan
93D4 **Sakākah** S Arabia
10C1 **Sakami,L** Can
100B2 **Sakania** Zaïre
101D3 **Sakaraha** Madag
60D5 **Sakarya** *R* Turk
58C1 **Sakasleja** Latvia
74D3 **Sakata** Japan
97C4 **Saketél** Benin
69G1 **Sakhalin** *I* Russian Fed
69E4 **Sakishima gunto** *Is* Japan
97A4 **Sal** *I* Cape Verde
61F4 **Sal** *R* Russian Fed
39H7 **Sala** Sweden
34D3 **Saladillo** Arg
34C2 **Saladillo** *R* Arg
34D3 **Salado** *R* Buenos Aires, Arg
34B3 **Salado** *R* Mendoza/San Luis, Arg
30D4 **Salado** *R* Sante Fe, Arg
97B4 **Salaga** Ghana
76C3 **Sala Hintoun** Camb
98B1 **Salal** Chad
81D4 **Şalālah** Oman
34A2 **Salamanca** Chile
23A1 **Salamanca** Mexico
50A1 **Salamanca** Spain
15C2 **Salamanca** USA
98B2 **Salamat** *R* Chad
71F4 **Salamaua** PNG
15C2 **Salamonica** USA
78D1 **Salang** Indon
38H5 **Salangen** Nor
30C3 **Salar de Arizaro** Arg
30C3 **Salar de Atacama** *Salt Pan* Chile
30C2 **Salar de Coipasa** *Salt Pan* Bol
30C3 **Salar de Uyuni** *Salt Pan* Bol
47C2 **Salasomaggiore** Italy
61J3 **Salavat** Russian Fed
70D4 **Salayar** Indon
105L5 **Sala y Gomez** *I* Pacific O
34C3 **Salazar** Arg
48C2 **Salbris** France
12E2 **Salcha** *R* USA
100A4 **Saldanha** S Africa
94C2 **Saldhad** Syria
34C3 **Saldungaray** Arg
58C1 **Saldus** Latvia
109C3 **Sale** Aust
18C2 **Salem** Illinois, USA
87B2 **Salem** India
16D1 **Salem** Massachusetts, USA
16B3 **Salem** New Jersey, USA
20B2 **Salem** Oregon, USA
78C4 **Salembu Besar** *I* Indon
39G6 **Salen** Sweden
53B2 **Salerno** Italy
42C3 **Salford** Eng
54A1 **Salgót** Hung
59B3 **Salgótarjan** Hung
31D3 **Salgueiro** Brazil
55C3 **Salihli** Turk
101C2 **Salima** Malawi
39K6 **Salimaa** *L* Fin
18A2 **Salina** Kansas, USA
53B3 **Salina** *I* Italy
23B2 **Salina Cruz** Mexico
30C3 **Salina de Arizato** Arg
34B3 **Salina Grande** *Salt pan* Arg
34B2 **Salina La Antigua** *Salt pan* Arg
35C1 **Salinas** Brazil
22B2 **Salinas** USA
22B2 **Salinas** *R* USA
34B3 **Salinas de Llancaneb** *Salt Pan* Arg
34B2 **Salinas Grandes** *Salt Pan* Arg
19B3 **Saline** *R* Arkansas, USA
27M2 **Salines,Pt** Grenada
31B2 **Salinópolis** Brazil
47A1 **Salins** France
Salisbury = Harare
43D4 **Salisbury** Eng
15C3 **Salisbury** Maryland, USA
6C3 **Salisbury I** Can
43D4 **Salisbury Plain** Eng
38K5 **Salla** Fin
47B2 **Sallanches** France
18B2 **Sallisaw** USA
6C3 **Salluit** Can
86A1 **Sallyana** Nepal
93D2 **Salmas** Iran
38L6 **Salmi** Russian Fed
20C1 **Salmo** Can
8B2 **Salmon** USA
13D2 **Salmon Arm** Can
8B2 **Salmon River Mts** USA
39J6 **Salo** Fin
47D2 **Salò** Italy
49D3 **Salon-de-Provence** France
Salonica = Thessaloníki
54B1 **Salonta** Rom
38K6 **Salpausselka** Region, Fin
34B2 **Salsacate** Arg
61F4 **Sal'sk** Russian Fed
94B2 **Salt** Jordan
30C3 **Salta** Arg
30C3 **Salta** State, Arg
24B2 **Saltillo** Mexico
8B2 **Salt Lake City** USA
34C2 **Salto** Arg
34D2 **Salto** Urug
32C3 **Salto Angostura** *Waterfall* Colombia
35D1 **Salto da Divisa** Brazil
33E2 **Salto del Angel** *Waterfall* Ven
30E3 **Salto del Guaira** *Waterfall* Brazil
32C4 **Salto Grande** *Waterfall* Colombia
84C2 **Salt Range** *Mts* Pak
27H2 **Salt River** Jamaica
17B1 **Saluda** USA
47B2 **Saluzzo** Italy
31D4 **Salvador** Brazil
19B4 **Salvador,L** USA
23A1 **Salvatierra** Mexico
91B5 **Salwah** Qatar
76B1 **Salween** *R* Burma
93E2 **Sal'yany** Azerbaijan
57C3 **Salzburg** Austria
56C2 **Salzgitter** Germany
56C2 **Salzwedel** Germany
68B1 **Samagaltay** Russian Fed
79B4 **Samales Group** *Is* Phil
27D3 **Samaná** Dom Rep
92C2 **Samandaği** Turk
84B1 **Samangan** Afghan
79C3 **Samar** *I* Phil
65G4 **Samara** Russian Fe
107E2 **Samarai** PNG
78D3 **Samarinda** Indon
80E2 **Samarkand** Uzbekistan
93D3 **Sāmarrā'** Iraq
79B3 **Samar S** Phil
86A2 **Sambalpur** India
78B2 **Sambas** Indon
101E2 **Sambava** Madag
84D3 **Sambhal** India
78D3 **Samboja** Indon
59C3 **Sambor** Ukraine
46B1 **Sambre** *R* France
74B3 **Samch'ŏk** S Korea
99D3 **Same** Tanz
47C1 **Samedan** Switz
46A1 **Samer** France
100B2 **Samfya** Zambia
76B1 **Samka** Burma
76C1 **Sam Neua** Laos
55C3 **Sámos** *I* Greece
55C2 **Samothráki** *I* Gree
34C2 **Sampacho** Arg
78D3 **Sampaga** Indon
78C3 **Sampit** Indon
78C3 **Sampit** *R* Indon
19B3 **Sam Rayburn Res** USA
76C3 **Samrong** Camb
56C1 **Samsø** *I* Den
92C1 **Samsun** Turk
97B3 **San** Mali
76D3 **San** *R* Camb
59C2 **San** *R* Pol
81C4 **Şan'ā'** Yemen
98B2 **Sanaga** *R* Cam
29C2 **San Agustín** Arg
79C4 **San Agustin,C** Phil
90A2 **Sanandaj** Iran
22B1 **San Andreas** USA
25C3 **San Andrés Tuxtla** Mexico
9C3 **San Angelo** USA
53A3 **San Antioco** Sardegna
53A3 **San Antioco** *I* Med S
34A2 **San Antonio** Chile
9C3 **San Antonio** New Mexico, USA
79B2 **San Antonio** Phil
9D4 **San Antonio** *R* Texas, USA
51C2 **San Antonio Abad** Spain
25D2 **San Antonio,C** Cub
26A2 **San Antonio de los Banos** Cuba
22D3 **San Antonio,Mt** U
29C4 **San Antonio Oeste** Arg
34D3 **San Augustin** Arg
34B2 **San Augustin de Valle Féril** Arg
85D4 **Sanawad** India
23A1 **San Bartolo** Mexic
24A3 **San Benedicto** *I* Mexico
22B2 **San Benito** *R* USA
22B2 **San Benito Mt** US
22D3 **San Bernardino** U
34A2 **San Bernardo** Chi
17A2 **San Blas,C** USA
34A3 **San Carlos** Chile
32A1 **San Carlos** Nic
79B2 **San Carlos** Phil

29B4 **San Carlos de Bariloche** Arg
69E4 **San-chung** Taiwan
61G2 **Sanchursk** Russian Fed
34A3 **San Clemente** Chile
22D4 **San Clemente** USA
21B3 **San Clemente I** USA
34C2 **San Cristóbal** Arg
25C3 **San Cristóbal** Mexico
32C2 **San Cristóbal** Ven
32J7 **San Cristóbal** *I* Ecuador
107F2 **San Cristobal** *I* Solomon Is
25E2 **Sancti Spíritus** Cuba
78C3 **Sandai** Indon
70C3 **Sandakan** Malay
44C2 **Sanday** *I* Scot
9C3 **Sanderson** USA
13F1 **Sandfly L** Can
21B3 **San Diego** USA
92B2 **Sandikli** Turk
86A1 **Sandila** India
39F7 **Sandnes** Nor
38G5 **Sandnessjøen** Nor
98C3 **Sandoa** Zaïre
59C2 **Sandomierz** Pol
38D3 **Sandoy** Føroyar
20C1 **Sandpoint** USA
49D2 **Sandrio** Italy
18A2 **Sand Springs** USA
106A3 **Sandstone** Aust
73C4 **Sandu** China
14B2 **Sandusky** USA
39H6 **Sandviken** Sweden
7A4 **Sandy L** Can
34C2 **San Elcano** Arg
9B3 **San Felipe** Baja Cal, Mexico
34A2 **San Felipe** Chile
23A1 **San Felipe** Guanajuato, Mexico
27D4 **San Felipe** Ven
51C1 **San Feliu de Guixols** Spain
28A5 **San Felix** *I* Pacific O
34A2 **San Fernando** Chile
79B2 **San Fernando** Phil
79B2 **San Fernando** Phil
50A2 **San Fernando** Spain
27E4 **San Fernando** Trinidad
22C3 **San Fernando** USA
32D2 **San Fernando** Ven
17B2 **Sanford** Florida, USA
12F2 **Sanford,Mt** USA
34C2 **San Francisco** Arg
27C3 **San Francisco** Dom Rep
22A2 **San Francisco** USA
22A2 **San Francisco B** USA
24B2 **San Francisco del Oro** Mexico
23A1 **San Francisco del Rincon** Mexico
22D3 **San Gabriel Mts** USA
85C5 **Sangamner** India
18C2 **Sangamon** *R* USA
71F2 **Sangan** *I* Pacific O
87B1 **Sangāreddi** India
78D4 **Sangeang** *I* Indon
22C2 **Sanger** USA
72C2 **Sanggan He** *R* China
78C2 **Sanggau** Indon
98B2 **Sangha** *R* Congo
85B3 **Sanghar** Pak
76B2 **Sangkhla Buri** Thai
78D2 **Sangkulirang** Indon
87A1 **Sāngli** India
98B2 **Sangmélima** Cam
9B3 **San Gorgonio Mt** USA
9C3 **Sangre de Cristo** *Mts* USA
34C2 **San Gregorio** Arg
22A2 **San Gregorio** USA
84D2 **Sangrūr** India
30E4 **San Ignacio** Arg
79B3 **San Isidro** Phil
32B2 **San Jacinto** Colombia
21B3 **San Jacinto Peak** *Mt* USA
34A3 **San Javier** Chile
34D2 **San Javier** Sante Fe, Arg
74D3 **Sanjō** *I* Japan
31C6 **San João del Rei** Brazil
22B2 **San Joaquin** *R* USA
22B2 **San Joaquin Valley** USA
32A1 **San José** Costa Rica
25C3 **San José** Guatemala
79B2 **San Jose** Luzon, Phil
79B3 **San Jose** Mindoro, Phil
22B2 **San Jose** USA
9B4 **San José** *I* Mexico
30D2 **San José de Chiquitos** Bol
34D2 **San José de Feliciano** Arg
34B2 **San José de Jachal** Arg
34C2 **San José de la Dormida** Arg
31B6 **San José do Rio Prêto** Brazil
24B2 **San José del Cabo** Mexico
34B2 **San Juan** Arg
27D3 **San Juan** Puerto Rico
34B2 **San Juan** State, Arg
27L1 **San Juan** Trinidad
32D2 **San Juan** Ven
26B2 **San Juan** *Mt* Cuba
8C3 **San Juan** *Mts* USA
34B2 **San Juan** *R* Arg
23B2 **San Juan** *R* Mexico
25D3 **San Juan** *R* Nic/Costa Rica
23B2 **San Juan Bautista** Mexico
30E4 **San Juan Bautista** Par
22B2 **San Juan Bautista** USA
25D3 **San Juan del Norte** Nic
27D4 **San Juan de los Cayos** Ven
23A1 **San Juan de loz Lagoz** Mexico
23A1 **San Juan del Rio** Mexico
25D3 **San Juan del Sur** Nic
20B1 **San Juan Is** USA
23B2 **San Juan Tepozcolula** Mexico
29C5 **San Julián** Arg
34C2 **San Justo** Arg
60D2 **Sankt-Peterburg** Russian Fed
98C3 **Sankuru** *R* Zaïre
22A2 **San Leandro** USA
93C2 **Şanlıurfa** Turk
32B3 **San Lorenzo** Ecuador
34C2 **San Lorenzo** Arg
22B2 **San Lucas** USA
34B2 **San Luis** Arg
34B2 **San Luis** State, Arg
23A1 **San Luis de la Paz** Mexico
21A2 **San Luis Obispo** USA
23A1 **San Luis Potosi** Mexico
22B2 **San Luis Res** USA
53A3 **Sanluri** Sardegna
33D2 **San Maigualida** *Mts* Ven
34D3 **San Manuel** Arg
34A2 **San Marcos** Chile
23B2 **San Marcos** Mexico
52B2 **San Marino** Republic, Europe
34B2 **San Martin** Mendoza, Arg
112C3 **San Martin** *Base* Ant
47D1 **San Martino di Castroza** Italy
23B2 **San Martin Tuxmelucan** Mexico
22A2 **San Mateo** USA
30E2 **San Matias** Bol
72C3 **Sanmenxia** China
25D3 **San Miguel** El Salvador
22B3 **San Miguel** *I* USA
23A1 **San Miguel del Allende** Mexico
34D3 **San Miguel del Monte** Arg
30C4 **San Miguel de Tucumán** Arg
73D4 **Sanming** China
9B3 **San Nicolas** *I* USA
34C2 **San Nicolás de los Arroyos** Arg
101G1 **Sannieshof** S Africa
97B4 **Sanniquellie** Lib
59C3 **Sanok** Pol
26B5 **San Onofore** Colombia
22D4 **San Onofre** USA
79B3 **San Pablo** Phil
22A1 **San Pablo B** USA
34D2 **San Pedro** Buenos Aires, Arg
97B4 **San Pédro** Ivory Coast
30D3 **San Pedro** Jujuy, Arg
30E3 **San Pedro** Par
22C4 **San Pedro Chan** USA
9C4 **San Pedro de los Colonias** Mexico
25D3 **San Pedro Sula** Honduras
53A3 **San Pietro** *I* Medit S
24A1 **San Quintin** Mexico
34B2 **San Rafael** Arg
22A2 **San Rafael** USA
22C3 **San Rafael Mts** USA
49D3 **San Remo** Italy
34D2 **San Salvador** Arg
26C2 **San Salvador** *I* Caribbean S
32J7 **San Salvador** *I* Ecuador
30C3 **San Salvador de Jujuy** Arg
51B1 **San Sebastian** Spain
53C2 **San Severo** Italy
30C2 **Santa Ana** Bol
25C3 **Santa Ana** Guatemala
22D4 **Santa Ana** USA
22D4 **Santa Ana Mts** USA
34A3 **Santa Bárbara** Chile
24B2 **Santa Barbara** Mexico
22C3 **Santa Barbara** USA
22C4 **Santa Barbara** *I* USA
22B3 **Santa Barbara Chan** USA
22C3 **Santa Barbara Res** USA
22C4 **Santa Catalina** *I* USA
22C4 **Santa Catalina,G of** USA
30F4 **Santa Catarina** State, Brazil
26B2 **Santa Clara** Cuba
22B2 **Santa Clara** USA
22C3 **Santa Clara** *R* USA
29C6 **Santa Cruz** Arg
30D2 **Santa Cruz** Bol
34A2 **Santa Cruz** Chile
79B3 **Santa Cruz** Phil
29B5 **Santa Cruz** State, Arg
22A2 **Santa Cruz** USA
22C4 **Santa Cruz** *I* USA
35D1 **Santa Cruz Cabrália** Brazil
22C3 **Santa Cruz Chan** USA
96A2 **Santa Cruz de la Palma** Canary Is
26B2 **Santa Cruz del Sur** Cuba
96A2 **Santa Cruz de Tenerife** Canary Is
100B2 **Santa Cruz do Cuando** Angola
35B2 **Santa Cruz do Rio Pardo** Brazil
22A2 **Santa Cruz Mts** USA
34D2 **Santa Elena** Arg
33E3 **Santa Elena** Ven
34C2 **Santa Fe** Arg
34C2 **Santa Fe** State, Arg
9C3 **Santa Fe** USA
35A1 **Santa Helena de Goiás** Brazil
73B3 **Santai** China
29B6 **Santa Inés** *I* Chile
34B3 **Santa Isabel** La Pampa, Arg
34C2 **Santa Isabel** Sante Fe, Arg
107E1 **Santa Isabel** *I* Solomon Is
21A2 **Santa Lucia** *Ra* USA
21A2 **Santa Lucia Range** *Mts* USA
97A4 **Santa Luzia** *I* Cape Verde
9B4 **Santa Margarita** *I* Mexico
22D4 **Santa Margarita** *R* USA
30F4 **Santa Maria** Brazil
26C4 **Santa Maria** Colombia
21A3 **Santa Maria** USA
96A1 **Santa Maria** *I* Açores
23B1 **Santa Maria** *R* Queretaro, Mexico
23A1 **Santa Maria del Rio** Mexico
32C1 **Santa Marta** Colombia
22C3 **Santa Monica** USA
22C4 **Santa Monica B** USA
29E2 **Santana do Livramento** Brazil
32B3 **Santander** Colombia
50B1 **Santander** Spain
51C2 **Santañy** Spain
22C3 **Santa Paula** USA
31C2 **Santa Quitéria** Brazil
33G4 **Santarem** Brazil
50A2 **Santarém** Port
22A1 **Santa Rosa** California, USA
25D3 **Santa Rosa** Honduras
34C3 **Santa Rosa** La Pampa, Arg
34B2 **Santa Rosa** Mendoza, Arg
34B2 **Santa Rosa** San Luis, Arg
22B3 **Santa Rosa** *I* USA
24A2 **Santa Rosalía** Mexico
20C2 **Santa Rosa Range** *Mts* USA
31D3 **Santa Talhada** Brazil
35C1 **Santa Teresa** Brazil
53A2 **Santa Teresa di Gallura** Sardegna
22B3 **Santa Ynez** *R* USA
22B3 **Santa Ynez Mts** USA
17C1 **Santee** *R* USA
47C2 **Santhia** Italy
34A2 **Santiago** Chile
27C3 **Santiago** Dom Rep
32A2 **Santiago** Panama
79B2 **Santiago** Phil
32B4 **Santiago** *R* Peru
50A1 **Santiago de Compostela** Spain
26B2 **Santiago de Cuba** Cuba
30D4 **Santiago del Estero** Arg
30D4 **Santiago del Estero** State, Arg
22D4 **Santiago Peak** *Mt* USA
31C5 **Santo** State, Brazil
35A2 **Santo Anastatácio** Brazil
30F4 **Santo Angelo** Brazil
97A4 **Santo Antão** *I* Cape Verde
35A2 **Santo Antonio da Platina** Brazil
27D3 **Santo Domingo** Dom Rep

35B2 **Santos** Brazil
35C2 **Santos Dumont** Brazil
30E4 **Santo Tomé** Arg
29B5 **San Valentin** *Mt* Chile
34A2 **San Vicente** Chile
98B3 **Sanza Pomba** Angola
30E4 **São Borja** Brazil
35B2 **São Carlos** Brazil
33G5 **São Félix** Mato Grosso, Brazil
35C2 **São Fidélis** Brazil
35C1 **São Francisco** Brazil
31D3 **São Francisco** *R* Brazil
30G4 **São Francisco do Sul** Brazil
35B1 **São Gotardo** Brazil
99D3 **Sao Hill** Tanz
35C2 **São João da Barra** Brazil
35B2 **São João da Boa Vista** Brazil
35C1 **São João da Ponte** Brazil
35C2 **São João del Rei** Brazil
35B2 **São Joaquim da Barra** Brazil
96A1 **São Jorge** *I* Açores
35B2 **São José do Rio Prêto** Brazil
35B2 **São José dos Campos** Brazil
31C2 **São Luis** Brazil
35B1 **São Marcos** *R* Brazil
35C1 **São Maria do Suaçui** Brazil
35D1 **São Mateus** Brazil
35C1 **São Mateus** *R* Brazil
96A1 **São Miguel** *I* Açores
49C2 **Saône** *R* France
97A4 **São Nicolau** *I* Cape Verde
35B2 **São Paulo** Brazil
35A2 **São Paulo** State, Brazil
31C3 **São Raimundo Nonato** Brazil
35B1 **São Romão** Brazil
35B2 **São Sebastia do Paraiso** Brazil
35A1 **São Simão** Goias, Brazil
35B2 **São Simão** Sao Paulo, Brazil
97A4 **São Tiago** *I* Cape Verde
97C4 **São Tomé** *I* W Africa
97C4 **São Tomé and Principe** Republic, W Africa
96B2 **Saoura** *Watercourse* Alg
35B2 **São Vicente** Brazil
97A4 **São Vincente** *I* Cape Verde
55C2 **Sápai** Greece
78D4 **Sape** Indon
97C4 **Sapele** Nig
74E2 **Sapporo** Japan
53C2 **Sapri** Italy
18A2 **Sapulpa** USA
90A2 **Saqqez** Iran
10C2 **Saquenay** *R* Can
90A2 **Sarāb** Iran
54A2 **Sarajevo** Bosnia-Herzegovina
90D2 **Sarakhs** Iran
61J3 **Saraktash** Russian Fed
63A2 **Sarala** Russian Fed
15D2 **Saranac L** USA
15D2 **Saranac Lake** USA
55B3 **Sarandë** Alb
79C4 **Sarangani Is** Phil
61G3 **Saransk** Russian Fed
61H2 **Sarapul** Russian Fed
17B2 **Sarasota** USA
54C1 **Sarata** Ukraine
15D2 **Saratoga Springs** USA
78C2 **Saratok** Malay
61G3 **Saratov** Russian Fed
61G3 **Saratovskoye Vodokhranilishche** *Res* Russian Fed
67F4 **Sarawak** State, Malay
92A2 **Saraykoy** Turk
90C3 **Sarbisheh** Iran
47D1 **Sarca** *R* Italy
95A2 **Sardalas** Libya
90A2 **Sar Dasht** Iran
52A2 **Sardegna** *I* Medit S
Sardinia = Sardegna
38H5 **Sarektjåkkå** *Mt* Sweden
84C2 **Sargodha** Pak
98B2 **Sarh** Chad
90B2 **Sārī** Iran
94B2 **Sarida** *R* Isreal
93D1 **Sarikamiş** Turk
107D3 **Sarina** Aust
47B1 **Sarine** *R* Switz
84B1 **Sar-i-Pul** Afghan
95B2 **Sarīr** Libya
95A2 **Sarir Tibesti** *Desert* Libya
74B3 **Sariwŏn** N Korea
48B2 **Sark** *I* UK
92C2 **Sarkišla** Turk
71E4 **Sarmi** Indon
29C5 **Sarmiento** Arg
39G6 **Särna** Sweden
47C1 **Sarnen** Switz
14B2 **Sarnia** Can
58D2 **Sarny** Ukraine
6E2 **Saroaq** Greenland
84B2 **Sarobi** Afghan
78A3 **Sarolangun** Indon
55B3 **Saronikós Kólpos** *G* Greece
47C2 **Saronno** Italy
55C2 **Saros Körfezi** *B* Turk
39G7 **Sarpsborg** Nor
46D2 **Sarralbe** France
46D2 **Sarrebourg** France
46D2 **Sarreguemines** France
46D2 **Sarre-Union** France
51B1 **Sarrion** Spain
85B3 **Sartanahu** Pak
53A2 **Sartène** Corse
48B2 **Sarthe** *R* France
61H4 **Sarykamys** Kazakhstan
65H5 **Sarysu** *R* Kazakhstan
86A2 **Sasarām** India
74B4 **Sasebo** Japan
5H4 **Saskatchewan** Province, Can
5H4 **Saskatchewan** *R* Can
13F2 **Saskatoon** Can
101G1 **Sasolburg** S Africa
61F3 **Sasovo** Russian Fed
97B4 **Sassandra** Ivory Coast
97B4 **Sassandra** *R* Ivory Coast
53A2 **Sassari** Sardegna
56C2 **Sassnitz** Germany
47D2 **Sassuolo** Italy
34C2 **Sastre** Arg
87A1 **Sātāra** India
4G2 **Satellite B** Can
78D4 **Satengar** *Is* Indon
39H6 **Säter** Sweden
17B1 **Satilla** *R* USA
61J2 **Satka** Russian Fed
84D2 **Satluj** *R* India
86A2 **Satna** India
85C4 **Sātpura Range** *Mts* India
54B1 **Satu Mare** Rom
34D2 **Sauce** Arg
39F7 **Sauda** Nor
80C3 **Saudi Arabia** Kingdom, Arabian Pen
46D2 **Sauer** *R* Germany/Lux
46D1 **Sauerland** Region, Germany
38B1 **Sauðárkrókur** Iceland
14A2 **Saugatuck** USA
16C1 **Saugerties** USA
13B2 **Saugstad,Mt** Can
7B5 **Sault Sainte Marie** Can
14B1 **Sault Ste Marie** Can
14B1 **Sault Ste Marie** USA
71E4 **Saumlaki** Indon
48B2 **Saumur** France
98C3 **Saurimo** Angola
27M2 **Sauteurs** Grenada
54A2 **Sava** *R* Serbia, Yugos
97C4 **Savalou** Benin
17B1 **Savannah** Georgia, USA
17B1 **Savannah** *R* USA
76C2 **Savannakhet** Laos
26B3 **Savanna la Mar** Jamaica
7A4 **Savant Lake** Can
76D2 **Savarane** Laos
97C4 **Savé** Benin
101C3 **Save** *R* Mozam
90B3 **Sāveh** Iran
46D2 **Saverne** France
47B2 **Savigliano** Italy
46B2 **Savigny** France
49D2 **Savoie** *Region* France
49D3 **Savona** Italy
38K6 **Savonlinna** Fin
4A3 **Savoonga** USA
38K5 **Savukoski** Fin
71D4 **Savu S** Indon
76A1 **Saw** Burma
85D3 **Sawai Mādhopur** India
78A2 **Sawang** Indon
76B2 **Sawankhalok** Thai
75C1 **Sawara** Japan
12E1 **Sawtooth Mt** USA
106B2 **Sawu** *I* Indon
97C3 **Say** Niger
84B1 **Sayghan** Afghan
91B5 **Sayhūt** Yemen
61G4 **Saykhin** Kazakhstan
68D2 **Saynshand** Mongolia
61H5 **Say-Utes** Kazakhstan
16C2 **Sayville** USA
13B2 **Sayward** Can
57C3 **Sázava** *R* Czech Republic
51C2 **Sbisseb** *R* Alg
42C2 **Scafell Pike** *Mt* Eng
44E1 **Scalloway** Scot
44C2 **Scapa Flow** *Sd* Scot
15C2 **Scarborough** Can
42D2 **Scarborough** Eng
27E4 **Scarborough** Tobago
44A2 **Scarp** *I* Scot
45B2 **Scarriff** Irish Rep
52A1 **Schaffhausen** Switz
57C3 **Scharding** Austria
46D1 **Scharteberg** *Mt* Germany
7D4 **Schefferville** Can
46B1 **Schelde** *R* Belg
10C2 **Schenectady** USA
47D2 **Schio** Italy
46D1 **Schleiden** Germany
56B2 **Schleswig** Germany
56B2 **Schleswig Holstein** State, Germany
16B1 **Schoharie** USA
71F4 **Schouten** *Is* PNG
7B5 **Schreiber** Can
21B2 **Schurz** USA
16A2 **Schuykill Haven** USA
16B2 **Schuylkill** *R* USA
57B3 **Schwabische Alb** *Upland* Germany
57B3 **Schwarzwald** *Upland* Germany
12C1 **Schwatka Mts** USA
47D1 **Schwaz** Austria
57C2 **Schweinfurt** Germany
101G1 **Schweizer Reneke** S Africa
56C2 **Schwerin** Germany
47C1 **Schwyz** Switz
53B3 **Sciacca** Italy
14B3 **Scioto** *R* USA
109D2 **Scone** Aust
6H2 **Scoresby Sd** Greenland
103F7 **Scotia Ridge** Atlantic O
103F7 **Scotia S** Atlantic O
44B3 **Scotland** Country, UK
112B7 **Scott** *Base* Ant
13B2 **Scott,C** Can
9C2 **Scott City** USA
112C6 **Scott I** Ant
6C2 **Scott Inlet** *B* Can
20B2 **Scott,Mt** USA
106B2 **Scott Reef** Timor S
8C2 **Scottsbluff** USA
17A1 **Scottsboro** USA
109C4 **Scottsdale** Aust
10C2 **Scranton** USA
47D1 **Scuol** Switz
Scutari = Shkodër
5J4 **Seal** *R* Can
108B3 **Sea Lake** Aust
18B2 **Searcy** USA
22B2 **Seaside** California, USA
20B1 **Seaside** Oregon, USA
16B3 **Seaside Park** USA
20B1 **Seattle** USA
22A1 **Sebastopol** USA
58D1 **Sebez** Russian Fed
17B2 **Sebring** USA
111A3 **Secretary I** NZ
18B2 **Sedalia** USA
46C2 **Sedan** France
111B2 **Seddonville** NZ
94B3 **Sede Boqer** Israel
94B3 **Sederot** Israel
97A3 **Sédhiou** Sen
94B3 **Sedom** Israel
100A3 **Seeheim** Namibia
111B2 **Sefton,Mt** NZ
77C5 **Segamat** Malay
51B2 **Segorbe** Spain
97B3 **Ségou** Mali
Segovia = Coco
50B1 **Segovia** Spain
51C1 **Segre** *R* Spain
97B4 **Séguéla** Ivory Coas
96A2 **Seguia el Hamra** *Watercourse* Mor
34C2 **Segundo** *R* Arg
78D2 **Seguntur** Indon
50B2 **Segura** *R* Spain
85B3 **Sehwan** Pak
46D2 **Seille** *R* France
38J6 **Seinäjoki** Fin
48C2 **Seine** *R* France
46B2 **Seine-et-Marne** Department, France
99D3 **Sekenke** Tanz
99D1 **Sek'ot'a** Eth
20B1 **Selah** USA
71E4 **Selaru** *I* Indon
78D4 **Selat Alas** *Str* Indo
78B3 **Selat Bangka** *Str* Indon
78A3 **Selat Berhala** *B* Indon
71E4 **Selat Dampier** *Str* Indon
78B3 **Selat Gaspar** *Str* Indon
78D4 **Selat Lombok** *Str* Indon
78D4 **Selat Sape** *Str* Ind
78B4 **Selat Sunda** *Str* Indon
71D4 **Selat Wetar** *Chan* Indon
12B1 **Selawik** USA
12C1 **Selawik** *R* USA
12B1 **Selawik L** USA
42D3 **Selby** Eng
55C3 **Selçuk** Turk
12D3 **Seldovia** USA
100B3 **Selebi Pikwe** Botswana
6H3 **Selfoss** Iceland
95B2 **Selima Oasis** Suda
5J4 **Selkirk** Can
42C2 **Selkirk** Scot

13D2 **Selkirk Mts** Can
22C2 **Selma** California, USA
50B2 **Selouane** Mor
12H2 **Selous,Mt** Can
78B3 **Selta Karimata** *Str* Indon
32C5 **Selvas** Region, Brazil
07D3 **Selwyn** Aust
4E3 **Selwyn Mts** Can
78C4 **Semarang** Indon
61E2 **Semenov** Russian Fed
12C3 **Semidi Is** USA
60E3 **Semiluki** Russian Fed
19A2 **Seminole** Oklahoma, USA
17B1 **Seminole,L** USA
65K4 **Semipalatinsk** Kazakhstan
79B3 **Semirara Is** Phil
90B3 **Semirom** Iran
78C2 **Semitau** Indon
90B2 **Semnān** Iran
46C2 **Semois** *R* Belg
23B2 **Sempoala** Hist Site, Mexico
32D5 **Sena Madureira** Brazil
00B2 **Senanga** Zambia
19C3 **Senatobia** USA
74E3 **Sendai** Honshū, Japan
74C4 **Sendai** Kyūshū, Japan
85D4 **Sendwha** India
15C2 **Seneca Falls** USA
97A3 **Senegal** Republic, Africa
97A3 **Sénégal** *R* Maur Sen
1G1 **Senekal** S Africa
31D4 **Senhor do Bonfim** Brazil
52B2 **Senigallia** Italy
52C2 **Senj** Croatia
69E4 **Senkaku Gunto** *Is* Japan
46B2 **Senlis** France
99D1 **Sennar** Sudan
7C5 **Senneterre** Can
49C2 **Sens** France
54A1 **Senta** Serbia, Yugos
98C3 **Sentery** Zaïre
13C2 **Sentinel Peak** *Mt* Can
85D4 **Seoni** India
Seoul = Soul
0B2 **Separation Pt** NZ
6D2 **Sepone** Laos
7D4 **Sept-Iles** Can
5A2 **Séquédine** Niger
21B2 **Sequoia** Nat Pk, USA
71D4 **Seram** *I* Indon
78B4 **Serang** Indon
78B2 **Serasan** *I* Indon
54A2 **Serbia** Republic, Yugos
61F3 **Serdobsk** Russian Fed
7C5 **Seremban** Malay
9D3 **Serengeti Nat Pk** Tanz
0C2 **Serenje** Zambia
9D3 **Seret** *R* Ukraine
1G2 **Sergach** Russian Fed
5H3 **Sergino** Russian Fed
1D4 **Sergipe** State, Brazil
0E2 **Segiyev Posad** Russian Fed
8C2 **Seria** Brunei
8C2 **Serian** Malay
5B3 **Sérifos** *I* Greece
7C2 **Serio** *R* Italy
5B2 **Serir Calanscio** *Desert* Libya
6C2 **Sermaize-les-Bains** France
1D4 **Sermata** *I* Indon
1H3 **Sernovodsk** Russian Fed
5H4 **Serov** Russian Fed
0B3 **Serowe** Botswana
0A2 **Serpa** Port
60E3 **Serpukhov** Russian Fed
35B2 **Serra da Canastra** *Mts* Brazil
50A1 **Serra da Estrela** *Mts* Port
35B2 **Serra da Mantiqueira** *Mts* Brazil
35A1 **Serra da Mombuca** Brazil
35C1 **Serra do Cabral** *Mt* Brazil
33F5 **Serra do Cachimbo** *Mts* Brazil
35A1 **Serra do Caiapó** *Mts* Brazil
35A2 **Serra do Cantu** *Mts* Brazil
35C2 **Serra do Caparaó** *Mts* Brazil
31C5 **Serra do Chifre** Brazil
35C1 **Serra do Espinhaço** *Mts* Brazil
35B2 **Serra do Mar** *Mts* Brazil
35A2 **Serra do Mirante** *Mts* Brazil
33G3 **Serra do Navio** Brazil
35B2 **Serra do Paranapiacaba** *Mts* Brazil
33F6 **Serra dos Caiabis** *Mts* Brazil
35A2 **Serra dos Dourados** *Mts* Brazil
33E6 **Serra dos Parecis** *Mts* Brazil
35B1 **Serra dos Pilões** *Mts* Brazil
35A1 **Serra Dourada** *Mts* Brazil
33F6 **Serra Formosa** *Mts* Brazil
55B2 **Sérrai** Greece
25D3 **Serrana Bank** *Is* Caribbean S
51B1 **Serrana de Cuenca** *Mts* Spain
35A1 **Serranópolis** Brazil
33E3 **Serra Pacaraima** *Mts* Brazil/Ven
33E3 **Serra Parima** *Mts* Brazil
33G3 **Serra Tumucumaque** Brazil
46B2 **Serre** *R* France
34B2 **Serrezuela** Arg
31D4 **Serrinha** Brazil
6G3 **Serrmilik** Greenland
35C1 **Serro** Brazil
35A2 **Sertanópolis** Brazil
72A3 **Sêrtar** China
78C3 **Seruyan** *R* Indon
100A2 **Sesfontein** Namibia
100B2 **Sesheke** Zambia
47B2 **Sestriere** Italy
74D2 **Setana** Japan
49C3 **Sète** France
35C1 **Sete Lagoas** Brazil
96C1 **Sétif** Alg
75B1 **Seto** Japan
75A2 **Seto Naikai** *S* Japan
96B1 **Settat** Mor
42C2 **Settle** Eng
5G4 **Settler** Can
50A2 **Sêtúbal** Port
93E1 **Sevan,Oz** *L* Armenia
60D5 **Sevastopol'** Ukraine
7B4 **Severn** *R* Can
43C3 **Severn** *R* Eng
1B9 **Severnaya Zemlya** *I* Russian Fed
63C2 **Severo-Baykalskoye Nagorye** *Mts* Russian Fed
60E4 **Severo Donets** Ukraine
64E3 **Severodvinsk** Russian Fed
64H3 **Severo Sos'va** *R* Russian Fed
8B3 **Sevier** *R* USA
8B3 **Sevier L** USA
50A2 **Sevilla** Spain
Seville = Sevilla
54C2 **Sevlievo** Bulg
97A4 **Sewa** *R* Sierra Leone
12E2 **Seward** Alaska, USA
18A1 **Seward** Nebraska, USA
12A1 **Seward Pen** USA
13D1 **Sexsmith** Can
89K8 **Seychelles** *Is* Indian O
38C1 **Seyðisfjörður** Iceland
92C2 **Seyhan** Turk
60E3 **Seym** *R* Russian Fed
108C3 **Seymour** Aust
16C2 **Seymour** Connecticut, USA
14A3 **Seymour** Indiana, USA
46B2 **Sézanne** France
96D1 **Sfax** Tunisia
54C1 **Sfînto Gheorghe** Rom
56A2 **'s-Gravenhage** Neth
72B3 **Shaanxi** Province, China
98C3 **Shabunda** Zaïre
82B2 **Shache** China
112C9 **Shackleton Ice Shelf** Ant
85B3 **Shadadkot** Pak
91B3 **Shādhām** *R* Iran
43C4 **Shaftesbury** Eng
29G8 **Shag Rocks** *Is* South Georgia
90A3 **Shāhabād** Iran
94C2 **Shahbā** Syria
91C3 **Shahdap** Iran
86A2 **Shahdol** India
90A2 **Shāhīn Dezh** Iran
90C3 **Shāh Kūh** Iran
91C3 **Shahr-e Bābak** Iran
Shahresa = Qomisheh
90B3 **Shahr Kord** Iran
87B1 **Shājābād** India
84D3 **Shājahānpur** India
85D4 **Shājāpur** India
61F4 **Shakhty** Russian Fed
61G2 **Shakhun'ya** Russian Fed
97C4 **Shaki** Nig
12B2 **Shaktoolik** USA
61J2 **Shamary** Russian Fed
99D2 **Shambe** Sudan
16A2 **Shamokin** USA
16B1 **Shandaken** USA
72D2 **Shandong** Province, China
73C5 **Shangchuan Dao** *I* China
72C1 **Shangdu** China
73E3 **Shanghai** China
72C3 **Shangnan** China
100B2 **Shangombo** Zambia
73D4 **Shangra** China
73B5 **Shangsi** China
72C3 **Shang Xian** China
41B3 **Shannon** *R* Irish Rep
72D3 **Shanqiu** China
74B2 **Shansonggang** China
63F2 **Shantarskiye Ostrova** *I* Russian Fed
73D5 **Shantou** China
72C2 **Shanxi** Province, China
72D3 **Shan Xian** China
73C5 **Shaoguan** China
73E4 **Shaoxing** China
73C4 **Shaoyang** China
44C2 **Shapinsay** *I* Scot
94C2 **Shaqqā** Syria
72A1 **Sharhulsan** Mongolia
90C2 **Sharīfābād** Iran
91C4 **Sharjah** UAE
106A3 **Shark B** Aust
90C2 **Sharlauk** Turkmenistan
94B2 **Sharon,Plain of** Israel
61G2 **Sharya** Russian Fed
99D2 **Shashemanē** Eth
73C3 **Shashi** China
20B2 **Shasta L** USA
20B2 **Shasta,Mt** USA
93E3 **Shaṭṭ al Gharrat** *R* Iraq
94B3 **Shaubak** Jordan
13F3 **Shaunavon** Can
22C2 **Shaver L** USA
16B2 **Shawangunk Mt** USA
15D1 **Shawinigan** Can
19A2 **Shawnee** Oklahoma, USA
73D4 **Sha Xian** China
106B3 **Shay Gap** Aust
94C2 **Shaykh Miskīn** Syria
99E1 **Shaykh 'Uthmān** Yemen
60E3 **Shchekino** Russian Fed
60E3 **Shchigry** Russian Fed
60D3 **Shchors** Ukraine
65J4 **Shchuchinsk** Kazakhstan
99E2 **Shebele** *R* Eth
14A2 **Sheboygan** USA
98B2 **Shebshi** *Mts* Nig
12F1 **Sheenjek** *R* USA
45C1 **Sheep Haven** *Estuary* Irish Rep
43E4 **Sheerness** Eng
94B2 **Shefar'am** Israel
42D3 **Sheffield** Eng
84C2 **Shekhupura** Pak
13B1 **Shelagyote Peak** *Mt* Can
16C1 **Shelburne Falls** USA
14A2 **Shelby** Michigan, USA
8B2 **Shelby** Montana, USA
14A3 **Shelbyville** Indiana, USA
12H2 **Sheldon,Mt** Can
12D3 **Shelikof Str** USA
109D2 **Shellharbour** Aust
111A3 **Shelter Pt** NZ
20B1 **Shelton** USA
93E1 **Shemakha** Azerbaijan
18A1 **Shenandoah** USA
15C3 **Shenandoah** *R* USA
15C3 **Shenandoah Nat Pk** USA
97C4 **Shendam** Nig
95C2 **Shendi** Sudan
72C2 **Shenmu** China
72E1 **Shenyang** China
73C5 **Shenzhen** China
85D3 **Sheopur** India
59D2 **Shepetovka** Ukraine
108C3 **Shepparton** Aust
6B2 **Sherard,C** Can
43C4 **Sherborne** Eng
97A4 **Sherbro I** Sierra Leone
15D1 **Sherbrooke** Can
85C3 **Shergarh** India
19B3 **Sheridan** Arkansas, USA
8C2 **Sheridan** Wyoming, USA
19A3 **Sherman** USA
56B2 **s-Hertogenbosh** Neth
12H3 **Sheslay** Can
40C1 **Shetland** *Is* Scot
Shevchenko = Aktau
91B4 **Sheyk Sho'eyb** *I* Iran
69H2 **Shiashkotan** *I* Russian Fed
84B1 **Shibarghan** Afghan
74D3 **Shibata** Japan
95C1 **Shibin el Kom** Egypt
75B1 **Shibukawa** Japan
72C2 **Shijiazhuang** China
84B3 **Shikarpur** Pak
67G3 **Shikoku** *I* Japan
75A2 **Shikoku-sanchi** *Mts* Japan
86B1 **Shiliguri** India
68D1 **Shilka** Russian Fed
68D1 **Shilka** *R* Russian Fed
16B2 **Shillington** USA
86C1 **Shillong** India
61F3 **Shilovo** Russian Fed
75A2 **Shimabara** Japan

75B2 **Shimada** Japan
69E1 **Shimanovsk** Russian Fed
74D3 **Shimizu** Japan
84D2 **Shimla** India
75B2 **Shimoda** Japan
87B2 **Shimoga** India
74C4 **Shimonoseki** Japan
75B1 **Shinano** *R* Japan
91C5 **Shināş** Oman
74D4 **Shingū** Japan
75C1 **Shinjō** Japan
74D3 **Shinminato** Japan
94C1 **Shinshār** Syria
99D3 **Shinyanga** Tanz
74E3 **Shiogama** Japan
75B2 **Shiono-misaki** *C* Japan
73A5 **Shiping** China
16A2 **Shippensburg** USA
72B3 **Shiquan** China
75C1 **Shirakawa** Japan
75B1 **Shirane-san** *Mt* Japan
75B1 **Shirani-san** *Mt* Japan
91B4 **Shīraz** Iran
90B3 **Shīr Kūh** Iran
75B1 **Shirotori** Japan
90C2 **Shirvān** Iran
12A1 **Shishmaref** USA
12A1 **Shishmaref Inlet** USA
4B3 **Shishmaret** USA
72B2 **Shitanjing** China
14A3 **Shively** USA
85D3 **Shivpuri** India
94B3 **Shivta** *Hist Site* Israel
101C2 **Shiwa Ngandu** Zambia
72C3 **Shiyan** China
72B2 **Shizuishan** China
75B1 **Shizuoka** Japan
54A2 **Shkodër** Alb
109D2 **Shoalhaven** *R* Aust
75A2 **Shobara** Japan
87B2 **Shoranūr** India
87B1 **Shorāpur** India
21B2 **Shoshone Mts** USA
60D3 **Shostka** Ukraine
19B3 **Shreveport** USA
43C3 **Shrewsbury** Eng
43C3 **Shropshire** County, Eng
72E1 **Shuanglia** China
69F2 **Shuangyashan** China
61J4 **Shubar-Kuduk** Kazakhstan
72D2 **Shu He** *R* China
73A4 **Shuicheng** China
84C3 **Shujaabad** Pak
85D4 **Shujālpur** India
68B2 **Shule He** China
54C2 **Shumen** Bulg
61G2 **Shumerlya** Russian Fed
73D4 **Shuncheng** China
12C1 **Shungnak** USA
72C2 **Shuo Xian** China
91C4 **Shūr Gaz** Iran
100B2 **Shurugwi** Zim
13D2 **Shuswap L** Can
61F2 **Shuya** Russian Fed
12D3 **Shuyak I** USA
82D3 **Shwebo** Burma
76B2 **Shwegyin** Burma
84A2 **Siah Koh** *Mts* Afghan
84C2 **Sialkot** Pak
Sian = Xi'an
79C4 **Siarao** *I* Phil
79B4 **Şiaton** Phil
58C1 **Šiauliai** Lithuania
65G4 **Sibay** Russian Fed
101H1 **Şibayi L** S Africa
52C2 **Šibenik** Croatia
70A4 **Siberut** *I* Indon
84B3 **Sibi** Pak
68C1 **Sibirskoye** Russian Fed
98B3 **Sibiti** Congo
99D3 **Sibiti** *R* Tanz
54B1 **Sibiu** Rom
70A3 **Sibolga** Indon
86C1 **Sibsāgār** India
78C2 **Sibu** Malay
79B4 **Sibuguay B** Phil
98B2 **Sibut** CAR
79B3 **Sibuyan** *I* Phil
79B3 **Sibuyan S** Phil
73A3 **Sichuan** Province, China
53B3 **Sicilia** *I* Medit S
53B3 **Sicilian** *Chan* Italy/Tunisia
Sicily = Sicilia
32C6 **Sicuani** Peru
85C4 **Siddhapur** India
87B1 **Siddipet** India
86A2 **Sidhi** India
95B1 **Sidi Barrani** Egypt
96B1 **Sidi Bel Abbès** Alg
96B1 **Sidi Kacem** Mor
44C3 **Sidlaw Hills** Scot
112B5 **Sidley,Mt** Ant
20B1 **Sidney** Can
8C2 **Sidney** Nebraska, USA
15C2 **Sidney** New York, USA
14B2 **Sidney** Ohio, USA
17B1 **Sidney Lanier,L** USA
Sidon = Săida
58C2 **Siedlce** Pol
46D1 **Sieg** *R* Germany
46D1 **Siegburg** Germany
46D1 **Siegen** Germany
76C3 **Siem Reap** Camb
52B2 **Siena** Italy
58B2 **Sierpc** Pol
23B2 **Sierra Andrés Tuxtla** Mexico
34B3 **Sierra Auca Mahuida** *Mts* Arg
9C3 **Sierra Blanca** USA
51B1 **Sierra de Albarracin** *Mts* Spain
50B2 **Sierra de Alcaraz** *Mts* Spain
34B2 **Sierra de Cordoba** *Mts* Arg
50A1 **Sierra de Gredos** *Mts* Spain
50A2 **Sierra de Guadalupe** *Mts* Spain
50B1 **Sierra de Guadarrama** *Mts* Spain
51B1 **Sierra de Guara** *Mts* Spain
51B1 **Sierra de Gudar** *Mts* Spain
23B2 **Sierra de Juárez** Mexico
34C3 **Sierra de la Ventana** *Mts* Arg
51C1 **Sierra del Codi** *Mts* Spain
34B2 **Sierra del Morro** *Mt* Arg
34B3 **Sierra del Nevado** *Mts* Arg
24B2 **Sierra de los Alamitos** *Mts* Mexico
50B2 **Sierra de los Filabres** Spain
23A1 **Sierra de los Huicholes** Mexico
23B2 **Sierra de Miahuatlán** Mexico
23A1 **Sierra de Morones** *Mts* Mexico
50A2 **Sierra de Ronda** *Mts* Spain
34B2 **Sierra de San Luis** *Mts* Arg
50B2 **Sierra de Segura** *Mts* Spain
50B1 **Sierra de Urbion** *Mts* Spain
34B2 **Sierra de Uspallata** *Mts* Arg
34B2 **Sierra de Valle Fértil** *Mts* Arg
23B2 **Sierra de Zongolica** Mexico
34C2 **Sierra Grande** *Mts* Arg
97A4 **Sierra Leone** Republic, Africa
97A4 **Sierra Leone,C** Sierra Leone
79B2 **Sierra Madre** *Mts* Phil
23A2 **Sierra Madre del Sur** *Mts* Mexico
24B2 **Sierra Madre Occidental** *Mts* Mexico
24C2 **Sierra Madre Oriental** *Mts* Mexico
34B2 **Sierra Malanzan** *Mts* Arg
9C4 **Sierra Mojada** Mexico
50A2 **Sierra Morena** *Mts* Spain
50B2 **Sierra Nevada** *Mts* Spain
21A2 **Sierra Nevada** *Mts* USA
32C1 **Sierra Nevada de Santa Marta** *Mts* Colombia
34B2 **Sierra Pié de Palo** *Mts* Arg
47B1 **Sierre** Switz
55B3 **Sífnos** *I* Greece
59C3 **Sighetu Marmaţiei** Rom
54B1 **Sighişoara** Rom
38B1 **Siglufjörður** Iceland
50B1 **Sigüenza** Spain
97B3 **Siguiri** Guinea
Sihanoukville = Kompong Som
85E4 **Sihora** India
93D2 **Siirt** Turk
68B3 **Sikai Hu** *L* China
85D3 **Sīkar** India
84B2 **Sikaram** *Mt* Afghan
97B3 **Sikasso** Mali
18C2 **Sikeston** USA
55C3 **Síkinos** *I* Greece
55B3 **Sikionía** Greece
86B1 **Sikkim** State, India
50A1 **Sil** *R* Spain
47D1 **Silandro** Italy
23A1 **Silao** Mexico
79B3 **Silay** Phil
86C2 **Silchar** India
96C2 **Silet** Alg
86A1 **Silgarhi** Nepal
92B2 **Silifke** Turk
82C2 **Siling Co** *L* China
54C2 **Silistra** Bulg
39F7 **Silkeborg** Den
47E1 **Sillian** Austria
18B2 **Siloam Springs** USA
19B3 **Silsbee** USA
95A3 **Şiltou** *Well* Chad
58C1 **Šilute** Lithuania
93D2 **Silvan** Turk
35B1 **Silvania** Brazil
85C4 **Silvassa** India
21B2 **Silver City** Nevada, USA
9C3 **Silver City** New Mexico, USA
20B2 **Silver Lake** USA
16A3 **Silver Spring** USA
13B2 **Silverthrone Mt** Can
108B2 **Silverton** Aust
47C1 **Silvretta** *Mts* Austria/Switz
78C2 **Simanggang** Malay
76C1 **Simao** China
90A3 **Simareh** *R* Iran
55C3 **Simav** Turk
55C3 **Simav** *R* Turk
61G3 **Simbirsk** Russian Fed
15C2 **Simcoe,L** Can
70A3 **Simeulue** *I* Indon
60D5 **Simferopol'** Ukraine
55C3 **Sími** *I* Greece
46D1 **Simmern** Germany
13B2 **Simoon Sound** Can
49D2 **Simplon** *Mt* Switz
47C1 **Simplon** *P* Switz
4C2 **Simpson,C** USA
106C3 **Simpson Desert** Au
6B3 **Simpson Pen** Can
39G7 **Simrishamn** Swede
69H2 **Simushir** *I* Russian Fed
99E2 **Sina Dhaqa** Somali
92B4 **Sinai** *Pen* Egypt
32B2 **Sincelejo** Colombia
17B1 **Sinclair,L** USA
85D3 **Sind** *R* India
85B3 **Sindh** Region, Pak
55C3 **Sindirği** Turk
86B2 **Sindri** India
50A2 **Sines** Port
99D1 **Singa** Sudan
77C5 **Singapore** Republic S E Asia
77C5 **Singapore,Str of** S E Asia
78D4 **Singaraja** Indon
99D3 **Singida** Tanz
78B2 **Singkawang** Indon
109D2 **Singleton** Aust
78A3 **Singtep** *I* Indon
76B1 **Singu** Burma
53A2 **Siniscola** Sardgena
93D2 **Sinjár** Iraq
84B2 **Sinkai Hills** *Mts* Afghan
95C3 **Sinkat** Sudan
82C1 **Sinkiang** Autonomous Regio China
33G2 **Sinnamary** French Guiana
92C1 **Sinop** Turk
54B1 **Sîntana** Rom
78C2 **Sintang** Indon
50A2 **Sintra** Port
32B2 **Sinú** *R* Colombia
74A2 **Sinŭiju** N Korea
59B3 **Siofok** Hung
47B1 **Sion** Switz
8D2 **Sioux City** USA
8D2 **Sioux Falls** USA
10A2 **Sioux Lookout** Ca
79B4 **Sipalay** Phil
27L1 **Siparia** Trinidad
69E2 **Siping** China
112B3 **Siple** *Base* Ant
112B5 **Siple I** Ant
79B3 **Sipocot** Phil
70A4 **Sipora** Indon
79B4 **Siquijor** *I* Phil
87B2 **Sira** India
53C3 **Siracusa** Italy
86B2 **Sirajganj** Bang
13C2 **Sir Alexander,Mt**
91B5 **Sīr Banī Yās** *I* UA
106C2 **Sir Edward Pellew Group** *Is* Aust
54C1 **Siret** *R* Rom
12J2 **Sir James McBrien,Mt** Can
87B2 **Sir Kālahasti** India
13D2 **Sir Laurier,Mt** Car
93D2 **Şirnak** Turk
85C4 **Sirohi** India
87B1 **Sironcha** India
85D4 **Sironj** India
55B3 **Síros** *I* Greece
91B4 **Sirri** *I* Iran
84D3 **Sirsa** India
13D2 **Sir Sandford,Mt** C
87A2 **Sirsi** India
95A1 **Sirte Desert** Libya
95A1 **Sirte,G of** Libya
52C1 **Sisak** Croatia
76C2 **Sisaket** Thai
76C3 **Sisophon** Camb
46B2 **Sissonne** France
90D3 **Sistan** Region, Ira Afghan
49D3 **Sisteron** France
63B2 **Sistig Khem** Russian Fed
86A1 **Sītāpur** India
55C3 **Sitia** Greece
4E4 **Sitka** USA
12D3 **Sitkalidak I** USA
12D3 **Sitkinak** *I* USA

76B2 **Sittang** *R* Burma
46C1 **Sittard** Neth
86C2 **Sittwe** Burma
78C4 **Situbondo** Indon
92C2 **Sivas** Turk
93C2 **Siverek** Turk
92B2 **Sivrihisar** Turk
95B2 **Siwa** Egypt
84D2 **Siwalik Range** *Mts* India
86A1 **Siwalik Range** *Mts* Nepal
72D3 **Siyang** China
56C1 **Sjaelland** *I* Den
39G7 **Skagen** Den
39F7 **Skagerrak** *Str* Nor/ Den
20B1 **Skagit** *R* USA
20B1 **Skagit Mt** Can
4E4 **Skagway** USA
39G7 **Skara** Sweden
59C2 **Skarzysko-Kamlenna** Pol
5F4 **Skeena** *R* Can
13B1 **Skeena Mts** Can
4D3 **Skeenjek** *R* USA
42E3 **Skegness** Eng
38H5 **Skellefte** *R* Sweden
38J6 **Skellefteå** Sweden
55B3 **Skíathos** *I* Greece
45B3 **Skibbereen** Irish Rep
5E4 **Skidegate** Can
58C2 **Skiemiewice** Pol
39F7 **Skien** Nor
96C1 **Skikda** Alg
74C4 **Skikoku** *I* Japan
42D3 **Skipton** Eng
55B3 **Skiros** *I* Greece
39F7 **Skive** Den
56B1 **Skjern** Den
6F3 **Skjoldungen** Greenland
14A2 **Skokie** USA
55B3 **Skópelos** *I* Greece
54B2 **Skopje** Macedonia
39G7 **Skövde** Sweden
63E2 **Skovorodino** Russian Fed
4C3 **Skwentna** USA
58B2 **Skwierzyna** Pol
40B2 **Skye** *I* Scot
39G7 **Slagelse** Den
45C2 **Slaney** *R* Irish Rep
54B2 **Slatina** Rom
78C4 **Slaung** Indon
5G3 **Slave** *R* Can
13E1 **Slave Lake** Can
65J4 **Slavgorod** Russian Fed
59D2 **Slavuta** Ukraine
60E4 **Slavyansk** Ukraine
44B3 **Sleat,Sound of** *Chan* Scot
12C2 **Sleetmute** USA
45C2 **Sleeve Bloom** *Mts* Irish Rep
19C3 **Slidell** USA
16B2 **Slide Mt** USA
45B1 **Sligo** County, Irish Rep
41B3 **Sligo** Irish Rep
41B3 **Sligo** *B* Irish Rep
54C2 **Sliven** Bulg
54C2 **Slobozia** Rom
3D3 **Slocan** Can
58D2 **Slonim** Belorussia
43D4 **Slough** Eng
22B2 **Slough** *R* USA
59B3 **Slovakia** Republic, Europe
52B1 **Slovenia** Republic, Europe
56C2 **Slubice** Pol
59D2 **Sluch'** *R* Ukraine
58B2 **Słupsk** Pol
58D2 **Slutsk** Belorussia
58D2 **Slutsk** *R* Belorussia
41A3 **Slyne Head** *Pt* Irish Rep
63C2 **Slyudyanka** Russian Fed
7D4 **Smallwood Res** Can
54B2 **Smederevo** Serbia, Yugos
54B2 **Smederevska Palanka** Serbia, Yugos
60D4 **Smela** Ukraine
15C2 **Smethport** USA
13E1 **Smith** Can
4F3 **Smith Arm** *B* Can
13B2 **Smithers** Can
7C3 **Smith I** Can
13B2 **Smith Sd** Can
15C2 **Smiths Falls** Can
109C4 **Smithton** Aust
13D1 **Smoky** *R* Can
109D2 **Smoky C** Aust
13E2 **Smoky Lake** Can
38F6 **Smøla** *I* Nor
60D3 **Smolensk** Russian Fed
55B2 **Smólikas** *Mt* Greece
54B2 **Smolyan** Bulg
58D2 **Smorgon'** Belorussia
16B3 **Smyrna** Delaware, USA
17B1 **Smyrna** Georgia, USA
42B2 **Snaefell** *Mt* Eng
38B2 **Snafell** *Mt* Iceland
8B2 **Snake** *R* USA
8B2 **Snake River Canyon** USA
56B2 **Sneek** Neth
45B3 **Sneem** Irish Rep
22B2 **Snelling** USA
59B2 **Sněžka** *Mt* Pol/ Czech Republic
38F6 **Snøhetta** *Mt* Nor
20B1 **Snohomish** USA
20B1 **Snoqualmie P** USA
76D3 **Snoul** Camb
43B3 **Snowdon** *Mt* Wales
43B3 **Snowdonia Nat Pk** Wales
4G3 **Snowdrift** Can
5H4 **Snow Lake** Can
108A2 **Snowtown** Aust
109C3 **Snowy Mts** Aust
9C3 **Snyder** USA
74B4 **Soan-kundo** *I* S Korea
99D2 **Sobat** *R* Sudan
31C2 **Sobral** Brazil
58C2 **Sochaczew** Pol
61E5 **Sochi** Russian Fed
9C3 **Socorro** USA
24A3 **Socorro** *I* Mexico
34A2 **Socos** Chile
81D4 **Socotra** *I* Yemen
38K5 **Sodankylä** Fin
39H6 **Soderhamn** Sweden
39H7 **Södertälje** Sweden
99C1 **Sodiri** Sudan
99D2 **Sodo** Eth
46E1 **Soest** Germany
101C2 **Sofala** Mozam
Sofia = Sofiya
54B2 **Sofiya** Bulg
69G4 **Sofu Gan** *I* Japan
32C2 **Sogamoso** Colombia
39F6 **Sognefjorden** *Inlet* Nor
82D2 **Sog Xian** China
95C2 **Sohâg** Egypt
84D3 **Sohīpat** India
46B1 **Soignies** Belg
46B2 **Soissons** France
85C3 **Sojat** India
74A3 **Sŏjosŏn-man** *B* N Korea
92A2 **Söke** Turk
97C4 **Sokodé** Togo
61E2 **Sokol** Russian Fed
58C2 **Sokołka** Pol
97B3 **Sokolo** Mali
6H3 **Søkongens Øy** *I* Greenland
99D1 **Sokota** Eth
97C3 **Sokoto** Nig
97C3 **Sokoto** *R* Nig
111A3 **Solander I** NZ
79B2 **Solano** Phil
87B1 **Solapur** India
47D1 **Solbad Hall** Austria
47D1 **Sölden** Austria
12D2 **Soldotna** USA
26C4 **Soledad** Colombia
43D4 **Solent** *Sd* Eng
46B1 **Solesmes** France
58D2 **Soligorsk** Belorussia
61J2 **Solikamsk** Russian Fed
32C4 **Solimões** *R* Peru
46D1 **Solingen** Germany
38H6 **Sollefteå** Sweden
61H3 **Sol'Iletsk** Russian Fed
70B4 **Solok** Indon
105G4 **Solomon** *Is* Pacific O
47B1 **Solothurn** Switz
39F8 **Soltau** Germany
22B3 **Solvang** USA
42C2 **Solway Firth** *Estuary* Eng/Scot
100B2 **Solwezi** Zambia
75C1 **Sōma** Japan
55C3 **Soma** Turk
81C5 **Somalia** Republic, E Africa
54A1 **Sombor** Serbia, Yugos
107D2 **Somerset** Aust
43C4 **Somerset** County, Eng
16D2 **Somerset** Massachusetts, USA
15C2 **Somerset** Pennsylvania, USA
100B4 **Somerset East** S Africa
6A2 **Somerset I** Can
16B3 **Somers Point** USA
16B2 **Somerville** USA
19A3 **Somerville Res** USA
54B1 **Somes** *R* Rom
46B2 **Somme** Department, France
46B2 **Somme** *R* France
46C2 **Sommesous** France
86A2 **Son** *R* India
74A3 **Sonch'ŏn** N Korea
39F8 **Sønderborg** Den
6E3 **Søndre Strømfjord** Greenland
47C1 **Sondrio** Italy
76D3 **Song Ba** *R* Viet
76D3 **Song Cau** Viet
101C2 **Songea** Tanz
73E3 **Songjiang** China
77C4 **Songkhla** Thai
74B3 **Songnim** N Korea
77C5 **Sông Pahang** *R* Malay
72A3 **Songpan** China
72C1 **Sonid Youqi** China
76C1 **Son La** Viet
85B3 **Sonmiani** Pak
85B3 **Sonmiani Bay** Pak
22A1 **Sonoma** USA
22B2 **Sonora** California, USA
24A2 **Sonora** *R* Mexico
9B3 **Sonoran Desert** USA
22C1 **Sonora P** USA
25D3 **Sonsonate** El Salvador
71E3 **Sonsorol** *I* Pacific O
10B2 **Soo Canals** Can/USA
13C3 **Sooke** Can
58B2 **Sopot** Pol
59B3 **Sopron** Hung
22B2 **Soquel** USA
53B2 **Sora** Italy
94B3 **Sored** *R* Israel
15D1 **Sorel** Can
109C4 **Sorell** Aust
92C2 **Sorgun** Turk
50B1 **Soria** Spain
38J5 **Sørkjosen** Nor
64C2 **Sørksop** *I* Barents S
61H4 **Sor Mertvyy Kultuk** *Plain* Kazakhstan
35B2 **Sorocaba** Brazil
61H3 **Sorochinsk** Russian Fed
71F3 **Soroi** *I* Pacific O
60C4 **Soroki** Moldova
71E4 **Sorong** Indon
71E4 **Sorong** Province, Indon
99D2 **Soroti** Uganda
38J4 **Sørøya** *I* Nor
53B2 **Sorrento** Italy
38K5 **Sorsatunturi** *Mt* Fin
38H5 **Sorsele** Sweden
79B3 **Sorsogon** Phil
38L6 **Sortavala** Russian Fed
74B3 **Sŏsan** S Korea
59B2 **Sosnowiec** Pol
65H4 **Sos'va** Russian Fed
98B2 **Souanké** Congo
97B4 **Soubré** Ivory Coast
16B2 **Souderton** USA
27P2 **Soufrière** St Lucia
27N2 **Soufrière** *Mt* St Vincent and the Grenadines
48C3 **Souillac** France
96C1 **Souk Ahras** Alg
74B3 **Soul** S Korea
51C2 **Soummam** *R* Alg
Sour = Tyr
101G1 **Sources,Mt aux** Lesotho
31D3 **Sousa** Brazil
96D1 **Sousse** Tunisia
100B4 **South Africa** Republic, Africa
16B2 **South Amboy** USA
14B2 **Southampton** Can
43D4 **Southampton** Eng
16C2 **Southampton** USA
6B3 **Southampton I** Can
28F6 **South Atlantic O**
7D4 **South Aulatsivik I** Can
106C3 **South Australia** State, Aust
104E5 **South Australian Basin** Indian O
19C3 **Southaven** USA
17B2 **South Bay** USA
14B1 **South Baymouth** Can
14A2 **South Bend** Indiana, USA
20B1 **South Bend** Washington, USA
16D1 **Southbridge** USA
South Cape = Ka Lae
11B3 **South Carolina** State, USA
70C2 **South China S** S E Asia
8C2 **South Dakota** State, USA
16C1 **South Deerfield** USA
43D4 **South Downs** Eng
109C4 **South East C** Aust
111A2 **Southen Alps** *Mts* NZ
5H4 **Southend** Can
43E4 **Southend-on-Sea** Eng
111A2 **Southern Alps** *Mts* NZ
106A4 **Southern Cross** Aust
5J4 **Southern Indian L** Can
27H2 **Southfield** Jamaica
105G5 **South Fiji Basin** Pacific O
12D2 **South Fork** *R* Alaska, USA
22B1 **South Fork** *R* California, USA
28F8 **South Georgia** *I* S Atlantic O
43C4 **South Glamorgan** County, Wales
14A2 **South Haven** USA
5J3 **South Henik L** Can
104F3 **South Honshu Ridge** Pacific O
111A2 **South I** NZ
16C2 **Southington** USA
74B3 **South Korea** Republic, S E Asia
21A2 **South Lake Tahoe** USA
112C8 **South Magnetic Pole** Ant
17B2 **South Miami** USA
16A3 **South Mt** USA

4F3 **South Nahanni** *R* Can
26G1 **South Negril Pt** Jamaica
103F8 **South Orkney** *Is* Atlantic O
8C2 **South Platte** *R* USA
80E **South Pole** Ant
42C3 **Southport** Eng
27R3 **South Pt** Barbados
16B2 **South River** USA
44C2 **South Ronaldsay** *I* Scot
103G7 **South Sandwich Trench** Atlantic O
22A2 **South San Francisco** USA
5H4 **South Saskatchewan** *R* Can
42D2 **South Shields** Eng
110B1 **South Taranaki Bight** *B* NZ
44A3 **South Uist** *I* Scot
South West Africa = Namibia
107D5 **South West C** Aust
105J5 **South West Pacific Basin** Pacific O
103D5 **South West Peru Ridge** Pacific O
43D3 **South Yorkshire** County, Eng
58C1 **Sovetsk** Russian Fed
61G2 **Sovetsk** Russian Fed
101G1 **Soweto** S Africa
98B3 **Soyo Congo** Angola
60D3 **Sozh** *R* Belorussia
46C1 **Spa** Belg
50A1 **Spain** Kingdom
Spalato = Split
43D3 **Spalding** Eng
14B1 **Spanish** *R* Can
26B3 **Spanish Town** Jamaica
21B2 **Sparks** USA
11B3 **Spartanburg** USA
55B3 **Spartí** Greece
69F2 **Spassk Dal'niy** Russian Fed
27R3 **Speightstown** Barbados
12E2 **Spenard** USA
14A3 **Spencer** Indiana, USA
8D2 **Spencer** Iowa, USA
6A3 **Spencer Bay** Can
108A3 **Spencer,C** Aust
108A2 **Spencer G** Aust
6C3 **Spencer I** Can
111B2 **Spenser Mts** NZ
45C1 **Sperrin** *Mts* N Ire
44C3 **Spey** *R* Scot
57B3 **Speyer** Germany
27K1 **Speyside** Tobago
47B1 **Spiez** Switz
12F1 **Spike Mt** USA
20C1 **Spirit Lake** USA
5G4 **Spirit River** Can
Spitsbergen = Svalbard
64C2 **Spitsbergen** *I* Barents S
57C3 **Spittal** Austria
38F6 **Spjelkavik** Nor
52C2 **Split** Croatia
47C1 **Splügen** Switz
20C1 **Spokane** USA
55C3 **Sporádhes** *Is* Greece
20C2 **Spray** USA
56C2 **Spree** *R* Germany
100A3 **Springbok** S Africa
18B2 **Springdale** USA
10B3 **Springfield** Illinois, USA
10C2 **Springfield** Massachusetts, USA
18B2 **Springfield** Missouri, USA
14B3 **Springfield** Ohio, USA
20B2 **Springfield** Oregon, USA
15D2 **Springfield** Vermont, USA
100B4 **Springfontein** S Africa
101G1 **Springs** S Africa
41D3 **Spurn Head** *Pt* Eng
13C3 **Squamish** Can
60E3 **Sredne-Russkaya Vozvyshennost** *Upland* Russian Fed
63B1 **Sredne Sibirskoye Ploskogorve** *Tableland* Russian Fed
61J2 **Sredniy Ural** *Mts* Russian Fed
76D3 **Srepok** *R* Camb
68D1 **Sretensk** Russian Fed
76C3 **Sre Umbell** Camb
83C5 **Sri Lanka** Republic, S Asia
84C2 **Srinagar** Pak
87A1 **Śrīvardhan** India
58B2 **Šroda Wlk.** Pol
30H6 **Sta Clara** *I* Chile
32J7 **Sta Cruz** *I* Ecuador
56B2 **Stade** Germany
44A3 **Staffa** *I* Scot
43C3 **Stafford** County, Eng
43C3 **Stafford** Eng
16C2 **Stafford Springs** USA
Stalingrad = Volgograd
6A1 **Stallworthy,C** Can
59C2 **Stalowa Wola** Pol
32J7 **Sta Maria** *I* Ecuador
16C2 **Stamford** Connecticut, USA
16B1 **Stamford** New York, USA
100A3 **Stampriet** Namibia
101G1 **Standerton** S Africa
14B2 **Standish** USA
101H1 **Stanger** S Africa
22B2 **Stanislaus** *R* USA
54B2 **Stanke Dimitrov** Bulg
109C4 **Stanley** Aust
29E6 **Stanley** Falkland Is
87B2 **Stanley Res** India
Stanleyville = Kisangani
25D3 **Stann Creek** Belize
63E2 **Stanovoy Khrebet** *Mts* Russian Fed
47C1 **Stans** Switz
109D1 **Stanthorpe** Aust
59C2 **Starachowice** Pol
54B2 **Stara Planiná** *Mts* Bulg
60D2 **Staraya Russa** Russian Fed
54C2 **Stara Zagora** Bulg
58B2 **Stargard Szczecinski** Pol
19C3 **Starkville** USA
57C3 **Starnberg** Germany
58B2 **Starogard Gdanski** Pol
59D3 **Starokonstantinov** Ukraine
43C4 **Start Pt** Eng
60E3 **Staryy Oskol** Russian Fed
15C2 **State College** USA
16B2 **Staten I** USA
17B1 **Statesboro** USA
15C3 **Staunton** USA
39F7 **Stavanger** Nor
46C1 **Stavelot** Belg
61F4 **Stavropol'** Russian Fed
108B3 **Stawell** Aust
58B2 **Stawno** Pol
20B2 **Stayton** USA
12B2 **Stebbins** USA
12F2 **Steele,Mt** Can
16A2 **Steelton** USA
20C2 **Steens Mt** USA
6E2 **Steenstrups Gletscher** *Gl* Greenland
4H2 **Stefansson I** Can
101H1 **Stegi** Swaziland
47D1 **Steinach** Austria
8D2 **Steinback** Can
38G6 **Steinkjer** Nor
13C2 **Stein Mt** Can
23B2 **Stemaco** Mexico
46C2 **Stenay** France
56C2 **Stendal** Germany
110B2 **Stephens,C** NZ
108B2 **Stephens Creek** Aust
14A1 **Stephenson** USA
12H3 **Stephens Pass** USA
7E5 **Stephenville** Can
100B4 **Sterkstroom** S Africa
8C2 **Sterling** Colorado, USA
14B2 **Sterling Heights** USA
61J3 **Sterlitamak** Russian Fed
13E2 **Stettler** Can
14B2 **Steubenville** USA
4D3 **Stevens Village** USA
13B1 **Stewart** Can
21B2 **Stewart** USA
12G2 **Stewart** *R* Can
12G2 **Stewart Crossing** Can
111A3 **Stewart I** NZ
107F1 **Stewart Is** Solomon Is
4E3 **Stewart River** Can
16A3 **Stewartstown** USA
101G1 **Steyn** S Africa
57C3 **Steyr** Austria
12G3 **Stika** USA
12H3 **Stikine** *R* Can
12H3 **Stikine Ranges** *Mts* Can
18A2 **Stillwater** Oklahoma, USA
21B2 **Stillwater Range** *Mts* USA
108A2 **Stirling** Aust
44C3 **Stirling** Scot
16C1 **Stockbridge** USA
59B3 **Stockerau** Austria
39H7 **Stockholm** Sweden
42C3 **Stockport** Eng
22B2 **Stockton** California, USA
42D2 **Stockton** Eng
18B2 **Stockton L** USA
43C3 **Stoke-on-Trent** Eng
38A2 **Stokkseyri** Iceland
38G5 **Stokmarknes** Nor
39K8 **Stolbtsy** Belorussia
58D2 **Stolin** Belorussia
16B3 **Stone Harbor** USA
44C3 **Stonehaven** Scot
19A3 **Stonewall** USA
12D2 **Stony** *R* USA
38H5 **Storavan** *L* Sweden
38G6 **Støren** Nor
109C4 **Storm B** Aust
44A2 **Stornoway** Scot
59D3 **Storozhinets** Ukraine
16C2 **Storrs** USA
38G6 **Stors168jon** *L* Sweden
38H5 **Storuman** Sweden
16D1 **Stoughton** USA
43E3 **Stowmarket** Eng
45C1 **Strablane** N Ire
109C4 **Strahan** Aust
56C2 **Stralsund** Germany
38F6 **Stranda** Nor
39H7 **Strängnäs** Sweden
42B2 **Stranraer** Scot
49D2 **Strasbourg** France
15C3 **Strasburg** USA
14B2 **Stratford** Can
16C2 **Stratford** Connecticut, USA
110B1 **Stratford** NZ
43D3 **Stratford-on-Avon** Eng
108A3 **Strathalbyn** Aust
42B2 **Strathclyde** Region, Scot
13E2 **Strathmore** Can
18C1 **Streator** USA
47C2 **Stresa** Italy
53C3 **Stretto de Messina** *Str* Italy/Sicily
38D3 **Streymoy** Føroyar
53C3 **Stroboli** *I* Italy
6E3 **Strømfjord** Greenland
44C2 **Stromness** Scot
18A1 **Stromsburg** USA
38H6 **Stromsund** Sweden
38G6 **Ströms Vattudal** *L* Sweden
44C2 **Stronsay** *I* Scot
43C4 **Stroud** Eng
16B2 **Stroudsburg** USA
54B2 **Struma** *R* Bulg
43B3 **Strumble Head** *Pt* Wales
55B2 **Strumica** Macedoni
59C3 **Stryy** Ukraine
59C3 **Stryy** *R* Ukraine
108B1 **Strzelecki Creek** *R* Aust
17B2 **Stuart** Florida, USA
13C2 **Stuart** *R* Can
12B2 **Stuart I** USA
13C2 **Stuart L** Can
47D1 **Stubaier Alpen** *Mts* Austria
76D3 **Stung Sen** Camb
76D3 **Stung Treng** Camb
52A2 **Stura** *R* Italy
112C7 **Sturge I** Ant
14A2 **Sturgeon Bay** USA
14C1 **Sturgeon Falls** Can
18C2 **Sturgis** Kentucky, USA
14A2 **Sturgis** Michigan, USA
106B2 **Sturt Creek** *R* Aust
108B1 **Sturt Desert** Aust
100B4 **Stuttemeim** S Afric
19B3 **Stuttgart** USA
57B3 **Stuttgart** Germany
38A1 **Stykkishólmur** Iceland
59D2 **Styr'** *R* Ukraine
35C1 **Suaçuí Grande** *R* Brazil
81B4 **Suakin** Sudan
73E5 **Su-ao** Taiwan
34C2 **Suardi** Arg
78B2 **Subi** *I* Indon
54A1 **Subotica** Serbia, Yugos
60C4 **Suceava** Rom
45B2 **Suck** *R* Irish Rep
30C2 **Sucre** Bol
35A1 **Sucuriú** *R* Brazil
98C1 **Sudan** Republic, Africa
14B1 **Sudbury** Can
43E3 **Sudbury** Eng
99C2 **Sudd** *Swamp* Sud
33F2 **Suddie** Guyana
98C2 **Sue** *R* Sudan
4H2 **Suerdrup Is** Can
92B4 **Suez** Egypt
92B3 **Suez Canal** Egypt
92B4 **Suez,G of** Egypt
16B2 **Suffern** USA
43E3 **Suffolk** County, Er
109D2 **Sugarloaf Pt** Aust
91C5 **Suhār** Oman
68C1 **Sühbaatar** Mongo
84B3 **Sui** Pak
72C2 **Suide** China
69E2 **Suihua** China
73B3 **Suining** China
46C2 **Suippes** France
41B3 **Suir** *R* Irish Rep
73C3 **Sui Xian** China
72E1 **Suizhong** China
85C3 **Sujāngarh** India
78B4 **Sukabumi** Indon
78C3 **Sukadana** Borneo, Indon
78B4 **Sukadana** Sumatr Indon
74E3 **Sukagawa** Japan
78C3 **Sukaraya** Indon
60E3 **Sukhinichi** Russian Fed
61F2 **Sukhona** *R* Russian Fed
61F5 **Sukhumi** Georgia
6E3 **Sukkertoppen** Greenland

6E3 **Sukkertoppen** *L* Greenland
38L6 **Sukkozero** Russian Fed
85B3 **Sukkur** Pak
87C1 **Sukma** India
95A2 **Sūknah** Libya
00A3 **Sukses** Namibia
75A2 **Sukumo** Japan
13C1 **Sukunka** *R* Can
60E3 **Sula** *R* Russian Fed
84B3 **Sulaiman Range** *Mts* Pak
70C4 **Sulawesi** *I* Indon
54C1 **Sulina** Rom
38H5 **Sulitjelma** Nor
32A4 **Sullana** Peru
18B2 **Sullivan** USA
13B2 **Sullivan Bay** Can
13E2 **Sullivan L** Can
52B2 **Sulmona** Italy
19B3 **Sulphur** Louisiana, USA
19A3 **Sulphur** Oklahoma, USA
19A3 **Sulphur Springs** USA
86A1 **Sultānpur** India
79B4 **Sulu Arch** Phil
70C3 **Sulu S** Philip
30D4 **Sumampa** Arg
70B4 **Sumatera** *I* Indon
70C4 **Sumba** *I* Indon
78D4 **Sumbawa** *I* Indon
78D4 **Sumbawa Besar** Indon
99D3 **Sumbawanga** Tanz
00A2 **Sumbe** Angola
44E2 **Sumburgh Head** *Pt* Scot
78C4 **Sumenep** Indon
69G3 **Sumisu** *I* Japan
13D3 **Summerland** Can
5F4 **Summit Lake** Can
21B2 **Summit Mt** USA
11B2 **Sumner,L** NZ
75A2 **Sumoto** Japan
17B1 **Sumter** USA
60D3 **Sumy** Ukraine
16A2 **Sunbury** USA
34C2 **Sunchales** Arg
74B3 **Sunch'ŏn** N Korea
74B4 **Sunch'ŏn** S Korea
36A2 **Sundargarh** India
36B2 **Sunderbans** *Swamp* India
42D2 **Sunderland** Eng
13E2 **Sundre** Can
15C1 **Sundridge** Can
38H6 **Sundsvall** Sweden
38D3 **Suduroy** Føroyar
78D3 **Sungaianyar** Indon
78A3 **Sungaisalak** Indon
20C1 **Sunnyside** USA
21A2 **Sunnyvale** USA
53D1 **Suntar** Russian Fed
97B4 **Sunyani** Ghana
75A2 **Suō-nada** *B* Japan
38K6 **Suonejoki** Fin
36B1 **Supaul** India
18A1 **Superior** Nebraska, USA
10A2 **Superior** Wisconsin, USA
10B2 **Superior,L** Can/USA
76C3 **Suphan Buri** Thai
93D2 **Süphan Dağ** Turk
71E4 **Supiori** *I* Indon
93E3 **Suq ash Suyukh** Iraq
72D3 **Suqian** China
Suqutra = Socotra
91C5 **Sūr** Oman
61G3 **Sura** *R* Russian Fed
78C4 **Surabaya** Indon
75B2 **Suraga-wan** *B* Japan
78C4 **Surakarta** Indon
09C1 **Surat** Aust
85C4 **Sūrat** India
84C3 **Sūratgarh** India
77B4 **Surat Thani** Thai
85C4 **Surendranagar** India
16B3 **Surf City** USA
64J3 **Surgut** Russian Fed
87B1 **Suriāpet** India
9D2 **Sürich** Switz
79C4 **Surigao** Phil
76C3 **Surin** Thai
33F3 **Surinam** Republic, S America
43D4 **Surrey** County, Eng
47C1 **Sursee** Switz
95A1 **Surt** Libya
38A2 **Surtsey** *I* Iceland
78A3 **Surulangan** Indon
47B2 **Susa** Italy
75A2 **Susa** Japan
75A2 **Susaki** Japan
21A1 **Susanville** USA
47D1 **Süsch** Switz
12E2 **Susitna** *R* USA
16A3 **Susquehanna** *R* USA
16B2 **Sussex** USA
43D4 **Sussex West** Eng
13B1 **Sustut Peak** *Mt* Can
100B4 **Sutherland** S Africa
84C2 **Sutlej** *R* Pak
21A2 **Sutter Creek** USA
14B3 **Sutton** USA
12C3 **Sutwik I** USA
74D3 **Suwa** Japan
58C2 **Suwałki** Pol
17B2 **Suwannee** *R* USA
94B2 **Suweilih** Jordan
74B3 **Suwŏn** S Korea
72D3 **Su Xian** China
75B1 **Suzaka** Japan
73E3 **Suzhou** China
74D3 **Suzu** Japan
75B2 **Suzuka** Japan
75B1 **Suzu-misaki** *C* Japan
64C2 **Svalbard** *Is* Barents S
59C3 **Svalyava** Ukraine
38G5 **Svartisen** *Mt* Nor
76D3 **Svay Rieng** Camb
38G6 **Sveg** Sweden
39G7 **Svendborg** Den
Sverdlovsk = Yekaterinburg
6A1 **Sverdrup Chan** Can
69F2 **Svetlaya** Russian Fed
58C2 **Svetlogorsk** Russian Fed
39K6 **Svetogorsk** Russian Fed
54B2 **Svetozarevo** Serbia, Yugos
54C2 **Svilengrad** Bulg
58D2 **Svir'** Belorussia
59B3 **Svitavy** Czech Republic
69E1 **Svobodnyy** Russian Fed
38G5 **Svolvaer** Nor
107E3 **Swain Reefs** Aust
17B1 **Swainsboro** USA
100A3 **Swakopmund** Namibia
42D2 **Swale** *R* Eng
70C3 **Swallow Reef** *I* S E Asia
87B2 **Swāmihalli** India
25D3 **Swan** *I* Honduras
43D4 **Swanage** Eng
108B3 **Swan Hill** Aust
13D2 **Swan Hills** Can
13D2 **Swan Hills** *Mts* Can
26A3 **Swan I** Caribbean S
5H4 **Swan River** Can
43C4 **Swansea** Wales
43C4 **Swansea B** Wales
101G1 **Swartruggens** S Africa
Swatow = Shantou
101H1 **Swaziland** Kingdom, S Africa
39G7 **Sweden** Kingdom, N Europe
20B2 **Sweet Home** USA
9C3 **Sweetwater** USA
100B4 **Swellendam** S Africa
59B2 **Świdnica** Pol
58B2 **Świdwin** Pol
58B2 **Świebodzin** Pol
58B2 **Świecie** Pol
5H4 **Swift Current** Can
43D4 **Swindon** Eng
45B2 **Swinford** Irish Rep
56C2 **Świnoujście** Pol
49D2 **Switzerland** Federal Republic, Europe
45C2 **Swords** Irish Rep
109D2 **Sydney** Aust
7D5 **Sydney** Can
64G3 **Syktyvkar** Russian Fed
17A1 **Sylacauga** USA
38G6 **Sylarna** *Mt* Sweden
86C2 **Sylhet** Bang
56B1 **Sylt** *I* Germany
14B2 **Sylvania** USA
112C11 **Syowa** *Base* Ant
Syracuse = Siracusa
15C2 **Syracuse** USA
65H5 **Syr Darya** *R* Kazakhstan
93C2 **Syria** Republic, S W Asia
61J2 **Sysert'** Russian Fed
61G3 **Syzran'** Russian Fed
56C2 **Szczecin** Pol
58B2 **Szczecinek** Pol
58C2 **Szczytno** Pol
59C3 **Szeged** Hung
59B3 **Székesfehérvar** Hung
59B3 **Szekszard** Hung
59B3 **Szolnok** Hung
59B3 **Szombathely** Hung
58B2 **Szprotawa** Pol

T

90C3 **Tabas** Iran
23A1 **Tabasco** Mexico
32D4 **Tabatinga** Brazil
96B2 **Tabelbala** Alg
76C3 **Tabeng** Camb
13E2 **Taber** Can
79B3 **Tablas** *I* Phil
100A4 **Table Mt** S Africa
12F1 **Table Mt** USA
18B2 **Table Rock Res** USA
78B3 **Taboali** Indon
57C3 **Tábor** Czech Republic
99D3 **Tabora** Tanz
97B4 **Tabou** Ivory Coast
90A2 **Tabrīz** Iran
92C4 **Tabūk** S Arabia
23A2 **Tacámbaro** Mexico
82C1 **Tacheng** China
79C3 **Tacloban** Phil
30B2 **Tacna** Peru
8A2 **Tacoma** USA
99E1 **Tadjoura** Djibouti
87B2 **Tādpatri** India
74B3 **Taebaek Sanmaek** *Mts* S Korea
74B3 **Taegu** S Korea
74B4 **Taehŭksan** *I* S Korea
74B3 **Taejŏn** S Korea
51B1 **Tafalla** Spain
96C2 **Tafasaset** *Watercourse* Alg
43C4 **Taff** *R* Wales
94B3 **Tafila** Jordan
60E4 **Taganrog** Ukraine
97A3 **Tagant** Region, Maur
79B4 **Tagbilaran** Phil
96B2 **Taguenout Hagguerete** *Well* Maur
107E2 **Tagula** *I* Solomon Is
79C4 **Tagum** Phil
Tagus = Tejo
96C2 **Tahat** *Mt* Alg
105J4 **Tahiti** *I* Pacific O
18A2 **Tahlequah** USA
21A2 **Tahoe City** USA
21A2 **Tahoe,L** USA
97C3 **Tahoua** Niger
71D3 **Tahuna** Indon
72D2 **Tai'an** China
72B3 **Taibai Shan** *Mt* China
72D1 **Taibus Qi** China
73E5 **T'ai-chung** Taiwan
111B3 **Taieri** *R* NZ
72C2 **Taihang Shan** China
110C1 **Taihape** NZ
72E3 **Tai Hu** *L* China
108A3 **Tailem Bend** Aust
44B3 **Tain** Scot
73E5 **T'ai-nan** Taiwan
35C1 **Taiobeiras** Brazil
73E5 **T'ai pei** Taiwan
77C5 **Taiping** Malay
75C1 **Taira** Japan
78A3 **Tais** Indon
75A1 **Taisha** Japan
29B5 **Taitao,Pen de** Chile
73E5 **T'ai-tung** Taiwan
38K5 **Taivelkoski** Fin
69E4 **Taiwan** Republic, China
Taiwan Haixia = Formosa Str
72C2 **Taiyuan** China
72D3 **Taizhou** China
81C4 **Ta'izz** Yemen
82A2 **Tajikistan** Republic, Asia
50B1 **Tajo** *R* Spain
76B2 **Tak** Thai
74D3 **Takada** Japan
75A2 **Takahashi** Japan
110B2 **Takaka** NZ
74C4 **Takamatsu** Japan
74D3 **Takaoka** Japan
110B1 **Takapuna** NZ
74D3 **Takasaki** Japan
75B1 **Takayama** Japan
74D3 **Takefu** Japan
70A3 **Takengon** Indon
76C3 **Takeo** Camb
75A2 **Takeo** Japan
Take-shima = Tok-do
90A2 **Takestān** Iran
75A2 **Taketa** Japan
4G3 **Takjvak L** Can
99D1 **Takkaze** *R* Eritrea/Eth
13B1 **Takla L** Can
13B1 **Takla Landing** Can
12B2 **Takslesluk L** USA
12H2 **Taku Arm** *R* Can
23A1 **Tala** Mexico
59B3 **Talabanya** Hung
84C2 **Talagang** Pak
34A2 **Talagante** Chile
87B3 **Talaimannar** Sri Lanka
97C3 **Talak** *Desert* Region, Niger
78A3 **Talangbetutu** Indon
32A4 **Talara** Peru
50B2 **Talavera de la Reina** Spain
34A3 **Talca** Chile
34A3 **Talcahuano** Chile
86B2 **Tālcher** India
82B1 **Taldy Kurgan** Kazakhstan
71D4 **Taliabu** Indon
84B1 **Taligan** Afghan
99D2 **Tali Post** Sudan
78D4 **Taliwang** Indon
12D2 **Talkeetna** USA
12E2 **Talkeetna Mts** USA
17A1 **Talladega** USA
93D2 **Tall 'Afar** Iraq
17B1 **Tallahassee** USA
94C1 **Tall Bīsah** Syria
60B2 **Tallinn** Estonia
92C3 **Tall Kalakh** Syria
19B3 **Tallulah** USA
60D4 **Tal'noye** Ukraine
58C2 **Talpaki** Russian Fed
30B4 **Taltal** Chile
109C1 **Talwood** Aust
78D1 **Tamabo Range** *Mts* Malay
97B4 **Tamale** Ghana
96C2 **Tamanrasset** Alg
96C2 **Tamanrasset** *Watercourse* Alg
16B2 **Tamaqua** USA
Tamatave = Toamasina
23A2 **Tamazula** Jalisco, Mexico
23B2 **Tamazulapán** Mexico
23B1 **Tamazunchale** Mexico
97A3 **Tambacounda** Sen
61F3 **Tambov** Russian Fed
50A1 **Tambre** *R* Spain
98C2 **Tambura** Sudan

97A3 **Tamchaket** Maur
50A1 **Tamega** *R* Port
23B1 **Tamiahua** Mexico
87B2 **Tamil Nādu** State, India
76D2 **Tam Ky** Viet
17B2 **Tampa** USA
17B2 **Tampa B** USA
39J6 **Tampere** Fin
23B1 **Tampico** Mexico
68D2 **Tamsagbulag** Mongolia
86C2 **Tamu** Burma
23B1 **Tamuis** Mexico
109D2 **Tamworth** Aust
43D3 **Tamworth** Eng
38K4 **Tana** Nor
99D1 **Tana** *L* Eth
99E3 **Tana** *R* Kenya
38K5 **Tana** *R* Nor/Fin
75B2 **Tanabe** Japan
38K4 **Tanafjord** *Inlet* Nor
78D3 **Tanahgrogot** Indon
71E4 **Tanahmerah** Indon
12D1 **Tanana** USA
12E2 **Tanana** *R* USA
Tananarive = Antananarivo
47C2 **Tanaro** *R* Italy
74B2 **Tanch'ŏn** N Korea
34D3 **Tandil** Arg
78B2 **Tandjong Datu** *Pt* Indon
71E4 **Tandjung d'Urville** *C* Indon
78D3 **Tandjung Layar** *C* Indon
78B3 **Tandjung Lumut** *C* Indon
78D2 **Tandjung Mangkalihet** *C* Indon
78C3 **Tandjung Sambar** *C* Indon
78C2 **Tandjung Sirik** *C* Malay
71E4 **Tandjung Vals** *C* Indon
85B3 **Tando Adam** Pak
85B3 **Tando Muhammad Khan** Pak
108B2 **Tandou L** Aust
87B1 **Tāndūr** India
110C1 **Taneatua** NZ
76B2 **Tanen Range** *Mts* Burma/Thai
96B2 **Tanezrouft** *Desert Region* Alg
91C4 **Tang** Iran
99D3 **Tanga** Tanz
60E4 **Tanganrog** Russian Fed
99C3 **Tanganyika,L** Tanz/Zaïre
96B1 **Tanger** Mor
82C2 **Tanggula Shan** *Mts* China
Tangier = Tanger
78A2 **Tangjungpinang** Indon
82C2 **Tangra Yumco** *L* China
72D2 **Tangshan** China
79B4 **Tangub** Phil
63C2 **Tanguy** Russian Fed
Tanintharyi = Tenasserim
79B4 **Tanjay** Phil
101D3 **Tanjona Ankaboa** *C* Madag
101D2 **Tanjona Babaomby** *C* Madag
101D2 **Tanjona Vilanandro** *C* Madag
101D3 **Tanjona Vohimena** *C* Madag
78C4 **Tanjong Bugel** *C* Indon
78B4 **Tanjong Cangkuang** *C* Indon
78C3 **Tanjong Puting** *C* Indon
78C3 **Tanjong Selatan** *C* Indon
78D3 **Tanjung** Indon
70A3 **Tanjungbalai** Indon
78A3 **Tanjung Jabung** *Pt* Indon
78B3 **Tanjungpandan** Indon
78B4 **Tanjung Priok** Indon
78D2 **Tanjungredeb** Indon
78D2 **Tanjungselor** Indon
84C2 **Tank** Pak
68B1 **Tannu Ola** *Mts* Russian Fed
97B4 **Tano** *R* Ghana
97C3 **Tanout** Niger
23B1 **Tanquián** Mexico
73E4 **Tan-shui** Taiwan
86A1 **Tansing** Nepal
95C1 **Tanta** Egypt
96A2 **Tan-Tan** Mor
4B3 **Tanunak** USA
99D3 **Tanzania** Republic, Africa
72A3 **Tao He** *R* China
72B2 **Taole** China
96B1 **Taourirt** Mor
60C2 **Tapa** Estonia
25C3 **Tapachula** Mexico
33F4 **Tapajós** *R* Brazil
34C3 **Tapalquén** Arg
70B4 **Tapan** Indon
111A3 **Tapanui** NZ
32D5 **Tapauá** *R* Brazil
85D4 **Tapi** *R* India
86B1 **Taplejung** Nepal
111B2 **Tapuaeniku** *Mt* NZ
35B2 **Tapuaritinga** Brazil
79B4 **Tapul Group** *Is* Phil
33E4 **Tapurucuara** Brazil
109D1 **Tara** Aust
65J4 **Tara** Russian Fed
65J4 **Tara** *R* Russian Fed
54A2 **Tara** *R* Bosnia-Herzegovina/Montenegro, Yugos
97D4 **Taraba** *R* Nig
30D2 **Tarabuco** Bol
Tarābulus = Tripoli
50B1 **Taracón** Spain
110C1 **Taradale** NZ
78D2 **Tarakan** Indon
44A3 **Taransay** *I* Scot
53C2 **Taranto** Italy
32B5 **Tarapoto** Peru
49C2 **Tarare** France
110C2 **Tararua Range** *Mts* NZ
96C2 **Tarat** Alg
110C1 **Tarawera** NZ
51B1 **Tarazona** Spain
44C3 **Tarbat Ness** *Pen* Scot
84C2 **Tarbela Res** Pak
42B2 **Tarbert** Strathclyde, Scot
44A3 **Tarbert** Western Isles, Scot
48C3 **Tarbes** France
106C4 **Tarcoola** Aust
109C2 **Tarcoon** Aust
109D2 **Taree** Aust
96A2 **Tarfaya** Mor
95A1 **Tarhūnah** Libya
91B5 **Tarif** UAE
30D3 **Tarija** Bol
87B2 **Tarikere** India
81C4 **Tarim** Yemen
99D3 **Tarime** Tanz
82C1 **Tarim He** *R* China
82C2 **Tarim Pendi** *Basin* China
84B2 **Tarin Kut** Afghan
18A1 **Tarkio** USA
79B2 **Tarlac** Phil
32B6 **Tarma** Peru
49C3 **Tarn** *R* France
59C2 **Tarnobrzeg** Pol
59C3 **Tarnów** Pol
107D3 **Taroom** Aust
51C1 **Tarragona** Spain
109C4 **Tarraleah** Aust
51C1 **Tarrasa** Spain
16C2 **Tarrytown** USA
92B2 **Tarsus** Turk
44D2 **Tartan** *Oilfield* N Sea
47D2 **Tartaro** *R* Italy
60C2 **Tartu** Estonia
92C3 **Tartūs** Syria
35C1 **Tarumirim** Brazil
70A3 **Tarutung** Indon
52B1 **Tarvisio** Italy
80D1 **Tashauz** Turkmenistan
86C1 **Tashigang** Bhutan
82A1 **Tashkent** Uzbekistan
65K4 **Tashtagol** Russian Fed
63A2 **Tashtyp** Russian Fed
78B4 **Tasikmalaya** Indon
94B2 **Tasīl** Syria
6E2 **Tasiussaq** Greenland
95A3 **Tasker** *Well* Niger
110B2 **Tasman B** NZ
107D5 **Tasmania** *I* Aust
111B2 **Tasman Mts** NZ
109C4 **Tasman Pen** Aust
107E4 **Tasman S** NZ Aust
92C1 **Taşova** Turk
96C2 **Tassili du Hoggar** *Desert* Region, Alg
96C2 **Tassili N'jjer** *Desert* Region, Alg
96B2 **Tata** Mor
96D1 **Tataouine** Tunisia
65J4 **Tatarsk** Russian Fed
69G2 **Tatarskiy Proliv** *Str* Russian Fed
61G2 **Tatarstan** Russian Fed
75B1 **Tateyama** Japan
5G3 **Tathlina L** Can
12E2 **Tatitlek** USA
13C2 **Tatla Lake** Can
59B3 **Tatry** *Mts* Pol/Slovakia
75A2 **Tatsuno** Japan
85B4 **Tatta** Pak
35B2 **Tatuí** Brazil
93D2 **Tatvan** Turk
31C3 **Tauá** Brazil
35B2 **Taubaté** Brazil
110C1 **Taumarunui** NZ
101F1 **Taung** S Africa
76B2 **Taungdwingyi** Burma
76B1 **Taung-gyi** Burma
76A2 **Taungup** Burma
84C2 **Taunsa** Pak
43C4 **Taunton** Eng
16D2 **Taunton** USA
46E1 **Taunus** Region, Germany
110C1 **Taupo** NZ
110C1 **Taupo,L** NZ
58C1 **Taurage** Lithuania
110C1 **Tauranga** NZ
110C1 **Tauranga Harbour** *B* NZ
110B1 **Tauroa Pt** NZ
7A3 **Tavani** Can
7A3 **Tavani** Can
65H4 **Tavda** *R* Russian Fed
43B4 **Tavistock** Eng
76B3 **Tavoy** Burma
76B3 **Tavoy Pt** Burma
92A2 **Tavsanli** Turk
111B2 **Tawa** NZ
19A3 **Tawakoni,L** USA
14B2 **Tawas City** USA
70C3 **Tawau** Malay
98C1 **Taweisha** Sudan
79B4 **Tawitawi** *I* Phil
79B4 **Tawitawi Group** *Is* Phil
23B2 **Taxco** Mexico
23B2 **Taxcoco** Mexico
44C3 **Tay** *R* Scot
78C3 **Tayan** Indon
12B1 **Taylor** Alaska, USA
13C1 **Taylor** Can
14B2 **Taylor** Michigan, USA
19A3 **Taylor** Texas, USA
18C2 **Taylorville** USA
80B3 **Taymā'** S Arabia
63B1 **Taymura** *R* Russian Fed
76D3 **Tay Ninh** Viet
63B2 **Tayshet** Russian Fed
68B2 **Tayshir** Mongolia
44C3 **Tayside** Region, Scc
79A3 **Taytay** Phil
90D3 **Tayyebāt** Iran
96B1 **Taza** Mor
95B2 **Tazirbu** Libya
12E2 **Tazlina L** USA
64J3 **Tazovskiy** Russian Fed
65F5 **Tbilisi** Georgia
98B3 **Tchibanga** Gabon
95A2 **Tchigai,Plat du** Nige
97C3 **Tchin Tabaradene** Niger
98B2 **Tcholliré** Cam
58B2 **Tczew** Pol
111A3 **Te Anau** NZ
111A3 **Te Anau,L** NZ
110C1 **Te Aroha** NZ
110C1 **Te Awamutu** NZ
96C1 **Tébessa** Alg
23A2 **Teboman** Mexico
23A2 **Tecailtlān** Mexico
21B3 **Tecate** Mexico
61K2 **Techa** *R* Russian Fed
23A1 **Tecolotlán** Mexico
23A2 **Tecpan** Mexico
54C1 **Tecuci** Rom
18A1 **Tecumseh** USA
80E2 **Tedzhen** Turkmenistan
65H6 **Tedzhen** *R* Turkmenistan
42D2 **Tees** *R* Eng
33E4 **Tefé** Brazil
78B4 **Tegal** Indon
78B4 **Tegineneng** Indon
25D3 **Tegucigalpa** Honduras
21B3 **Tehachapi Mts** US/
21B2 **Tehachapi P** USA
4J3 **Tehek L** Can
90B2 **Tehrān** Iran
23B2 **Tehuacán** Mexico
23B2 **Tehuantepec** Mexi
23B2 **Tehuitzingo** Mexic
43B3 **Teifi** *R* Wales
50A2 **Tejo** *R* Port
23A2 **Tejupilco** Mexico
111B2 **Tekapo,L** NZ
82B1 **Tekeli** Kazakhstan
92A1 **Tekirdağ** Turk
55C2 **Tekir Dağlari** *Mts* Turk
86C2 **Teknaf** Bang
110C1 **Te Kuiti** NZ
25D3 **Tela** Honduras
94B2 **Tel Aviv Yafo** Israe
34B3 **Telén** Arg
21B2 **Telescope Peak** *Mt* USA
33F5 **Teles Pires** *R* Braz
47D1 **Telfs** Austria
63A2 **Teli** Russian Fed
94B3 **Tell el Meise** *Mt* Jordan
12A1 **Teller** USA
87B2 **Tellicherry** India
77C5 **Telok Anson** Mala
78D2 **Tělok Darvel** Mala
71E4 **Tělok Flamingo** *B* Indon
78C3 **Tělok Kumai** *B* In
78B4 **Tělok Pelabuanrat** Indon
78D4 **Tělok Saleh** *B* Ind
78C3 **Tělok Sampit** *B* Indon
78B3 **Tělok Sukadona** *B* Indon
23B2 **Teloloapán** Mexico
64G3 **Tel'pos-iz** *Mt* Russian Fed
58C1 **Telšiai** Lithuania
78C3 **Telukbatang** Indo
71E4 **Teluk Berau** *B* Inc
78B4 **Telukbetung** Indo
70D4 **Teluk Bone** *B* Ind
71E4 **Teluk Cendrawasil** Indon
78D3 **Teluk Mandar** *B* Indon
71D4 **Teluk Tolo** *B* Indo

70D3 **Teluk Tomini** *B* Indon
71D3 **Tĕluk Weda** *B* Indon
14B1 **Temagami,L** Can
23B2 **Temascal** Mexico
78A3 **Tembesi** *R* Indon
78A3 **Tembilahan** Indon
27E5 **Temblador** Ven
77C5 **Temerloh** Malay
65G5 **Temir** Kazakhstan
65J4 **Temirtau** Kazakhstan
15C1 **Temiscaming** Can
09C2 **Temora** Aust
9B3 **Tempe** USA
19A3 **Temple** USA
45C2 **Templemore** Irish Rep
23B1 **Tempoal** Mexico
34A3 **Temuco** Chile
11B2 **Temuka** NZ
32B4 **Tena** Ecuador
87C1 **Tenāli** India
23B2 **Tenancingo** Mexico
76B3 **Tenasserim** Burma
43B4 **Tenby** Wales
99E1 **Tendaho** Eth
83D5 **Ten Degree Chan** Indian O
98B1 **Ténéré** *Desert Region* Niger
96A2 **Tenerife** *I* Canary Is
76B1 **Teng** *R* Burma
78D3 **Tenggarong** Indon
72A2 **Tengger Shamo** *Desert* China
12C2 **Teniente Jubany** *Base* Ant
12C2 **Teniente Rodolfo Marsh Martin** *Base* Ant
87B3 **Tenkāsi** India
0B2 **Tenke** Zaïre
97B3 **Tenkodogo** Burkina
06C2 **Tennant Creek** Aust
11B3 **Tennessee** State, USA
18C2 **Tennessee** *R* USA
34A2 **Teno** Chile
8D1 **Tenom** Malay
25C3 **Tenosique** Mexico
9D1 **Tenterfield** Aust
17B2 **Ten Thousand Is** USA
3A1 **Teocaltiche** Mexico
35C1 **Teófilo Otôni** Brazil
23B2 **Teotihiucan** Hist Site, Mexico
3B2 **Teotitlan** Mexico
3A1 **Tepatitlan** Mexico
24B2 **Tepehuanes** Mexico
3B2 **Tepeji** Mexico
3A1 **Tepic** Mexico
7C2 **Teplice** Czech Republic
0C1 **Te Puke** NZ
3A1 **Tequila** Mexico
3B2 **Tequistepec** Mexico
1C1 **Ter** *R* Spain
7C3 **Téra** Niger
5B1 **Teradomari** Japan
2B2 **Teramo** Italy
6A1 **Terceira** *I* Açores
9D3 **Terebovlya** Ukraine
1C3 **Teresina** Brazil
5C2 **Teresópolis** Brazil
2C1 **Terme** Turk
0E2 **Termez** Uzbekistan
2B2 **Termoli** Italy
1D3 **Ternate** Indon
2B2 **Terni** Italy
9D3 **Ternopol** Ukraine
3B2 **Terrace** Can
3B2 **Terracina** Italy
0B3 **Terrafirma** S Africa
2C8 **Terre Adélie** Region, Ant
9B4 **Terre Bonne B** USA
4A3 **Terre Haute** USA
9A3 **Terrell** USA
6B2 **Terschelling** *I* Neth
1B1 **Teruel** Spain
4C2 **Teshekpuk** USA
4C2 **Teshekpuk L** USA
4E2 **Teshio** *R* Japan
68B2 **Tesiyn Gol** *Mts* Mongolia
12H2 **Teslin** Can
12H3 **Teslin** *R* Can
12H2 **Teslin L** Can
63B3 **Teslyn Gol** *R* Mongolia
96C2 **Tessalit** Mali
97C3 **Tessaoua** Niger
101C2 **Tete** Mozam
23A2 **Tetela** Mexico
96B1 **Tetouan** Mor
61G2 **Tetyushi** Russian Fed
30D3 **Teuco** *R* Arg
23A1 **Teúl de Gonzalez Ortega** Mexico
71D4 **Teun** *I* Indon
52B2 **Tevere** *R* Italy
42C2 **Teviot** *R* Scot
65J4 **Tevriz** Russian Fed
111A3 **Te Waewae B** NZ
78C3 **Tewah** Indon
109D1 **Tewantin** Aust
72A3 **Têwo** China
19B3 **Texarkana** USA
19B3 **Texarkana,L** USA
109D1 **Texas** Aust
9C3 **Texas** State, USA
19B4 **Texas City** USA
56A2 **Texel** *I* Neth
19A3 **Texoma,L** USA
101G1 **Teyateyaneng** Lesotho
23B2 **Teziutlán** Mexico
86C1 **Tezpur** India
76C1 **Tha** Laos
101G1 **Thabana Ntlenyana** *Mt* Lesotho
101G1 **Thaba Putsoa** *Mt* Lesotho
76B3 **Thagyettaw** Burma
76D1 **Thai Binh** Viet
76C2 **Thailand** Kingdom, S E Asia
76C3 **Thailand,G of** Thai
76D1 **Thai Nguyen** Viet
76C2 **Thakhek** Laos
84C2 **Thal** Pak
77C4 **Thale Luang** *L* Thai
109C1 **Thallon** Aust
110C1 **Thames** NZ
43E4 **Thames** *R* Eng
76D2 **Thanh Hoah** Viet
87B2 **Thanjavur** India
Thanlwin = Salween
85C3 **Thar Desert** India
108B1 **Thargomindah** Aust
55B2 **Thásos** *I* Greece
76B2 **Thaton** Burma
76B2 **Thayetmyo** Burma
5F5 **The Dalles** USA
91B4 **The Gulf** S W Asia
4H3 **Thelon** *R* Can
107E3 **Theodore** Aust
9B3 **Theodore Roosevelt L** USA
55B2 **Thermaïkós Kólpos** *G* Greece
8C2 **Thermopolis** USA
4F2 **Thesiger B** Can
14B1 **Thessalon** Can
55B2 **Thessaloníki** Greece
43E3 **Thetford** Eng
15D1 **Thetford Mines** Can
101G1 **Theunissen** S Africa
19B4 **Thibodaux** USA
5J4 **Thicket Portage** Can
8D2 **Thief River Falls** USA
20B2 **Thielsen,Mt** USA
49C2 **Thiers** France
97A3 **Thiès** Sen
99D3 **Thika** Kenya
86B1 **Thimphu** Bhutan
49D2 **Thionville** France
55C3 **Thíra** *I* Greece
42D2 **Thirsk** Eng
Thiruvananthapuram = Trivandrum
39F7 **Thisted** Den
55B3 **Thívai** Greece
48C2 **Thiviers** France
17B1 **Thomaston** Georgia, USA
45C2 **Thomastown** Irish Rep
17B1 **Thomasville** Georgia, USA
6A2 **Thom Bay** Can
5J4 **Thompson** Can
18B1 **Thompson** *R* USA
4G3 **Thompson Landing** Can
13C2 **Thompson R** Can
16C2 **Thompsonville** USA
17B1 **Thomson** USA
107D3 **Thomson** *R* Aust
76C3 **Thon Buri** Thai
76B2 **Thongwa** Burma
47B1 **Thonon-les-Bains** France
42C2 **Thornhill** Scot
48B2 **Thouars** France
15C2 **Thousand Is** Can/USA
13E2 **Three Hills** Can
7G4 **Three Kings Is** NZ
76B2 **Three Pagodas P** Thai
14A2 **Three Rivers** Michigan, USA
20B2 **Three Sisters** *Mt* USA
Thrissur = Trichūr
6D2 **Thule** Greenland
47B1 **Thun** Switz
10B2 **Thunder Bay** Can
47B1 **Thuner See** *L* Switz
77B4 **Thung Song** Thai
47C1 **Thur** *R* Switz
57C2 **Thüringen** State, Germany
57C2 **Thüringen Wald** *Upland* Germany
45C2 **Thurles** Irish Rep
71F5 **Thursday I** Aust
44C2 **Thurso** Scot
112B4 **Thurston I** Ant
47C1 **Thusis** Switz
108B1 **Thylungra** Aust
73B5 **Tiandong** China
73B5 **Tian'e** China
72D2 **Tianjin** China
73B5 **Tianlin** China
82C1 **Tiān Shan** *Mts* C Asia
72B3 **Tianshui** China
72A2 **Tianzhu** China
96C1 **Tiaret** Alg
35A2 **Tibagi** *R* Brazil
94B2 **Tiberias** Israel
94B2 **Tiberias,L** Israel
Tiber,R = Tevere,R
95A2 **Tibesti** *Mountain Region* Chad
82C2 **Tibet** Autonomous Region, China
108B1 **Tibooburra** Aust
86A1 **Tibrikot** Nepal
24A2 **Tiburón** *I* Mexico
97B3 **Tichitt** Maur
96A2 **Tichla** Mor
47C2 **Ticino** *R* Italy/Switz
15D2 **Ticonderoga** USA
25D2 **Ticul** Mexico
97A3 **Tidjikja** Maur
47C1 **Tiefencastel** Switz
74A2 **Tieling** China
46B1 **Tielt** Belg
40C1 **Tienen** Belg
65J5 **Tien Shan** *Mts* China/Kirghizia
72D2 **Tientsin** China
39H6 **Tierp** Sweden
23B2 **Tierra Blanca** Mexico
23B2 **Tierra Colorada** Mexico
29C6 **Tierra del Fuego** Territory, Arg
28C8 **Tierra del Fuego** *I* Arg/Chile
35B2 **Tietê** Brazil
35A2 **Tiete** *R* Brazil
14B2 **Tiffin** USA
17B1 **Tifton** USA
32B4 **Tigre** *R* Peru
33E2 **Tigre** *R* Ven
93E3 **Tigris** *R* Iraq
23B1 **Tihuatlán** Mexico
21B3 **Tijuana** Mexico
85D4 **Tikamgarh** India
60D2 **Tikhin** Russian Fed
61F4 **Tikhoretsk** Russian Fed
93D3 **Tikrīt** Iraq
1B8 **Tiksi** Russian Fed
46C1 **Tilburg** Neth
43E4 **Tilbury** Eng
30C3 **Tilcara** Arg
108B1 **Tilcha** Aust
76A1 **Tilin** Burma
97C3 **Tillabéri** Niger
20B1 **Tillamook** USA
97C3 **Tillia** Niger
55C3 **Tílos** *I* Greece
108B2 **Tilpa** Aust
32B3 **Tiluá** Colombia
64G3 **Timanskiy Kryazh** *Mts* Russian Fed
111B2 **Timaru** NZ
60E4 **Timashevsk** Russian Fed
55B3 **Timbákion** Greece
19B4 **Timbalier B** USA
97B3 **Timbédra** Maur
Timbuktu = Tombouctou
97B3 **Timétrine Monts** *Mts* Mali
97C3 **Timia** Niger
96C2 **Timis** *R* Rom
54B1 **Timişoara** Rom
10B2 **Timmins** Can
106B1 **Timor** *I* Indon
106B2 **Timor S** Aust/Indon
34C3 **Timote** Arg
79C4 **Tinaca Pt** Phil
27D5 **Tinaco** Ven
87B2 **Tindivanam** India
96B2 **Tindouf** Alg
96B2 **Tinfouchy** Alg
96C2 **Tin Fouye** Alg
6F3 **Tingmiarmiut** Greenland
32B5 **Tingo Maria** Peru
97B3 **Tingrela** Ivory Coast
86B1 **Tingri** China
71F2 **Tinian** Pacific O
30C4 **Tinogasta** Arg
55C3 **Tínos** *I* Greece
43B4 **Tintagel Head** *Pt* Eng
96C2 **Tin Tarabine** *Watercourse* Alg
108B3 **Tintinara** Aust
96C2 **Tin Zaouaten** Alg
22C2 **Tioga P** USA
77C5 **Tioman** *I* Malay
47D1 **Tione** Italy
45C2 **Tipperary** County, Irish Rep
41B3 **Tipperary** Irish Rep
18B2 **Tipton** Missouri, USA
87B2 **Tiptūr** India
23A2 **Tiquicheo** Mexico
55A2 **Tiranë** Alb
47D1 **Tirano** Italy
60C4 **Tiraspol** Moldova
87B2 **Tirchchirāppalli** India
55C3 **Tire** Turk
93C1 **Tirebolu** Turk
44A3 **Tiree** *I* Scot
54C2 **Tirgovişte** Rom
54B1 **Tirgu Jiu** Rom
54B1 **Tirgu Mureş** Rom
84C1 **Tirich Mir** *Mt* Pak
96A2 **Tiris** Region, Mor
61J3 **Tirlyanskiy** Russian Fed
54B1 **Tirnăveni** Rom
55B3 **Tírnavos** Greece
85D4 **Tirodi** India
47D1 **Tirol** Province, Austria
53A2 **Tirso** *R* Sardegna
87B3 **Tiruchchendūr** India
87B3 **Tirunelveli** India
87B2 **Tirupati** India
87B2 **Tiruppattūr** India
87B2 **Tiruppur** India
87B2 **Tiruvannamalai** India
19A3 **Tishomingo** USA

94C2 Tisīyah Syria
59C3 Tisza R Hung
86A2 Titlagarh India
54B2 Titov Veles Macedonia
98C2 Titule Zaïre
17B2 Titusville USA
43C4 Tiverton Eng
52B2 Tivoli Italy
23B2 Tixtla Mexico
99E2 Tiyeglow Somalia
23B2 Tizayuca Mexico
25D2 Tizimin Mexico
96C1 Tizi Ouzou Alg
96B2 Tiznit Mor
23A1 Tizpan el Alto Mexico
23B2 Tlacolula Mexico
23B2 Tlacotalpan Mexico
23A2 Tlalchana Mexico
23B2 Tlalnepantla Mexico
23B2 Tlalpan Mexico
23A1 Tlaltenango Mexico
23B2 Tlancualpicán Mexico
23B2 Tlapa Mexico
23B2 Tlapacoyan Mexico
23A1 Tlaquepaque Mexico
23B2 Tlaxcala Mexico
23B2 Tlaxcala State, Mexico
23B2 Tlaxiaco Mexico
96B1 Tlemcem Alg
101D2 Toamasina Madag
34C3 Toay Arg
75B2 Toba Japan
84B2 Toba and Kakar Ranges Mts Pak
27E4 Tobago I Caribbean S
13C2 Toba Inlet Sd Can
71D3 Tobelo Indon
14B1 Tobermory Can
44A3 Tobermory Scot
71E3 Tobi I Pacific O
21B1 Tobin,Mt USA
65H4 Tobol R Kazakhstan
70D4 Toboli Indon
65H4 Tobol'sk Russian Fed
Tobruk = Tubruq
31B2 Tocantins R Brazil
31B3 Tocantins State, Brazil
17B1 Toccoa USA
47C1 Toce R Italy
30B3 Tocopilla Chile
30C3 Tocorpuri Mt Chile
32D1 Tocuyo R Ven
85D3 Toda India
47C1 Tödi Mt Switz
75A1 Todong S Korea
9B4 Todos Santos Mexico
13E2 Tofield Can
13B3 Tofino Can
12B3 Togiak USA
12B3 Togiak B USA
97C4 Togo Republic, Africa
72C1 Togtoh China
12F2 Tok USA
74E2 Tokachi R Japan
75B1 Tokamachi Japan
95C3 Tokar Sudan
69E4 Tokara Retto Arch Japan
92C1 Tokat Turk
74B3 Tŏkchŏk-kundo Arch S Korea
75A1 Tok-do I S Korea
82B1 Tokmak Kirghizia
110C1 Tokomaru Bay NZ
12H3 Toku R Can/USA
78C3 Tokung Indon
69E4 Tokuno I Japan
74C4 Tokushima Japan
75A2 Tokuyama Japan
74D3 Tōkyō Japan
110C1 Tolaga Bay NZ
101D3 Tôlanaro Madag
30F3 Toledo Brazil
50B2 Toledo Spain
14B2 Toledo USA
19B3 Toledo Bend Res USA
101D3 Toliara Madag
23B1 Toliman Mexico
32B3 Tolina Mt Colombia
51B1 Tolosa Spain
29B3 Toltén Chile
23B2 Toluca Mexico
61G3 Tol'yatti Russian Fed
74E2 Tomakomai Japan
78D1 Tomani Malay
58C2 Tomaszów Mazowiecka Pol
11B3 Tombigbee R USA
98B3 Tomboco Angola
35C2 Tombos Brazil
97B3 Tombouctou Mali
100A2 Tombua Angola
34A3 Tomé Chile
50B2 Tomelloso Spain
50A2 Tomer Port
106B3 Tomkinson Range Mts Aust
63E2 Tommot Russian Fed
55B2 Tomorrit Mt Alb
65K4 Tomsk Russian Fed
16B3 Toms River USA
25C3 Tonalá Mexico
20C1 Tonasket USA
15C2 Tonawanda USA
105H4 Tonga Is Pacific O
101H1 Tongaat S Africa
73D3 Tongcheng China
72B2 Tongchuan China
72A2 Tongde China
46C1 Tongeren Belg
76E2 Tonggu Jiao I China
73A5 Tonghai China
74B2 Tonghua China
74B3 Tongjosŏn-man N Korea
76D1 Tongkin,G of China/Viet
72E1 Tonglia China
73D3 Tongling China
108B2 Tongo Aust
34A2 Tongoy Chile
73B4 Tongren Guizhou, China
72A2 Tongren Qinghai, China
86C1 Tongsa Bhutan
76B1 Tongta Burma
68B3 Tongtian He R China
44B2 Tongue Scot
72D2 Tong Xian China
72B2 Tongxin China
73B4 Tongzi China
9C4 Tonich Mexico
99C2 Tonj Sudan
85D3 Tonk India
18A2 Tonkawa USA
76C3 Tonle Sap L Camb
21B2 Tonopah USA
12E2 Tonsina USA
8B2 Tooele USA
109D1 Toogoolawah Aust
108B1 Toompine Aust
109D1 Toowoomba Aust
22C1 Topaz L USA
18A2 Topeka USA
9C4 Topolobampo Mexico
20B1 Toppenish USA
99D2 Tor Eth
55C3 Torbali Turk
90C2 Torbat-e-Heydarīyeh Iran
90D2 Torbat-e Jām Iran
12D2 Torbert,Mt USA
50A1 Tordesillas Spain
56C2 Torgau Germany
46B1 Torhout Belg
69G3 Tori I Japan
47B2 Torino Italy
99D2 Torit Sudan
35A1 Torixoreu Brazil
50A1 Tormes R Spain
13E2 Tornado Mt Can
38J5 Torne L Sweden
38H5 Torneträsk Sweden
7D4 Torngat Mts Can
38J5 Tornio Fin
34C3 Tornquist Arg
15C2 Toronto Can
60D2 Toropets Russian Fed
99D2 Tororo Uganda
92B2 Toros Dağlari Mts Turk
43C4 Torquay Eng
22C4 Torrance USA
50A2 Torrão Port
51C1 Torreblanca Spain
53B2 Torre del Greco Italy
50B1 Torrelavega Spain
50B2 Torremolinos Spain
108A2 Torrens,L Aust
24B2 Torreón Mexico
47B2 Torre Pellice Italy
107D2 Torres Str Aust
50A2 Torres Vedras Port
16C2 Torrington Connecticut, USA
8C2 Torrington Wyoming, USA
9C4 Torrón Mexico
38D3 Tórshavn Føroyar
47C2 Tortona Italy
51C1 Tortosa Spain
90C2 Torūd Iran
58B2 Toruń Pol
40B2 Tory I Irish Rep
60D2 Torzhok Russian Fed
75A2 Tosa Japan
74C4 Tosa-shimizu Japan
74C4 Tosa-wan B Japan
75B2 To-shima I Japan
Toshkent = Tashkent
60D2 Tosno Russian Fed
75A2 Tosu Japan
92B1 Tosya Turk
61F1 Tot'ma Russian Fed
43C4 Totnes Eng
33F2 Totness Surinam
23B2 Totolapan Mexico
51B2 Totona Spain
109C2 Tottenham Aust
74C3 Tottori Japan
97B4 Touba Ivory Coast
97A3 Touba Sen
96B1 Toubkal Mt Mor
97B3 Tougan Burkina
96C1 Touggourt Alg
97A3 Tougué Guinea
46C2 Toul France
49D3 Toulon France
48C3 Toulouse France
97B4 Toumodi Ivory Coast
76B2 Toungoo Burma
46B1 Tourcoing France
96A2 Tourine Maur
46B1 Tournai Belg
48C2 Tours France
74E2 Towada Japan
74E2 Towada-ko L Japan
15C2 Towanda USA
107D2 Townsville Aust
16A3 Towson USA
43C4 Towy R Wales
74D3 Toyama Japan
75B1 Toyama-wan B Japan
75B2 Toyohashi Japan
75B2 Toyonaka Japan
75A1 Toyooka Japan
74D3 Toyota Japan
96C1 Tozeur Tunisia
46D2 Traben-Trarbach Germany
93C1 Trabzon Turk
22B2 Tracy California, USA
34A3 Traiguén Chile
13D3 Trail Can
41B3 Tralee Irish Rep
45B2 Tralee B Irish Rep
45C2 Tramore Irish Rep
39G7 Tranås Sweden
77B4 Trang Thai
71E4 Trangan I Indon
109C2 Trangie Aust
12E2 Transalaskan Pipeline USA
Transylvanian Alps = Munţii Carpaţii Meridionali
53B3 Trapani Italy
109C3 Traralgon Aust
97A3 Trarza Region, Mau
76C3 Trat Thai
108B2 Traveller's L Aust
56C2 Travemünde Germany
14A2 Traverse City USA
12C1 Traverse Peak Mt USA
111B2 Travers,Mt NZ
47C2 Trebbia R Italy
59B3 Třebíč Czech Republic
54A2 Trebinje Bosnia-Herzegovina
57C3 Trebon Czech Republic
29F2 Treinta y Tres Urug
29C4 Trelew Arg
39G7 Trelleborg Sweden
43B3 Tremadog B Wales
15D1 Tremblant,Mt Can
13C2 Trembleur L Can
16A2 Tremont USA
59B3 Trenčin Slovakia
34C3 Trenque Lauquén Arg
43D3 Trent R Eng
47D1 Trentino Region, Italy
47D1 Trento Italy
15C2 Trenton Can
18B1 Trenton Missouri, USA
16B2 Trenton New Jerse[y], USA
7E5 Trepassey Can
34C3 Tres Arroyos Arg
35B2 Tres Corações Bra[zil]
30F3 Três Lagoas Brazil
34C3 Tres Lomas Arg
22B2 Tres Pinos USA
35C2 Três Rios Brazil
47C2 Treviglio Italy
47E2 Treviso Italy
47C2 Trezzo Italy
87B2 Trichūr India
108C2 Trida Aust
46D2 Trier Germany
52B1 Trieste Italy
45C2 Trim Irish Rep
87C3 Trincomalee Sri Lanka
33E6 Trinidad Bol
29E2 Trinidad Urug
9C3 Trinidad USA
34C3 Trinidad I Arg
27E4 Trinidad I Caribbean S
103G6 Trindade I Atlanti[c]
27E4 Trinidad & Tobago Republic Caribbea[n]
19A3 Trinity USA
9D3 Trinity R USA
7E5 Trinity B Can
12D3 Trinity Is USA
17A1 Trion USA
94B1 Tripoli Leb
95A1 Tripoli Libya
55B3 Trípolis Greece
86C2 Tripura State, Indi[a]
103H6 Tristan da Cunha Atlantic O
87B3 Trivandrum India
59B3 Trnava Slovakia
107E1 Trobriand Is PNG
15D1 Trois-Riviéres Ca[n]
65H4 Troitsk Russian F[ed]
39G7 Trollhättan Swed[en]
38F6 Trollheimen Mt N[or]
89K9 Tromelin I Indian
38H5 Tromsø Nor
38G6 Trondheim Nor
38G6 Trondheimfjord I[nlet] Nor
42B2 Troon Scot
102J3 Tropic of Cancer
103J6 Tropic of Capricor[n]
96B2 Troudenni Mali
7A4 Trout L Ontario, C[an]
17A1 Troy Alabama, US[A]
16C1 Troy New York, U[SA]
14B2 Troy Ohio, USA
54B2 Troyan Bulg
49C2 Troyes France

91B5 **Trucial Coast** Region, UAE
21A2 **Truckee** *R* USA
25D3 **Trujillo** Honduras
32B5 **Trujillo** Peru
50A2 **Trujillo** Spain
32C2 **Trujillo** Ven
109C2 **Trundle** Aust
7D5 **Truro** Can
43B4 **Truro** Eng
68B2 **Tsagaan Nuur** *L* Mongolia
68B1 **Tsagan-Tologoy** Russian Fed
101D2 **Tsaratanana** Madag
100B3 **Tsau** Botswana
99D3 **Tsavo** Kenya
99D3 **Tsavo Nat Pk** Kenya
65J4 **Tselinograd** Kazakhstan
100A3 **Tses** Namibia
68C2 **Tsetserleg** Mongolia
97C4 **Tsévié** Togo
100B3 **Tshabong** Botswana
100B3 **Tshane** Botswana
98B3 **Tshela** Zaïre
98C3 **Tshibala** Zaïre
98C3 **Tshikapa** Zaïre
98C3 **Tshuapa** *R* Zaïre
101D3 **Tsihombe** Madag
61F4 **Tsimlyanskoye Vodokhranilishche** *Res* Russian Fed
Tsinan = Jinan
Tsingtao = Qingdao
101D2 **Tsiroanomandidy** Madag
13B2 **Tsitsutl Peak** *Mt* Can
58D2 **Tsna** *R* Belorussia
72B1 **Tsogt Ovoo** Mongolia
68C2 **Tsomog** Mongolia
75B2 **Tsu** Japan
75B1 **Tsubata** Japan
74E3 **Tsuchira** Japan
74E2 **Tsugaru-kaikyō** *Str* Japan
100A2 **Tsumeb** Namibia
100A3 **Tsumis** Namibia
75B1 **Tsunugi** Japan
74D3 **Tsuruga** Japan
74D3 **Tsuruoka** Japan
75B1 **Tsushima** Japan
74B4 **Tsushima** *I* Japan
74C3 **Tsuyama** Japan
50A1 **Tua** *R* Port
45B2 **Tuam** Irish Rep
60E5 **Tuapse** Russian Fed
111A3 **Tuatapere** NZ
30G4 **Tubarão** Brazil
94B2 **Tubas** Israel
79A4 **Tubbataha Reefs** *Is* Phil
57B3 **Tübingen** Germany
95B1 **Tubruq** Libya
16B3 **Tuckerton** USA
9B3 **Tucson** USA
30C4 **Tucumán** State, Arg
34B2 **Tucunuco** Arg
33E2 **Tucupita** Ven
51B1 **Tudela** Spain
93C3 **Tudmur** Syria
101H1 **Tugela** *R* S Africa
109D2 **Tuggerah** *L* Aust
12D3 **Tugidak** *I* USA
79B2 **Tuguegarao** Phil
63F2 **Tugur** Russian Fed
72D2 **Tuhai He** *R* China
4E3 **Tuktoyaktuk** USA
58C1 **Tukums** Latvia
99D3 **Tukuyu** Tanz
84B1 **Tukzar** Afghan
60E3 **Tula** Russian Fed
23B1 **Tulancingo** Mexico
78A3 **Tulangbawang** *R* Indon
32B3 **Tulcán** Colombia
60C5 **Tulcea** Rom
100B3 **Tuli** Zim
94B2 **Tulkarm** Israel
48C2 **Tulle** France
19B3 **Tullos** USA
45C2 **Tullow** Irish Rep
18A2 **Tulsa** USA
93C3 **Tulūl ash Shāmīyah** *Desert Region* Syria/S Arabia
63C2 **Tulun** Russian Fed
78C4 **Tulungagung** Indon
32B3 **Tumaco** Colombia
109C3 **Tumbarumba** Aust
32A4 **Tumbes** Ecuador
108A2 **Tumby Bay** Aust
74B2 **Tumen** China
87B2 **Tumkūr** India
77C4 **Tumpat** Malay
85D4 **Tumsar** India
97B3 **Tumu** Ghana
109C3 **Tumut** Aust
109C3 **Tumut** *R* Aust
27L1 **Tunapuna** Trinidad
93C2 **Tunceli** Turk
99D3 **Tunduma** Zambia
101C2 **Tunduru** Tanz
54C2 **Tundzha** *R* Bulg
87B1 **Tungabhadra** *R* India
68D4 **Tung-Chiang** Taiwan
38B2 **Tungnafellsjökull** *Mts* Iceland
12J2 **Tungsten** Can
63B1 **Tunguska** *R* Russian Fed
87C1 **Tuni** India
96D1 **Tunis** Tunisia
88E4 **Tunisia** Republic, N Africa
32C2 **Tunja** Colombia
12B2 **Tuntutuliak** USA
12B2 **Tununak** USA
34B2 **Tunuyán** Arg
34B2 **Tunuyán** *R* Arg
22C2 **Tuolumne Meadows** USA
35A2 **Tupã** Brazil
35B1 **Tupaciguara** Brazil
19C3 **Tupelo** USA
30C3 **Tupiza** Bol
15D2 **Tupper Lake** USA
34B2 **Tupungato** Arg
29C2 **Tupungato** *Mt* Arg
86C1 **Tura** India
63C1 **Tura** Russian Fed
61K2 **Tura** *R* Russian Fed
90C2 **Turān** Iran
63B2 **Turan** Russian Fed
93C3 **Turayf** S Arabia
80E3 **Turbat** Pak
32B2 **Turbo** Colombia
54B1 **Turda** Rom
63A3 **Turfan Depression** China
65H4 **Turgay** Kazakhstan
63B3 **Turgen Uul** *Mt* Mongolia
54C2 **Turgovishte** Bulg
92A2 **Turgutlu** Turk
92C1 **Turhal** Turk
39K7 **Türi** Estonia
51B2 **Turia** *R* Spain
Turin = Torino
61K2 **Turinsk** Russian Fed
69F2 **Turiy Rog** Russian Fed
99D2 **Turkana,L** Kenya/Eth
80E1 **Turkestan** Region, C Asia
82A1 **Turkestan** Kazakhstan
92C2 **Turkey** Republic, W Asia
80D1 **Turkmenistan** Republic, Asia
90B2 **Turkmenskiy Zaliv** *B* Turkmenistan
27C2 **Turks Is** Caribbean S
39J6 **Turku** Fin
99D2 **Turkwel** *R* Kenya
22B2 **Turlock** USA
22B2 **Turlock L** USA
110C2 **Turnagain,C** NZ
25D3 **Turneffe I** Belize
16C1 **Turners Falls** USA
46C1 **Turnhout** Belg
13F1 **Turnor L** Can
54B2 **Turnu Măgurele** Rom
63A3 **Turpan** China
26B2 **Turquino** *Mt* Cuba
80E1 **Turtkul'** Uzbekistan
18A2 **Turtle Creek Res** USA
13F2 **Turtle L** Can
63A1 **Turukhansk** Russian Fed
68C1 **Turuntayevo** Russian Fed
35A1 **Turvo** *R* Goias, Brazil
35B2 **Turvo** *R* São Paulo, Brazil
58C2 **Tur'ya** *R* Ukraine
19C3 **Tuscaloosa** USA
18C2 **Tuscola** USA
90C3 **Tusharík** Iran
Tutera = Tudela
87B3 **Tuticorin** India
54C2 **Tutrakan** Bulg
57B3 **Tuttlingen** Germany
68C2 **Tuul Gol** *R* Mongolia
105G4 **Tuvalu** *Is* Pacific O
63B2 **Tuvinskaya Respublika,** Russian Fed
23A2 **Tuxpan** Jalisco, Mexico
24B2 **Tuxpan** Nayarit, Mexico
23B1 **Tuxpan** Veracruz, Mexico
23B2 **Tuxtepec** Mexico
25C3 **Tuxtla Gutiérrez** Mexico
50A1 **Túy** Spain
76D3 **Tuy Hoa** Viet
92B2 **Tuz Gölü** *Salt L* Turk
93D3 **Tuz Khurmātū** Iraq
54A2 **Tuzla** Bosnia-Herzegovina
60E2 **Tver'** Russian Fed
42C2 **Tweed** *R* Eng/Scot
109D1 **Tweed Heads** Aust
42C2 **Tweedsmuir Hills** Scot
7E5 **Twillingate** Can
8B2 **Twin Falls** USA
111B2 **Twins,The** *Mt* NZ
14A2 **Two Rivers** USA
63E2 **Tygda** Russian Fed
19A3 **Tyler** USA
65K3 **Tym** *R* Russian Fed
69G1 **Tymovskoye** Russian Fed
42D2 **Tyne** *R* Eng
42D2 **Tyne and Wear** Metropolitan County, Eng
42D2 **Tynemouth** Eng
38G6 **Tynset** Nor
12D3 **Tyonek** USA
94B2 **Tyr** Leb
Tyre = Tyr
45C1 **Tyrone** County, N Ire
108B3 **Tyrrell,L** Aust
53B2 **Tyrrhenian S** Italy
65H4 **Tyumen'** Russian Fed
43B3 **Tywyn** Wales
55B3 **Tzoumérka** *Mt* Greece

U

99E2 **Uarsciek** Somalia
35C2 **Ubá** Brazil
35C1 **Ubaí** Brazil
98B2 **Ubangi** *R* CAR
47B2 **Ubaye** *R* France
75A2 **Ube** Japan
50B2 **Ubeda** Spain
6E2 **Ubekendt Ejland** *I* Greenland
35B1 **Uberaba** Brazil
35B1 **Uberlândia** Brazil
76C2 **Ubon Ratchathani** Thai
58D2 **Ubort** *R* Belorussia
98C3 **Ubundi** Zaïre
32C5 **Ucayali** *R* Peru
84C3 **Uch** Pak
63F2 **Uchar** *R* Russian Fed
74E2 **Uchiura-wan** *B* Japan
63B2 **Uda** *R* Russian Fed
85C4 **Udaipur** India
86B1 **Udaipur Garhi** Nepal
34D3 **Udaquoila** Arg
39G7 **Uddevalla** Sweden
38H5 **Uddjaur** *L* Sweden
87B1 **Udgir** India
84D2 **Udhampur** India
61H2 **Udmurtskaya Respublika,** Russian Fed
76C2 **Udon Thani** Thai
63F2 **Udskaya Guba** *B* Russian Fed
87A2 **Udupi** India
75B1 **Ueda** Japan
99C2 **Uele** *R* Zaïre
56C2 **Uelzen** Germany
98C2 **Uere** *R* Zaïre
61J3 **Ufa** Russian Fed
61J2 **Ufa** *R* Russian Fed
100A3 **Ugab** *R* Namibia
99D3 **Ugaila** *R* Tanz
12D3 **Ugak B** USA
99D2 **Uganda** Republic, Africa
12C3 **Ugashik B** USA
12C3 **Ugashik L** USA
47B2 **Ugine** France
69G2 **Uglegorsk** Russian Fed
60E2 **Uglich** Russian Fed
60E3 **Ugra** *R* Russian Fed
44A3 **Uig** Scot
98B3 **Uige** Angola
61H4 **Uil** Kazakhstan
8B2 **Uinta Mts** USA
100B4 **Uitenhage** S Africa
59C3 **Ujfehértó** Hung
75B2 **Uji** Japan
99C3 **Ujiji** Tanz
30C3 **Ujina** Chile
85D4 **Ujjain** India
70C4 **Ujung Pandang** Indon
99D3 **Ukerewe** *I* Tanz
86C1 **Ukhrul** India
21A2 **Ukiah** California, USA
20C1 **Ukiah** Oregon, USA
58C1 **Ukmerge** Lithuania
60C4 **Ukraine** Republic, Europe
68C2 **Ulaanbaatar** Mongolia
68B2 **Ulaangom** Mongolia
72C1 **Ulaan Uul** Mongolia
82C1 **Ulangar Hu** *L* China
68C1 **Ulan Ude** Russian Fed
68B3 **Ulan Ul Hu** *L* China
34B2 **Ulapes** Arg
74B3 **Ulchin** S Korea
54A2 **Ulcinj** Montenegro, Yugos
68D2 **Uldz** Mongolia
68B2 **Uliastay** Mongolia
58D1 **Ulla** Lithuania
109D3 **Ulladulla** Aust
44B3 **Ullapool** Scot
38H5 **Ullsfjorden** *Inlet* Nor
42C2 **Ullswater** *L* Eng
74C3 **Ullung-do** *I* S Korea
57C3 **Ulm** Germany
108A1 **Uloowaranie,L** Aust
74B3 **Ulsan** S Korea
45C1 **Ulster** Region, N Ire
65K5 **Ulungur He** *R* China
65K5 **Ulungur Hu** *L* China
44A3 **Ulva** *I* Scot
42C2 **Ulverston** Eng
109C4 **Ulverstone** Aust
63G2 **Ulya** *R* Russian Fed
60D4 **Uman** Ukraine
6E2 **Umanak** Greenland
86A2 **Umaria** India
85B3 **Umarkot** Pak
108A1 **Umaroona,L** Aust
20C1 **Umatilla** USA
38L5 **Umba** Russian Fed
99D3 **Umba** *R* Tanz
38H6 **Ume** *R* Sweden
38J6 **Umea** Sweden
101H1 **Umfolozi** *R* S Africa
4C3 **Umiat** USA
91C4 **Umm al Qaiwain** UAE

91C5 **Umm as Samīm** *Salt Marsh* Oman
99C1 **Umm Bell** Sudan
98C1 **Umm Keddada** Sudan
99D1 **Umm Ruwaba** Sudan
91B5 **Umm Sa'id** Qatar
20B2 **Umpqua** *R* USA
85D4 **Umred** India
100B4 **Umtata** S Africa
35A2 **Umuarama** Brazil
52C1 **Una** *R* Bosnia-Herzegovina/Croatia
35B1 **Unai** Brazil
12B2 **Unalakleet** USA
80C3 **Unayzah** S Arabia
16C2 **Uncasville** USA
101G1 **Underberg** S Africa
60D3 **Unecha** Russian Fed
94B3 **Uneisa** Jordan
7D4 **Ungava B** Can
30F4 **União de Vitória** Brazil
34B3 **Unión** Arg
18B2 **Union** Missouri, USA
17B1 **Union** S Carolina, USA
14C2 **Union City** Pennsylvania, USA
17A1 **Union Springs** USA
15C3 **Uniontown** USA
91B5 **United Arab Emirates** Arabian Pen
36C3 **United Kingdom** Kingdom, W Europe
2H4 **United States of America**
6B1 **United States Range** *Mts* Can
13F2 **Unity** Can
20C2 **Unity** USA
46D1 **Unna** Germany
86A1 **Unnão** India
44E1 **Unst** *I* Scot
13A1 **Unuk** *R* USA
92C1 **Ünye** Turk
61F2 **Unzha** *R* Russian Fed
33E2 **Upata** Ven
98C3 **Upemba Nat Pk** Zaïre
6E2 **Upernavik** Greenland
22D3 **Upland** USA
100B3 **Uplington** S Africa
14B2 **Upper Arlington** USA
13D2 **Upper Arrow L** Can
111C2 **Upper Hutt** NZ
20B2 **Upper Klamath L** USA
20B2 **Upper L** USA
45C1 **Upper Lough Erne** *L* N Ire
27L1 **Upper Manzanilla** Trinidad
39H7 **Uppsala** Sweden
72B1 **Urad Qianqi** China
91A4 **Urairah** S Arabia
61H3 **Ural** *R* Kazakhstan
109D2 **Uralla** Aust
61H3 **Ural'sk** Kazakhstan
65G4 **Uralskiy Khrebet** *Mts* Russian Fed
5H4 **Uranium City** Can
75B1 **Urawa** Japan
18C1 **Urbana** Illinois, USA
14B2 **Urbana** Ohio, USA
52B2 **Urbino** Italy
42C2 **Ure** *R* Eng
61G2 **Uren'** Russian Fed
80E1 **Urgench** Uzbekistan
84B2 **Urgun** Afghan
55C3 **Urla** Turk
54B2 **Uroševac** Serbia, Yugos
31B4 **Uruaçu** Brazil
23A2 **Uruapan** Mexico
35B1 **Urucuia** *R* Brazil
30E4 **Uruguaiana** Brazil
29E2 **Uruguay** Republic, S America
29E2 **Uruguay** *R* Urug
82C1 **Ürümqi** China
69H2 **Urup** *I* Russian Fed
84B2 **Uruzgan** Afghan
61F3 **Uryupinsk** Russian Fed
61H2 **Urzhum** Russian Fed
54C2 **Urziceni** Rom
82C1 **Usa** China
75A2 **Usa** Japan
64G3 **Usa** *R* Russian Fed
92A2 **Uşak** Turk
100A3 **Usakos** Namibia
99D3 **Ushashi** Tanz
65J5 **Ush Tobe** Kazakhstan
29C6 **Ushuaia** Arg
63E2 **Ushumun** Russian Fed
43C4 **Usk** *R* Wales
92A1 **Üsküdar** Turk
63C2 **Usolye Sibirskoye** Russian Fed
34B2 **Uspallata** Arg
69F2 **Ussuriysk** Russian Fed
47C1 **Uster** Switz
53B3 **Ustica** *I* Italy
57C2 **Ústí nad Labem** Czech Republic
65J4 **Ust'Ishim** Russian Fed
58B2 **Ustka** Pol
65K5 **Ust'-Kamenogorsk** Kazakhstan
63B2 **Ust Karabula** Russian Fed
61J2 **Ust'Katav** Russian Fed
63C2 **Ust'-Kut** Russian Fed
61E4 **Ust Labinsk** Russian Fed
63F1 **Ust'Maya** Russian Fed
1C8 **Ust'Nera** Russian Fed
63E2 **Ust'Nyukzha** Russian Fed
63C2 **Ust'Ordynskiy** Russian Fed
64G3 **Ust'Tsil'ma** Russian Fed
63F2 **Ust'Umal'ta** Russian Fed
75A2 **Usuki** Japan
25C3 **Usumacinta** *R* Guatemala/Mexico
101H1 **Usutu** *R* Swaziland
8B3 **Utah** State, USA
8B2 **Utah L** USA
58D1 **Utena** Russian Fed
85B3 **Uthal** Pak
10C2 **Utica** USA
51B2 **Utiel** Spain
13D1 **Utikuma L** Can
56B2 **Utrecht** Neth
101H1 **Utrecht** S Africa
50A2 **Utrera** Spain
38K5 **Utsjoki** Fin
74D3 **Utsunomiya** Japan
76C2 **Uttaradit** Thai
86A1 **Uttar Pradesh** State, India
65H4 **Uval** Russian Fed
107F3 **Uvéa** *I* Nouvelle Calédonie
99D3 **Uvinza** Tanz
99C3 **Uvira** Zaïre
6E2 **Uvkusigssat** Greenland
39J6 **Uvsikaupunki** Fin
68B1 **Uvs Nuur** *L* China
74C4 **Uwajima** Japan
72B2 **Uxin Qi** China
63B2 **Uyar** Russian Fed
30C3 **Uyuni** Bol
80E1 **Uzbekistan** Republic, Asia
48C2 **Uzerche** France
59C3 **Uzhgorod** Ukraine
54A2 **Užice** Serbia, Yugos
60E3 **Uzlovaya** Russian Fed
92A1 **Uzunköprü** Turk

V

101F1 **Vaal** *R* S Africa
101G1 **Vaal Dam** *Res* S Africa
100B3 **Vaalwater** S Africa
38J6 **Vaasa** Fin
59B3 **Vác** Hung
30F4 **Vacaria** Brazil
35C1 **Vacaria** *R* Minas Gerais, Brazil
21A2 **Vacaville** USA
85C4 **Vadodara** India
38K4 **Vadsø** Nor
47C1 **Vaduz** Leichtenstein
38D3 **Vágar** Føroyar
29E3 **Va Gesell** Arg
59B3 **Váh** *R* Slovakia
87B2 **Vaigai** *R* India
65K3 **Vakh** *R* Russian Fed
60B4 **Vâlcea** Rom
29C4 **Valcheta** Arg
47D2 **Valdagno** Italy
60D2 **Valday** Russian Fed
60D2 **Valdayskaya Vozvyshennost'** *Upland* Russian Fed
32D2 **Val de la Pascua** Ven
50B2 **Valdepeñas** Spain
12E2 **Valdez** USA
29B3 **Valdivia** Chile
46B2 **Val d'Oise** *Department* France
17B1 **Valdosta** USA
20C2 **Vale** USA
13D2 **Valemount** Can
31D4 **Valença** Bahia, Brazil
35C2 **Valença** Rio de Janeiro, Brazil
49C3 **Valence** France
51B2 **Valencia** Region, Spain
51B2 **Valencia** Spain
32D1 **Valencia** Ven
45A3 **Valencia** *I* Irish Rep
50A2 **Valencia de Alcantara** Spain
46B1 **Valenciennes** France
47C2 **Valenza** Italy
32C2 **Valera** Ven
39K7 **Valga** Estonia
54A2 **Valjevo** Serbia, Yugos
Valka = Valga
39J6 **Valkeakoski** Fin
25D2 **Valladolid** Mexico
50B1 **Valladolid** Spain
47B2 **Valle d'Aosta** Region, Italy
27D5 **Valle de la Pascua** Ven
23A1 **Valle de Santiago** Mexico
47B2 **Valle d'Isére** France
32C1 **Valledupar** Colombia
97C3 **Vallée de l'Azaouak** *V* Niger
97C3 **Vallée Tilemis** *V* Mali
30D2 **Valle Grande** Bol
22A1 **Vallejo** USA
30B4 **Vallenar** Chile
53B3 **Valletta** Malta
8D2 **Valley City** USA
20B2 **Valley Falls** USA
15D1 **Valleyfield** Can
13D1 **Valleyview** Can
47E2 **Valli di Comacchio** *Lg* Italy
51C1 **Valls** Spain
58D1 **Valmiera** Latvia
35A2 **Valparaiso** Brazil
34A2 **Valparaiso** Chile
23A1 **Valparaiso** Mexico
17A1 **Valparaiso** USA
101G1 **Vals** *R* S Africa
85C4 **Valsād** India
60E3 **Valuyki** Russian Fed
50A2 **Valverde del Camino** Spain
38J6 **Vammala** Fin
93D2 **Van** Turk
63C1 **Vanavara** Russian Fed
18B2 **Van Buren** Arkansas, USA
13C3 **Vancouver** Can
20B1 **Vancouver** USA
5F5 **Vancouver I** Can
12G2 **Vancouver,Mt** Can
18C2 **Vandalia** Illinois, USA
14B3 **Vandalia** Ohio, USA
13C2 **Vanderhoof** Can
106C2 **Van Diemen G** *Gulf* Aust
39G7 **Vänern** *L* Sweden
39G7 **Vänersborg** Sweden
101D3 **Vangaindrano** Madag
93D2 **Van Gölü** *Salt L* Turk
76C2 **Vang Vieng** Laos
9C3 **Van Horn** USA
15C1 **Vanier** Can
1C6 **Vankarem** Russian Fed
38H6 **Vännäs** Sweden
48B2 **Vannes** France
47B2 **Vanoise** *Mts* France
100A4 **Vanrhynsdorp** S Africa
6B3 **Vansittart I** Can
105G4 **Vanuatu** *Is* Pacific O
14B2 **Van Wert** USA
47C2 **Varallo** Italy
90B2 **Varāmīn** Iran
86A1 **Vārānasi** India
38K4 **Varangerfjord** *Inlet* Nor
38K4 **Varangerhalvøya** *Pe* Nor
52C1 **Varazdin** Croatia
39G7 **Varberg** Sweden
39F7 **Varde** Den
38L4 **Vardø** Nor
58C2 **Varéna** Lithuania
47C2 **Varenna** Italy
47C2 **Varese** Italy
35B2 **Varginha** Brazil
38K6 **Varkaus** Fin
54C2 **Varna** Bulg
39G7 **Värnamo** Sweden
17B1 **Varnville** USA
35C1 **Várzea da Palma** Brazil
47C2 **Varzi** Italy
50B1 **Vascongadas** Region, Spain
60D3 **Vasil'kov** Ukraine
14B2 **Vassar** USA
39H7 **Västerås** Sweden
39H7 **Västervik** Sweden
52B2 **Vasto** Italy
65J4 **Vasyugan** *R* Russian Fed
38B2 **Vatnajökull** *Mts* Iceland
38A1 **Vatneyri** Iceland
54C1 **Vatra Dornei** Rom
39G7 **Vättern** *L* Sweden
9C3 **Vaughn** USA
32C3 **Vaupés** *R* Colombia
13E2 **Vauxhall** Can
87C3 **Vavunija** Sri Lanka
39G7 **Växjö** Sweden
64G2 **Vaygach, Ostrov** *I* Russian Fed
34C2 **Vedia** Arg
38G5 **Vega** *I* Nor
13E2 **Vegreville** Can
50A2 **Vejer de la Frontera** Spain
39F7 **Vejle** Den
52C2 **Velebit** *Mts* Croatia
52C1 **Velenje** Slovenia
35C1 **Velhas** *R* Brazil
39K7 **Velikaya** *R* Russian Fed
60D2 **Velikiye Luki** Russian Fed
61G1 **Velikiy Ustyug** Russian Fed
54C2 **Veliko Tŭrnovo** Bul
97A3 **Vélingara** Sen
87B2 **Vellore** India
61F1 **Vel'sk** Russian Fed
87B3 **Vembanad L** India
34C2 **Venado Tuerto** Arg
35B2 **Vençeslau Braz** Bra
49C2 **Vendôme** France
12E1 **Venetie** USA
47D2 **Veneto** Region, Ita
47E2 **Venezia** Italy

32D2 **Venezuela** Republic, S America
87A1 **Vengurla** India
12C3 **Veniaminof V** USA
Venice = Venezia
87B2 **Venkatagiri** India
56B2 **Venlo** Neth
58C1 **Venta** *R* Latvia
101G1 **Ventersburg** S Africa
58C1 **Ventspils** Latvia
32D3 **Ventuari** *R* Ven
22C3 **Ventura** USA
60D1 **Vepsovskaya Vozvyshennost'** *Upland* Russian Fed
30D4 **Vera** Arg
51B2 **Vera** Spain
23B2 **Veracruz** Mexico
23B1 **Veracruz** State, Mexico
85C4 **Verāval** India
47C2 **Verbania** Italy
47C2 **Vercelli** Italy
35A1 **Verde** *R* Goias, Brazil
23A1 **Verde** *R* Jalisco, Mexico
35A1 **Verde** *R* Mato Grosso do Sul, Brazil
23B2 **Verde** *R* Oaxaca, Mexico
Verde,C = Cap Vert
35C1 **Verde Grande** *R* Brazil
34C3 **Verde,Pen** Arg
49D3 **Verdon** *R* France
46C2 **Verdun** France
101G1 **Vereeniging** S Africa
61H2 **Vereshchagino** Russian Fed
97A3 **Verga,C** Guinea
34D3 **Vergara** Arg
50A1 **Verin** Spain
63D2 **Verkh Angara** *R* Russian Fed
61J3 **Verkhneural'sk** Russian Fed
63E1 **Verkhnevilyuysk** Russian Fed
1C8 **Verkhoyansk** Russian Fed
35A1 **Vermelho** *R* Brazil
13E2 **Vermilion** Can
10C2 **Vermont** State, USA
22B2 **Vernalis** USA
13D2 **Vernon** Can
46A2 **Vernon** France
9D3 **Vernon** USA
17B2 **Vero Beach** USA
54B2 **Veroia** Greece
47D2 **Verolanuova** Italy
47D2 **Verona** Italy
46B2 **Versailles** France
01H1 **Verulam** S Africa
46C1 **Verviers** Belg
46B2 **Vervins** France
46C2 **Vesle** *R* France
49D2 **Vesoul** France
38G5 **Vesterålen** *Is* Nor
38G5 **Vestfjorden** *Inlet* Nor
38A2 **Vestmannaeyjar** Iceland
53B2 **Vesuvio** *Mt* Italy
59B3 **Veszprém** Hung
39H7 **Vetlanda** Sweden
61F2 **Vetluga** *R* Russian Fed
46B1 **Veurne** Belg
47B1 **Vevey** Switz
46A2 **Vexin** Region, France
47A2 **Veynes** France
50A1 **Viana do Castelo** Port
Viangchan = Vientiane
49E3 **Viareggio** Italy
39F7 **Viborg** Den
53C3 **Vibo Valentia** Italy
Vic = Vich
12C2 **Vicecomodoro Marambio** *Base* Ant
52B1 **Vicenza** Italy
51C1 **Vich** Spain
32D3 **Vichada** *R* Colombia
61F2 **Vichuga** Russian Fed
49C2 **Vichy** France
19B3 **Vicksburg** USA
35C2 **Vicosa** Brazil
106C4 **Victor Harbour** Aust
34C2 **Victoria** Arg
13C3 **Victoria** Can
34A3 **Victoria** Chile
78D1 **Victoria** Malay
108B3 **Victoria** State, Aust
9D4 **Victoria** USA
106C2 **Victoria** *R* Aust
26B2 **Victoria de las Tunas** Cuba
100B2 **Victoria Falls** Zambia/Zim
4G2 **Victoria I** Can
108B2 **Victoria,L** Aust
99D3 **Victoria,L** C Africa
112B7 **Victoria Land** Region, Ant
86C2 **Victoria,Mt** Burma
99D2 **Victoria Nile** *R* Uganda
111B2 **Victoria Range** *Mts* NZ
106C2 **Victoria River Downs** Aust
4H3 **Victoria Str** Can
15D1 **Victoriaville** Can
100B4 **Victoria West** S Africa
34B3 **Victorica** Arg
21B3 **Victorville** USA
34A2 **Vicuña** Chile
34C2 **Vicuña Mackenna** Arg
17B1 **Vidalia** USA
54C2 **Videle** Rom
54B2 **Vidin** Bulg
85D4 **Vidisha** India
58D1 **Vidzy** Belorussia
29D4 **Viedma** Arg
26A4 **Viéjo** Costa Rica
Vielha = Viella
51C1 **Viella** Spain
Vienna = Wien
18C2 **Vienna** Illinois, USA
14B3 **Vienna** W Virginia, USA
49C2 **Vienne** France
48C2 **Vienne** *R* France
76C2 **Vientiane** Laos
47C1 **Vierwaldstätter See** *L* Switz
48C2 **Vierzon** France
53C2 **Vieste** Italy
70B2 **Vietnam** Republic, S E Asia
76D1 **Vietri** Viet
27P2 **Vieux Fort** St Lucia
79B2 **Vigan** Phil
47C2 **Vigevano** Italy
48B3 **Vignemale** *Mt* France
50A1 **Vigo** Spain
87C1 **Vijayawāda** India
55A2 **Vijosë** *R* Alb
38B2 **Vik** Iceland
54B2 **Vikhren** *Mt* Bulg
13E2 **Viking** Can
38G6 **Vikna** *I* Nor
101C2 **Vila da Maganja** Mozam
101C2 **Vila Machado** Mozam
101C3 **Vilanculos** Mozam
Vilanova i la Geltrú = Villanueva-y-Geltrú
50A1 **Vila Real** Port
101C2 **Vila Vasco da Gama** Mozam
35C2 **Vila Velha** Brazil
58D2 **Vileyka** Belorussia
38H6 **Vilhelmina** Sweden
33E6 **Vilhena** Brazil
60C2 **Viljandi** Estonia
101G1 **Viljoenskroon** S Africa
9C3 **Villa Ahumada** Mexico
34B2 **Villa Atuel** Arg
50A1 **Villaba** Spain
23A2 **Villa Carranza** Mexico
52B1 **Villach** Austria
34B2 **Villa Colon** Arg
34C2 **Villa Constitución** Arg
34C1 **Villa de Maria** Arg
23A1 **Villa de Reyes** Mexico
34B2 **Villa Dolores** Arg
47D2 **Villafranca di Verona** Italy
34C2 **Villa General Mitre** Arg
34B2 **Villa General Roca** Arg
34D2 **Villaguay** Arg
25C3 **Villahermosa** Mexico
23A1 **Villa Hidalgo** Mexico
34C2 **Villa Huidobro** Arg
34C3 **Villa Iris** Arg
34C2 **Villa Maria** Arg
30D3 **Villa Montes** Bol
23A1 **Villaneuva** Mexico
50A1 **Villa Nova de Gaia** Port
50A2 **Villanueva de la Serena** Spain
51C1 **Villanueva-y-Geltrú** Spain
34B3 **Villa Regina** Arg
51B2 **Villarreal** Spain
29B3 **Villarrica** Chile
30E4 **Villarrica** Par
50B2 **Villarrobledo** Spain
34D2 **Villa San José** Arg
34C2 **Villa Valeria** Arg
32C3 **Villavicencio** Colombia
49C2 **Villefranche** France
7C5 **Ville-Marie** Can
51B2 **Villena** Spain
46B2 **Villeneuve-St-Georges** France
48C3 **Villeneuve-sur-Lot** France
19B3 **Ville Platte** USA
46B2 **Villers-Cotterêts** France
49C2 **Villeurbanne** France
101G1 **Villiers** S Africa
87B2 **Villupuram** India
58D2 **Vilnius** Lithuania
63D1 **Vilyuy** *R* Russian Fed
63E1 **Vilyuysk** Russian Fed
34A2 **Viña del Mar** Chile
51C1 **Vinaroz** Spain
14A3 **Vincennes** USA
38H5 **Vindel** *R* Sweden
85D4 **Vindhya Range** *Mts* India
16B3 **Vineland** USA
16D2 **Vineyard Haven** USA
76D2 **Vinh** Viet
76D3 **Vinh Cam Ranh** *B* Viet
77D4 **Vinh Loi** Viet
77D3 **Vinh Long** Viet
18A2 **Vinita** USA
54A1 **Vinkovci** Croatia
60C4 **Vinnitsa** Ukraine
112B3 **Vinson Massif** *Upland* Ant
100A3 **Vioolsdrift** S Africa
47D1 **Vipiteno** Italy
79B3 **Virac** Phil
87B2 **Virddhāchalam** India
100A2 **Virei** Angola
35C1 **Virgem da Lapa** Brazil
101G1 **Virginia** S Africa
10C3 **Virginia** State, USA
10A2 **Virginia** USA
21B2 **Virginia City** USA
27E3 **Virgin Is** Caribbean S
52C1 **Virovitica** Croatia
46C2 **Virton** Belg
87B3 **Virudunagar** India
52C2 **Vis** *I* Croatia
21B2 **Visalia** USA
79B3 **Visayan S** Phil
39H7 **Visby** Sweden
4H2 **Viscount Melville Sd** Can
54A2 **Višegrad** Bosnia-Herzegovina
50A1 **Viseu** Port
83C4 **Vishākhapatnam** India
47B1 **Visp** Switz
49C1 **Vissingen** Neth
21B3 **Vista** USA
Vistula = Wisla
57C3 **Vitavia** *R* Czech Republic
87A1 **Vite** India
60D2 **Vitebsk** Belorussia
52B2 **Viterbo** Italy
50A1 **Vitigudino** Spain
63D2 **Vitim** *R* Russian Fed
50B1 **Vitora** Spain
31C6 **Vitória** Brazil
31C4 **Vitória da Conquista** Brazil
48B2 **Vitré** France
46C2 **Vitry-le-Francois** France
38J5 **Vittangi** Sweden
53B3 **Vittoria** Italy
47E2 **Vittorio Veneto** Italy
69H2 **Vityaz Depth** Pacific O
50A1 **Vivero** Spain
63B1 **Vivi** *R* Russian Fed
34D3 **Vivorata** Arg
63C2 **Vizhne-Angarsk** Russian Fed
83C4 **Vizianagaram** India
54B1 **Vlădeasa** *Mt* Rom
61F5 **Vladikavkaz** Russian Fed
65F4 **Vladimir** Russian Fed
59C2 **Vladimir Volynskiy** Ukraine
74C2 **Vladivostok** Russian Fed
56A2 **Vlieland** *I* Neth
46B1 **Vlissingen** Neth
55A2 **Vlorë** Alb
57C3 **Vöcklabruck** Austria
76D3 **Voeune Sai** Camb
47C2 **Voghera** Italy
101D2 **Vohibinany** Madag
101E2 **Vohimarina** Madag
99D3 **Voi** Kenya
97B4 **Voinjama** Lib
49D2 **Voiron** France
54A1 **Vojvodina** *Aut Republic* Serbia, Yugos
26A5 **Volcán Baru** *Mt* Panama
23B2 **Volcán Citlaltepetl** *Mt* Mexico
30C3 **Volcán Lullaillaco** *Mt* Chile
34A3 **Volcáno Copahue** *Mt* Chile
34A3 **Volcáno Domuyo** *Mt* Arg
Volcano Is = Kazan Retto
29B3 **Volcáno Lanin** *Mt* Arg
30C3 **Volcán Ollagüe** *Mt* Chile
34A3 **Volcáno Llaima** *Mt* Chile
34B2 **Volcáno Maipo** *Mt* Arg
34A3 **Volcáno Peteroa** *Mt* Chile
34B3 **Volcáno Tromen** *V* Arg
23A2 **Volcán Paracutin** *Mt* Mexico
32B3 **Volcán Puraće** *Mt* Colombia
34A2 **Volcán Tinguiririca** *Mt* Arg/Chile
61J2 **Volchansk** Russian Fed
61G4 **Volga** *R* Russian Fed
61F4 **Volgodonsk** Russian Fed

61F4 **Volgograd** Russian Fed
61G3 **Volgogradskoye Vodokhranilishche** *Res* Russian Fed
60D2 **Volkhov** Russian Fed
60D2 **Volkhov** *R* Russian Fed
58C2 **Volkovysk** Belorussia
101G1 **Volksrust** S Africa
61F2 **Vologda** Russian Fed
48B2 **Vologne̲s** France
55B3 **Vólos** Greece
61G3 **Vol'sk** Russian Fed
22B2 **Volta** USA
97B3 **Volta Blanche** *R* Burkina
97B4 **Volta,L** Ghana
97B3 **Volta Noire** *R* Burkina
35C2 **Volta Redonda** Brazil
97B3 **Volta Rouge** *R* Burkina
61F4 **Volzhskiy** Russian Fed
12D2 **Von Frank Mt** USA
6J3 **Vopnafjörður** Iceland
47C1 **Voralberg** Province, Austria
47C1 **Vorder Rhein** *R* Switz
56C1 **Vordingborg** Den
64H3 **Vorkuta** Russian Fed
39G6 **Vorma** *R* Nor
60E3 **Voronezh** Russian Fed
38M5 **Voron'ya** *R* Russian Fed
39K7 **Võru** Estonia
49D2 **Vosges** *Mt* France
39F6 **Voss** Nor
63B2 **Vostochnyy Sayan** *Mts* Russian Fed
112B9 **Vostok** *Base* Ant
61H2 **Votkinsk** Russian Fed
46C2 **Vouziers** France
60D4 **Voznesensk** Ukraine
54B2 **Vranje** Serbia, Yugos
54B2 **Vratsa** Bulg
54A1 **Vrbas** Serbia, Yugos
52C2 **Vrbas** *R* Serbia, Yugos
52B1 **Vrbovsko** Bosnia-Herzegovina
101G1 **Vrede** S Africa
33F2 **Vreed en Hoop** Guyana
54B1 **Vršac** Serbia, Yugos
52C2 **Vrtoče** Bosnia-Herzegovina
100B3 **Vryburg** S Africa
101H1 **Vryheid** S Africa
54A1 **Vukovar** Croatia
13E2 **Vulcan** Can
53B3 **Vulcano** *I* Italy
77D3 **Vung Tau** Viet
38J5 **Vuollerim** Sweden
38L6 **Vyartsilya** Russian Fed
61H2 **Vyatka** *R* Russian Fed
69F2 **Vyazemskiy** Russian Fed
60D2 **Vyaz'ma** Russian Fed
61F2 **Vyazniki** Russian Fed
60C1 **Vyborg** Russian Fed
64G3 **Vym'** *R* Russian Fed
43C3 **Vyrnwy** *R* Wales
60D2 **Vyshiy Volochek** Russian Fed
59B3 **Vyškov** Czech Republic
60E1 **Vytegra** Russian Fed

W

97B3 **Wa** Ghana
13E1 **Wabasca** Can
5G4 **Wabasca** *R* Can
13E1 **Wabasca L** Can
14A2 **Wabash** USA
14A3 **Wabash** *R* USA
5J4 **Wabowden** Can
7D4 **Wabush** Can
17B2 **Waccasassa B** USA
16D1 **Wachusett Res** USA
19A3 **Waco** USA
85B3 **Wad** Pak
95A2 **Waddān** Libya
5F4 **Waddington,Mt** Can
93E4 **Wadi al Bātin** *Watercourse* Iraq
93D3 **Wadi al Ghudāf** *Watercourse* Iraq
94C2 **Wadi al Harīr** *V* Syria
93D3 **Wadi al Mirah** *Watercourse* Iraq/ S Arabia
93D3 **Wadi al Ubayyid** *Watercourse* Iraq
93D3 **Wadi Ar'ar** *Watercourse* S Arabia
91A5 **Wadi as Hsabā'** *Watercourse* S Arabia
92C3 **Wadi as Sirhān** *V* Jordan/S Arabia
94C2 **Wadi az Zaydi** *V* Syria
94C3 **Wadi edh Dhab'i** *V* Jordan
94A3 **Wadi el 'Arish** *V* Egypt
94C3 **Wadi el Ghadaf** *V* Jordan
94B3 **Wadi el Hasa** *V* Jordan
94C3 **Wadi el Janab** *V* Jordan
94B3 **Wadi el Jeib** *V* Israel/ Jordan
95B3 **Wadi el Milk** *Watercourse* Sudan
92A3 **Wadi el Natrun** *Watercourse* Egypt
94B3 **Wadi es Sir** Jordan
94B3 **Wadi Fidan** *V* Jordan
94B3 **Wadi Hareidin** *V* Egypt
93D3 **Wadi Hawrān** *R* Iraq
95B3 **Wadi Howa** *Watercourse* Sudan
98C1 **Wadi Ibra** *Watercourse* Sudan
94C2 **Wadi Luhfi** *Watercourse* Jordan
94B3 **Wadi Mujib** *V* Jordan
94B3 **Wadi Qitaiya** *V* Egypt
80B3 **Wadi Sha'it** *Watercourse* Egypt
99D1 **Wad Medani** Sudan
93E4 **Wafra** Kuwait
6B3 **Wager B** Can
6A3 **Wager Bay** Can
109C3 **Wagga Wagga** Aust
106A4 **Wagin** Aust
95A2 **Wāḥa** Libya
21C4 **Wahaiwa** Hawaiian Is
18A1 **Wahoo** USA
8D2 **Wahpeton** USA
87A1 **Wai** India
111B2 **Waiau** NZ
111A3 **Waiau** *R* NZ
111B2 **Waiau** *R* NZ
71E3 **Waigeo** *I* Indon
110C1 **Waihi** NZ
110C1 **Waikaremoana,L** NZ
110C1 **Waikato** *R* NZ
108A2 **Waikerie** Aust
111B3 **Waikouaiti** NZ
21C4 **Wailuku** Hawaiian Is
111B2 **Waimakariri** *R* NZ
111B2 **Waimate** NZ
21C4 **Waimea** Hawaiian Is
106B1 **Waingapu** Indon
13E2 **Wainwright** Can
4B2 **Wainwright** USA
111B2 **Waipara** NZ
110C2 **Waipukurau** NZ
111C2 **Wairarapa,L** NZ
111B2 **Wairau** *R* NZ
110C1 **Wairoa** NZ
110C1 **Wairoa** *R* NZ
111B2 **Waitaki** *R* NZ
110B1 **Waitara** NZ
110C1 **Waitomo** NZ
110B1 **Waiuku** NZ
75B1 **Wajima** Japan
99E2 **Wajir** Kenya
75B1 **Wakasa-wan** *B* Japan
111A3 **Wakatipu,L** NZ
74D4 **Wakayama** Japan
42D3 **Wakefield** Eng
27H1 **Wakefield** Jamaica
16D2 **Wakefield** Rhode Island, USA
76B2 **Wakema** Burma
69G2 **Wakkanai** Japan
108B3 **Wakool** *R* Aust
59B2 **Walbrzych** Pol
109D2 **Walcha** Aust
58B2 **Walcz** Pol
46D1 **Waldbröl** Germany
16B2 **Walden** USA
43C3 **Wales** Country, UK
12A1 **Wales** USA
6B3 **Wales I** Can
109C2 **Walgett** Aust
112B4 **Walgreen Coast** Region, Ant
99C3 **Walikale** Zaïre
21B2 **Walker** *L* USA
14B2 **Walkerton** Can
8B2 **Wallace** USA
108A2 **Wallaroo** Aust
109C3 **Walla Walla** Aust
20C1 **Walla Walla** USA
16C2 **Wallingford** USA
105H4 **Wallis and Futuna** *Is* Pacific O
20C1 **Wallowa** USA
20C1 **Wallowa Mts** *Mts* USA
109C1 **Wallumbilla** Aust
18B2 **Walnut Ridge** USA
110C1 **Walouru** NZ
43D3 **Walsall** Eng
9C3 **Walsenburg** USA
9C3 **Walsenburgh** USA
17B1 **Walterboro** USA
17A1 **Walter F George Res** USA
16D1 **Waltham** USA
100A3 **Walvis Bay** Namibia
103J6 **Walvis Ridge** Atlantic O
97C4 **Wamba** Nig
98B3 **Wamba** *R* Zaïre
18A2 **Wamego** USA
84B2 **Wana** Pak
108B1 **Wanaaring** Aust
111A2 **Wanaka** NZ
111A2 **Wanaka,L** NZ
14B1 **Wanapitei L** Can
109C1 **Wandoan** Aust
108B3 **Wanganella** Aust
110C1 **Wanganui** NZ
110C1 **Wanganui** *R* NZ
109C3 **Wangaratta** Aust
99E2 **Wanle Weyne** Somalia
76E2 **Wanning** China
87B1 **Wanparti** India
73B3 **Wanxian** China
73B3 **Wanyuan** China
13D2 **Wapiti** *R* Can
18B2 **Wappapello,L** USA
16C2 **Wappingers Falls** USA
87B1 **Warangal** India
109C4 **Waratah** Aust
108C3 **Waratah B** Aust
108C3 **Warburton** Aust
108A1 **Warburton** *R* Aust
109C1 **Ward** *R* Aust
101G1 **Warden** S Africa
99E2 **Warder** Eth
85D4 **Wardha** India
111A3 **Ward,Mt** NZ
5F4 **Ware** Can
16C1 **Ware** USA
16D2 **Wareham** USA
109D1 **Warialda** Aust
76C2 **Warin Chamrap** Thai
100B3 **Warmbad** S Africa
16B2 **Warminster** USA
21B2 **Warm Springs** USA
56C2 **Warnemünde** Germany
20B2 **Warner Mts** USA
17B1 **Warner Robins** USA
108B3 **Warracknabeal** Aust
108A1 **Warrandirinna,L** Aus
107D3 **Warrego** *R* Aust
19B3 **Warren** Arkansas, USA
109C2 **Warren** Aust
16D2 **Warren** Massachusetts, USA
14B2 **Warren** Ohio, USA
15C2 **Warren** Pennsylvania, USA
45C1 **Warrenpoint** N Ire
18B2 **Warrensburg** USA
101F1 **Warrenton** S Africa
15C3 **Warrenton** USA
97C4 **Warri** Nig
108A1 **Warrina** Aust
42C3 **Warrington** Eng
108B3 **Warrnambool** Aust
Warsaw = Warszawa
58C2 **Warszawa** Pol
59B2 **Warta** *R* Pol
109D1 **Warwick** Aust
43D3 **Warwick** County, Eng
43D3 **Warwick** Eng
16B2 **Warwick** New York, USA
16D2 **Warwick** Rhode Island, USA
8B3 **Wasatch Range** *Mts* USA
101H1 **Wasbank** S Africa
21B2 **Wasco** USA
4H2 **Washburn L** Can
85D4 **Wāshīm** India
10C3 **Washington** District of Columbia, USA
17B1 **Washington** Georgi USA
14A3 **Washington** Indiana USA
18B2 **Washington** Missouri, USA
16B2 **Washington** New Jersey, USA
14B2 **Washington** Pennsylvania, USA
8A2 **Washington** State, USA
14B3 **Washington Court House** USA
6D1 **Washington Land** Can
15D2 **Washington,Mt** US
43E3 **Wash,The** Eng
85A3 **Washuk** Pak
12E2 **Wasilla** USA
7C4 **Waskaganish** Can
26A4 **Waspán** Nic
70D4 **Watampone** Indon
16C2 **Waterbury** USA
45C2 **Waterford** County, Irish Rep
41B3 **Waterford** Irish Rep
45C2 **Waterford Harbour** Irish Rep
46C1 **Waterloo** Belg
10A2 **Waterloo** USA
15C2 **Watertown** New York, USA
101H1 **Waterval-Boven** S Africa
10D2 **Waterville** Maine, USA
16C1 **Watervliet** USA
5G4 **Waterways** Can
43D4 **Watford** Eng
15C2 **Watkins Glen** USA
8C1 **Watrous** Can
99C2 **Watsa** Zaïre
12J2 **Watson Lake** Can
22B2 **Watsonville** USA
71F4 **Wau** PNG
99C2 **Wau** Sudan
7B5 **Waua** Can
109D2 **Wauchope** Aust
17B2 **Wauchula** USA
14A2 **Waukegan** USA
10B2 **Wausau** USA

14A2 **Wauwatosa** USA
106C2 **Wave Hill** Aust
43E3 **Waveney** *R* Eng
14B3 **Waverly** Ohio, USA
46C1 **Wavre** Belg
10B2 **Wawa** Can
95A2 **Wāw Al Kabīr** Libya
95A2 **Wāw an Nāmūs** *Well* Libya
22C2 **Wawona** USA
19A3 **Waxahachie** USA
17B1 **Waycross** USA
17B1 **Waynesboro** Georgia, USA
19C3 **Waynesboro** Mississippi, USA
16A3 **Waynesboro** Pennsylvania, USA
15C3 **Waynesboro** Virginia, USA
18B2 **Waynesville** Missouri, USA
84B2 **Wazi Khwa** Afghan
43E4 **Weald,The** *Upland* Eng
42C2 **Wear** *R* Eng
19A3 **Weatherford** Texas, USA
20B2 **Weaverville** USA
14B1 **Webbwood** Can
16D1 **Webster** USA
18B2 **Webster Groves** USA
29D6 **Weddell I** Falkland Is
12C2 **Weddell S** Ant
13C2 **Wedge Mt** Can
20B2 **Weed** USA
01H1 **Weenen** S Africa
09C2 **Wee Waa** Aust
72D1 **Weichang** China
57C3 **Weiden** Germany
72D2 **Weifang** China
72E2 **Weihai** China
72C3 **Wei He** *R* Henan, China
72C2 **Wei He** *R* Shaanxi, China
09C1 **Weilmoringle** Aust
73A4 **Weining** China
07D2 **Weipa** Aust
14B2 **Weirton** USA
20C2 **Weiser** USA
72D3 **Weishan Hu** *L* China
57C2 **Weissenfels** Germany
7A1 **Weiss L** USA
99D1 **Weldiya** Eth
01G1 **Welkom** S Africa
15C2 **Welland** Can
43D3 **Welland** *R* Eng
06C2 **Wellesley Is** Aust
12G2 **Wellesley L** Can
43D3 **Wellingborough** Eng
09C2 **Wellington** Aust
18A2 **Wellington** Kansas, USA
11B2 **Wellington** NZ
6A2 **Wellington Chan** Can
13C2 **Wells** Can
43C4 **Wells** Eng
10B1 **Wellsford** NZ
06B3 **Wells,L** Aust
57C3 **Wels** Austria
43C3 **Welshpool** Wales
13D1 **Wembley** Can
7C4 **Wemindji** Can
20B1 **Wenatchee** USA
20C1 **Wenatchee** *R* USA
97B4 **Wenchi** Ghana
72E2 **Wenden** China
73E4 **Wenling** China
32J7 **Wenman** *I* Ecuador
73A5 **Wenshan** China
07D4 **Wenthaggi** Aust
08B2 **Wentworth** Aust
72A3 **Wen Xian** China
73E4 **Wenzhou** China
73C4 **Wenzhu** China
01G1 **Wepener** S Africa
2G1 **Wernecke Mts** Can
57C2 **Werra** *R* Germany
09D2 **Werris Creek** Aust
56B2 **Wesel** Germany
6B2 **Weser** *R* Germany
06C2 **Wessel Is** Aust
14A2 **West Allis** USA
104C4 **West Australian Basin** Indian O
104C5 **West Australian Ridge** Indian O
19C3 **West B** USA
86B2 **West Bengal** State, India
43D3 **West Bromwich** Eng
16B3 **West Chester** USA
46D1 **Westerburg** Germany
56B2 **Westerland** Germany
16D2 **Westerly** USA
106A3 **Western Australia** State, Aust
87A1 **Western Ghats** *Mts* India
44A3 **Western Isles** Scot
96A2 **Western Sahara** Region, Mor
105H4 **Western Samoa** *Is* Pacific O
46B1 **Westerschelde** *Estuary* Neth
46D1 **Westerwald** Region, Germany
49D1 **Westfalen** Region, Germany
29D6 **West Falkland** *I* Falkland Is
16C1 **Westfield** Massachusetts, USA
15C2 **Westfield** New York, USA
18C2 **West Frankfort** USA
109C1 **Westgate** Aust
43C4 **West Glamorgan** County, Wales
102E3 **West Indies** *Is* Caribbean S
13E2 **Westlock** Can
14B2 **West Lorne** Can
45C2 **Westmeath** County, Irish Rep
18B2 **West Memphis** USA
43D3 **West Midlands** County, Eng
43D4 **Westminster** Eng
16A3 **Westminster** Maryland, USA
17B1 **Westminster** S Carolina, USA
100B3 **West Nicholson** Zim
78D1 **Weston** Malay
14B3 **Weston** USA
43C4 **Weston-super-Mare** Eng
17B2 **West Palm Beach** USA
18B2 **West Plains** USA
22B1 **West Point** California, USA
19C3 **West Point** Mississippi, USA
16C2 **West Point** New York, USA
12F2 **West Point** *Mt* USA
45B2 **Westport** Irish Rep
111B2 **Westport** NZ
40C2 **Westray** *I* Scot
13C2 **West Road** *R* Can
42E3 **West Sole** *Oilfield* N Sea
11B3 **West Virginia** State, USA
22C1 **West Walker** *R* USA
109C2 **West Wyalong** Aust
42D3 **West Yorkshire** County, Eng
71D4 **Wetar** *I* Indon
13E2 **Wetaskiwin** Can
99D3 **Wete** Tanz
46E1 **Wetzlar** Germany
Wevok = Cape Lisburne
71F4 **Wewak** PNG
19A2 **Wewoka** USA
45C2 **Wexford** County, Irish Rep
45C2 **Wexford** Irish Rep
5H5 **Weyburn** Can
43C4 **Weymouth** Eng
16D1 **Weymouth** USA
110C1 **Whakatane** NZ
110C1 **Whakatane** *R* NZ
44E1 **Whalsay** *I* Scot
110B1 **Whangarei** NZ
42D3 **Wharfe** *R* Eng
19A4 **Wharton** USA
111B2 **Whataroa** NZ
16A3 **Wheaton** Maryland, USA
8B3 **Wheeler Peak** *Mt* Nevada, USA
9C3 **Wheeler Peak** *Mt* New Mexico, USA
14B2 **Wheeling** USA
13C3 **Whistler** Can
15C2 **Whitby** Can
42D2 **Whitby** Eng
18B2 **White** *R* Arkansas, USA
12F2 **White** *R* Can
14A3 **White** *R* Indiana, USA
8C2 **White** *R* S Dakota, USA
7E4 **White B** Can
108B2 **White Cliffs** Aust
40C2 **White Coomb** *Mt* Scot
13D2 **Whitecourt** Can
14A1 **Whitefish Pt** USA
7D4 **Whitegull L** Can
15D2 **Whitehall** New York, USA
16B2 **Whitehall** Pennsylvania, USA
42C2 **Whitehaven** Eng
12G2 **Whitehorse** Can
110C1 **White I** NZ
19B4 **White L** USA
109C4 **Whitemark** Aust
21B2 **White Mountain Peak** *Mt* USA
12E1 **White Mts** Alaska, USA
15D2 **White Mts** New Hampshire, USA
99D1 **White Nile** *R* Sudan
16C2 **White Plains** USA
7B5 **White River** Can
15D2 **White River Junction** USA
White S = Beloye More
13B2 **Whitesail L** Can
20B1 **White Salmon** USA
17C1 **Whiteville** USA
97B4 **White Volta** *R* Ghana
42B2 **Whithorn** Scot
17B1 **Whitmire** USA
21B2 **Whitney,Mt** USA
12E2 **Whittier** Alaska, USA
22C4 **Whittier** California, USA
5H3 **Wholdia L** Can
108A2 **Whyalla** Aust
14B2 **Wiarton** Can
18A2 **Wichita** USA
9D3 **Wichita Falls** USA
44C2 **Wick** Scot
45C2 **Wicklow** County, Irish Rep
45C2 **Wicklow** Irish Rep
45C2 **Wicklow** *Mts* Irish Rep
109C1 **Widgeegoara** *R* Aust
46D1 **Wied** *R* Germany
59B2 **Wielun** Pol
59B3 **Wien** Austria
59B3 **Wiener Neustadt** Austria
58C2 **Wieprz** *R* Pol
46E1 **Wiesbaden** Germany
42C3 **Wigan** Eng
19C3 **Wiggins** USA
42B2 **Wigtown** Scot
42B2 **Wigtown B** Scot
47C1 **Wil** Switz
20C1 **Wilbur** USA
108B2 **Wilcannia** Aust
21B2 **Wildcat Peak** *Mt* USA
47B1 **Wildhorn** *Mt* Switz
13E2 **Wild Horse** Can
47D1 **Wildspitze** *Mt* Austria
17B2 **Wildwood** Florida, USA
16B3 **Wildwood** New Jersey, USA
101G1 **Wilge** *R* S Africa
56B2 **Wilhelmshaven** Germany
15C2 **Wilkes-Barre** USA
112B8 **Wilkes Land** Ant
13F2 **Wilkie** Can
20B2 **Willamette** *R* USA
108B2 **Willandra** *R* Aust
20B1 **Willapa B** USA
9C3 **Willcox** USA
27D4 **Willemstad** Curaçao
108A1 **William Creek** Aust
108B3 **William,Mt** Aust
21A2 **Williams** California, USA
13C2 **Williams Lake** Can
15C2 **Williamsport** USA
16C1 **Williamstown** Massachusetts, USA
14B3 **Williamstown** W Virginia, USA
16C2 **Willimantic** USA
16B2 **Willingboro** USA
13D2 **Willingdon,Mt** Can
107E2 **Willis Group** *Is* Aust
17B2 **Williston** Florida, USA
100B4 **Williston** S Africa
13C1 **Williston L** Can
8D2 **Willmar** USA
108A3 **Willoughby,C** Aust
13C2 **Willow** *R* Can
20B2 **Willow Ranch** USA
21A2 **Willows** USA
18B2 **Willow Springs** USA
108A2 **Wilmington** Aust
16B3 **Wilmington** Delaware, USA
17C1 **Wilmington** N Carolina, USA
7A5 **Wilnona** USA
11C3 **Wilson** USA
108B1 **Wilson** *R* Aust
6B3 **Wilson,C** Can
22C3 **Wilson,Mt** California, USA
20B1 **Wilson,Mt** Oregon, USA
109C3 **Wilsons Promontory** *Pen* Aust
43D4 **Wiltshire** County, Eng
46C2 **Wiltz** Lux
106B3 **Wiluna** Aust
14A2 **Winamac** USA
101G1 **Winburg** S Africa
16C1 **Winchendon** USA
15C1 **Winchester** Can
43D4 **Winchester** Eng
16C1 **Winchester** New Hampshire, USA
15C3 **Winchester** Virginia, USA
42C2 **Windermere** Eng
100A3 **Windhoek** Namibia
107D3 **Windorah** Aust
8C2 **Wind River Range** *Mts* USA
109D2 **Windsor** Aust
16C2 **Windsor** Connecticut, USA
43D4 **Windsor** Eng
7D5 **Windsor** Nova Scotia, Can
14B2 **Windsor** Ontario, Can
15D1 **Windsor** Quebec, Can
17B1 **Windsor Forest** USA
16C2 **Windsor Locks** USA
27E4 **Windward Is** Caribbean S
26C3 **Windward Pass** Caribbean S
13E1 **Winefred L** Can
18A2 **Winfield** Kansas, USA
109D2 **Wingham** Aust

34C3 **Winifreda** Arg
7B4 **Winisk** *R* Can
7B4 **Winisk L** Can
76B2 **Winkana** Burma
20B1 **Winlock** USA
97B4 **Winneba** Ghana
14A2 **Winnebago,L** USA
20C2 **Winnemucca** USA
19B3 **Winnfield** USA
5J4 **Winnipeg** Can
5J4 **Winnipeg,L** Can
5J4 **Winnipegosis** Can
4J4 **Winnipegosis,L** Can
15D2 **Winnipesaukee,L** USA
10A2 **Winona** Minnesota, USA
19C3 **Winona** Mississippi, USA
15D2 **Winooski** USA
9B3 **Winslow** USA
16C2 **Winsted** USA
11B3 **Winston-Salem** USA
46E1 **Winterberg** Germany
17B2 **Winter Garden** USA
17B2 **Winter Park** USA
22B1 **Winters** USA
47C1 **Winterthur** Switz
107D3 **Winton** Aust
111A3 **Winton** NZ
43E3 **Wisbech** Eng
10B2 **Wisconsin** State, USA
7B5 **Wisconsin Rapids** USA
12D1 **Wiseman** USA
58B2 **Wisla** *R* Pol
56C2 **Wismar** Germany
33F2 **Witagron** Surinam
101G1 **Witbank** S Africa
9D3 **Witchita Falls** USA
43D3 **Witham** *R* Eng
42E3 **Withernsea** Eng
43D4 **Witney** Eng
46D1 **Witten** Germany
56C2 **Wittenberg** Germany
106A3 **Wittenoom** Aust
46D1 **Wittlich** Germany
58B2 **Wladyslawowo** Pol
58B2 **Włocławek** Pol
58C2 **Włodawa** Pol
109C3 **Wodonga** Aust
47C1 **Wohlen** Switz
71E4 **Wokam** Indon
43D4 **Woking** Eng
71F3 **Woleai** *I* Pacific O
20B2 **Wolf Creek** USA
8C2 **Wolf Point** USA
57C3 **Wolfsberg** Austria
56C2 **Wolfsburg** Germany
5H4 **Wollaston L** Can
5H4 **Wollaston Lake** Can
4G3 **Wollaston Pen** Can
109D2 **Wollongong** Aust
101G1 **Wolmaransstad** S Africa
59B2 **Wolow** Pol
108B3 **Wolseley** Aust
43C3 **Wolverhampton** Eng
16A2 **Womelsdorf** USA
109D1 **Wondai** Aust
74B3 **Wŏnju** S Korea
108B2 **Wonominta** *R* Aust
13C1 **Wonowon** Can
74B3 **Wŏnsan** N Korea
108C3 **Wonthaggi** Aust
108A2 **Woocalla** Aust
16B3 **Woodbine** USA
15C3 **Woodbridge** USA
5G4 **Wood Buffalo Nat Pk** Can
109D1 **Woodburn** Aust
20B1 **Woodburn** USA
16B3 **Woodbury** USA
12F1 **Woodchopper** USA
21A2 **Woodland** California, USA
20B1 **Woodland** Washington, USA
107E1 **Woodlark** *I* PNG
106C4 **Woodmera** Aust
106C3 **Woodroffe,Mt** Aust
14B2 **Woodstock** Ontario, Can
16B3 **Woodstown** USA
110C2 **Woodville** NZ
19B3 **Woodville** USA
108A2 **Woomera** Aust
15D2 **Woonsocket** USA
14B2 **Wooster** USA
43C3 **Worcester** Eng
100A4 **Worcester** S Africa
16D1 **Worcester** USA
47E1 **Wörgl** Austria
42C2 **Workington** Eng
8C2 **Worland** USA
46E2 **Worms** Germany
43B4 **Worms Head** *Pt* Wales
43D4 **Worthing** Eng
8D2 **Worthington** USA
71D4 **Wowoni** *I* Indon
12H3 **Wrangell** USA
12H3 **Wrangell I** USA
12F2 **Wrangell Mts** USA
40B2 **Wrath,C** Scot
43C3 **Wrexham** Wales
17B1 **Wrightsville** USA
22D3 **Wrightwood** USA
4F3 **Wrigley** Can
59B2 **Wrocław** Pol
58B2 **Września** Pol
69E2 **Wuchang** China
76E1 **Wuchuan** China
72E2 **Wuda** China
72C2 **Wuding He** *R* China
72A3 **Wudu** China
73C4 **Wugang** China
72B2 **Wuhai** China
73C3 **Wuhan** China
73D3 **Wuhu** China
73D5 **Wuhua** China
84D2 **Wūjang** China
72B1 **Wujia He** *R* China
73B4 **Wu Jiang** *R* China
97C4 **Wukari** Nig
73B4 **Wuling Shan** *Mts* China
97D4 **Wum** Cam
73A4 **Wumeng Shan** *Upland* China
46D1 **Wuppertal** Germany
72B2 **Wuqi** China
72D2 **Wuqing** China
57B3 **Würzburg** Germany
57C2 **Wurzen** Germany
72C2 **Wutai Shan** *Mt* China
71F4 **Wuvulu** *I* Pacific O
72A2 **Wuwei** China
73E3 **Wuxi** China
73E3 **Wuxing** China
72C2 **Wuyang** China
73D4 **Wuyi Shan** *Mts* China
72B1 **Wuyuan** China
76D2 **Wuzhi Shan** *Mts* China
72B2 **Wuzhong** China
73C5 **Wuzhou** China
14B2 **Wyandotte** USA
109C1 **Wyandra** Aust
43C4 **Wye** *R* Eng
43C4 **Wylye** *R* Eng
43E3 **Wymondham** Eng
106B2 **Wyndham** Aust
18B2 **Wynne** USA
4G2 **Wynniatt B** Can
109C4 **Wynyard** Aust
8C2 **Wyoming** State, USA
14A2 **Wyoming** USA
109D2 **Wyong** Aust

X

84D1 **Xaidulla** China
72D1 **Xai Moron He** *R* China
101C3 **Xai Xai** Mozam
23B2 **Xaltinguis** Mexico
100A2 **Xangongo** Angola
46D1 **Xanten** Germany
55B2 **Xánthi** Greece
100B3 **Xau,L** Botswana
14B3 **Xenia** USA
72A2 **Xiahe** China
73D5 **Xiamen** China
72B3 **Xi'an** China
73B4 **Xianfeng** China
73C3 **Xiangfan** China
73C4 **Xiang Jiang** *R* China
73C4 **Xiangtan** Province, China
73C4 **Xianning** China
72B3 **Xianyang** China
73C4 **Xiao Shui** *R* China
73D4 **Xiapu** China
73A4 **Xichang** China
23B1 **Xicotepec** Mexico
76C2 **Xieng Khouang** Laos
73B4 **Xifeng** China
86B1 **Xigazê** China
72A1 **Xi He** *R* China
72B2 **Xiji** China
73C5 **Xi Jiang** *R* China
72E1 **Xiliao He** *R* China
73B5 **Xilin** China
23B1 **Xilitla** Mexico
73D4 **Xinfeng** China
72C1 **Xinghe** China
73D5 **Xingning** China
73B4 **Xingren** China
72C2 **Xingtai** China
33G4 **Xingu** *R* Brazil
68B2 **Xingxingxia** China
73A4 **Xingyi** China
72A2 **Xining** China
72E2 **Xinjin** Liaoning, China
73A3 **Xinjin** Sichuan, China
72D2 **Xinwen** China
72C2 **Xin Xian** China
72C2 **Xinxiang** China
73C3 **Xinyang** China
73C5 **Xinyi** Guangdong, China
72D3 **Xinyi** Jiangsu, China
72D1 **Xi Ujimqin Qi** China
74A2 **Xiuyan** China
23B2 **Xochimilco** Mexico
73D3 **Xuancheng** China
73B3 **Xuanhan** China
72D1 **Xuanhua** China
73A4 **Xuanwei** China
72C3 **Xuchang** China
99E2 **Xuddur** Somalia
72A2 **Xunhua** China
73C5 **Xun Jiang** *R* China
69E2 **Xunke** China
73D5 **Xunwu** China
73C4 **Xupu** China
76E1 **Xuwen** China
73B4 **Xuyong** China
72D3 **Xuzhou** China

Y

73A4 **Ya'an** China
108B3 **Yaapeet** Aust
98B2 **Yabassi** Cam
68C1 **Yablonovyy Khrebet** *Mts* Russian Fed
94C2 **Yabrūd** Syria
20B2 **Yachats** USA
30D3 **Yacuiba** Bol
87B1 **Yādgīr** India
95A1 **Yafran** Libya
23A1 **Yahualica** Mexico
98C2 **Yahuma** Zaïre
75B1 **Yaita** Japan
75B2 **Yaizu** Japan
73A4 **Yajiang** China
20B1 **Yakima** USA
20B1 **Yakima** *R* USA
97B3 **Yako** Burkina
98C2 **Yakoma** Zaïre
74E2 **Yakumo** Japan
12G3 **Yakutat** USA
12G3 **Yakutat B** USA
63E1 **Yakutsk** Russian Fed
77C4 **Yala** Thai
23B2 **Yalalag** Mexico
98C2 **Yalinga** CAR
109C3 **Yallourn** Aust
68B3 **Yalong** *R* China
73A4 **Yalong Jiang** *R* China
54C2 **Yalova** Turk
60D5 **Yalta** Ukraine
74B2 **Yalu Jiang** *R* China
74D3 **Yamagata** Japan
74C4 **Yamaguchi** Japan
68D1 **Yamarovka** Russian Fed
109D1 **Yamba** New S Wale[s] Aust
108B2 **Yamba** S Australia, Aust
99C2 **Yambio** Sudan
54C2 **Yambol** Bulg
71E4 **Yamdena** *I* Indon
Yam Kinneret = **Tiberias,L**
108B1 **Yamma Yamma,L** Aust
97B4 **Yamoussoukro** Ivor[y] Coast
85D3 **Yamuna** *R* India
86C1 **Yamzho Yumco** *L* China
63F1 **Yana** *R* Russian Fe[d]
108B3 **Yanac** Aust
75A2 **Yanagawa** Japan
87C1 **Yanam** India
72B2 **Yan'an** China
80B3 **Yanbu'al Bahr** S Arabia
108B2 **Yancannia** Aust
72E3 **Yancheng** China
72B2 **Yanchi** China
108B1 **Yandama** *R* Aust
98C2 **Yangambi** Zaïre
72C1 **Yang He** *R* China
73C5 **Yangjiang** China
76B2 **Yangon** Burma
72C2 **Yangquan** China
73C5 **Yangshan** China
73C3 **Yangtze Gorges** China
72E3 **Yangtze,Mouths of the** China
72D3 **Yangzhou** China
73B4 **Yanhe** China
74B2 **Yanji** China
108C3 **Yanko** *R* Aust
8D2 **Yankton** USA
68A2 **Yanqqi** China
72D1 **Yan Shan** *Hills*
108B1 **Yantabulla** Aust
72E2 **Yantai** China
72D2 **Yanzhou** China
98B2 **Yaoundé** Cam
71E4 **Yapen** *I* Indon
71E3 **Yap Is** Pacific O
24B2 **Yaqui** *R* Mexico
61G2 **Yaransk** Russian F[ed]
32C3 **Yari** *R* Colombia
74D3 **Yariga-dake** *Mt* Japan
82B2 **Yarkant He** *R* Chin[a]
86C1 **Yarlung Zangbo Jiang** *R* China
7D5 **Yarmouth** Can
94B2 **Yarmūk** *R* Syria/ Jordan
61E2 **Yaroslavl'** Russian Fed
94B2 **Yarqon** *R* Israel
109C3 **Yarram** Aust
109D1 **Yarraman** Aust
109C3 **Yarrawonga** Aust
60D2 **Yartsevo** Russian Fed
63B1 **Yartsevo** Russian Fed
32B2 **Yarumal** Colombi[a]
97C3 **Yashi** Nig
97C4 **Yashikera** Nig
61F4 **Yashkul'** Russian Fed
84C1 **Yasin** Pak
59C3 **Yasinya** Ukraine
109C2 **Yass** Aust
109C2 **Yass** *R* Aust
75A1 **Yasugi** Japan
18A2 **Yates Center** USA
98C2 **Yatolema** Zaïre
74C4 **Yatsushiro** Japan
94B3 **Yatta** Israel
32C4 **Yavari** Peru
85D4 **Yavatmāl** India
74C4 **Yawatahama** Jap[an]
76D2 **Ya Xian** China
90B3 **Yazd** Iran
90B3 **Yazd-e Khvāst** Ira[n]
19B3 **Yazoo** *R* USA

19B3 **Yazoo City** USA
76B2 **Ye** Burma
59D3 **Yedintsy** Moldova
08A2 **Yeelanna** Aust
60E3 **Yefremov** Russian Fed
61F4 **Yegorlyk** *R* Russian Fed
99D2 **Yei** Sudan
65H4 **Yekaterinburg** Russian Fed
60E3 **Yelets** Russian Fed
44E1 **Yell** *I* Scot
87C1 **Yellandu** India
Yellow = Huang He
8B1 **Yellowhead P** Can
4G3 **Yellowknife** Can
5G4 **Yellowmead P** Can
09C2 **Yellow Mt** Aust
69E3 **Yellow Sea** China/Korea
8C2 **Yellowstone** *R* USA
8B2 **Yellowstone L** USA
6B1 **Yelverton B** Can
97C3 **Yelwa** Nig
81C4 **Yemen** Republic, Arabian Pen
76C1 **Yen Bai** Viet
97B4 **Yendi** Ghana
76B1 **Yengan** Burma
63B2 **Yeniseysk** Russian Fed
63B1 **Yeniseyskiy Kryazh** *Ridge* Russian Fed
64J2 **Yeniseyskiy Zal** *B* Russian Fed
12D2 **Yentna** *R* USA
43C4 **Yeo** *R* Eng
09C2 **Yeoval** Aust
43C4 **Yeovil** Eng
63C1 **Yerbogachen** Russian Fed
65F5 **Yerevan** Armenia
21B2 **Yerington** USA
21B3 **Yermo** USA
69E1 **Yerofey-Pavlovich** Russian Fed
94B3 **Yeroham** Israel
61G3 **Yershov** Russian Fed
Yerushalayim = Jerusalem
92C1 **Yeşil** *R* Turk
94B2 **Yesud Hama'ala** Israel
09D1 **Yetman** Aust
96B2 **Yetti** Maur
93E1 **Yevlakh** Azerbaijan
60D4 **Yevpatoriya** Ukraine
72E2 **Ye Xian** China
60E4 **Yeysk** Russian Fed
55B2 **Yiannitsá** Greece
73A4 **Yibin** China
73C3 **Yichang** China
69E2 **Yichun** China
72B2 **Yijun** China
54C2 **Yildiz Dağlari** *Upland* Turk
92C2 **Yıldızeli** Turk
73A5 **Yiliang** China
72B2 **Yinchuan** China
72D3 **Ying He** *R* China
72E1 **Yingkou** China
73D3 **Yingshan** Hubei, China
72B3 **Yingshan** Sichuan, China
73D4 **Yingtan** China
82C1 **Yining** China
72B1 **Yin Shan** *Upland* China
9D2 **Yirga Alem** Eth
9D2 **Yirol** Sudan
63D3 **Yirshi** China
73B5 **Yishan** China
72D2 **Yishui** China
55B3 **Yíthion** Greece
38J6 **Yivieska** Fin
73C4 **Yiyang** China
38K5 **Yli-Kitka** *L* Fin
38J5 **Ylilornio** Sweden
9A4 **Yoakum** USA
23B2 **Yogope** Mexico
78C4 **Yogyakarta** Indon
13D2 **Yoho Nat Pk** Can
98B2 **Yokadouma** Cam
75B2 **Yokkaichi** Japan
75B1 **Yokohama** Japan
75B1 **Yokosuka** Japan
74C3 **Yonago** Japan
74E3 **Yonezawa** Japan
73D4 **Yong'an** China
72A2 **Yongchang** China
74B3 **Yŏngch'on** S Korea
73B4 **Yongchuan** China
72A2 **Yongdeng** China
73D5 **Yongding** China
72D2 **Yongding He** *R* China
74B3 **Yŏngdŏk** S Korea
74B3 **Yŏnghŭng** N Korea
74B3 **Yongju** S Korea
72B2 **Yongning** China
16C2 **Yonkers** USA
49C2 **Yonne** *R* France
42D3 **York** Eng
18A1 **York** Nebraska, USA
16A3 **York** Pennsylvania, USA
107D2 **York,C** Aust
108A2 **Yorke Pen** Aust
108A3 **Yorketown** Aust
7A4 **York Factory** Can
41C3 **Yorkshire Moors** *Moorland* Eng
42D2 **Yorkshire Wolds** *Upland* Eng
5H4 **Yorkton** Can
22B2 **Yosemite L** USA
22C1 **Yosemite Nat Pk** USA
75A2 **Yoshii** *R* Japan
75A2 **Yoshino** *R* Japan
61G2 **Yoshkar Ola** Russian Fed
74B4 **Yŏsu** S Korea
41B3 **Youghal** Irish Rep
45C3 **Youghal Harb** Irish Rep
73B5 **You Jiang** *R* China
109C2 **Young** Aust
34D2 **Young** Urug
111A2 **Young Range** *Mts* NZ
13E2 **Youngstown** Can
14B2 **Youngstown** Ohio, USA
22A1 **Yountville** USA
73B4 **Youyang** China
92B2 **Yozgat** Turk
20B2 **Yreka** USA
39G7 **Ystad** Sweden
43C3 **Ystwyth** *R* Wales
44C3 **Ythan** *R* Scot
73C4 **Yuan Jiang** *R* Hunan, China
73A5 **Yuan Jiang** *R* Yunnan, China
73A4 **Yuanmu** China
72C2 **Yuanping** China
21A2 **Yuba City** USA
74E2 **Yūbari** Japan
25D3 **Yucatan** *Pen* Mexico
25D2 **Yucatan Chan** Mexico/Cuba
72C2 **Yuci** China
63F2 **Yudoma** *R* Russian Fed
73D4 **Yudu** China
73A4 **Yuexi** China
73C4 **Yueyang** China
54A2 **Yugoslavia** Republic, Europe
73B5 **Yu Jiang** *R* China
12C2 **Yukon** *R* Can/USA
4E3 **Yukon Territory** Can
76E1 **Yulin** Guangdong, China
73C5 **Yulin** Guangxi, China
72B2 **Yulin** Shaanxi, China
9B3 **Yuma** USA
68B3 **Yumen** China
72D2 **Yunan** China
34A3 **Yungay** Chile
73C5 **Yunkai Dashan** *Hills* China
108A2 **Yunta** Aust
72C3 **Yunxi** China
72C3 **Yun Xian** China
73B3 **Yunyang** China
32B5 **Yurimaguas** Peru
73E5 **Yu Shan** *Mt* Taiwan
38L6 **Yushkozero** Russian Fed
82D2 **Yushu** Tibet, China
73A5 **Yuxi** China
74F2 **Yuzhno-Kuril'sk** Russian Fed
69G2 **Yuzhno-Sakhalinsk** Russian Fed
61J3 **Yuzh Ural** *Mts* Russian Fed
46A2 **Yvelines** Department, France
47B1 **Yverdon** Switz

Z

56A2 **Zaandam** Neth
93D2 **Zāb al Babir** *R* Iraq
93D2 **Zāb as Şaghīr** *R* Iraq
68D2 **Zabaykal'sk** Russian Fed
59B3 **Zabreh** Czech Republic
59B2 **Zabrze** Pol
23A2 **Zacapu** Mexico
24B2 **Zacatecas** Mexico
23B2 **Zacatepec** Morelos, Mexico
23B2 **Zacatepec** Oaxaca, Mexico
23B2 **Zacatlan** Mexico
23A1 **Zacoalco** Mexico
23B1 **Zacualtipan** Mexico
52C2 **Zadar** Croatia
76B3 **Zadetkyi** *I* Burma
50A2 **Zafra** Spain
95C1 **Zagazig** Egypt
96B1 **Zagora** Mor
52C1 **Zagreb** Croatia
91D4 **Zāhedān** Iran
94B2 **Zahle** Leb
51C2 **Zahrez Chergui** *Marshland* Alg
61H2 **Zainsk** Russian Fed
98C3 **Zaïre** Republic, Africa
98B3 **Zaïre** *R* Zaïre/Congo
54B2 **Zaječar** Yugos
68C1 **Zakamensk** Russian Fed
93D2 **Zakho** Iraq
55B3 **Zákinthos** *I* Greece
59B3 **Zakopane** Pol
59B3 **Zalaegerszeg** Hung
54B1 **Zalău** Rom
56C2 **Zalew Szczeciński** *Lg* Pol
98C1 **Zalingei** Sudan
63F2 **Zaliv Akademii** *B* Russian Fed
65G5 **Zaliv Kara-Bogaz Gol** *B* Turkmenistan
74C2 **Zaliv Petra Velikogo** *B* Russian Fed
69G2 **Zaliv Turpeniya** *B* Russian Fed
95A2 **Zaltan** Libya
89H9 **Zambesi** *R* Mozam
100B2 **Zambezi** Zambia
100B2 **Zambezi** *R* Zambia
100B2 **Zambia** Republic, Africa
79B4 **Zamboanga** Phil
79B4 **Zamboanga Pen** Phil
58C2 **Zambrów** Pol
32B4 **Zamora** Ecuador
23A2 **Zamora** Mexico
50A1 **Zamora** Spain
59C2 **Zamość** Pol
72A3 **Zamtang** China
98B3 **Zanaga** Congo
50B2 **Záncara** *R* Spain
84D2 **Zanda** China
14B3 **Zanesville** USA
84D2 **Zangla** India
90A2 **Zanjān** Iran
34B2 **Zanjitas** Arg
34B2 **Zanjon** *R* Arg
99D3 **Zanzibar** Tanz
99D3 **Zanzibar** *I* Tanz
96C2 **Zaouatallaz** Alg
72D3 **Zaozhuang** China
93D2 **Zap** *R* Turk
39K7 **Zapadnaja Dvina** *R* Russian Fed
65H3 **Zapadno-Sibirskaya Nizmennost'** *Lowland* Russian Fed
63B2 **Zapadnyy Sayan** *Mts* Russian Fed
34A3 **Zapala** Arg
60E4 **Zaporozh'ye** Ukraine
93C2 **Zara** Turk
23A1 **Zaragoza** Mexico
50B1 **Zaragoza** Spain
90B2 **Zarand** Iran
90C3 **Zarand** Iran
80E2 **Zaranj** Afghan
33D2 **Zarara** Ven
58D1 **Zarasai** Lithuania
34D2 **Zárate** Arg
90B3 **Zard Kuh** *Mt* Iran
12H3 **Zarembo I** USA
84B2 **Zarghun Shahr** Afghan
84B2 **Zargun** *Mt* Pak
97C3 **Zaria** Nig
92C3 **Zarqa** Jordan
94B2 **Zarqa** *R* Jordan
32B4 **Zaruma** Ecuador
58B2 **Zary** Pol
96D1 **Zarzis** Tunisia
84D2 **Zāskār** *Mts* India
84D2 **Zāskār** *R* India
94C2 **Zatara** *R* Jordan
Zatoka Gdańska = Gdańsk,G of
69E1 **Zavitinsk** Russian Fed
59B2 **Zawiercie** Pol
63C2 **Zayarsk** Russian Fed
65K5 **Zaysan** Kazakhstan
82D3 **Zayü** China
68B4 **Zayü** *Mt* China
58B2 **Zduńska Wola** Pol
46B1 **Zeebrugge** Belg
94B3 **Zeelim** Israel
101G1 **Zeerust** S Africa
94B2 **Zefat** Israel
97C3 **Zegueren** *Watercourse* Mali
99E1 **Zeila** Somalia
57C2 **Zeitz** Germany
72A2 **Zekog** China
61G2 **Zelenodol'sk** Russian Fed
39K6 **Zelenogorsk** Russian Fed
47D1 **Zell** Austria
98C2 **Zemio** CAR
64F1 **Zemlya Aleksandry** *I* Barents S
64F2 **Zemlya Frantsa Iosifa** *Is* Barents S
64F1 **Zemlya Georga** *I* Barents S
64H1 **Zemlya Vil'cheka** *I* Barents S
73B4 **Zenning** China
47B1 **Zermatt** Switz
63E2 **Zeya** Russian Fed
63E2 **Zeya** *Res* Russian Fed
50A1 **Zézere** *R* Port
94B1 **Zghorta** Leb
58B2 **Zgierz** Pol
72D1 **Zhangjiakou** China
73D4 **Zhangping** China
72D2 **Zhangwei He** *R* China
72E1 **Zhangwu** China
72A2 **Zhangye** China
73D5 **Zhangzhou** China
73C5 **Zhanjiang** China
73A4 **Zhanyi** China
73C5 **Zhaoqing** China
73A4 **Zhaotong** China
72D2 **Zhaoyang Hu** *L* China
61J4 **Zharkamys** Russian Fed
63E1 **Zhatay** Russian Fed
73D4 **Zhejiang** Province, China
67F3 **Zhengou** China

72C3 **Zhengzhou** China
72D3 **Zhenjiang** China
73A4 **Zhenxiong** China
73B4 **Zhenyuan** China
61F3 **Zherdevka** Russian Fed
73C3 **Zhicheng** China
68C1 **Zhigalovo** Russian Fed
73B4 **Zhijin** China
58D2 **Zhitkovichi** Belorussia
60C3 **Zhitomir** Ukraine
60D3 **Zhlobin** Belorussia
60C4 **Zhmerinka** Ukraine
84B2 **Zhob** Pak
58D2 **Zhodino** Latvia
72B2 **Zhongning** China
112C10 **Zhongshan** *Base* Ant
73C5 **Zhongshan** China
72B2 **Zhongwei** China
68B4 **Zhougdian** China
73E3 **Zhoushan Quandao** *Arch* China
72E2 **Zhuanghe** China
72A3 **Zhugqu** China
73C3 **Zhushan** China
73C4 **Zhuzhou** China
72D2 **Zibo** China
106C3 **Ziel,Mt** Aust
58B2 **Zielona Góra** Pol
76A1 **Zigaing** Burma
73A4 **Zigong** China
97A3 **Ziguinchor** Sen
23A2 **Zihuatanejo** Mexico
94B2 **Zikhron Ya'aqov** Israel
59B3 **Žilina** Slovakia
95A2 **Zillah** Libya
47D1 **Ziller** *R* Austria
47D1 **Zillertaler Alpen** *Mts* Austria
58D1 **Zilupe** Russian Fed
63C2 **Zima** Russian Fed
23B1 **Zimapan** Mexico
23B2 **Zimatlan** Mexico
100B2 **Zimbabwe** Republic, Africa
94B3 **Zin** *R* Israel
23B2 **Zinacatepec** Mexico
23A2 **Zinapécuaro** Mexico
97C3 **Zinder** Niger
73C4 **Zi Shui** China
23A2 **Zitácuaro** Mexico
57C2 **Zittau** Germany
72D2 **Ziya He** *R* China
72A3 **Ziyang** China
61J2 **Zlatoust** Russian Fed
59B3 **Zlin** Czech Republic
65K4 **Zmeinogorsk** Russian Fed
58B2 **Znin** Pol
59B3 **Znoimo** Czech Republic
100B3 **Zoekmekaar** S Africa
47B1 **Zofinger** Switz
72A3 **Zoigê** China
59D3 **Zolochev** Ukraine
101C2 **Zomba** Malawi
98B2 **Zongo** Zaïre
92B1 **Zonguldak** Turk
97B4 **Zorzor** Lib
96A2 **Zouerate** Maur
54B1 **Zrenjanin** Serbia, Yugos
47C1 **Zug** Switz
47D1 **Zugspitze** *Mt* Germany
50A2 **Zújar** *R* Spain
100C2 **Zumbo** Mozam
23B2 **Zumpango** Mexico
97C4 **Zungeru** Nig
73B4 **Zunyi** China
76D1 **Zuo** *R* China
73B5 **Zuo Jiang** *R* China
47C1 **Zürich** Switz
47C1 **Zürichsee** *L* Switz
95A1 **Zuwārah** Libya
95A2 **Zuwaylah** Libya
61H2 **Zuyevka** Russian Fed
100B4 **Zvishavane** Zim
59B3 **Zvolen** Slovakia
54A2 **Zvornik** Bosnia-Herzegovina
97B4 **Zwedru** Lib
46D2 **Zweibrücken** Germany
47B1 **Zweisimmen** Switz
57C2 **Zwickau** Germany
56B2 **Zwolle** Neth
58C2 **Zyrardów** Pol
65K5 **Zyryanovsk** Kazakhstan
59B3 **Żywiec** Pol
94A1 **Zyyi** Cyprus